Tragic Mountains

Tragic

**INDIANA
UNIVERSITY
PRESS**

Bloomington
and
Indianapolis

Mountains

The
Hmong,
the
Americans,
and the
Secret Wars
for Laos,
1942–1992

Jane Hamilton-Merritt

The paper used in this publication meets the minimum requirements of American National Standard for Information Sciences—Permanence of Paper for Printed Library Materials, ANSI Z39.48-1984.

Manufactured in the United States of America

Library of Congress Cataloging-in-Publication Data

Hamilton-Merritt, Jane.
    Tragic mountains : the Hmong, the Americans, and the secret wars for Laos, 1942-1992 / Jane Hamilton-Merritt.
       p.   cm.
    Includes bibliographical references and index.
    ISBN 0-253-32731-8 (alk. paper).
    1. Hmong (Asian people)—Wars.   2. Hmong (Asian people)—Government policy—Laos.   3. Hmong (Asian people)—History—20th century.   4. Laos—Politics and government.   5. Laos—History—20th century.   I. Title.
DS555.45.M5H36   1992
959.4'00495—dc20   92-28970

1 2 3 4 5 96 95 94 93

Hmong textile art, *pa'ndau*, found on the title page and on the part titles are examples of traditional Hmong designs.

In memory of
all Hmong who
died defending
their families and
homelands.

CONTENTS

■■■■■■■■■■■■■■■■■■■■■■■■■■

Maps

PREFACE

In the mid-1960s when I arrived in Southeast Asia as a journalist and photographer, the Indochina peninsula was at war. North Vietnam, supported by its Soviet, Chinese, and Eastern Bloc allies, fought against South Vietnam and the United States and their allies from South Korea, Australia, New Zealand, and Thailand. Some of the critical battlefields of this struggle were in the remote northeastern mountainous areas of Laos inhabited by the tribal minorities. This war pitted the highly trained and well-equipped North Vietnamese Army and its allies against the mountain men of Laos, primarily of the Hmong tribe, but also those of the Kmhmu and Mien groups. While some Hmong joined with the communist forces, most Hmong elected to join the fight to eject North Vietnam from Laos.

The remote hills where this war was being fought were forbidden to journalists. Those of us who spent time in Laos lived on the edge of this story. During this time, I covered the Vietnam War for midwestern and Asian newspapers and magazines. I knew of the "secret war" being fought in northern Laos, but I could not write about it then. It was embargoed.

While reporters were forbidden in northeastern Laos, they were allowed and even encouraged to visit the lowland Lao villages to report on economic development and medical projects. Several times, I had tried to visit the northern Lao province of Xieng Khouang. Since this area included Long Chieng, Hmong General Vang Pao's headquarters, the CIA paramilitary base of operations, and was the province with the heavy fighting, my requests were denied. It was easy to control who went to General Vang Pao's area since those hills were accessible only by aircraft. Permission had to be obtained from U.S. authorities. Journalists found such authorization difficult to obtain. As a result, few of them spent meaningful time in Laos. Secrecy and restrictions made significant stories diffi-

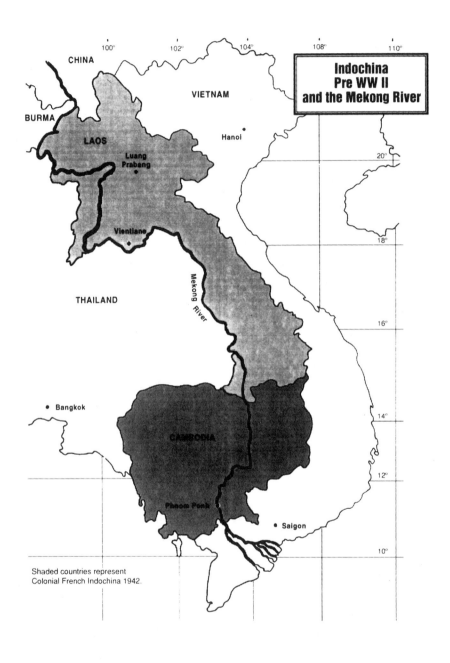

Shaded countries represent
Colonial French Indochina 1942.

Laos: Political Map

Ou Neua

PHONG

• Phong Saly

SALY

Dien Bien
• Phu

Sop Nao •

Nam Tha •

NAM THA.

Muong Sai •

Ban Nam
• Bac

Ban Houei
• Sai

LUANG PRABANG

Sam Neua •

Luang Prabang •

XIENG
KHOUANG

SAM NEUA

Ban Ban •

Phong
Savan •

Khang
Khay

Nong Het •

Sala Phou •
Khoun

Xieng Khouang •

Sayaboury •

Muong •
Kassi

Ban
Sorn •

Padong •

Tha
• Thom

• Vang Vieng

SAYABOURY

Hin •
Heup

BORIKHANE

Paksane

VIENTIANE

Vientiane •

KHAMMOUANE

• Udorn

• Mahaxay

Thakhek

Vinh •

Demillitarized
Zone*

THAILAND

Séno •

• Savannakhet

Tchepone •

Khe
Sanh •

Hué •

SAVANNAKHET

SARAVANE

WAPIKHANTHONG

Saravane •

• Ubon

Pakse

SEDONE

ATTOPEU

CHAMPASSAK

Attopeu •

SITHANDONE

• Khong Island

NORTH VIETNAM

Hanoi •

Haiphong •

GULF OF
TONKIN

*Geneva Accords separate Vietnam at
17th parallel creating North and South Vietnam,
July 22, 1954

cult to document. Most journalists concluded that the accolades and prizes would go to those who covered Vietnam. And they were correct.

We few journalists who did venture into Laos found a home at the Constellation Hotel in Vientiane, run by Maurice Cavalerie, a smiling Frenchman who always seemed to have his trouser cuffs rolled up. The Constellation, old, decrepit, hot, mosquito-infested, with one toilet per floor, had little to recommend it, but it was a home to us of the wandering press. Journalists, usually dressed alike in khaki bush jackets and trousers, often waited in the Constellation "lobby," hunched forward on the red plastic chairs, sipping cool drinks to kill the heat of the day. The press corps, accustomed to U.S. military assistance in getting to a story and the freedom allowed them in South Vietnam, found little largesse in Laos.

I had wanted to explore the limestone caves which had been used by unknown peoples as burial grounds and the high plateau called the Plaine des Jarres in Xieng Khouang Province in Military Region II, but could not get permission. On this plain, known to Americans as the "PDJ," stood mysterious brown jars that some experts concluded were burial urns of peoples long forgotten. (The Kmhmu, also called Lao Teung, believe they are the native people of Laos and claim these stone jars were carved by their heroes centuries ago before they were driven to the mountains by the Lao and Thai people when they moved south from China into Laos sometime after 1300.) The PDJ was a cherished piece of real estate with its rolling hills, moderate climate, fertile soil, and vistas of the surrounding mountains. Here on this plain was Xieng Khouang town, the population center of the province and the heart of the ancient Kingdom of Xieng Khouang.

Partly as a result of the information blackout on northern Military Region II, the press labeled the town of Long Chieng in northern Laos the "CIA Secret Base," the fighting in Laos as the "CIA Secret War," and General Vang Pao and his soldiers as a "CIA Secret Army." These "secret" labels stuck, branding the Hmong incorrectly as mercenaries and shielding their true story.

I have known the Hmong for over two decades. I have lived with them in refugee camps in Thailand. Often I was the only Westerner in these camps after sundown. Infiltrated by enemy agents, the camps were dangerous places, particularly at night. On several occasions, Hmong boys, armed with knives and clubs, slept with me on the same wooden platform bed to protect me. Several times in Ban Vinai camp, I found myself in very dangerous situations. One time, heavily armed Thai camp guards, determined to expel or jail me for entering the camp, held me captive.

Hmong interceded and put their lives on the line by protecting and sheltering me. I have been with the Hmong resistance many times. I have also spent considerable time living with Hmong families in every major Hmong community in the U.S. and in France. From 1982 to 1985, I served as an expert-consultant on Highland Lao (hilltribe people) to the U.S. Department of State's U.S. Ambassador-at-Large and Coordinator for Refugee Affairs.

Tragically for the people of Laos, too few people know about the events that took place on the historic Plaine des Jarres, or along the Ho Chi Minh Trail complex in Laos, or in the tribal villages and on the mountaintops of Laos in the first long-term "secret" war that the U.S. had ever fought. And even fewer people know about the Lao "killing fields" that took the lives of thousands after the communist takeover.

In my research, I discovered that much of what we, the public, had heard about the "secret war" in Laos during the 1960s and 1970s and of what happened to the Hmong under the communist rule of the Lao People's Democratic Republic was often rumor, innuendo, propaganda, and disinformation.

Laboriously I tracked down an assortment of individuals who had known Laos firsthand since the 1940s to piece together the history of their times. Some of these witnesses are French commandos who fought in a secret operation with the Hmong during World War II against the Japanese and through the time of the French defeat by the Viet Minh at Dien Bien Phu and after the cease-fire when the French remained to train the Royal Lao Army. Other eyewitnesses are the pilots and crews of Air America and Continental Air Services—the "CIA airlines," fighter pilots, spotter pilots, Thai and U.S. military advisors to the Hmong "special forces" and to the Royal Lao Armed Forces. Others are aid, rural development, and medical personnel from the U.S., Canada, Thailand, Australia, and the Philippines. I interviewed diplomats, cabinet ministers, and advisors in the governments of Laos, Thailand, and the U.S.

Still others I interviewed were CIA field advisors to the Hmong, CIA administrators in Southeast Asia, and CIA officials in Washington headquarters during those years of the "secret war." The CIA men who worked the Lao problems for years had remained silent. Now that many of them are retired and advancing in years, several who had key roles over long periods of time in Laos wanted to speak out, shedding light and meaningful detail on America's longest covert war—a war that ended in tragedy and defeat.

I have also extensively interviewed medical personnel involved with the care of Hmong victims of chemical-biological toxin warfare and scientists from around the world involved in identifying some of these lethal agents—some were eventually documented as man-made trichothecene mycotoxins, bleeding agents.

The principal witnesses of this history are the Hmong themselves: the men, women, and children—the students, schoolteachers, foot soldiers, officers, pilots, intelligence personnel, tribal chiefs, district officers, farmers, victims of chemical-biological toxin warfare, torture, and breeding camps, survivors of the brutal "seminar camps," and those who were repatriated to Laos who then *re-escaped* to document what happened to them when they were returned to communist Laos.

After the 1975 communist takeover of Laos, when floods of frightened people fled to Thailand, I returned many times seeking information about the fate of friends and later to learn what was going on in Laos. There was much confusion, worry, and fear. Families had been separated. Some had fled the country. Others who feared for their lives had opted to hide in Laos rather than to try to escape. Northern Thailand was dotted with refugee camps with ethnic Lao and minority peoples seeking sanctuary from the harsh regime of the new rulers in Laos. Information on life in interior Laos brought out by refugees was terrifying. Those Hmong who had sided with the Royal Lao Government and the United States during the American involvement in Vietnam and against the communists—the North Vietnamese and the Pathet Lao—were being hunted down, imprisoned, and eliminated by the Lao People's Democratic Republic, headed by Kaysone Phomvihane.

From 1976 to 1992 I visited various United Nations–sponsored refugee camps in Thailand, seeking information about the fate of those whom I had known in Laos before the communists took over. In camp after camp, I had listened to accounts by refugees from many areas in Laos. They described the events after the U.S. withdrawal and General Vang Pao's forced evacuation. They recalled the dramatic coming to power of the Marxist Lao People's Democratic Republic and the brutality that followed.

People fleeing Laos to Thailand told of concentration camps—called "seminar camps," of torture, of forced labor, and of starvation. Their homeland, Lao refugees reported, had slipped behind a formidable and sinister curtain of communism which had closed its borders to all except those who were disposed toward the new regime.

For *Tragic Mountains* I have conducted research at the Chateau de Vincennes, which houses the French Army Archives, in Vincennes, France;

the Foreign Ministry Office in Bangkok, Thailand; the National Archives in Washington, D.C.; the Lyndon B. Johnson Presidential Library in Austin, Texas; the U.S. Air Force Historical Research Center at Maxwell Air Force Base, Montgomery, Alabama; the Office of Air Force History at Bolling Air Force Base, Washington, D.C.; and the U.S. State Department Archives. Under the Freedom of Information Act, I have sought materials from the Defense Intelligence Agency, the Central Intelligence Agency, the Department of State, the U.S. Air Force and the Johnson Library.

Since U.S. activities in Laos were "secret," Laos received little meaningful U.S. press during the Vietnam War era. Americans were confused about this faraway place with reported "secret armies" of tribal people and "secret CIA bases" hidden in remote mountains. This ignorance, coupled with the barrage of disinformation and propaganda extolling the virtues of the new communist regime in Laos and the evils of the American imperialists and their "running dog" allies, turned many people away from taking a studied interest in Laos, a little known country halfway around the world, and its "primitive" tribal peoples. Most Americans are largely oblivious of the contributions made by the Hmong during the U.S. "secret war" and of their extraordinary losses.

Some Hmong who escaped the "killing fields" in Laos and became refugees have been—and continue to be—brusquely transported by jet halfway around the world to reestablish themselves in totally alien cultures of the West, resulting in the breakdown and loss of Hmong culture and life as they had known it for centuries.

In 1992, over 125,000 Hmong refugees lived in the U.S. Their resettlement has been dramatic, troublesome, and for many unsuccessful. Over 50,000 more could be on their way as the situation in Laos remains unsettled. Hmong, determined to retake their homeland from the communists, continue a ragtag but determined resistance against the communist regime of Kaysone Phomvihane. In the unrelenting fighting, communist Lao and Vietnamese forces continued into 1991 to use lethal poisons against resistance areas.

Many details of the American involvement in Laos remain secret to this day. As a result of this secrecy, some recent books on Laos that have been promoted in the media and in films have been based on limited research and with little or no input from significant participants in the events in Laos. As a result, some of these sensational tales bear little resemblance to truth, making the events and people seem more like comic book material or potential misfits and criminals than heroic individuals—American and Asian—who fought bravely and honorably.

I have interviewed Lao, Kmhmu, Mien, Lahu as well as Hmong from many factions. I interviewed communist Hmong once loyal to Phay Dang, Hmong loyal to Touby LyFong, to Vang Pao, to Pao Kao Her, and to other factions. In addition, I have interviewed Hmong from all the major clans on three continents.

Tragic Mountains focuses primarily on the lives of those Hmong who sided with the French in the 1940s, the Royal Lao government following independence, and later with the Americans during the time of the Vietnam War. They constituted the majority of the Hmong in Laos. This is the story of Hmong, communist, anticommunist, and those who just wanted simply to live traditional, peaceful lives in the mountains, who were abused and suffered under the communist regime of Kaysone Phoumvihane.

I have interviewed hundreds of Hmong—all with compelling stories. Since it was impossible to include all these testimonies, I decided to select those representative of typical experiences of many Hmong—farmers, children-soldiers, wives and war widows, students, teachers, fighter pilots, Forward Air Guides, "special forces," low-ranking soldiers, senior military officers, clan elders, Prisoners of War (POWs), anticommunist resistance fighters, survivors of chemical-biological toxin warfare, refugees in camps in Thailand, and forced repatriates to Laos who re-escaped. This, I hoped, would be the Hmong *voice*.

ACKNOWLEDGMENTS

It has taken me almost fourteen years to research and write this book. During this long, difficult journey, a number of people have stepped forward to assist. Without their support, I would not have been able to complete this enormous undertaking. First, I want to thank the Smith-Richardson Foundation and The American Spectator Educational Foundation for the research grant that was so critical during the initial stages of my work. Special thanks go to several experts: Arthur J. Dommen, the Lao historian, for reading and checking my manuscript for accuracy; Professor William Leary, University of Georgia historian on Air America, for his assistance on Air America in Laos; Professor Earl H. Tilford, Jr., Air Force historian, for checking the accuracy of the U.S. air war over Laos; Gary Crocker, an expert on chemical-biological toxins, who over the years has been very helpful; Moua Lia and Vang Tou Fu for helping me sort out Hmong history and then reading and rereading my manuscript for accuracy. To Vang Na for his steadfastness in being an accurate interpreter. Special thanks to Professor John C. Pratt, who over the years has encouraged me to continue the struggle; to the late Michael V. Forrestal, who was especially helpful in piecing together the Kennedy administration's efforts in Laos, and to General Paul Aussaresses, whose assistance in providing access to archival French records and in introducing me to Frenchmen who had worked with the Hmong during and after World War II and others in intelligence was of great importance.

To Ed Thompson, David Minter, H. Eugene Douglas, Elisabeth Weickert Douglas, Gayle Morrison, James Tyson, Elizabeth Sewell, Roy Fairfield, Joseph Goulden, John Del Vecchio, Al Santoli, Kenneth Adelman, Ray S. Cline, George Plimpton, Cordelia Jason, Charles Kinsolving, Lee Thomas, Sandy Broyard, Nancy Whitney Lutz, Stephen Kurtz, Douglas Pike, Joe P. Dunn, Julian Bach, Marianne and George Henderson, William Colby, Dean Echenberg, Norm Wagner, Mary Lou Conrad, Bob Congdon, Mary and John Taylor, Gloria Smith, John and Lucy Hartwell,

Irene Hixon Whitney, Peter and Nicole Stroh, Devon Gaffney, Dave and Ruthie Dodge, Dorothy and Bruce Dines, George and Joan Anderman, Fred and Jan Mayer, Bill Whitley, Mary Ann Drury, Craig Morrison, Lynn Kohrn, Susan Snow, Hal Sutphen, James McClatchy, Bernard François-Poncet, Jenks and Lydia Middleton, and J. Philip Smith, I thank you for your support and assistance over the years.

I also want to thank those men and women—Asian and American—whose names cannot appear in this book but whose personal recollections of events in Laos have been enormously helpful in piecing together the story of the relationships between the Hmong and the Americans, the role of Laos in the Vietnam War, and the rationale for the secrecy of this war.

I am indebted to many writers' "best friends": librarians. Particularly helpful were Archie Difante of the Alfred F. Simpson Historical Research Center, Maxwell Air Force Base, Montgomery, Alabama; Wayne Thompson and Sheldon A. Goldberg at the Office of Air Force History at Bolling Air Force Base, Washington, D.C.; David C. Humphrey, Ted Gittinger, and the staff at the Lyndon B. Johnson Library, Austin, Texas; and to Nancy Wilford, Amnesty International librarian; Daniel L. Wade, librarian at the Yale Law School Library; and Paul Holmer, Shirley Cavanagh, Liza Bennett, Claire Bennett, Tom Claire, Mary Hargan, and Helen Stauderman.

These days, writers must include among their "best friends" those who can solve computer problems. Thanks to Chris Hoeffel and Laura Swenson for always being there in a crisis.

Chris Powell and Patricia Barker took on the enormous tasks of transcribing interviews, researching obscure documents, and filing all of this in meaningful ways. Laura Swenson and Kelly Hitt diligently created the maps.

I am grateful to Professor Drew S. Days III, Director of the Schell Center for International Human Rights at the Yale Law School, for understanding the importance of holding a conference on human rights in Laos and for continuing to work on behalf of Hmong refugees in Thailand and those returned to Laos. Thanks also to Susana Martins and Paul Boudreau for indispensable work on this conference.

Thanks also to Rosemary Ozminkowski, my travel agent, who often seemed to find cheap air tickets, ones I could almost afford.

In Thailand, I always found warm and brilliant assistance from Jeranai Lunsucheep, Nongnart Phenjati, Dr. Suvit Yodmani, and William Young. I am grateful to these friends of so many years for so many reasons.

Often in my memory is my dear friend and sometime mentor Josephine Stanton, wife of Edwin Stanton, the first U.S. Ambassador to Thailand after World War II. I benefited greatly from Josie's wisdom, humanity, and deep understanding of the peoples of Southeast Asia.

To John Gallman, my editor, for your wise and sophisticated editorial suggestions and for your courage and commitment to publish this book and to the Indiana University Press marketing and sales staff, particularly Mary Beth Haas, Sue Havlish, Shelly Davis, and Kathleen Ketterman for your understanding of the importance of this book and your commitment to its wide readership.

To Buzz for his long-suffering patience and help on this book—particularly for his excellent editing suggestions and his willingness to read the many drafts of this complicated manuscript. And to Schuyler, who learned at an early age about a writer's world, human tragedy, and the beauty of Hmong friendships. And to my parents, who taught me the values of hard and responsible work and the satisfaction to be found in the often simple and unexpected.

I also want to thank the many Hmong—in Thailand refugee camps, in France, in Australia, and in the U.S.—who spent hours—sometimes days—with me relating their experiences. Between 1976 and 1992, I made more than 25 trips to the refugee camps in northern Thailand to interview escapees from the Lao People's Democratic Republic. These camps included Mae Jarim, Pua, Ban Nam Yao, Ban Vinai, Chiang Kham, Pinat Nikom, Na Pho, Nong Khai, Ban Thong. I spent time in every major Hmong community in the U.S. from the eastern states of Rhode Island and Massachusetts to the midwestern states of Michigan, Wisconsin, Minnesota, Illinois, Ohio, and Indiana, to the southern states of North Carolina and Georgia, to the western states of Montana, Colorado, Washington, and Oregon and in the large Hmong communities in the Central Valley of California.

Everywhere, Hmong families graciously extended traditional hospitality that is an integral part of Hmong culture. They always found room for me to stay the night with them in their humble homes. Long into the night, Hmong gathered to tell me about life in Laos, about terrifying escapes from Laos, about life in refugee camps, and about their deep sadness over the loss of their homelands and the deaths of many relatives. They told of recurring nightmares in which they relived the days of terror in Laos under the communists. Many admitted that they suffered tormented guilt for abandoning family members in Laos. I know of only a few families that did not lose close relatives to the communists. In spite of deep grief and mental and physical devastation and aided by a keen sense of humor and wit and the ability to laugh at themselves, the Hmong maintain a steady purpose in caring for their loved ones and in facing their uncertain future with determination.

CHRONOLOGY

1893   France assumes control over Kingdom of Laos.

1940   France surrenders to Nazi Germany. Japan takes control of French Indochina, including Laos.

1945   Lao king, under pressure, issues proclamation joining Laos to Japan's Co-Prosperity Sphere. President Roosevelt dies. Truman becomes President. Ho Chi Minh proclaims Democratic Republic of Vietnam in September. Free Lao movement forms Lao Issara, promoting total independence from France.

1946   Nationalist Chinese, sent to disarm Japanese, withdraw. French reoccupation troops enter Laos in March. In August Viet Minh establishes Resistance Committee of Eastern Laos in Hmong homelands.

1947   Laos becomes independent state within the French Union. In December George Kennan, U.S. State Department, publishes his theory on "containment of communism" which becomes U.S. policy.

1949   Laos becomes member of United Nations.

1950   In June North Korea invades South Korea. U.S. troops sent to Korea under U.N. auspices.

1952   Dwight D. Eisenhower elected President.

1953   Viet Minh invade Hmong homelands in northern Laos. Korean War ends in July. Korea remains divided at 38th parallel. France grants full independence to Kingdom of Laos as member of French Union.

1954   Viet Minh siege of French at Dien Bien Phu begins in January. Dien Bien Phu falls in early May. Geneva Conference establishes cease-fire between France and Ho's Viet Minh, divides North and South Vietnam at 17th parallel and establishes Laos as a neutral, sovereign state.

1955   U.S. military advisors provide covert training to Lao Army through Program Evaluation Office (PEO).

1959   Ho travels to Moscow seeking Soviet aid.

1960   April elections oust coalition government of Souvanna Phouma and bring in pro-American, anticommunist government. In August U.S.-trained Kong Le overthrows American-backed government, returning power to Souvanna Phouma. In October, Soviets announce aid to Souvanna Phouma's government. John Kennedy elected President.

1961   Khrushchev declares Soviet support for wars of national liberation. Geneva Conference on Laos opens in May under false assumption that a cease-fire is in place.

1962   In July Geneva Accords reaffirm Laos as a neutral state and prohibit foreign bases and troops. North Vietnam, denying it has troops in Laos, does not withdraw its soldiers.

1963   In November South Vietnamese Premier Diem and U.S. President Kennedy assassinated. Lyndon Johnson becomes President.

1964   North Vietnamese and Pathet Lao occupy Plaine des Jarres. China explodes first atomic bomb. Khrushchev ousted. Replaced by Brezhnev and Kosygin.

1965   Mao Zedong begins Great Proletarian Cultural Revolution. At Udorn Air Base in Thailand, U.S. 2nd Air Division/13th Air Force activated to provide air support in the secret fight for Laos.

1967   U.S. installs top-secret equipment atop Phou Pha Thi in Laos to provide 24-hour all-weather precision bombing against targets in northern Laos and North Vietnam.

1968   North Koreans capture USS *Pueblo.* On January 31, North Vietnamese General Giap launches Tet Offensive throughout

South Vietnam. Khe Sanh, U.S. Marine base, in northern South Vietnam under siege. Johnson announces he will not seek re-election. Richard Nixon elected President of U.S.

1969   In June Nixon announces troop withdrawal from South Vietnam. In September, Ho Chi Minh dies. In October, Senator Stuart Symington conducts secret hearings on Laos. Senator William Fulbright reveals CIA runs military operation in Laos.

1970   In February B-52 bombers used for first time in northern Laos and Henry Kissinger begins U.S. secret talks with North Vietnamese in Paris. In March, Nixon acknowledges U.S. involvement in Laos. In Cambodia, Prince Sihanouk overthrown by General Lon Nol.

1971   In June U.S. Senate passes Mansfield amendment, calling on president to withdraw all forces from Southeast Asia within nine months providing Hanoi releases American POWs. In December North Vietnam launches massive attack against Hmong base in northern Laos.

1972   Nixon visits People's Republic of China. Nixon signs Biological and Toxin Convention banning such weapons. Nixon re-elected.

1973   January 27, cease-fire agreements signed in Paris. "The Agreement on Ending the War and Restoring Peace in Vietnam" takes effect. In February, Royal Lao government signs "Agreement on the Restoration of Peace and Reconciliation in Laos." In November Congress passes War Powers Act, rendering presidential retaliation for violation of peace treaties impossible.

1974   In June last Air America plane and last U.S. military personnel leave Laos. Over 40,000 North Vietnamese troops remain in Laos. President Nixon resigns as result of Watergate scandal; replaced by Gerald Ford.

1975   In January U.S. ratifies Biological and Toxin Convention. In the same month, North Vietnam launches offensive against South Vietnam. Ford's request for military equipment for South Vietnam denied by Congress. Soviet Union ratifies Biological and Toxin Convention. North Vietnamese Army (NVA) and Pathet Lao capture Royal Lao positions. In May Cambodia falls to Pol Pot's communist Khmer Rouge. Last U.S. evacuation helicopter leaves U.S. Embassy in Saigon as South Vietnam falls to communist North Vietnam. Hmong General Vang Pao evacuated by air to Thailand; thousands of Hmong left behind. Pathet Lao publicly announce plans to "wipe out" Hmong. In June U.S. Air Force deactivated in Thailand. In July former senior Royal Lao civilians and military rounded up for "seminar" (concentration) camps. Lao border closes in August. In December the Lao People's Revolutionary Party takes power. Monarchy abolished. Laos becomes a communist state, known as the Lao People's Democratic Republic (LPDR).

1976   LPDR forces and People's Army of Vietnam (PAVN) use chemical-biological toxin warfare against Hmong in Laos. Lao royal family arrested and imprisoned in "seminar" camps. Jimmy Carter defeats Gerald Ford in presidential elections.

1977   In March, Carter administration begins talks with Vietnamese to explore U.S. recognition of communist Vietnam. Treaty of Friendship and Cooperation between the Lao People's Democratic Republic and the Socialist Republic of Vietnam reaffirms commitment to Marxism-Leninism and provides legal basis for extensive Vietnamese involvement in Laos.

1978   Communists, using conventional and chemical-biological toxin weapons, massacre Hmong in Phou Bia area. Survivors, fleeing the terror in Laos, seek sanctuary in Thailand. In December Vietnam invades Chinese-backed Pol Pot's Khmer Rouge in Cambodia.

1979   In February, China invades Vietnam. In April explosion at Sverdlovsk in Soviet Union at secret military compound releases lethal toxins, causing deaths. Soviet Union denies existence of biological research facility. Soviet Union invades Afghanistan in December.

1980   Iran takes American hostages. Ronald Reagan easily defeats

Jimmy Carter in presidential election. U.N. General Assembly adopts resolution to investigate use of chemical-biological warfare in Laos, Cambodia, and Afghanistan.

1981   Western scientists identify lethal agents being used against Hmong and in Cambodia and Afghanistan. Experts say agents used in Laos came from Soviet Union. U.S. Senate holds hearings on use of chemical-biological toxins by Vietnamese in Laos and Cambodia and Soviets in Afghanistan. Lao leaders in exile form United Lao National Liberation Front (ULNLF).

1982   U.S. House of Representatives holds Hearings on chemical-biological weapons use in Laos, Cambodia, and Afghanistan.

1984   Ronald Reagan re-elected President.

1985   Thailand begins "pushing back" Hmong refugees to LPDR.

1986   Thailand's National Security Chief reports LPDR involved in heroin trafficking.

1988   Narcotics-related corruption by LPDR causes President Reagan to determine LPDR not eligible for U.S. assistance. George Bush defeats Michael Dukakis in presidential election.

1989   Kaysone Phomvihane, head of LPDR, commends China for crackdown on students at Tiananmen Square. LPDR makes clear linkage between cooperation with U.S. on POW/MIAs and on narcotics issues. In November the Berlin Wall comes down. In December ULNLF announces creation of "Provisional Democratic Government" inside Laos with an army of some 10,000.

1990   LPDR remains major opium-heroin trafficking state. In July Lao resistance radio begins daily broadcasting. In October, LPDR jails communist cabinet vice-ministers for calling for multi-party system. *Glasnost* and *perestroika* movement dominates Eastern Europe. Soviet economic support for LPDR diminishes.

1991   In March, Fifth Lao Party Congress in Vientiane reaffirms commitment to Marxism-Leninism. In June LPDR signs agreement with Thais and U.N. to repatriate Hmong refugees from Thailand to the LPDR. Soviet Union collapses. Soviet aid to LPDR ends.

1992   LPDR remains one of world's largest producers of opium-heroin. Involvement by LPDR officials in drug trafficking persists. U.S. grants aid, offers helicopters, and upgrades diplomatic mission to LPDR. U.S. and Western commercial interests seek support for business ventures in LPDR. U.N.-Thai forced repatriation of Hmong to LPDR intensifies, with U.S. support.

U.S. Senate Select Committee holds hearings on American POWs with particular attention to Americans lost in Laos. U.S. presidential candidate Ross Perot testifies that a Pathet Lao official had admitted to him that American POWs were held in Laos.

Part One

The Fight
for the
Control of
Indochina

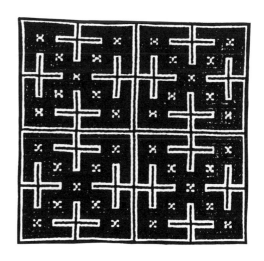

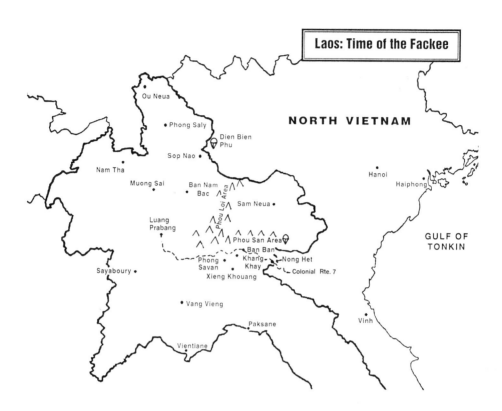

Laos: Time of the Fackee

Ou Neua

• Phong Saly

Dien Bien
Phu

Sop Nao •

NORTH VIETNAM

Nam Tha

Muong Sai
•

Ban Nam
Bac
•

Sam Neua •

Hanoi
•

Haiphong

Luang
Prabang

Phou Loi Area

Phou San Area

GULF OF
TONKIN

Sayaboury •

Phong
Savan
Xieng Khouang

Ban Ban
Khang
Khay

Nong Het

Colonial Rte. 7

• Vang Vieng

Paksane

Vinh
•

Vientiane

1.

Massacre on the Mekong

The communists know that we were the Americans' hands, arms,
feet and mouths. That's why they believe they must kill all
Hmong—soldiers, farmers, children. We suffer and die just like the
Jews in World War II, but the world ignores us.

—Ly Chai, a Hmong survivor resettled in the U.S., in a 1980 interview

The Hmong have a 4,000-year-old culture which treasures concepts of
honor, commitment, loyalty, and freedom. For years, Hmong have lived
in China, Vietnam, Laos, and Thailand. According to Catholic priest and
Hmong scholar Yves Bertrais, who spent over forty years working with
the Hmong and compiling two Hmong dictionaries, the word "Hmong"
has the connotation of "free people" or "those who must have their
freedom and independence."[1] While there are several explanations of
the origins and meanings of the often used word "Meo," to the Hmong
of Laos the word "Meo" is pejorative. The five million Hmong in China
are called "Miao." For the Lao Hmong, the words "Meo" or "Miao"
imply slavery and contempt.

While the Hmong in Laos may have seemed "primitive" to casual
observers, those who knew them well knew that these were tough,
strong, truthful, committed people whose stories, legends, and textile
arts, virtually unknown in the West, were not "primitive" and whose
social structure and customs were in many ways sophisticated.

Laos, a small, land-locked country, until recently known as the "Kingdom of a Million Elephants and a White Parasol," played a strategically
pivotal, though secret, role for both the North Vietnamese and the
Americans during their 15-year-long fight for the control of Indochina.
In Laos, the North Vietnamese built and developed their critical supply

route complex to South Vietnam and later to Cambodia, known as the Ho Chi Minh Trail.

In Laos, the Americans, with strong commitments to contain communism at the borders of "Red China" and to keep the first domino from falling, and the Hmong, with their dislike of the Vietnamese and their desire to be free, came together in a common cause to stop the North Vietnamese in their quest for hegemony throughout Indochina. The lengthy and bloody effort failed. The Americans lost and retreated across the ocean; the Hmong remained behind to be savaged by the conquerors.

During the time of the Americans, Laos was at least two countries— the river valley settlements of ethnic Lao and the highland plateaus and mountain villages of the ethnic minorities who speak their own tribal languages. The Hmong were different ethnically, culturally, religiously, and linguistically from the lowland Lao peoples who governed Laos. Historically the ethnic Lao have lived in the villages and towns located principally in the fertile lands along the Mekong River, growing wet rice and leading a life of comparative ease. Before the communist takeover, the ethnic Lao were predominantly Theravada Buddhist. The ethnic minorities, not traditionally Buddhist, practiced animism, a belief that the elements of nature have spirits which need to be respected and propitiated.

In the rugged and forested mountains, purple karsts, stalagmite formations of rocks, thrust skyward in mysterious shapes like ancient stone sentinels on guard. Constant fog draped many of the higher peaks, softening their lavenders, heavy azures, evening dark greens, and dry season browns. In these highlands, houses of split bamboo and thatch sat on the ground, unlike the stilted houses of the Lao. The tribal inhabitants wore dark clothes adorned with bright yarns, intricate needlework, beads and old silver French coins.

The Hmong expressed their history, legends, and animistic beliefs in their art which appeared in their jewelry and in the intricate and colorful designs with which they embellished their everyday dress—on belts, headdresses, purses, hats, and baby carriers. These they brought down to the markets in Luang Prabang and Vientiane to sell. In Hmong tradition, these needle arts were of much more than commercial value. Ingenuity in needlework brought status—and to a maiden perhaps an influential husband. Passed on through the centuries, these traditional designs were rich in meaning.

Babies were prized possessions. Carried everywhere in their colorful slings on the backs of adults or older siblings, the children were adorned with lavish hats of embroidery and colonial French silver coins that protected their sensitive heads and warded off evil. Older children were taught to farm, to care for animals, to embroider, to make guns and silver jewelry. Special attention was paid to teaching children clan taboos and the Hmong values of truthfulness, bravery, and loyalty.

Hmong life in the highlands was difficult, but Hmong life had never been easy. History tells us of ancient Hmong homelands in China and of a people proud and fiercely independent with a culture dating back to at least 2,000 B.C. Over the centuries the Chinese tried to conquer and control its minorities, but many Hmong resisted.

In the eighteenth century the Hmong had entered into a fateful understanding with the Chinese. Many Hmong lived in the mountains in south China and the expanding Chinese wanted Hmong lands. Never able to subdue militarily the fiercely independent Hmong, or *Miao* as the Chinese called them, the Chinese generals had tricked them instead.

Sonom, the last recorded Hmong king in China, and his entire court were prevailed upon to surrender with honor on the condition that peace would come. The king and his court agreed to be taken to Peking where, upon their arrival, they discovered a plot: they were to be tortured and killed as part of a festival. The Hmong military leader with the delegation begged the Chinese Emperor for the life of young King Sonom. He protested that the Hmong could have sold their lives at a high price, yet they surrendered upon the assurance of the emperor's mercy. He spoke in vain.

At a signal from the emperor, the tortures began. With gags in their mouths, King Sonom, his advisors, his doctors, and his aunt were cut into small pieces. Their heads were exhibited in cages with signs designating their names and titles. On following days, those of lesser rank were executed. Of this delegation only a few survived and they were given to the victorious Chinese officers as slaves.[2]

To remain conqueror, the victor kept the vanquished weak and unable to resist. The attempts by the Chinese to separate the Hmong into groups and to destroy Hmong culture were effective. Eventually, Chinese generals, assigned to subdue the Hmong, split them into groups and forced them to wear identifying clothing—in a sense branding them. This may explain why there are Green Hmong, White Hmong, Black Hmong, Flowery Hmong, and Striped Hmong with dialectic and sartorial differences.[3]

The Chinese forbade Hmong upon penalty of death to use their written language. Women cleverly kept their alphabet alive by including its letters in intricate, hieroglyphic-like patterns passed on generation after generation from mother to daughter to adorn tribal dress. During the years of fleeing and disruption, however, the Hmong lost the ability to use their written language. Many twentieth-century Hmong women, who still painstakingly embroider or batik ancient symbols and ideographs of historical events, are not able to read or write the language which their needles preserved. As a result of continued Chinese attempts to subjugate the remaining independent-minded Miao, many clan leaders moved their people southward into North Vietnam, Laos, and eventually into Thailand.

These peoples, who practiced slash-and-burn farming, never considered integrating into the main ethnic societies of their new homelands until after World War II. They practiced their own customs, spoke their own language, and followed their own religious beliefs. In the 1960s and 1970s, Hmong General Vang Pao promoted the Lao language, respect for Lao culture and religion, and integration into the dominant Lao society.

Among the Hmong who migrated from China to Laos beginning in the nineteenth century, the major clans include: Chang (or Cheng), Chue, Fang (or Feng), Hang, Her, Kue, Moua, Ly (or Lee), Lo (or Lao or Lor), Pha, Thao, Vang, Vue, Yang, and Xiong. Most continue the tradition of placing the clan name first with given names following. Hmong women keep the clan names of their fathers, although once married they belong to the clan of their husbands as do their children.

In the name Vang Pao, Vang is the clan name and Pao, meaning "to protect," is the given name. In Moua Chia, Moua is the clan name and Chia, meaning "scissors," is the given name. Names are often descriptive. Chee means "to create," Lia is "red," and Lue means "to wave." Some are named after objects: Chue means "bell," Chou is "a rice-steamer," and Lhi is "moon." In addition, Hmong often carry descriptive nicknames that become "official" names. Na, meaning "mouse," was given to a tiny baby boy. Though he grew up not to be tiny at all, everyone still knows him by "Na," the "mouse."

A Hmong man, after marriage, several children, and establishing himself with fields, is given an "adult" or ordination name by his father-in-law or mother-in-law in a special ceremony that confers upon him a special name, recognizing his status as an adult member of the community. In the name Moua Cher Pao—Moua is the clan name, Pao is the given name, and Cher is the ordination name which precedes the given name.

Not every male is given an ordination name. General Vang Pao, the military and Hmong tribal leader for the past 30 years, and Moua Lia, who became the superintendent of schools in Military Region II in Laos, have no ordination names. The Hmong say that these cases were exceptions—they did not need adult names.

7   Massacre on the Mekong

When the Americans arrived in Laos in the late 1950s, Laos, "The Kingdom of a Million Elephants and a White Parasol," was newly independent from France. King Savang Vatthana, the reigning Lao sovereign, traced his lineage to the beginning of recorded history in Laos in 1353 and beyond back to the eighth century. Buddhist temples with glittering upturned finials, saffron-robed monks with alms bowls, white-garbed Lao officials with their rows of garish medals and ribbons, embassies sprouting antennas, and the Lao version of the Arc de Triomphe backgrounded international intrigue, underdevelopment, and tropical ennui. The Laos of this time gave few clues that it had once been a major Southeast Asian power. Vientiane, its major city with a population of about 70,000, was a dusty, humid, uninspired town hugging the north bank of the Mekong River.

In the 1960s and 1970s, the great powers—the Soviets, Americans, and Chinese—and the not-so-great powers had established embassies in Vientiane to pursue their interests in the spoils of Laos. Embassy compounds, heavily guarded, stood as reminders of the power struggles that were being played out in Southeast Asia. Communist Pathet Lao headquarters was patrolled by several dour-looking armed guards who protected the officials of their third of the 1962 Geneva conference-contrived tripartite government. The Pathet Lao claimed control of the two northeastern provinces of Phong Saly and Sam Neua; the royalists and neutralists claimed the rest of the country.

Embassies from the Eastern and Western blocs entertained each other with flourish and high-minded toasts that mocked reality. President Kennedy was dead, but some American officials honored the false hope held by Kennedy and his men that the Soviet Union had no interest in Laos other than its neutralization. The U.S. mission excelled in air-conditioned offices, acronyms, and antennas. While the U.S. ambassador approved U.S. airstrikes in Laos, the international intelligence community stationed in Vientiane agreed in the mid-1960s upon a ten-kilometer area around this intrigue-filled town as a safe zone—one in which there would be no violence, no assassination. Intelligence agents, particularly those from communist countries, devoted considerable energies to espionage, to counterintelligence, to luring potential defectors, and to successfully recruiting a cadre of young, educated Lao and Hmong. The chatter of the international diplomatic community was filled with rumors of coups and counter-coups. Many laughed at the comic strip shenanigans. Laos, this "Land of Oz," as some called it, consistently produced the unusual, bizarre, and unthinkable.

Young Caucasians, many long-haired and dirty Americans, loitered in the streets and in the lobbies of cheap hotels, hoping to connect with their next purchase of marijuana, opium, or heroin. After the French and their opium monopoly were gone, others—Lao, Chinese, Corsicans—had moved into this lucrative business. Hmong grew opium poppies and used opium as a natural medication for diarrhea, stomach disorders, fevers, and pain, but they were not involved in the laboratory conversion of opium into heroin or in international drug trafficking. Those in control would never allow minorities to participate. There was money to be made—big money—in the narcotics business that flourished out of the Golden Triangle, an area where Laos, Burma and Thailand border. Processing opium into heroin and trafficking it belonged to Kuomintang soldiers, remnants of Chiang Kai-shek's army still holding out in the mountains of Burma and Thailand—and corrupt Lao, Thai, and Chinese.[4] In the 1960s, however, opium and heroin were cheap and easy to obtain by anyone in Vientiane—even by children of Americans working in Laos.

A curious assortment of Americans worked in Laos. There were those dressed in tan bush outfits, who ran the extensive USAID programs. There were Air America, Bird Air, and Continental Air Services pilots and their crews. There were also the invisible people: the CIA paramilitary advisors and the U.S. military men on temporary duty assignments to the U.S. Embassy in Vientiane who helped to direct the air war in Laos. These men were ordered to avoid contact with strangers, particularly journalists.

The clasped-hands symbol of the United States aid mission to Laos appeared everywhere—on electric ceiling fans in hotel rooms, open-air restaurants, and office buildings, on bags of cement, sacks of rice, furniture, medicine, and gasoline cans.

To make life more comfortable for the American USAID workers and their families who were to "develop" and "save" Laos, the U.S. built a large compound outside of Vientiane at Kilometer 6. This settlement, known as "K-6," included an olympic-size swimming pool, air conditioned Western-style ranch houses, a gymnasium, a school, and a paved road, a luxury in Laos.

One could learn something about the "secret war" being fought in northern Laos in the bar-restaurants in Vientiane, where cold San Miguel and Budweiser beer, along with aged French wine, could be purchased cheaply. Here American civilian pilots, their crews, and paramilitary advisors hung out and talked of their problems. Tanned American flyers, wearing Rolex and Seiko watches and heavy gold link chains, complained of unpredictable weather and dangerous air strips. They talked about "Lima sites," dry and wet season offensives, the NVA (North Vietnamese Army) on the PDJ (Plaine des Jarres), special operations, and Long Chieng. If they thought outsiders were listening, they called Long Chieng "Happy Valley," "20 Alternate," or just "Alternate."

Always they talked about the "little guys," as the Americans called the hilltribe people, caught in the tough fighting. They complained that many Lao soldiers were hopeless, running away before or during a fight, but the "little guys"—the only ones who could be counted on to fight the communists—managed to hang on to fight another day, time and time again. And no conversation about the "little guys" was complete without new stories about the exploits of the "big little guy"—Hmong General Vang Pao, the Royal Lao Army commander of Military Region II.

They talked about the "Chi-Com" (Chinese Communist) roads that extended from the Chinese border south into central Laos, protected by Chinese antiaircraft guns; of NVA battalions, well-equipped, disciplined, and determined, pushing brazenly in from North Vietnam along National Route 7 through Xieng Khouang Province and the PDJ, the Hmong homelands, to the heartland of Laos.

They talked about Hanoi's strategy to occupy the eastern provinces of Laos in order to protect its vital supply and troop reinforcement route— the Ho Chi Minh trail complex in Laos—which supplied the Viet Cong in South Vietnam. Reconnaissance pilots reported that much of the trail system had been converted into an all-weather road system. Portions of the trail were ingeniously camouflaged by netting covered with vegetation, making it difficult for pilots to spot convoys.

They talked about Hanoi's successful denial that it had troops or operations in Laos. Part of Hanoi's success, they argued, was the failure of the naive, stupid, corrupt, and ham-strung International Control Commission (ICC), established by the Geneva Conference, to investigate cease-fire violations.

The communist Pathet Lao (also known as the P.L.) described themselves as "peace-loving people" whose soldiers became the "people's patriotic defense forces" or "volunteers" who cleared "bandits" from areas to "liberate" the suffering people from the "imperialistic" and "aggressive" Americans who sought to establish military bases in Laos in order to attack China. It was doubtful that the Pathet Lao were capable of such sophistication without the aid of their comrades in Hanoi, Peking, and Moscow.

While it was impossible for journalists to know the military situation, much could be learned by watching the skies. Daily, U.S. C-47s, C-123s, H-34 helicopters, Helio-Couriers, Pilatus Porters, and small Cessnas took off from Vientiane's Wattay airport for destinations in the highlands. Frequently, gray-green camouflaged U.S. fighter jets, usually in pairs, lifted off airbases across the Mekong River in Thailand and streaked low across the horizon pulling behind them droning wails of speed. Sometimes within minutes, these same aircraft returned and like birds in autumn flew low and nestled effortlessly onto one of the several joint U.S.-Thai airbases constructed in the rice paddies of Thailand. Sometimes, only a single jet returned and like a single Canada goose whose mate has been shot down, the lone jet's high whine mourned a casualty.

Occasionally, the giant HH-3E and HH-53 rescue helicopters—called "Jolly Green Giants"—like airborne water buffalo ploddingly whopped across the Mekong from bases in Thailand. They, too, headed northeast—toward General Vang Pao's Region II and the secret war.

After the defeat of the United States in Southeast Asia in 1975, the communists came to power in South Vietnam, Cambodia, and Laos. The men in Hanoi took control, directly or indirectly, of Laos. While the Vietnam War was over for the Americans, the fighting continued for the indigenous people, as the new regimes tried to eliminate opposition. The United States paid little attention to the plight of its former allies. Most Americans wanted to forget the conflict which had divided the nation. For many Americans, the only reminder of that war was the resettlement in the United States of tens of thousands of refugees from Laos, Cambodia, and Vietnam.

Soon after the Jimmy Carter administration came to power in 1977, it actively sought U.S. restoration of diplomatic recognition of Vietnam. Assistant Secretary of State Richard Holbrooke initiated talks with Vietnamese officials in March 1977. In June 1978, Vietnam joined Comecon, the East European economic community. On December 25, 1978, Vietnam invaded and occupied Pol Pot's Cambodia, installing a pro-Hanoi government and pushing the murderous Pol Pot regime into the countryside. In now unified Vietnam, repression against the large Chinese community created Chinese refugees, known as the "boat people," who had begun to flee Vietnam in late 1978. In February 1979, China invaded Vietnam, but the tough Vietnamese military mauled the Chinese forces. That same month, Carter's attention turned to Iran where anti-Shah forces threatened a revolution which endangered some 35,000 Americans who worked there. In the late summer of 1979, neither the White House nor most

Americans were interested in Southeast Asia. Few knew anything about Laos, much less about the Hmong.

* * *

On the morning of July 27, 1979, I stood on the banks of the Mekong River in northern Thailand. Across the river was Laos. As I looked at the swirling, reddish muddy waters, I thought about recent times when I had seen the bloated bodies of Hmong women and girls—slain by the communist Pathet Lao and Vietnamese river patrols—held afloat by their heavy and tough hemp skirts snagged in drifting debris. I thought about the genocide taking place in the interior of Laos. I thought about the terror and the political implications of the deadly and mysterious new weapons—the poison rains—being used so effectively against these friends of the United States by the Lao communist regime and its mentors in Hanoi.

Mists miraged the expanding waters of the river. Through my binoculars, I searched the grayness for the people whose sounds I heard, but found no one. The sun finally forced the mists to retreat, revealing a group of about two hundred Hmong—some men, but mostly women and children—sitting silently by the edge of a narrow sandbar river-island, far from the Thai bank and safety.

Later I saw them gathering vines to weave into ropes which they attached to patches of river reeds to make a link to shore and safety. The river was visibly rising and storm clouds hung over the mountains to the north. They could all drown if the river rose much higher. There was little time.

Believing themselves out of Lao territory, they built fires and boiled water in old U.S. Army canteens. Women removed their dark blouses, leaving themselves bare-breasted, and, with sticks for frames, made cloth shelters for the sick, the babies, and the old women. I saw them force fingers full of rice into the small mouths of their children—many only skeletons. Adults did not eat, saving the last of the rice for the children.

Thai soldiers appeared on the Thai bank, with a machine gun bolted to the body of a jeep. Soon two Thai patrol boats landed on the island. I knew they were there to inform the Hmong leader that he must return to Laos. Thailand had been accepting refugees from Laos, but recently Thai authorities had cracked down, saying that there were too many refugees in Thailand. The Thai ordered the Hmong not to cross into Thailand, but to return to Laos. I later learned that the Hmong told the Thai soldiers that they would build bamboo rafts and leave during the night. The

Hmong huddled on the Thai side of the island, hoping that soldiers from the higher Lao banks would not see them. Later that afternoon, Thai soldiers in boats slashed the vines, severing the Hmong lifeline to freedom.

Night fell. The Hmong took up guard. They had no food and the river was still rising.

Daybreak. The Hmong continued to build rafts, not, as the Thai soldiers wanted, to cross back to Laos, but to go downstream in the hope of passing undiscovered into Thailand beyond the sight of the Thai patrol. I knew the Hmong realized that if they were forced back to Laos they would all be killed—including the children.

About midday, a man in a boat paddled from the Thai side to the island, ignoring the warning of the Thai soldiers. The Hmong leader gave him a note to take to Vang Yee, chief of the Hmong refugees in the nearby Ban Vinai refugee camp, just inside the northern Thai border in Loei Province. The note was turned over to me and I read it. It told of their two months' trek out of Laos and of their desperate situation now that the Thai soldiers would not allow them to cross into Thailand and safety. The note urgently requested that the chief at the camp obtain permission for the 189 on the island to enter Thailand before it was too late.

I took the message to Vang Yee. He read it, folded it into a small square, and walked away from me.

The next day was hot. Many Hmong on the island appeared to be sick or starving. Through field glasses, I saw those who were able eating grass and drinking boiled water. Thai soldiers came again and insisted that they leave that night. The Hmong—so I was told—explained that they did not have enough rafts to ferry all the people back across to the Lao side, but the Thais insisted.

The following day I saw less movement from the blouse lean-tos. The waters of the Mekong lapped ever higher on the island. As I watched the island prisoners, I thought about the power—physical and geopolitical—of this mighty river.

The Mekong flows for thousands of miles from the high mountains of Tibet, through the western edge of China's Yunnan Province that borders northern Burma, into western Laos, through Cambodia and into Vietnam. It tumbles down mountain rapids, cuts into hillsides, and sweeps through rich valleys, dragging fertile soils southward to spill onto lands populated by Shan, Lao, Thai, Cambodians and Vietnamese. As the river reaches lower altitudes, it sometimes widens as it meanders through wide valleys to touch the historical Asian towns and cities of Luang Prabang, Vientiane, and Phnom Penh before flowing into the South China Sea.

One of the great rivers of the world, the Mekong had escaped white man's probing until quite recently. It was not until April 1867 that a French exploration team, headed by Commander Doudart de Lagrée, passed this very spot in its attempts to chart the Mekong for France in anticipation that this river would provide for the French empire a trade route to the riches of China. As I thought about the French expedition struggling along this portion of the river, I realized how little had changed in the ensuing hundred years. The Lao side of the Mekong remained inhospitable with its mountains edging dramatically to the riverbank. The river, now in a torrent due to flooding, threatened those in her waters and along her banks, just as it had threatened the French expedition. Large stretches of the Mekong remained unnavigable for anything but small boats; no bridge spanned the river as it passed through Thailand and Laos; shorelines which the French described as under the jurisdiction of "petty kings" were little changed now in the mid-20th century; and the Mekong, at least this stretch of it, remained as unfamiliar to most of the world as it was in the days of Lagrée and his French expedition.

Under the communist regime, the Mekong River had become a Berlin Wall, dividing communist Laos from non-communist Thailand. Heavily armed Vietnamese and Pathet Lao patrols—sometimes in helicopters—shot and killed those fleeing across the Mekong to Thailand.

On the fifth day, the morning sky brought signs of another torrid day. The Mekong continued to rise. The Thai soldiers remained vigilant. Many bamboo rafts had been built on the island. The stranded Hmong apparently believed that Vang Yee would send help soon—that he would be able to convince the Thai authorities to allow the people to leave the river island to safety in Thailand. They did not know what I knew—that Vang Yee, once a military leader and teacher, was now only a helpless and vulnerable detainee in a squalid refugee camp.

As I stood helplessly on the bank gazing at those marooned on the island, I remembered the stories told me by so many Hmong who, like those out in the river, had fled Laos under the most terrifying circumstances. Drumming in my head were the words of one young Hmong man who only recently had said to me: "I feel so sad for my wife. She's sick from the poison rains, yet she cares for my brother's five children. The youngest is four. He's so weak he cannot stand; she must carry him strapped to her back. Our baby is tied to her breast. My brother is dead from the poison gas. His wife disappeared while searching for food. I often think of my American friends. In Laos when we were fighting together, they gave me their addresses but I've lost them. We've been running and hiding for four years in Laos. I have nothing left. It seems so long ago General Vang Pao and the Americans left. Now the fighting is even more difficult, with so few weapons and no one to help us. We Hmong are so tired, so frightened. So many are dead. We Hmong are so pitiful.''

Two days later—on August 2, 1979—I heard that a group of thirty to forty Pathet Lao soldiers had landed on the river island. Shooting broke out and the Hmong were massacred. I never learned whether there were any survivors.

Later that day, I reported this to Chief Vang Yee in Ban Vinai camp. He had known from the beginning, I suspected, that there was no hope for those trapped in the river. Now, when I reported that it was all over, he looked north beyond me into the distance toward Laos. Finally, he returned from that reverie. ''We Hmong fight, work like buffalo, run, starve, and die—and no one knows.'' He said it softly and it lingered on the sticky air as an epitaph for all those slain that day.

*   *   *

This was not my first trip to Ban Vinai refugee camp. I had been here many times since the camp was constructed in 1976. It was now the largest Hmong settlement in Southeast Asia holding some 40,000 refugees. The Laos of yesteryear with its ''never mind'' attitude, Chinese gold shops, French wine and American beer, alming monks, and royal family was no more.

Gone were the spangle and daring of American adventure of the 1960s and 1970s. Gone were the sleek American jets that once screamed overhead. Gone were the daring fighter pilots who flew down North Vietnam's Red River Valley in ''Operation Rolling Thunder'' to strike targets in ''Route Pack Six.'' Gone were the American chopper rescue pilots and their crews who often defied enemy guns to pick up downed airmen. Gone were ''Alley Cat'' and ''Cricket,'' airborne electronic command planes that circled twenty-four hours a day over northern Laos to direct U.S. air strikes. Gone were the American advisors and their vast stocks of supplies. Gone were the power and the glory of U.S. hi-technology and the ''can do'' attitude.

Where were the Americans who worked and played in Laos during ''the American time''? Where were the USAID workers and their families who once inhabited the modern American compound at Kilometer 6? Where were the Bird Air, Air America, and Continental Air Service pilots with their heavy gold link bracelets, their big salaries, and their daring? Where were the Raven spotter pilots who flew clandestinely in Laos to direct airstrikes in support of Hmong soldiers on the ground? Where were the CIA paramilitary advisors, with their gusto for counter-insurgency, women, drink, and freedom, who had worked intimately with the Hmong since 1961? Had they just walked away and abandoned their friends of 15 years?

Here in this refugee camp was the pitiful human residue of the U.S.-backed war in Laos. Here were some of the "little guys" who had survived the holocaust in Laos. They were crying for help and few were listening.

The Hmong who had worked so closely with the Americans repeatedly asked for their American friends. They wanted to find their CIA advisors like Colonel Billy, Kayak, Bamboo, Mr. Clean and American civilian pilots who had worked long, difficult years with them and who had shared fears, triumphs, and defeats. They thought that those who knew them best would surely help them; those who knew them to be people of honor who could testify that they had been trained in intelligence by the U.S. and that the Hmong word was reliable. They were certain that these men—as they had done in the past—could get desperately needed food and medicines to those still in Laos. Sadly, the names by which the Hmong had known them were only code-names or nick-names. Locating their American friends was impossible.

Hmong clan leaders in Ban Vinai begged for someone to alert the world to the atrocities taking place in their homelands, particularly the poison rains. They were sure that if the world knew about these poisons from the sky, then responsible countries would force the Vietnamese and Pathet Lao to stop.

There were Americans in Ban Vinai camp as relief workers, but the Hmong said they were different from the ones they had known in Laos. Many were young, with little knowledge of the history of Laos or of the Hmong. Many had sympathy for the Pathet Lao and North Vietnamese. This came as a great shock to the Hmong who, with Americans, had been fighting these forces for more than fifteen years.

*   *   *

I entered the bowels of the camp into a tangle of refugee huts. Here, where outsiders seldom ventured, the narrow and steep paths, made slippery and treacherous by the rain, often forced those of us who ventured out to crawl.

Red sticky mud slopped against my legs and sucked on my feet. Children, naked except for an occasional festive tribal hat and neck amulets of old French coins, beads and animal teeth, clung to mothers' nipples, cried, or played in the ocher mud as other children might play in seashore sands. Dark adult eyes glared from darker doorways. Men in black tribal dress sat on tree stumps, staring. For years, I had seen these same men sitting on these same stumps. I noticed a handsome Hmong grandmother wearing a dirty Western-donated T-shirt that read, "I Can Make It With You." Since she was pre-literate, she could not read the words that mocked her dignity.

Ahead, the drums of Hmong shamans beat out impending death for those who were victims of the poison rains. I followed the quickening beat of one down into a small valley. As I approached, moaning and sobbing filtered through a wailing musical lament played on a bamboo pipe. In the thatch darkness, a boy child lay motionless on a makeshift bamboo stretcher. He was dead. His father and uncle, kneeling beside him on the floor, rubbed his stiff body. All their other children had already been killed either by mysterious poisons or by the communist guns in Laos. I paid my respects and eased out of the crowded hut.

I spent the day interviewing recent arrivals from Laos. Time passed quickly. Soon the hazy monsoon sun dropped behind the nearby hill, signaling imminent darkness and a camp curfew which extended from late dusk until sunrise. Night was dangerous in this camp. Refugees were slain in their huts by mysterious assailants who were never caught. Thai soldiers and police, assigned to keep order, seemed helpless or, more likely, uninterested. The Hmong, stripped of all weapons by Thai authorities, were defenseless against those who prowled the camp to murder their leaders. It was believed that communist agents slipped into the camp under cover of darkness, undetected by inept guards, to kill at will.

Like the refugees, I had to observe curfew. I walked to the thatch building on the hill behind the hospital—sleeping quarters offered me by a camp doctor. A purpleness slipped over this valley, caused, I thought, by the smoke from the ubiquitous charcoal fires sputtering beneath pots of rice gruel which became trapped in the heavy moisture of the monsoon season.

My hut, unused for some time, reeked of mold, making breathing difficult. Yards of spider webs, laced with dust and grime, filled all corners and hung from the ceiling. Alerted by my intrusion, beetles scurried noisily about in the thatch. Sleeping in refugee camps was always difficult. I knew tonight would be no different. All the troublesome ingredients were present—bugs, mosquitoes, heat, and worry.

The next day dawned hot. Today, I would interview more survivors. I made my way to the camp hospital. Hundreds of Hmong—young and old—littered the grounds, lying beneath trees and bushes to avoid the sun. On the cement slab outside the hospital buildings, Hmong, most wearing torn, faded, and soiled tribal clothes, were lying in neat rows. Inside, two and three Hmong, many dirty and in rags, rested on each high wooden slab that passed as a hospital bed. Beneath each and in all aisles other Hmong—many mothers suckling scrawny babies—waited silently, staring.

Refugee workers ladled out rice to adults who tended to naked and cadaverous children whose waxen faces were drawn so tightly that their teeth were bared. Parents forced rice between their tight lips. The children could only vomit it back and cry thin wails of impending death. Everyone was weak, even those tending to gravely ill relatives. Fear dominated and the pervasive silence prompted me to think that there must have been such a quiet in Nazi concentration camps when prisoners were forced to look upon and care for those who had been brutalized.

A young Philippine doctor moved from bed to bed, followed by teenage Hmong boys who, without any experience or schooling, played critical roles as para-medics. The thin, dark-haired doctor occasionally closed his eyes. He was either searching his mind for medical clues that would allow him to treat these sick people—or he was praying.

Outside Ward I, a 13-year-old girl, eyes rolled back, rested on a straw mat. Blood flowed from her nose and mouth. Bubbles of perspiration dotted her face and neck. Her mother, fear in her dull, dark eyes, rubbed the child and beat the heavy air with a thatch fan. She called for help from a passing boy medic. He stopped briefly to examine the girl. In a few minutes, he returned with the doctor who knelt on the cement, his leg resting in the expanding pool of blood from her mouth. He ordered an I.V.

As the Hmong medic slipped the I.V. needle into her thin arm, the doctor stood erect and looked about him at the scores of Hmong patients, many of whom were watching him. I asked him the nature of this girl's medical problem. With a fatigued expression and a shrug of his shoulders, he admitted that he did not know, but that she would die.

He too had heard the escapees' reports of the mysterious and lethal poisons dropped from the skies by communist planes, or launched from enemy mortars, or placed in food and water supplies by Pathet Lao and Vietnamese soldiers. In spite of his impossible medical task, he took photographs of the survivors, as did I. Neither the doctor nor I had any idea what poisons were being used. We wondered if it were biological warfare. If that were the case, were we all exposed? Would we become ill and die as the Hmong were dying? Would we be carriers of unknown and untreatable epidemics that would infect other populations?

As I watched the doctor, several European and Philippine nurses, and the Hmong medics trying desperately and unsuccessfully to save lives, I thought about all those who refused to believe Hmong reports of atrocities in Laos. Some disbelievers claimed that the Hmong were seeking sympathy in an effort to persuade the U.S. to re-arm them. Others insisted that the Hmong were merely suffering from traditional diseases such as dengue fever, hemorrhagic fever, malaria, T.B. and worms. Still others declared that they were the primitive dupes of the CIA which had set them up to discredit the communist government of Laos. Others said that it was all propaganda; that neither the North Vietnamese, who directly controlled Laos, nor the Soviets, who backed the Vietnamese, were capable of such inhumane actions. And a few denied that the Soviets could be involved since they had signed the 1972 Biological and Toxin Weapons Convention that banned the use of such weapons.

Clan relatives of another skeletal girl who had just died at the hospital arrived to take her away. I watched her funeral party snake down the hill to the jumble of refugee huts where she would be prepared for burial on the hillside at the edge of the camp. Within minutes after the procession disappeared into the camp, the sound of her death drum, vigorous and angry in its rhythm, questioning the soul—which way to go, which way to turn—reverberated in the oppressive air.

As I stood on the hill listening to the driving, unrelenting drum beats echoing each other from various sections of the camp, I knew that the truth of what had happened in Laos since World War II and after the communist victory in 1975 was in this camp.

When I asked older Hmong men to explain the events that initiated this terror, many answered that their tragic story had begun during the time of the "Fackee," as the Hmong call the French.

2.

The Time of the Fackee

During 1945, when the Japanese . . . gained control of Asia, some
French survivors took refuge in the mountains; the Hmong, without
thought for the consequences, went to the aid of these white fugi-
tives. In keeping with their traditional hospitality, they welcomed
them, nursed them, fed them, and hid them in caves so the Japanese patrols would not see them. The Hmong did not know that
this action, which for them was strictly humanitarian, would pro-
voke political consequences to the extent of bringing about the
deaths of thousands of them, and destroying the social and economic balance that they had attempted to preserve through the
ages.

—Doua Yang, "The Story of Why the Hmong Escaped from Laos"

The French had penetrated Indochina by 1858. By 1864, they had an-
nexed Cochin China (southern Vietnam), and established a protectorate
over Cambodia. By 1884, they had successfully integrated Tonkin (northern Vietnam) and Annam (central Vietnam) into protectorates. It was not
until near the end of the nineteenth century that Laos came under
French colonial rule.

French rule rested lightly on Laos. The Lao elite gave advice to the
French, who in turn used their services and those of the various tribal
groups. The French encountered few problems in Laos. One arose when
the French used Vietnamese as civil servants. Intense dislike and mistrust
of the Vietnamese chafed the Lao. Otherwise, French control over Laos
prior to World War II was relatively peaceful. The French found it necessary to use military force only three times, once against the Hmong, led
by Paj Chai, who with a combination of charisma and mysticism, rallied
his kinsmen to fight the French in 1919. This group called itself Chao

Fa—"Prince of the Sky." The rebellion was short-lived, and by the 1920s most Hmong considered their relationship with the colonial French to be to their advantage. The Hmong and other minority groups, whose combined populations outnumbered the ethnic Lao who ran the country, were generally disliked and discriminated against by lowland Lao and by the Vietnamese. This attitude was absent in the colonial French. By the 1930s, many Hmong believed that since the French had education, an advanced economy, laws, a military capability to provide security, and technology—particularly aviation—they could guide them to a better life and improve their status in Laos.

While colonial French authorities and Hmong leaders had worked out a relationship amenable to both parties, there was still discrimination against and mistreatment of the Hmong by Lao and Vietnamese bureaucrats, whose perceived aggressive Vietnamese personality and hostility toward the Hmong conflicted with Hmong values. Hmong observed that when the French brought Vietnamese soldiers with them, the French did not allow the Vietnamese to harm them. However, when Vietnamese soldiers came without French officers, they killed Hmong animals, entered Hmong houses, took whatever they wanted without paying, and called them insulting names.

Nong Het, nestled in a 4,500-foot mountain pass on the Vietnam-Lao border, was a major market town, a French military outpost, a center of Hmong culture, and the home of the young Hmong chieftain Touby of the Ly clan. Educated in French schools in Vinh in northern Vietnam and in Vientiane, Touby and his brothers were the first formally educated Hmong in the area. Touby, who modified his clan name of Ly to LyFong, was the pro-French Hmong leader in the area. (Frenchmen called him Touby. Later the Americans would call him Touby LyFong, placing his given name first in Western style.) Hmong who claimed allegiance to Touby lived both in Laos and in northern Vietnam. National boundaries were unknown to the Hmong who farmed these highlands. In Nong Het, Hmong, who had lost their written Hmong language many years before, studied in French in an open-air school and became knowledgeable about the world. Touby believed that only through education could his people achieve equality and respect. This town of approximately 3,000 people was most proud of its school.

Not all Hmong were loyal to Touby or pro-French. One anti-French and anti-Touby Hmong was Phay Dang, from the Lo clan. A bloody dispute had erupted between the Ly and Lo clans over which clan should receive the honor of being Tasseng, a district officer in charge of many villages. This dispute had its origins with the Hmong king, Lo Pa Sy. Sometime in the mid-1800s, Lo Pa Sy brought his followers out of China to escape persecution. In Laos, he and his son Lo Blia Yao, who reigned as the Hmong leader from 1920 to 1935, were acknowledged by the French as the local authority and given the prestigious and coveted title of Tasseng. As Tasseng, the Lo clan leader reported directly to the French authorities, giving the Lo clan the highest possible status among the Hmong. The Lo clan assumed that clansman Phay Dang, who was next in line, would become Tasseng following the death of Blia Yao. Phay Dang even made a pilgrimage to Luang Prabang, the royal capital, to see Lao Prince Phetsarath Ratanavongsa to convince him to plead his case with the French. So important was the title of Tasseng that Phay Dang gave the Lao prince a gift more powerful than money: his father's rhinoceros horn, which was believed to hold extraordinary protective powers. Phay Dang's pilgrimage and gift were unavailing. In 1938, Touby, in his twenties, was appointed Tasseng by the French. The Lo clan had lost prestige, and Phay Dang developed a hatred for Touby that would consume him for a lifetime and result in deadly battles between the Ly and Lo clans. Phay Dang's passionate dislike of the French and of Touby drove him to become guide and collaborator for the Japanese and the anti-French Vietnamese, soon to be called the Viet Minh.

The Hmong also had problems with a Lao named Phoumi Vongvichit who had gained influence by becoming secretary to the French Resident in Xieng Khouang Province, a rich agricultural area with a large Hmong population, and a tax collector for the French. In his tax-collecting role, Phoumi Vongvichit charged more than ten times what the French ordered. When Hmong tried to complain to the French Resident about this Lao's corruption and cruelty to those who could not pay, Vongvichit blocked their access to the French. The Hmong finally managed to speak directly to the French Resident about him. The French were about to take action against Vongvichit when the Japanese invaded. Vongvichit immediately allied himself with the Japanese garrisoned at Xieng Khouang and became one of their most important collaborators.[1]

* * *

In 1940, France's surrender to the Nazis brought the Vichy collaborators to power. Under the Vichy regime, the French military and civilian apparatus stayed in place in Indochina. Frenchmen were instructed to do nothing to interfere with Japanese military activities and administrative desires. Soon Japan controlled all of French Indochina, the former British colonies of Malaya and Burma, and, important for Laos, neighboring Thailand through a collaborating regime.

France, now a fallen nation itself, no longer had the means to fulfill its obligations to provide protection of any kind to Laos. Japanese soldiers entered Laos from northern Vietnam—called Tonkin at the time—along Colonial Route 7, the road constructed by the French to connect northern Vietnam with the heartland of Laos. This main east-west route passed through Nong Het, the major Hmong enclave.

Route 7 twisted westerly and a bit south from Nong Het through the Plaine des Jarres, passing clusters of massive stone jars, those mysterious artifacts of an ancient culture, through towns named Ban Ban, Khang Khay, Xieng Khouang, Muong Soui, primarily inhabited by ethnic Lao. Hmong lived in the fog-draped mountains overlooking these lower settlements.

The belief that the French could guide the Hmong to a better life had seemed reasonable until the Japanese army arrived. Life under the Japanese was quite different from life under the French. The French had operated the Pa Heo silver mine near Muang Cha and hired Hmong to work it. When the Japanese took it over, they forced Hmong men, women, and children to work it as slave laborers and to sleep in the mine shafts. One night a mine shaft collapsed, killing over 200 Hmong. Instead of closing the unsafe mine, the Japanese rounded up more Hmong to work it—and more Hmong died. Word about Japanese cruelty spread quickly. Hmong remained in their mountains, trying to avoid contact.

Under Japanese occupation, French Indochina was cut off from the West, resulting in an intelligence void that crippled allied military planning to liberate the area. In 1944, a daring top-secret plan unfolded for the liberation of Indochina using the Plaine des Jarres in Xieng Khouang Province as a staging area. It was so secret that the men who were to parachute clandestinely into Laos were not told of the plan or their roles. One of those men was Free French Second Lieutenant Maurice Gauthier.

Near Calcutta, this 23-year-old Frenchman, who knew little about Laos and nothing about the Hmong, trained. Four years earlier, when he was 19, Gauthier's family had been killed in a German air raid against his hometown. For the next six months, he lived by his wits, scavenging off the streets. He made his way to unoccupied France and joined General Charles de Gaulle's resistance. Sent to North Africa, he trained as a commando in the Corps Leger d'Intervention. In the spring of 1944, he volunteered for Special Service Action and a top secret mission. On June

1, 1944, the bespectacled Gauthier, only 5 feet 3 inches tall, departed Cairo on a C-47 heading for India.[2]

In India, Gauthier, code-named "Phidias" after a Greek sculptor, was assigned to Force 136, a clandestine operation commanded by the British to train commandos who could be dropped into occupied countries to collect intelligence, disrupt enemy communications, and organize and train indigenous peoples as resistance fighters. While each man learned all phases of commando operations so that the team could split up if necessary, each also had a specialty. Gauthier was the team's intelligence specialist. Initial training took place on the shores of Lake Karakwasla near Poona. For security reasons, trainees were divided into teams of ten men, isolated by barbed wire, and forbidden to see or talk to others in the camp.

In September 1944, Gauthier's team arrived at Chaklala Air Base in Rawalpindi for parachute training. There they made only three jumps, two during daylight and one at night. While in training, Gauthier learned of the liberation of Paris and the Normandy Invasion.

The ten French commandos were ready, but they had no idea where they would be sent. Since they were repeatedly told there would be no outside assistance, they knew the assignment would be dangerous. The night after Christmas in 1944, Gauthier's team gathered at the airfield at Jessore, near Calcutta. Moonlight touched the wings and propellers of two American B-24 Liberators, long-distance four-engine bombers. Gauthier, dressed in coveralls hiding a French Army of Indochina uniform, fully armed, waited and looked at the moon. "We all knew that a full moon was needed for night-dropping. We assumed tonight we would begin our secret mission."

Gauthier's commanding officer spoke briefly. His simple instructions heralded danger. Tonight this team and thousands of pounds of ammunition and explosives would be night-parachuted into Xieng Khouang Province in Laos. Each plane would carry five men responsible for its cargo. As his commanding officer spoke, Gauthier searched his mind for information on Xieng Khouang Province and Laos. Xieng Khouang meant nothing; Laos meant little more.

"Our orders were brief: jump over the fire signal, hide the parachutes, guns and explosives, then make contact with the French garrison at Khang Khay on the Plaine des Jarres. Once in place, we were to gather intelligence and communicate that in code back to headquarters in India on our newly developed transmitters. Simultaneously, we were to organize indigenous resistance to the Japanese."

Then Gauthier learned that their ultimate mission was to secure the Plaine des Jarres for an allied airborne invasion of Indochina to be staged from India. The invasion date was not mentioned, but from his commander's orders he believed it would be soon.

Gauthier wondered how ten men could secure a Japanese-occupied area and hold it so that an airborne invasion force could land. Without asking, he climbed into a Liberator to be flown to a place about which he knew very little to conduct a mission that seemed impossible.

All night the team flew. "We flew over Burma, occupied by the Japanese, without an escort. We droned on and on through the night. We waited for the pilot to locate the signal—a burning reverse L—which supposedly would be lit by a Frenchman earlier night-dropped into Laos. While the moon was full, a cloud cover prevented our British pilots from finding the ground signal. We returned to base in India in time for breakfast. We tried again two nights later. Once again our pilot was unable to locate the signal and he flew us back to India for breakfast. At our base, we learned that the other pilot had dropped his five men and their cargo."

For Gauthier's five-man team it was too late to try again in December. Since they needed a full moon, his team was now forced to wait another month. "Now that we were briefed about the mission we were virtually under arrest. We were all young men who knew waiting a month in India in isolation would be unbearable. We pleaded for leave. It was turned down. Then we threatened to resign. Since we were volunteers, we could withdraw from Force 136. We pledged we would keep the secret and finally the authorities relented. We spent a month in Bombay and never said a word about our mission."

On January 23, 1945, Gauthier climbed into a Liberator for his third attempt to parachute into Laos. He remembered this night vividly: "Once again, the British pilot was unable to locate the ground signal and as before we returned to base in India in time for breakfast. Two days later on January 25, we boarded the plane for our fourth attempt. This time our pilot, a Royal Canadian Air Force pilot, told us after takeoff: 'I'm not bringing you fellows back for breakfast. You're going in.'" The five commandos sat silently in the noisy and dark fuselage of the converted bomber as it droned through the night across Japanese-occupied Burma. For Gauthier, the waiting and false attempts had taken a toll. He was thrilled when he heard the pilot announce, "Prepare to jump!"

"Within seconds, we got into the slides, the door opened, and out we went into the darkness. As soon as my parachute opened, I looked below.

That wasn't a signal fire down there; it was a raging forest fire. Five men and several tons of explosives were plummeting into a fire! Luckily, we landed a bit short of the 'signal.' None of us was hurt. We quickly dragged the explosives away from the fire and worked the rest of the night and the next day to bury and hide the supplies."

Years later Gauthier learned that the French mission working with Force 136 had entered on its records in red ink, beside the name of each man on the team, the date of his jump and a code-word indicating that he was not recoverable. The French never expected to retrieve any of these men.

After hiding the supplies, the men buried their coveralls. Wearing their French Army of Indochina uniforms, they unpacked topographical maps and surveying equipment which would provide cover for their clandestine mission. "If anyone questioned us, we were to say 'hello' and act the fool, saying we were the French experts sent in from Saigon to survey and map northern Laos. This would have been logical since at this time northern Laos had not yet been surveyed."

Their initial worry was not protecting their cover, but determining their location. "We had no idea where we were. Our reception committee—the five men who had parachuted in the previous month—were not there to greet us. We were supposed to be on the Plaine des Jarres, but we were in mountains, not on a plain. Since we had no fix, we didn't know which way to walk. We didn't know if the Japanese knew of our arrival and might be looking for us, so we waited one more night before we moved out. After five hours of walking through the jungle, we came to a road. We knew that if we were in Laos, which wasn't certain, there was only one road it could be—Colonial Route 7 which ran east-west through Laos. After some discussion, we decided to turn right. We walked the remainder of the night and into the next day. Then we came upon a signpost with two arrows and two names. Above the arrow pointing in the direction from which we had just come we read the word 'Vientiane.' Over the other arrow, we happily read 'Xieng Khouang'—a major town on the Plaine des Jarres, our destination. We had landed forty miles west of our target."

Their next challenge was to contact the French garrison at Khang Khay. The soldiers stationed here were supposedly loyal to the Vichy and the Japanese. Making contact with the garrison turned out to be relatively easy because there were no Japanese soldiers stationed at Khang Khay. The Japanese were based at Xieng Khouang town several miles away. The garrison was manned by one French Army company, a mix of

French, French Foreign Legion, and local soldiers, commanded by Captain Battestini, a Corsican.

The commandos learned that Khang Khay, designated as a main resupply base for the airborne invasion, already held enough petrol, aviation gas, ammunition, artillery shells, and bombs to keep the French Expeditionary Force in Indochina fighting for weeks.

Gauthier surveyed the undulating Plaine des Jarres where his team was supposed to find a suitable landing area for the initial wave of gliders. The gliders would carry troops to build a landing field and to secure it for propeller-driven aircraft to fly in artillery shells, bombs, and more troops. It seemed an enormous task for these few men, but they were young and determined.

The five commandos who had jumped in December came in from the jungle. The reassembled team, code-named "Polaire," moved into an isolated and uninhabited stone house near Route 7 north of the Plaine des Jarres that belonged to French General Leclerc's family. The team intended to use it as its main communications base to house its special B-2 radios to report intelligence assessments to headquarters and receive instructions.

The B-2 radios, capable of transmitting in Morse code thousands of miles, were their lifelines. They were not, however, easily portable. To move one radio required separating it into two parts. It took two strong men, each packing a portion on his back, to move it any distance.

The team soon received a coded message to prepare drop zones for night deliveries of weapons, ammunition, and high explosives which were to be channeled to French garrisons throughout Indochina in preparation for the upcoming invasion and liberation. All of this required total secrecy. If the Japanese and their collaborators suspected any preparations for an invasion, the allied operation would fail. Much to Gauthier's amazement, several senior French officers visited his team. Then the Catholic bishop based in Saigon brazenly drove to the Plaine des Jarres to meet the clandestine commandos. The men agreed that their operation would be exposed if they stayed at Leclerc's house. Giving no notice, the team simply disappeared. From then on, the commandos lived and operated in the jungle.

Critical to the success of the allied invasion was reliable and current intelligence on enemy activities. French Inspector Doussineau, who oversaw the Provincial Police Force and knew everyone of importance in Xieng Khouang Province, introduced Gauthier to French-educated Chao (Prince) Sai Kham, the last descendent of the royal house of the Kingdom of Xieng Khouang. This kingdom, which predated the Kingdom of Luang Prabang, was famous for its succulent oranges and peaches, its moderate climate, its beautiful mountains, and its plateau filled with ancient and mysterious stone jars. In the early 1900s, the French had decreed Xieng Khouang part of Laos.

The Japanese placated the king in Luang Prabang for his loss to Thailand of Sayaboury Province by giving him the independent Kingdom of Xieng Khouang. On August 29, 1941, Xieng Khouang and two other provinces—Houei Sai and Vientiane—were turned over to the Kingdom of Luang Prabang. Prince Sai Kham's family had been cast aside.

When the French commandos asked Prince Sai Kham to provide intelligence on the Japanese and collaborators like tax collector Vongvichit, he quickly agreed to assist. But the commandos needed more than Prince Sai Kham's spying. They needed men. Inspector Doussineau advised them to recruit Hmong through their chieftain Touby who lived at Nong Het, far to the north on the Vietnam border.

Gauthier needed a guide to take him to Nong Het. He found a Frenchman who called himself simply Tisserand. A crusty former French Legionnaire with a checkered past, Tisserand, whom the Hmong called Haje, had married a Lao and was farming a small plot near Ban Ban when Gauthier demanded at gunpoint that he join the resistance. Tisserand agreed to guide Gauthier to Nong Het to meet Touby.

Touby had been under heavy pressure from the Japanese to cooperate with them. The local Japanese commander had ordered him to provide food for his troops. Touby selected a boy from the local primary school, who spoke good French and had a reputation as a resourceful and bright student, to work with the local Japanese commander to obtain the food, particularly meat. This alert, smiling boy who knew the mountains so well was named Vang Pao.

When Gauthier arrived at Nong Het, he found Touby living in the only stone house. He wore Western dress and spoke excellent French. With a round face and coal-black hair, he stood a bit taller than Gauthier and was straight-backed and athletic. Gauthier lost no time in recruiting him. "My initial conversation with Touby was straightforward. I told him the allies were considering invading the area, more troops would be arriving and we were preparing to fight the Japanese. I asked him what he thought, and he said, 'I'm with you.' He said he was willing to cooperate and bring his people into the fight together with us. We agreed to give weapons to his people, train them to use them, and lead them into the fight. There was no question of money; there was no question of mercenaries. I think Touby saw in this an opportunity of gaining better positions for his people, politically."

By the end of the meeting, Touby had agreed to provide guides and messengers for the French commandos, men to porter and hide the night-dropped supplies, and men to be trained in guerrilla warfare. Joining Touby was his brother Tou Geu and another Hmong from the Moua clan—Chia Xang. These three became the leadership core of the pro-French Hmong who provided support and logistics for the French resistance.

Touby recommended that the French use Phou San, an extended mountain massif inhabited by Hmong, as an operational base. Phou San stretched from near Ban Ban, not far from Tisserand's small farm, west to the northern edge of the Plaine des Jarres. Since this range was near the strategic Route 7, by operating on Phou San they could watch it for enemy convoys. Phou San's tall trees would provide good cover for resistance activities.

Led by Hmong guides provided by Touby, Gauthier set off on foot for Phou San. He observed that life in this beautiful land was often harsh. It was not easy to earn a living from the steep mountainside fields. Women and children toiled from before sunrise until sunset to produce enough to feed their families and animals. Farmers hoped there would be extra vegetables to trade for salt, pots, Chinese needles, and silk cloth. Many families tended patches of opium poppies, which grow best at over 3,000 feet. For many, raw opium was their only cash crop.

Traditionally, Hmong used opium as a natural medication, particularly for diarrhea, stomach disorders, fevers, and pain. Hmong either grew their own opium or traded for it. Elderly Hmong sometimes smoked opium to induce sleep or to ease the aches and pains of age. While as a rule Hmong were not drug abusers, addiction did occur, but it was frowned upon. An opium addict was a burden to his family, his village, and his clan.

This was the dry season and time to harvest the opium pods. Women and children, using small curved knives, made two or three slits on each hardened poppy pod. White sap oozed from the cuts. Exposed to air, the strong-smelling sap turned dark. This was raw opium. Harvesters, often with their noses and mouths covered to protect themselves from the strong odor of the sap, moved slowly through hillside poppy fields, laboriously scraping small bubbles of sap from pods into leaves. Each pod produced only a minuscule amount of sap. A family poppy field could not provide much income. Gauthier was surprised at how much effort was required to harvest a small field of poppies which produced, if the weather was just right, one to two kilograms of opium.

Gauthier's guides took him to Phou Duu village where he met a remarkable Hmong who was about his age and an inch shorter. Moua Chong Toua, a proud, barefoot, and clever man, had been born into the Vang clan, orphaned, then adopted by the Moua clan.

Chong Toua always wore Hmong traditional clothes: black floppy trousers, a tight-fitting black jacket, and a large silver necklace. Gauthier smoked tobacco and Chong Toua smoked opium, but both remained vigorous men. Chong Toua could not read or write, but he had learned to speak a broken French that allowed him to communicate effectively with Gauthier and other Frenchmen. Chong Toua would become the young Frenchman's close friend and a hero of the Free French Resistance in Laos.

Chong Toua, like the other heads of households at Phou Duu, was a slash-and-burn farmer. Hmong farmers staked out a hillside, then cut down the trees and vegetation. When the downed plants and trees dried, they set fire to them, creating an enriched residue in which they planted dry hill rice, corn, vegetables, and opium. When fields became infertile, the village headman sought unused land. Again, the men slashed and burned to create their fields, which were worked by the women and children. Villagers always hoped that new fields could be reached from their old villages. If not, the villagers packed up their possessions, moved to the new location and built new houses.

Gauthier studied the faces of the Hmong in this village. Some resembled the round faces of the Chinese, the males often sporting wisps of whiskers. Others resembled descendants of Ghengis Khan. Still others had slender faces, narrow noses, and high cheekbones.

Barefoot Hmong women, burdened by their back-baskets of wood and vegetables or their sleeping children tied to their backs in cloth slings, walked quickly in single file along mountain paths. Some women wore heavy silver necklaces. Hmong kept their wealth in silver jewelry and silver bars. They had little interest in gold, except for the gold-tipped teeth itinerant Chinese dentists put in their mouths.

In early 1945, there was no time for the men of Phou Duu to create new villages or work in fields. They labored with the French commandos to prepare drop zones. Women and children, raising pigs, chickens, ponies, and sometimes cows and water buffalo, could not count on any help from the men. After the Hmong hacked out a drop zone, the commandos radioed the coordinates to Force 136 headquarters in

India. A coded message came back, giving the date and approximate drop time.

On the eve of a drop, Gauthier and his team prepared four signal flares in the form of a reverse L—with three flares in a row and one to the left of the first. Since there were no navigational aids, pilots depended upon ground flares to guide them to drop zones, often only a few yards in length, at altitudes of 4,000 to 6,000 feet. Once the flares were in place, 40 to 50 Hmong, barefoot and wearing tribal dress, waited nearby. Farther away other armed Hmong waited in the darkness in case of a Japanese attack.

Liberator pilots dared not fly over Japanese-occupied Burma during daylight hours. Since it was a six-hour flight from the secret airfield in India to Phou San in Laos, pilots lifted off at dusk, reaching their target about midnight. The window of opportunity over Lao targets was small. Pilots had to find their drop zones, drop their cargoes, and fly back over Burma during darkness to India without refueling.

When the men on the ground heard the Liberators' engines, they lit the flares. Gauthier turned on his Eureka radio signal, intended to direct the pilots in but which, according to Gauthier, rarely functioned. As a pilot approached, he lined up on the three flares, keeping the single flare to his left.

If the weather was clear and the pilots on course, a flight of three to five Liberators swooped down one after the other, dropping tons of cargo, including high explosives. The men on the ground had only the darkness hours to hide the supplies in nearby caves and ravines or porter them to rendezvous points along Route 7, where they would be picked up and taken to French garrisons at Vinh and Hanoi.

Since this was the dry season, the weather was usually good, allowing drops to continue night after night. However, some nights fog shrouded the mountains. Then the resistance heard the pilots flying around and around, searching in vain for the signal flares. Unable to see them and with the Eureka system not functioning, these pilots often returned to Jessore to try again, though never at the same drop zone. The "Polaire" team never used the same drop zone in successive operations, believing that invited discovery.

The commandos faced many problems, but the most persistent was keeping the B-2 radios charged. These radios operated on batteries which were not available in the jungle and had to be constantly recharged. Since electricity was nonexistent, recharging required considerable ingenuity. The commandos invented a "steam machine," an awkward, improvised contraption which burned wood to create steam that turned a homemade generator that produced power to recharge the batteries. It took two men to carry the radio and one to carry the "steam machine."

While the Frenchmen could communicate by radio with India over a thousand miles away, communication within Laos was by foot. Messengers, usually young boys, ran up and down the mountains delivering instructions from French commandos to Hmong chiefs responsible for organizing men to help with the supply drops and for recruiting men for weapons and commando training.

Gauthier, who had never heard of the Hmong until recently, was impressed with their hard work and the fact that they never asked for anything in exchange for their efforts. He showed his gratitude by giving the silk parachutes to the men, whose wives and mothers turned them into clothing. He also noticed that they cherished their homemade flintlock rifles, so he gave them modern guns.

Military man Gauthier was most impressed with Hmong speed, toughness, and endurance. He recalled: "The Hmong could walk eight to ten miles an hour for 48 hours. I considered myself in top physical shape, but in the early days I had great difficulty in keeping the Hmong pace. In the jungle, I struggled to follow the pace of the man before me. I was amazed that the Hmong approached a mountaintop by heading straight for its peak. None of this winding up the mountain. One day, I asked the men with me why they always walked straight to the top of the mountain. All of them looked at me in disbelief. One man answered simply: 'That's where we're going.'"

In February, Gauthier observed Chinese caravans moving through Hmong territory, buying Hmong opium. Chinese caravans had always plied this wilderness, but since the French government had decided to give up its opium monopoly, Chinese traders now had access to the entire opium production of Laos.

While stockpiling for the allied invasion moved ahead swiftly, training of Hmong to operate modern guns took place in small groups in the mountains around the Plaine des Jarres, particularly on Phou San. Once trained, Hmong taught others who, in turn, trained others. There were no uniforms, no salaries, and time was short.

Suddenly the Frenchmen found themselves victims of Yalta, where Roosevelt, in February 1945, indicated to Stalin that the U.S. would not assist the French in returning to Indochina. Gauthier remembered the result of that session. "President Roosevelt wanted the French out of Indochina. Shortly after Yalta, we received word from Force 136 in India that there would be no further actions and no assistance whatsoever for any French actions. Supplies from Force 136 were to end immediately. We were to be cut off, stranded in Laos. However, someone in Force 136 managed to authorize dropping some more supplies after this ultimatum."

The commandos and the Hmong constantly feared that the Japanese would discover their operation. Touby feared that Phay Dang, the anti-French Hmong, and his followers would notice the night drops or the movement of supplies and alert the Japanese command. This fear became reality on the night of March 9, 1945, when the Japanese staged a *coup de main* with attacks against French installations, both civilian and military, throughout Indochina. Within days, troops of the Rising Sun had imprisoned thousands of French soldiers and civilians and taken over all major Indochina cities, including Saigon, Hanoi, Vientiane, and Xieng Khouang.

Some garrisons fought back. Others retreated in cowardly fashion. French fatalities were high, as were the number of French taken to concentration camps. Some soldiers eluded the Japanese and took to the jungle, intending to walk to China to find the Americans or to join the resistance in the mountains. One soldier who found the French resistance was from the Khang Khay garrison. He told Gauthier that when Captain Battestini, commander of the garrison, heard there was fighting in the cities, he packed his belongings on horses and headed north with his men, abandoning the garrison's massive supplies.

After hearing this information, Gauthier and the team's demolition expert hurried to Khang Khay. "The reserve supplies for the whole of the French Army in case we had to make a final stand were stored here. We couldn't let the enemy have these supplies. We had to destroy them. We boobytrapped the garrison so that when the Japanese arrived both the supplies and the Japanese would be blown up together. On March 14, 1945, the explosions began and they continued for half a day."

The allied invasion that intended to use the high plateau of the Plaine des Jarres to liberate Indochina from the Japanese had been preempted. No longer did Japanese patrols allow French soldiers to pass. Now they aggressively combed the countryside searching for Frenchmen who had eluded imprisonment. The Japanese and the Free French were at war in Indochina.

Assigned by Touby to gather intelligence on the enemy, Vue Sai Long, a slim Hmong in his twenties with an aristocratic, high-bridged nose, witnessed the Japanese treatment of the French. One day at the market town of Ban Ban, Vue Sai Long heard scuffling and shouting in the distance. Then he saw Japanese soldiers moving up the dusty street. After several silent strutting soldiers passed, he saw five "Fackee" soldiers, each followed by a bellowing Japanese soldier. The Frenchmen, dirty and staggering, were bent over. Every few steps they suddenly jerked upright and screamed. The Japanese seemed to be controlling their erratic movements. As they neared, Vue saw that the Japanese had run strings through the nostrils of all the French soldiers and were driving them like water buffaloes. Blood spurted from their noses as the Japanese jerked them from side to side while shouting to the Hmong onlookers. "Their noses are too long," the Japanese snarled. "See this, we are showing you these French who are not humans. They are only ghosts and they can't control this country."[3]

As Vue Sai Long watched, he recalled the harsh treatment of the Hmong by the Japanese. If suspected of working with the French, the Japanese didn't bother to torture the Hmong; they simply shot them, saying: "Since your noses are not too high or too long, we will just kill you right now."

Kicking, beating, and jerking their prisoners, the Japanese paraded their captives. As the helpless French passed they cried to the Hmong to help them. The Hmong could say nothing because the Japanese had forbidden the Hmong to associate with the "Fackee." Vue Sai Long and other Hmong, trying not to show their fear, watched and remembered. Demonstrations like this convinced many Hmong that they must help the French—whom most considered to be friends—to defeat the invaders. Hmong volunteered to resist the Japanese and to protect and hide French soldiers. At great risk to themselves and their villagers, Hmong moved Frenchmen from cave to cave and mountaintop to mountaintop. Vue Sai Long and his group hid five French soldiers—including one officer named Jean and another named Blond—in a cave atop Phou Lhat.

While the Japanese combed the countryside looking for French soldiers and civilians, Gauthier's team trained men to fight the Japanese, whose numbers were increasing. More Frenchmen were needed. In Jessore, more commandos trained.

Near Phou Duu, Gauthier, two other Frenchmen, and Chong Toua, with his Hmong fighters, prepared for their first ambush. A Japanese convoy with a dozen trucks headed west along Route 7 near Ban Ban. As the convoy passed, the three Frenchmen flicked their submachine and Sten guns to automatic. Volleys of bullets struck the lead trucks. Soldiers in the last truck, unharmed by the attack, jumped out, firing. Suddenly,

Gauthier sensed that too few guns were firing. He looked around to discover no Hmong in sight. He signaled for retreat. The Frenchmen, greatly outnumbered, took off running for Phou Duu. There they found Chong Toua and his men waiting. Gauthier asked Chong Toua what had happened. "He admitted the noise of the fast firing had frightened them—and they had fled."

The Fackee commando explained they should not worry about the noise and that there was no need to run as long as "we are giving the bullets to the enemy." After several hit and run operations, the men of Phou Duu lost their fear of automatic weapons fire.

Gauthier never used the term "soldiers" when referring to Chong Toua's men or the other Hmong who took up arms to fight. "I always called them 'warriors.' For me, the word 'soldier' implied disciplined men who responded to commands and orders. The Hmong fought as individuals. They were brave and tough, but they were not soldiers; they were 'warriors.' If the men didn't think a particular fight was worthwhile, they didn't show up. The Hmong fought on their own terms, not on mine."

The Hmong, who referred to the short commando as the "Little Fackee," were impressed with his ability to live with them. When they were sick or wounded, he tended to them. When soldiers were killed, he gave their widows, who never asked for compensation, a sum of money. To honor Gauthier, they held *ba-sii* ceremonies, animist rituals during which Hmong tied white cords around his wrists and called on the spirits to protect him and to keep his soul inside his body. Little Fackee often sat in a circle with them to drink homemade corn whiskey. He had learned a few words of Hmong and Prince Sai Kham was teaching him Lao.

In late March 1945, Gauthier's commandos, operating northeast of Ban Ban, found an American near death. "It was clear that the American was in the last stages of starvation and exhaustion. He was Air Force Captain Hughett (his first name and the correct spelling of his last name is not known by the Hmong), from Texas—a relative, he said, of General Stillwell. He had fled the Philippines when it fell to the Japanese and made his way by ship to Indochina. He arrived in Saigon about the time of the March 9 Japanese attacks against the French and he was captured. He escaped and headed north on foot to try to reach China when he become lost near Ban Ban."

Chong Toua's wife cared for this American flyer, fed him, and nursed him back to health.*

After Hughett recovered, the French offered to send him to China with a Hmong guide, but he wanted to stay and fight. "Soon after he joined us, he was wounded in a firefight. We had to run so we made a stretcher and carried him to a spot near a small stream, tended to his wounds, left him some medical supplies to dress his wounds, some water, and one Hmong to find him food. We then abandoned him. We told him that we would be back in one month. In a month we returned. He was still there. The Hmong had taken good care of him. His wound had healed. This time when we offered to send him to China with a Hmong guide, he accepted."

Japanese supplies coming in from the docks at Haiphong passed into Laos through the mountain pass at Nong Het and along Colonial Route 7 through Ban Ban. To deny the Japanese the use of Route 7, Little Fackee and his guerrillas repeatedly blew up the Ban Ban bridge. Always the Japanese rebuilt it. "The first time we blew it, the Japanese had no guards. Then a couple of soldiers patrolled it on foot. We still blew it up. Then Japanese machine gun crews protected the bridge. Still we blew it up."

They hit convoys, ambushed patrols, and blew bridges effectively and often. Hmong teams moving fast hit one target, moved to another many miles away, struck it, and perhaps still hit a third target in the same day. The Japanese thought the French had parachuted in thousands of soldiers. They tried to locate the nonexistent secret French base from which they thought these teams operated. The effective harassment of the Japanese Imperial Army was conducted by barefoot mountain men assisted by an odd assortment of French Army stragglers directed by a few French commandos.

On April 8, 1945, the Lao king, under pressure from the Japanese, from Prince Souphanouvong, and from Lao Issara (Free Lao) leaders, issued a royal proclamation joining Laos to Japan's Co-Prosperity Sphere: "from this day forward, our Kingdom of Laos, formerly a colony of France, is now an independent nation . . . and will join with neighboring countries to build prosperity and progress following the principles

---

*Forty-two years later, this woman, living as a refugee in Limoges, France, told me that the American had promised that one day he would pay her for the chickens he had eaten, and complained that all this time she has been waiting for repayment.

of the Greater East-Asia Co-Prosperity Sphere. . . . I hereby declare that our Kingdom has agreed to cooperate in all things with Japan."[4]

On April 12, as columns of Viet Minh troops moved toward Laos, Japanese-armed Vietnamese at Khang Khay announced the area belonged to Annam—the central part of Vietnam. Though this attempt to take part of Laos failed, the intent was clear. The Viet Minh wanted control of Laos.

At the end of May, orders came for Gauthier's team to split up. With the Allied invasion plan abandoned, the men were needed in other areas to gather intelligence and to train men to fight. One commando went to Sam Neua Province. Others moved to southern provinces in Laos. One went to Dien Bien Phu. Gauthier remained alone in Xieng Khouang waiting for Force 136 to drop in a new commando, Captain René Bichelot, and a radio operator.

Over clandestine radios, Hmong resistance fighters monitored the progress of the Allied Forces' war effort against the Japanese. When they heard that the U.S. had dropped an atomic bomb on Hiroshima and Japan would soon surrender, they sent runners to tell the French whom they were hiding. The French cheered and shouted that they would soon be back in control.

Vue Sai Long did not know about Hiroshima or the impending Japanese surrender. In mid-August 1945, his group watched a Japanese encampment near Kasak on the Luang Prabang–Xieng Khouang border. On this day, Vue Sai Long observed the Japanese officers as they sat beneath a parachute propped into a tent, eating noodles and listening to a radio. The radio blared loudly. Then suddenly the senior officer stopped eating, reached for a knife, and committed *hara-kiri*. Other officers— about 50 of them—grouped themselves into small circles, placed hand grenades in their armpits, and pulled the pins. The Hmong, startled by this bizarre behavior, abandoned the scene of the mass suicide—a tangle of parachute silks, radio equipment, maps, guns, food, and bodies—leaving it as a reminder of the Japanese occupation.

Not all Japanese soldiers decided to commit *hara-kiri*. Some turned over their supplies to Viet Minh. Others went to North Vietnam to join the Viet Minh. One young Japanese officer asked Gauthier for a job— any job—because he could never return to Japan. Gauthier refused. Others headed west where the Hmong said they "disappeared with the wind."

3.

The Rise of the Viet Minh

The Communists have developed *a new kind of aggression in which one country sponsors internal war within another.* Communist-sponsored internal war is clearly international aggression, but a form of aggression that frequently eludes the traditional definitions of international law. It means the use of native and imported guerrillas to serve the interests of Communist nations.

—Roger Hilsman, in a foreword to General Vo Nguyen Giap's *People's War People's Army: The Viet Cong Insurrection Manual for Underdeveloped Countries*

A few hundred miles away from Xieng Khouang, in Hanoi, Archimedes Patti, a U.S. Army major assigned to the Office of Strategic Services (OSS), the predecessor of the CIA, prepared to meet with a Vietnamese communist who had taken the revolutionary name of Ho Chi Minh. Ho had recently returned after a 30-year absence during which he had studied Marxism in France and the Soviet Union, worked in the Comintern International, and learned the revolutionary tactics of Mao Zedong in China. In 1930, he had attended the Communist International Conference in Hong Kong that united the communist parties in Indochina into one party called the Communist Party of Indochina. It was now 1945, and Ho had approached U.S. intelligence offering information on the Japanese and on American POWs. Archimedes Patti would befriend him.

With brilliant timing, Ho Chi Minh took advantage of the power vacuum and confusion following the Japanese defeat and departure. The French military in Indochina, weakened by the Japanese imprisonment of its men, was pathetic. During Nazi occupation, France and its far-flung empire had eroded to a shadow of its former prominence. President Roosevelt was determined to prevent a French colonial return to Indochina. After World War II, the French held on in Indochina, but France was economically destitute and politically divided.

On September 2, 1945, less than a month after the Japanese surrender, Ho Chi Minh, with Major Patti present, proclaimed his Democratic Republic of Vietnam. Photographers documented the moment, showing Patti and two of his aides standing beside Viet Minh military leader Vo Nguyen Giap, saluting the communist flag as it was hoisted over the Citadel, a French colonial office building in Hanoi. As Ho talked, a flight of American aircraft dipped down over the gathered crowd. Many onlookers interpreted this overflight as a symbolic salute by the United States to Ho and his new republic.[1]

There was no such intent. The overflight was pure coincidence. Patti later admitted he had been naive and that Ho had used him. "I knew he was using us, and I didn't mind frankly because the use he made of us was more one of image rather than substance. Really what he was trying to do was to say: 'Well, look, even the Americans believe in my cause'—when speaking to the Vietnamese."[2]

Patti did not recognize the value of image over substance. This apparent American backing of Ho influenced many Vietnamese. Tran Van Don, later a general in the South Vietnamese Army, was one of those influenced. "His name [Ho Chi Minh] was only known in 1945. People like myself discovered that there was a leader, who came and took over control of Hanoi, with the name of Ho Chi Minh, leading an organization. We didn't know how big, but especially we knew at that time that his organization was backed by the Americans."[3]

Through this kind of manipulation, Ho won legitimacy by first winning recognition outside his native country. Virtually unknown to the Vietnamese at the time, Ho managed to ride to national notice by cleverly associating himself with the American victors of World War II. His manipulation of Major Patti might be considered Ho's first successful attempt at "guerrilla diplomacy," which he would employ so adroitly in the years to come. But he did not rely totally on images to promote himself. He violently eliminated those nationalists who competed against him.

The Japanese surrender also created a power vacuum in Laos. Both the Vietnamese and the Chinese took advantage of the situation. Over 30,000 Vietnamese lived in the Lao river towns, working as senior administrators for the French, especially in the police force, or as merchants. In general, the Vietnamese were disdainful of the Lao. For most Vietnamese living in Laos, their first allegiance was to Vietnam. Many were anti-French and pro-independence. After the Japanese coup on March 9, the Vietnamese in two Lao towns hoisted the flag of Ho's newly declared republic.[4]

Also anti-French in sentiment was the previously clandestine Free Lao movement which promoted total Lao independence and which on October 12, 1945, publicly and officially formed the Lao Issara. Prominent leaders of the Lao Issara included three princely half-brothers: Prince Souphanouvong, married to a pro–Viet Minh Vietnamese; Prince Souvanna Phouma, married to a Frenchwoman and worried about Vietnamese interference in Laos; and Prince Phetsarath, an older half-brother who vigorously sought an independent Laos and seemed always in competition with the king. The Lao Issara, unhappy about the king's desire to return Laos to the French following the Japanese surrender, allied with Nationalist Chinese troops, who entered Laos under the terms of an Allied agreement reached at the Potsdam Conference, to topple the king.

While the Lao Issara and the royal family squabbled, in remote Xieng Khouang Province Maurice Gauthier, René Bichelot, and the radioman continued to fight the Viet Minh. Surprised and disgusted by the reported American support of Ho and his new republic, the three-man French team in Xieng Khouang Province had no intention of abandoning the area or the people to the Viet Minh.

Lao Prince Souphanouvong along with a party of Viet Minh arrived in Laos in October of 1945 to receive the title of Commander-in-Chief of the Armed Forces. One of Souphanouvong's first acts was to agree to a "Military Convention" with Hanoi which in effect gave Hanoi through its "technical advisors" extraordinary power in Laos. These cadre had decisive input at all levels of the military, and later the police and intelligence.[5] Gauthier and Bichelot received daily reports of Viet Minh infiltration and activity. They also learned that Phoumi Vongvichit, the corrupt Lao tax collector and Japanese collaborator, was working with the Viet Minh.

The two French officers decided to act. While Captain Bichelot remained in Xieng Khouang town with a small contingent of French soldiers and civilians, Gauthier and his radio operator hurried to Nong Het to monitor enemy traffic coming into Laos from Vietnam. To observe what passed along this road, Gauthier used Touby's stone house. "I knew the Chinese merchants probably carried information to the enemy that there was a foreigner in Touby's house. So at night Touby, his brother Tou Geu, some Hmong 'warriors,' my radio-operator and I slept on a nearby hill overlooking the house. We had information that a column of soldiers was heading toward Nong Het. We were certain an attack would come.''

On the night of November 22, Gauthier and Touby's men as usual climbed the hill outside Nong Het to spend the night. Just before dawn, Gauthier awoke to a heavy barrage of gunfire below. ''We couldn't see who was firing, so we waited in the darkness. The shooting alerted the Hmong in the nearby hills, who ran to our position with their weapons. Under cover of darkness, we sent men out to encircle the enemy. When dawn came, we saw about 100 heavily armed enemy soldiers, some with machine guns, surrounding Touby's house. Some had dug in. The enemy intended to stay. But we had them encircled. There would be no escape.''

Touby's men and boys opened fire. In the initial surprise the Hmong ''warriors,'' many of them good shots, killed or wounded a number of enemy soldiers. At noon, only one enemy machine gunner fired. After a burst of gunfire from the Hmong, that gun was silenced. Expecting a trap, Gauthier and his men slowly descended and moved toward Touby's house. ''The Hmong examined the dead and wounded to discover they were Vietnamese from Vinh,'' recalled Gauthier. ''One machine gunner was Japanese as was his gun. There were other former Japanese soldiers in this group. Many of their weapons were Japanese. The Japanese soldiers acted as advisors to the Viet Minh.''

While Gauthier and the Hmong had prevented this Viet Minh detachment from reaching Xieng Khouang town, other Viet Minh units had already arrived. At Xieng Khouang, Bichelot assessed the situation and concluded that the enemy force was superior. He decided to evacuate. The only available vehicle was an old, prewar French car. Since there was no gasoline, Bichelot had resourcefully found a way of distilling rotten rice into alcohol which fueled his car. The consumption was terrible—about one liter per kilometer, but that did not matter.

With Tisserand driving, Bichelot sped out of Xieng Khouang, hoping to put some distance between himself and the enemy before abandoning the car and heading for the safety of the Hmong hills. Once there, he intended to regroup and organize the Hmong fighters to retake the town. Only a few miles out, the Viet Minh ambushed them, seriously wounding Bichelot in the back. The car, although hit by gunfire, continued to run, so Tisserand sped on for several more miles before abandoning it. Bichelot, now in shock, could not walk. Tisserand put him on his shoulders and carried him through the jungle up to Phou Duu village.

When Chong Toua saw Bichelot's condition, he dispatched a runner with a message for Gauthier. Gauthier immediately set out to help

Bichelot. When he arrived, he found Bichelot could not be moved. "I concluded it would take weeks before his wound would heal. I decided I would stay with Bichelot. I ordered everyone to keep a low profile until he recovered."

Soon Touby joined Gauthier. As the two men waited, they schemed together, making plans for future military actions. Touby told Gauthier about his dreams of educating his people. He believed that education would make life better for the minorities. It would be the first step in obtaining equality in Laos. They talked about the need for more modern medicine and public health.

Repeatedly Gauthier tried to convince Chong Toua that a weekly bath was healthy. Chong Toua listened, but argued that the layer of dirt that covered his skin protected him from disease. Chong Toua approved of Western medicine for malaria, but he, like many of his kinsmen, believed in the shamans who had the ability to appease the spirits. Shamans functioned as healers of both the body and the mind. Some were charlatans; others, renowned for the knowledge of herbal medicines and psychological stresses, successfully healed people.

In the coolness of the mountaintop village, other Hmong joined Touby and Gauthier. Everyone talked about the better life when peace returned. To achieve that peace, Gauthier believed that the French had to regain their credibility. France had not protected Laos from the Japanese invaders. Now it seemed unable to stop the Viet Minh ambushes and their recruitment of local people to fight the French. Gauthier decided that if the French hit the Viet Minh hard, they could regain standing with the local people.

Gauthier and Touby made plans. "We decided that our target would be Lat Boua, a big Lao village west of Phou Duu," recalled Gauthier. "Lat Boua, heavily fortified with deep trenches surrounding it, was used by the Viet Minh as an operational base."

The warriors grew restless, waiting for Bichelot to recover. Touby and Gauthier decided that they could wait no longer. With several hundred Hmong warriors, and without Bichelot, they led a successful commando attack against the Viet Minh base at Lat Boua.

Christmas came and still Bichelot remained weak and unable to be moved. Touby, Gauthier, Moua Chia Xang, Chong Toua, and Prince Sai Kham planned an action to retake Xieng Khouang town from the Viet Minh. Moua Chia Xang was picked to infiltrate the town to spy on the Viet Minh positions, estimate the number of troops, and ask Prince Sai Kham's father to recruit local citizens to join in the attack.

While the men waited for Moua Chia Xang's return, a Hmong patrol brought five lost Frenchmen in tatters to Phou Duu. The commander, a major, code-named "Mutin," explained that they had been in Sam Neua Province when they were assigned to the retaking of Hanoi. Mutin had decided the mission was unrealistic; instead of following orders he had headed south on foot toward Saigon.

Gauthier never forgot this countryman. "Mutin and his men stayed with us for a few days. We explained the situation to Mutin and told him a bit of our plans to recapture Xieng Khouang town. Mutin assured us that the situation was hopeless. He urged us to save ourselves and march in the direction of Saigon. He believed that to remain meant certain death or capture by the Viet Minh." Gauthier revealed to Bichelot, who could now stand, some technicalities of their plan to retake Xieng Khouang. "Bichelot thought about it and said it was risky, but it could work. Mutin, who was the highest ranking soldier with us, laughed and said, 'By God, you're crazy. It won't work and I won't be part of it!'"

Mutin pressured Bichelot to move out with him. Bichelot contemplated abandoning his position. Finally, Gauthier told Bichelot: "'You go with Mutin. I'll stay here with the Hmong. We have to take Xieng Khouang back. It's the provincial capital.' Finally, Bichelot agreed to stay with me." Energized by Bichelot's decision and angered by Major Mutin's defeatist attitude, Gauthier decided to attack early on January 26, 1946.

Touby sent runners to tell the Hmong men and boys to assemble at Phou Duu village. Hmong arrived carrying an odd assortment of weapons—old French guns, Sten guns, and rifles. Gauthier was surprised at the turnout. "Within 24 hours, Touby had assembled a Hmong force of 3,000 to 3,500 men. It was unbelievable to me. I wasn't certain that we could muster 100 men because the Hmong only fought when they thought it was a good idea." As the Hmong assembled, Major Mutin prepared to leave. He told Bichelot and Gauthier: "'I'll watch your deaths from the top of the mountain.'"

That night, the Hmong, dressed in their dark tribal clothes, moved through the blackness down from the hills and surrounded the town. Bichelot, Gauthier, Chong Toua, Moua Chia Xang, and five other Hmong listened one more time to Prince Sai Kham describe the route to the temple, located on the highest hillock, where Viet Minh gunners manned two heavy machine guns and a mortar on its roof. From this strategic location, they could easily defend the town. The resistance had to capture the temple, the weapons, and the enemy gunners without a sound.

Dark shadows moved undetected in the darkness. Prince Sai Kham led ten men to the top of the hillock, into the temple, and up to its roof to rush the enemy. All were killed soundlessly with knives. The most important position in town with its machine guns and a mortar now belonged to the resistance.

About eight in the morning, Touby's men, encircling the town, attacked from every direction, shouting and firing. The men in the temple turned the machine guns and mortar on Viet Minh positions. The recapture of the town was not easy, but after several hours of fighting, including hand-to-hand combat, the surviving Viet Minh signaled for a cease-fire. Gauthier came down from the temple and met up with Touby. "We tied up the prisoners, then marched to the French governor's residence and hoisted the French flag. I was elated. Our group of guerrilla fighters had done the impossible. We had retaken the provincial capital."

After the fighting, Major Mutin came down from the mountain pass where he had been waiting to see the defeat of Bichelot and Gauthier. "Believe it or not, he actually had the courage to return. That was unfortunate for us because then Major Mutin was the highest-ranking French officer at Xieng Khouang. As the senior officer, Mutin signed the report on our action and added in writing that he had participated in this battle.[6] Few people knew that he had no part of this action and had only watched from a safe distance, expecting us to be defeated."

Hmong "warriors" guarded the recaptured governor's residence in Xieng Khouang against Viet Minh revenge.

On February 14, Gauthier arrived in Saigon to request reinforcements and awards for those who had assisted the French in retaking Xieng Khouang. A French officer told him he could not give him any reinforcements—not even a battalion. "I quickly responded that I didn't want a battalion. If he could give me just one dozen men, that would multiply my force four times. He sent out an order for volunteers to be parachuted into Xieng Khouang. The next morning, a hundred men from a cavalry regiment volunteered. I chose one dozen of them. None had seen a parachute. On February 17, with no training in parachuting, we jumped into Xieng Khouang."

It was a joyful return for Gauthier. He had twelve more men, and in his pockets he carried the awards. In front of the French governor's residence, the entire population of the town and hundreds of Hmong "warriors" from the surrounding hills, assembled. Prince Sai Kham and Touby wore Western dress. As expected, Chong Toua wore tribal clothes and his big silver necklace. In recognition of their unfaltering and faithful actions to help the French "restore the peace," Prince Sai Kham and Touby were awarded the French Legion of Honor. Chong Toua, Moua Chia Xang, and every Hmong clan leader involved in the retaking of Xieng Khouang town received the Croix de Guerre, the highest French decoration for combat valor.

Soon after, a Vietnamese, about 30 and a former sergeant in the French Army, came to the governor's residence seeking work. A few days after he was hired, he warned Gauthier that the Viet Minh intended to kill him. He had been ordered to poison him. Gauthier remembered: "In the end, he couldn't betray me. He committed suicide—put a rifle in his mouth. He had no choice; they would have killed him for not killing me."

A short time after the liberation of Xieng Khouang town, some of the "warriors" were appointed to Lao government positions. It was the first time Hmong had held even minor government positions. They were pleased. Chong Toua was made the *Nai Khong*, or headman, of Phou Duu.

In March, the Nationalist Chinese troops began withdrawing under terms reached between France and China. French reoccupation forces entered Laos. Free Lao leaders, who controlled Luang Prabang but who had no army, realized that they would have to negotiate with the French if they were to be successful in gaining some degree of independence.

In Xieng Khouang Province, the battles between the Viet Minh and the forces of Touby and the French continued. Hmong reported Viet Minh activities to Gauthier. "The Viet Minh agents were well trained and politically strong men who preached communist ideology and who used every means—including threats and force—to persuade the population to go with them. The masses of the people were not for the Viet Minh and were afraid of them."

Gauthier visited French headquarters in Saigon to discover that the promises he had made to the Hmong—that the French would push for more minority rights and opportunities, more schools, and better health care—were of little interest to those in high places. To Gauthier, it seemed that the French had quickly forgotten those who so recently had been recognized with France's highest decorations. Frustrated and disillusioned, Lt. Maurice Gauthier contemplated resigning from the military.

The French, hard pressed for money, rescinded their preferential tax treatment of the Hmong. The Hmong, also ravaged by years of warfare, faced food shortages and hard times. The French told the Hmong that since they had spent considerable money on the construction of roads, airfields, and market places, they would have to tax them to pay back these monies. The French taxed each Hmong household seven *kip* in silver per year plus a house tax of five *bee.* The Hmong considered this new tax a heavy burden and paid it grudgingly, often in opium, thus the phrase "opium tax." Some sold their children to pay the taxes. A child could be sold for fourteen *kip* in silver. This taxation made many Hmong think that perhaps the French should go home. It was fuel for Viet Minh propaganda.[7]

In August 1946, Crown Prince Savang Vatthana signed a "modus vivendi" that provided for a Franco-Lao commission to study the future of Laos and its relationship to France. An election for representatives to prepare a constitution was to take place within the year. At the same time, the Viet Minh set up a Resistance Committee of Eastern Laos in the Hmong lands.[8] By autumn, Viet Minh forces had infiltrated Xieng Khouang Province and Xieng Khouang town with the intention of occupying and controlling the area.

In December, although harassed by the Viet Minh, voters elected 44 delegates who, with French assistance, were to draft a Lao constitution that would grant limited independence to Laos. For the French, a major crisis had passed. Laos would remain within the French domain.

That same month, Gauthier's resignation from the French military became official. He moved to Saigon, where he built a truck from bits and pieces of war scrap and began hauling much-needed foodstuffs from Cambodia to Saigon. "No place outside of Saigon was safe at this time, but I drove my old truck weekly through dangerous territory to and from Cambodian border towns. I was heavily armed, as was a friend who rode in the cab with me. Many vehicles were ambushed. We were lucky; we were never attacked. I made lots of money trucking, but I also spent lots of money."

Prince Souphanouvong was disillusioned. Many Lao Issara were satisfied with the negotiated independence that put Laos in the French Union. Instead of joining his countrymen to build a newly constituted Laos, he took his small band of followers—soon to be known as the Pathet Lao—to the mountains of northeast Laos in Hmong homelands to join Ho's Marxist-Leninist-Maoist Viet Minh in their "wars of national liberation."

The decision by most Hmong leaders—with the exception of Phay

Dang—to side with the French against the Japanese and their collabora-tors had been a political watershed. By protecting French soldiers, pro-viding intelligence for the French, and conducting guerrilla warfare against the Japanese and the Viet Minh, Touby's Hmong had chosen sides in the battles to come.[9]

4.

The Time of the Viet Minh

[The Hmong possessed] understanding of the country and of its possibilities, their adaptation to the conditions of the local life, their primitive instinct for acute danger, their potential to suffer much more than we. They can often find a solution that a European is incapable of imagining.

—French Colonel Roger Trinquier, commander of the Groupe de Commandos Mixtes Aéroportés (GCMA), French special forces, who had overall command of the partisan groups fighting the Viet Minh, from his book *Les Maquis d'Indochine*

In early 1947, pink and red bougainvillea bloomed along the main street of Prince Sai Kham's Xieng Khouang town, where only a year earlier he, Gauthier, and the Hmong had driven out the Viet Minh. Yet a threat remained. Vendors from the countryside brought troublesome news that the Viet Minh were recruiting rural people to their cause. He hoped the Lao government, with French military assistance, would push all the Viet Minh out of Laos. The Viet Minh, however, had other ideas. Their political commissar, a tough Vietnamese captain, and thousands of Vietnamese soldiers and political cadre had moved permanently into Laos where they worked with Prince Souphanouvong and his followers.

While the Viet Minh prepared to take over northeastern Laos, Sisavang Vong, the Lao king, on May 11, 1947, promulgated a constitution, drafted by elected delegates, that declared Laos an independent state within the French Union. In reality, Laos was not totally independent, and its voice in the French Union was weak; but it was a step toward total independence.

At Nong Het, so remote from Paris and even from Vientiane, the influence of the new Lao government was minimal. Here the Viet Minh were the dominant force, although most Hmong wanted Laos to be part of the French Union and wanted the French military to stop the Viet Minh from harassing and killing those loyal to the French.

Even in these unsettled times, Chief Touby continued to urge Hmong parents to send their bright male children to the open-air Nong Het school. Here Moua Lia, the freckle-faced son of the decorated warrior Moua Chia Xang, and a stocky boy named Vang Chou, whose father gathered intelligence for the French, studied with a couple of dozen other boys.

In 1947, Vang Chou, at age 11, had his first encounter with the communists. He was sitting in the doorway of his home while his mother prepared the evening meal when a Viet Minh convoy arrived. Always interested in mathematics, Chou counted the soldiers as they passed. He had counted over 500—and more were coming—when a Hmong informer for the Viet Minh noticed him. ''You're spying for the Fackee!'' he shouted at the boy. ''Off to jail!''[1] The informant grabbed Vang Chou and dragged him along the street for all to see, shouting ''Spy! Spy! A spy of the Fackee!'' At the edge of town, the Viet Minh supporter threw the boy into a dark cave that functioned as the local jail. Vang Chou was frightened. His father was pro-Fackee and anti–Viet Minh. At night messengers often visited his father with reports on the Viet Minh which his father passed on to the French. Within several hours Chou was released, but he never forgot the incident, intended as a warning to his father. Vang Chou's father took the Viet Minh warning seriously and moved into the mountains. He sent his family to a village near Xieng Khouang town.

Within days of the convoy's arrival, farmers reported to Chou's father that there were thousands of Vietnamese soldiers and cadre in the area, under the command of a Vietnamese colonel, Du Ku Thai. Viet Minh cadre explained their presence, telling the farmers that their goal was to send the French back to Europe and to clear out the Hmong who supported the French so there could be peace.

The war in Laos that would continue into the 1990s—almost half a century—was under way. Vang Chou's father would become a leader in the *Meo* (Hmong) *Maquis,* Hmong partisans organized by the French to fight the Viet Minh. Vang Chou and his schoolmate Moua Lia would become major participants in this long and deadly struggle.

At the end of 1947, Maurice Gauthier, disillusioned and penniless, left

Saigon to return to France. He would eventually marry a Frenchwoman and become involved in the jewelry business.

*   *   *

Responding to Lao demands for more independence and to the growing Viet Minh threat in Laos and Vietnam, France granted more rights to Laos, including the right to its own Territorial Army to be trained and commanded by Frenchmen. During World War II, the Hmong had learned a valuable lesson. They were now keenly aware of the need to protect Hmong lands. Those like Vue Sai Long, who had only been partisans during the Japanese occupation, now joined the military. This way, the Hmong reasoned, they would have the necessary training and modern weapons to protect themselves.

In Paris in July 1949, King Sisavang Vong signed a treaty with the French, whereupon Lao proudly unfurled a new Lao flag, a three-headed white elephant standing on the five Buddhist precepts under a white parasol. Laos would also have a seat in the United Nations. The man responsible for setting up the Lao U.N. mission in New York would be Prince Sisouk na Champassak, the French-educated son of the politically important Champassak family of southern Laos. Prince Sisouk would become the first Lao Ambassador to the United Nations.

On October 1, 1949, Mao Zedong's revolutionary forces marched into Beijing to establish communist control over China. In Washington, a furor arose: China was lost. Mao's victory was also felt in northern Laos. Some Hmong living in China fled his revolution and trekked to Laos where they told their kinsmen of the harsh life under communism.

In that same month, after Laos had gained major independence concessions, the Lao Issara announced its dissolution, but Prince Souphanouvong and his followers refused to disband, calling themselves the Pathet Lao, meaning Country of Lao, and claiming to be the successors of the Free Lao. Soon after, Prince Souphanouvong visited Ho's Tonkin headquarters, where he was warmly received by Ho and Vo Nguyen Giap, commander-in-chief of the Viet Minh forces. Before the Lao prince departed, the Viet Minh designated him the head of a Lao Liberation Committee. Ho, determined that the Vietnamese would replace the French throughout Indochina, needed a Lao prince on his side in Laos.

On January 14, 1950, Ho appealed for recognition of his self-styled people's democratic republic. Communist governments in Beijing and Moscow complied. The U.S. responded by recognizing the French-sponsored governments in Vientiane, Phnom Penh, and Hanoi and by sending economic and military assistance. This assistance went through the French who were reluctant to allow the U.S. to negotiate directly with these countries.

At Phou Duu, Chong Toua, already a legend, added to his stature by purchasing a jeep and learning to drive it. After Touby, he was the first Hmong to own a vehicle. In May 1950, after the opium harvest, Chong Toua, in his position as *Nai Khong,* loaded his jeep with opium to pay his village's taxes. Although Chong Toua was a Lao government official, he insisted on wearing Hmong clothes and his big heavy silver necklace. Today was no exception. He and his three passengers, including one of his sons, headed for Xieng Khouang town to turn over the "opium tax" to Touby. In 1946, Touby had become the first deputy provincial governor and in this position collected Hmong taxes. Chong Toua delivered the tax and stayed to visit. It was dark when he began the treacherous journey home. While the distance was only 60 kilometers, it was a long, tough drive up the rutted track to Phou Duu. At 11 p.m., Chong Toua neared the last stretch of the narrow, steep mountain trail. Suddenly his engine lost power, jerking, stalling, and then rolling backward down the hill. Chong Toua pulled the hand brake. It did not hold. As the jeep careened backwards down the steep incline, his three passengers jumped out. Realizing he could not stop the jeep, Chong Toua also attempted to jump out. In the darkness, the jeep crashed into a large tree.

His three passengers were bleeding, but not seriously hurt. They rushed to the jeep. Chong Toua was still in the driver's seat. His large silver necklace, entangled in the steering wheel, held his head close to it at an odd angle. Blia Vue, his son, saw that his father was unconscious. The Hmong believed that an unconscious person must immediately be given a drop of urine to "bring the person back." Blia Vue gave his father a drop of his own urine. Chong Toua momentarily regained consciousness. He told his son his neck hurt and to get help. Blia Vue ran to the house of "Haje" Tisserand, the ex–Foreign Legionnaire, who lived close to the crash site.

At five in the morning, Chong Toua, unconscious, was moved from the crash site and taken to the Plaine des Jarres, where he was airlifted by a C-47 to Seno and then on to Saigon. As Chong Toua's plane approached Saigon, he died.

Much to the dismay of his family, Chong Toua, wearing his silver necklace, was buried in a Saigon cemetery. His grieving relatives begged the authorities to return his body. Finally, after 29 days in the ground,

Chong Toua's body was exhumed and returned to Laos. Hmong from all over northern Laos assembled for the burial ceremony to honor one of their bravest warriors.

*   *   *

On June 25, 1950, North Korean communist forces plunged over the 38th parallel into South Korea. Four days later, communist forces held Seoul. This invasion and Mao Zedong's revolutionary forces perched on the borders of Vietnam, Laos, and Burma dramatically changed U.S. policy toward Asia. The spread of communism, with its wars of national liberation, was perceived as a threat to all of Asia and had to be stopped—or at least contained.

While the U.S. had initially deplored France's return to influence in Indochina, continued problems with the Soviet Union in Europe and then the communist invasion of South Korea moderated that view. The U.S. needed its NATO ally France both in Europe and in Indochina. As many policymakers contended, France had moved, though perhaps slowly, toward granting independence to its former colonies in Indochina, albeit within a French Union. France, they argued, was far preferable to the communist alternative. In Asia, the "cold" war became a series of "hot" wars. In the U.S., the "Red Menace" scare brought Senator Joseph McCarthy's hearings and "brinksmanship" diplomacy. The Iron Curtain was drawn across Europe, securing Eastern Europe in the Soviet bloc.

In this environment, the U.S. decision to back France in Indochina seemed logical. On June 29, 1950, the first U.S. supplies arrived in Saigon to aid the French in their fight against General Giap's Chinese-backed Viet Minh.

*   *   *

In 1952, Viet Minh in Laos regularly ambushed the French, inflicting heavy casualties. Since Frenchmen, with rare exceptions, could not endure long stretches in the jungle, master indigenous languages, or slip unnoticed into a village to gather information, they lacked adequate intelligence and therefore had little choice but to turn to the indigenous people for assistance.

The French commander at Muang Ngan ordered Vang Pao, by then a soldier without rank in the Lao Territorial Army, to learn all Viet Minh troop locations in his area and their attack plans. [2] Vang Pao told the officer that he could not guarantee anything since the French had been working for weeks on this problem with no success. But the Frenchmen urged him to try, and finally Vang Pao agreed. The officer did not know that this Hmong, whom they had recruited to tackle a problem that totally baffled them, was only 18.

Two days later, armed with French small automatic weapons and thirty rounds of ammunition, Vang Pao, with a small group of Hmong, departed the post to search for the elusive Viet Minh and the information the French needed. Vang Pao knew the trails had been mined by the Viet Minh, so he and his men headed for the jungle. Unlike the French, who were unfamiliar with the mountains and stuck to main roads and trails, the Hmong avoided the Viet Minh by using the jungle and a compass.

After several days' walk, they reached the area where Vang Pao believed he would find the enemy. Here he came upon a young Hmong couple working their mountainside cornfield. Stopping to talk to them, he learned that they had just married. Using a technique that became a Vang Pao trademark, he sat down and listened to them. After hearing about their marriage and their families, he said he was sorry to have missed their wedding and offered them good wishes and presents of aspirin and silver. They talked for four or five hours without Vang Pao mentioning the enemy. Finally, he broached the subject of his mission, asking the bride if she knew anything about a group of 13 Viet Minh in this area who were organizing the people. She told Vang Pao where they were camped and drew him a map.

With the bridegroom as a guide, Vang Pao's team neared the Viet Minh encampment in darkness by coming down a mountainside—an approach unsuspected and unprotected. While his men waited in the bamboo forest, Vang Pao crept close enough to the suspected hut to see through its split bamboo walls. Around a glowing fire, 13 Viet Minh soldiers talked and relaxed, unaware that they were being watched.

Since the Hmong had only small arms and 30 rounds of ammunition, Vang Pao had to attack at close range. His team quietly surrounded the hut. They fired into its walls. Then all was quiet. As they approached, an enemy soldier darted out the door and into the darkness. Vang Pao ran after him, capturing him after a 300-meter chase. In the hut, Vang Pao found important documents and maps describing impending military actions against French posts.

The weary Hmong returned to Muang Ngan only to learn that the French, while pleased with their efforts, proposed another immediate action. They had received information that the Viet Minh planned to attack Sop Nao as soon as additional troops arrived. Vang Pao's mission was to interdict these reinforcements. The French commander ordered Vang Pao to leave that night. Vang Pao protested, explaining that his men were too tired. The commander insisted, pointing out that only the Hmong could maintain the pace necessary to intercept the advancing troops.

Vang Pao relented. Restocked with ammunition and a machine gun, he marshaled his tired men. After walking all night, they came upon soldiers preparing breakfast. With binoculars, he studied them. They were Viet Minh. Vang Pao set up a machine gun. Those with small arms crawled closer. His machine-gun fire toppled the unsuspecting soldiers. As the team rushed forward, one soldier scrambled to his feet and up the bank on the far side of the road. Vang Pao took off after the enemy soldier, who had a considerable lead. After chasing him for over a kilometer, Vang Pao began gaining on him. Suddenly, the tiring Viet Minh turned and lobbed a hand grenade that exploded near Vang Pao. Without breaking stride, Vang Pao, unharmed, pursued and captured the exhausted enemy soldier. Again, Vang Pao's team found significant military documents.

Vang Pao returned to report another successful mission, with no friendly casualties. The French commander, Captain Fiet, was impressed. Vang Pao never forgot their conversation: "The French commander said to me, 'Vang Pao, I hope you are not just a soldier. I hope you are an officer.' I told the commander, 'I am not an officer. I am only a lowly soldier without any rank.' The French commander was surprised. Then he announced: 'Vang Pao, you have to become an officer.' With no hesitation, I answered, 'O.K. I agree.'"

Over a hand-cranked communications system, Captain Fiet contacted authorities in Vientiane. The next day a plane air-dropped an entrance examination for officers' training school. Although Vang Pao had completed only a few years of education at the Nong Het primary school, within two months he was attending Dong Hene officers' school in southern Laos where the French trained a Lao army. Vang Pao, the only Hmong among 56 newcomers in the class, struggled with the written assignments, but when it came to tactics and operations he was at the top of his class. He graduated seventh in his class. In March 1952 he received his cadet officer's stripes from King Sisavang Vong.[3]

*   *   *

In November 1952, Viet Minh forces occupied Dien Bien Phu, an obscure market town just inside the North Vietnamese border, only 125 miles from Luang Prabang, the religious capital and home of the Lao royal family, and used it to launch an April offensive against Laos. Meeting little resistance, they pushed rapidly westward. Vang Pao rushed to protect Luang Prabang and the king by blocking the road. The Viet Minh withdrew without an engagement and moved into "liberated zones," as they called territories they overran, to wait and to deploy their political cadre to erode local French support by recruiting people, often brutally.

After the April invasion, most remaining Nong Het Hmong trekked south to Xieng Khouang town, where they sought Touby's protection. Touby, realizing the town could not accommodate so many refugees, moved some to Lat Houang, due west in the mountains. At Lat Houang, a rich agricultural plateau famous for its citrus, Hmong prepared fields and built a school. Others sought refuge on Phou San, the elongated mountain ridge where Gauthier had operated with Touby during World War II.

* * *

On July 27, 1953, after 37 months of bitter fighting pitting the South Koreans and U.S. and other United Nations forces against the invading Soviet-backed North Korean Army and the Red Chinese Army "volunteers," the Korean War ended where it had begun. Korea remained divided at the 38th parallel. The U.S. policy of limited warfare, initiated by President Truman in the defense of Korea, endured under President Eisenhower. It would be soon repeated in Southeast Asia.

In a speech on September 2, 1953, Ho Chi Minh declared the stalemate in the Korean War a victory for peace and democracy and a victory for the Chinese and Koreans. Ho said: "The U.S. imperialists and the U.S. side had to agree to the cease-fire because they failed bitterly, and could not carry on the fight. Therefore, the Chinese and Korean armies and peoples and the world camp for peace and democracy as a whole must struggle and be vigilant against sabotaging schemes of the imperialists and their lackeys."

* * *

General Henri Navarre, French commander-in-chief in Indochina, understood the defense of Laos as a moral obligation. After the Viet Minh 1953 spring invasion into Laos, he began to formulate plans that would eliminate the Viet Minh threat both in Vietnam and Laos.

In October 1953, Captain Jean Sassi, a French commando trained by Force 136 during World War II who had night-parachuted into Laos in June 1945 to help French commandos already there, returned to Laos after a tour in Africa and Vietnam. This time, Sassi was assigned to the French special forces Groupe de Commandos Mixtes Aéroportés (GCMA). Sassi deployed to Laos as a commando in the 8th Choc. He was to train, arm, and lead indigenous forces, to be called the Meo Maquis, in the fight against the Viet Minh.

At the Khang Khay garrison, Sassi renewed his friendship with Touby, whom he had met in 1945. Here he also met Vang Pao, now a commissioned second lieutenant who was serving with French Lieutenant Max Mesnier, chief of the Meo Maquis.

Soon after Sassi's arrival, he and Vang Pao conducted missions together. Sassi was impressed with the young Hmong officer. "Vang Pao's eyes, darting and quick, saw all. He reminded me of a panther. On one of our first treks, he suddenly stopped, silencing the rest of us, and pointed to the underbrush. I couldn't see anything. He motioned again. I still couldn't see anything. He raised his carbine, shot, and a bird fell to the ground. He and his men could see things that none of the Frenchmen could see. Vang Pao and his men were 'magnifique' in the jungle. The jungle was their habitat and they thrived in it."[4]

In the fall of 1953, the French High Command in Indochina initiated a plan that would not only protect Laos but would trap General Vo Nguyen Giap and his Viet Minh forces. In late November 1953, French paratroopers retook Dien Bien Phu to deny the Viet Minh this base from which they could invade Laos. Here in this remote valley, a few miles from the Lao border in northern Vietnam and two hundred miles from French supply bases in Hanoi and Haiphong, General Navarre set his trap. Here, he believed, he would strike the devastating final blow to Ho's intentions of taking over French Indochina by luring General Giap's divisions into the surrounding mountains and pounding them with air strikes and long-range artillery. The French concluded that Dien Bien Phu, defended and supplied by the French Air Force, was impregnable. Some nicknamed it "the Hedgehog" because it bristled with French military might.

By Christmas, the Dien Bien Phu trap held 12,000 men, including some 200 Hmong, and bristled with tanks, howitzers, mortars, airfields, command posts, and a field hospital. As Navarre had predicted, Giap's forces occupied the higher ground roundabout.

Yang Cheng Leng, a Hmong from Vietnam, served inside Dien Bien Phu, as did his relative Yang Mi Cha. Cheng Leng's battalion, composed of French, Hmong, and Thai Dam soldiers, protected the main airfield with 37mm mortars, machine guns, and small arms. Chong Toua's son Tou Lue, who had joined the Maquis in 1953 at the urging of Touby, was positioned on a nearby mountain and could see the lights of Dien Bien Phu. For several weeks, tribal scouts like Tou Lue had reported that the enemy monitored every French move. It seemed to him that the French did not care.[5]

General Navarre flew to Dien Bien Phu for Christmas Eve. He gave presents to his field commanders, but apparently he said nothing about the enormous military threat mushrooming in the hills fencing in the French bastion. Nor did he mention the decoded military intelligence intercepts indicating that Giap had long-range guns, either in place or about to be put in place, in the encircling mountains, and that escape from the Hedgehog might soon be impossible.

That night, French Expeditionary Corps soldiers sang Christmas carols in their native tongues of French, German, and English as machine guns burped on the perimeters. Hmong soldiers watched in amazement. They knew their camp lights could be seen for miles, and songs of religious celebration carried throughout the valley and into the mountains.

Throughout northern Laos, French officers like Sassi, working with tribal leaders, clandestinely recruited and trained resistance forces. During late 1953, many Hmong had volunteered for the Maquis. Like the French underground resistance during World War II, it was important that these forces remain secret.

As Maquis were trained, they were put into the field encadred by French commandos. At Tha Li Noi, Moua Chia Xang organized a Maquis unit, consisting of 104 Hmong, one French sergeant, and a radio operator. Vang Pao organized units at Nam Khan and Pa Pong which eventually formed into Commando Group (GC) 204 under Sassi's command.*

On March 13, 1954, the earth shook around Dien Bien Phu. General Giap's 50,000 troops attacked with over one hundred 105mm howitzers and eighty antiaircraft guns, most supplied by Communist China complete with Chinese advisors and gunners. By April 1, the Viet Minh in savage fighting had established a foothold inside the perimeters of the Hedgehog, the main base. Giap's antiaircraft guns and howitzers now denied the French Air Force use of the garrison's airfields. Supplies had to be air-dropped at considerable risk to pilots. The easy victory envisioned by the French military command did not come. The trap had sprung on the French.

---

*Frenchmen Malo and Servan, with Hmong leader Sangsue, formed Commando Group (GC) 200, totaling 4,000 men.

Captain Jean Sassi, the veteran commando, understood the gravity of the situation at Dien Bien Phu. Working with Touby, he refined a plan to use his Meo Maquis to break the siege. Code-named "Operation D" (for Dien Bien Phu), Sassi's plan was simple. The Maquis would arrive quickly and get as close as possible to Dien Bien Phu. Then they would harass the Viet Minh rear with small-group guerrilla action. This was to cause the enemy to lessen its pressure on the besieged garrison, permitting some trapped men to break out. After the breakout, the Maquis would regroup the escapees and protect them in the jungle. Sassi's plan called for a battalion of paratroopers to reinforce the escapees. They would serve as the framework of the Maquis groups needed to hold the mobile defense perimeter until larger forces could arrive and resupply efforts could occur.[6]

In Washington, policymakers feared that Maoist China might move south—as had happened previously in Korea—from Yunnan Province to overrun Laos, Thailand, and Cambodia. This fear grew with reports of a possible victory by Ho's Maoist-backed forces at Dien Bien Phu. The U.S. was already heavily supplying the French forces in Indochina. Now, President Eisenhower authorized supplies for the besieged garrison. The U.S. hired Civil Air Transport (CAT) planes to deliver them. American civilian pilots were recruited by CAT to fly C-119s, known as "Flying Boxcars," from Haiphong to Dien Bien Phu to deliver supplies.

As the Viet Minh's stranglehold on Dien Bien Phu tightened, some French pilots refused to fly the suicidal supply drops. American crews also hesitated, but twice daily, at eight in the morning and one in the afternoon, the CAT pilots, sitting exposed in bubble cockpits, roared off the airfield at Haiphong in unarmed C-119s for the most dangerous missions many of these veterans had ever flown.

On April 12, Fred Walker landed at Haiphong to fly the Dien Bien Phu run. Walker, a veteran of World War II, had deep roots in New England. His father was a doctor in Boston. His ancestors had participated in the founding of Maine's Colby College, and the family owned farmland in rural Maine. Tall and taciturn, Walker was a meticulous notetaker. He used his flight logbooks as diaries to record cargo, passengers, weather, and the major events of each day. Now 35, Walker had plenty of flying experience. During World War II, he had flown 60 missions from India over the "Hump"—the Himalayas—and mountains of Burma into southern China. With Mao Zedong's soldiers shooting at him, he flew one of the last U.S. planes out of China.

At Dien Bien Phu, Walker quickly learned about true terror. Some say it was on these missions that he perfected his whispered, almost reverent, "Jes-us Christ" which he unconsciously used when the odds were against him. By the time Walker arrived to fly Dien Bien Phu, it was no longer called the Hedgehog. Now it was called the "Chamber Pot" or worse.

On April 16, Captain Sassi went to Saigon to discuss his Operation D with the French command. "I proposed my plan to Colonel Trinquier, commander of the GCMA, and I asked approval and requested logistical and troop support for my Maquis, and a paratrooper battalion."[7] Sassi's plan received positive attention. Four days later, Sassi returned to the Khang Khay garrison "to complete the mobilization orders and to prepare for the departure of the Maquis." By activating them, he removed the Maquis units from secrecy.

General Navarre had agreed to provide a bar of silver for each Hmong who joined with the French in this dramatic last-minute expedition to attempt a breakout at Dien Bien Phu. But Touby refused the silver—much cherished by the Hmong—saying that they had no need for silver. It was their duty to help. This show of loyalty touched the French, causing Colonel Trinquier to write, "I had already experienced the loyalty of the Meo. This however for me was an amazing verification of the loyalty of Touby and all the Meo."[8]

For Sassi, it was impossible to accept without response the death or capture of his countrymen and the loss of the French base at Dien Bien Phu. Hmong leaders shared Sassi's sentiments. Each Maquis group committed forces for Operation D, making a combined force of about 2,000 men.

As Operation D prepared to launch, Sassi learned that only the Maquis would participate. The paratrooper battalion had been denied. Sassi angrily changed the meaning of Operation D to "Operation Desperate." He and Touby decided to go ahead without the paratroopers. Touby remained at Khang Khay while Sassi, with Vang Pao as his adjutant, began a forced march from the Plaine des Jarres to the besieged garrison at Dien Bien Phu. Both Sassi and Vang Pao believed that they had no choice. Frenchmen and Hmong were trapped inside and they had to help. Before leaving the Plaine des Jarres in mid-April, Vang Pao estimated that, if Operation D could avoid enemy ambushes and the rains held off, his group would reach Dien Bien Phu by mid-May, maybe earlier.

In an odd assortment of tribal clothes and French military uniforms, Operation D moved north-northeast, under radio silence. Although this silence denied them information on the situation at Dien Bien Phu, daily they heard aircraft overhead and knew the battle still raged.

During the last week of April, there were renewed hopes of U.S. military intervention. A U.S. B-29 squadron in the Philippines waited for orders to bomb the enemy surrounding Dien Bien Phu. But the order to lift off never came; perhaps the U.S. decided it could not undertake such a mission without the approval of its major ally, Britain, which refused to change its policy of nonintervention in Indochina.

Maquis scouts like Tou Lue, already in mountain positions overlooking Dien Bien Phu, watched the battle. "I was close enough that I saw paratroopers jump and land on punji sticks [booby traps made of pointed sticks laced with dung or poison to disable or kill those who step on them] put there by the Viet Minh. I saw air-drops and planes hit by Viet Minh guns. It was so pitiful."

By the first of May, the situation at Dien Bien Phu was extremely grave. Enemy gunners knew how to target the resupply aircraft. CAT crews flew, but not without serious complaint that it was too dangerous. On the ground heading for Dien Bien Phu, the men of Operation D, dirty and tired, had walked 19 days with little rest, pushing doggedly in driving rain squalls through rugged high country toward the besieged position. Advance patrols reported distant pounding of heavy guns. Vang Pao urged his men to hurry along the slippery trails and through the chilling rain.

On May 5, Fred Walker joined the 23 CAT pilots for the usual 12:30 briefing. "Hugh Marsh, our chief CAT pilot, said he had an important announcement. 'Men,' he said, 'we're going to run a low level drop over Isabelle today at 4,500 feet instead of the usual 9,000 feet.' Isabelle was one of the last remaining outposts not overrun by the Viets. It was quiet. Then someone piped up and said, 'Jesus Christ! You trying to commit suicide?' Marsh answered: 'Shut up! I'll be leading the parade!' That was the end of that rebellion."[9]

Then James MacGovern, famous for his bright flowered shirts, his thundering voice, his aerial prowess, and his outrageous nickname of "Earthquake McGoon," complained about Fred Walker being assigned to him as copilot. "Earthquake said though he had nothing against me he had been flying with Wally Buford for six weeks. Since this was going to be a red-hot drop, he argued it was no time to be training new men. He wanted someone he knew in the cockpit for this dangerous mission. He wanted Buford. Buford, he got. That crew change was fine with me. I had been flying with Stu Dew since my arrival. I didn't want to change either. That day, we had eight airplanes scheduled to go over Isabelle. They scratched the last airplane—that was Stu Dew and myself."

With this news, Walker and Al Judson, another CAT pilot, headed for downtown Haiphong and a sidewalk cafe for a drink. They did not want to be located in case someone decided another flight was needed. As Walker savored a cool beer, he heard the C-119s heading west for Dien Bien Phu and Isabelle.

At 3 p.m., a CAT employee found Judson and Walker at the cafe. "He ordered us to get out to the airport—RIGHT NOW—to get cranked up and get out to the vicinity of Dien Bien Phu. Earthquake was down. We raced to the airport, started our engines. Then someone called us on the radio, 'Shut down. Never mind. He's down and dead.'"

Earl MacGovern, hit by enemy fire over Dien Bien Phu, had turned his plane toward Laos. He crashed 23 miles north of Sam Neua, Pathet Lao headquarters of Souphanouvong, the Red Prince. He had tried to land along a river bank. A wing tip caught and the airplane cartwheeled, crashed, and burned, killing Earthquake and his copilot, Wallace Buford. With the first cartwheel, the two cargo kickers in the back were thrown out the open door. Both survived.

The next morning, May 6, Walker and the other CAT pilots stood down. They were dismayed over losing a crew and refused to fly. Vice President of Operations Robert Rousselot arrived from Taipei to give them a pep talk. Walker remembered his solemn message: "He told us that when we took this contract we were expecting some fatalities. We've had one and we are going to continue operating. Then he said, 'If anyone doesn't want to fly down there anymore, I'm leaving at 7 o'clock tomorrow morning for Taipei. I'll be in my room from 7 until 10 tonight. You can signify your desires.' Dutch Brongersma asked, 'What's going to be our disposition if we refuse to fly and go back to Taipei?' We knew it was grounds for termination. Rousselot answered, 'Well, that policy hasn't been determined yet.' I knew what he was thinking. If all 24 pilots quit, he couldn't fire all of us without crippling the airline. If two or three guys quit, they would probably be canned. I understand seven guys took him up on his offer. I didn't blame them. It was the damnedest operation I've ever been in in my life. It was terrible. Terrible!"

At Dien Bien Phu that night, the earth shook as explosives planted inside the French perimeter by Viet Minh tunnel sappers tore open the turf. Preparation for the final Viet Minh assault was underway. During the night, 24 French Dakota aircraft dropped 70 tons of supplies to Dien Bien Phu during its death throes. Most drops fell into enemy hands.

Giap's forces were everywhere. Viet Minh jumped from tunnels bringing them up inside the French perimeter. The glow of burning tanks, jeeps, and supplies silhouetted Viet Minh darting around the camp, blowing up bunkers, collecting abandoned weapons, and planting the Viet Minh flag. Defenders with ammunition continued firing.[10] Several French colonels prepared to break out—with or without Sassi's promised Operation D reinforcements advancing by ground. Operation D noticed an orange glow in the northern horizon and picked up the pace.

At dawn, Fred Walker awoke with a sinking feeling in his stomach as he thought about the two upcoming missions over Dien Bien Phu. Mechanically he walked into the breakfast room. "First thing that I heard was that the place had fallen. I said to myself, 'Thank Christ!' That was the best news I've had before or since. The best news of my life. The very best."

The men of Operation D, dirty and tired, struggled along Phou Loi, some miles south of Dien Bien Phu. Some noted they had heard no airplanes this morning, but they marched on, maintaining radio silence. Early the next day, the radioman of Operation D raced to join Sassi and Vang Pao. "Listen!" he shouted. "Listen!" He held the radio before him and the words filled the air: *"Dien Bien Phu est tombé! Dien Bien Phu est tombé! Tombé!"*[11]

Sassi and Vang Pao listened in silence as the message was repeated several times. Finally, Sassi acknowledged and asked for instructions. "Return to the Plaine des Jarres!" the voice on the radio ordered. Vang Pao and his men fell by the side of the trail, exhausted, confused, and worried. What would this defeat mean for those who had helped the French? Giap had timed it perfectly. The Geneva Conference was scheduled to open on May 8, the next day.

After 55 days of unrelenting battle, 2,000 French Expeditionary Corps soldiers lay dead. Almost 12,000 men from the garrison, including Hmong, were taken prisoner. Yang Cheng Leng, whose battalion was assigned to protect the airfield, slipped away during the confusion of rounding up the prisoners and headed west. Many Hmong, perhaps as many as 2,000, including both those at Dien Bien Phu and those captured in the hills, were taken prisoner.

Sassi, furious that the French High Command had not agreed to support his Operation Dien Bien Phu and that the Viet Minh had taken the base, again changed the code-name of his operation from "Operation Desperate" to "Operation Deception." He did not, however, change his mission. "Our mission had not changed: to harass the Viets' rear, to gather up survivors, to harass the Viets—again and always. We believed we would win in the end. The Hmong thought the same thing. We were disturbed, overwhelmed by what would happen to the DBP survivors, but for us, we remained completely confident of victory."

Shortly after the defeat, Tou Lue's unit received an emergency radio message: "We were to immediately lead a group of 300 Frenchmen who had escaped from Dien Bien Phu to Xieng Khouang. We met up with the Frenchmen who were pitiful. Almost immediately the Viet Minh saw us and began chasing us. We could not stop to sleep. Some Frenchmen could not go on. We left them behind with their guns. Along the way we were ambushed, 100 men were killed, including seven Hmong." Three months after leaving the Dien Bien Phu area, Tou Lue's group arrived at Xieng Khouang. Only 30 French had survived. "A lot of Fackee soldiers died during the escape because we had no food," remembered Tou Lue. "We had to eat leaves, bamboo, and bananas. The Fackee were not used to our food and died. Most Fackee no longer had shoes. Their feet were sore and bleeding. They couldn't continue to walk barefoot as we did."

Moua Chia Xang's Tha Li Noi Maquis rescued 19 French soldiers, including Captain Desphases, who had escaped from Sam Neua, and six other French soldiers from Nong Het, including Captain Debon.[12]

On May 11, Sassi received formal orders to return to base. He returned to Khang Khay, but the Maquis of Operation D stayed on to look for survivors. "More than 200 escapees owed their lives to the Hmong of Operation D." reported Sassi.

General Giap's booty included a major cache of weapons and supplies. His forces captured 11,721 French Union soldiers and released 3,290. Most of these were French nationals. The other 7,801 prisoners were unaccounted for—presumably killed or kept as POWs. But the most important spoil of this war was his victory over the white man.

Hmong taken prisoner during the battle for Dien Bien Phu were held in captivity by the Vietnamese communists until 1979 when the Chinese invaded Vietnam. Then, the Vietnamese, fearing that these prisoners of war would be found by the Chinese, released those still alive. One of those released in 1979 was Yang Mi Cha, now in his late 50s.[13] The Viet Minh had captured him as he tried to defend the French headquarters at Dien Bien Phu and held him for 25 years. Many of his fellow prisoners died during their quarter of a century of imprisonment. During all this time, apparently no international agency tried to secure the release of these POWs.

* * *

In the beautiful city of Geneva, in May 1954, France, the Democratic Republic of Vietnam, the noncommunist Associated States of Vietnam (South Vietnam), Laos, and Cambodia, the United States, Britain, the People's Republic of China, and the Soviet Union assembled to negotiate a cease-fire and to forge an "acceptable peace."

Here the Viet Minh employed their "guerrilla diplomacy" by requesting the conference to seat representatives of their resistance groups in Cambodia and in Laos. At the time, the Pathet Lao numbered only a few hundred members, and the Pathet Lao delegate came to Geneva on a North Vietnamese passport. The conference did not seat him.

The Viet Minh delegation deftly denied that it had any troops in Laos. In fact, thousands operated there. This deception turned out to be an important victory, for it allowed the Viet Minh to keep in place in Laos its political cadre and its armed soldiers.

Ho Chi Minh's guerrilla diplomacy included the ingenious concept of *hoa de tien* or fighting to negotiate whereby treaties or agreements are not intended to be honored but are useful only to buy time to reorganize and to reequip one's own forces while disarming and weakening enemy forces.

* * *

While diplomats convened in Geneva for the conference, CAT pilot Fred Walker remained based at Haiphong. Now he flew C-119 supply missions over Laos. During May, he dropped tons of barbed wire, fence pickets, parachutes, and rice into Laos, often on the Plaine des Jarres and at Vientiane. Walker humorously concluded that maybe Laos expected trouble and was considering fencing off the entire country. Being the "good soldier," he never asked why Laos needed all that barbed wire and all those pickets.

In early June, Walker was reassigned to Vietnam for a few days to fly Viet Minh POWs. Then he returned to flying supplies to Laos, including foodstuffs and roofing. On June 12, 1954, his cargo changed dramatically. In his logbook, he recorded a delivery of 11,700 pounds of 81mm mortar shells with fuses to Seno in southern Laos. On each of the next two days, he delivered 13,500 pounds of 60mm mortar shells. Then he returned to air-dropping food, parachutes, barbed wire, and fenceposts, which had replaced the less substantial pickets. Serious American involvement in Laos had begun.

In July, France and Ho's Democratic Republic signed armistice agreements that theoretically ended the fighting in Laos, Cambodia, and Vietnam. The Accords recognized Laos as an independent entity. Conference participants spoke of Laos as a neutral state and buffer zone between communist North Vietnam and noncommunist Thailand and Cambodia.

The accords permitted agreements that Laos had negotiated before the Geneva Conference to remain in place, including the economic development assistance and military aid agreements between Laos and the U.S. The accords also let stand the Treaty of Amity and Association between France and Laos that obligated France to protect Laos against aggression and allowed French officers such as Captain Jean Sassi to stay on to train and to advise the Royal Lao Armed Forces. The accords did prohibit the introduction of foreign troops, "except for the purpose of the effective defense" of Lao territory, and also prohibited the establishment of "foreign bases."

Sam Neua and Phong Saly were designated as regrouping zones for the Pathet Lao. Nothing was noted about the withdrawal of Viet Minh forces from Laos because the Viet Minh had successfully denied they had troops there.

While the accords specified that it was the "sovereign right of the Royal Government to establish its administration in the two northern provinces [Phong Saly and Sam Neua] and this right is undisputed," the Pathet Lao and Viet Minh, in defiance, set up schools in their "liberated" zone, printed textbooks, appointed headmen and district officials, dealt out punishment as determined by the discipline of the communist party, recruited a local army—called "volunteers"—and acted as if these two provinces were a Pathet Lao state.

The accords also created an International Control Commission (ICC) charged with monitoring cease-fire violations. Procedures to reintegrate Pathet Lao troops were left for future negotiation.

Since the accords did not deal with Viet Minh troops in Laos, or with a reintegration procedure, the Viet Minh troops were not withdrawn and the Pathet Lao troops were not reintegrated. Circumvention of the intent of the Geneva Accords foreshadowed disaster for the Royal Lao government.

Hmong leaders concluded that the accords meant nothing to the Vietnamese who, they believed, intended to take over Laos. A warning by one of their elders circulated: "Do not worry about the words in Geneva, they are only words. Worry about the Vietnamese soldiers in Laos, they are real."

Viet Minh soldiers, cadre, and their student Pathet Lao surrogates divided and frightened the Hmong. In villages in Sam Neua and Phong Saly, communist cadre persuaded, coerced, and terrorized villagers into cooperation—into becoming "volunteers." Villages became cells which were divided into smaller cells. Women's groups, youth groups, and other groups—of weavers, potters, silversmiths, gunsmiths, and farmers —were dominated by cadre. Through such organizational control, communist dominance was total.

In some areas entire Hmong villages performed slave labor. They worked as porters or built roads. The Hmong who had worked as *corvée* labor for the colonial French had listened to communist cadres only a few years earlier telling them that the French must be forced out because they demanded 15 days of free labor annually for civic work, building roads, marketplaces, and sometimes commercial ventures such as mining. Under the Viet Minh, forced labor was promoted as a "volunteer" activity, a patriotic cause, and could last for months. For those who disobeyed, punishment was severe. Offenders were often sent to North Vietnam for reeducation. Many never returned.

The Lao government, isolated from the villages where the Viet Minh operated, could do little to protect its citizens. Protecting citizens and fighting Viet Minh remained the burden of the Maquis.

Lao officials also lacked political savvy in dealing with the communists. Prince Souvanna Phouma naively believed that he could work out "something" with his communist half-brother Souphanouvong. Laos also lacked experienced personnel to govern this extremely underdeveloped nation which functioned primarily on a barter system. Few Lao had experience running their own country because during colonial times the French had used Vietnamese bureaucrats to administer Laos. Even the Lao military was short of experienced personnel. Under the French, most officers had been French; most noncommissioned officers had been Vietnamese.

Captain Sassi, now an official military counselor to the Royal Lao government, collaborated with Lt. Vang Pao to transfer Maquis into the regular Lao forces. Concerned about abandoning the Hmong as the French curtailed their involvement in the area, Sassi regularly sent his junior officers to Hanoi to recover munitions and equipment for his Maquis in case the departing French authorities decided to disarm them. "Tons of replacement material were given to the Maquis who were positioned on the PDJ to be restored, reconditioned, and camouflaged with great dispatch and secrecy. As a result, there was to be no question that I would leave my Hmong friends disarmed facing the Viet hordes that we kept on fighting after the cease-fire and until my departure.''

In early 1955, Captain Jean Sassi prepared to leave Laos. His tour of duty ended in March. In those final weeks, he knew there was much to do, but he took comfort in some of his accomplishments: ''When I left Laos, it was independent, it had preserved its king, its government, its army. Numerous French military advisors were still there. The ICC created by the Geneva Accords to monitor the situation had an office there. In Laos, the Viets were not in the big cities. They had not won any battle, quite the opposite. Our Maquis had everywhere thrown them back. The Viets were everywhere completely insecure. American forces were stationed in Vientiane, apparently ready to relieve us.''

Just before Sassi departed, he traveled to the Plaine des Jarres to visit Touby and Vang Pao, now commander of all Hmong forces in upper Laos. ''It was naturally hard for me to leave my Hmong and Lao brothers in arms. Our good-bye, on the PDJ, was in the nature of 'au revoir'— until we meet again.'' That was never to happen.

The Fackee were gone; only the Americans represented any challenge to Hanoi's dreams of expansionism.

Part Two

Laos:
The First
Domino

5.

The Time of the Americans

Despite its remoteness, we were determined to preserve the independence of Laos against a take-over backed by its neighbors to the north—Communist China and North Vietnam. For the fall of Laos to Communism could mean the subsequent fall—like a tumbling row of dominoes—of its still-free neighbors, Cambodia and South Vietnam and, in all probability, Thailand and Burma. Such a chain of events would open the way to Communist seizure of all Southeast Asia.

—President Dwight D. Eisenhower in *Waging the Peace*

Laos, hanging on the belly of an aggressive communist China, was an obvious key domino. The Eisenhower administration had no intention of allowing Laos to fall to communism, setting the stage for the loss to the West of strategically important Southeast Asia. Laos would be a test case—a dramatic struggle, pitting the U.S. against the forces of communism. To keep the Lao domino from falling, the Eisenhower administration initiated a large-scale military, economic, and political strategy in that country in the wake of the armistice at Geneva. Although the first Indochina War was over, few believed that the Vietnamese communists would leave their neighbors alone.

Although the Royal Lao government had declared its intent not to allow foreign military bases on its territory, and Laos was not a member of the Southeast Asia Treaty Organization (SEATO) founded by the United States and five other nations in September 1954, Laos, along with Cambodia and South Vietnam, was designated in a protocol to the treaty as a country where the mutual security provisions of the treaty would apply in the event of aggression.

The U.S. also took over a large share of the responsibility of training, equipping, and paying the Royal Lao Army with the aim of enabling it to cope with the continued presence of the Pathet Lao armed units regrouped in Sam Neua and Phong Saly provinces. To circumvent the prohibition against a foreign military presence in Laos, this mission was entrusted to a new organization, the Programs Evaluation Office (PEO) which began functioning in 1955. PEO consisted of U.S. military personnel transferred to temporary civilian status, headed by a general.

While some Hmong had recently joined the Royal Lao Army, most without rank, the majority in the army were ethnic Lao. It is ironic that an army whose principal mission was to enforce the government's right of sovereignty in two border provinces contained few members of those minorities whose villages were in contest. In these provinces, sporadic skirmishing between the Royal Lao Army and the Pathet Lao continued unabated.

An economic aid program was undertaken by the U.S. in the years after 1954 which soon became the largest such program anywhere in the world in terms of aid received per capita. Much of this aid was intended to prevent the inflationary pressures on the tiny Lao economy stemming from paying the army. The net effect of much of this aid, however, was to create an opportunity for graft and corruption by government officials and merchants. Lao farmers and hill people received little, if anything, from the U.S. largesse during the 1950s, while corrupt individuals grew rich in the towns.

The Eisenhower administration's strategy in Laos was motivated by fear that the Lao leaders in Vientiane would invite the communists in by the back door by agreeing to form a coalition government which included the Pathet Lao. The Pathet Lao had demanded a coalition in exchange for their agreement to relinquish their exclusive control over the two northern provinces. After Prince Souvanna Phouma's rise to prime minister in 1956, negotiations with the Pathet Lao would proceed over the objections of the American Embassy in Vientiane, which would result in the formation in November 1957 of the first coalition government with two Pathet Lao ministers. From Washington's perspective, the situation would worsen further during 1958, when in supplemental elections Pathet Lao or leftist candidates won a majority of the contested National Assembly seats. Alarmed by the trend and fearful that the Lao domino was toppling, the Eisenhower administration would embark on a program of sabotaging the coalition, counting on the army and such irregular forces as it could find in the country to stabilize the situation.

*   *   *

In September 1955, CAT pilot Fred Walker was assigned six weeks' temporary duty (TDY) to Saigon, although he actually operated out of Udorn Air Force Base in northern Thailand. Flying a C-46, he air-dropped bags of rice along the Lao-China border and the Lao–North Vietnam border at remote places like Ban Ban and Phou Pha Thi, a dramatic 5,500-foot-high mountain about 15 miles west of the North Vietnamese border.[1] During October of that year, Walker flew many missions over Laos. Sometimes he flew low-level missions scattering propaganda pamphlets over communist territory. On October 27, as Walker prepared to return to Taipei after his TDY assignment, he wrote in his logbook: "Said goodbye to the International Control Commission. It takes them two weeks to show when there is trouble." Walker's sarcasm reflected the disdain and frustration that many Americans felt toward the hamstrung commission established by the Geneva Accords to monitor the cease-fire in Laos.

On November 23, 1956, Walker departed Kadena Air Force Base in Japan for Vientiane. In his logbook, he wrote: "Kadena, Clark, Taipei, Vientiane. 8,100 pounds of medical supplies. Ha. Ha." He had not been loaded with medicines: he had been hauling ammunition. During 1957, he often flew to Thailand, Vietnam, and Laos under contract to U.S. government agencies. On July 19, he flew to Laos, recording in his logbook: "More medical supplies. More sick people." In September, his cargo to Vientiane included a number of CIA personnel and military supplies.

As the American effort increased, so did the communist rhetoric and effective word mirages. Advised by their Vietnamese backers, who mimicked their Maoist mentors in China, the Pathet Lao lexicon portrayed its supporters falsely as the "majority group" and the Royal Lao government as a "minority" group of American "lackeys." The communist "people's patriotic defense forces" heroically and continually "liberated" the suffering people from the "imperialistic" Americans, who sought to establish military bases in Laos to attack China and financially exploit the local people. The propaganda value of corrupting U.S. aid fit nicely with the Pathet Lao anti-American campaign that emphasized the imperialistic, exploitative nature of American neocolonialism. Communist radio broadcasts and leaflets labeled the American efforts in Laos as "cash and violence." The cash part was true. It was, however, the Pathet Lao who effectively used violence, assassinating key provincial leaders and terrorizing people into cooperation.

The U.S. and the Royal Lao government responded to this propaganda with air-dropped leaflets designed to rally the opposition to the government side. Pilots like Fred Walker who flew leaflet drops doubted that they produced many defectors.

As communist control of villages tightened, Hmong found it difficult to gather intelligence. "The Northern Warrior," Moua Cher Pao, who had fought with the French against the Viet Minh at Phou San, had a solid reputation for stubbornness, toughness, courage, and a willingness to try to outwit the Vietnamese. This short, wiry man, with frizzy, raven-black hair, had two wives. His second wife was Vue Mee, widow of his best friend, Lor Chong Tou. When he married Mee, she had several small children, including a beautiful daughter named Chia. By his first wife, he had three boys and six girls. Nhia, the sixth child, resembled her father both physically and emotionally. A spirited, dark-eyed girl, she had a frizz to her hair, too.

To penetrate the communist-controlled areas, he organized his own special intelligence team, consisting of his spindle-legged eight-year-old daughter, Nhia, and several of her friends—girls and boys. It was their assignment to gather information from Hmong in communist enclaves. Nhia, as leader of this gaggle of children, continued a Hmong tradition of operating behind enemy lines. These youngsters, with their back-baskets filled with bamboo shoots, considered a delicacy, set out for communist-controlled villages. Viet Minh harshly questioned the children as to their reasons for coming. Nhia was totally unafraid. "I politely and happily told the soldiers we had come to sell them the very best bamboo shoots. After the questioning, the Viet Minh soldiers always let us sell our shoots. While we were selling to Hmong, we asked in our Hmong language how many soldiers in the area, what plans the enemy had, and whether they could escape. When we had the information and had sold our bamboo, we left to tell our own soldiers the news about the communists. My reports to my father were often the same: 'The people are afraid and when the communists are not watching they intend to leave.'"[2]

In communist villages, Nhia's customers paid in Viet Minh scrip, useless on the Lao economy. This disappointed her until she learned that the Americans, who were interested in Viet Minh money, would give her Lao *kip* in exchange.

In March 1958, Walker for the third time returned to flying C-46 missions over Laos. Walker and CAT's fleet of World War II C-46s and 47s droned daily through Lao skies, searching for remote drop-zones. That month he flew 127 hours, making air drops of rice and salt at places like Muong Sai, Sam Chiau, Sam Neua, Ban Na, and Phong Saly. Operation Brotherhood, a medical operation staffed largely by men from the Philippines, ran several bush hospitals, one in Phong Saly. Walker regularly dropped medical supplies to the "O.B." teams. Occasionally he airlifted Royal Lao troops. On March 21, flying northeast of Vientiane, he logged his two-millionth mile. He considered this a great feat, but he was yet to fly thousands of miles more—many of them over Laos.

In the spring of 1959, China called the fighting in Laos a "civil war." Hanoi echoed China. The phrase "civil war" conveyed less cruelty and belligerence and conferred a heroic dimension on those who fought against the established power—in this case the Royal Lao government.

On July 2, 1959, North Vietnamese leader Ho Chi Minh traveled to Moscow to talk to Soviet Premier Nikita Khrushchev. While he was in the Soviet Union, North Vietnamese Army (NVA) troops attacked Lao government outposts in Sam Neua and Phong Saly provinces. On July 31, Ho left the Soviet Union for the People's Republic of China for a three-week visit while his troops fought in Laos in a "civil war." During this fighting, CAT pilots flew military advisors and intelligence experts from the Pentagon throughout Laos so they could assess the military situation first-hand. Fearful that it might have to use American troops in Laos, the U.S. ordered Task Force 116 to stand alert on Okinawa.

* * *

Prince Sai Kham, now the governor of Xieng Khouang Province, and young men like Moua Lia and Vang Chou listened to refugees and soldiers such as Vang Pao tell of the fighting in the countryside. Vang Pao, by this time a major in the Royal Lao Army, continued to earn accolades for his successful, unorthodox skirmishes with the enemy. Moua Lia had graduated from a Lao teacher's training school, taken a wife, and was teaching grade six in the Groupe Scolaire—the middle school at Xieng Khouang town. Vang Chou, now a member of the provincial police force, had never forgotten his frightening childhood experience with the Viet Minh at Nong Het in 1947. Twelve years later the North Vietnamese still threatened his people.

In late 1959, life changed dramatically for Fred Walker. He and his wife separated. They had been living in Taipei near CAT headquarters. She returned to the U.S. with their children. Walker took a month's leave in Hawaii to think. While there, CAT headquarters called, telling him he was being transferred to Vientiane, Laos. Walker protested, but finally agreed to the transfer, calling Laos the "Siberia of CAT." Although he had flown many miles in Lao skies, he had spent little time on the ground and knew little about Laos. He had usually bunked in Saigon, Udorn, or Bangkok. Those days were over. His permanent base was now Vientiane. In Laos, CAT changed its name to Air America.

Walker's permanent transfer to Laos reflected the U.S. decision that Laos would henceforth be a front line in the containment of communism in Southeast Asia. Leaders in neighboring Thailand pointed out that it was better to fight communism on Lao soil than Thai soil. The Thai also thought it prudent to have the U.S. deeply involved in that fight.

As the U.S. moved to further prop up the Lao domino, it mobilized men, money, and machines to meet the challenge. If Laos intended to build a nation and fight an insurgency it had to overcome the lack of roads and a communications system. Construction of a network of roads would take years and was financially prohibitive. In the short term, helicopters seemed the answer, but helicopters were too expensive to purchase and to operate. CIA planners recommended the Helio-Courier, a Short Take Off and Landing (STOL) aircraft, which was relatively inexpensive to buy and operate. With its turbocharged engine, it could land supplies and personnel on short, dirt airstrips at high altitudes. The CIA sent several Helios to Laos.

Lt. Col. Harry C. "Heine" Aderholt, who had worked in the Birmingham, Alabama, steel mills as a youth, was a tough, no-nonsense World War II and Korean War combat pilot who had been the officer in command of the Tibetan airlift. Aderholt, an aerial supply expert, was based in Okinawa. In January 1960, he was assigned to temporary duty in Thailand, where he commanded the 1095th Operational Evaluation Training Group. "I had sent the Helio to Laos and Thailand as part of evacuation plans for the King and Queen of Thailand and of Laos and for their key followers when the Eisenhower Administration thought that Laos and Thailand were about to fall. When I arrived in Thailand, I learned that the Helios delivered to Laos usually sat idle because Air America pilots, unfamiliar with their performance capabilities, neglected them. Since we had no rescue and recovery system in Laos, these pilots were reluctant to fly these single-engine planes."[3]

To demonstrate the Helio, Aderholt asked Air America pilots to identify the most difficult landing strip in Laos. They nominated the 4,500-foot-high strip at Phong Saly, only a few miles from the Chinese border. Aderholt invited Air America's chief pilot to fly with him. "I knew that if I could convince Eddie Sims that the Helio could get into Phong Saly, then pilots could be recruited and trained to fly into hastily constructed strips in the mountains."

Sims accepted Aderholt's invitation. Unfamiliar with northern Laos, Aderholt headed north from Vientiane, navigating with the only chart available—a partially accurate old French road map. Lieutenant Gauthier's commando team had never gotten around to mapping northern Laos. Aderholt knew there were no accurate maps and that the only means of communication in the provinces was the old manually cranked wireless radios that transmitted both voice and typed code. He hoped he would not have an emergency on this flight.

Aderholt and Sims headed north. Misty peaks jutted through fog banks, resembling Chinese mountainscapes. Finding a remote strip in Laos by dead reckoning time and distance did not overly trouble this veteran pilot. As a man who always planned ahead, he pondered what he would tell the communist Chinese if he cracked up in China. He could not think of anything they would believe, so he returned to studying his French road map until he found Phong Saly. He flew over the strip to size it up. Not only was it short and narrow, but about midway it had a 15 to 20-degree turn. With considerable concern, Aderholt dropped the Helio onto the dirt strip, impressing Sims. Aderholt's arrival did not, however, impress the local Pathet Lao commander, who rushed out to capture the two Americans. After an unpleasant forced overnight stay, Aderholt and Sims lifted off the following morning and headed for Vientiane. Aderholt had convinced Sims. The Helio would be the short-term substitute for cars and trucks in Laos and crude landing strips, called "Lima Sites," would substitute for roads.

Later, pilots laughed at their initial concerns about using STOL aircraft in Laos. Within a few years, pilots regularly jammed Helios and Pilatus Porters, another STOL aircraft, onto airstrips shorter and higher than Phong Saly.

In the early days of 1960, Walker flew CIA personnel and senior military men such as Army General John A. Heintges, head of the PEO program, the cover for the U.S. military training mission in Laos, and Army Secretary Wilber Brucker, who were trying to assess the situation in Laos and to formulate a U.S. response. On February 20, 1960, Walker wrote plaintively in his logbook: "To the Boondocks for One Year?" He was still bemoaning his fate and wondered if he could hang on for an entire year. In fact, this was to be his first year in a decade of flying cargo in Laos.

In those days, most cargo was air-dropped from C-46s and C-47s. This required considerable skill and coordination between the pilot and his cargo-handling "kickers" in the rear. After a pilot had lined up on a drop zone, he signaled the kickers in the back of the aircraft by punching a bell. When the bell rang, the kickers manually released the cargo pallets while the pilot pulled the nose up. In this nose-up configuration, the cargo was "kicked" out. To prevent falling out with the cargo, the kickers wore harnesses attached to the cargo bay. One of Walker's kickers was Jerry Daniels, a good-looking Montana youth in his early 20s. Daniels had been an experienced mountain smoke-jumper, parachutist, and firefighter when the CIA recruited him from the Montana Forest Service to work in aerial resupply in Asia. Daniels, one of the first smoke-jumpers to fly the Tibetan airlift, had flown numerous missions over Tibet before he was assigned to Laos.

In anticipation of the April national election, the Lao government distributed leaflets, gerrymandered districts, and raised educational standards for candidates thereby reducing the number of eligible Pathet Lao. It also detained Prince Souphanouvong and several deputies of Neo Lao Hak Sat, the overt political Pathet Lao party, accused of offenses against the security of the state.

Flying village chiefs to talk to government officials ranked as a major campaign tactic. Walker flew a number of these missions. His C-46 theoretically held 38 passengers. On some of these campaign flights, he carried almost twice that number. He was often overloaded, not by weight but by head count. At these meetings, government representatives urged—and in some cases demanded—that headmen rally the vote for the government candidates. The Pathet Lao and their Viet Minh cadre instructors had often and successfully used this technique; now the Pathet Lao accused the Lao government of coercion.

In the final weeks before the election, the Royal Lao government recalled some troops from the fighting in the north to take the offensive in southern Laos to "mop up" the Pathet Lao. U.S.-trained Captain Kong Le, commanding a battalion of crack paratroopers, parachuted into southern Laos as part of this "mopping up." During the first week of March, his paratrooper battalion reported itself lost. It radioed its location and requested assistance. The Lao Air Force searched in vain. After a week, the paratroopers radioed Vientiane, threatening to kill some of their officers unless they were rescued.

On March 13, Fred Walker became an instant hero. He was summoned to fly Jack Matthews, U.S. advisor to this battalion, and Army Colonel Arthur "Bull" Simons (who in 1970 would lead the raid on the Son Tay POW camp in North Vietnam) to look for Kong Le. Walker listened to the Americans describe the situation. "I decided that we should start a square search. I flew along the Mekong where the battalion had jumped. I started to fly the first grid. Within two minutes, I had located Kong Le's lost battalion.''

Walker's elation at finding the lost paratroopers dissipated in the grinding hours of flying routine missions. During the month of March, Walker flew salt, soldiers, rice, an assistant U.S. air attaché, Operation Brotherhood supplies, leaflets, village chiefs, and Father Lucien Buchard, a Catholic priest who usually walked everywhere, but occasionally bummed a ride with Walker.

Laos was turning out not to be the desultory backwater that Walker had imagined. He was flying 30 days a month. In March, he logged 195 hours. In April and May, Walker carried sweaters to Luang Prabang, medical supplies for Operation Brotherhood, sheet roofing, shovels, fuel drums, gas, wheelbarrow frames, empty bottles, rice, salt, lumber, and Coca Cola. He also flew visiting celebrities, including radio and TV personality Arthur Godfrey. Since there were no airfield lights and no navigational aids, Walker's missions were strictly daylight operations. His nights were usually spent in Vientiane, a town which he would soon come to consider home and to know intimately.

In Xieng Khouang, Moua Chia Xang, Lia's father, a popular man, campaigned actively for a seat in the National Assembly. In the final days before the voting, he was ambushed and assassinated. Some say the communists ambushed him. Some say he was assassinated* by forces loyal to Touby LyFong. Others say the Lao did not want a Hmong for a representative and arranged for his death.[4]

In the election, rightist candidates scored a substantial victory. A pro-American and anticommunist government was installed in Vientiane. The coalition government headed by Prince Souvanna Phouma had lost. The Pathet Lao charged government fraud, proclaiming again that the Royal Lao government officials were only the ''lackeys'' of the ''imperialistic, neocolonialist'' Americans. In May 1960, Prince Souphanouvong and other Pathet Lao leaders detained in a Vientiane jail escaped during a rain squall. It was generally believed that the escape was prearranged so that the newly elected government would not have to deal with the politics of their trial.

Walker was interested in airplanes and flying, not in local politics. He

---

*Jean Deuve has written that Moua Chia Xang (Chang) was not assassinated but bought off and withdrew his candidacy; this enraged Touby, but he was bought off in return with a promised nomination to the King's Council. Jean Deuve, *Le Royaume du Laos, 1949–1965* (Paris: 1984), p. 148. His son Moua Lia insists he was ambushed and killed.

knew in minute detail the workings of seemingly all parts of the planes he flew and the nuances of the maximum and minimum performances of each. When it came to Lao politicians and Lao VIPs, he knew who they were, but that was about it. He did admit, however, that he enjoyed "matching wits with the Reds." On July 13, Walker paid attention to a local soldier brought on board his Helio by Ralph Johnson, who worked for the CIA. In his logbook, Walker recorded his cargo: "medical supplies for O.B., salt, three pigs, Ralph Johnson, and a Major Pao." Walker made special note of the major (Vang Pao) because he seemed important to Johnson.

On August 9, 1960, U.S.-supported Captain Kong Le, with his recently "lost" Second Paratrooper Battalion, overthrew the American-backed Lao government, installed only a few months earlier. Kong Le insisted that corruption had inspired him to take this bold act—an act that would change the destiny of Laos.

In the skies over northern Thailand, a tanned and trim brown-haired American dressed in khaki sat in the right seat of an unmarked American C-46 piloted by a Chinese-American, John Lee. Lee suddenly gestured to his passenger to put on earphones. He stared fixedly ahead as he listened to the traffic from Vientiane describing Kong Le's coup. A quiet, almost shy man, "Colonel Billy" appeared emotionless. He knew this was the signal. He had never met Captain Kong Le, but instinctively he knew serious trouble was ahead for fragile Laos. His ten years of training to fight communist insurgency in Southeast Asia would be needed. Laos could indeed become the tottering central piece of Eisenhower's domino theory of the vulnerability of Southeast Asia to communism.[5]

Like many young Americans during World War II, at 18, Colonel Billy had joined the army. Fighting in Germany during the waning days of the war, he had been negatively impressed with the Russian troops and reported home to his widowed mother that the Soviet Union would be trouble for the U.S. In 1951, when he had arrived in Thailand, the communist threat seemed to be everywhere in Asia—in Korea, Malaysia, Vietnam, Laos, even in Thailand. Only months before his arrival, communist Chinese troops had marched ruthlessly against defenseless Tibetans and conquered an ancient kingdom. U.S. intelligence warned that Chinese plans included expansion of cadre south into Thailand and possibly invasion. In 1954, he had followed the defeat of the French at Dien Bien Phu. He would never forget the human drama of those trapped there.

His initial mission had been to train the Thai in counterinsurgency should Thailand be overrun by the "Red" Chinese. Though this had not materialized, the Thais decided to keep together this elite group and had asked Colonel Billy to form from it a mobile force of highly skilled communications, intelligence, and weapons experts who could train others. Each man would be in top physical condition, be an experienced parachutist, and speak a second language—Vietnamese, Cambodian, or Lao. Each team, with its own medic, would be operationally self-sufficient. These were to be known as the Thai PARU, Police Aerial Reinforcement Units. The Thai bestowed upon this quiet American PARU advisor the rank of colonel—an exceptional honor for a foreigner.

PARU training and capability resembled that of Force 136 of Gauthier and Sassi during World War II. Colonel Billy had never met Lieutenant Gauthier or Captain Sassi, or even heard of them. All three were similar—quiet, tough, thoughtful, and expertly trained in guerrilla warfare and counterinsurgency. It was unfortunate they had never met. The Frenchmen could have told Colonel Billy about their experiences and disappointment when their government abandoned the Hmong.

In Vientiane, Kong Le, celebrating his successful coup against the U.S.-supported minister of defense, General Phoumi Nosavan, announced over a loudspeaker that he was a "Neutralist." He pledged to deny all foreign interference in his country, eliminate corruption in officialdom, and commit Laos to a path of neutrality. This meant reinstating Prince Souvanna Phouma as a Neutralist prime minister.

There followed a rapidly changing and confusing set of shifting alliances. Souvanna Phouma, appointed prime minister by the newly assembled cabinet, proclaimed support of Kong Le and his Neutralist position. Prince Souphanouvong's communist Pathet Lao announced its support of Kong Le's coup. Communist troops attacked government positions. General Phoumi, strongly anticommunist, whose soldiers had previously received CIA support, headquartered himself in Savannakhet in southern Laos. He was a relative of Marshall Sarit, the anticommunist, pro-American prime minister of Thailand. Both men disapproved of appeasing the communists.

On August 16, Souvanna Phouma's government received Western recognition. Four days later, Fred Walker and all Air America employees evacuated to Thailand. Ten days later, they returned quietly to Vientiane to wait until the situation became clearer.

On September 18, Walker was summoned to the flight line to ferry six Kong Le paratroopers to Sam Neua. Walker puzzled over this order. Only weeks earlier, the U.S. had backed the government that Kong Le overthrew. Now he was to fly the coup-maker's troops. None of this made sense to him. As he lifted off the runway at Vientiane, he wondered what kind of reception he might receive at Sam Neua. He was met by submachine-gun-armed soldiers and their commander, who, Walker quickly discovered, was not a supporter of Kong Le. The commander refused to allow Kong Le's soldiers to speak or to disembark. As he harshly lectured them, some Operation Brotherhood hospital staff arrived at the airstrip. Walker got their attention and formed the words on his lips: "Do you want to leave?" They shrugged their shoulders, indicating they did not understand the situation any more than Walker did.

That night, a Saturday night in Vientiane, Walker played poker with other Americans. At 2:55 a.m., an explosion near the town's water works interrupted the poker game. Walker concluded Kong Le would have trouble staying in power.

While Lao leaders maneuvered and jockeyed for positions and influence after Kong Le's coup, Pathet Lao and North Vietnamese Army troops launched successful military initiatives against Royalist troops in Sam Neua and Xieng Khouang provinces. As Sam Neua fell to the communists on September 28, the Operation Brotherhood staff set off on foot with Father Buchard, the itinerant Catholic priest, leading them.

As the situation worsened, John Lee flew Colonel Billy to Savannakhet to confer with General Phoumi, who made it clear that any accommodation with the Pathet Lao, such as a coalition government, was unwarranted and would play into the communists' plan to gain more power. Instead of accommodation, he intended a countercoup.

In late September 1960, word leaked out that the Soviets planned to open an embassy in Vientiane. U.S. embassy staff were startled. About the same time, Washington decided to stop its cash-grant aid to the Lao government, which now paid both Kong Le's and General Phoumi's opposing soldiers.

In Xieng Khouang, far from the twittering diplomats in Vientiane, senior Lao Army officers had turned their allegiances to Souvanna Phouma and his policy of negotiation and accommodation with the communists. Hmong Chieftain Touby LyFong and Major Vang Pao, now garrisoned at Xieng Khouang, strongly disapproved of accommodation. Governor Prince Sai Kham, while gravely concerned about communist support of Kong Le, advised the Hmong not to take action, but to wait. Respecting the advice of their long-time friend, they waited.

Vang Pao, who had been fighting the communists for so long, grew impatient. In October, he decided to act. He needed money to feed his men; they had not been paid since the August coup. It was his duty to take care of them. Otherwise, they would no longer follow him. An astrologer advised him on winning numbers in the upcoming lottery, and Vang Pao won. With his windfall, he bought and slaughtered a bull to feast his men. Though winning a lottery and feeding hungry soldiers brought him praise, it did not solve the larger problem—the lack of consistent pay for his men. As a junior officer and a member of a minority group, he had no power and no military might. He did have guile and ingenuity.

When Lao General Amkha Soukhavong, the area commander who supported Kong Le, flew to Vientiane, Vang Pao made his move. During his absence, Vang Pao organized some 200 Hmong civilians and brought them to the airport. Once assembled, he announced that they were going to make a *coup d'état*. The civilians asked how they could do that without weapons. "Don't be afraid," he answered. "We will make a *coup d'état*."

When Amkha disembarked from his plane upon his return, Vang Pao and his mostly unarmed compatriots surrounded the general and his aides on the air field. Vang Pao sent a radio message to General Phoumi Nosavan. His demand was simple: You can have General Amkha in exchange for our back pay. General Phoumi liked the idea. His soldiers' salary arrived promptly. General Amkha was taken to Savannakhet, where Phoumi put him under house arrest. Vang Pao was promoted to lieutenant colonel in the Royal-Lao Army, the only Hmong to hold such high rank. After Vang Pao's bloodless coup and promotion, he became the military chief of Xieng Khouang Province. General Amkha was eventually released and served again with the Royal Lao Army. He never held personal animosity toward Vang Pao, and later they became friends.

Word of this obscure soldier's weaponless and bold coup reached Colonel Billy. He asked Lao Army officers about Vang Pao. While a few had heard of him, no one knew him well or was very enthusiastic about him since he was an ethnic minority—a "Meo," the word the Lao used when referring to the Hmong.

On October 13, Prime Minister Souvanna Phouma asked the new Soviet Ambassador for military assistance for his "Neutralist" government. Also in October, North Vietnamese Army and Pathet Lao units joined to take the town of Ban Ban on Route 7. Other locations fell as the communist forces asserted control in northern and eastern Laos. Phou Duu school closed. Warrior Moua Cher Pao moved his soldiers to Bouam Loung. Nhia and her mother left Phou Duu to join relatives at the tiny village of Phou Ang. Frightened Hmong fled areas invaded by the North Vietnamese to areas like Lat Houang where Hmong leaders lived, thinking they would be safe.

In the midst of this uncertainty, a retired American farmer, who would become a legend, arrived in Laos to work as a $65-a-month volunteer with a small agricultural project funded by U.S. aid monies and run by International Voluntary Services (IVS). This man was Edgar "Pop" Buell from Hamilton, Indiana. His assignment was Lat Houang, a town of about 1,000. The one dusty street had a few more stores than it did in 1953 when the Hmong refugees from the Viet Minh invasion resettled here. It had a school where Ly Lue, the only Hmong teacher among several Lao teachers, taught Hmong boys.

One of Ly Lue's fifth-grade students was 15-year-old Lo Ma. To reach grade five was a considerable accomplishment. While Phay Dang of the Lo clan continued his personal vendetta against Touby of the Ly clan, this boy from the Lo clan looked upon his teacher from the Ly clan as a mentor. Lo Ma revered Ly Lue, not just because both had been born in the village of Phou Peng, but because he was a good teacher.[6]

Lat Houang sported an open-air restaurant and a small bar operated by Corsicans, known as The Million Elephants, which also functioned as an opium trading center. During colonial times, the French government monopoly had purchased the crop to convert it into medicinal opiates with morphine bases. After independence, the high-grade opium grown in the Lao highlands belonged to the highest bidders. In Xieng Khouang Province, Corsicans controlled the trade.

While Pop Buell settled in the IVS compound with its white picket fence, intending to teach Lat Houang farmers modern agricultural methods, Fred Walker flew wounded Lao soldiers to Bangkok for treatment, ferried fresh paratroopers into battle, and dropped carbines and ammunition. On November 27, Walker delivered rice, 300 carbines, 57mm shells, and whiskey to the Xieng Khouang airstrip. The whiskey was a gift to help celebrate Hmong New Year which began with the waxing of the 12th moon.

Hmong New Year had to be a glorious occasion—even during war. Most Hmong believed that in a time of threat it was especially important to honor ancient traditions to usher in an auspicious year. Because old men and respected shamans warned of trouble, special ceremonies to propitiate spirits and to honor ancestors preceded the arrival of this 12th moon. The times, they said, were similar to 1954, when the armies of the French and the Viet Minh prepared for battle at Dien Bien Phu.

In spite of the threat of war, Hmong celebrated. At Lat Houang, Hmong in holiday dress created montaged swirls of fuchsia, red, green, black, and silver as they moved in clusters along the street. Old silver French coins sewn to sashes, jackets, purses, and headdresses jingled softly. A *khene* player, clad in black trousers and jacket trimmed with a red embroidered sash and a silver necklace, stomped the ground while blowing tunes on his bamboo pipe. Those around him laughed and cheered as he performed a series of acrobatic stunts, never losing the pipe from his mouth or missing a note.

Unmarried youth, wearing their finest clothes and jewelry, played "ball toss," a courting ritual. In two rows facing each other—the boys on one side and the girls on the other—they tossed cotton balls and sang traditional and extemporaneous poetry to each other. Admiring adults gathered around those who were particularly clever at creating original poems. Lo Ma's poems brought smiles to the faces of listening adults, including his teacher, Ly Lue. Girls giggled and whispered about tall, handsome, and educated Vang Chou. Many wished he would ask them to ball-toss, but he seemed only slightly interested in the giggling maidens. He was more concerned about the increasing enemy buildup.

During these festive days, children temporarily forgot the dreaded *Tchaw Gee*—a derogatory Hmong term for the Vietnamese which, loosely translated, meant "those who eat gall bladders." The words frightened all Hmong children because they had been told about the fierce Vietnamese soldiers who had invaded Hmong lands. While children may have momentarily forgotten the *Tchaw Gee,* adults had not. Hmong like Vue Sai Long, wearing a combination of old French uniforms and tribal dress, carried carbines and scanned the crowds. Vang Pao had ordered all Hmong with guns to be on the alert since North Vietnamese Army troops were reported throughout the province.

Amidst the celebrants were those who had fled the communist regime in China. Most Hmong in Laos had decided they did not want that way of life, particularly if it were to be administered by traditional enemies— the Chinese or the Vietnamese. Many Hmong believed that the leaders in Hanoi needed Lao land to feed the stomachs of overcrowded and underproductive North Vietnam. They believed Hanoi did not need or want people other than those who would help accomplish this goal. Hmong feared the elimination of the local population, a military tactic often used in the area. Elders discussed how the Hmong, armed only with aged carbines and homemade rifles, could protect themselves against the heavily armed and much more experienced North Vietnamese. They recalled how at Dien Bien Phu the Viet Minh had mauled the French, who had airplanes.

Vang Pao predicted that increased fighting would break out soon on the Plaine des Jarres. When the attack came, he believed the Hmong should go to the hills. Soon after Kong Le's coup, Vang Pao had begun developing a secret plan to move Hmong to several mountains surrounding the PDJ. From these locations, they would run interdiction and sabotage missions against the larger, better-equipped enemy forces. They could harass the enemy and cut its supply lines, just as they had done so successfully against the Japanese and the Viet Minh.

As far into the night leaders discussed Hmong plans to fight the North Vietnamese, *khene* players blew dirge-like songs, portending dangerous times.

On December 3, 1960, a ceremony at the Vientiane Airport inaugurated Soviet flights between Hanoi and Vientiane. The first planes, reportedly just in from Africa where they had been flying cargo and troops into the Congo, carried critically needed oil.

In Savannakhet, General Phoumi, with U.S. arms, prepared to move against Kong Le in Vientiane. Souvanna Phouma's request to U.S. Ambassador Winthrop G. Brown to stop General Phoumi was fruitless. Souvanna Phouma visited Kong Le and his red-armbanded troops, then delegated his powers to a Lao general and on December 9 exiled himself to Cambodia.

On December 10, Quinim Pholsena, one of Souvanna Phouma's ministers, flew to Hanoi where he concluded a bargain with the Soviets to arm and supply those fighting General Phoumi—if Kong Le and the Pathet Lao agreed on a formal alliance.[7]

The next day, Soviet Ilyushin air crews landed at Vientiane and unloaded six 105 howitzers along with North Vietnamese gun crews. Neither Kong Le nor the Pathet Lao had men who could operate these big guns. Daily, Soviet planes flew in more weapons and munitions for Kong Le as stunned Americans watched.

Fred Walker, interested in the Soviet aircraft, studied their planes and crews. "Those planes were copies of our C-47 and Convair 240. The Convair copy looked like it was made of stove iron and it performed that way, too. I watched these guys take off in an empty airplane. They ate up a lot of runway. When they got up, they didn't climb very well. If it had been a spectacular performer, these pilots would have laid on a show. These guys never did. I remember looking at the crews. These were the elite of the Russian Air Force in that they could be let out of the country without fear that they would defect. They were in civvies. Their clothes were shoddy; their shoes were shoddy."

On December 13, General Phoumi launched his countercoup. Kong Le defended with his U.S.-equipped troops and his newly delivered Soviet artillery manned by North Vietnamese gunners. After three days of bloody fighting, Kong Le began a retreat to the Plaine des Jarres, taking with him five of the powerful Soviet howitzers. As he made his way north, the Soviets and North Vietnamese turned the Plaine des Jarres into an armed camp.

Hmong district official Ly Neng Tong lived in the area and witnessed the gigantic North Vietnamese and Soviet buildup. ''Big dark airplanes bigger than the Dakotas, bearing a Russian flag, dropped parachutists and military equipment from noon of that day until dark. Each flight consisted of five planes. The sky was filled with 'mushrooms' sending men and equipment to our area. We Hmong were never afraid of the Lao, nor of Kong Le. We knew the Lao well and we knew that the Lao can never defeat the Hmong. But the black aircraft which we had never seen before and the many parachutists and supplies that the planes dropped scared us. These soldiers were not Lao. They were well-armed. We were not.''[8] He suspected they were Vietnamese and their foreign advisors.

Word of the Soviet air drop quickly reached Lat Houang. Ly Lue calmly continued teaching as elders talked of the growing military threat. Lo Ma studied his teacher for a hint that he was afraid.

As Kong Le retreated, Colonel ''Heine'' Aderholt, at Takhli air base in Thailand, received orders to stand alert. His squadron of loaded B-26s waited for orders to bomb Kong Le: ''There was much discussion at high levels on whether to bomb him. We could have done it. Finally the decision was made to allow him to move to the PDJ to join the Pathet Lao.''

Khang Kho, Tasseng Yang's mountain village, sat on an escape route from communist-controlled areas further north. Families with few possessions and no food had straggled into Khang Kho, seeking protection, food, and assistance to retake their villages. They reported the North Vietnamese Army in hot pursuit. Tasseng Yang was overwhelmed. In the final days of 1960, some 2,000 fearful Hmong waited in his village. Yang Mino was one of them. He was from northern Vietnam and had fought with the Maquis. After the French defeat at Dien Bien Phu, he, afraid of Viet Minh reprisals against those who allied with the French, had abandoned his possessions and fled to Lat Houang with his family. When the fighting started in Laos, he and his family, including his daughters Mai and My, first hid in the mountains nearby. When it soon become too dangerous there, they once again abandoned possessions and fields, and fled to Khang Kho.[9]

Tasseng Yang, believing that an attack against his unarmed village was imminent, repeatedly sent urgent messages over a manually cranked wireless to Vientiane, but no one responded. His young assistants, who had rigged up a bicycle-style crank, spelled each other as each cranked faster and faster, hoping to generate enough current to transmit their distress signal. The Tasseng and the refugees had almost given up hope when a helicopter, flying high, approached from the southwest. The children, including Yang My, watched. It dropped into the mountain valley and headed for a dry rice paddy near the village, then it suddenly pulled upward, creating swirls of grit and debris. Hmong wiped their eyes and watched in alarm as the helicopter flew away. They shouted and cried for it to come back. Then they heard a flopping sound echoing in the hills. It was returning. Tasseng Yang's gold-tipped teeth showed as he grimaced and shaded his eyes from the penetrating dirt blown by the helicopter. Broad shouldered and stout, he stood motionless, facing the noise.

This time the U.S. Marine helicopter landed. Before the blades stopped spinning, two men emerged. As they walked toward the Tasseng, he ordered his modest house readied to receive the visitors—one American, wearing glasses and dressed in khaki pants and jacket, who introduced himself as Colonel Billy, and one Thai, dressed identically, who called himself Colonel Khouphan.

Over cups of Chinese tea, Tasseng Yang explained the desperate situation. Policeman Vang Chou, sent by Vang Pao to help the Tasseng, also listened. As details were given, Colonel Billy studied those in the room. He wondered if he and his Thai colleague had walked into a trap. The Hmong, wearing tribal black floppy pants and tight-fitting jackets, carried a few old guns and milled about, obviously agitated.

The Hmong asked the American if he could give them guns. He did not answer directly. First he wanted to know if all the Hmong waiting at Khang Kho wanted to fight the communists. The Hmong insisted that if they had weapons they would fight. Tasseng Yang remembered that meeting. "Colonel Billy told us that the Americans had guns but it would take time to get them. In the meantime, Colonel Billy said that he wanted to find a Hmong officer named Vang Pao. Could we take him to Vang Pao? He said that if Vang Pao agreed that we needed guns and would fight the communists, then in eight days, we would have 500 guns."[10]

Colonel Billy's true mission was to locate Vang Pao and determine if the hill people—primarily the Hmong—wanted to fight the Pathet Lao and North Vietnamese and, if they did, to assess their potential.

After much discussion as to Lt. Col. Vang Pao's exact location, it was decided that the Tasseng and several Hmong leaders would go by helicopter with the American and the Thai to find him. After loading, the helicopter lifted slowly off the ground, covering the village in dust. It hung in the air only a few feet off the ground. The inexperienced pilot, Clarence Abadie, pulled the chopper skyward, heading toward a nearby mountain ridge. As the Hmong on the ground watched, the chopper blades whacked into tall trees, then somersaulted down the mountain, ripping off pieces of metal.

Yang My, the young Hmong from North Vietnam, stood near the Tasseng's second wife. As the helicopter tumbled down the mountain, his wife ran toward it, screaming, "My husband! My dear husband!" Others followed. The helicopter came to rest not far from where it had lifted off. The moment the helicopter stopped rolling, Colonel Billy leaped from the copilot's seat, clearing the aircraft on a run. Afraid of an explosion, he ran a few hundred yards before stopping to look back. When he did, he saw no one following him. He shouted for the others to get out. The stunned passengers tumbled out one by one. Finally, Tasseng Yang emerged. None aboard was seriously injured.

Abadie climbed out slowly, stumbled to a nearby tree, sat down, and burst into tears. Colonel Billy rushed to him, thinking he was hurt. He sniffled that he feared he would lose his job. Colonel Billy assured him he would not. Aberdee stayed on and later commanded Air America's helicopter program.

In the Tasseng's house, one young man frantically cranked the wireless while another one shouted into the headset and occasionally banged the keys to send Colonel Billy's message to Savannakhet that his helicopter was down. Finally, a reply came back in code, "What parts do you need to make it fly?" Everyone laughed. The helicopter needed more than parts, since it had broken into several pieces. The radio operators responded again with cranking, shouting, and banging the keys to tell the authorities to send another helicopter. Colonel Billy, Colonel Khouphan, and Aberdee spent the night sleeping on the hard wooden beds in the Tasseng's house. The next day, another chopper came to pick up Colonel Billy and the pilot. The Thai colonel stayed with the Hmong to locate Vang Pao. Then he would send for Colonel Billy.

Earlier, Colonel Billy had visited Okinawa, where the CIA stockpiled World War II weapons, including mortars, bazookas, recoilless rifles, M-1 30-caliber machine guns, and M-1 carbines. If these were needed in Laos, he knew Colonel Aderholt, the aerial supply expert, could muster the aircraft and the expertise to drop weapons packs to the Hmong.

*   *   *

The youthful Vang Pao wore khaki fatigues, a floppy bush hat, and tan French Army jungle boots resembling tennis shoes. The Hmong runner had told him that the important American would come today, but where was he? Those who knew Vang Pao knew his fetish for punctuality. It was no surprise to those standing with him at the Ta Vieng encampment that he was impatient—particularly with the enemy on the attack. He scanned the Plaine des Jarres, ringed by purple mountains now partly obscured by smoke from fires farmers set to clear the land for the next rice planting.

First Vang Pao heard it, then the others—the sound of a helicopter. A dusty green Marine H-34 dropped from the sky, swirling up the dust. As the brown cloud dissipated, Colonel Billy emerged, followed by Colonel Khouphan. Vang Pao stood at attention. As they neared, he saluted smartly. The American returned his salute, then gave a *whai,* the customary Lao and Thai greeting, by holding his hands in prayer fashion before his face.

As Colonel Billy followed Vang Pao, the American's pulse quickened. Would this youthful-looking soldier be capable of organizing, inspiring, and leading his people to resist a communist takeover of their homeland?

The two men, so different in background and personality, sat in the coolness of a thatch shack. Vang Pao, an experienced mountain guerrilla fighter with only a few years' formal education, spoke with vigor and impatience, gesturing to make his points. A fifth-generation Texan from the panhandle area, Colonel Billy had graduated from Texas A&M College. A thoughtful man, he routinely hesitated before speaking in his slow Texas drawl.

Though Colonel Billy had never been a guerrilla fighter, he knew counterinsurgency techniques and theories from his training with the CIA and from his experiences in Thailand. To be effective, counterinsurgency needed irregular forces—or special guerrilla units (SGUs) as they were later called—who were determined, motivated, and knew the terrain intimately. The American contribution to these irregular forces would be to arm and train those already motivated to fight communist aggression.

Vang Pao listened and observed, sizing up the man before him who explained in the northern Thai language that he had been working with the Thai government and hilltribe people inside Thailand. He agreed with Vang Pao that the communist advance in Laos had to be stopped short of Luang Prabang, the royal capital, and Vientiane. If these two major towns fell, the rest of Laos would tumble. He did not tell Vang Pao that many Americans had concluded that the Royal Lao Army could not hold against the communist forces.

Meeting on this mountain, so near the communist encampment on the Plaine des Jarres, the seriousness of the situation energized the participants. Vang Pao assured Colonel Billy that his people hated the communists—particularly the Vietnamese—and would fight. He pledged: "For me, I can't live with communism. I must either leave or fight. I prefer to fight." These were key words for Colonel Billy. He was pleased with Vang Pao's determination.

Vang Pao explained that many Hmong Maquis fighters had been captured by the Viet Minh after Dien Bien Phu and remained prisoners, but there were others willing to fight if they had weapons. He was quick to point out that his people needed food, salt, and medicine, and asked the American for emergency assistance.

Colonel Billy, always cautious in his promises, told Vang Pao that he believed the U.S. could provide refugee assistance and, if the Hmong committed themselves to fight the communists, also weapons and training. After several hours of talking with Colonel Billy and Colonel Khouphan, Vang Pao and his men discussed the American's plan in the Hmong language, which neither the American nor the Thai understood. Then Vang Pao explained that while he favored the plan, he had to seek the support of his people by consulting with clan leaders, as was the Hmong custom. Colonel Billy urged Vang Pao to consult the men immediately since the current crisis threatened to topple the Royal Lao government.

On the flight back to Vientiane, Colonel Billy reviewed his meeting with Vang Pao. One of his overriding principles was to keep any U.S. involvement to a minimum. He was devoted to the idea of providing indigenous people with training and weapons to protect their own homelands at a minimal cost. The Hmong appeared determined to fight—they only wanted arms, training, and food. This seemed an ideal situation for "The Third Option," a CIA strategy to fight insurgencies with counterinsurgency.

Soon after Colonel Billy departed, Vang Pao, with a small contingent including the Thai colonel, departed on foot to seek approval from clan leaders. Living as they did in scattered, often isolated villages, Hmong society seemed decentralized, but such was not the case. The estimated 350,000 to 500,000 Hmong had no single government or ruler but were organized by clans. Clan leaders were the most important men in Hmong society. For example, Lo clan members wherever they lived respected and followed the decisions of Lo clan leaders. These men, in turn, sought counsel from lesser clan leaders so that a major decision reflected the thinking of all Lo clan leadership. At the village level with several clans present, representatives from each clan met with the village chief to resolve problems. Hmong decisions were reached by long discussions leading to a consensus. In a most democratic way, all clans had equal voice in the discussions, which continued until all points of view had been heard, reviewed, and contemplated. Finally—in a way only understood by the Hmong—a decision was reached.

Although, in the past, outside rule had been colonial France and, after Lao independence, it had become the Lao government and its provincial agencies, the real governing influence on the Hmong continued to be the clans.

Clan leaders reminded Vang Pao of Hmong Maquis languishing in North Vietnamese prisons, taken prisoner by Giap's forces, and pointed out that the Fackee had done nothing to seek their release. They also recalled the sudden French departure, leaving the Viet Minh to harass and kill those who had worked with the Fackee. Would the Americans be different? They wanted to know the details of the treaty proposed by the American. Elders talked about "treaties" much as Native American leaders talked about "treaties" with the white man, believing that written agreements were only words on paper and that spoken promises were more important. But they too had to be watched. There were historical reasons in the Hmong past to be cautious of treaties with foreigners.

Vang Pao, not yet a clan leader but becoming an orator of note, urged the elders to accept the American's plan by speaking about the history he knew: the 1947 installation in Xieng Khouang Province of a Vietnamese political commissar, thousands of Vietnamese soldiers and civilians sent to occupy their lands, and the Vietnamese refusal to leave Laos in defiance of the 1954 Geneva Accords. Many Hmong, driven from their villages by the communists, lacked food and shelter. If the Hmong joined with the Americans, the refugees would receive rice and salt until new fields could be found and readied for planting. The American had also promised arms, training, and a commitment to stop communism in Laos.

From Colonel Billy's perspective, the Lao domino would surely fall unless irregular forces could be mobilized in time to hold the North Vietnamese. At last, word arrived for him to return. At their meeting, Vang Pao pledged that with training and weapons equal to those of the enemy, his men could push the Vietnamese back across the border. Vang Pao unveiled his strategy of placing his men on the mountains surrounding the Plaine des Jarres to harass the enemy. He would orchestrate this from a headquarters at Padong, a high mountain overlooking the plain, where tea had been grown under the French and which had a small dirt airstrip.

As Colonel Billy listened to the enthusiastic Vang Pao, he contemplated the realities of arming his men. As soon as enemy forces saw arms air-dropped they would attack the positions being supplied. He asked Vang Pao a critical question: How long would it take the enemy to get to Padong? Vang Pao thought for a moment and answered, "Three days."

"Three days." Colonel Billy repeated it several times, wondering if his PARU teams could teach the Hmong men and boys to operate new weapons to defend themselves in three days.

That night, Lt. Col. Vang Pao and his officers sat with Colonel Billy and Colonel Khouphan in a dark room lit only by candles surrounding a five-tiered *ba-sii* offering to the spirits. Vang Pao admired the large and colorful offering constructed from fresh banana leaves filled with small oranges, bananas, wild orchids, smoldering incense, and topped with a duck egg. Vang Pao's mother and his two wives, with the help of a shaman, had created it. He searched the dark corners, certain the women were waiting in the shadows, out of sight of the men, just in case something was needed.

The shaman intoned a chant in which he beseeched the spirits to protect the souls of these men and to bring good fortune. As he mumbled the magic words, he tied quick knots in three strands of white cotton thread and bound the wrists of each man, thus tying in their souls and their good fortune. As the ceremony ended, he pressed into the hand of each man a hard-boiled duck egg, symbolizing vitality and strength. Then Vang Pao, with his men following his lead, tied still more strings around the wrists of the American and the Thai, asking the spirits to protect them.

From the dark doorway, a Hmong bamboo pipe wailed a mournful song. Clad in black and wearing an elaborate silver necklace, the musician moved into the light. With a slow, stomping rhythm created by his bare feet on the cool mud floor, he moved hypnotically in circles, playing the haunting pipe music that stirs Hmong souls.*

---

*The *ba-sii* ceremony described in this chapter was conducted many times with the Americans assigned to work with the Hmong. None of the participants in this particular *ba-sii* can remember the exact details because too much time has passed, but the ceremony remains virtually unchanged even today as the Hmong continue this tradition in the U.S.

With this ceremony, the fate of the Hmong was irrevocably linked to the Americans. Training would start at Padong. USAID-organized relief supplies would be given to Hmong in need.

A few days later, Colonel Billy, Colonel Khouphan, and Lt. Col. Vang Pao arrived at Khang Kho. Tasseng Yang and other clan leaders wanted to hear directly from the American the details of the U.S. commitment. Tasseng Yang remembered that day: "I asked, 'If we defeat the Vietnamese, how will you help us?' Colonel Billy answered: "'If Hmong people beat the Vietnamese, then we will help the Hmong people as much as we can. If the Hmong people lose, we will find a new place where we can help the Hmong people.' That promise pleased us. After this discussion, Colonel Billy, Colonel Khouphan, Vang Pao, and I signed a paper that said that in eight days, American people would send us 500 guns."

On December 30, North Vietnamese tanks and soldiers attacked General Phoumi's forces protecting Route 7 near Ban Ban. Unable to contact the general, local Lao Army units and a Hmong contingent detailed to defend Route 7 concluded they were cut off and fled in panic. North Vietnamese Army artillery barrages also scared off the Lao Army and its American advisors stationed at the Khang Khay garrison.

On December 31, fighting broke out on the Plaine des Jarres between the combined forces of the Neutralists and communists and General Phoumi's rightist troops. It was immediately clear that Nosavan's forces would not be able to retake the PDJ. This was the signal for the Hmong. In 200 Hmong villages, men, women, and children moved to seven friendly mountains surrounding the Plaine des Jarres. Vang Pao headed for Padong to establish his headquarters.

In Xieng Khouang town, there was panic. Prince Sai Kham hurriedly packed provincial records. Moua Lia rushed to his house to get his young wife and his month-old daughter. Moua Lia remembered his fear on that fateful day. "We could see the massive Soviet airlift to the Plaine des Jarres and we heard that Kong Le was moving toward us with heavily armed troops. We had no weapons. We had to flee immediately. Our group of about 300 people, including Prince Sai Kham, had no weapons and no food. Vang Pao told us to get to Ta Vieng as fast as possible and make an airstrip so we could get help."

A few miles away at Lat Houang, it was late afternoon on December 31 when gunfire sent frightened villagers, schoolchildren and their teachers to the hills. Pop Buell and IVS workers fled to the nearby Phong Savan airport, where they scrambled aboard a C-47 sent to pick up the U.S. military advisors who had abandoned the Khang Khay garrison. The U.S. military advisors and the IVS volunteers were safely evacuated. The

Hmong who remained in the area were on their own. Farmers abandoned fields, livestock, and possessions and took to the high jungle or moved west to avoid enemy forces. North Vietnamese soldiers took over the IVS compound with its white picket fence. The communists were to convert it into a prison, where they held U.S. Army "White Star" special forces advisory team member Captain Walter "Wallie" Moon, who was captured 30 miles north of Vang Vieng on April 22, 1961, and executed on July 22 after being wounded in an escape attempt.

Moua Lia's group moved silently along trails where orchids, thriving in the foggy mountain moisture, perfumed the air and colorful, exotic birds called from bamboo and pine groves. Today, no one saw beauty in this. No children mimicked the jungle bird calls which adults used as secret signals. Pushed by fear, they reached Ta Vieng after a full day of hard walking and immediately began making a landing strip. With light from burning faggots, everyone worked day and night, digging and cutting a clearing. Under Vang Pao's direction, they finished the strip and waited for a plane and help.

On Phou San, Hmong also watched the Soviet airlift. Moua Cher Pao and Moua Sue, his warrior son, led about 5,000 people from there to Bouam Loung, a high mountain bowl lying northeast. Chong Toua's two sons Blia Vue and Teu Lu decided not to leave. They did not want to lose their livestock, opium fields, or their orchards lower down the mountain. Besides, Phou San had always protected Hmong.[11]

On January 6, 1961—in the final hours of the Eisenhower administration—Soviet Premier Nikita Khrushchev declared, for the benefit of youthful incoming President John F. Kennedy, that the Soviet Union would back all wars of national liberation around the world. This Soviet threat echoed those of the Chinese and the North Vietnamese.

The Soviet Union's quick intervention in Laos under the guise of supporting Kong Le and Prince Souvanna Phouma—the "Neutralists"—had been brilliant. Between December 15 and January 2, U.S. intelligence estimated the Soviets flew 184 missions in northern Laos. The massive Soviet airlift to support Kong Le and his Pathet Lao allies provided a way to supply the communist forces, while on the surface appearing to arm neutralists. The Pathet Lao, who before the Soviet involvement used homemade weaponry or relied on Chinese weapons given to Hanoi, now possessed sophisticated Soviet arms. The addition of Kong Le's men, heavily armed with American equipment, made the combined communist-neutralist force on the Plaine des Jarres most formidable.

When Kong Le arrived on the PDJ to join the Pathet Lao, it belonged to the Soviets and the North Vietnamese. At Phong Savan airfield—

where only a few days earlier an American C-47 had evacuated U.S. advisors and IVS workers—a dozen Soviet flight technicians maintained Soviet airlift planes. At Phong Savan town, North Vietnamese opened "information" offices and erected a field hospital. At Khang Khay, Soviet, Chinese, North Vietnamese, and Pathet Lao military delegations headquartered. At Xieng Khouang town, Mao Zedong's representatives, calling themselves members of an economic and cultural delegation, moved in.

As Tasseng Yang waited for the promised guns, Colonel "Heine" Aderholt organized planes and pilots for the pack drops of World War II guns and munitions taken out of storage in Okinawa. The Tasseng counted the days. "We knew that the Vietnamese were very close. On day eight, a Dakota dropped 300 guns by parachute. We waited two more days, and three more Dakotas dropped another 200 guns and ammunition. The Americans had kept their promise to help the Hmong. By January 13, 1961, we had received the promised weapons. On this same day, the communists attacked us near Khang Kho."

Within a week, Eisenhower would leave the White House and Kennedy would be inaugurated. In Eisenhower's final remarks to Kennedy, he warned that Laos would be his most serious problem. It was, he believed, "the key to the entire area of Southeast Asia" and intervention by U.S. combat troops might be required.*

---

*The Eisenhower administration, believing that it might have to go to war with China or the Soviet Union or both, planned to use long range strategic bombers, B-47s, believed capable of penetrating enemy borders. In the days before aerial refueling, the B-47 pilots, if ordered to strike China or the Soviet Union, would be on one-way missions. After striking their targets, the pilots would head for safe havens like Thailand and bail out. Inventors and intelligence men, working in secrecy, struggled to develop recovery techniques to extract these pilots. One idea was an inflatable airplane in which a downed airman could fly 50 to 60 miles to a safe area for rescue. Another was a small aircraft capable of short take-off and landings on rough terrain fields at high altitudes. This craft would not only rescue airmen but could be used to infiltrate and exfiltrate behind enemy lines. It would evacuate key personnel and heads of state in case of a communist takeover. The inflatable aircraft, however, was not used in Southeast Asia.

6.

Camelot and the Land of Oz

On March 22 1955, the People's Party of Laos (now the Lao People's Revolutionary Party) was set up. . . . It was the successor to the splendid cause of the Communist Party of Indochina in Laos, taking on the historic task of guiding the people of Laos in their struggle to liberate their motherland, and against the American imperialists. . . . 1954–1963 were years of struggle against the hypocritical counter-revolutionary strategy of the American imperialists and their henchmen. . . .

—Kaysone Phomvihane, *Revolution in Laos,* 1981

Vang Pao's force—consisting of less than 7,000 volunteer soldiers—would be the bulwark of freedom. The Americans reasoned that these "little guys," with U.S. assistance and training, would hold off the North Vietnamese Army of "national liberation" to buy time to try for a political solution in Laos and, more importantly, to buy time for Thailand. Thailand needed to improve its infrastructure—to build roads and dams, provide rural development, and provide education for all its citizens—to respond to the winds of change blowing across Asia.

President Kennedy's men had opted not to send U.S. ground troops to Laos. Instead they continued "The Third Option" begun under Eisenhower to fight an unconventional war in the highlands with the CIA's newly developed counterinsurgency techniques, strategies, and experts.

Yellow, orange, and blue parachutes fluttered atop Padong, protecting men and supplies from the weather. Here Colonel Billy's Thai PARU teams, U.S. Army White Star advisory teams, and CIA paramilitary advisors worked with Vang Pao to train a counterinsurgency force. From Padong's 4,500-foot-high vantage point overlooking the Plaine des Jarres, Vang Pao viewed much of the Hmong traditional homelands, now occupied by the enemy with its Molotova trucks, armored cars, Soviet 37mm guns, and antiaircraft guns.

At Padong, Lima Site 5, Thai PARU teams conducted initial training to transform farmers into an effective guerrilla force. CIA paramilitary advisors and White Star teams assisted in the training and functioned as liaison between their positions and U.S. agency offices in Vientiane responsible for obtaining and distributing supplies to the mountain outposts. Colonel Arthur "Bull" Simons, of the Army's 77th Special Forces, commanded the White Star teams. Simons, a former journalist, was already a respected military figure when he was tapped to organize a clandestine group of 107 military men to advise the Lao Army.

American advisors at Padong included a young West Point graduate, a demolitions expert, a radio man, a mechanic, a medic, a young man with paratrooper experience who spoke Lao and several tribal languages, and a couple of crusty, hard-living veterans of World War II, Korea, and Tibet who thrived on Scotch and beer.

It was Vang Pao, recently promoted to full colonel, who was the man of the moment. Not because he was the Hmong tribal leader—that role still belonged to Touby LyFong—but because the Hmong believed only Vang Pao, who had fought the Vietnamese since the late 1940s, was clever enough to outsmart them.

Vang Pao, an erect and solitary figure, paced between campfires, occasionally stopping to listen to problems. Everyone atop Padong was a refugee, having abandoned homes, fields, and animals. Prince Sai Kham, Moua Lia, and Vang Chou were here, as was Lo Ma. Teacher Ly Lue had finished his three days of PARU training and had moved out to a mountain position. Most volunteers needed more than the three-day training course, but there was no time for additional training. Men were needed to fight. After training, helicopters airlifted some to their positions. Others walked.

Volunteers seeking arms and training came to Padong with their families, swelling the encampment to some 10,000 people. While it seemed that all the Hmong of Xieng Khouang Province were here, many had been killed or lost in the jungle as they fled communist forces.

Vang Pao had been successful on the battlefield, but his domestic life held sadness and frustration. His first wife from the Thao clan had died, leaving him with several small children. Soon after her death, he married her younger sister to have someone to look after the children. Known as Nhia Thao, this woman became his senior wife. During the time of the Viet Minh, he had married a second wife, Ly True. According to Hmong custom, men did not divorce their wives. The marriage to Ly True had been a political marriage to unite the powerful Ly clan to his Vang clan. It was not a happy relationship and there were no children from this marriage. Only days before he moved to Padong, he married Moua Chia, the spirited, beautiful, and courageous stepdaughter of "Northern Warrior" Moua Cher Pao. It was reported to be a marriage of love. Moua Chia stayed with her husband at Padong on the front lines. The Americans referred to her as his battlefield wife.

No one could remember who first thought of Vang Pao as the "Wizard" and Laos as the "Land of Oz." U.S. officialdom in Vientiane did not approve of Laos being called the "Land of Oz" or "Never-Never Land," but those in the field considered the nomenclature brilliant.

Americans, assigned code-names, forbidden to have cameras, and restricted from talking to the press who worked at places like Padong, witnessed mysterious comings and goings of U.S. personnel and North Vietnamese denials of military and political operations in Laos. They joked about this country with a king in Luang Prabang, two princely brothers— one communist and one neutralist—who operated out of self-proclaimed capitals in two separate provinces; a conservative general backed by the CIA headquartered in yet another town; and a coup-making American-trained paratrooper who called himself a neutralist and whose troops, supplied by both the U.S. and the Soviet Union, shelled Vang Pao and his Thai and American advisors. This had to be "Oz."

The Hmong, however, did not call Vang Pao the "Wizard." They addressed him either by his military rank or as "Uncle," a Hmong term of respect. Some advisors called him "V.P." But no name seemed so descriptive as the "Wizard." Vang Pao's canny—seemingly omniscient—understanding of his enemy mystified his American advisors. They knew that he had better intelligence than they had, and it irritated them.

Fred Walker had taken leave and missed the New Year's Eve offensive. He returned in January with a promotion to chief pilot for Air America's operations in Laos to discover that Padong was the center of action in northern Laos and that the "little guys" were taking a beating. Walker helped evacuate wounded in a Helio.

He soon learned that Vang Pao could be harsh. One day, he walked into Vang Pao's mess tent to find two prisoners squatting in a corner tied with ropes. "One guy was about 45 or 50 years old and he looked like

'I've just seen my last sunrise.' The other guy was about 21 and looked like 'You haven't got anything on me.' Vang Pao's aide said the two guys had been at Xieng Khouang telling the enemy about our troops. Where they are and how many. The colonel didn't like that!'"[1]

The next day, Walker returned to the mess tent for lunch. "The young guy was there and the old guy was gone. I asked the aide what happened to the old guy. 'The colonel let him go,' he said. Colonel Vang Pao comes in and eats lunch. While he's eating, one of his aides comes over and says something and points to the young guy squatting in the corner. Suddenly, Vang Pao spit out the sound 'Ba!' A couple of soldiers stood up and took the prisoner outside. Vang Pao continued eating. A few minutes later, I heard four shots. Traitors were dealt with harshly in Laos."

A few days later, Walker saw another side of Vang Pao. "He and I were walking along at Padong when a woman came up to him. They talked for quite a while, then V.P. reached into his pocket and peeled off about $50 in *kip* notes and gave them to her. After she left, I asked, 'What was that?' He explained that her husband had been killed in the fighting. 'She needed money, so I gave her money.' Fifty dollars was a lot of money in Laos."

Like fabled U.S. General George Patton in World War II, Vang Pao had the ability to think like his enemy. Vang Pao, however, was no Patton. He did not command great armies, nor did he have tank battalions or any other sophisticated 20th century military equipment. He did not stride about in jack boots, carry a riding crop, or have a dog as a mascot. In northern Laos, without all-weather roads, telephones, and electricity, he commanded men and boys who wore homespun clothes and took their wives and children to battle. They would fight with their crossbows and flintlocks if they had to—Vang Pao knew that.

This man of seemingly indomitable spirit and boundless energy, who slept only a few hours a night, faced enormous problems. Thousands of starving and displaced people who fled the fighting foraged from the jungle. They needed help. USAID promised assistance, but first those in need had to be located. Lack of communications bedeviled rescue efforts. Vang Pao solved this problem by taking to the air. He often flew with Walker in Helio 835. With his face pressed against the scratched window, he strained to locate refugees and friendly villages. When he found a group of a village, he scribbled a message, often telling them to clear an area as a drop zone or landing strip. He put his message in a canteen and as the pilot made a low pass, he tossed it out the window. Upon receipt of a message, those on the ground dug clearings in the jungle to receive assistance.

USAID's emergency relief program brought Pop Buell back to Laos after his evacuation to Thailand when the Plaine des Jarres fell. This retired Indiana farmer teamed up with several young Hmong assistants from Lat Houang to locate lost refugees. Once found, Pop alerted USAID officials who requested Air America pilots to drop life-saving cargoes of rice, salt, and medicines, often to newly cleared drop zones.

As more Hmong were trained and the fighting increased, those who became full-time irregular forces and could therefore no longer tend to their fields would be given a small salary provided by the CIA. Those trained to fight but who stayed in their villages and continued farming did not need salaries.

Since the situation called for more reconnaissance and resupply aircraft, William Bird, an American whose construction company operated in Laos, created Bird Air. Bill Bird lured Robert L. "Dutch" Brongersma from Air America and made him chief pilot for Bird Air. Brongersma, like Walker, had flown with CAT at Dien Bien Phu.

Bird Air owned a PB-2, a World War II patrol bomber rigged for aerial resupply and photo-reconnaissance. This PB-2, which Brongersma flew, had been taken to the "Skunk Works" at Lockheed, where the U-2, and SR-71 had been built, to be equipped with the latest cameras. Brongersma told Walker that the Skunk Works was so secret he was not allowed inside, nor would they tell him anything about the cameras they installed. His only instruction was to flip a yellow toggle switch exposing the camera and it would run until he turned it off.

The U.S. monitored communications in and out of Hanoi. In February, intercepts gave details of an upcoming visit by Red Prince Souphanouvong to the Plaine des Jarres. Initially it was proposed that his plane would be attacked in the air or after landing. Later this was ruled out and replaced with a directive to photograph Souphanouvong's involvement with the North Vietnamese on the PDJ. The assignment went to Bird Air and its specially equipped PB-2. Brongersma took off from Vientiane and loitered on an intercept course until he picked up the Soviet plane with Souphanouvong aboard on its approach to land on the PDJ.

Brongersma flew over just when Souphanouvong was being formally greeted by his hosts. He made a 180 and tried another pass. This time, he took small arms fire in the nose section, igniting an electrical fire which burned all the way to Vientiane, where he made an emergency landing.

He had, however, accomplished his mission: he had perfect, identifiable photos of the event.[2]

On March 9, 1961, within two months of the start of the Kennedy presidency, forces of Kong Le, the Pathet Lao, and the North Vietnamese stopped General Phoumi's attempt to retake the Plaine des Jarres. By the end of March, the communists held territory in six provinces: from Phong Saly, Sam Neua, Xieng Khouang, Luang Prabang, and Vientiane to Khammouane in the southern panhandle. The communists claimed these were "liberated zones."

The fighting and disruption in the northern provinces sent thousands more southward to seek safety. Many sought sanctuary at Padong, including the Khang Kho defenders who had fought the North Vietnamese Army for two months. After a valiant stand, these untrained men realized they could not fight the more sophisticated enemy. Tasseng Yang led them, including the family of Yang My and Mai, to Padong.

But the mountain base at Padong was not safe either. It was surrounded and under almost constant attack, as were most of the friendly mountain sites. At San Tiau, Lima Site 2, situated inside a bowl atop a 5,000 foot mountain, some 200 Hmong trainees, their Thai PARU instructors, and two CIA paramilitary advisors, Jack Shirley and Tom Ahern, waited for an attack. Five North Vietnamese Army companies, supported by several howitzer batteries, were within ten miles.

On March 23, Fred Walker landed his Helio hard at Site 2, cracking his landing gear. Unable to get out, Walker spent the next two nights at Shirley's camp with his Garand semiautomatic rifle as his companion.

The war in Laos was not a war Americans easily understood. In South Korea, North Koreans had invaded. That was easy to comprehend and to fight. But in Laos, the war had invisible battle lines, insurgents, "wars of national liberation," "people's armies," and bureaus of propaganda—considered more important than military divisions—that excelled in disinformation, double talk, and subversion. In addition to the Soviet Union's supplying the so-called Neutralists on the Plaine des Jarres, North Vietnam armed, trained, and advised the Pathet Lao, who proclaimed they were the patriotic forces. The North Vietnamese Army (soon to be known as the NVA) fought the main battles, but gave credit to the Pathet Lao, since North Vietnamese troops were prohibited from being in Laos by the Geneva Accords. In northern Laos, armed communist Chinese work crews constructed roads that some thought would link China to the Mekong River and access to the fertile and natural resource–rich lands of Thailand and Cambodia. China also supplied weapons to the NVA and Pathet Lao fighting in Laos.

President Kennedy detailed W. Averell Harriman, former U.S. ambassador to Moscow, to investigate the possibility of a negotiated resolution. Harriman, who often operated without permission or direction from the State Department, found Prince Souvanna Phouma touring in India. Harriman liked him and decided he could work with him to neutralize Laos. The U.S. went along with a plan to have the United Kingdom and the Soviet Union, co-chairs of the 1954 Geneva Conference, convene a new enlarged conference to deal with the Laos crisis.

Harriman, the chief negotiator at Geneva, was convinced that the Soviets were the key to solving the Lao problem or to at least buying time. A seasoned diplomat, he intended to use the diplomatic apparatus of the Geneva Conference to create a "neutralized" Laos. The terminology had changed from "neutral" to "neutralized." The difference was significant. Harriman believed that the United States, with the help of the Soviet Union, could force into existence a neutralized country removed from the ideological struggle for control over Southeast Asia.

State Department experts argued that Souphanouvong, the Red Prince, and Souvanna Phouma, the Neutralist prince, would ultimately reach an accord for a coalition government that would include the anticommunist faction as well. This envisioned coalition government would be headed by Souvanna Phouma, who had the support of Soviet-armed Kong Le and of the North Vietnamese-backed Pathet Lao. Under the aegis of these two princes, they reasoned, the Kingdom of Laos could remain outside the communist bloc.

Leonard Unger, the number two man in the U.S. Embassy in Bangkok, was scheduled to become the ambassador to Laos to usher in the Kennedy neutralization policy. According to Unger, "We really believed that by neutralizing Laos, we could lift it out of the fray and fighting in the area. Since Laos was so weak, we thought it was the only way it could be saved."[3]

On April 17, 1961, CIA-backed Cuban exiles landed at the Bay of Pigs to overthrow the Soviet-backed regime of Fidel Castro. They suffered a resounding defeat which humiliated the U.S. and angered President Kennedy. Under extreme pressure to counter-challenge Khrushchev, Kennedy demonstrated toughness—at least symbolically—in Laos. Two days later, to their disbelief, he ordered White Star advisors, who had been operating covertly, to wear military attire and to operate openly. The value of this directive was not clear, other than to prove that the U.S. was violating the Geneva Accords.

Also on April 19, Fred Walker received an urgent radio message from Jack Shirley at Site 2. "He reported they were in a hell of a fire-fight and called for a load of 81 millimeter mortar shells. Then he called for 60 millimeter mortar shells. The next day, he reported casualties and ordered a load of 30 caliber machine gun ammunition. It was obvious the enemy was getting closer and closer."

Three days later, Jack Shirley called Walker to order a load of hand grenades. "My crews rigged and loaded Dutch Brongersma. During his parachute drops, Dutch had the misfortune to have a malfunction," recalled Walker. "A parachute went over the top of his horizontal stabilizer while a load of grenades went under. So there he was. About the same time, his left engine caught fire, forcing him to shut it down. Well, the average guy in these circumstances would immediately discontinue the drop and head for home. Not Dutch. He finished dropping his load and headed for Paksane, the nearest suitable airfield, with grenades hanging from his tail. Dutch landed dragging grenades the length of the runway. None exploded." Earlier, Jack Shirley had complained angrily that Aderholt was dropping him corroded ammo. Apparently the load of grenades hanging from Brongersma's tail were "duds."

Walker flew Colonel Billy around Site 2 and Padong for a first-hand look. That night Walker wrote in his logbook: "Stand-by to evacuate Jack Shirley. Situation deteriorating at Padong."

On April 23, Shirley, Ahern, and the remaining Hmong defenders could no longer hold San Tiau, Site 2. They took off on a predetermined escape route south, through a mine field they had laid. Every now and then they stopped to rig booby traps. Behind them they occasionally heard explosions triggered by their pursuers.

Air America pilots were airborne immediately looking for them. The next day, Ron Sutphin, flying a Helio, spotted them south of Site 2. He radioed their location and two Air America helicopters took out Shirley, Ahern, and other high-ranking people. Shirley told the remaining men to head west to a friendly site—to Padong if possible.

On April 24, Britain and the Soviet Union issued invitations for the convening of a new conference on the Lao situation. The conference was scheduled to begin in mid-May in Geneva. Talks between the two sides had already begun in order to arrange a cease-fire.

With San Tiau overrun, the North Vietnamese "fighting to negotiate" as usual, intensified their attacks against Padong. Artillery from North

Vietnamese and Kong Le gun positions on the Plaine des Jarres slammed into Vang Pao's mountain base.

Shells ripped into the colorful parachute tents of the American advisors, who ducked incoming artillery to scramble for the trenches. Shirley, dressed in pajama bottoms and shower shoes, stood with a beer in his hand, shouting over and over that the damned Viets were not running him off this mountain. No commie bastard scared him. He and his men were staying.

Surrounded by NVA with token Pathet Lao soldiers and Kong Le's men, the Padong defenders did not have the military might to strike back. The enemy shelled Padong with little concern for retaliation. U.S. guns given to the Hmong lacked the range to reach the enemy. The Hmong dug deeper trenches.

Ed Dearborn, a rugged, tall former Marine rifleman who had been wounded three times in Korea and had received a field promotion to sergeant before he was 20, flew another Air America Helio. He remembered the confusion at the time. "Hmong villages and locations were overrun, causing lots of refugees. At the same time, the Hmong were trying to prepare to fight back. I often flew Vang Pao so he could monitor enemy troop movement and get into remote positions to talk to his people. There were no air charts, and the Hmong-made airstrips were barely usable. Weather permitting, Vang Pao was airborne almost every day."[4]

Hmong who wanted to join the fight signaled their need for weapons and food by digging narrow gouges—which they called landing strips—into mountaintops and onto hillsides. Men, women, and children using their farming tools pushed and pulled the earth, felled trees, and rolled boulders to open a patch of dirt on which they thought a plane could land. These mountain airstrips were always dangerous, usually crooked, frequently uphill, and occasionally dog-legged. One was constructed over a small wooden bridge. One extended over the edge of a mountain. Here villagers, determined to have an airstrip on their mountainside, felled large trees and dragged them into place to construct a cantilevered runway. While these ingeniously constructed mile-high airfields opened up isolated mountain settlements, they demanded more use of STOL aircraft and consummate pilot skill. Throughout Hmong territory, many gouges appeared, announcing village decisions to join the fight.

Vang Pao, aware that Colonel "Heine" Aderholt was partly responsible for the air drops of weapons, found an opportunity to thank him. One day after Aderholt had flown him on an aerial search for landing strip sites, Vang Pao invited him to Padong.

Aderholt, who disapproved of military men drinking in a combat area, never forgot his first Hmong party. "It was my first trip to Padong. We all sat in a hut around a big churn of white lightning—and that's worse than any drinkin' you'll ever do out of a Scotch bottle. There was one long stem for all of us. We passed the stem around and sucked on it. The old guy next to me had betel nut running out of the corners of his mouth; another guy had a big goiter. We were all sitting there getting drunk on this white lightning in my honor and talking about how we would whip the North Vietnamese."[5] They would soon realize that whipping the North Vietnamese would take more than white lightning.

Colonel Billy worried about the Kennedy push for a neutralized Laos held together by a coalition government. He wondered if in Washington they really understood the situation in Laos. If policymakers were as uninformed about Laos and Southeast Asia as they appeared, the U.S. might become entrapped in foolhardy policies and strategies.

The Kennedy men assigned to resolve the Lao crisis did lack knowledge not only of Laos but of the cultural and political nuances of the area. Many Kennedy advisors were Eastern Establishment with a European focus. Words like "flexible response" and "brush-fire" conflicts punctuated their language as they sought to deal with the fighting in "developing nations." George Ball, Kennedy advisor, described the chaotic Lao situation as a "Kung Fu movie."[6] President Kennedy mispronounced the word Laos—making it rhyme with "chaos" instead of "mouse." (Native Lao spoke of themselves as "Lao" and their country as "Lao." The "s" was added during French rule for reasons that remain unclear.) Vang Pao predicted that the negotiations in Geneva would end up just like the Accords of 1954 by producing a piece of paper which the North Vietnamese had no intention of honoring. Vang Pao had never trusted the North Vietnamese, about whom he knew so much; nor did he trust their students—the Pathet Lao— who numbered at this time about 3,000 regular troops and another 3,000 part-time soldiers.

One day in early May, a Vietnamese-speaking Hmong monitoring NVA radios shouted for Colonel Vang Pao. He dashed to the radio tent to hear NVA instructions to position their big guns against Padong. Vang Pao yelled for everyone to take cover. Shells blasted into Padong, spewing the mountainside into the air. Vang Pao grabbed a mortar and began firing, all the time shouting encouragement and instructions to his men. His diminutive wife, Moua Chia, appeared from the safety of a bunker and ran to Vang Pao's position. Without a word, she passed him ammunition. Newly trained boy-medics ran in and out of the maze of trenches responding to calls for help. When the shelling stopped, American advisors ordered the men and women of Padong to dig in deeper.

Territorial holdings were now critical bargaining chips in the negotiations at Geneva. The more experienced forces of North Vietnam and Kong Le easily gained ground. The Royal Lao Army had already been pushed off the Plaine des Jarres. Determined to take as much territory as possible before any negotiations at Geneva, the enemy aggressively overran government outposts. Isolated Hmong mountain outposts in Xieng Khouang and Sam Neua provinces reported NVA troop movements, shelling, and more refugees. Could Padong hold out until an actual cease-fire could be put in place?

Vang Pao, remembering the French abandonment of the Hmong, repeatedly asked his U.S. advisors for assurances that the Americans intended to stay and fight and not abandon them to their enemies. Captain Bill Chance, a West Point man on the White Star team at Padong, always reassured him that the U.S. had a fervent commitment to help them fight the communists.

A reconnaissance patrol of barefoot tribesmen carrying homemade guns and World War II carbines gathered around Vang Pao. The team leader reported NVA and Kong Le troops, using Pathet Lao as coolie laborers, were inching up the mountain by digging terraced trenches, lifting their artillery ever closer to Padong. Vang Pao shouted angrily, asking if Kong Le intended to attack with weapons given him by the U.S. He switched on his field radio to hear an order in Vietnamese to move forward. Vang Pao, who could speak some Vietnamese, grabbed his radio intending to deliver a verbal assault, then decided against it. He vented his insults into the morning air. For all his bravado, he knew the assault was imminent.

If Padong were to hold, it needed critical air supply. Air America pilots needed good weather, but monsoon rains threatened and dense fog drifted over Padong, sealing it in gray isolation for days at a time. Walker told Vang Pao he doubted his pilots could keep Padong supplied during the upcoming rains. On May 6, Walker aborted his flight to Padong, not because of bad weather but because it was being shelled. The communists with their 85mm guns outgunned the Hmong, whose only heavy weapons were 4.2-in. mortars.

The diplomats at Geneva had reactivated the International Control Commission (ICC) created by the 1954 Geneva Accords to monitor and supervise. As in the past, the ICC, comprised of members from Canada, India, and Poland, was to prove ineffective. Without being able to conduct on-site inspections in communist-controlled territory, the ICC would have to take the word of the Pathet Lao that a cease-fire was in effect.

On May 11, the ICC—after witnessing a meeting of delegates from the three Lao factions at the small town of Ban Namone—telegraphed Geneva that a cease-fire was in effect and that the Conference could begin. Immediately the U.S. faced serious problems. Ignoring U.S. objections, the Pathet Lao delegation, referred to by the communist participants as the Patriotic Alliance of Laos, was seated as if it were a country.

The U.S. and Royal Lao delegations at Geneva complained about cease-fire violations at Padong. The Pathet Lao delegation brazenly responded in double-talk, proclaiming that Padong was entirely within its territory and the fighting was necessary to protect the local people from "imported bandits"—the Hmong. Responding to a report in the French press about some 10,000 husky Hmong fighters holding out at Padong, the Pathet Lao responded that this was simply American fiction. They changed the focus of debate by accusing the U.S. of conducting raids on villages and press-ganging villagers to fight.

The Chinese, belligerently anti-American, accused the U.S. of delaying the conference by requesting ICC verifications of nonexistent cease-fire violations. The Chinese mission ran an effective propaganda campaign against the U.S., using the assembled international press to carry its anti-American sentiments worldwide. U.S. diplomats, inexperienced in guerrilla diplomacy, responded limply and ineffectively to masterful salvos by the North Vietnamese and the Chinese. In spite of communist assertions at Geneva, no cease-fire existed. Communist forces continued attacks against Royal Lao government and Hmong positions.

On May 12, there was trouble at Moung Ngai, Lima Site 1. Here, in a mile-high mountain valley, a four-man Thai PARU team trained 80 Hmong. A crude, short airstrip ran alongside a series of volcanic cones littering the valley floor. The only cover was knee-high grass. On one of the cone-shaped hills, the men set up a position, protecting it by digging deep trenches all around the cone and positioning three 50-caliber machine guns to cover the field. Fred Walker talked to the Thai PARU team at 7:30 that evening. This would be his last contact.

At 4 the next morning, the pre-dawn darkness split with the sounds of crashing cymbals and trilling whistles. Under the cover of NVA 57s pounding the position, some 1,000 screaming NVA troops stormed Site 1. Hmong and PARU gunners mowed many down with machine gun fire. Still the enemy advanced, some reaching the battlements. Defenders fought with gun butts, knives, fists, and pistols. The position held; the NVA retreated.

The retreat was only temporary. Between the initial pre-dawn attack and 4 in the afternoon, the NVA ran three more frontal assaults on Site 1. Forty of the 80 Hmong were killed. The remaining 40 all suffered wounds. One Thai PARU was seriously wounded by a 57 burst that exploded near him, caving in his chest; he was also shot in the hip and leg.

During the fourth assault, the PARU team leader told the Hmong chief they were leaving. They could not get caught in Laos because the Premier of Thailand had said that except for a mercenary or two there were no Thai troops in Laos. Two days later, Dutch Brongersma spotted the PARU team and radioed Udorn requesting Air America choppers for a rescue. Within hours, the PARUs were out.

Nothing more was heard of the 40 wounded Hmong left behind. Walker believed the wounded were killed. "We lost the place," remembered Walker. "The Pathet Lao or North Vietnamese would shoot people rather than take them prisoner."

After the fall of Site 1, Walker, on alert for any unusual activity, spotted a Soviet PT-76 tank near Muong Soui leading a 15-truck convoy west toward Luang Prabang. Walker flew a couple of miles away to monitor the convoy while he alerted Flight Information of his sighting.

ICC requests to inspect violations were denied. The Pathet Lao claimed these incidents were not cease-fire violations, but police actions requested by local officials. They claimed that help had been sent in the form of Pathet Lao soldiers to restore order.

The ICC was in an impossible situation: it had to have unanimous agreement from the three Lao factions—the neutralists, the communists, and the anticommunists—for on-site inspections. The Pathet Lao derailed any investigation by claiming there were no violations, or transportation was not available, or it insisted the ICC visit areas in which there had been no action for some time. Cease-fire violations were reported to the ICC in Laos and to the American mission at Geneva, but protests voiced by the Americans had little effect.

On May 15, the day before the conference opened, the NVA laid down a deadly artillery barrage on Padong. A NVA ground attack was imminent. On May 17, Fred Walker tried unsuccessfully again to land. It would be his last attempt to resupply Vang Pao at Padong. On May 21, he departed for Taipei, not to return until July.

At Padong, the situation worsened. Throughout May 26 and 27, for 48 hours straight, communist artillery pounded the camp. Padong had been under daily attack for nearly a month. The Hmong, Thai, Americans, and some newly arrived and frightened Lao gunners dug themselves deeper into the trenches. White Star officer Bill Chance frequently radioed Vientiane with the continuing bad news. Cease-fire or not, he told the Americans in Vientiane, the "bad guys" had no intention of leaving until Padong and Vang Pao were eliminated.[7] He repeated requests for inspections by the ICC team, but such were not on the ICC schedule nor on the schedule of Marek Thee, the Polish delegate to the ICC. This man had other plans. He had accepted Hanoi's invitation for a visit with North Vietnamese leaders "to exchange views."

On the night of May 29, Hmong and Americans at Padong studied the dark, starless sky. Fog protected the camp from enemy artillery, but day fog or monsoon clouds also meant chopper pilots would have difficulty getting in.

On the morning of May 30, puffs of mist clung to Padong. Sent up in tandem from Vientiane, helicopter pilots often flew in marginal weather with no navigational aids. Pressed by the needs of those on the ground, they sometimes pushed their flying limits in dangerous weather situations. Vue Sai Long, who had sheltered French soldiers from the Japanese, worked with "Tip," a young Lao-speaking American CIA advisor, to load pallets with carbines, plastique explosives, and other supplies desperately needed in remote positions. One H-34 helicopter found a hole in the thick clouds, dropped down, loaded, and took off.[8] Both heard the second chopper coming in and looked up momentarily, but saw nothing. The chopper was hidden in the mists. Then they heard a strange whop-whop of blades, then a whine, followed by a screaming transmission as it raced out of control.

Men dashed toward the crash site. Vue Sai Long and several other Hmong crawled up the steep terrain to reach the crash site before Tip and West Pointer Bill Chance. The cockpit hung in a tree. A Hmong, already in the cockpit, called for help. He could see the pilot, a large man, bleeding from his mouth and ears and gurgling in his own blood. The copilot was cut into several pieces.

The deaths of these two men cast a sense of doom over those encamped on Padong. They were the first Americans killed in Laos.*

---

*On August 13, 1961, a C-46 delivering ammunition to Vang Pao at Pha Khao went down, killing all five crew members, including the pilot, Woody Forte, and three young CIA-hired "kickers." At Takhli, Colonel Aderholt received an urgent message that Forte was dead. Forte had trained in Okinawa with the Fulton "Sky Hook" Recovery System designed to

The next day, the Geneva Conference broke for the June 4 summit meeting in Vienna between President Kennedy and Soviet Premier Khrushchev. It was a tough meeting for Kennedy. Michael Forrestal, a member of Kennedy's National Security Council, remembered: "Kennedy had a terrible and scary fight with Khrushchev in Vienna. They seemed to agree on only one thing—that there was no need for Russian and American soldiers to fight in Laos. Only later would we understand why Khrushchev had made this remark. The truth was that China and North Vietnam were in control of the communist efforts in Laos at that time—not the Soviet Union."[9] Kennedy, however, took Khrushchev's comment at face value. According to Forrestal, after that Vienna meeting, Kennedy told Averell Harriman to negotiate a troop reduction and to reach a settlement in Laos.

On the same day that Kennedy and Khrushchev met in Vienna, Vang Pao departed Padong by helicopter for Pha Khao and Yat Mo in search of food for the Padong defenders. At Yat Mo he discovered several thousand refugees totally without food. At Pha Khao things were a bit better, but food was short.

On June 6—two days after the Kennedy-Khrushchev Vienna summit—storm clouds rolled over Padong. Vang Pao tried several times to return to his base, but it remained weathered in. His inability to return probably sealed the fate of Padong.

Enemy barrages against Padong had been so heavy that most women and children had been evacuated, though Vang Pao's young bride, Moua Chia, remained. Since the Wizard's intelligence and sixth sense told him that a ground attack was imminent, he had backed his men not critical to the defense of the base to the far side of the mountain, leaving forward posts manned by soldiers with machine guns and mortars.

A Hmong patrol reported to Captain Chance that they had sighted telephone wires above the Hmong base. When he heard this, he warned that the enemy was in position for a ground attack directed from higher up the mountain.

Nineteen-year-old Vang Chou, who, as a child, had been thrown in jail as a Fackee spy because he counted a Viet Minh convoy as it passed

---

retrieve American pilot Al Pope, condemned to death, from an Indonesian prison. With Forte's death, the plan to snatch Pope from prison was scrapped. Forte had been the only pilot trained to use the Fulton Recovery System. Also killed were two "kickers," Johnny Lewis and Darrell Eubanks, high school friends from Lampasas, Texas, recruited by the CIA from the U.S. Forest Service.

through Nong Het, now manned a frontline post. "My position was high. Rain clouds rolled against my position, blinding my view. I knew the enemy was out there in the rain and the clouds. I could sense they were there. Sometimes I could hear them."[10] As Vang Chou waited in the shivering dampness, he wondered if the enemy knew that Vang Pao was unable to return to Padong because of bad weather. He guessed that they did.

About 3 p.m.—only two days after Kennedy and Khrushchev had agreed that the two countries should not fight over Laos—small arms fire erupted from above. Soviet-made howitzers and mortars slammed into Padong with deadly accuracy, spewing into the air tents, pallets, shelters, and people. Vang Chou fired his mortar into the grayness. Hmong on the front lines fought back while those at the rear withdrew with the remaining civilians and the White Star team. Before retreating, Chance barked orders to throw dirt into Padong's guns, to set fire to supplies, to destroy everything. In their panic, many did not keep to the escape route and ventured into the mine fields laid to protect Padong.

The NVA increased its attack. In front of Vang Chou, three Lao soldiers manning a mortar received a direct and lethal hit, spewing their blood and flesh into the air. Vang Chou fired, defending the perimeter. Rain squalls reduced visibility to only a few yards, yet the attack continued. He and the five Hmong manning this forward position set up two 30mm machine guns only recently air-dropped. Darkness came. The North Vietnamese shelling continued.

Suddenly Chou realized his position was the only one firing. He and his five companions were the last defenders of Padong. In a lull in the shooting, they abandoned their position, taking with them two machine guns and as much ammunition as they could carry to repel pursuing Vietnamese. As they moved through the camp, they picked up two wounded men. Passing Vang Pao's thatch headquarters, they checked it for sensitive materials. They grabbed the colonel's much prized tape-recorder and a heavy silver necklace belonging to his wife Moua Chia, who had stayed until the end. Heavily burdened, they retreated in the darkness and chilling rains, struggling with their weapons and aiding the wounded. In the slippery mud, the group pushed through the darkness, crossed streams and gullies to climb down Padong and up another mountain to reach Yat Mo.

On June 7, troops belonging to North Vietnam, Kong Le, and the Pathet Lao witnessed the arrival of dawn at Padong. As the victors celebrated atop Padong and at Geneva, the last defenders of Padong moved in a dark thin line toward Yat Mo. In Geneva, the North Vietnamese delegation vehemently denied that it had soldiers in Laos.

Late on this morning of June 7, the Pathet Lao gave the ICC permission to inspect reported cease-fire violations at Padong. American elation quickly turned to anger when they learned that Padong had been overrun the night before.

At Yat Mo, Vang Chou's group was told to move on for another tough 24-hour walk to Pha Khao, 20 miles south of the communist controlled PDJ.

Colonel Vang Pao stood atop Pha Khao, which would be his new base, and searched between lingering clouds for his Padong defenders. He greeted his tired men by announcing that all was not lost. They would regroup here to fight another day.

Soviet Ilyushin aircraft based on the Plaine des Jarres formed a critical air bridge between Laos and North Vietnam. On June 9, Marek Thee, the Pole on the ICC team, boarded a Hanoi bound plane on the PDJ that would take him to meetings to which Hanoi's officialdom had invited him a few days earlier. Years later, this Polish ICC delegate would write about that important trip: "I was met by old friends, party and government officials. I was received as a guest of the Foreign Ministry and was allotted a comfortable villa in the center of town. I learned most at a meeting with the Acting Prime Minister, Pham Hung. . . . He spoke with strong inner conviction. Basic national interests were involved [in Laos]. Laos and Vietnam were bound by fate. For Pham Hung this was historical inevitability."[11]

In various meetings with high-level Hanoi officials, the Polish ICC delegate learned more about the North Vietnamese involvement in Laos. "Hanoi kept very close contact with the Pathet Lao and strategical planning was a joint enterprise. Listening to the information presented by my Vietnamese hosts, I realized how much of the brunt of efforts in Laos was being carried by Hanoi. This was so in many fields: military support, economic and technical help, political counsel. In Hanoi an interdepartmental body was in constant touch with Laos. . . . North Vietnam provided the nucleus for assault units in the main battles. Vietnamese staff officers aided in military planning. Both the battles at Tha Thom and Ban Padong had been won with Vietnamese support. About twenty thousand Vietnamese were employed in clearing and repairing roads, while about one thousand Vietnamese drivers were in Laotian service."

The denial of this information to the Geneva participants spelled disaster for any meaningful negotiations on Laos. It was not until 12 years later in 1973—after the U.S. had decided to abandon Laos and the fate of Laos was sealed—that ICC delegate Marek Thee made it available in a book published in the U.S.

Marek Thee was not the only person to know of the heavy North Vietnamese involvement in Laos. The Soviets knew, the Chinese knew, and the Hmong knew.

At the conference, the communist delegations had been energized by their initial diplomatic victory of seating the Pathet Lao, by their propaganda against the U.S., by their victories at Padong and other Lao government locations following the May cease-fire, and by their ability to control the ICC.

In Geneva, Harriman faced the "guerrilla diplomacy" of the feisty North Vietnamese. Not to be cowed by their rhetoric, Harriman responded with his "water torture" techniques. Harriman's aides (William Sullivan, Michael Forrestal, Chester Cooper, Paul Nitze) recounted some of his tactics for Walter Isaacson and Evan Thomas in their book *The Wise Men:* "He would make the same point over and over, letting it drip down until his adversaries gave in. He would use scorn judiciously. When the North Vietnamese, the most devious of the lot, spoke, Harriman would ostentatiously read the *New York Times.* When a North Vietnamese representative began calling the U.S. a warmonger, Harriman 'accidentally' hit the 'talk' button on his microphone and said to an aide, 'Did that little bastard say we started World War II?'"[12]

7.

The Charade of Neutralization

For the Communist side, neutralization of Laos was a screen for *de facto* partition which, in turn, became a screen for a slow invasion of South Vietnam.

—Norman Hannah, *Key to Failure: Laos and the Vietnam War*

In Washington, men prepared for the Geneva Conference and a neutralized Laos. Not all those working on the Lao problem agreed that the U.S. sought a neutralized Laos. Some believed that Kennedy was only trying to buy time. While neutralization efforts were under way, Kennedy also undertook military initiatives. He created the Green Berets, put Task Force 116 with its specially trained troops in Okinawa on alert for deployment to Laos, ordered the Seventh Fleet to move into the Gulf of Siam, considered an American airborne invasion to occupy the Plaine des Jarres, and sent a squadron of helicopters to Udorn Air Base in Thailand to stand-by for action in Laos.

While American diplomats circled the globe seeking support for a conference on Laos, Hanoi continued its strategy of "fighting to negotiate." In neighboring South Vietnam, communist insurgency increased. Unbeknownst to the Americans, in late 1960 Hanoi had given the signal to its people in South Vietnam to begin the violent stage of the struggle to unite Vietnam under the North Vietnamese regime. Critical to this goal was the trail complex being constructed by the North Vietnamese inside Laos. This system of supply arteries—which would become known as the Ho Chi Minh Trail—would provide the means to infiltrate agents, provide secure communication, and funnel the weapons, medicines, machines, and troops necessary for a communist victory in South Vietnam.

This goal had to remain secret for two important reasons. If detected, North Vietnam would be violating the 1954 Geneva Accords that prohibited it from using a second country (Laos) in order to fight in yet another country (South Vietnam). Second, since the strategy was to create an image of an indigenous, struggling Viet Cong independent of North Vietnam, the detection of massive assistance from the North would destroy this popular and effective underdog, grassroots image.

As the Geneva Conference dragged along into autumn, fighting continued in Laos. Communist landgrabbing created tens of thousands of refugees from all ethnic groups throughout Laos. More aircraft were needed to ferry refugee supplies and newly trained Hmong irregulars into mountain positions. Helicopters that Kennedy earlier had ordered to Udorn Air Base in Thailand began flying in Laos. Colonel "Heine" Aderholt was in Udorn when the Marine helicopter squadron arrived. "They arrived from Okinawa to work in Laos in September 1961. The Marines got into operation and then they pulled out, leaving their helicopters. The men who wanted to fly resigned from the Marines and volunteered. We had until October to replace the regular duty Marines with civilians. That's when Air America picked up the recruitment and converted some Marines over to their operation."[1] By resigning from active duty, these Marine pilots theoretically were not defying the Geneva Accords which prohibited foreign military personnel from serving in Laos.

As more aircraft arrived, Air America pilot Ed Dearborn was delegated to name and map both those airstrips ordered by Colonel Vang Pao and those built spontaneously by villagers. One day Dearborn landed on one of these new strips. "With an interpreter, I paced off the field, took a compass heading, and recorded the condition of the landing field which had huge trees at either end, rocks on the surface, and was crooked. I carried a form on which I recorded these details which would become a page in the pilots' landing site book. When I got to the space on the form for the name of the site, the villagers told me there was no name. I told them that I had to have a name or we couldn't log this strip onto the map. The villagers insisted that there was no name. So I declared that this strip—Lima Site 100—would be known henceforth as Ban [village] Beecher, named after Beecher Strother Stowe, my grandfather, who was a trial lawyer in Los Angeles whom I adored."[2]

Because of the fluidity of the situation and lack of communication with landing sites to determine which side was in control, pilots were instructed never to land if the signal—pieces of white cloth held down by rocks assembled in the form of a predetermined code letter—was already in place. Pilots were to land *only* if they observed the signal being put into place.

One day in early 1962, Dearborn loaded his Helio with a tall Texan and his survey equipment. The Texan had been sent from the U.S. to improve on Dearborn's rough mapping of Lima Site airfields. Usually, Dearborn checked with Vang Pao's men to get the latest intelligence reports. "This morning I didn't bother since I had recently been to this area and I was in a hurry. As I approached the site, I saw the signal indicating it was safe already in place, which should have warned me of trouble. The other signs that the field was safe and in friendly hands were in place—women were building fires and children and dogs were playing. Violating our basic rule that the pilot had to witness the code letter being put in place, I dropped onto the site. I kept the motor running while the Texan unloaded his equipment. I noticed that some soldiers were wearing the puffy caps of the Pathet Lao, but no one came forward or raised a gun, so I concluded that they weren't the enemy. Then I took off to drop off other cargo. At noon, I returned to Pha Khao for lunch at Vang Pao's headquarters. He asked me where I had flown this morning. I told him. He stopped eating and asked again where I had been. 'No! No! Enemy strip,' he insisted. 'Enemy take last night!'

"I assured him that the Texan was busily at work surveying and everything was fine. Vang Pao insisted that the enemy held the strip and the American was in danger. I hoped he was wrong, but Vang Pao was never wrong on enemy locations. I knew that. So, I got in my plane and flew back to the site. The signal was still out. I could see the Texan working down there with a crowd of people around him. There seemed to be more men with the putty hats and guns.

"I landed, expecting gunfire. As I taxied to a stop, I waved frantically to the Texan to come. He shouted back that he wasn't finished. I shouted to him that he *was* finished! This was an enemy field! He ground out his cigar, collected his equipment, and walked toward the plane. He was struggling to get his equipment into the plane when I saw a puffy-hatted soldier running toward us with a bag. I shouted to the Texan to get in and close the door. Before he could get the door latched, the soldier forced it open and threw a bag inside. I knew it was a grenade and waited for the explosion. When it didn't explode, I grabbed the bag and tore it open. Inside was mail. We took it back to Pha Khao. It turned out that the mail was messages for the communist commanders in the region. Apparently, the enemy soldiers took us to be Soviets and decided that distributing orders by air was a lot easier than by foot. The military data collected that day represented a significant coup for Vang Pao. After this experience, I never relied on anyone but Vang Pao for military information."

During the Geneva negotiations, town after town was overrun by the communists. The Royal Lao Army often responded to enemy attacks, but was usually defeated. White Star teams stayed with their Lao and tribal forces, trying to prevent defeat. The Lao government could not cope with the growing number of refugees. Air America pilots flew rice drops to them and to besieged outposts. Overall, it was a deteriorating situation.

*   *   *

Not all Asian leaders agreed with Kennedy's idea that a coalition government representing the neutralists, the communists, and rightists was a viable resolution to the Lao crisis. General Phoumi Nosavan, whom the CIA had backed, opposed such an arrangement, as did the leaders of South Vietnam and Thailand.

Since the U.S. neutralization strategy was based on a coalition government representing the three factions, Washington decided it was necessary to convince General Phoumi to step aside to allow the return of Prince Souvanna Phouma as head of a neutralized Laos. Prince Souvanna Phouma was Kennedy's man; General Phoumi had to go.

In March 1962, during a recess in the Geneva negotiations, Harriman sent foreign service officer William Sullivan, his deputy at Geneva and later U.S. Ambassador to Laos, and Michael Forrestal, a member of Kennedy's National Security Staff, to Laos to persuade General Phoumi to end his resistance to a coalition government. They soon discovered the assignment was beyond their abilities. They were forced finally to call in Harriman himself to convince Phoumi.

While awaiting Harriman's arrival, Forrestal and Sullivan flew to the Plaine des Jarres to meet Kong Le and Vang Pao to convince them to work together. These two knights of Camelot in the "Land of Oz" flew in a Soviet aircraft to the Plaine des Jarres, now occupied by Soviet-equipped Pathet Lao and North Vietnamese soldiers, to talk with American-trained and equipped Kong Le who had joined with the communist troops and who actively fought Vang Pao's CIA-equipped soldiers. Reportedly, U.S. aid provided the fuel for Soviet planes and for housing of the Soviet pilots who trained Lao pilots to fly Soviet aircraft.[3]

Forrestal described that meeting at the Plaine des Jarres airport. "Kong Le, a small man in meticulous paratrooper dress, presented himself to our delegation wearing his red beret, a yellow scarf and smelling of perfume. Speaking in French in front of Vang Pao [who could speak five languages, including French], Kong Le quickly pointed out that the tribal minorities were not really people, that they were incapable of thinking and very capable of moving away overnight from their positions.''[4]

Like Colonel Vang Pao, Captain Kong Le had been recruited by the French to fight the Viet Minh and had served in the Territorial Army. He stood only 5 foot 1 inch, a couple of inches shorter than Vang Pao, but Forrestal observed that Vang Pao seemed much taller.

Vang Pao made an impression on Forrestal. "He had arrived from his Pha Khao base and he smelled of sweat and garlic. He had with him his senior officers who wore tribal clothes and carried primitive weapons. While Kong Le spoke of the failings of the tribal people, Vang Pao remained silent and self-assured. After Kong Le spoke, Vang Pao, also speaking in French, energetically registered his complaints to us about Kong Le and his Lao forces. He said they were untrustworthy and unreliable because they easily abandoned positions, leaving others behind to be shot.''

Forrestal concluded that neither Kong Le nor Vang Pao was prepared for a joint venture. He concluded that Vang Pao was the stronger leader. Back in Vientiane, Forrestal asked U.S. authorities why Vang Pao did not have modern weapons like Kong Le. He was told that the Hmong leader did have a few modern weapons but had probably chosen not to bring them down from his mountain location for fear that Kong Le might take them away. The Plaine des Jarres, after all, was enemy territory. Forrestal concluded there was more to it than that. "I deduced that Vang Pao was hoping to impress the Americans by appearing as a rag-tag army leader who had no time for perfumes and scarves. He hoped that the U.S. delegation might be influenced to recommend that he should be better equipped.''

Forrestal's observation was astute. Vang Pao's soldiers were always outgunned. While the North Vietnamese had the latest Soviet and Chinese military weapons and Kong Le had modern U.S. equipment, Vang Pao had World War II weapons and munitions, often corroded and useless.

While some American observers evaluated Kong Le as an effective and well-liked battalion commander, he was also generally considered extremely naive. He had demonstrated that naivete in front of Forrestal by his verbal assault on Vang Pao.

In anticipation of Harriman's arrival, Forrestal and Sullivan spoke to the Lao notables—basically the families who ran the lowland valley areas and formed much of the Lao cabinet. Harriman arrived. Lao leaders, dressed in white ceremonial uniforms, draped with gold and red braid and decorated with garish medals indicating service to the Kingdom of a Million Elephants and a White Parasol, assembled in Vientiane in a building along the banks of the Mekong River. When Harriman spoke, the ministers did not seem particularly pleased with his proposals for neutralization and the return of Prince Souvanna Phouma as prime minister, or with his threat to cut aid to Laos and Thailand if they did not cooperate.

At one point, Harriman looked out the window at the broad expanse of the Mekong River rushing by and said to the Lao dignitaries: "See that river out there? It's wide and running fast. If you think that you can swim across that river when you have to, then I'll go home." The Lao giggled nervously, but Harriman persisted. In spite of embarrassed fidgeting and uncomfortable bursts of laughter by the Lao who considered his behavior rude, Harriman pressed them. He faced each cabinet member, asked each the same question, and waited for an answer.

Most of the Lao present were not physically in shape for a half-mile swim through strong currents. The Mekong was a dangerous river; they all knew that. The cabinet members had no choice but to mumble something to Harriman about not wanting to swim the Mekong. After eliciting a response from each, Harriman continued: "If you will agree with us and give us some time, maybe we can arrange something so that you won't have to leave your country—or swim that river."[5]

Within a week, General Phoumi agreed to step aside.

*   *   *

In the spring of 1962, Air America operations received a U.S. Army Caribou, C-7, which Fred Walker, as chief pilot in Laos for Air America, would test. This twin-engine cargo plane, designed for heavy loads and short-field landings and take-offs, would become the workhorse of the Vietnam War era. On May 12, 1962, Walker landed it at a newly constructed airstrip tucked in a mountain valley with a dangerous approach and karst at the far end of the runway. In his logbook, he recorded it as Lima Site 30. Walker had landed at Long Chieng, destined to become infamous in the press as a "CIA secret base."[6] In reality, Long Chieng became a forward-staging area for CIA-supported operations in Laos. CIA headquarters, the real "secret base," would be located in northern Thailand, where it went unnoticed by the media. The Americans rarely referred to Long Chieng as Lima Site 30, which was its actual site number. Later on, to confuse the enemy and outsiders, they called it "20 Alternate" or "Alternate."

On June 23, one month before the signing of the Geneva Agreement on Laos, the U.S., to show good faith, began pulling out its White Star advisory teams. One month later, the fourteen nations meeting in Geneva signed a declaration and a protocol on the neutrality of Laos. Prince Souvanna Phouma became prime minister, heading a tripartite government. The language of the accords reiterated the words of the 1954 accords, proclaiming the need to "build a peaceful, neutral, independent, democratic, unified, and prosperous Laos." The treaty also stipulated that foreign troops, regular and irregular, and paramilitary and military personnel were to be withdrawn under ICC oversight. Foreign bases would be prohibited as well as the introduction of armaments, munitions and war material except that deemed necessary by the Royal Lao government for national defense. Signatories would "not use the territory of the Kingdom of Laos for interference in the internal affairs of other countries" and would "not use the territory of any country, including their own, for interference in the internal affairs of the Kingdom of Laos." Signing were: Burma, Cambodia, Thailand, South Vietnam, France, India, Poland, Canada, United Kingdom, United States, Soviet Union, China, North Vietnam, and Laos.

With this signing, Washington officially decreed that the Lao crisis had been resolved—at least on paper. On July 27, Prince Souvanna Phouma visited President Kennedy in Washington. Kennedy's Lao policy of neutralization was in place. Ambassador Leonard Unger prepared to move into the American Embassy in Vientiane to usher in this new era.

While Washington celebrated the neutralization of Laos, thousands of Hmong on mountaintops and in refugee camps waited to see if the communists would honor the agreement. Vang Pao warned that the "treaty" was only paper and predicted that if the Americans withdrew from Laos without an equivalent withdrawal by the North Vietnamese, the anti–North Vietnamese Hmong faced extermination.

Soon after the signing, Vang Pao expressed his doubts to Souvanna Phouma. "I told him: 'We are happy on the outside that there has been an international conference on Laos in Geneva, but on the inside we know already that any conference will be a profit for the Vietnamese. We already know that they will make an agreement with no intention to follow it.' Souvanna Phouma listened but said nothing."[7]

Between the July 23 signing of the documents and the October 7 deadline for withdrawal of all foreign troops, the U.S. withdrew 666 military men, accounted for at ICC check points. By the deadline, the only American military men remaining in Laos were the military attaché at the embassy and his staff. The Americans had withdrawn their military personnel. Colonel Billy moved across the Mekong to the small Thai town of Nong Khai and waited.

Hanoi grandstanded with an ICC-monitored public withdrawal of "technicians," "experts," and "advisors," continuing to deny that it had any troops in Laos. These were advisory cadre. In total, the North Vietnamese withdrew 13 officers, 17 noncommissioned officers, five experts, and five men wearing fatigues bearing no rank or insignia: 40 men, from an estimated 7,000-to-9,000-man force.

William Colby, then assigned by the CIA to Southeast Asia, recalled that Harriman insisted the Americans not violate the Geneva agreement by supplying the rightist faction. He demanded to be told of every shipment of food and nonmilitary supplies sent into Laos and insisted on approving each flight.[8]

Roger Hilsman, Kennedy's Director of the Bureau of Intelligence and Research in the State Department, emphasized the Kennedy administration's adherence to the agreements: "The policy of the Kennedy administration was to neutralize Laos and live by it. We really did that—with a few exceptions of air drops to supply Pop Buell and some mercy missions for the Meo [Hmong]. We cut contacts. It was only after Kennedy was killed and we [some Kennedy advisors, including Hilsman] were kicked out and Johnson came in and started bombing the North that all the contacts with the Meo were reactivated."[9]

But in the summer of 1962, CIA training facilities at Marana, Arizona, bustled with activity. A number of those trained there would serve in Laos. Some had already worked in Laos. Ed Dearborn was there briefly that summer for more flight training. So were Jerry Daniels, a cargo-kicker on the C-46s operating in Laos, and Toby Scott, a smoke-jumper like Daniels. In their free time, Daniels and Scott rode bulls and broncos in a local rodeo circuit. Scott remembered those macho days: "We didn't win any prize money, but we had a hell of time with lots of girls in tight-fitting pants, who followed us around. Then one of our men got injured. That was it. The boss said either work for the Agency [CIA] or ride bulls. We quit the rodeo."[10] Scott would be sent to South Vietnam. Daniels would be assigned to the Hmong as a paramilitary advisor.

The Hmong soon found out what the communists intended for those who opposed them. In late August 1962, one month after the signing of the second Geneva Agreement, North Vietnamese soldiers attacked the area around Ban Ban, home to about 6,000 Lao, Kmhmu, and Hmong. Unable to defend themselves, lightly armed villagers fled southward with their attackers in pursuit. After 18 hours of flight, they sought refuge in a high mountain bowl to rest. About midnight, communist soldiers rushed the sleeping camp. "The ambushers, fiercely armed and more than four hundred strong, ran screaming down the hillsides and slithered down the faces of the limestone cliffs surrounding the bowl. Then they launched into an unspeakable orgy of bloodletting," remembered one survivor.[11]

People panicked, fleeing herd-like out of the bowl with their attackers pursuing all night. "Children were snatched from their mothers' arms and hurled with head-crushing force against rocks. Old men and women were shot in the legs and left to die alone, abandoned both by their young and by their executioners. Women were raped, then disemboweled."[12]

The orgy ended about noon of the next day with 1,300 Hmong, Lao, and Kmhmu dead, many wounded, and 200—mostly young men—captured and taken away by the enemy. News of the attack reached Phou Ang, where Nhia, several of her siblings, and her mother were hiding. Within minutes, they evacuated. "My mother told us not to make any noise and walk quickly. We obeyed. The first night, we found a small, friendly village on Phou San where they had rice for us. The following day, before dark, we reached Bouam Loung and my father, Moua Cher Pao."[13]

Survivors walked into Muong Meo, some 40 miles from the site of the atrocities, to describe the massacre. The 20,000 refugees at Muong Meo had to be dispersed. Using Air America planes, half were flown southwest across several mountains to a village called Muang Cha. Here villagers had already hacked down trees to clear a swatch for an airstrip, to be Lima Site 113.[14]

Pop Buell and USAID personnel hoped these refugees could start again at Muang Cha, but dysentery struck, killing 30 to 50 people daily. American doctor Charles Louis "Jiggs" Weldon and partially trained Hmong paramedics tended to ill bodies and terrorized minds. Vang Pao often visited the Muang Cha encampment to give encouragement to survivors.

Also in August, approximately six weeks after the signing of the Protocol, an American photo-reconnaissance jet on a routine surveillance flight filmed an NVA convoy coming into Laos along Route 7, heading for the PDJ. Photos revealed tanks, armored cars, a small number of towed artillery pieces, and trucks loaded with Vietnamese troops.[15] By the end of August, U.S. intelligence estimated that there were 10,000 NVA in Laos.

The State Department did not file a formal protest with the ICC. Instead, it turned to the Soviet Union with its concerns. To allay U.S. anxieties, the Soviet Union gave assurances that the North Vietnamese troops would disappear into the jungle and counseled the U.S. not to worry. The Americans still did not understand that the Soviets had little influence with Hanoi. Kennedy and Harriman mistakenly continued to view Khrushchev as the North Vietnamese enforcer and to operate under the guidance of the vague, verbal understanding between Kennedy and Khrushchev at Vienna.

Photo surveillance of the NVA buildup was not made public by the State Department until 1964. The decision to ignore Hanoi's violations and to keep this critical information secret would come to haunt the U.S. Many involved at this time believed that if State had made this information public, it could have exposed Hanoi's true intentions at an early date. That did not happen, adding to the secrecy, intrigue, and lack of public knowledge of the Lao situation.

That same month, an estimated 200,000 refugees, mostly Hmong, were displaced by communist military actions in northern Laos. Vang Pao watched as more enemy trucks, tanks, and artillery pieces were assembled and camouflaged. He knew these weapons were intended to be used against him. The Hmong situation was bleak. The communists demanded that all American assistance to the Hmong be stopped. Without U.S.-supplied rice, salt, and weaponry, they could easily be wiped out.

On September 10, Ambassador Leonard Unger, at the request of Prime Minister Souvanna Phouma, recommended that the U.S. resume deliveries of military supplies to the rightist army.

In mid-October 1962, Kennedy and the Soviet Union entered a tense period of "brinkmanship." Aerial reconnaissance revealed that the Soviets had offensive missiles in Cuba. Kennedy had made it clear earlier that he would not tolerate Soviet missiles in Cuba. Khrushchev was testing Kennedy once again. Kennedy responded by putting the Strategic Air Command, with its nuclear bombing capability, on alert and announced that he was "quarantining" Cuba until the Soviet Union withdrew its missiles. For a week, Americans talked of nothing but the possibility of war on U.S. soil. Then Khrushchev backed down. Soviet missiles were removed from Cuba.

In Laos, George Ball's "Kung Fu movie" played on. Kong Le's neutralist army, or "centrist" army as Washington was now calling his forces, depended upon Soviet-bloc weapons airlifted in by Soviet planes. In November, the Soviets terminated their airlift to Kong Le, leaving him totally dependent upon the North Vietnamese for supplies.

On November 27, an Air America Caribou, ferrying supplies to Kong Le's neutralists on the Plaine des Jarres, was shot down by an antiaircraft gun under Kong Le's command. Two Americans were killed. To avoid another shootdown, the U.S. gave Souvanna Phouma several cargo planes to supply Kong Le. Since no Lao pilots at the time were trained to fly these transport planes, American crews were necessary.

At the same time, Ilyushin-14s, used since 1960 to supply troops on the PDJ, were turned over to the North Vietnamese who could determine which factions received supplies. All along, the Pathet Lao and North Vietnamese had skimmed supplies intended for Kong Le. Unbeknownst to him, the communists intended to weaken his forces, then drive him off the PDJ.

Late in 1962, when it became obvious that the North Vietnamese had no intention of leaving Laos, the CIA returned to its "Third Option"—counterinsurgency and guerrilla warfare. Vang Pao moved his headquarters from Pha Khao to nearby Long Chieng. The CIA, code-named CAS (Controlled American Source), also set up a field base at Long Chieng. CAS headquarters was across the Mekong River on the Royal Thai Air Force Base at Udorn. Here Colonel Billy worked in a modest open-air office in a nondescript Thai-style building, monitoring events in Laos and in South Vietnam. He strongly disapproved of the American buildup in South Vietnam and of the huge sums of money being spent to arm, dress, and shoe the South Vietnamese Army. He believed that a successful counterinsurgency effort had to be one that could, if necessary, be financed entirely by local people. Soldiers had to be fielded on only a few cents a day.[16]

Determined to keep the Lao operation running on a minimal budget, he studied the French jungle boot, which resembled a tennis shoe, and various uniforms to determine the best kind of footwear and clothing for mountainous Laos. Instead of using the expensive American-made shoes and fatigues which the U.S. issued in South Vietnam, he commissioned Chinese merchants in Thailand to make combat clothes and shoes for the irregulars. He outfitted his counterinsurgency force at a fraction of the per capita cost of outfitting the South Vietnamese Army.

In these days, Vang Pao took great pride in personally delivering the pay to his troops. Ed Dearborn often flew Vang Pao on his payroll runs. "Because we used the Helio for carrying cargo, we had no seats in the back. One day, 'V.P.' was sitting on the floor in the back, holding the payroll as I approached a site. It was a difficult airstrip, sitting at 5,600 feet with severe wind drafts on approach. There was not enough land for the runway which ran up the mountain. The villagers had extended the runway over the edge of the mountain by building an extension from tree logs and filling it with dirt. With the extension, it was only 600 feet long. On approach, a draft sucked the plane down. I jammed on the power, but the tail caught the edge of the logs with a jolt. We skidded to a halt. When we stopped, I looked back. The tail section of the plane was gone. There sat Vang Pao on the floor, still holding the payroll, looking out the huge hole at the rear. Before I could say anything, not concerned that he had just missed death, he asked: 'When we leave? Must deliver payroll.'

"There was no way we could leave. We had only half a plane. Later that day, a chopper came in to pick 'V.P.' up so he could continue his rounds. Many days later we managed to repair and fly the wounded bird out."

In early April, Pathet Lao forces attacked Kong Le, forcing him to abandon his positions at Khang Khay, the Neutralist capital, and at Xieng Khouang town. On May 12, the State Department ordered delivery of arms and ammunition to Kong Le. Walker's Air America pilots responded, air-dropping supplies to Kong Le, clinging to the edge of the Plaine des Jarres. The U.S. was supplying Kong Le's troops while simultaneously supporting Vang Pao's soldiers who found themselves in firefights with him. Years later, American advisors concluded that the U.S. armed and pampered Kong Le to keep him from joining the communists.*

Vang Pao took advantage of the communist focus on eliminating Kong Le and launched a series of stinging attacks against enemy troops positioned in the mountains. His guerrilla operations drove many enemy troops to the PDJ to the protection of the armed camp there.

Vang Pao's men, with the backing of the CIA and the use of the Air America fleet to keep them supplied, retook about 75 percent of Xieng Khouang Province. While the PDJ remained in the hands of the communists, Americans had plenty of evidence that the "Third Option" was working.

Under the "Third Option," civilian needs had to be met as well. At

---

*The U.S. even gave Kong Le his own plane and assigned him a personal American pilot.

Sam Thong, Lima Site 20, a mountain ridge almost a day's walk from Long Chieng, refugees from Sam Neua and Xieng Khouang provinces waited. Here Prince Sai Kham carried on a civilian government for them. This was also Pop Buell's home base, and USAID warehoused refugee supplies here. Before the influx of refugees, this small community, whose Lao name meant "Copper Marsh," had been an agriculturally rich Hmong community of long standing. Now the orchards, wet rice lands, and water supply could not sustain the thousands of refugees collected here.

The Hmong desire to educate their children had also to be addressed. Vang Pao knew that education had to be available or the Hmong might follow Touby LyFong to Vientiane, where he worked in a Lao government ministry. Pop Buell wanted to educate all children, boys and girls, including those of ordinary folks. In Laos, this was a revolutionary thought. Prince Sai Kham joined Pop in promoting this bold idea. The man called upon to implement primary schools throughout Xieng Khouang Province was Moua Lia, who had recently completed some teacher training in France.[17]

Moua Lia discovered that in 1963 in the entire Xieng Khouang Province only 1,200 students attended school in grades one through three. No girl students were enrolled in official government schools. A few girls attended makeshift schools—like Nhia, who attended a school at Bouam Loung initiated by her father. Nhia was extremely lucky. Most Hmong girls and women remained uneducated and illiterate.

Since teachers were scarce, Vang Pao ordered his officers who could read and write to man the primary classrooms. Ly Lue no longer taught. He and his former student Lo Ma served as infantrymen in the Royal Lao Army. After the fall of Padong, Lo Ma had tried to enroll in a Lao school in Vientiane to continue his studies. Denied access, he had stayed in Vientiane and for one year had studied English in a U.S.-sponsored English as a Second Language program. At 16, he had joined the Army where he earned $14 a month.

While Moua Lia struggled with the enormous task of trying to educate Hmong children, NVA activities increased in Laos. Communist cease-fire violations were reported to the ICC; again and again the ICC was immobilized by its Polish member, Marek Thee.

On November 2, 1963, South Vietnam's Premier Ngo Dinh Diem was assassinated, reportedly with acquiescence of the Kennedy administration. As a result, the situation in South Vietnam worsened. In four months, South Vietnam would have three changes of government. Less than three weeks after Diem's death, President John Kennedy was assassinated. The U.S. had 16,300 military personnel and a number of civilians serving in South Vietnam when Lyndon Johnson became President. The Johnson administration became mired in confusion, in conflicting data and advice, in guilt over Diem's assassination, and in the tumultuous, emotional aftermath of Kennedy's death.

Capitalizing on the turmoil caused by the death of these two heads of state, Hanoi accelerated its plans for "liberating" South Vietnam and Laos. Hanoi used the "Harriman Memorial Highway," as some Americans bitterly called the Ho Chi Minh Trail. The Trail was, in fact, a system of trails leading from North Vietnam through Laos into South Vietnam, which were used to infiltrate more men and supplies into South Vietnam. Hanoi's use of one country—Laos—to overthrow the government of yet another country—South Vietnam—was in direct violation of the Geneva Accords.

On December 16, Souvanna Phouma told Seymour Topping of the *New York Times* that Hanoi had made it clear that "it is supporting the Chinese Communist ideology and that Peking has acknowledged that all Indochina is to be considered North Vietnam's sphere of influence." This bold statement prompted Souvanna Phouma to criticize U.S. understanding in understatement: "I fear that the Soviet influence on Hanoi is not totally effective."[18]

By now, the ephemeral and utopian scheme for a neutralized Laos with the Soviet Union and the United States acting as enforcers should have been discredited. Incredibly, however, the charade continued. Laos remained the Land of Oz.

Part Three

Secret War
in Laos:
The Johnson
Years

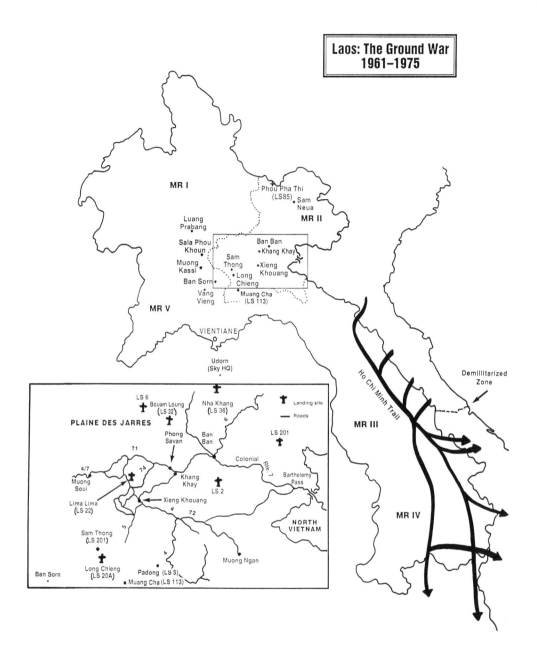

Laos: The Ground War
1961–1975

MR I

Phou Pha Thi
(LS85) • Sam
Neua

MR II

Luang
Prabang

Sala Phou
Khoun

Ban Ban
• Khang Khay

Muong
Kassi

Sam
Thong

• Xieng
Khouang

Ban Sorn•

• Long
Chieng

MR V

Vang
Vieng

Muang Cha
(LS 113)

VIENTIANE

Udorn
(Sky HQ)

Ho Chi Minh Trail

Demilitarized
Zone

LS 6
Bouam Loung
(LS 32)

Nha Khang
(LS 36)

Landing site

PLAINE DES JARRES

Phong
Savan

Ban
Ban

LS 201

Roads

MR III

71

4/7

74

Colonial

Rte. 1

Barthelemy
Pass

Muong
Soui

Khang
Khay

Lima Lima
(LS 22)

LS 2

← Xieng Khouang

72

NORTH
VIETNAM

MR IV

Sam Thong
(LS 201)

Long Chieng
(LS 20A)

Padong (LS 5)

Muang Cha (LS 113)

Muong Ngan

Ban Sorn
•

Laos: The Air War 1964–1973

NORTH VIETNAM

Dien Bien Phu

Hanoi

Haiphong

Muong Sai

Ban Nam Bac

Phou Bha Thi (LS 85) ✳

Sam Neua

Na Khang (LS 36) ✳

GULF OF TONKIN

Bouam Loung (LS 32) ✳

Luang Prabang

Ban Ban

Skyline Ridge (LS 20A) ✳

Khang Khay

Nong Het

Sayaboury

Ban Sorn

Padong

Vang Vieng

Vinh

Paksane

Vientiane

Udorn

Nakhon Phanom (NKP)

Demilitarized Zone

Nam Phong

Séno

Savannakhet

Tchepone

Khe Sanh

Hué

THAILAND

Ubon

Pakse

Takhli

Korat

Attopeu

Bangkok/Don Muang

U Taphao (B-52 Base)

▲ Thai airforce bases used by USAF

✳ Navigational sites used by U.S. Military to direct air operations over North Vietnam and northern Laos

Spellings coincide with official U.S. Government usage of the period

8.

CIA Operations at Long Chieng

Foreigners should know why we fight for so long in Military Region II. We fight not for another country, not for another person. We are not the mercenaries of the Americans or English or French. No! We fight to defend our own freedom. We know that the land belongs to us. We were born there so we fight against the communists. Who are the communists? The Vietnamese. We continue to fight the North Vietnamese until we withdrew from our land. We fight from the 1940s.

—Moua Lia, who was responsible for Hmong education during the 1960s and 1970s

Long Chieng, which would be mislabeled "the Secret CIA Base," was located in a long, narrow, high plateau basin not far from Padong. Long Chieng meant "Clear Valley," but it was not always clear, as pilots discovered. It was often socked in by monsoon rains and mountain fogs.

Soon to become one of the most famous airfields in Southeast Asia, "Alternate," as pilots called Long Chieng's field, was just one runway. It ran northwest-southeast at an altitude of 3,200 feet. Alternate had only one approach because the northern end abruptly terminated at two large purple karsts dramatically jutting skyward, denying air access from that side. In 1963, pilot "site books" listed this runway as 1,520 feet long. In 1972, it would be listed at 2,200 feet, adequate to handle slower, tactical planes. In fact, it was 4,200 feet long and capable of handling fighters in an emergency situation.[1]

A serrated mountain rim known to the Americans as "Skyline Ridge" provided natural fortification to the east. Here the U.S. installed a Tactical Air Navigation (TACAN) facility. South of Skyline several jagged, purple mountain peaks loomed. The highest, known to Americans as the "dreaded mountain," was constantly contested. Whoever occupied the dreaded mountain controlled the approach to the "dreaded valley," Alternate's vulnerable landing site. If enemy troops occupied the purple peaks of the dreaded mountain, they could call in long-range artillery to destroy the runway and Long Chieng.

Dramatic limestone karsts jutted hundreds of feet into the air from the valley floor. Critical installations and supply depots were constructed on the western side of the karsts, taking advantage of these natural protective sentinels.

Vang Pao, headquartered at Long Chieng, was now a general, with the code-name "White Star." Colonel Billy was pleased when Vang Pao, at age 34, received his general's star, the only Hmong to achieve such a distinction in the Royal Lao Army, which was composed largely of ethnic Lao. Colonel Billy viewed his promotion as a positive step toward the integration of Hmong into Lao society.

In the spring of 1964, NVA and Pathet Lao forces attacked Kong Le, driving him from the Plaine des Jarres. In April Souvanna Phouma visited Hanoi, where he learned that the attack against Kong Le was no aberration. He "became fully aware for the first time of the serious intent of the leaders in Hanoi to acquire the hegemony over Indochina that the French possessed, regardless of the cost to themselves and to the native peoples. General Giap told Souvanna Phouma bluntly they could not tolerate the presence of troops on the Plain of Jars other than those of the Pathet Lao."[2]

With this knowledge, Souvanna Phouma, in June 1964, authorized unarmed U.S. reconnaissance flights over the Plaine des Jarres. On June 6, communist antiaircraft guns shot one down. Three days later, President Johnson retaliated by deploying eight F-100s to silence the communist antiaircraft battery at Xieng Khouang.

* * *

At Eglin Air Force Base in Florida, Colonel "Heine" Aderholt, commander of the 1st Air Commando Wing, prepared Detachment 6 for its deployment to Udorn Air Base in Thailand. Aderholt, known for his resourcefulness in solving difficult problems, continued to pioneer in unconventional warfare and special operations. He helped formulate counterinsurgency roles for Air Force personnel and aircraft. Aderholt believed that fast-moving jets were inappropriate for counterinsurgency warfare where targets were small, often moving, and usually cleverly camouflaged. Jets moved too fast for pilots to see these targets, much less hit them.

Aderholt's air commandos would advise and train indigenous men to fight insurgency. At their Thai base in Udorn, they initially would train Lao pilots to fly T-28s, the old but powerful single-engine fighter-bombers used by the U.S. Navy as training craft, and would assist with aircraft maintenance.

On August 4, Johnson, whose advisors still included many of Kennedy's men, ordered the first air strikes against North Vietnam in retaliation for the Gulf of Tonkin incident in which an American destroyer, the *Maddox,* reportedly was fired upon by North Vietnamese gunboats. On August 7, Congress passed the Gulf of Tonkin Resolution, granting Johnson almost unlimited authority to act as he saw fit in Southeast Asia. Earlier Pentagon planners had refined plans to bomb North Vietnam. Both Hanoi and Washington had decided to escalate the conflict.

In October, China exploded its first atomic bomb and joined the nuclear powers. That same month, Soviet Premier Khrushchev fell from power and was replaced by Leonid Brezhnev and Aleksei Kosygin, who increased aid to Hanoi.

Having thoroughly defeated Goldwater in the November 1964 election, Johnson, empowered by the Gulf of Tonkin Resolution, became more aggressive. In 1965, American ground troops arrived in South Vietnam. Air Force fighter squadrons deployed to bases in northern Thailand.

*   *   *

The once relatively quiet Royal Thai Air Force base at Udorn, where previously Air America cargo planes, World War II B-26 bombers, a few helicopters, and training aircraft lazily operated, now reverberated with the thunderous jet engines of the fastest fighter aircraft in the U.S. Air Force arsenal. Air-conditioned barracks, officers' and noncom clubs, cafeterias, communications and maintenance shacks, a modern hospital, and headquarters buildings for the commander of what soon would be designated the 7/13th Air Force popped up around Colonel Billy's simple office which, for years, had run the CIA operation in Laos.

The Hmong referred to their CIA advisors as "SKY" or "SKY men." SKY advisors had explicit orders never to engage in combat. They could, of course, defend themselves if attacked, but their orders and their mission forbade fighting. They trained irregulars in the use of weapons and counterinsurgency and functioned as paymasters for these forces. To avoid skimming of funds by middlemen in Vientiane, the irregulars were paid directly by their battalion commanders with funds provided by the CIA. In addition to their paramilitary roles, SKY advisors were responsible for the civilians in their areas and directed airlifts of food supplies to them.

Living conditions for the SKY men were primitive and dangerous. Often a makeshift bunker or a Hmong-style hole dug into the ground provided the only protection. At Long Chieng, SKY personnel, often wearing blue jeans or khaki pants and T-shirts, operated out of a building on the rising slope west of the landing strip. From this simple structure, sprouting with antennas, SKY personnel directed and supplied those assigned to the field and coordinated with their clandestine base across the Mekong River. Contact with Long Chieng or Udorn—locations of SKY bases—was by radio, usually in code.

The SKY men had code-names—the only names by which the Hmong knew most of them. Military operations, military sites, and types of aircraft all had code-names. The clandestine nature of activities produced a fetish for exotic code-names, unusual behavior and dress, and secrecy. Some worked hard to find a code-name for themselves. Colonel Billy was code-named "Cigar." His replacement was known as "The Little General" or "Fats." Air America pilots referred to the CIA paramilitary advisors as "The Customer."

Jerry Daniels, the Montana smoke-jumper and former cargo kicker on Fred Walker's flights, had been recruited by the CIA to return to Laos as a paramilitary advisor to General Vang Pao in Military Region II. Daniels was the CIA man in the northern zones of Xieng Khouang Province and in Sam Neua Province, the province in which the Pathet Lao had its headquarters and which it considered its territory. Daniels' main base at Na Khang, Lima Site 36, was essentially behind enemy lines.

Daniels' code-name was "Hog." Ed Dearborn, a friend about the same age, knew why he chose that name. "It was his way of saying that all this code-name business was overblown and that most of us took it much too seriously. Hog wanted to be down in the trenches where life itself was irreverent. In Jerry Daniels, the Agency had found someone special— intelligent, clever, resourceful, a clean-cut college graduate. He was different from the other guys. He worked at fostering his image of being irreverent. He was irreverent towards anything and anyone—good friends, war, soldiers, pilots, and, though he loved them, toward women.

He tried to assume the image of a 'bad guy.' But he never made it since he didn't have a mean streak in him. He never even showed anger."[3]

Hmong who worked with Daniels found it difficult to call this mild-mannered, nice-looking man Hog. Not wanting to be impolite, some called him *Tan Hog*, meaning "Mr. Hog," or "Mr. Jerry."

Every SKY man had a radioman who could speak English, Lao, Hmong, and maybe some Vietnamese. Since the SKY usually did not speak local languages well—if at all—these men were critically important. Lo Ma, who had served in the Lao Army for three years earning $14 a month, decided to use his knowledge of English and volunteered to work with the Americans. At 19, he became Daniels' interpreter and radioman. His pay improved considerably. Now he earned $2 a day in salary plus a $40 per month food allowance.

In December, a month after Johnson's election, the U.S. Air Force launched "Operation Barrel Roll." From bases in Thailand, fighter jets lifted off for air strikes against enemy targets in northern Laos to support Vang Pao's ground actions. The U.S. air war against communist forces in Laos had begun. In the years to come, American pilots would fly thousands of air strikes against targets in Laos. Most remained secret.

As fighting in Laos increased, Long Chieng mushroomed into a major Hmong settlement. Many inhabitants were refugees from the war. Like a Colorado gold rush town, it grew in a haphazard way along the town's main feature—the runway. In this village of wooden and thatch houses were many defenders of Padong, many of whom now held rank and commissions in the Royal Lao Army. The primary school was overcrowded with its 300 male and almost 100 female students, among them Nhia from Bouam Loung. Moua Cher Pao, her father, determined that his daughter be educated, arranged for her to stay with a relative at Long Chieng so she could go to school.

On March 2, 1965, U.S. war planes struck North Vietnam in "Rolling Thunder," the operational name for air strikes over the North. No longer would the U.S. launch only retaliatory air strikes. Now it would regularly bomb military targets "Up North." This, it was reasoned, would make the war more costly for Hanoi and bolster the morale of the South Vietnamese. Rolling Thunder strikes against North Vietnam would continue for almost four years.

Rolling Thunder implied vast, unlimited, unpredictable, destructive power. In reality, pilots flying Rolling Thunder quickly learned that their missions were extremely limited. They were fighting a limited war. Many targets were off limits. U.S. pilots watched the construction of a

SAM (Surface-to-air Missile) site southeast of Hanoi in April 1965, but were denied permission to take it out until it had been operational for three months, after it had shot down an F-4C. Soviet and Chinese supply ships offloading war material in Haiphong harbor were also placed off limits to American pilots.

Fearing war with China and the Soviet Union, President Johnson took control of the air war over North Vietnam, insisting on personally approving important targets. In a procedural labyrinth resembling the bureaucracy in the Land of Oz, Johnson's target decisions were transmitted through Secretary of Defense Robert McNamara to the Joint Chiefs of Staff, who then issued strike directives to CINCPAC (Commander in Chief, Pacific Command), headquartered in Hawaii. That staff then apportioned fixed targets and armed reconnaissance routes between the U.S. Air Force, the U.S. Navy, and the Vietnamese Air Force.[4] This cumbersome, time-consuming procedure eliminated the important tactical element of surprise. In addition, the White House exempted from attack sanctuary areas around Hanoi and Haiphong, a buffer zone along the China border, and SAM sites and MiG bases located within the Hanoi-Haiphong area. It was Johnson's policy to minimize civilian casualties.

In addition to restrictive rules of engagement and the Neanderthal chain of command that eliminated surprise and mandated targets often two weeks old, the Commander of the 2nd Air Division, headquartered in Saigon, had to coordinate with local Navy and Army commanders and with U.S. ambassadors in Saigon, Bangkok, and Vientiane. In the initial years, although aircraft based in Thailand could fly strikes against North Vietnam and Laos, they could not be used against targets in South Vietnam.

In Laos, the situation was even more complex. In most wars the conduct of war belongs to military leaders. In South Vietnam the war was conducted by American and South Vietnamese generals. In Laos a U.S. ambassador conducted the American part of the war. The U.S. was not officially fighting in Laos, so there was no need for command staff military personnel as there was in South Vietnam. To make things even more bizarre, U.S. strike aircraft which the ambassador controlled were based not in Laos, but in neighboring Thailand.*

In 1965, when the air war against North Vietnam and Laos began,

---

*In 1961, President Kennedy designated the ambassador as the head of each U.S. diplomatic mission. As head of the "Country Team," the ambassador had ultimate responsibility for all U.S. activities, programs, and personnel, including the CIA. In Laos where the CIA's

William Sullivan headed the Country Team, as the embassy senior staff was known. Ironically, it was Sullivan who had assisted Averell Harriman in 1961–1962 to neutralize Laos—although the Laos which had greeted Sullivan was far from neutralized. Sullivan, however, carried on as if such a state existed. He continued to believe that the U.S. could count on Moscow's ability to influence Hanoi and, conversely, that the U.S. could discount China's ability to influence leaders in North Vietnam. In truth, Soviet influence over Hanoi had diminished considerably by the time Hanoi decided that Kong Le would no longer receive Soviet supplies.

Ambassador Sullivan's Country Team meetings included Colonel Billy and representatives from the Air Force command based at Udorn. Also present were staff from USIA, USAID, Army, and Air Force attachés, the CIA Station Chief in Vientiane, diplomats assigned to Thailand, and of course people from the Ambassador's staff. "The Mission," as the Americans more commonly called the embassy staff, was run by the State Department. This was often a point of discontent and discord. As the fighting in Laos escalated, military men thought they, not the diplomatic corps, should be running the war. The CIA disagreed. It did not want Laos to become another South Vietnam. It did not want military bureaucrats taking over and Americanizing its covert counterinsurgency operation.

More and more, the Americans turned to General Vang Pao's forces to hold the NVA at bay in Laos. The harder Vang Pao defended his territory, the more aggressive the NVA strikes. Vang Pao always intended to retake the Plaine des Jarres, clear Route 7 from the North Vietnam border to Luang Prabang, retake the Ban Ban area, and push the Vietnamese back through the Nong Het pass to North Vietnam.

Drawing upon years of guerrilla warfare experience against the Japanese and Viet Minh, Vang Pao made full use of the advantages of unpredictability. Sometimes he ordered one aircraft readied for a mission. At the last moment, he jumped into another and took off. He had recently discovered that it was easier to direct firefights by radio from the right seat of a slow-moving plane, flying at high altitudes to avoid enemy fire. As visible as he was to his enemies, he remained a fast-moving, elusive, and unpredictable target. Needing little sleep, he thought and fought with the energy of several men. Both enemy and ally found it difficult to outguess him.

"Third Option" operated with assistance from Air America aircraft and eventually U.S. Air Force aircraft and personnel, the ambassador was in charge.

Vang Pao's command, Military Region II (MR II), was the most difficult in Laos. His region included the northern provinces of Sam Neua and Xieng Khouang—the areas of intense fighting. As a general in the Lao Army, he commanded regular Lao Army troops, Special Guerrilla Units (SGUs), and hilltribe irregulars, including Kmhmu, armed and trained under the auspices of the CIA. He had under his command approximately 15,000 fighters. He was not only the senior military man in this large, war-torn area, but also responsible for much of civilian life as well. He worked with the various groups—Hmong, Lao, Kmhmu—living in Region II. He also worked with the Royal Lao government bureaucracy, USAID personnel, Lao generals in Vientiane, and sometimes with King Savang Vatthana in Luang Prabang.

In South Vietnam, South Vietnamese and American forces held the towns and cities. In Region II in Laos, it was the opposite. Pathet Lao and NVA forces held centers of population and main routes while the Hmong irregulars with their families held the high points—the mountains. From these mountains, tribal soldiers observed, gathered intelligence, and struck the enemy with hit and run missions. Their jungle mobility was their best asset. Initially, at least, few defended fixed positions.

From his headquarters base at Long Chieng, General Vang Pao orchestrated frontline defenses for the royal capital at Luang Prabang and the administrative capital at Vientiane. The plan was to keep the enemy away from the vulnerable and populated plain that surrounded Vientiane. The Americans reasoned that if Region II fell to the communists, Laos was lost. The Hmong irregulars remained the front lines and the shield on which the Americans and the Lao depended. Ironically, the Hmong—who were deprecated by the Lao—protected the Lao-populated Mekong River valley and the two major Lao towns by fighting the enemy in the mountains.

With the advent of Rolling Thunder in 1965, General Vang Pao's soldiers played critical roles in rescues of flyers downed by communist guns. From mountaintop positions, Hmong watched the skies and monitored their radios for crippled aircraft and bail-outs. They stood ready to rescue the downed pilots or secure an area for a rescue chopper to pick up the men. The U.S. military knew that a downed airman had to be picked up almost immediately or his chances of a rescue were greatly reduced. Because time was so critical, the Air Force wanted its search and rescue forward operation as close as possible to strike areas.

Na Khang, Lima Site 36, became a forward staging base for these search and rescue operations. Each morning, big U.S. rescue helicopters—"Jolly Green Giants"—flew from Thai bases to Na Khang to stand-by. Prior to this, Air America had orchestrated most search and rescue operations.

At Udorn, Colonel Billy worried about the increasing American presence in Laos and Thailand. He was staggered by the massive, rapid American buildup in neighboring South Vietnam. He feared the same would happen in Laos. His fears were about to be realized. As the war escalated, the U.S. mission in Vientiane expanded dramatically. The roles of the Hmong multiplied, requiring more CIA advisors, technicians, and support aircraft. Increased fighting brought increasing numbers of refugees and more USAID personnel to aid them. Air cargo volume soared, enticing Continental Air Services, a private company, to bid successfully against Air America for USAID and CIA contracts. In mid-1965, Ed Dearborn joined Continental Air Services as its chief pilot. Fred Walker, chief pilot for Air America in Laos, flew only 80 to 85 hours a month because he had to manage a growing fleet of planes and the crews to operate and maintain them.

Colonel Billy, who had received intelligence on a suspected NVA offensive, flew to Long Chieng to talk with Vang Pao. His small plane spiraled down through the approach gap into the dreaded valley at Alternate. As it taxied, an Air America C-47 landed and lumbered to the edge of the runway. The door opened. Out tumbled refugees, crying children, chickens, and several squeaking piglets.

Before heading for General Vang Pao's house, Colonel Billy decided to walk through Long Chieng village. Evidence of war was everywhere—in the faces of the women, in the footless and legless who hobbled about on improvised stick crutches fashioned from tree branches, and in refugee shacks often assembled from flattened red and blue aviation petrol drums and USAID cast-off rice sacks.

Never had so many Hmong lived in one place before. Feeding such large numbers became a major USAID problem. Alternative means of producing food for those denied their mountainside fields had to be found. One of Long Chieng's two prized bulldozers worked to make fish ponds, promoted by USAID as a means of supplementing the Hmong diet. The other bulldozer leveled off a nearby hillside to make a small field. Water resources were limited. Ground wells dug by hand were often polluted.

In Long Chieng's ramshackle open-air market, women and old men sold lettuce, cucumbers, tomatoes, onions, and eggs. Some vendors sold yard goods or raw opium, a common Hmong medicine, packaged in used whiskey bottles.

As Colonel Billy walked back across the runway toward Vang Pao's house, he remembered that it had been almost five years since he had first met Vang Pao. The general had not changed much. He lived in a simple wooden house on the western side of the runway. This building, with its add-ons, stretched and meandered to accommodate clan meetings, visiting American officials, daily military briefings and debriefings, and Vang Pao's growing family—which included three wives and a strong-willed mother to whom he was devoted. Clustered around Vang Pao's house were dozens of outbuildings that functioned as temporary housing for soldiers and sleeping quarters for kinsmen and visitors.

An *aide de camp* ushered the American inside. As usual, Vang Pao greeted Colonel Billy with exuberance, offering him a seat at his table where nearly a hundred men ate a noon meal of sticky rice balls, soup, and chicken. This was no special occasion. Daily, Vang Pao provided the noon meal for his officers and anyone else who wanted to see him.

Near Vang Pao was his crackling sideband UHF radio with which he admitted he ran his entire war. From the men at his table, he learned about current enemy activities, problems and needs of local villages, and assessments of military requirements. While many were civilians, others were members of SGUs and irregular units that Colonel Billy's PARUs had begun training five years earlier. Hmong who were not in the Royal Lao Army but who fought the war anyway never called themselves "irregulars." That word offended them; they called themselves "special forces."

A short, wiry man with raven-black frizzy hair, who energetically spoke out and sometimes interrupted Vang Pao, caught Colonel Billy's attention. This was Moua Cher Pao, the famous "Northern Warrior" who bragged that the Vietnamese would never take his position at Bouam Loung. Colonel Billy knew of Commander Moua and his men who often staged dangerous missions behind enemy lines. He also knew that Vang Pao's third wife, Moua Chia, who had been with him at Padong, was Moua's stepdaughter.

Vang Pao listened to men from several reconnaissance units, which the Hmong called "teams looking for news." One team had just arrived from Hog Daniels' area, Lima Site 36, to report increased enemy activities. Another team had returned from a stake-out on Route 7. Vang Seng, a soft-spoken team member, reported that he saw enemy troop movements, an increased number of enemy truck convoys, and had several near-misses with the enemy. He believed, probably correctly, that the NVA listened to his radio messages.

Several men reported on the difficult life for families who remained on mountaintops to watch the enemy and to organize hit-and-run strikes. Living in enemy territory and unable to tend fields, they sometimes had to resort to eating berries, roots, and wild plants. Often the day came when they had eaten everything around them. That was the case now in several villages.

As Colonel Billy listened to Hmong describe their harsh life, he wondered again—as he had wondered so often in past weeks—if the Hmong were being asked to do more than they were capable of doing. The Hmong could not fight a conventional war against the North Vietnamese Army. The Hmong were neither equipped nor trained to defend a permanent location.

Much had changed for the Hmong since 1961 on Padong when volunteers wore tribal trousers and jackets, went barefoot, and carried flintlocks or World War II carbines. Now they wore camouflage uniforms, combat boots, and red berets; they responded to code-names, carried foreign guns, and worked with SKY advisors.

Colonel Billy noticed a damaged plastic funeral wreath in a corner of the dining hall which also served as a ceremonial room where those killed were prepared for burial and where family and friends wailed songs of death. As he thought about the last funeral he had attended in this room, he studied the worried faces of those around the table. He recalled his first meeting with Vang Pao at Ta Vieng and the emotional words of the young Hmong: "For me, I can't live with communism. I must either leave or fight. I prefer to fight." Vang Pao had not changed. He was as feisty and determined as ever.

Vang Pao interrupted Colonel Billy's reminiscences by announcing that Region II needed more "air." For months, Vang Pao's main request had been for more air support for his ground troops. This he simply called "air." Once again, he energetically and loudly told Colonel Billy he needed "air." And he needed his own men flying the "air" because only they knew the territory and the enemy, and could talk to the troops on the ground.

Colonel Billy agreed. But getting Hmong in the air posed considerable problems. He had been unable to convince Americans, including Captain Richard Secord, who would become an Air Force General, that Hmong could fly. They argued that these primitive tribesmen who had only a few years of schooling were not capable of handling planes, and certainly not sophisticated equipment such as the T-28. Opposition came also from Lao generals who were reluctant to allow General Vang Pao to have his own T-28 pilots and thus more power. Vang Pao, after all, was not ethnic Lao.

As if Vang Pao had orchestrated it, in walked Vang Chou, who wanted to be a pilot, carrying a gallon thermos and announcing he was hungry. Vang Chou, one of the last Hmong defenders of Vang Pao's Padong headquarters, was now a captain in the Lao Army, flying as a "backseater"—a spotter—on air strikes and reconnaissance missions with Thai-based American and Thai pilots in T-28s and in A-26s. His sweaty shirt clung to his broad shoulders as he nudged into a place at the crowded table. He had just completed an airborne reconnaissance mission along Route 7 near Ban Ban, where enemy troop movements had been spotted.

Since 1963, Vang Chou had flown almost daily because he knew every valley, stream, mountain, and karst in Region II, his homeland. As a result of this knowledge, Thai and American pilots with whom he flew tagged him "General Direction" because he seemed to be the only man who knew villages and targets in all directions.

Vang Chou took full advantage of the SKY Chief's presence to stress the need for more Hmong in the air. "I told him that since early 1963, I've flown almost every day. There's blood in my urine and still I fly. I spend my life in the air and I'm always so tired. As a backseater, I've smelled T-28 gasoline far too long."[5]

Stocky and tall for a Hmong—almost 5 feet 8—Vang Chou had the look of a Hopi Indian chief. Tufts of his dark, shiny hair stood straight up, tortured into this position by the radio headset worn all day. His earlobes, slightly elongated, resembled those on Buddha images in Lao temples. Vang Chou had married Yang Mai, whose father had fought with the Meo Maquis in North Vietnam during the time of Dien Bien Phu and had fled to Laos after the French defeat. Chou had received complaints and kidding about marrying a "Black" Hmong, a tribal subgroup from North Vietnam, who was Catholic. Although not for Vang Chou, the Yangs' Catholic connection was paying off for their younger brother, Dao. With the support of his sisters, Mai and My, Dao was privileged to attend a French Catholic school in Vientiane.*

---

*It would indeed pay off for Dao. Later he would be financed by General Vang Pao to study in France where he would become the first Hmong from Laos to earn a Ph.D.

In Colonel Billy's mind, men like Vang Chou, if given the opportunity, could not only defeat the communists but contribute to modernizing Laos. He agreed that Vang Chou should not have to smell aviation gas from a back seat. If all had gone according to plan, he should have been flying T-28s by now.

Chou had been part of Colonel Billy's earlier aborted plan to train Hmong pilots. The previous year, when Colonel Billy told Vang Pao that he was trying to arrange for two Hmong to learn to fly turboprop T-28s, Vang Pao eagerly agreed. Immediately he asked Vang Chou to join in the first class since he already had flown thousands of missions as a back-seater in several kinds of aircraft.

Chou and five other men, including infantryman Ly Lue, the former schoolteacher who was now in his 30s, volunteered. None had experience with the sciences or modern technology. Ly Lue could not drive a car when he volunteered. These six men reported to Udorn Air Base in Thailand, ready and very eager. There they met frustration. For one year, they were kept in ground school with no plane to fly. At Udorn, bureaucracy and discrimination prevailed.

Finally two small, two-seat Piper Cub aircraft arrived. Chou never forgot the Piper Cubs which the Hmong trainees eventually learned to fly. After less than 20 hours of flying time, they had all soloed and were ready for T-28 flight training. Lao and Thai candidates were sent to Hua Hin in Thailand for more training and then were airborne. Not the Hmong. They cried when they realized they had been politically and bureaucratically grounded. They grew restless and angry, knowing that General Vang Pao needed them. Colonel Billy was almost as disappointed as the Hmong, but he did not give up on the idea of Hmong pilots and more Hmong Forward Air Guides (FAGs), men on the ground who called in air strikes.[6]

Finally, the last man at the table had his turn to talk. Colonel Billy excused himself and went outside. Children, many belonging to Vang Pao, played in the compound. Colonel Billy watched as soldiers looked after the children. One soldier, wearing a camouflage uniform, whittled wooden wheels for a child's wagon fashioned from a bomb crate. Another soldier swooped up a sobbing child and gently dried his tears with his shirtsleeve.

As the afternoon sun moved low in the horizon, Vang Pao and Colonel Billy walked together across Alternate. Vang Pao pointed with pride to the Buddhist temple in the distance that the Hmong were building. Historical Lao distrust of the Hmong was exacerbated by the growing power and influence of Vang Pao and by the responsibilities given Vang Pao and the Hmong by the Americans. To show respect for and loyalty to the Lao king and Buddhism, the Hmong, who were not Buddhist but animist, were constructing near the approach to Alternate a whitewashed Buddhist temple with upturned finials soon to be trimmed in glittering glasswork.

They also intended to build a summer bungalow for the king across the valley, not far from SKY headquarters. It would overlook Alternate, the Buddhist temple, and the growing Hmong town to remind both Hmong and foreigners working here that this was Lao country.

General Vang Pao wanted to discuss with Colonel Billy his difficulties in appeasing the skeptical Lao and in formulating workable relationships with often feuding American agencies with activities touching both his life and the lives of his kinsmen. But he did not know how to do it without losing face.

As Colonel Billy prepared to board his plane for the flight back across the Mekong River, "the fence," to Udorn, Vang Pao did explain that Moua Lia still lacked trained teachers and school materials and that he was resisting Pop Buell's plan to train Hmong girls as nurses and medics because he was certain Hmong men would not approve. Colonel Billy knew that Pop was already secretly training girls to be nurses, but he said nothing about it to the general.

Colonel Billy departed Long Chieng with mixed thoughts. He was not reassured by the reports of Hmong suffering and increased enemy activity, particularly near Na Khang. He also worried about the number of American advisors appearing on the Lao scene. He believed that the fewer Americans the better and that there should never be more than one in any location. If there was more than one, then they would talk to each other and not with the local people to learn the problems. Opposed to Americans fighting someone else's war, he was depressed that 184,000 U.S. military personnel served in South Vietnam. He maintained that communist insurgency had to be fought with indigenous counterinsurgency efforts, with an absolute minimum number of Americans involved. If the tribal Hmong could hold off the NVA in Laos, why, he wondered, couldn't the South Vietnamese hold off the Viet Cong and NVA in their country?

That evening, the general gave Vang Seng's reconnaissance team a few days off before it returned to the Ban Ban area. Vang Chou had hoped to spend a few days with his wife at Long Chieng, but that was not to be. A somewhat garbled message ordered him back to Thailand where he was needed immediately for "general direction" work. That night, General Vang Pao worried about an enemy attack on Na Khang, Lima Site 36.

9.

Widening of the "Secret War"

If the Americans want us to bring the tiger home, then either the tiger must die or we must die.

—Hmong General Vang Pao, New Year's Celebration, 1987, reflecting on the U.S. involvement in Laos

Na Khang, 150 nautical miles west of Hanoi, was a critical base for the United States. It served as a forward staging area for U.S. search and rescue operations which tried to reach downed air crews before they were captured. Rescue crews of the "Jolly Green Giant" helicopters waited at Na Khang for American pilots to lift off from Thai airfields, aircraft carriers in the South China Sea, and bases in South Vietnam on missions over North Vietnam or Laos. Then the Jolly Greens orbited at 10,000 feet over the Lao-North Vietnam border, waiting to pick up downed American flyers. In 1966, U.S. helicopters had no aerial refueling capability, and since they could only hover for a couple of hours, Na Khang's fuel depot was critical to search and rescue missions.

These missions were important to the Americans because, apart from humanitarian concerns and the cost and time of training pilots, there were political considerations. The Johnson administration had decided not to make an issue of the fact that the North Vietnamese held American POWs, mostly air crews. Further, since the U.S. military was not officially in Laos, it would be embarrassing if air crews were lost in fighting over Laos. Those killed or captured in Laos were listed as missing in Indochina.

Airmen shot down over hostile territory had about fifteen minutes to be picked up. If the rescue took longer, chances of being captured or shot increased dramatically. To save American lives, it was necessary to base rescue aircraft and crews as close as possible to enemy territory.

There were no friendly forces in North Vietnam. Downed flyers were doomed to capture, cruelty, a cell in a POW camp, and sometimes death. If airmen bailed out over Laos, they had a chance of being found by friendly forces and of being rescued by Air America pilots in the early days and later by Air Force search and rescue teams.

Na Khang also functioned as General Vang Pao's most forward resupply base in Military Region II. Surrounded on three sides by mountains, SKY advisor Jerry Daniels and the Hmong had dug in along this 4,400-foot-high landing field that handled the rescue helicopters, C-123s, Helios, Porters, aviation gas, and troops. From here Vang Pao's soldiers and their supplies were airlifted almost daily to remote mountaintops.

Because of the importance of Na Khang to Vang Pao and the Americans, it was a primary NVA target. They had tried unsuccessfully several times to take it.

Only hours after Vang Chou, on a reconnaissance flight, spotted an enemy buildup around Na Khang, the communists attacked. Vang Pao, no armchair general, immediately ordered a helicopter to fly him to Na Khang. His frontline appearances inspired his men, and his unorthodox tactics, often demanding considerable bravery from his soldiers, confounded the enemy and terrified his SKY advisors. If Vang Pao were to be killed, the Americans reasoned that the war would be lost. Vang Pao had not trained a military successor.

Vang Pao landed as the enemy artillery pounded Na Khang. Air America choppers and big Chinooks were nearby to evacuate the defenders if necessary. Vang Pao moved from position to position, directing counterattacks and pinpointing enemy locations. Learning about one position pinned down by concealed guns, he choppered there to assess the situation. On the ground, he spotted a concealed enemy gun and turned sideways to shout instructions to his gunners. An enemy gunner fired, hitting him. Because he had turned sideways at the moment of the gun burst, he avoided a hole in his chest and death. Instead the rounds hit him in the side and arm. He was medevacked to Thailand for surgery. Seriously wounding Vang Pao was an important psychological victory for his enemy.

On February 17, while Vang Pao remained in the hospital, Na Khang radioed that it could no longer hold. Chinooks dropped onto the ridge positions and picked up Hmong soldiers. Fred Walker helped with the evacuation. "The loaders piled them in those choppers upright—200 men to a chopper. It looked like a New York City subway at 5 p.m., but they got them all out."[1] One American and eight Hmong were killed and 24 others were wounded. Jerry Daniels escaped unscathed.

With Vang Pao in a Thai hospital and the enemy probing other government positions, Touby LyFong initiated a coup attempt against him. Several officers of the Ly clan, responding to Touby's call, ordered troops under their commands to advance toward Long Chieng. Their troops, not knowing anything about a coup, moved out. As some units neared Long Chieng, they suspected a trick. Many, including soldiers from the Ly clan, refused to proceed when they learned the true intent of their advancement. Touby's coup dissolved before a shot was fired.

Learning of Touby's attempted coup, Vang Pao, from his hospital bed, taped a message which was played over the Long Chieng radio station. His voice, full of vigor and determination, calmed Hmong fears that he was dead or dying. Talk of replacing him subsided.

Vang Pao was determined to return to the front lines as soon as possible and to recapture Na Khang for the Americans. With his arm in a sling, he soon stood on a mountaintop position directing a firefight. He took no action against those who had thought of ousting him. He had his military eye on retaking Na Khang during the upcoming rainy season, the months of April through October.

A pattern had emerged in the fighting in Vang Pao's Region II. During the dry season, from November through March, the communists usually attacked. In this clear weather, the U.S. could use its air power to support Vang Pao's efforts by bombing enemy supply caches, diverting the enemy in its rear and slowing the NVA offensive.

During the rainy season months of April through October, the NVA units, with their heavy equipment and long logistical support lines often bogged down in the mud, preferred not to fight. That was when Vang Pao took the initiative. But at the beginning of this wet season, Vang Pao faced surgery. His arm had not healed properly and hung limply at his side. Instead of leading an attack against the North Vietnamese, he and Vang Chou boarded a U.S. military plane for Hawaii and surgery. Chou, whose English was better than Vang Pao's, went along to interpret, donate blood if necessary, and look after him while he recovered. At Hickham Air Force Hospital, well cared for by a female nursing staff, he recovered quickly.[2] Vang Pao returned to Laos renewed and in favor of female nurses. He told Pop Buell that it would be a good idea to train

Hmong women to be nurses. Pop then confessed that he had been train-ing them all along.

Vang Pao used the remaining months of the monsoon season to attack the NVA. With U.S. air destroying large quantities of enemy supplies, his irregulars retook Na Khang. By August 1966, his Region II forces, sup-ported by American air power, pushed on to Nam Bac, only 45 miles from the North Vietnamese border. This was a significant victory for Vang Pao, who repeatedly announced that pushing the NVA back into North Vietnam was his ultimate goal. Vang Pao continued to move northeast, clearing the enemy in his path. The communists, however, still held the Plaine des Jarres and considerable terrain protecting the vital Ho Chi Minh Trail complex.

Hanoi responded to Vang Pao's victories by sending an additional 14,000 well-trained soldiers, bringing the total of North Vietnamese forces in Laos to some 50,000. Vang Pao's force totaled less than 20,000, many untrained and young, with outdated weapons. With the onset of the fall and the dry season that year, these superior communist forces moved against Vang Pao in Sam Neua Province where Hmong occupied Lima Site 53, only 20 miles from Sam Neua town, headquarters of "Red Prince" Souphanouvong and his Pathet Lao. U.S. air strikes came to Vang Pao's aid, forcing the enemy to retreat.

The U.S. Air Force, desperate for better guidance systems to direct precise bombing missions over North Vietnam and northern Laos, that summer installed a TACAN facility on Phou Pha Thi, Lima Site 85, a remote mile-high location only 25 kilometers from the North Vietnam-ese border.

The Americans were extremely pleased with Vang Pao's efforts, partic-ularly in light of the miserable performance of the Neutralist forces, whose reputation for cowardice and defection were legendary.

Colonel Billy was still convinced that Hmong would be good pilots. With Vang Pao's victories and the increasing need for air power, he be-lieved that it was time to reinitiate Hmong pilot training. That was good news to Vang Pao. In a gesture of reconciliation, he and Touby LyFong, whom Vang Pao had always respected, called a joint meeting at Long Chieng to request two volunteers for pilot training.

Many men attended, including Vang Chou and all the others who had volunteered the first time. Vang Chou had only one child when he first went to Udorn with the hope of becoming a T-28 pilot. Now he had three. Regretfully, he gave up his dream of flying, preferring not to leave his family. Ly Lue, the former schoolteacher, and Vang Toua, who had done well in his Piper Cub training, would return to Udorn to learn to fly the T-28 attack bombers.

*   *   *

North Vietnamese convoys moved continuously along the Ho Chi Minh Trail complex in Laos, carrying massive amounts of war material to the Viet Cong in South Vietnam. In Washington, Johnson's men knew that to win the war in South Vietnam, these convoys had to be stopped. But interdiction of the Trail presented problems. Most traffic moved during darkness and inclement weather. Successful interdiction required the capability to fly night missions and launch strikes in all kinds of weather. While the U.S. Air Force did not have this capability, it was nonetheless given the interdiction task. Specifically, the assignment was given to the 7/13th Air Force, headquartered in Udorn, controlled by the 7th Air Force in Saigon.

On November 6, 1966, at Udorn, a top secret briefing on the Lao situation was given to visiting American VIPs by 7/13th Air Force personnel. This briefing was one of many given over the years to congressmen and senators. It highlighted the critical role of the "Meo," as the Americans called the Hmong, and the "Yao," more properly called the Mien. It was also a portent of events to come.

> Here [in Laos] we have a war that is confusing because so little is generally known about it. This dearth of knowledge reflects the self-effacing policy of the United States Government which does not want any publicity given to our very considerable activities there. . . .
>
> The government of Laos is willing to give us what amounts to a free hand in exploiting air power to interdict the Ho Chi Minh Trail in the Panhandle [southern Laos].
>
> However, if the capitals of Laos are ever threatened or it appears that the communists may take the Mekong valley, there is little doubt in the minds of those who have been working with the Lao Government for some time that the present government will seek an accommodation with the communists. With the communists in the government, we would no doubt lose the right to use Laotian air space in striking North Vietnam and the Ho Chi Minh Trail, and lose our right to strike in the Panhandle as well. . . . One efficient friendly force in Laos is the CAS [Controlled American Source, code-name for the CIA]-supported force of nearly 20,000 irregulars in Northern Laos. In the main these are ethnic tribal people— Meo [Hmong] and Yao [Mien] tribesmen. This small but . . . potentially significant force is young and growing. These guerrillas have shown the necessary will and desire . . . but they need time for maturing and developing their organization.

The briefer told the VIPs of the secret air war being fought in Laos.

The air offensive in Barrel Roll [U.S. air strikes over northern Laos launched in December 1964] remains different from other air operations in the theater. The key to the operation is the FAC [Forward Air Controller] flying an 01B aircraft [usually a single-engine unarmed plane] who takes into the air a detailed knowledge of the latest ground source and photographic intelligence in his operating area. The USAF FAC on occasion will carry with him the leader of a guerrilla team [Hmong] from the Barrel Roll area who will point out hiding places for troops and supplies that he himself ferreted out on the ground. As a result of this limited effort friendly forces have regained a large degree of their cohesion and confidence and have gone over to the offensive in separate ambushes and fire fights. . . . In this way, if time can be bought, our Laotian guerrilla forces can be developed and increased to a point where they can be considered better than a fair match for their opponent.

Additionally, CAS has inserted indigenous road watch teams [many were Hmong] which, by means of radio communication, are able to relay from ground-to-air and ground-to-ground information pertaining to the movement of traffic. . . . [3]

The Air Force briefer went on to tell the VIPs about various indigenous troops fighting on the ground and pilots flying "Operation Steel Tiger," the code-name for interdiction of the Ho Chi Minh Trail. One of those he talked about, although he did not mention him by name, was Colonel "Heine" Aderholt.

Aderholt, after serving a tour in South Vietnam, had returned to Thailand in late 1966 to activate an Air Commando Special Operations Wing. When Aderholt arrived, pilots, flying vintage World War II A-26s, call-sign "Nimrod," were taking heavy losses from antiaircraft gunfire along the Trail and in North Vietnam where they attempted to hit trucks ferrying supplies headed for South Vietnam. Aderholt obtained permission to commit a T-28 squadron to aid the Nimrods.[4] At Nakhon Phanom (NKP), a spartan air base not far from Udorn, he soon commanded a squadron of T-28s that flew low-level night interdiction missions in Operation Steel Tiger with the Nimrods and sometimes against targets "Up North."

Aderholt's slow-moving T-28s, call-sign "Zorro," carried 2,500 pounds of armament, including bombs, cluster bomb units (CBU), napalm, and 500 rounds of 50-caliber machine gun munitions. Almost nightly his T-28 pilots lifted off NKP, heading for the Trail—less than 50 miles due east. Once over the Trail, Aderholt and his wingman flew north and south searching for enemy truck traffic. These interdiction missions were extremely dangerous. If a plane was hit by enemy gunners, the pilot's chances of getting out were marginal. There were no ejection seats, and bailing out at low altitudes reduced survival chances.

Knowing that U.S. aircraft did not have the capability to bomb the Trail in the dark, the North Vietnamese moved at night. To interdict the Ho Chi Minh Trail, Aderholt's pilots needed a nighttime capability. Initially, C-130 flare ships, planes equipped to drop flares to light a target area, were used, but his pilots needed more. Flare ships alerted the enemy, eliminating the critical element of surprise. Aderholt and his pilots wanted to spot the enemy in advance, to retain the element of surprise. So they introduced the infantryman's starlight scope, a device allowing its operator to see in darkness, in the air. First, Aderholt jury-rigged a starlight scope into a C-123's forward fuselage hatch. The navigator, looking through this scope, searched roadways and trails for targets. When a target was sighted, he alerted the accompanying T-28 and A-26 pilots to the exact locations and types of targets. Then the C-123 flared and the attack pilots dove in for the kill.

But C-123s, many of them based in Taiwan, were not always available when needed. Aderholt commandeered his own C-123 and rigged it with a starlight scope. It worked well, until officials at 7th Air Force found out that this jury-rig had not been properly tested. "When they found out what I had done, it was like they had discovered a turd in a punch bowl," remembered Aderholt, who was reprimanded for improvising in the field.

Next, Aderholt, working with Captain Tom Deacon, put an observer with a starlight scope in an 0-1 Bird Dog, a single-engine spotter plane, also equipped to drop flares. Since the T-28s were faster than spotters, the T-28s flew nose up at a 45-degree angle in order to stay with the slower aircraft. The T-28s, which had no ability to see the enemy, hung about 25 to 30 feet above the wing of the smaller plane that could see. Night after night, one small spotter plane, flying at about 90 mph, lifted off the runway at NKP. After a few minutes, two T-28s roared off to rendezvous with it. This strange configuration—again, not approved Air Force procedure—proved effective.

While Aderholt's resourcefulness made him famous in the area and effective on the ground, the Air Force did not always officially approve, particularly if he had not sought prior authority—which he usually did not. The remoteness of NKP airstrip aided Aderholt's creative "make-do." One of the men who served with him later wrote, "It has been said, 'If Heine could have ordered a base, he would have ordered NKP.' There are others that firmly believe he did! Far enough in the jungle to make it an undesirable point for the brass and visiting firemen to have on their itineraries. Short enough runway to discourage anything that consumed kerosene [jets] from landing except in extreme emergency. Uncomfortable enough that the crews were happy to fly combat missions in return for an occasional motivating trip to Bangkok. And, finally, big enough to hide all the men and equipment purloined from other unsuspecting organizations throughout the world."[5] Aderholt's introduction of the starlight scope in the air allowed successful night interdiction of the Trail. Such success, however, brought bigger and more sophisticated enemy guns along the Trail.

Equally dangerous were the missions of the road watch teams, which radioed information on enemy supply movements to U.S. air operations, and the "teams looking for news." Road watch teams along the Ho Chi Minh Trail consisted mostly of Thai volunteers. Further north in Laos, they were usually Hmong men and boys who worked behind enemy lines for weeks at a time. As the war intensified and the casualty rate among Hmong soldiers increased, the "teams looking for news" also functioned as sabotage units and defended permanent observation outposts.

In the midst of war, Hmong celebrated the Lunar New Year. Nhia, the 15-year-old daughter of the Northern Warrior Moua Cher Pao, was living in Long Chieng with an uncle and attending school. At this special time when Hmong revere their ancestors, Nhia was thinking about her family in Bouam Loung. She knew about the heavy fighting there, but worried little about her father. He seemed invincible. She prepared to enjoy the local New Year celebration.

Nhia talked excitedly with her girl friends as they fussed with their hair and adjusted their elaborate headdresses. The old French coins that decorated Nhia's sash and headdress jingled pleasantly as she walked. She had borrowed a simple silver necklace to wear, not having one of her own, and looked splendid. She urged her friends to hurry—she was hoping to see the young soldier, a member of a "team looking for news," with whom she had tossed ball the day before.[6]

As the girls approached the soccer field near the runway, the celebration was already underway. Nhia did not see her soldier, so she joined a row of girls and tossed ball with a boy who lived near her uncle's house. Then her soldier arrived, dressed in camouflage fatigues. Nhia eagerly threw her ball to the soft-spoken and handsome youth named Vang Seng. All day they tossed the ball as they chanted poems to each other. Nhia had fallen in love. She knew that if Vang Seng was on an intelligence-gathering team behind enemy lines, he must be a courageous man.

Air America pilot Fred Walker also attended the Long Chieng New Year's party. He had flown in some American VIPs for the celebration. While he waited for them, Walker was repeatedly invited to join in the ball-toss courting and to drink Hmong whiskey. Not speaking Hmong, he declined their offers by flapping his arms as if he were trying to fly, to show that he was a pilot on duty. Hmong laughed as they watched the tall, shy Yankee fend off multiple offers of libations and opportunities to court young women.

Nhia and Vang Seng did not notice Walker. They concentrated on each other. Before the ten-day celebration ended, they had decided to marry. When Nhia told her father, he was furious, shouting that she was only a schoolgirl and did not know how to earn a living. Being an obedient Hmong child, she listened to her father's stern warnings, but in a few weeks she married Vang Seng. Nhia's father did not attend the late December wedding, saying he had to stay at Bouam Loung. Her uncle substituted. Five days after the wedding, Vang Seng departed with his team for a secret mission behind enemy lines. Nhia moved in with her new husband's family.

Meanwhile, Vang Pao, under pressure from the Lao to prove he loved the Lao people, and in a move to strengthen his power base, took a Lao girl for a wife through an arranged marriage in a Buddhist ceremony in her father's village. The Hmong called her Mae La, the Youngest Mother. She joined the other wives at the Long Chieng headquarters house. The Hmong say that the Lao people had more confidence in Vang Pao after he took a Lao wife.

Communist troops again attacked Na Khang. It took some bold flying by American pilots to save it. Under a low 200-foot ceiling, an A-1E pilot strafed and bombed the site to keep the NVA from overrunning the command post to which the defenders had retreated until the weather improved for air strikes. It was so reminiscent of a movie in which the U.S. Cavalry rescues the besieged fort at the last moment that thereafter Na Khang became known as "the Alamo." Daniels and a couple of other SKY men survived, but an American USAID worker and several Hmong were killed. NVA radiomen taunted the defenders of the Alamo, declaring they would take it next time.

After operating for some time along the North Vietnamese border, Vang Seng returned to his young bride. He confided to Nhia that being in enemy territory at night and sneaking close to enemy positions frightened him. He had decided to quit and become a pilot. Soon he and three other Hmong volunteers flew to Muang Cha for preliminary training.

On February 2, 1967, communist troops mortared the airfield at Luang Prabang, destroying eight aircraft and the operations center. At Udorn, Ly Lue and Vang Toua, in flight training, listened anxiously to news of the fighting in their homeland. They responded by working harder to win their wings so they could soon return to fight. Both were exemplary students. Their greatest problem was their small size. Since they were at least a foot shorter than the American flyers for whom the T-28s were designed, they had trouble reaching the rudders and seeing out. Instructor pilots solved the first problem by wiring 2x4s to the rudders so these trainees could reach them, and the trainees solved the second by sitting on several thick pillows so they could see out the windshields. Each morning, the two Hmong pilots headed for the flight line proudly wearing their new flight suits and carrying their helmets and their pillows.

Soon Ly Lue and Vang Toua were combat ready. Only their final check-rides remained. Colonel Aderholt had closely monitored the training of the Hmong pilots: "As the time for their final flight performance tests neared, I intended to show them off to local VIPs. With permission of the squadron commander, I invited General Vang Pao, Ambassador William Sullivan, Colonel Paul Pettigrew, the Air Attaché at the U.S. Embassy in Laos, and Colonel Billy as guests of honor. I had arranged to have Ly Lue and Vang Toua in the front seats of their T-28s and their two instructor pilots hidden down in the back seats so no one could see them. We stood out on the flight line watching as these pilots came down over the field, rolled their airplanes—right off the deck—took them up and rolled them again. Then they made another approach and landed. Watching the performance of his pilots, Vang Pao became eight feet tall. We didn't tell the VIPs until later that the instructor pilots were aboard, because those Hmong pilots were qualified to fly those airplanes. Ly Lue would become a great fighter pilot."

Ly Lue and Vang Toua immediately returned to Laos. They assumed the call-sign "Chaophakaow" (Lord White Buddha) given all T-28 pilots, whether Lao or Hmong. Colonel Billy's strategy had worked. It took three years, but it opened the way for Hmong to fly the skies over their homeland. Vang Pao now had "air" piloted by men who knew the terrain and could speak the language of the troops on the ground. Hmong pilots would fly only in Vang Pao's Region II.

Vang Toua, unfortunately, was shot down and killed soon after he took to the skies. After his death, Nhia's husband, Vang Seng, who had been studying English at Hua Hin in southern Thailand, transferred to

Udorn to begin flight training in Project Water Pump, the code-name given to the 56th Air Commando Wing flight training for indigenous pilots.

Now that the opportunity to fly was open to Hmong, many volunteered. For those who qualified, it was a great honor. After completion of flight training, each Hmong fighter pilot received his wings, a photo of himself dressed in a U.S. Air Force flight suit standing beside a T-28, and a celebration party. Five classes of Hmong pilots eventually graduated from Water Pump.

American pilots in Southeast Asia had six-month or one-year tours of duty, flying the war zones with periodic rest and recreation in Bangkok, Sydney, or Honolulu. American pilots flew 100 combat missions, celebrated with a champagne party, and went home with medals for bravery. Hmong pilots had no 100-mission parties with champagne, no R&R in faraway cities, and no end of tour. Instead, they flew until they were blown out of the sky. Heroes all, the Hmong said.

Hmong maiden, dressed in the Sam Neua Province style. Jacket
and hat trimmed with old French silver coins. (Photo credit:
Jane Hamilton-Merritt)

Hmong child, hat and bracelet decorated with old French silver
coins. (Photo credit: Jane Hamilton-Merritt)

Lieutenant Gauthier's Hmong warriors in front of the French Lega-
tion, Xieng Khouang, after their victory over the Viet Minh, 1945.
Left to right: Lyfong Geu Tou, Touby LyFong (LyFong Touby), Moua
Chia Xang, Moua Nao Lue, unidentified, Lor Bee Chou, Ly Neng
Tong, Ly Choua Va, unidentified, Jean (last name unknown), un-
identified, unidentified, unidentified. (Photo in the collection of
Maurice Gauthier)

French Commando Lt. Maurice Gauthier and Hmong warrior Chong Toua, Xieng Khouang, 1944. (Photo in the collection of Maurice Gauthier)

Air America pilot Fred Walker, atop Padong, Lima Site 5, in 1961. (Photo in the collection of F. F. Walker)

Prince Souvanna Phouma (with pipe), his son (center), and his half-brother, Souphanouvong, the "Red Prince," 1962. (Photo in the collection of the author)

Thai PARU, left, with Moua Cher Pao, the "Northern Warrior," 1962. (Photo in the collection of the author)

Col. "Heine" Aderholt in the cockpit of a T-28 on the runway at Nakhon Phanom (NKP) air base, Thailand. From this base he flew air strikes against targets on the Ho Chi Minh Trail in Laos. (Photo in the collection of Brig. Gen. Harry C. Aderholt)

Ed Dearborn, who flew first for Air America and then became chief pilot for Continental Air Services in Laos, in the cockpit of an Air America Caribou in April 1963 over the South China Sea on a North Vietnam reconnaissance flight. (Photo in the collection of Ed Dearborn)

Air America C-46 air drop at Pha Khao, Lima Site 14, 1961, after North Vietnamese Army (NVA) and Pathet Lao overran Padong. (Photo in the collection of Ed Dearborn)

Vang Pao in the early 1960s. Colonel Billy told the author that this is the way he wanted to remember Vang Pao—sitting on a mountaintop, planning how he would push the North Vietnamese Army out of the Hmong homelands in Laos. (Photo by Vint Lawrence)

General Vang Pao in white, Touby LyFong pointing; Long Chieng about 1964. (Photo in the collection of the author)

Long Chieng: headquarters for Hmong General Vang Pao's Military
Region II and the CIA "secret" base, which in reality was a forward
staging area in northeastern Laos. "Alternate," the code-name for
this landing strip, was set at an elevation of 3,120 feet in what pilots called the "dreaded valley." From the mid-1960s through the
early 1970s, Alternate bustled with war activity. Note the helicopters in the air at both ends of the runway. General Vang Pao's
home (bottom) doubled as his headquarters. The Hmong, most of
whom are not Buddhists, built the Buddhist temple (center) to show
respect for Lao culture and the Lao king. (Photo in the collection of
the author)

General Vang Pao, left, with Kong Le about 1965. According to an American who was there, at this time Kong Le was having second thoughts about his association with the communists and wanted a meeting. (Photo in the collection of the author)

Jerry "Hog" Daniels (with moustache, facing the camera), CIA SKY advisor to the Hmong. (Photo in the collection of the author)

Vang Chou, "General Direction," in flight suit before he was wounded near Ban Ban in 1968. (Photo in the collection of Vang Chou)

Flight over the Plaine des Jarres (PDJ), showing the ancient stone jars, an old French colonial road, and a karst in which the NVA stored its petrol and ammunition for the attack against Lima Lima. (Photo in the collection of Col. Bill Keeler)

Soviet PT-76 tank used by the NVA in attack against Lima Lima on the PDJ, 1970. (Photo in the collection of Col. Bill Keeler)

Hmong fighter-ace Ly Lue with his T 28.
(Photo in the collection of his family)

Rescue of downed American air crew in Laos. (Photo in the collection of Col. Bill Keeler)

Long Chieng, 1972: Raven "spotter" pilot Darrel Whitcomb and the man who saved his life: Hmong pilot Xiong Ly Tou, who was later killed defending Sala Phou Khoun as the communists came to power in Laos in 1975. (Photo in the collection of Col. Darrel Whitcomb)

Lao officer standing beside Hmong "carbine soldier" who manned a machine gun position at Lima Lima on the PDJ and killed many NVA commandos when they attacked the site in 1970. (Photo in the collection of Col. Bill Keeler)

Col. Moua Cher Pao's Bouam Loung, Lima Site 32, 1970. Aircraft is "Papa Hotel Foxtrot" in which Ed Dearborn flew night cover during the siege of Long Chieng on New Year's Eve, 1971. (Photo in the collection of Ed Dearborn)

Moua Lia, school superin-
tendent of Xieng Khouang
Province. (Photo in the collection of Moua Lia)

CIA SKY headquarters and
part of village at Long
Chieng, 1972. Note the an-
tenna on the SKY buildings.
(Photo in the collection of T.
J. Thompson)

Mie, a 6-year-old girl from Bouam Loung, who was hit by an NVA mortar round and gravely wounded, losing one leg. Shown with her mother and aerial SKY advisor T. J. Thompson, who helped and befriended her during her difficult recovery. After the communists took over, Thompson lost track of the two. (Photo in the collection of T. J. Thompson)

Party at Bouam Loung, 1973, celebrating the victory over the NVA, when it attacked and laid siege to Lima Site 32. General Vang Pao, wrists wrapped with *ba-sii* strings, toasts the defenders. To his right is Pat Landry, chief SKY advisor. (Photo in the collection of Col. Darrel Whitcomb)

The C-130 sent by Brigadier General Aderholt during the evacuation of the Hmong from Long Chieng, May 13, 1975, as the communists came to power. (Photo by Moua Blong)

10.

Phou Pha Thi Falls, "the Alamo" Holds

Every minute, hundreds of people die all over the world. The life or
death of a hundred, a thousand, or tens of thousands of human be-
ings, even if they are our compatriots, represents really very little.

—General Vo Nguyen Giap

In March 1967, General Vo Nguyen Giap, concerned about increasing
Viet Cong and North Vietnamese losses in South Vietnam, visited Moscow to seek additional assistance. The Soviets responded with more
planes, missiles, artillery, small arms, petrol, and food. These would be
delivered down the Ho Chi Minh Trail.

With preliminary talks in Paris stalemated, General William West-
moreland, head of the U.S. Military Command in South Vietnam,
warned President Johnson that "if we couldn't stop the flow of men and
material down the Ho Chi Minh Trail the war could go on indefinitely."[1]

In Washington, there was urgent talk of ways to deny North Vietnam
this critical strategic artery. Secretary of Defense Robert S. McNamara
promoted an electronically patrolled barrier that would extend along
the 17th parallel DMZ through Vietnam west through Laos, thus barring
Hanoi's use of the Trail. Johnson was concerned about accusations that
he was a "baby killer" and also about straying into Chinese airspace,
thus possibly triggering a war with China, the Soviet Union, or both.
Thus evolved the concept of surgical bombing—hitting only military
targets such as bridges, oil depots, and military complexes. To accomplish this, more sophisticated navigational equipment was needed to allow more precise bombing and enable pilots to avoid flying into

restricted airspace. The U.S., with its vast technological capability, ended up developing a formidable electronic battlefield. Included in that arsenal were instruments to be dropped along suspected infiltration routes, particularly the Ho Chi Minh Trail. Code-named "Igloo White," these seismic, sonar-based, voice-activated and other sensitive devices monitored enemy movement. The system required men on the ground near the devices. Once again the assignment was given to General Vang Pao's irregulars, often night-dropped behind enemy lines on "black missions" for weeks at a time to monitor and test the experimental equipment.

To stop the military traffic into South Vietnam, air strikes had to be flown in all kinds of weather and around the clock. A reliable all-weather, nighttime guidance facility to cover North Vietnam and northern Laos was needed. It had to be unobstructed and as close as possible to the target areas. The obvious place was Phou Pha Thi, Lima Site 85, where the U.S. Air Force had already installed a TACAN in the summer of 1966. Some 28 miles from the Pathet Lao headquarters at Sam Neua town and about 15 miles from the border, Phou Pha Thi was 5,500 feet high; from this mountaintop on a clear day one could see deep into North Vietnam. For years the Hmong had used it as a resupply base, and from it they ran intelligence gathering operations and hit and run strikes against NVA convoys.

In early 1967, General Hunter Harris, Commander in Chief of the Pacific Air Forces, came to Thailand for a meeting of Air Force and State Department officials at which he proposed Phou Pha Thi as the site for installing the new radar bombing technology—the TSQ-81, a modified version of the Strategic Air Command's radar bomb scoring system used by B-52s. Among those present were Colonel Billy and Richard Secord, then a major in the U.S. Air Force, detailed to the CIA to help in Laos. Based at Udorn, Secord worked under Colonel Billy.

Colonel Billy worried about the long-term security of this exposed installation and the new burdens it would place on the war-weary Hmong. They would be called upon to protect the site, which would certainly come under attack. He cautioned Air Force and State Department officials that while General Vang Pao could initially hold the facility, if the North Vietnamese made an all-out effort to take it he would have extreme difficulty. Nevertheless, the decision was made to proceed. Major Secord was given the overall staff responsibility for the site's defense.

That summer, in great secrecy, installation of the TSQ-81 began atop Phou Pha Thi. Equipment had to be modified so that it could be airlifted in small components by crane helicopters. Everything had to be chop-pered in—even water. This forlorn promontory, thought of by Air Amer-ica Captain Fred Walker as "the battleship," rose starkly into the sky with a cliff of almost 2,000 feet on one side. The Americans believed that the cliff would protect the site from attack from that quarter. About 600 yards down the other slope, the Hmong, under the direction of SKY advi-sors, chopped out a helipad that would allow helicopters to resupply, move troops, and evacuate quickly if necessary, dug bunkers, and built quarters for the technicians who would operate the facility.

In October, just before the equipment became fully operational, Hmong caught two Buddhist monks with a camera at the site. Following interrogation by Vang Pao's people, the two confessed to being enemy spies. Vang Pao was convinced the site had been compromised. The Air Force disagreed and concluded that "the suspects were in fact bona fide Buddhist monks,"[2] and went ahead with its plan to activate the TSQ.

*   *   *

On October 21, 1967, some 50,000 antiwar protesters, including au-thor Norman Mailer, "Yippie" Jerry Rubin, Dr. Benjamin Spock, and Yale University Chaplain Sloane Coffin, demonstrated at the Pentagon. Protesters shouted: "Hell, no, we won't go" and "Hey, hey, LBJ, how many kids did you kill today?" And in November, Bertrand Russell and his International War Crimes Tribunal opened its second session in Swe-den and captured the attention of the world press. The purpose of the mock tribunal, patterned after the Nuremberg Trials following World War II, was to document U.S. atrocities against the Vietnamese.

Johnson believed time was running out with the American public. His experts counseled that winning the war in South Vietnam still depended on winning the war in Laos—or at least denying the North the use of the Trail. To counter increased U.S. bombing of the Trail, the communists deployed more sophisticated defensive weapons. U.S. air losses in-creased. Washington remained convinced, however, that technology could keep losses down and bring a U.S. military victory.

*   *   *

The U.S. Air Force technicians who were to operate the site at Phou Pha Thi arrived at Udorn in Thailand. Since Lima Site 85 presented ultra-sensitive political concerns, they were undercover as civilian contract employees of the Air Force so as not to violate the 1962 Geneva Accords. Mostly they went unnoticed. The few at Udorn who knew of this top-secret operation were amazed that the technicians assigned to such a remote and vulnerable site were without weapons or survival training. At the last moment, some minimal survival training was provided.

In November 1967, Site 85's innovative hi-tech battle station, code-named "Commando Club," high in the tropical Lao sky, became fully operational. Technicians operating the TSQ-81 radar bombing equipment looked electronically down North Vietnam's Red River Valley, the route U.S. pilots flew on their bombing missions. Guided by the men atop Phou Pha Thi, they could fly precision bombing strikes in all kinds of weather, 24 hours a day, against enemy targets in both North Vietnam and northern Laos. Their equipment also allowed technicians to monitor the flight paths of U.S. crews to prevent them from violating Chinese airspace.

Guarded by Hmong soldiers and their families, this space-age site, housed in camouflaged metallic trailers painted with a dull, nonreflective paint and manned by 16 Americans, seemed secure. The Hmong, however, were not certain. They remembered the two spies disguised as Buddhist monks.

Xiong Xia Chia, code-named "Alex," who had worked his way from being a cook for one of the first American advisors to a lieutenant trained in intelligence, was one of the 200 soldiers protecting the technicians and equipment at Lima Site 85. "We knew that our mission was very important. We knew that we must defend it to the last man to protect it from the NVA. We worried a lot about defending this site, but we had patrols. Another 800 Hmong patrolled lower down the mountain. Our undefended side was safe because there was a cliff, straight down for about 2,000 feet. The Americans told us no one could approach from that direction."[3]

The site commanders were Jerry Daniels and another SKY man.[4] They rotated between Phou Pha Thi and Na Khang, spending a few days at each site. At Udorn, Major Richard Secord monitored enemy activity in their area.

As U.S. civilian and military policy emphasized stopping Hanoi's men and supplies from reaching South Vietnam, more responsibilities fell to those in Laos. Ambassador William Sullivan's "Mission" expanded. New buildings, often windowless and air-conditioned, cubicled increasing numbers of U.S. military personnel, who wore civilian clothes and worked out of the Air Attaché's office in the embassy.

At Udorn, Colonel Billy agonized over the new directives coming from Washington. "The CIA wanted to make our operation bigger and better. They thought if you put more money and more Americans in there, it would get bigger and better. They were wrong."[5] Colonel Billy's simple wooden office at the Udorn Air Base was upgraded. His superiors had accused him of running the Lao operation out of his hip pocket. He admitted that this was true: "In fact, I *did* run it out of my hip pocket. I had a small notebook that I carried in my pants pocket and it had everything in it. That changed in 1967 when architects from Washington came to Udorn. They came to build me a new office. I told him that my present small office was fine. I didn't need anything bigger. They argued, telling me that I needed a larger building for such a large operation. I designed a modest building that would cost about $100,000. This didn't satisfy them. Instead, they designed a big air-conditioned building that must have cost a million dollars. It had lots of rooms.

"You know what they did with all those empty rooms? They filled them with Americans, who sat at desks and created paper on the increasing number of Americans working in Laos. This is just what I wanted to avoid—a large American presence. That was the problem in South Vietnam, where the Americans had taken the war away from the South Vietnamese. Now the Americans were taking the war away from the Lao, the Hmong, and the Thai. I was bothered that the idea I had worked on during my whole career, which was to have a minimum American presence, was being destroyed."

Colonel Billy's pride in the successes of his counterinsurgency efforts and of Hmong pilots was being blunted by Washington policy changes toward Laos. He strongly believed that the number of Americans should remain at an absolute minimum, and that Thai involvement should increase if more men were necessary. He always imagined that the Thai would join with the Hmong and the Lao to fight their common enemy, the North Vietnamese.

Colonel Billy's mentor, Desmond FitzGerald, had been involved with Vietnam and Laos as the CIA's deputy director of plans for its Far Eastern Division in the early 1960s when Colonel Billy worked with the Thai PARU and Vang Pao. FitzGerald thought the same way Colonel Billy did. He was a champion of paramilitary counterinsurgency warfare with its measured, manageable efforts using indigenous forces. In 1965, FitzGerald became the CIA's deputy director of plans—an influential position. But in 1967, while playing tennis at his home in Virginia, he died of a heart attack. His death was a serious blow to Colonel Billy and his plans for the Hmong. Colonel Billy worried about the Hmong.

"Beginning in about 1968, we were asking them to do more than they were capable of handling. We asked them to take on more military responsibilities, particularly conventional, set-piece military battles. Vang Pao was at his best in pure guerrilla warfare. I don't know if he resisted the change to conventional warfare. I'm not sure he didn't believe that doing some of these things would be of advantage to his people in the future. He could have considered it as one way for his people to assume a bigger role in Laos without looking at the limitations. I could see we were making mistakes. I had spent years there, studying the situation. I knew the Hmong, their situation, and I knew they were best at being guerrillas, but that was being changed by the Americans."

After FitzGerald's death, Colonel Billy sensed that the CIA senior management began to focus on the counterinsurgency success in Laos, where the war had been fought so cheaply with irregular forces. This new concentration of official interest would put Colonel Billy at odds with the agency. "We had done so much in Laos at such a low cost. The success with Vang Pao was so good that everybody wanted to get into it. Reputations and big promotions were to be made for those Americans working with the Hmong. Washington sent the ones they thought were the hotshots and they began to do all those things which I didn't think were exactly right."

As the French and Colonel Billy knew, the Hmong genius as fighters was their quickness in striking and their superb knowledge of the terrain. Colonel Billy reminded his superiors in Washington of this Hmong capability. "I told them that the Hmong knew the terrain and could run up and down those hills without equal. They could run circles around the Vietnamese. The Hmong, sitting on those mountaintops, could strangle the enemy. They were doing to the North Vietnamese exactly what the communists were doing to us in South Vietnam. They were fighting a true guerrilla war and the Vietnamese couldn't come to grips with it."

Colonel Billy wasn't the only one dissatisfied. As the war escalated throughout Southeast Asia, military men thought that the State Department should abdicate its military role in Laos to the Department of Defense. This was a war; it should be run by military men, not ambassadors. Defense personnel looked upon the CIA counterinsurgency effort as inadequate to fight well-trained and armed NVA divisions. Counterinsurgency experts, like Colonel Billy, doubted that the U.S. military machine could achieve victory in South Vietnam or Laos; they resisted the military's efforts to take over. At the Country Team meetings of the Mission to Laos, men bickered and jockeyed for position, reflecting the confusion and frustrations of Washington policymakers.

Congressional teams sent to visit the Lao operation usually came away impressed. A trip to Long Chieng to visit General Vang Pao gave visitors a taste of the exotic and a few hours' exposure to life on the "front lines." It kept them talking about their experiences for months. Most were impressed not only by Hmong hospitality and exotic tribal ways, but also by the low cost of the military effort in Laos.

American involvement in South Vietnam cost billions, often with little to show for it. In Laos, an effective counterinsurgency operation cost little. Supporting Vang Pao's irregulars was, as some in Washington labeled it, "war on the cheap." Vang Pao's special or irregular forces, now officially known as Special Guerrilla Units (SGU) and later as *Groupes Mobiles* (GM), were funded directly by U.S. government-appropriated funds. Salaries were very low. It was estimated that his 20,000 men were paid ten cents a day per man, for a total of $2,000 per day or $60,000 per month to field forces that were holding their own against the NVA. This, compared to the exorbitant expenditures in South Vietnam, pleased Washington.[6] Village defense units, known as *Auto Défense de Choc* (ADC) and *Auto Défense Ordinaire* (ADO) forces, were organized by zones and paid by the Lao government. The ADC units received some training and weapons and salaries of 1,000 to 2,000 *kip*—$2 to $3—per month. ADO units were not trained or salaried but were provided with weapons and ammunition for village defense.

In Military Region II, Vang Pao paid his soldiers on the basis of merit. Their salaries depended upon the difficulty and hardship of their assignments. Soldiers fighting on the front lines received more than those sitting at desks keeping records.

Increasing numbers of Americans involved in Laos meant increasing attempts to Americanize the accepted and traditional ways. Several younger Americans believed that Vang Pao's system of merit pay was unfair; they thought all soldiers should receive the same pay whether they fought in a foxhole or pushed pencils in some rear position. They complained to the Mission in Vientiane, and were told that the merit pay system was preferred by the Hmong. But the hard-headed Americans pushed until they won. Vang Pao, wanting nothing to do with the new scheme, turned it over to the Americans.

To reflect the new American pay procedures, each man was given a pay number. Soldiers who had fought hard the previous month complained that their payment was not commensurate with their efforts. When told all soldiers in the same rank were receiving the same pay, they were furious and announced they would not fight unless paid as before. Eventually the increasing unhappiness of men in combat forced the Americans to relent. The merit pay system returned to Military Region II. (The soldiers, however, kept their American-issued pay numbers. Later, as refugees, they would give these numbers to refugee authorities, believing them to be U.S. military serial numbers and hence proof that as part of the American military they were entitled to veterans' benefits.)

* * *

The radar equipment at Phou Pha Thi was proving extremely successful. The TSQ-81 system directed and controlled attacking jet fighters and bombers to their targets, providing aircraft with precise bomb release points around the clock in all kinds of weather. Damage to non-military structures and harm to civilians were kept to a minimum.

But Major Richard Secord, responsible for the defense of Site 85, feared for the unarmed technicians' safety. "There were certain ground rules laid down about these people. They were supposed to be civilians operating on an Air Force contract. They of course were not. They were Air Force. They were supposed to be unarmed to be consistent with their cover. Ambassador Sullivan reaffirmed that order several times. I finally put on my military hat. Since I was the senior military officer in charge of all this, I countermanded his order and armed them."[7] So M-16s, fragmentation grenades, concussion grenades, and sidearms were choppered in to the technicians on Phou Pha Thi. The SKY men and Sgt. James Gary, an Air Commando combat air controller who had been assigned to Phou Pha Thi as the situation worsened, trained them to use these weapons.

U.S. photo-reconnaissance planes flew daily over the area. Colonel Billy studied the photos; they showed road construction inching up the mountain toward the Americans. He warned officials, including the U.S. Embassy, that the North Vietnamese intended to take Site 85 soon, and advised evacuation of the technicians. "Washington's response was that for each day Site 85 operated, it saved lots of American lives. So, it should operate as long as possible."

In Hanoi, General Giap prepared for a major offensive into South Vietnam to be launched in late January during the Tet New Year holiday, the most important Vietnamese celebration. Giap hoped to bolster morale of the communist forces in the South and to convince the South Vietnamese to join his forces. The success of this offensive depended upon the resupply of the Viet Cong and Giap's NVA troops fighting in South Vietnam. In order to accomplish this, he had to eliminate Lima Site 85 and outmaneuver the U.S. interdiction efforts along the vital Ho Chi Minh Trail.

"Heine" Aderholt flew interdiction strikes along the Trail. One dark, rainy night, he sat in the cockpit of a fully armed T-28 on the ramp at NKP. There were reports of heavy truck traffic on the Trail. Rain squalls rushed across the airfield, obscuring the runway. As Aderholt waited with his wingman, Col. Tom Deacon, to lift off, sweat ran down his back. Dressed in survival gear, parachute, and helmet, Aderholt cracked the canopy, but rain gusts forced him to close it. Finally Aderholt ordered the aircraft shut down. He called the flightline taxi, a truck. The two pilots climbed inside and took off their gear to wait out the storm. Suddenly there was a lull. They donned their gear and hurriedly climbed into their cockpits. Within minutes they were airborne, heading for the Trail.

Flares from a C-123 flare ship and tracers from antiaircraft laced the scudding clouds. As they neared the target, Airborne Command and Control Center (pronounced AB-Triple C) radioed Aderholt to stand down for a flight of Navy A-4 jets low on fuel so they could hit their targets. Aderholt and Deacon held near Tchepone. Radio chatter indicated many enemy gunners awaited them. As the Navy planes headed home to their carrier in the South China Sea, Aderholt and Deacon received clearance for their strike on the Trail.

On their first pass, Aderholt and Deacon each hit a truck, both of which burst into flames. Aderholt pulled up and went around for another pass. As he came off target, antiaircraft gun bursts followed him. In a steep climb, his engine sputtered and lost power. "My God! They've hit my engine," he shouted to Deacon over the radio. "I'm going over the side. I'm bailing out!" He pushed open the canopy, stood up to roll over the side, and reached for the D-ring on his parachute. "It wasn't there! In my dash to get off before another rain squall hit, I had buckled on my survival gear, but not my parachute. I sat down. Scared shitless, I pushed the stick forward. The engine took hold. It sputtered, regained some power. I called Deacon to take me home with my rough engine." Aderholt and Deacon flew off into the darkness, heading for NKP.

Meanwhile, Major Secord worried about the road coming up the mountain at Phou Pha Thi. "We overflew it every day and photographed it constantly. The NVA brought down a regiment of infantry and a full regiment of artillery from the homeland. We had them spotted." About Christmas, Secord began a campaign to interdict the road. "I screamed, bitched, moaned, griped, sent messages, and went to Saigon many times to complain to the 7th Air Force commander that we had to have air support to stop the construction of the road or we couldn't hold the site. . . . I knew, we all knew, that the NVA could move in heavy artillery, which would be the death knell for us.

"The long and short of it was that I couldn't get sufficient interdicting and close air support to hold the site. That seems a little bit ridiculous in that the Air Force demanded we hold it. Because of the way in which the Air Force fought that war from the central command position in Saigon, they had very little actual, first-hand knowledge of what was going on. The commander for the 7th Air Force [William Momyer] had his own priorities." The day before Christmas, a TACAN site in the central part of the Lao Panhandle, east of Savannakhet, was overrun. Secord recalled, "Although we didn't realize it immediately, this did signal the beginning of the Tet Offensive."

President Johnson ordered a Christmas pause in the bombing of North Vietnam, expecting Hanoi to agree to peace talks. In the final days of 1967, the Viet Cong and the South Vietnamese agreed to a U.S.-sponsored truce to take place during the celebration of Tet, the Vietnamese Lunar New Year, which would begin on January 31. Aderholt took advantage of the bombing pause to spend a few days with his family in the Philippines before being assigned as director of operations for the USAF Special Air Warfare Center at Eglin Air Force Base in Florida. There he would provide Air Operations officers for the U.S. Embassy in Vientiane and pilots for Project 404, Water Pump.

*   *   *

On January 1, 1968, Hanoi announced that it had agreed to talks with the U.S. if all bombing was stopped. Johnson extended the Christmas bombing pause. As the date for the Tet Offensive neared, the NVA gave top priority to the destruction of the Phou Pha Thi installation. If Lima Site 85 were eliminated, U.S. air power would be seriously crippled.

Jerry Daniels had rotated from Na Khang, "the Alamo," to Phou Pha Thi when, on January 12, two slow Soviet-built AN-2 biplanes surprised the mile-high site. Since their engines sounded like Air America aircraft, Hmong soldiers and their families moved about, unsuspecting. Over the site, NVA crews dropped 120mm mortar shells into makeshift tubes in the planes' floors. These shells armed themselves in the slipstream and detonated on impact. Meanwhile, the planes fired 57mm rockets from wing pods. As the biplanes bombed and rocketed the site, Daniels and the Hmong fired back at them with small arms. They peppered one plane on a low pass. It crashed into a nearby mountainside and burned. Daniels later insisted that he had brought down that first plane. Others claimed it as well.

The other plane continued its attack. An Air America Huey helicopter pilot, monitoring Site 85's radio, heard its call for help and responded. As he approached, he saw the biplane attacking. Unarmed except for an M-16 automatic rifle carried by a crewman, the chopper pilot headed for the biplane as if he were flying a strike plane. As he pulled alongside, a crew member sprayed the biplane with the M-16, scoring a hit. It staggered for a few miles, then crashed into a ridge. A helicopter crew had scored a "kill" with an M-16![8]

The defenders surveyed the damage: four Hmong dead, two men and two women. Several defenders were wounded, but there was no significant damage to the TSQ-81 trailers. Immediately Hmong ground teams were sent to the crash sites to look for survivors. At one, they found three North Vietnamese bodies. American intelligence personnel choppered in to examine this cropduster-type biplane and to photograph its conversion to an attack aircraft. At CIA headquarters at Udorn, Major Secord and others were astonished that the NVA had attacked Phou Pha Thi with jury-rigged, slow-moving biplanes. A biplane attack seemed crazy and comical. Their laughter, however, was short-lived. Secord knew this aerial attack showed that the enemy knew the importance of the site.

Colonel Billy and Major Secord continued to monitor the NVA road that headed from Sam Neua westward to the base of the mountain—Route 602, as the Americans called it. On January 19, a Hmong patrol reported five battalions of NVA and Pathet Lao troops moving toward Phou Pha Thi—one more than the four estimated by the defenders as necessary to take the site, if the enemy was willing to take heavy losses. Secord watched the Vietnamese progress against Site 85. "Everything was proceeding as normal in the North Vietnamese ant-like way. They are very methodical. They are easy to fight for that reason—if you have the goods to fight them." But Secord could not get the "goods" from 7th Air Force in Saigon, and the roadbuilding continued.

In the early hours of January 31, Giap's 1968 Tet Offensive was underway. Between then and February 10, communist forces attacked 36 of the 44 provincial capitals in South Vietnam. The South Vietnamese, however, did not rise up as a nation to join the communist forces as predicted by Hanoi. Instead they fought back, inflicting huge enemy losses. While most battles were short, the battle for Hue, the old imperial capital just south of the DMZ, turned into a protracted, bloody encounter. Here U.S. Marines joined the South Vietnamese Army in house-to-house fighting, finally defeating the enemy forces on February 25.

During this time, the U.S. Air Force continued bombing North Vietnam. In February, Lima Site 85's "Commando Club" directed 27 strikes against North Vietnam—55 percent of all missions against the North. With the increasing threat to the site, Vang Pao in early February assigned two of his top field commanders and 300 Hmong to defend it. NVA and Pathet Lao mortar attacks now reached the outer perimeters defended by Hmong lower down the mountain.

On February 18, these Hmong ambushed and killed an NVA artillery survey party and found a notebook with detailed plans for the attack on Phou Pha Thi. The battle plan included the use of four battalions, three North Vietnamese and one Pathet Lao, to take the site. Major Secord examined the captured documents. ''This was the single most important piece of intel that we got before the final clash. There was an NVA major leading the patrol—a major is a tall dog in the NVA—and they had maps all drawn up very neatly with standard military symbology. It looked like it came out of the French military academy. They had surveyed in a large number of weapons sites, artillery and heavy mortars.''

With this information and the knowledge that 7th Air Force had priorities other than sending air power to defend Site 85, planners at Udorn decided there was no choice but to pull out and blow the site before it was overrun. Major Secord attended those planning meetings. ''We had the site mined and prepared to blow it. Permission to blow it was denied by Washington at the highest levels—White House, Joint Chiefs of Staff, and the Director of Central Intelligence, Mr. Helms. 'Hold it,' they said. We said, 'We'll give it a whirl.' Following that directive, Theodore Shackley, CIA station chief in Laos, cabled Washington that based on patrol reports he did not believe Lima Site 85 could be held beyond March 10.''[9]

As the enemy net tightened, 50 Thai infantrymen, with two mortars and a howitzer, commanded by a Thai West Point captain, were choppered to Phou Pha Thi. The American TSQ site commander, Lt. Col. Clarence Blanton, received permission to direct air strikes in self-defense. SKY advisors, responsible for the Hmong defense of the site, stayed in close touch with Hmong patrols. Air Force Sergeant James Gary, Air Commando air controller based at the helipad lower down the slope, talked often to the CIA in Udorn. From February 20–29, Lima Site 85 directed 342 strikes within 30 kilometers of itself to disrupt the enemy buildup, but still the enemy advanced.

By March 9, Lima Site 85 was totally surrounded. By this time, Jerry Daniels had rotated from Site 85 to Na Khang, the Alamo. Because of the around-the-clock capability needed to defend the base, five more Air Force technicians had been airlifted in, bringing the number of technicians to 16. Since the site operated 24 hours a day, men rotated sleeping and working. During the first ten days of March, Phou Pha Thi directed some 90 percent of the U.S. air strikes in northern Laos.

On March 10, a helicopter from Long Chieng landed to take out several Hmong in intelligence to headquarters for new assignments. One of these called back to Long Chieng was "Alex"— Xiong Xia Chia. Just before dark, artillery and mortars, firing with extraordinary precision from a recently captured nearby Lima site, hit near the American living quarters and knocked out the lone 105mm Thai howitzer. The technicians grabbed weapons and ran to bunkers and trenches, abandoning their equipment and depriving themselves of the ability to direct air strikes against the attackers.

The SKY advisor at the helipad radioed the CIA at Udorn that Site 85 was under attack. Secord, who spent most of his time in the radio room during these days of increasing crisis, was having his hair cut in this room when the call came that the site was taking artillery and mortar fire.

At about the same time, down the hill below the helipad, Hmong defenders at a position 1 1/2 kilometers south of Site 85 encountered heavy fighting as the NVA attempted to reach Phou Pha Thi via the trails. The Hmong held their outposts along the trails leading to the top. This attack against the Hmong positions was a feint to cover the sapper assault that would doom Site 85.

At 7:45 p.m., the barrage against Site 85 ceased. Air Force Major Stanley J. Sliz, who was on Phou Pha Thi that evening, recalled that no Americans were injured during the first attack. After the shelling ceased, those on duty returned to the TSQ van to call in defensive strikes. Sliz and two young airmen took their sleeping bags from their damaged living quarters to an open area near a grotto south of the operations van. By 1 a.m., they were asleep.[10]

After the news of the attack reached General Vang Pao, he began moving a reserve battalion, headquartered at Long Chieng, to Na Khang. All night, Air America choppers ferried his troops from Alternate to the Alamo, in case a counterattack was needed.

After midnight, the land-line wires running from the helipad to the top of Phou Pha Thi were cut. At the helipad, they waited and watched. It was too quiet. They feared a ground attack.

About 2 a.m., the SKY advisor at the helipad reported to Secord and other CIA men in the radio room at Udorn that he had heard small arms fire from the top and that the helipad position had lost all communications with the men up there. Even their two-way radio was dead. Udorn ordered him to get as many Hmong as possible and prepare for a counterattack against the enemy.

About 3 a.m., Secord and his chief photo interpreter briefed Udorn-based A-1 Skyraider pilots on the critical situation at Phou Pha Thi and familiarized them with the locations of the trailers, the living quarters, and the helipad. The Skyraiders would fly cover for the evacuation of the Americans and for Vang Pao's counterattack.

At 4:15, Sliz and the two airmen were awakened by gunfire, grenades, and voices on the hill above them. They scrambled a few yards into the nearby grotto. Two other airmen were already there, armed with their M-16 rifles and a few grenades. They waited in silence. Six enemy soldiers neared the entrance of the cave. The sergeant guarding the entrance held his fire until they were close. With that first burst of fire, the NVA knew their location. For the next three hours, Sliz and the four other Americans trapped inside the grotto were attacked by NVA, using automatic weapons fire and hand grenades. "The boy on my right died almost instantly. The boy on his right had a broken leg from a bullet. There were at least a half dozen grenades tossed in through a small cavernous hole. We had no way of defending ourselves . . . except when the grenades came bouncing on in they would land in my proximity and I could grab them and throw them down the hill."[11]

As the crews prepared the Skyraiders for battle, the pilots worried about the weather. It was marginal. Just before dawn, it began to break. At 5:15 a.m., Ambassador Sullivan, in Vientiane, finally decided to remove all Americans from the site. The signal to go was given to the Skyraiders. In waves, the entire squadron lifted off at Udorn and flew north over the "fence." Sullivan announced that evacuation would take place at 7:15. He did not know that the Americans no longer manned the TSQ equipment.[12]

As the Skyraiders flew north, the SKY commander at the helipad and his Hmong troops moved quietly toward the beleaguered position above them. About first light, they reached the top and got their first view of the situation. The enemy had already set up a 12.7 antiaircraft gun in a sandbagged emplacement. There was no sign of any Americans.

General Vang Pao watched from an airborne position near Site 85 as the Skyraider pilots tried to knock out the antiaircraft gun and pin down the enemy soldiers so the rescue choppers could get in.

When the rescue choppers were in sight, Hmong soldiers, led by their SKY advisor, rushed the TACAN-TSQ site. NVA soldiers opened fire on them and on the rescue helicopters. As the Hmong and the NVA fired at each other, the SKY advisor shouted to the technicians that help was coming and asked them to identify their locations so he could rescue them. NVA gunfire responded to his plea. Blood spurted from his right thigh as he continued calling to the Americans. As he rounded one of the trailers, he saw the antiaircraft gun firing at the Skyraiders. He lobbed a grenade into the gun emplacement, killing two gunners. He and the Hmong located five technicians, all wounded, and hurried them down the slope to the helipad where Sergeant Gary was directing Skyraider strikes and rescue chopper pilots.

With the antiaircraft gun silent, a Skyraider dropped its bombs near the TSQ, forcing the enemy soldiers to take cover and allowing the first hovering Air America helicopter to land at the helipad where all the Americans waited. All Americans except Sergeant Gary were wounded. As the survivors were pulled and pushed aboard, enemy soldiers rushed down the slope toward them, firing automatic weapons. As the chopper lifted off, it took a burst to its belly, killing one of the wounded technicians. Overhead an Air America Volpar photo-reconnaissance plane also took hits. The NVA was in control of Site 85.

Of the 19 Americans at Lima Site 85, five Air Force technicians, including Major Sliz, two CIA SKY advisors, and Sergeant Gary, the Air Commando air controller, were extracted. Some of the American technicians were known to be dead. The fate of Lieutenant Colonel Blanton, the TSQ site commander, and the others remains unknown to this day.

As the rescue choppers headed south, the main NVA force, in unit formations, moved up the mountain on the front slope. Hmong held this trail system to the top until the choppers departed. Then, those who were not seriously wounded melted into the jungle to move to safer locations and await instructions. An unknown number of Hmong died trying to defend Phou Pha Thi and rescue the American technicians.

Soon after the rescue helicopters departed, Air Force jet fighters arrived. This time, Major Secord recalls, the Air Force responded to his call for help. "Dozens and dozens—maybe 100—jets flew north. They pounded the enemy force. It was no easy trip up the mountain for the enemy."[13]

In the confusion of the sudden NVA commando attack, the secret equipment at the site had not been blown. Secord had never counted on the enemy getting in among the technicians. "We expected to make a deliberate retreat. Instead, because of higher orders, we were forced to make a panicked exodus. As a result, they were in no shape to accomplish the destruction."

Blowing the site now became Secord's task. "I hoped to be able to knock it off through dive-bombing. As soon as we completed our rescue operation, I requested jet air strikes on that site. Unfortunately, it took three days to get a hit on it. On the third day, an Air Commando by the name of Bill Palank, who was on his third tour in Southeast Asia, hit it on his first pass in an A-1 Skyraider and cleaned it."

There remains much confusion about the final hours of Site 85. The official Air Force version is that the American technicians ran from their facilities into automatic weapons fire. Several died on the spot. Some managed to scramble to the cliff and climb into slings they had fashioned to hide in, by hanging from the cliff wall in these slings until rescued. The Hmong reported another version. Alex, the Hmong soldier who had departed the site shortly before the attack and who later talked to Hmong who were there, reported that dark-clothed NVA commandos scaled the cliff with mountain-climbing equipment, slipped undetected into the command center, and quietly slit the throats of the technicians on duty. This might explain why the Americans did not blow up their equipment. They had no warning. According to the Hmong version, some off-duty technicians, hearing the firing, apparently ran for the slings that hung over the cliff. Alex explained: "The Hmong did not know of the attack until the NVA commandos ran from the buildings, then the Hmong opened fire. Since the Americans told us that it was impossible to scale the cliff, the Hmong soldiers, who didn't know anything about mountain-climbing equipment, concentrated on protecting the position from artillery and rocket attacks and from ground troops, expected to come along the trails leading to the position."[14]

If the technicians did survive, their whereabouts remain unknown. Some have speculated that survivors were captured and kept as prisoners by the North Vietnamese and held in Laos or taken to the Soviet Union, where the Soviets questioned them on the technology deployed at Site 85. To date, none of the remains of any of the Air Force technicians* lost at Phou Pha Thi have been recovered.

From November 1, 1967, through March 11, 1968 when Lima Site 85 fell, 27 percent of Rolling Thunder and Barrel Roll strikes against North

---

*Those listed by the Department of Defense as missing in action after the fall of Phou Pha Thi, Lima Site 85, are: Lt. Col. Clarence Blanton, Master Sgt. James H. Calfee, Staff Sgt. James W. Davis, Staff Sgt. Henry G. Gish, Technical Sgt. Willis R. Hall, Technical Sgt. Melvin A. Holland, Staff Sgt. Herbert A. Kirk, Airman First Class David S. Price, Technical Sgt. Patrick L. Shannon, Technical Sgt. Donald K. Springsteadah, and Staff Sgt. Don Worley.

Vietnam and northern Laos were directed from Phou Pha Thi. During the first ten days of March, Site 85 directed 314 strikes in defense of itself, trying to stop truck convoys and porters resupplying troops encircling it. After the fall of Phou Pha Thi, no other facility existed to provide similar coverage for the U.S. Air Force. Many believe that the fall of this site critically affected the course of the war. In a few days, President Johnson announced he would halt the bombing of most of North Vietnam.

* * *

After the successful rout of the Americans and their technology from Phou Pha Thi, the enemy moved against Na Khang, the Alamo, 35 miles away. Major Secord monitored the situation there. "It was clear from our intelligence and from their actions that they were going to overrun Site 36. And it was clear that we were going to make a stand. We found ourselves by March 31 in a tremendous bind at 36. We had put a lot of Hmong in there and they couldn't get out. The Hmong really didn't like it because the place was surrounded by many lines of wire and mine fields. This was a set piece battle which they hated. We felt we had to hold 36. It was our last site in the north. We had to hold if we could because, if not, they would roll right on down through. We were stretching for the rainy season."[15]

On March 31, April Fool's day in Asia, President Johnson announced that he was not going to run for reelection. He also announced a bombing halt north of the 20th parallel, eliminating air strikes over the northern two-thirds of North Vietnam, in the hope that such unilateral action would lead to early peace talks. Johnson made no mention of the loss of the TSQ site at Phou Pha Thi.

At Udorn, Secord listened to the President and labeled it Johnson's April Fool's Day speech. "Most important for us," recalled Secord, "was the bombing pause north of the 20th parallel because this was interpreted by our military to mean north of the 20th parallel everywhere— not just in North Vietnam." Such an interpretation would deny U.S. air power to save the Alamo, Daniels, and its Hmong defenders. Secord argued that Johnson's bombing pause meant north of the 20th parallel in North Vietnam, NOT in Laos. "I argued that since we weren't in Laos officially, how could we have a bombing pause? But they stopped bombing in Laos for days."[16]

Secord believed that Na Khang, the northernmost friendly position in Laos with its critical rescue base and TACAN, would fall without air support. "So we took it all the way through the Director of Central Intelligence to the President, to the Joint Chiefs and said that this [bombing pause in Laos] is a catastrophe."

Defying Washington, Secord requested B-52 strikes to defend the Alamo. "In Washington, they were saying you can't have any more air. I was saying not only do we want more air, we want B-52s, for the first time in Laos, to hold this place. We were denied B-52s but given up to 300 fighter strikes a day until further notice—effective about the second or third of April. We got some air-controllers up there and started to methodically pound away on the concentrations. We had done a very good 'intel job,' through patrolling and other means, and had identified the locations of various enemy units. We literally pulverized the place and they finally retired. This was a tremendous fight compared to Phou Pha Thi. This was a big, protracted fight—close to a month."

Secord evaluated the defense of Na Khang as a significant victory for air power. "The bottom line there was that we really held the place for the first time, I think, in the annals of warfare through the use of air alone. This included the siege of Khe Sanh which was finally lifted by American troops going in there. But this one, the siege of Site 36 in 1968, was lifted through the application of tactical air power—in massive quantities.

"The important thing is that in 1968 we finally blunted the NVA drive to the south. I think what we did was burn up all the forces that the North Vietnamese High Command had been willing to commit to this offensive. They achieved their objectives at Phou Pha Thi and were stymied at the Alamo."

Johnson's March 31 announcement had concluded with a warning, echoing Kennedy's "bear any burden" speech. Johnson said: "But let men everywhere know, however, that a strong, a confident, and a vigilant America stands ready tonight to seek an honorable peace—and stands ready tonight to defend an honored cause—whatever the price, whatever the burden, whatever the sacrifices that duty may require." The Hmong took this to be a reaffirmation of the American commitment to their cause.

11.

Hmong in the Skies

UPI story from Vientiane . . . alleges that Prime Minister Prince
Souvanna Phouma admitted that US planes are bombing North Vietnamese troop concentrations and infiltration routes in Laos. Embassy Vientiane Reports Souvanna said our—meaning Royal Lao
Government—planes not US planes.

Present Defense Dept Policy for response on US operations in
Laos still applies and is quoted as follows: Quote. The preferable response to questions about air operations in Laos is no comment.

—Instructions from Commander of the Pacific Air Forces sent to
U.S. Air Force commanders in Thailand, February 15, 1969

The skies over northern Laos were filled with aircraft. Jets from six
major Thai Air Force bases across "the fence," as the pilots called the
Mekong River, and sometimes Navy planes launched from aircraft carriers in the South China Sea, screamed through the skies. To support the
fighter aircraft there were the reconnaissance planes, airborne jammer
planes, rescue helicopters, and refueling tankers. There were C-47s converted into gunships, known as "Spookies" because they often operated
at night, and airborne battle command and control craft, ABCCC, which
coordinated air activity operations in northern Laos, along the Ho Chi
Minh Trail, and in North Vietnam. Then there were Air America and
Continental Air Services C-47s and C-123s, the resupply workhorses, and
their single-engine Helios and Porters that could land on the short, high-
altitude Lima sites; Air America helicopters, which ferried troops and
supplies and were based in Udorn under contract to USAID in Laos, and
the fragile single-engine spotter planes that flew like drowsy autumn
mosquitoes over the tropical mountain vastness.

General Vang Pao, like most Hmong, loved aviation. He never earned a pilot's license, but he could fly a Cessna 185 or H-34 helicopter once airborne. His SKY advisors, however, strongly disapproved of the general flying himself. To expand Hmong aviation capability, he would eventually urge Hmong pilots to learn to fly C-46 and C-47 cargo planes so the Hmong could be self-sufficient in the air.

As U.S. interdiction sorties in Laos increased, the North Vietnamese responded by introducing more powerful weapons, including highly mobile and accurate 37, 57, 85, 100, and eventually 130mm guns that operated from over 3,000 gun emplacements in Laos. The NVA cleverly camouflaged their positions and guns, relying heavily on the security of caves to hide their men and weapons from U.S. aerial reconnaissance. In some cases, big guns were put on tracks and rolled out to fire and then rolled back into the caves.

The Americans and General Vang Pao countered this threat by putting men on the ground in enemy territory to ferret out the caves and the hidden positions and then to direct air strikes against these targets. These men were the Forward Air Guides—the FAGs. Inserted clandestinely into enemy territory by helicopters, they moved through the jungle day after day with only a survival supply of rice, a map, a compass, a strobe light, a call-sign, and a 15-pound back-carried PRC-25 field radio. Once a FAG sighted a target, he called either the airborne Forward Air Controller (FAC) pilot in the area, Long Chieng, or Udorn to report his find. Then he helped orchestrate the attack. In emergencies, he worked directly with ABCCC circling overhead to direct air strikes.

Hmong chosen as FAGs and FACs had to speak English in order to communicate with American pilots, American-crewed ABCCC aircraft, and often American personnel on the ground. Since FAG and FAC responsibilities were complicated and involved directing American air strikes, they also had to be highly intelligent and to possess extraordinary courage.

Vang Chou, who had been flying as a spotter pilot since the early days of the war, now flew with American Sam Deichelman as a FAC in one of the single-engine Cessnas, known as Bird Dogs, that carried the call-sign of "Raven."* Sam and Chou—"General Direction" as Sam called him—

---

*Before the Ravens, Air Commandos, based in northern Thailand, functioned as Forward Air Controllers (FACs) in Laos. Flying in the right seat, usually in Air America planes, these FACs, known as "Butterflies," communicated with pilots in fast moving strike aircraft directing them to targets. Butterfly FACs, steady, calm, and low-profile men—like James flew as Raven 22. Deichelman, the college-age son of a retired Air Force general, and Chou often drew the Ban Ban assignment because this was Chou's home area. As Chou looked for signs of the enemy, he thought, as he often did, about his childhood experiences at Nong Het and Padong with the North Vietnamese. As he remembered, he touched the holstered pistol strapped to his side. Then he reached behind his seat to doublecheck that the aircraft carried a bigger weapon just in case of a shootdown. His fingers touched an M-16. Chou knew, despite Hanoi's continued official pronouncements that it had no troops in Laos, that Soviet-supplied North Vietnam radar-controlled antiaircraft guns, tanks, and long range artillery spat deadly fire from Lao soil. Their plane maneuvered slowly over NVA-controlled Route 7 and Ban Ban, a dreaded and deadly stretch for pilots. Here the enemy's sophisticated and accurate guns had shot down many American, Thai, Lao, and Hmong flight crews.

In the 23 years since the Hmong and Gauthier had blown the Ban Ban bridge with charges to stop the Japanese, war technology had advanced. Now, to blow a bridge or hit an enemy convoy, a Raven crew ordered an air strike by calling ABCCC. Twenty-four hours a day, one ABCCC orbited over northern Laos, near Ban Ban, and another orbited over southern Laos. In the north, the daytime ABCCC was code-named "Cricket." At night, "Alley Cat" came on station.

Ravens were posted to each of the five Lao military regions. Usually five or six were assigned to fly Vang Pao's Region II. Flying as a FAC in Laos was a volunteer, clandestine, and dangerous six-month assignment. FACs were first assigned to Detachment 1 of the Air Commandos at Udorn where they were "sterilized" or "sheepdipped"—stripped of all vestiges of their Air Force connections. Once "sterilized," they were posted TDY (temporary duty) to the Air Attache's Office at the U.S. Embassy in Vientiane. They did not wear Air Force clothing but instead sported cowboy hats, bright-flowered Hawaiian shirts, and camouflage jackets. They toted guns and wore bandoliers of ammunition.

Vang Chou spotted something below—some kind of storage area, maybe petrol and ammo. Using a grease pencil, he noted on the wind-

---

Sanford and Charlie Jones—earned reputations for courage and skill. In 1967, Air Force senior officers discovered that the Butterfly FACs were enlisted men and not pilots. They reasoned that only pilots with experience in fighters and bombers would know how to guide air strikes. The Butterfly FAC program ended. The Air Force replaced them with pilots experienced in FAC flying in South Vietnam, or with jet pilots. Several were Air Force Academy graduates. These "gung-ho" pilots changed the call-sign from Butterfly to Raven.

shield the coordinates and drew a quick sketch of the terrain and location to be marked by a smoke rocket. Chou radioed in code that he had a target and its coordinates. He knew that Alternate's Hmong T-28s, the Chaophakaow, would scramble to bomb his target. He listened intently to the pilot chatter on the radio. He knew how many minutes from their liftoff to his position. He waited, then shouted to Sam, "Now!" The small Cessna stopped what appeared to be inattentive flying and headed for the target. Down low, fire the smoke rockets, pull up and away. Raven 22 had done it so many times. As the Cessna pulled up, a drifting pinkish smoke trail rose from the target.

"Chaophakaow Lead, Raven 22's got you some NVA ammo," announced Chou in Hmong over the radio while his plane rode a draft upward away from the target. "This is Chaophakaow Lead, we see the target," came the answer, also in Hmong. Chou recognized the voice. It was Lt. Ly Lue.[1]

Ly Lue's plane slipped out of the sky to drop two bombs directly on the target. His wingman followed with two more bombs. Explosions acknowledged their hits. Then over the radio burst a desperate call for "air." "Position Echo Charlie. Under attack by NVA! Need air! Now!" Ly Lue, on his way around to drop his two remaining bombs, headed for Echo Charlie. His wingman, who had only recently finished flight training, followed. It was always this way with Ly Lue. "Air" could save lives. When the call for "air" came in, Ly Lue always responded because he had once been an infantryman. He knew air strikes could save men on the ground.

Chou listened to the pilots switch call-signs, using their wives' names, to make the enemy think this was a different mission and that the Hmong had more planes and pilots than they did. Ly Lue flew with grace and competence. He seemed to have no fear when flying. So far the auspicious call-sign of Chaophakaow, "Lord White Buddha," had protected him. Chou knew that Chaophakaow pilots had more than auspicious call-signs to protect them; they were good pilots, especially Ly Lue. Weather permitting, Ly Lue and his fellow Hmong pilots flew seven days a week from sunup to sundown in support of Vang Pao's soldiers and Royal Lao troops. Flight pay was less than $100 per month. General Vang Pao also gave each pilot an additional 1,000 *kip*—U.S. $2—for each mission. Chou often wondered whether, if he had volunteered a second time for flight training, he might have become an ace like Ly Lue. He loved flying the T-28s and still did whenever he got a chance. But flying as a Raven, he reasoned, was just as dangerous or maybe more so, since he flew in unarmed, slow-moving aircraft at low altitudes.

Chou saw something and told Sam to change course. Sam rolled the plane and dropped down to take a closer look. Trucks, NVA trucks. Antiaircraft guns spit back. Raven 22 rolled the other way and climbed into a protecting cloud. It rode inside the cloud for a few seconds to confuse the gunners, then slipped out and dove for the ground to look again. Stretching forward in the cockpit, Chou searched for movement or the glint of metal. Flashes from NVA guns shot skyward from the dull green land below. He mentally landmarked the position and greased in the coordinates on the windshield. It was too late this day to launch another strike. Raven 22 would return tomorrow to mark the target for the Hmong pilots.

On his way home, Ly Lue, as he often did, buzzed Sam Thong, the ridge to the north of Long Chieng where his parents and cousins lived. Ly Lue knew his plane, knew its limits and aerobatic capabilities. Hmong screamed in delight as he came in low and fast, swept over their houses, pulled up and into a roll.

Raven 22, heading for home at Alternate, flew over Skyline Ridge. Hmong positions dotted the crest of this mountain ridge. All pilots habitually scanned Skyline on approach to Long Chieng, looking for the enemy. If enemy troops took position there, they could launch an attack on Long Chieng, knock out Hmong air power, destroy U.S.-warehoused weapons and supplies, and overrun the CIA command center.

Ly Lue landed ahead of Sam and Vang Chou. They taxied in parade toward flight operations, a Quonset hut midway along the runway. After tying down, Sam said good-night to General Direction and headed for the Raven hootch and dinner. General Direction headed for the Air Operations Center, the AOC. In this spartan office with its walls plastered with air maps, a blackboard, and metal lockers, flight crews and men in or about to enter flight training gathered almost daily. Awaiting the crews were three Hmong about to become pilots: ''Fackee,'' ''Coyote,'' and Vang Seng. Vang Bee, nicknamed Fackee because he was light-skinned and tall like a Frenchman, worked at the Long Chieng radio station where he announced the news, read messages to counter communist propaganda, and urged the Hmong to think of themselves as Lao nationals. Moua Chue was known as Coyote because he was sleek, fast, and the best Hmong soccer player. Coyote had given up his dream of playing professional soccer to enter T-28 pilot training. Eager to become a good pilot, he hung around AOC seeking rides on flights. Vang Seng, on home leave from training in Thailand to visit Nhia, who was pregnant again, joined the men in the hut. He did not talk much; he preferred listening to the banter of the others.

The pilots looked very Western in their American charcoal green flying suits with zippered pockets; the FAC backseaters, usually in a combination of Western and tribal clothes, did not. They joked and laughed as they put their seat pillows and flight gear into lockers. Relieved that no one had been shot down today and proud of their strikes, the air crews recalled the details of the day's battles and congratulated each other. They were alive to fly another day. Always, the pilots talked of the war. Today they concluded that it was going in their favor—as long as they had "air" available—Hmong "air" and American "air." The Hmong were capable of keeping the NVA off balance, but "air," they believed, was the only thing that could defeat the enemy.

Ly Lue's presence dominated the room. He sported a crew cut, mimicking American pilots, and a wide, appealing smile. Everyone there knew he was the best of the Hmong fighter pilots—maybe the best pilot in Laos. He had astounded even the Americans by chalking up 15 bombing missions in one day. An experienced American combat jet fighter pilot described him as "a man who knew that he was a damned good fighter pilot. In truth, he was even better than he thought he was." Seemingly easygoing, Ly Lue astonished his kinsmen with his cavalier attitude. Many had heard his advice to his worrying wife. "Don't cry. If you see my plane come back, you will be rich. If not, then you can cry."

But Ly Lue was not cavalier about the fact that the Hmong T-28s did not have ejection systems. He feared being hit and wounded and not having enough strength to open or break the canopy to get out. In somber moments, he confessed that he feared being trapped inside a burning plane. (Hmong T-28s were not outfitted with ejection seats until late 1968.)

Known for their sense of humor, backseaters could be counted on for stories about the American FAC pilots with whom they flew. While the American Raven pilots volunteered for a six-month tour of duty and then went home, Hmong flight crews flew as long as they lived. "Moonface," "Scar," and U Va Lee, all of them famous Hmong backseaters for American Raven pilots, died directing air strikes against the enemy. It was often terrifying to fly with the American pilots. Some backseaters refused to fly with certain American pilots who were considered too reckless—or too luckless. According to one: "Some American pilots were crazy. They didn't believe us when we said the enemy was everywhere. They always laughed when we said in our funny English—'Enemy to the north. Enemy to the east. Enemy to the west. Enemy everywhere!' It was true—the enemy was everywhere—but the Americans just laughed."

Fackee, as he did daily, reported the latest news on the peace negotiations that Johnson had initiated with Hanoi. There was nothing new to report. The North Vietnamese continued to argue about the shape of the conference table. This arrogant stalling tactic infuriated the flight crews. They understood Hanoi's devious strategy—even if the Americans did not. After the daily round of derogatory comments about the North Vietnamese, Fackee announced that he did have some important news: he had decided to leave the radio station to join the military. He joked: "Any soldier as tâll as I am will be a good target for the enemy, so I'm volunteering for pilot training." The flight crews smiled, knowing he was tempting fate by becoming one of them. Fackee and Coyote soon joined Vang Seng and seven Lao for T-28 flight training in project Water Pump at Udorn.

A Hmong from a line crew came in to report that an American had been around today to check T-28 gun sights. Everyone joked about American dedication to technology. Hmong pilots did not rely on their gun sights, which were often broken, but on their own eyes and their remarkable depth perception.

Coyote, who loved music and played the guitar and sang, picked up a *khene,* a Hmong reed pipe. Blowing the singsong notes, he danced, slowly lifting his legs stiffly in the Hmong tradition. Instead of floppy black pants and bare feet, he had trousers with zippered pockets bulging with survival knives, code-books, and map sections, and wore U.S. combat boots. His fellow flyers watched and laughed as he turned and twisted, reminding all of the two worlds which these men occupied. Many Hmong pilots were superb athletes, often excelling—like Coyote—in soccer, the national Lao sport. Sometimes to relieve the tension they organized pick-up soccer games on the edges of the airstrip. It was too late for soccer this evening.

As the men prepared to leave, Vang Chou told Ly Lue about sighting a truck convoy and said he had sighted trucks repeatedly in this area during late afternoons. They agreed to rendezvous the next afternoon at three near Ban Ban. Chou warned Chaophakaow Lead to be ready for fireworks. Ly Lue gave Chou the thumbs-up sign as he jumped into a jeep. Spinning his tires, he departed in a swirl of dirt. This ritual, learned from his American pilot friends at Udorn, was a Ly Lue trademark. He headed for the special housing provided him by General Vang Pao. Vang Seng walked briskly toward his parents' house where Nhia and the baby lived. Coyote and Fackee, still laughing and joking, walked away together. Vang Chou climbed on his bicycle for the ride across Alternate, past the general's house, to his home. He had promised his wife to work on their fish pond before bedtime.

Like all Hmong in Long Chieng, Chou watched the activities at Vang Pao's house. The general's Hmong-style house was being replaced by a two-story block structure. The new house would function as home for Vang Pao's growing family, tribal headquarters, guest house, communal dining hall, funeral home, and Region II military headquarters.

*   *   *

At dawn the next morning, Vang Chou, as usual, discussed with the AOC commander Hmong reports of enemy movement and helped chart schedules for the day's Raven flights. Soon Ly Lue lifted off Alternate, heading for Vientiane and minor repairs on his plane. Chou and Sam followed him off the field.

With Sam in the left seat and Chou in the right, they flew into the grayness of the early morning for another long and dangerous day searching for the enemy. By noon, Sam and Chou had successfully marked two strikes and refueled at Alternate for the afternoon flight. As the afternoon wore on, Chou flew the plane from the right seat. Sam seemed exhausted and pushed his seat back to relax and rest his eyes. Chou watched the weather and the time. He did not want to be late for the rendezvous with Ly Lue. As three o'clock approached, he headed toward heavily defended Ban Ban on Route 7.

Over the rendezvous site, Chou flew slowly at about 500 feet, looking for trucks. They were there just as he had predicted. Five of them. He radioed Ly Lue. No answer. He called again and again to Chaophakaow Lead. No answer. Chou knew that Ly Lue would come. He always kept his word. While keeping the five trucks in sight, he looked for more targets and noticed two bunkers dug into two facing hillsides. "I flew closer to see at least three 50 caliber machine guns. I radioed again to Ly Lue to tell him I had more than trucks; I had an NVA gun position. Still no answer.

"Stalling for time until Ly Lue flew into the area, I flew low over the NVA machine gun positions one more time. Midway in my second pass, machine gun fire burst through the plane, up through my body, through my right arm, through my chest, through the windshield. Blood and flesh splattered Sam and the cockpit control panel. Stunned but conscious, I realized I was critically wounded. I was bleeding heavily from my mouth.

"With the wind howling through the ragged hole in the windshield and not knowing the extent of the plane's damage, I told Sam to shoot all the smoke rockets. After he fired the rockets, Sam managed to find two morphine tablets for me.

"Sam was scared. We were both covered with blood. Sam took over the controls and radioed Cricket: 'We've been hit! My man General Direction is critical!' Cricket responded, 'Can you make it to Korat? There's a hospital there.' I knew Korat was more than two hours from our position. I shouted to Sam over the noise of the wind, 'No! Not Korat! No gas! Too far! I can't make it to Korat! Take me to Sam Thong!' The American voice from Cricket said: 'OK, do as he wants.'" With the cover of two Skyraiders, Sam flew Vang Chou in the damaged aircraft to Sam Thong where massive blood transfusions and surgery kept him alive.

Ly Lue never arrived for the Ban Ban rendezvous. In Vientiane, the American mechanic working on Ly Lue's T-28 had not finished with repairs until almost dark.

In the weeks that Vang Chou was hospitalized, Sam visited his man, General Direction, several times, bringing him gifts of canned fruit juice, considered a special treat in Laos. At the Sam Thong hospital, Chou was cared for by his wife and Moua Lia's wife, the Yang sisters, and by Hmong nurses trained under Pop Buell's program. Moua Lia and Vang Chou were first cousins, and each had married one of the Yang sisters, originally from North Vietnam. After this crisis, their friendship became closer.

A few weeks after General Direction was hit, Sam went to Saigon to pick up another Cessna to replace the damaged one. On his return trip, he was shot down over the Ho Chi Minh Trail. Officially reported missing in action on September 6, 1968, Sam Deichelman was never seen again.

Vang Chou's wounds resulted in permanent damage to his right arm and hand. His loss to the FAC roster came at a time when Hmong FAC pilots were desperately needed for the ever-increasing air war. After his release from the hospital, Chou tried several times to return to flying, but his attempts to fly a spotter plane with only his left hand were unsuccessful. Never one to surrender to adversity, Chou finally had to admit that his days as a Raven backseater were over. He would eventually be promoted to lieutenant colonel in the Royal Lao Army and until the end of the American involvement he would work with General Vang Pao, the American Embassy's air attachés in Vientiane, and the SKY air operations personnel to direct air strikes flown by Lao, Hmong, and American pilots.

12.

Vang Pao Goes to Washington

. . . Vang Pao is the head of the Meo [Hmong] irregular forces, now consisting of over 22,000 men, which have been the backbone of the resistance to Communist infiltration in Northern Laos. . . . They have killed or wounded during the nine months to 1 August 1968 a total of some 3,500 of the enemy at losses of 1,500 to themselves. Vang Pao is one of the two Lao "fighting generals" as well as being a most effective leader of his people. He is well thought of by both the King and Souvanna Phouma. Although he is primarily interested in the defense of his people and their highland living areas, he recognizes that in the long run the Meo will have to become integrated with the rest of Laos society and has already taken considerable steps to this end, including educating the young children in the Lao language and teaching them allegiance to the King.

—Richard Helms, Director of the CIA, writing to Walt W. Rostow, Special Assistant to President Johnson, introducing General Vang Pao, September 25, 1968

By 1968 everyone in Military Region II—soldiers, farmers, schoolteachers, students—was involved in the fight to defend Hmong homelands. Fathers killed in firefights were replaced by their sons, sometimes 11 and 12 years old. For Hmong soldiers there would be none of the glitter and tinsel of "R&R" trips given U.S. fighting men to glamorous, exotic cities and vacation retreats. In Region II, there was only war.

Widows married their brothers-in-law in tribal custom so they would have protection and not have to give up their children. Villagers, denied their fields by the communists, faced chronic malnutrition and sometimes starvation. Boys as tall as a carbine became "carbine soldiers" and abandoned school to fight. Other boys, shorter and younger, volunteered as cooks' helpers and went to the battlefields.

One was Vang Xeu, who had been in primary school when the North Vietnamese had threatened his village in 1953. Now, at age 13, he volunteered to fight. "Everyone knew that Vang Pao had been a soldier at 13, so many young boys volunteered to fight to protect our land. I was a small, weak boy but determined to help my people. After three months training in Pitsanoulouk in Thailand, we were sent back to Laos to fight. In my first fight, I discovered that I couldn't shoot my weapon by hand-holding it; it was too heavy. I had to find a rock or tree to steady it on before firing. That was dangerous. So, I asked General Vang Pao if I could be a paratrooper. He agreed and I trained for that. On my first jump, I was so light that I floated and floated and came down far from my unit. To solve my floating problem, the next time I jumped with a B-40 grenade launcher. That brought me down. But once on the ground, I wasn't strong enough to operate the B-40 effectively. I asked Vang Pao if I could be trained in intelligence. He agreed. That was the right place for me."[1]

Many Hmong trained at special camps in Thailand, at places called Hua Hin, Pitsanoulouk, and Lopburi, and were instructed by Thai and American soldiers. They learned to parachute, gather intelligence, use codes, operate clandestine radios and sophisticated electronic gear, read maps, chart air strikes, and refine sabotage techniques first learned from the French. Training was minimal, sometimes lasting only weeks or a few months, since these men and boys were needed in the front lines.

There was one bright spot—the new secondary school at Sam Thong. Due to prejudice and discrimination, Hmong students found it almost impossible to gain admission to the Lao higher educational system. General Vang Pao and teacher Moua Lia with help from Pop Buell and Prince Sai Kham decided to revive the Xieng Khouang School which they had abandoned in December 1960. Although they called it Sam Thong College, it was not a college in the American sense. As in the French system, it offered grades six through ten. From its opening in 1968, over the years, several hundred Hmong students would graduate from Sam Thong College and many would go on to earn degrees from colleges and universities in France and the U.S.

Colonel Billy, operating out of his new, large, Western-style, air-conditioned SKY headquarters at Udorn, continued to fret about the increasing Americanization of the war in Laos and the overuse of the Hmong, which resulted in high fatalities and the wounding and crippling of civilians and combatants. He warned American newcomers that "they were forcing the Hmong out of what they did best—pure guerrilla warfare—into a more conventional war which meant more casualties. When we began to helicopter them to fight pitched battles, we got away from what was their greatest capability—which was to hit and run and to use the country which they knew so well."[2] Disillusioned that his counterinsurgency strategy had been abandoned and realizing that the burden being placed on the Hmong would be devastating, Colonel Billy requested and was granted a transfer.

In Paris, Averell Harriman, Johnson's envoy, confronted with the North Vietnamese stalling tactics, failed to accomplish a breakthrough in negotiations before the Democratic Convention. In July, he suggested that Johnson halt all bombing of North Vietnam in an effort to get negotiations started.

Johnson also wanted a breakthrough. If he offered a total cessation of the bombing to induce serious negotiations, he, not trusting Hanoi, needed the capability to electronically monitor North Vietnamese military activities. This brought renewed attention to Northern Warrior Moua Cher Pao's Bouam Loung, Lima Site 32, from where, it was thought, sophisticated electronic equipment could monitor conversations and activities in North Vietnam. By early May, five enemy battalions threatened the Alamo, Lima Site 36, and its 1,500 defenders. SKY advisors reported to Udorn that General Giap intended to take Site 36. A fallback position was needed. Americans studied maps of northern Laos for a defendable location which could be used to monitor NVA activities, to guide air strikes if necessary, and to function as a base from which to launch "black missions" across the border into North Vietnam. American strategists asked question after question about Bouam Loung—just in case the Alamo fell.

Bouam Loung* sat deep in enemy territory. Soldiers operating behind enemy lines often were airlifted out of here by helicopter and then resupplied from this base. Though not as high as Phou Pha Thi, the rim of Bouam Loung at almost 5,000 feet allowed Moua's men to see for miles. From this position, they monitored Routes 6 and 7 coming in from North Vietnam, the enemy's major resupply and weapons infiltration routes.

---

*In the Lao language, Bouam Loung means "mistaken or confused pond" because inside this mountain bowl, natural springs created several ponds—unexpected at the top of a mountain of this altitude. Since most high mountains in Laos had no water source, it was considered a natural mistake to find springs so high, thus its name.

Bouam Loung was only a few miles northwest of Phou San where Lieutenant Gauthier and the Hmong, twenty years earlier, had headquartered for their fight against the Japanese and later the Viet Minh. Now Soviet trucks carried North Vietnamese soldiers with their Soviet and Chinese weapons along these two roads where once Japanese trucks had carried them. Hmong who had patrolled this area in those times, now older, still moved through the high mountainous jungle looking for an opportunity to blow up a convoy just as they had done against the occupying Japanese Imperial Army and later the Viet Minh.

Moua Cher Pao knew his position was vulnerable since it was in enemy territory, but he assured General Vang Pao and his SKY advisors that it was different from Na Khang and Phou Pha Thi. It was not, he believed, compromised by enemy agents, and he intended to ask his followers to defend Bouam Loung to the death. He assembled his defenders, including a representative from each household, to participate in the powerful "drinking of the water" ceremony, in which, one by one, the defenders drank water from a special vessel, binding them together in the defense of this position no matter what the odds.

After Colonel Billy departed for the U.S., SKY field personnel in Laos increased. Men bearing the code-names Bag, Mr. Clean, Pigpen, Bamboo, Ringo, Digger, Kayak, Mule, Lumberjack, Hardnose, and Redcoat joined Jerry "Hog" Daniels. Some of these men were young and adventuresome; they enjoyed the world of code-names and secret operations. Others were older—more professional, they thought—with experience from other wars and other exotic places. All were thrust into a world of shadows where the distinctions between warrior and outcast, patriot and mercenary became confused. All claimed they were "can-do" men and proudly believed that they, in fact, could do anything. Many were unfamiliar with the Hmong, their backgrounds, and their capabilities. Some had lost sight of, or perhaps never knew, the original American goals in Laos.

As more SKY men arrived at Long Chieng, their quarters grew. More antennas sprouted from the SKY headquarters. There were more comings and goings by Americans, who walked up the hill near Vang Pao's house to talk to the SKY men. The Americans were concerned about the lack of courage and discipline of the Royal Lao Army whose troops often ran when the enemy approached, abandoning post after post and leaving behind ammunition, weapons, medical supplies, communications equipment, and food. Time and again the task of retaking key positions, abandoned by Royal Lao troops, fell to General Vang Pao and his "special forces," who suffered many casualties in the process.

The harder Vang Pao defended his territory, the more aggressive became the NVA strikes against his troops. Vang Pao's primary goal remained to retake the Plaine des Jarres, then push the North Vietnamese back through the Nong Het pass—back to North Vietnam.

Attempts to kill or capture White Star, one of Vang Pao's code-names, consumed the enemy and worried the Americans. Vang Pao knew there was an extraordinary price on his head, but paid little attention. The Soviets had assured the Americans in Vientiane that they did not intend to kill Vang Pao because without him they reasoned the Hmong could not be controlled. That did not deter Hanoi's desire to eliminate him. Vang Pao's SKY advisors constantly sought to keep him out of dangerous military situations—an impossible task. He remained his own man—stubborn, sometimes irascible, and sometimes taking poor advice—much to the consternation of the Americans. While communists called Vang Pao the American puppet, those who worked with him knew well that he was no one's puppet. He was feisty, determined, and in the end did what he thought had to be done even if it meant defying everyone, including the American Ambassador in Vientiane.

Vang Pao was undeterred by danger and always wanted to be with his men on the front lines, even though he had been seriously wounded once and crash-landed many times. During the repeated shellings of Long Chieng, his house never took a serious hit. Often he and his assistants worked there during attacks, confident that they were safe. He only used the bunkers near his headquarters when the shelling was heavy.

Having escaped death so often, Vang Pao came to believe that his life was protected. Unlike many Lao soldiers, he wore no Buddha images or amulets for protection. In the field, he dressed simply, often not even wearing his general's stars. Everyone knew who he was. He needed no insignia.

While Touby LyFong remained a respected elder Hmong chieftain, Vang Pao, as a general with enormous influence with the Americans and often with the Lao, clearly was the man making decisions for the Hmong. Few Americans were aware of the dimensions of Vang Pao's civil responsibilities to his people. The moral and ethical obligations of his two roles weighed heavily on him. These he bore alone. No Americans could advise him on his Hmong duties.

Some short-timers in Laos, unfamiliar with Hmong culture, misjudged Vang Pao and labeled him a warlord, as did his enemies. While it was true that Vang Pao was unpredictable, emotional, quick-tempered, tough on his troops, and often extremely harsh with his enemies, he constantly sought to honor the trust his people had given him—no easy task in the milieu of a nasty war, conducted in a brutal manner, with complex and vacillating political dimensions beyond his control.

Since it was Vang Pao who had convinced the clan leaders to fight with American assistance and since they, in turn, had recruited others to join the irregulars, it was Vang Pao's responsibility to take care of those who followed him. The role of a Hmong chief is to lead, to demonstrate Hmong values, and to provide for and look after those who follow. This last required wealth. Vang Pao was not a wealthy man; he had been a soldier all his life.

The U.S. funded the Royal Lao Army through congressional appropriations and the CIA funded the irregular forces, so Vang Pao's personal lack of financial resources was usually not a problem. SKY provided him with a contingency fund to carry out his dual functions of military and tribal leader. His enemies said he was corrupt and misused American funds. Those who worked closely with him remain convinced he was not corrupt—that his troops and his people were actually the principal beneficiaries of U.S. funds.

By 1968, Vang Pao, fearing U.S. aid might cease, decided to store arms for the day when the Hmong might have to operate on their own. He bulldozed a field at the northern end of Alternate into a supply depot. Munitions were stockpiled between two purple karsts near the USAID building.

Vang Pao's new two-story house east of the runway at Alternate dwarfed the other dwellings. While it was grand for Hmong housing, it was also quite simple and functioned much like a Native American long house. The balconies in the style of southern France, its distinguishing feature, protected the interior from the intense tropical sun. Here, as he had done in the other house, he served meals to his field officers, Hmong pilots, clan leaders, SKY advisors, USAID workers, and all visitors—official and ordinary.

After the 1968 Democratic Convention in Chicago, General Vang Pao accepted an official but secret invitation from the CIA to visit the United States. On hand to greet Vang Pao was his old friend Colonel Billy. The two men did not talk about the things they had spoken of in the past. Now they talked about schooling for the Hmong and about their own children. Vang Pao had more than a dozen. Colonel Billy took him on a tour of Disneyland and Colonial Williamsburg in Virginia. Vang Pao did not like Disneyland. Maybe its unreality reminded him of wartime Laos—the Land of Oz. He was impressed with Williamsburg because what he saw there was the same kind of life that his people were living now. He wanted to learn how the people of Williamsburg progressed so quickly. He wanted the same thing to happen to his people.

Another host was Colonel "Heine" Aderholt, now at Eglin Air Force Base in Florida. The men were delighted to see each other. Aderholt and his wife, Jessie, feted the general with an outdoor barbeque attended by about 100 people, many of whom had worked in Laos. Jessie Aderholt entertained Nhia Thao, the general's senior wife, by demonstrating her dishwasher, washing machine, and electric stove. Dressed in a Lao sarong skirt and high-heeled shoes, Nhia Thao looked more Lao than Hmong.[3] Vang Pao, wearing a dark suit, white shirt, tie, and black shoes, seemed uncomfortable out of his fatigues or dress uniform. On the battlefield, where he was totally in charge, he was a commanding figure. Visiting tourist sites in the U.S., he appeared narrow-shouldered, small, and shy.

On October 1, 1968, in secret meetings, Vang Pao visited with Johnson White House officials, including Special Assistant to the President Walt Rostow. These were heady days for this tribal man, born on a remote mountain in Laos with only a few years formal education, now talking with the leaders of one of the most powerful countries in the world. He considered his invitation to the White House a high honor and a recognition of the extraordinary relationship and friendship that he perceived existed between the government of the U.S. and the Hmong. Following Hmong etiquette, Vang Pao brought a gift for President Johnson—a handcrafted Hmong rifle.

His jubilant return to Laos was dampened when he learned that the communist forces now had 200 radar-guided antiaircraft positions in Laos and longer-range and more accurate artillery. He complained to the Americans that he was outgunned and outnumbered by enemy forces. He needed more "air" to give his troops an advantage.

On October 31, 1968, President Johnson, hoping that Hanoi would agree to peace negotiations, announced a complete halt to "all air, naval, and artillery bombardment of North Vietnam." Communications intercepts obtained from Bouam Loung allowed the U.S. the critical capability to listen in on Hanoi's military leaders.

On November 5, Richard M. Nixon was elected President of the United States. A few days later, President Johnson wrote a thank-you note to General Vang Pao on White House stationery. "I very much appreciate your kindness in giving me the handsome flintlock Meo rifle. I will cherish it as a reminder of a brave people and a gallant leader who are determined to defend their freedom with whatever weapons are at hand. It is that kind of courage which is the ultimate guarantee of freedom." It was dated November 14, 1968, and was signed "LBJ."[4]

In December, Vang Pao moved against the enemy holding Phou Pha Thi, Lima Site 85. When his troops stalled under heavy enemy fire, 7th Air Force allocated 50 sorties a day for five days.[5]

Daily, Ly Lue bored through the clear skies, heading for Sam Neua Province and the scarred cliff of Lima Site 85 to support Hmong on the ground. In less than two years since he had earned his wings, Ly Lue had flown several thousand combat sorties, an extraordinary feat. On Phou Pha Thi enemy gunners, monitoring Hmong radios, knew that Ly Lue led the air strikes. On the third day of the battle, Ly Lue's plane was hit. He managed to get his canopy open, stand up, and roll over the side of his T-28. His plane exploded into a fireball. Rescued quickly by Air America, Ly Lue was returned to Long Chieng. He was airborne the next day in a new plane. This shootdown changed Ly Lue's attitude. He confided to his friends that it was not the same any more; he had a new plane, but it didn't respond like the old one.

In late December, Air America Captain Fred Walker flew to Alternate to say a quiet good-bye to General Vang Pao. He told him he was being transferred to Bangkok. Vang Pao expressed great disappointment. Only months before, Colonel Billy had departed; now Captain Fred, whom he had known for nine years, was leaving. As a parting gift, Vang Pao gave Walker a magnificent silver Hmong necklace weighing almost four pounds.[6]

On January 16, 1969, four days before Richard Nixon's inauguration, American and North Vietnamese negotiators in Paris announced that an agreement on the shape of the conference table had been reached. The table would be round.

Men like Averell Harriman, Michael Forrestal, Roger Hilsman, Robert McNamara, McGeorge Bundy, and Walt Rostow who had set in motion the Kennedy plan for Laos were gone. Nixon replaced them with individuals who had no personal experience with Laos, General Vang Pao, or the Hmong. Like those preceding him, the man in the Nixon administration primarily responsible for determining the fate of Laos and the Hmong would be a man whose main focus was Europe—Henry A. Kissinger. Kissinger was appointed national security advisor and later secretary of state. This Harvard professor would replace Harriman at the round table in Paris as Nixon's chief negotiator.

By late February 1969, communist troops again threatened the Alamo with its TACAN facility and staging base for air search and rescue operations. Enemy forces pinned down the Hmong and their SKY advisors. Then the SKY were finally evacuated. U.S. planes from Thai bases tried unsuccessfully to bomb the enemy from its perimeters. Finally, on March 1, after all Hmong and Lao officers had been killed, the remaining forces fled. Na Khang, the Alamo, which Hmong had fought so hard to hold for so many years, had fallen.

With Na Khang lost, search and rescue operations staged out of Long Chieng and Bouam Loung became Vang Pao's northernmost major position. A TACAN was installed at Bouam Loung to guide strike sorties, resupply, and photo surveillance missions.

Jerry "Hog" Daniels, who had been operating out of the Alamo, moved to Bouam Loung. Lo Ma, now 22 and one of the best Hmong ground air controllers, became Daniels' radio man. Daniels had an ability to understand Hmong, but he could only speak a few words. Lo Ma, who spoke good English, functioned as his interpreter and liaison with the Hmong. They set up a command bunker at Bouam Loung and dug "holes" for themselves, knowing that the NVA had no intention of backing off on their threat to eliminate Moua Cher Pao's position.[7]

While Hmong considered their defense of Bouam Loung as critical, it is doubtful that they knew the importance of the electronic surveillance equipment they guarded. The intelligence gathered from the Bouam Loung installation would be so important that a direct National Security Agency hookup was made. A U.S. intelligence officer who knew the quality of these intercepts later verified the importance of the Bouam Loung listening post. "The military information gathered at Bouam Loung about Hanoi's plans saved the lives of many American soldiers fighting in South Vietnam. This was another major Hmong contribution to us. By keeping Lima Site 32 operating so we could monitor the enemy, they saved the lives of American fighting men in South Vietnam. The Hmong should be very proud of this accomplishment."[8]

To dislodge the intrepid Moua Cher Pao from Bouam Loung had for years been a major NVA military objective. Year after year, NVA soldiers boasted over their field radios that they would take Bouam Loung. Their boasts remained hollow. The ability of the Bouam Loung defenders to continue to exist inside enemy territory became a psychological defeat for the NVA and a source of considerable pride for the Hmong. Now that Na Khang had fallen, the NVA and the Pathet Lao increased pressure on Bouam Loung.

It was during this time that General Vang Pao announced to the Americans in Vientiane that his people had earned the right to be called

"Hmong" rather than "Meo," as was the American inclination. An American intelligence officer with Vang Pao at the time remembered his announcement. "It was late one night—about 3 or 4 in the morning—after Vang Pao had finished a brilliant briefing to an Air Force officer at the embassy in Vientiane, when he announced, 'The time has come to call my people Hmong.' He explained that the word 'Meo' meant slave in Chinese. [While the word in Chinese does not mean slave per se, the Hmong who had fled China because of mistreatment and slavery hated the Chinese term for them. It might as well have meant slave.] He told us that he had thought about this for some time and had decided that when his people had made major accomplishments, then it would be time to ask everyone to call them by their proper name. According to Vang Pao, the time had now come and he asked that the Americans call his people 'Hmong.'"[9]

Such was not to happen, however. The Americans and the Lao continued to use the word "Meo." With the flux in American personnel, the numbers of short-termers assigned to Laos, and the Lao insistence on using the word "Meo," the transition to "Hmong" did not come during the American period but only after the Americans had departed and the Hmong were refugees.

Part Four

The Nixon-Kissinger Years

13.

Men of Courage

Many Hmong died trying to rescue the American pilots who were
shot down. Often the communists had already captured the pilots or
killed them. So, the communists hid their positions waiting for
Vang Pao's soldiers to come to the area. They knew we would come
and then they could kill us. Many Hmong died like this, trying to
save the Americans.

—Sgt. Moua Paje, a Hmong soldier with Vang Pao's forces who
helped rescue downed American pilots

The war in Laos produced many Hmong heroes. None typified this heroism better than Lt. Ly Lue, Sgt. Moua Paje, and Vang Kai.

Soon after the capture of Na Khang, communist forces moved toward
Vang Pao's headquarters at Long Chieng. Furious that Na Khang had
fallen, he proposed a bold plan to retake the Plaine des Jarres. The U.S.
Mission in Vientiane did not share the general's enthusiasm. Most of his
advisors thought that it would be impossible to push the NVA and Pathet
Lao from their large and heavily defended positions on the Plaine des
Jarres. Vang Pao insisted, however, and on March 23 a scaled-down version of his original U.S. air-supported battle plan went into effect. American pilots flew 730 sorties against PDJ targets. Lao and Hmong T-28
pilots bombed day after day in support of ground forces. Moua Cher
Pao's men from Bouam Loung fought a rear action and interdiction behind enemy lines.

The general's intelligence teams reported an enemy buildup near
Muong Soui, Site 108, the high plateau Lao town that sat just at the edge
of the Plaine des Jarres on the road to Luang Prabang, the royal capital.
Muong Soui was defended by 4,000 Neutralist troops whose reputation

for cowardice was a subject for joking among Hmong soldiers. The Hmong had never forgiven Kong Le and his Neutralists for joining the Pathet Lao and NVA in 1960. The Americans believed that if Muong Soui fell it would be a serious defeat for Souvanna Phouma's Royal Lao government. To stiffen the Muong Soui defenses, Thailand, with urging from the U.S., sent a 300-man artillery unit.

In March 1969 Nixon approved, without public discussion, bombing of North Vietnamese and Viet Cong sanctuaries in Cambodia, which he believed necessary to enable the South Vietnamese Army to hold its own against the communists. When this became public, a fire storm of protests resulted. This action became known as Nixon's "secret bombing of Cambodia." In May, Nixon proposed a simultaneous withdrawal of both U.S. and NVA forces from South Vietnam. Then, on June 8, he announced the unilateral withdrawal of 25,000 U.S. troops from South Vietnam. Several months later, he announced that an additional 35,000 would be withdrawn.

Swept up in the escalating war in Laos and the death of so many of his men, General Vang Pao listened numbly to BBC radio reports of Nixon's steps toward U.S. military disengagement in Southeast Asia— the de-Americanization of the war which became known as "Vietnamization." Nixon's announcements seemed to Vang Pao to overlook the fact that infiltration of North Vietnamese troops and supplies into the South through Laos continued to increase, as did the North Vietnamese presence in his country. How could the U.S. withdraw its support when the fighting in Laos was worse than ever? What would Nixon's Vietnamization and disengagement mean for Laos? But Nixon said little about Laos. Colonel Billy was no longer around to answer questions. Ambassador William Sullivan had left Laos in mid-March. His replacement, G. McMurtrie Godley, had not yet arrived. Vang Pao could not discuss these political issues or what was really happening in Washington with any of the other paramilitary SKY advisors assigned to Region II. They were either too young, too long in Asia, or too uninterested in international politics. He was certain about one thing: whatever Washington was up to, it was all *"politique,"* following his penchant for employing French when using diplomatic terminology. The general was correct, although he knew nothing of Henry Kissinger's intentions to establish secret negotiations with Hanoi.

NVA tanks approached Muong Soui. Vang Pao and the Hmong were again needed to bolster the frightened Lao troops. As always, the burden on the Hmong would be heavy, this time particularly so.

On June 24, 1969, NVA, with tanks, attacked Muong Soui, immediately capturing some artillery and controlling the landing strip. When the fighting died down, U.S. helicopters extracted the frightened Neutralists and the Thai artillery unit. The NVA victors bunkered in to stay at Muong Soui.

After this incident, the Thai, fearing that their troops would be captured in Laos with negative international repercussions, withdrew their regular units and switched to recruiting "volunteers." The Thai involvement in Laos grew as a result of the U.S.-sponsored Vietnamization process in South Vietnam. The U.S. worked secretly with Thailand for a "Thaization" of the Lao theatre. "Arrangements for the actual recruiting of Thais were made at the Ambassadorial level in Bangkok. These arrangements were then translated into quotas which were assigned to the various Royal Thai Army units. It was then up to the unit commander to fill the quota. Most frequently, squads, platoons, or whole companies volunteered as units. These volunteers were then sent to a CAS [CIA] training center at Koke Kathiem, where they were organized into battalions and Mobile Groups. While serving in Laos, these troops received regular pay, benefits, longevity, promotions, and a substantial pay supplement."[1]

The loss of Muong Soui was significant. The Lao government needed this strategic village with its airfield. On July 1, about 1,000 Lao troops with U.S. air support were committed to rout the NVA from Muong Soui. At the critical time, the Lao troops failed to move and bad weather kept most U.S. air support grounded in Thailand. General Vang Pao announced that he alone would retake Muong Soui. He would use his own Hmong "air"—his "flying artillery," as he called strike aircraft. His Hmong pilots would dislodge the entrenched NVA.

His reliance on his T-28 pilots had grown to an obsession. He often personally directed his T-28 pilots on bombing missions. Some critics say that he depended too much on "air." On the other hand, air support was available and extremely useful against the superior forces of the North Vietnamese. He believed his Hmong pilots were braver and more accurate than the Lao, the Thai, and even the American pilots. The Hmong pilots agreed with him. Since they flew to protect their own people and their own country, they considered it a fight to the death. Defeat was unthinkable.

This day, the general directed an attack against an enemy mountain command post near Muong Soui. He radioed Long Chieng for a T-28 strike against bunkered-in NVA. Ly Lue and Vang Sue responded, scrambling two T-28s already loaded and waiting at Alternate. Ly Lue, flying as Chaophakaow Lead, lifted off, followed by his wingman, Vang Sue, who had little combat experience. The veteran pilot dared the communists to shoot him down, taking risks far exceeding those of American pilots flying in Laos. Almost daily he dove his T-28, strafing and bombing the enemy. Disregarding the danger to his own life, he always responded when his fellow Hmong were under attack.

Standing at a 3,000-foot-high vantage point that overlooked enemy positions, Vang Pao talked by radio to Ly Lue, directing him to a precise position. Ly Lue approached the target with assurance and dove with a strafing and bomb run against the NVA. As he pulled up, Vang Pao observed the results of the strike through field glasses. He shouted to Ly Lue that he had not hit the NVA command bunker. The enemy was in the bunker, Vang Pao told his T-28 pilot. "There are lots of enemy in the bunker. Go again, Ly Lue! Go again!" the general shouted.

Ly Lue answered that he did not have the proper ordnance to penetrate an entrenched position. He told Vang Pao he would fly to Vientiane, load up with the big bombs needed to destroy a bunker, and return. Instead of listening to his most experienced pilot, Vang Pao ordered Ly Lue to go around again. Ly Lue protested, but Vang Pao commanded he go in now and go in low—very low—and get the damned North Vietnamese in the bunker.

"Don't be afraid, Ly Lue. Don't be afraid. I'm praying for you. Go low! Go low! Now! Lower! Lower, Ly Lue! I'm praying for you!" Vang Pao shouted over the radio to his pilot. Devoted to his commander, Ly Lue dove his plane directly at the NVA bunker with his wing guns firing. Over the target, he dropped his remaining two bombs. It was a good hit. As he was pulling up, a buried and previously undetected NVA gun fired directly at him.

From his mountain post, Vang Pao's bravado shouts of congratulations ceased. Ly Lue's plane, climbing skyward, appeared out of control and heading into enemy territory. "Ly Lue, south! Head south! Ly Lue! South!" Vang Pao screamed over his radio. If Ly Lue were to parachute or crash in NVA territory, the North Vietnamese would torture him most cruelly, for he was known as the best Hmong pilot and responsible for heavy damage to communist convoys and positions.

There was no answer. The plane, out of control and losing altitude, made lazy half-circles in the sky, still heading for enemy terrain. Vang Pao shouted again and again, begging his pilot to head south to friendly territory. Slowly the disabled plane stopped its confused meandering and headed south. As General Vang Pao watched, it headed directly toward his position, crashing only a few hundred feet from him.

Vang Pao and his men bolted to the plane. Ly Lue, mangled by the impact, still gripped the controls. They tried desperately to free his body from the wreckage, but could not. Vang Pao stared incredulously at his dead pilot. Ly Lue was not dressed in the familiar gray-green American-style flight suit. He wore his formal khaki dress uniform with all his medals. Vang Pao began to cry. Ly Lue, who was up for promotion to captain, had been about to leave the operations center with Vang Chou to have photographs taken for their promotion files when Vang Pao's order came for a scramble of T-28s. Ly Lue had jumped into his plane without changing into his flight suit.

Sobbing, General Vang Pao radioed for assistance in evacuating his finest pilot. He flew back to Alternate. Even there, with many of his soldiers around him, he found it difficult to stay the tears. A Lao Army officer who happened to be at Long Chieng warned him it would be bad for his men's morale to see him cry, but the warning had no effect. Vang Chou also saw the general's grief and offered advice: "In this war, we are all throwing water. Some of us will get wet. It must be so." The general looked at Vang Chou, his former backseater now disabled, another of his finest men, nodded his head in agreement, and turned away.

Crowds of Hmong came to pay their respects to Ly Lue, their hero, the Hmong ace. After the traditional Hmong ceremonies conducted by relatives and friends, after the wailing and touching of Ly Lue by his relatives, after the pipe and the drum had directed his spirit, came the journey to the pilot burial grounds.

Ly Lue's casket, covered with an elaborate handmade tower of brightly colored paper flowers, was gently lifted onto the open bed of a truck to join his wife, Vang You, his four children, and other family members. On foot, preceding the truck, other pilots, Hmong commanders, and more relatives led the procession. Vang Seng, Nhia's pilot husband, had flown in from Udorn where he was nearing completion of his T-28 training. Dressed in his flight suit, he walked near the head of the funeral parade. Nhia, pregnant with her second child, hoped she would never have to travel the dirt path around Alternate to the grave site to bury Vang Seng. Lo Ma, who had come to pay respects to his former teacher, followed behind Vang Seng. Moua Lia, who had trudged over the mountain ridge from Sam Thong, joined the SKY men and a representative from the U.S. Air Attaché's office in the U.S. Embassy in Vientiane, who carried a large wreath. The Americans, standing awkwardly tall amidst the Hmong, seemed out of place with their long noses, whitish skin, gangly arms and legs, and ill-fitting clothes. Vang Pao led the procession. The ceremonial journey moved slowly along the small dirt access road running beside Alternate. It crossed the end of the runway where Ly Lue had landed his T-28 thousands of times, then it doubled back to the other side, past the hospital, and wound up the hill to the burial site.

Vang Pao personally oversaw the lowering of Ly Lue's elaborate coffin, with its ornate corners resembling up-turned Buddhist temple roofs, into the red earth. When it came to rest he walked to the edge of the grave, looked down at the coffin, and gave a slow salute in farewell.

No Hmong could forget the legendary bravery of Ly Lue—the first Hmong ace—and his mystical, ominous crash in full dress uniform at the feet of the general who had directed his last mission. Ly Lue's logbook recording over 5,000 missions was given to his family.

General Vang Pao's grief over the death of Ly Lue converted into what most considered an outrageous plan to obtain his military goal: retake all the Plaine des Jarres from the North Vietnamese and push them back across the border. By eliminating the NVA from Laos, Vang Pao could avenge Ly Lue's death.

*   *   *

Vang Pao and his senior officers studied the map of the Plaine des Jarres. The NVA occupied the area where once Lt. Maurice Gauthier and Free French forces clandestinely operated with the Hmong to oust the Japanese Army. Vang Pao thought about Lima Lima, not far from Xieng Khouang town, where the French had built an airfield. It was unusable, grown over by grass and pocked with bomb craters. The French hangars had been destroyed, exposing old shell casings once stored there. He knew well this airfield and its surrounding trenches and fortifications. He had helped dig them. A few nautical miles to the north of Lima Lima was Khang Khay, the Neutralist capital created by Kong Le and Souvanna Phouma in the early 1960s. The Chinese Cultural Mission in Khang Khay, although a known enemy storage area, had been placed off limits to U.S. air strikes by the U.S. Embassy in Vientiane.

General Vang Pao's unfolding plan to take Lima Lima called for Lao government troops to reestablish a presence on the southern edges of the Plaine des Jarres while his soldiers disrupted enemy supplies to the north. Hmong operating out of Bouam Loung would work behind enemy lines to harass the enemy and to interdict enemy supply lines, particularly Route 7. With supply lines cut, NVA troops on the PDJ could be isolated. Then Vang Pao would strike. Using his "flying artillery" to force the enemy into a retreat, he would deploy, by air, additional troops to occupy terrain and establish a Royal Lao government presence on the Plaine des Jarres. He called this mission "Operation About Face." Of course, it was risky to launch such a major offensive during the monsoon season, when heavy rains and violent weather could ground air support. But the rainy season was also a time for enemy trucks and tanks to get bogged down in the mud. While his special forces excelled at penetrating enemy territory and locating enemy missiles, guns, tanks and convoys, they needed assistance in destroying them. Vang Pao again needed "air." The U.S. Air Force promised 200 sorties daily, diverting them from Barrel Roll, to support Lao-based T-28s.

In early August, Vang Pao gave the signal to retake the PDJ. Operation About Face was launched. Hmong operating out of San Chiau, Lima Site 2, Phou Vieng, Lima Site 6, and Bouam Loung, Lima Site 32, attacked enemy supply lines, disappearing into the jungle to strike again and again.

While thousands of men on the ground moved through rain and foul weather, many of Barrel Roll's 200 committed daily sorties were not flown because of the monsoons. By mid-August, the weather improved enough to permit the 200 sorties a day. Enemy gunners fired at friendly pilots as they attacked. Planes were shot down. Hundreds of Americans and Thais and thousands of Hmong participated in About Face, including Sgt. Moua Paje, one of two known survivors of his original unit.

Moua Paje had joined the French military as a boy of about 13 or 14—as he remembered, as soon as he was able to shoot a gun. Now almost 30, stout, and just over five feet tall, he manned a shoulder-held 57mm mortar. Repeated firing of this weapon would render him partially deaf. He was often dropped behind enemy lines in small spy or sabotage groups. Men like Moua Paje who worked behind enemy lines called themselves by the Lao words *Tahaan Su Tai*—"soldiers willing to die." Others called them *men of courage.*

Moua Paje and his team of 30 manned a mountain position near Khang Khay, overlooking the fighting on the Plaine des Jarres. He watched an A1-E Skyraider bomb an enemy position. Suddenly over the radio Sergeant Moua heard the excited voice of the American pilot calling SKY for more planes! More T-28s! More bombs! As the Skyraider pilot called for help, he made another pass over the target. NVA guns ripped through his plane. Almost immediately, Sergeant Moua saw two parachutes. "The pilots jumped from their plane directly into enemy territory. Moua Pha, our team leader, ordered us to run to the pilots. We picked up our radio and weapons and ran, watching the parachutes to see exactly where the pilots would land. We knew that the enemy also watched the parachutes. Maybe they would be there first and ambush us. Moua Pha urged us to run faster."[2]

After running for about an hour and a half, they neared the parachutes. They looked for signs or sounds of Vietnamese soldiers, but noticed nothing unusual. "That worried us. We knew there were many Vietnamese soldiers in this area. Then we came to an open space. As we started across it, the Vietnamese opened fire on us, seriously wounding four of our team. The Vietnamese had been waiting for us. They knew we would come to save the American pilots."

Sergeant Moua and his men dropped to the ground, crawling and scrambling for cover. For over an hour they fought the Vietnamese force. Then they decided to retreat since they were so outnumbered. They slipped back into the jungle to discuss what to do and to tend to the four wounded men. "From our position, we could see the two parachutes. At first, we thought we should retreat because the Vietnamese forces were too great for us. As we talked, we all watched the parachutes and wondered if the Americans might be alive. Then we discussed some more. We said that either we die or the pilots die—one or the other will die. We didn't know if the pilots were alive or not, but we had to take the risk to see. We decided that we had to make a second attempt—and we would take our wounded along.

"Now it was between life and death for us. First we had to fight the Vietnamese force. We found the enemy and watched them. We concluded that they thought they had defeated us. So we attacked. We fought hard for about 30 minutes. Then quietness. We moved forward slowly expecting an ambush, but all we saw was blood on the trails, leading into the jungle. Still we waited for an ambush, but none came. Then we realized the Vietnamese had run away."

Those not wounded raced toward the parachutes, hoping they were the first to arrive. The wounded lagged behind, having spent their last energies in the fire fight.

The men cautiously approached one parachute hanging in a tree, anticipating an ambush. They moved closer and closer. Still only quiet. Finally, one of them called out the password, "Tahaan Vang Pao!" [soldiers of Vang Pao]. A voice speaking Thai answered, "Is it true or not? Are you Vang Pao soldiers?" Sergeant Moua and his men quickly assured him that they were soldiers of Vang Pao. "Our leader asked him if the other pilot was Thai as well. He said the other pilot was an American and pointed to where he thought the American had landed."

Sixteen Hmong stayed with the Thai pilot to protect him while ten men, including Sergeant Moua, took off running to find the American. "We ran for another few minutes before finding the second parachute. We could see no one. I wondered if the Vietnamese had already captured him. We waited and listened. No noise. Then we had no choice. We had to call out the code words identifying ourselves as Vang Pao soldiers as we moved closer. Then we saw him, hiding behind a big tree, a pistol in his hands, pointing it at us. The American pilot didn't say anything. Our leader continued saying the code words—'Tahaan Vang Pao.' Maybe the American hadn't learned the code-words, or maybe he didn't believe us. He motioned for only one man to come toward him. We asked each other who was going to volunteer. We didn't know if he would shoot us or take us prisoner. I was brave and young then, so I volunteered.

"I walked slowly toward him with my M-16 pointed toward the ground. When I got close to him, he shouted, 'Number!' and pointed at my gun. I raised my gun slowly, putting the side with the serial number facing him. He took the longest time to look at the serial number. He still pointed his gun at me. He could have killed me at any moment. Finally, he said, 'Vang Pao! Vang Pao!'

"I was happy. I motioned to the other men. Nine of the 16 men approached us. We could not talk English. So with our hands, we told the American that we would carry his things for him, that the enemy was everywhere, and that we had to go immediately."

The team moved out quickly with the Thai and American in the middle to protect them in case of attack. The day was hot and the terrain difficult. After about three hours of walking, the pilots said they could not walk any more. Sergeant Moua and his team insisted that they keep moving because the area belonged to the enemy. They had to reach a safe area to call in a rescue chopper. But the pilots said they could not continue. "We cut sticks for the pilots to help them walk. We were climbing a mountain when they got so tired. One of our men pushed from the back while another one pulled from the front. We thought about carrying them, but they were too big."

Sergeant Moua's team decided they had no choice but to call in a chopper—even in enemy territory. The pilots' inability to continue could mean death for everyone. "We were now in the high jungle near Phou Keng. We sent 20 men to cut an opening and then secure it so the chopper could get in. After we called in the coordinates, we waited for two hours. Then we saw a Raven appear overhead guiding a chopper. The chopper dropped down and picked up the two pilots and took off in a burst of dust."

The rescue chopper had pinpointed the location of Sergeant Moua's team for the enemy. Exhausted and with four seriously wounded in their party, they moved out, hoping to avoid contact with the enemy. "We continued walking, the wounded dragging themselves along. We walked until dark, heading south to try to get away from the enemy. The next dawn, we decided the four wounded men had to get to a hospital. Nine of our team went with them to try to reach the hospital at Sam Thong. Now we were 17 men. Over the radio, we received our new orders. It took us seven days of walking to join our new battalion. Our new position was on Padong." This time, no Hmong had been killed while trying to rescue pilots. On other rescue attempts, Sergeant Moua had seen men die trying to save Americans.

* * *

Aerial reconnaissance showed that the interdiction of fuel and ammunition supplies had caused the enemy to abandon tanks and trucks on the PDJ. Determined to keep the enemy short of supplies, Vang Pao had units staked out along all supply routes, particularly along Route 7 and in the Ban Ban area. Vang Kai, who had joined the Hmong "special forces" a year earlier at age 16, and who would eventually gain the rank of lieutenant, was a member of one of these 100-man units. His unit operated near Lat Sen, not far from Ban Ban. Vang Kai knew it was his duty to rescue American pilots. The order, as he understood it, was to make any sacrifice to get them out. There was never any quibbling about this order. He and other Hmong considered it their duty to save Americans.

NVA forces surrounded Vang Kai's unit. Radios screeched with frightened men calling for "air." American jets responded, swooping in on enemy positions with bombs and strafing runs. During one day of heavy fighting, Vang Kai noticed smoke coming from an American jet. "Two pilots parachuted. Everyone, including the enemy, could see them. As we watched, an urgent message came over our radio: 'Get the American pilots before the Vietnamese!' Quickly coordinates were given to our radio man. It was our turn to rescue Americans.'

"Since there were so many Vietnamese in this area, we knew we would have to fight to get there. We knew we had to be fast to reach the Americans before the Vietnamese did. Our rescue party of 100 started to run. We ran! Fighting! Running! Fighting! More than an hour of running and fighting. We reached the area first, but the Vietnamese were chasing us. One American pilot was hurt from the waist down; the other was also wounded, but could walk. We could not secure the area for the rescue chopper to get in. There were too many Vietnamese—shooting and closing in on us. They would kill us all. We must take the Americans and run. We took turns carrying the one who could not walk. He was big and heavy. We ran, carrying him, until the two men carrying him couldn't run any more. Then two other Hmong would pick him up and run. We ran like this, carrying one wounded American and helping the other. Still the Vietnamese chased us, firing. For several hours, we ran and fought.

"Finally, we outran the Vietnamese and got to the Lat Sen position. We secured the airstrip long enough to call in a chopper to take out the wounded pilots. When we got to Lat Sen, there were only 40 men left in our rescue party. The rest were lost."

Years later when I asked Lt. Vang Kai, who was then living in Montana as a refugee, about the extraordinary loss of Hmong life to save the two Americans, he explained: "When the Americans arrived in Laos, the Hmong respected them and called them 'sir.' We were friends. We had a *ba-sii* ceremony for every American who came to live and work with us. We did everything we could to help the Americans. When the Americans were in trouble, we Hmong made a path with our blood to save them."

There are no public American records of Sergeant Moua's participation in the rescue of two pilots or of the heroic sacrifices of Vang Kai's group to save two other American flyers. It is not likely that these pilots or others rescued by the Hmong ever realized that Hmong lives were sacrificed to save theirs. Data on men missing or killed in Laos remain sketchy. For years, such men killed in Laos were listed as missing or killed in "Southeast Asia," because theoretically the U.S. military was not in Laos. During both the Kennedy and Johnson administrations, there was little official mention of American POWs held in North Vietnam, South Vietnam, or Laos. This silence on POWs lasted until 1969 when Nixon became president. As a result of this secrecy and lack of documents, it is almost impossible to know how many Americans were lost in Laos, or how many saved. The U.S. Defense Department imposed a total blackout on information about American aircraft losses in Laos for almost ten years—from June 7, 1964, to March 10, 1974. There was no concerted U.S. effort to record rescue details. Hmong, of course, kept no formal records; their mission was to get the Americans out quickly and safely, not to record aircraft tail numbers, pilots' names, serial numbers, or their squadron numbers.*

One Hmong who worked as an interpreter and aide to General Vang Pao knew of the American reluctance to keep records on aircraft losses. ''Because the air war in Laos was secret, records of lost aircraft and pilots were also kept secret. I've seen the Americans write the details of crashed planes on their hands with ball point pens. Then spit on their hands and wipe away the losses as if they never happened.''[4]

How many Americans did the Hmong rescue or assist in rescuing? According to General Vang Pao, Hmong soldiers were involved in some way in saving the lives of hundreds of American airmen. While there may be no U.S. archival records of Hmong-assisted rescue, Hmong records of rescues reside vividly in the minds of those who called themselves *Tahaan Su Tai*—soldiers willing to die.

There were many men and boys like Moua Paje and Vang Kai who stoically and with great sacrifice accomplished their missions. There were many Hmong of high courage and commitment who had no high rank or title other than these simple, descriptive words—*men of courage*—conferred upon them by their countrymen.

*   *   *

When Vang Pao learned on September 3, 1969, that Ho Chi Minh had died, he stopped to contemplate what it might mean for Laos and for the Hmong, but decided not to be distracted by speculation. He needed to concentrate on retaking the PDJ. On September 12, 1969, he did what the experts had said was impossible: he retook Xieng Khouang town and the airfield at Lima Lima, which had been held by the communists since the early 1960s—since the days of Captain Kong Le, the Soviet airlift, and Averell Harriman. He captured more than three million rounds of ammunition, 150,000 gallons of gasoline, 12 tanks, 30 trucks, and 13 jeeps.[5]

Sixteen days later, Muong Soui, Site 108, where Ly Lue had been shot down, was retaken, but not by a major battle. The NVA, with their supply lines interrupted, were temporarily without adequate supplies and with-

---

*My efforts to locate American airmen rescued directly or indirectly in Laos by indigenous troops were unsuccessful. Air Force and Navy archival staffs, while willing to assist in this search, need certain data to access their files. They need information that the Hmong do not have. After this book is published, I hope that Americans rescued in Laos will come forward.

drew. Once again, the airfield at Muong Soui belonged to the Royal Lao government.

Bill Keeler, an Air Force officer and pilot who had served as director of the Air Operations Center in the Air Attaché's Office in Vientiane in 1966 when William Sullivan was Ambassador, returned to Laos in 1969 to serve a second tour. This time he would serve under Ambassador G. McMurtrie Godley who, on July 24, had replaced Sullivan. Godley, a big, burly man, had served in the Congo as both deputy chief of mission and ambassador. He had a reputation as a hard driving man who knew something about paramilitary operations. Before arriving in Laos, Godley had served in Washington as deputy assistant secretary of state for Far Eastern affairs. Vang Pao and Godley, both strong personalities, would clash.

Since the U.S. involvement in Laos remained secret, Keeler was under orders to keep his rank unknown. During Keeler's first tour as a major, Lao who worked with him called him "Sir" even though this was against regulations. Now promoted to lieutenant colonel, they addressed him as "Super Sir."

Vang Pao constantly complained to Keeler about his lack of "air," pointing out that Lao and Thai piloted T-28s and the American-flown A-1s based in Thailand only flew two missions a day to support him. The enemy knew this and took advantage of it. Because some T-28s were stationed at Luang Prabang, some at Vientiane, and the A-1s in Thailand, these planes, based far from his operations, could handle only a few missions a day—not enough to effectively support his men. He suggested basing T-28s at Muong Soui, Lima Site 108.

Keeler knew T-28s could use the airfield there although the strip had two problems. The Neutralist forces assigned to protect it seemed unable to hold it for long periods or even to keep it secure when they did. Also, the excessive dirt and dust damaged engines and fogged pilot vision. Trying to solve the dust problem, Keeler spent considerable time at Muong Soui. One morning, he found scrawled on his hootch the words "Death to the Americans." Keeler had little time to worry about the author of these words. He had to keep the strip wet so it was usable. "I had a helluva time keeping it hosed down. Finally, with great difficulty, I got a water truck in there. I was so proud of that water truck and the job it was doing in keeping the dirt down."[6]

Vang Pao and Keeler discussed repairing the old French runway at Lima Lima, located in the midst of the enemy. From here, pilots could fly fifteen missions a day instead of the two currently being flown. Keeler listened as Vang Pao talked more and more about returning to guerrilla tactics with a new twist—integrating T-28s into his operations. These slow-moving T-28s could provide close ground support for his troops. Keeler also listened to enthusiastic CIA comments about Vang Pao's idea to conduct air strikes from the Plaine des Jarres.

While Vang Pao might have temporarily retaken Muong Soui and Lima Lima in Operation About Face, the North Vietnamese had no intention of losing control of the strategic Plaine des Jarres. They had every intention of whipping the Hmong general.

14.

The U.S. Betrays the Hmong

General [Vang] Pao does know what democracy is. He is a very
highly self-educated man. . . . I would like to say it like I heard a
general from the U.S. about 1965 or '66. After we got run down
from the north, [the U.S. general] asked what did [Vang Pao] need,
did he want a lot of men—this was the third time they got offered
men, I mean GIs from the United States—did he want that, what
did he need to help; and his answer to this man was: "Sir, we don't
need your boys; all I need is for you to supply me . . . and you will
not have to send your boys. . . . I feel what I am doing is my part
of the fighting for what the free world is fighting for."

—Edgar "Pop" Buell, in his testimony before the House Committee
on Internal Security, May 25, 1972*

On Monday, October 20, 1969, less than a month after Vang Pao's
recapture of the Plaine des Jarres and five days after a massive antiwar
demonstration in Washington, Senator Stuart Symington opened secret
hearings on Laos. Symington, chairman of the Senate Foreign Relations
Committee's Subcommittee on U.S. Security Agreements and Commitments Abroad, had visited Laos several times and had been extensively
and repeatedly briefed on U.S. activities there.

The heated hearings opened with comments by Symington: "Specula-
tive news stories, Communist propaganda, irresponsible political

---

*"The Theory and Practice of Communism in 1972 [Southeast Asia]," Part I, Hearings
before the Committee on Internal Security, House of Representatives, 92nd Cong., 2nd
sess., May 25 and July 20, 1972, p. 7770.

charges, are poor substitutes for reliable information on a subject of such importance. If whatever it is that we have done there is right, the American people deserve to know it. If whatever has been wrong, secrecy can only compound that wrong rather than right it." Symington promised to make public a declassified transcript of the hearings. But the transcript would remain classified for another six months and when it was released, under pressure, only a portion would be declassified.

A number of those working for various U.S. agencies flew in from Laos to appear before the committee. The principal witness was William Sullivan, who had served as U.S. Ambassador to Laos from late 1964 until March 18, 1969, and earlier as a senior aide to Averell Harriman during negotiations of the Geneva Agreements in 1962. At the time of the hearings, Sullivan was Deputy Assistant Secretary of State for East Asian and Pacific Affairs. In three explosive days of hearings, some extraordinary views emerged—particularly from Sullivan. They foretold disaster for the Hmong. Under repeated questioning by Symington, Senator J. W. Fulbright, and the Committee Counsel, Roland A. Paul, Sullivan maintained that the U.S. had no moral commitment of any kind to Laos, no written, verbal, or moral obligation to the Royal Lao government or to General Vang Pao and his Hmong soldiers. He pointed out that Laos was not a member of the Southeast Asia Treaty Organization (SEATO); therefore the U.S. had no treaty commitment to defend Laos as it had Thailand. Paul questioned Sullivan at length about U.S. moral commitments to General Vang Pao.

Mr. Paul: "Another aspect that could be considered a moral commitment is what we have done for General Vang Pao, and in urging him to continue the effort that he has made. Do you see any obligation on the part of the United States for the safety or well being of General Vang Pao and his people?"

Mr. Sullivan: "No formal obligation upon the United States; no."

Mr. Paul: "You referred earlier this afternoon specifically to the case of urging General Vang Pao to continue the effort when he was willing, perhaps, to move his people away from the frontlines to avoid the high attrition rate which they have been subject to. . . . As a result of this urging of General Vang Pao to carry on we do not owe him any obligation?"

Mr. Sullivan: "I am not particularly familiar with this conversation that was testified to today. I have known General Vang Pao over the years, know that he is somewhat mercurial in his statements and temperament. I think it should be quite clear that General Vang Pao and his people are concerned with and defending territory that they consider their own, their own not only in terms of the areas that they have traditionally lived in, but areas because of their nature and terrain which would provide them with a traditional form of life. They are hill people, and I think that General Vang Pao's decisions and the Meo [Hmong] people's decisions about where they will remain and where they will defend and where they will sustain, are decisions that they are going to make themselves.

"In short, I do not think we are dealing with people in this region for whom the world has any great illusions, and they have seen lots of white faces, lots of round eyes, and I don't believe that their attitudes in dealing with us are disposed upon matters of sentiment or moral obligations."

The Staff Counsel continued to press Sullivan about U.S. commitments to Laos. Perhaps unwittingly, Sullivan admitted that the U.S. was prepared to walk away from Laos within hours.

Mr. Paul: "So the presence of American military forces in Laos is not in itself a commitment generating factor?"

Mr. Sullivan: "We do not consider that it is a commitment."

Mr. Paul: "Would this mean that we could increase our military presence in stages in Laos with the ability to terminate that augmentation at any time?"

Mr. Sullivan: "I believe that we have that ability currently. In fact, we used to use as rule of thumb our ability to make it reversible and terminate it within 8 hours. It would probably take 24 hours now, but it still could be done."

During this hearing, Senator Fulbright, who would say later that he did not know that there was a war in Laos until this session, asked Sullivan why the war was officially secret. Sullivan responded that it was a way to keep intact the Kennedy-Khrushchev understanding of Vienna in June 1961.

Mr. Sullivan: " . . . a senior Soviet official, for example, has said that insofar as he reads things in newspapers or hears statements and allegations about U.S. operations, he does not have to take any official cognizance of them, and this will color, to some extent, the Soviet attitude toward Souvanna Phouma's neutrality and toward the retention of the understandings which underlie the agreement between ourselves and the Soviets for the neutrality of Laos.

"One other feature that enters into this was the fact . . . that the mechanism for determining and bringing to public attention gross violations by the North Vietnamese of the Lao neutrality are frustrated because the ICC [International Control Commission] are not able to move into areas and ascertain exactly what is going on there.

"The North Vietnamese operate with enormous numbers of forces in Laos, totally clandestinely. They deny that their people are there, and this, therefore, in terms of the mechanism of the 1962 agreements, gives them a totally unfair, totally legal protection. Part of the concern being our desire to maintain the framework of the 1962 agreements, so that eventually they can reestablish and put back into function, we have therefore been concerned in attempting to avoid those actions or those statements which would result in the mechanism being deployed in relation to us."[1]

Senator Fulbright: " . . . you talked about its effect [acknowledging publicly what is going on in Laos] on the Russians. I do not know why it would. The Russians know it. What in the world would the Russians do, could or would do, if you acknowledged tomorrow morning exactly what you were doing? We did not pretend we were not bombing North Vietnam, and the Russians didn't do any more than they were doing, that is, they gave the assistance they thought appropriate?

"What do you think they would be doing in Laos?"

Mr. Sullivan: "I think our concern would be primarily with the attitude of the Soviets toward continuing a respect for the Prime Minister of Laos as a neutralist."

The Land of Oz had moved to the Senate chambers. Symington interrupted to ask, "why is it that we do not allow bombing in North Vietnam, preferring to work it out with ground troops in South Vietnam, but do not have ground troops in Laos, preferring to work it out with bombing?" Fulbright interrupted Symington to ask Sullivan, "Doesn't this ever strike you as sort of an absurdity? They are pretending they are not there and we are pretending we are not there. What does it all lead to?" Sullivan was undeterred in his assessment of this Soviet-U.S. understanding which, importantly, was not in writing but only based on a conversation between Kennedy and Khrushchev.

On the last day of the hearings, Sullivan reiterated the need to keep the war in Laos officially secret. "When President Kennedy and Mr. Khrushchev in June of 1961 met in Vienna they reached agreement, and it was one of the few understandings we had had with the Soviets which we think has endured, that it would serve the interests of the United States and the Soviet Union both if Laos could be an independent neutral country . . . we do believe in our estimate of the Soviets that it continues to be their policy to assume that a neutral Laos would serve their interest more."[2]

So the U.S. commitment was to the Soviets—not to Laos and not to General Vang Pao and the Hmong.

The drama playing out in the Senate chambers resembled a Greek tragedy in which an unseen chorus whines a warning of dreadful events to come. Ambassador Sullivan's testimony on the lack of U.S. commitment to Laos and to General Vang Pao foretold a fate for the Hmong that neither the general nor Colonel Billy could ever have imagined.

Vang Pao and his Hmong would have been horrified if they had heard Sullivan's words. Unlike Sullivan, Vang Pao had a commitment to his people and his country, and beyond that he had a commitment to the Americans. It was during Sullivan's tenure in Laos that visiting American generals had offered Vang Pao U.S. soldiers to help fight the North Vietnamese. He had always refused, explaining to the Americans that he and the Hmong were helping the U.S. in its fight for freedom around the world, particularly against communism in Laos, and thus preventing American soldiers from dying there.

15.

Lima Lima

While Air America provided the airlift and Vang Pao had great latitude through the Agency in getting stuff where he wanted it, when it came down to the wire and he needed close air support, he was at the mercy of the 7th Air Force in Saigon.

—U.S. Air Force Brigadier General Harry "Heine" Aderholt

Richard Nixon was determined to make his "Vietnamization" work and Hanoi was just as determined to derail it. Victory for either side would in part be determined by who controlled the Ho Chi Minh Trail. By now, the Trail network, greatly expanded and improved, allowed high-volume traffic to move quickly through certain portions. To hide Trail traffic, roads were camouflaged with netting laced with branches. Underwater bridges, decoy trucks, and blinking lights misled U.S. pilots, while surface to air missiles, some 600 antiaircraft guns, and 45,000 NVA protected it. As a result of heavy Trail traffic, the U.S. shifted its air strike capability from Vang Pao's area to interdicting the Trail further south.

The NVA, taking advantage of the lack of air coverage in Region II, brought in supplies and fresh troops to attack Moua Cher Pao's interdiction units operating around Ban Ban. With Vang Pao's forces hurting and U.S. air strikes curtailed, NVA supplies rolled into Laos for its upcoming offensive to retake territory lost to Vang Pao in Operation About Face on the Plaine des Jarres.

By early 1970 the NVA had two divisions in northeast Laos. Ambassador Godley and General Vang Pao watched the massive buildup. On January 23, Godley requested B-52 strikes from Washington. His request set in motion a month-long series of bizarre attempts to authorize the use of

B-52s and yet have no agency responsible for this action. Henry Kissinger described it as "a stately bureaucratic minuet . . . that told much about the state of mind of our government. We were caught between officials seeking to protect American forces for which they felt a responsibility and a merciless Congressional onslaught that rattled these officials in their deliberations."[1] To minimize disclosure, Kissinger brought Godley's B-52 request before Nixon's Washington Special Actions Group (WSAG), which included representatives of Defense, CIA, State, and the White House, for approval. It was feared that leaks about bombing in Laos would bring an outcry from the antiwar critics.

Vang Pao, knowing that previously requested B-52 strikes had been denied, pushed his people to repair the airfield at Lima Lima so he could bring in his T-28s. He also decided to defy the American ban on bombing the Chinese Cultural Mission at Khang Khay, which housed a huge cache of weapons. For years Vang Pao had insisted that this enemy arsenal be destroyed, but the U.S., afraid of China, had prohibited air strikes against it. Now he took action.

When Major General Andrew Evans, commander of the 7/13th Air Force at Udorn, learned that Vang Pao's T-28s had destroyed the Chinese Cultural Mission, he was furious. He announced that he wanted Vang Pao at Udorn immediately. His aides advised that if he wanted to talk to Vang Pao, he would have to go to Long Chieng. General Evans did not want to do that. He next decided to ground Vang Pao's T-28s, but a staff member reminded him that these planes were not under his command. Still, Evans wanted Vang Pao punished. He decided to deny the Hmong general aviation fuel. While the American commander of the 7/13th devised ways to punish his ally, Beijing chose to ignore the destruction of its disguised arsenal. Thus, later, when fighting on the PDJ increased and Vang Pao's T-28s were needed to stem the NVA, Evans forgot Vang Pao's transgressions.[2]

While Washington's policymakers delayed a decision on Godley's request, people at Lima Lima shoveled, raked, and hauled heavy baskets of dirt to repair the runway. Once a short landing strip was readied, Porters, Helios, and helicopters ferried in small USAID construction equipment, ammunition, and troops to defend the site. Lao Special Guerrilla Units (SGUs), commanded by a Lao called Cowboy because he wore a Texas cowboy hat, moved in to protect one side of the airstrip.

The NVA watched. It was clear that Vang Pao intended to stay on the PDJ. That was unacceptable. NVA gunners nightly harassed the site, damaging the runway. Hmong teams operating near these enemy gun positions crept close to pinpoint their exact positions for the Thai artillery gunners.

Soon C-47s and C-123s carrying heavy weapons and ammunition landed at Lima Lima. The 123 crews kept their engines running when they came in. They landed, taxied to the end of the runway, opened the hatch, and spun around. The cargo, on rollers, spewed out the back as they took off in the opposite direction.

With cargo planes landing munitions, Vang Pao brought in his "flying artillery" for close ground support of his troops and to pound away at the enemy. A minimum of four T-28s worked out of this site, often to support Moua Cher Pao's men or to respond to FAGs who had spotted enemy positions. By reloading here, each T-28 pilot could fly twelve to fifteen missions a day instead of two or three if based elsewhere. Since it was too dangerous to leave any aircraft overnight, the T-28s departed at dusk for either Long Chieng or Vientiane. As the tempo of the fighting increased, Lao and Thai T-28 pilots joined the Hmong crews.

On the morning of February 11, 1970, Air Force Colonel Bill Keeler, responding to an urgent message from Vang Pao to get to Lima Lima as fast as possible, departed Vientiane in a T-28. As he approached the PDJ, he again admired the lavender beauty of this gently rolling plain surrounded by dramatic mountains. He was never certain why the NVA was so determined to occupy this high plateau. But he *was* certain why Vang Pao wanted it—it belonged to the Hmong. Keeler coveted it too—at least part of it. He wanted to build a golf course here. As he neared the site, he heard the excited radio chatter of Hmong pilots. He called Lima Lima. In broken English, a voice warned, "Enemy close to runway." Acknowledging the warning, Keeler came in fast. As he landed, those repairing the runway grabbed their baskets and shovels and scrambled to the side.[3]

Keeler climbed out of the cockpit as a T-28 roared off, banked left, pulled up on downwind, and dropped its bombs. Keeler was surprised at the closeness of the enemy. He watched this pilot return and taxi to the rearming area. With his engines running, the pilot motioned to ground crews to rearm his plane. As he reloaded, another T-28 took off. Keeler watched as the second T-28 pilot dropped his bombs. He estimated the enemy was less than a mile away. This was indeed Vang Pao's "flying artillery."

Parachutes fluttered over gun positions to protect the gunners from the sun. Empty shell casings, fuel drums, pieces of packing platforms, and other debris of war littered the site. Men piled sandbags higher around slit trenches and bunkers. Lao SGU soldiers unraveled another string of barbed wire around an artillery position. Black pots of rice sat on smoldering fires.

Keeler enjoyed the cool, invigorating climate of the plateaued PDJ. This morning, he felt great. With buoyancy in his step, he searched for Vang Pao and found him standing alone at the barbed wire perimeter, looking northeast. Wearing his Ranger hat and a pistol strapped to his waist, Vang Pao did not hear Keeler approaching. He startled the distracted general by shouting to him to be careful not to walk into the nearby mine fields.

The general did not greet Keeler. Instead, he pointed his finger at a small valley in the distance and announced, "They come through there. They bring their equipment in through there." Keeler's eyes followed Vang Pao's finger. He looked, but could see nothing significant. "I didn't see a damn thing. I told him I thought the attack would come 90 degrees from where he was pointing—from the tree line not more than a few hundred yards away where the NVA were taking potshots at most planes that took off or landed."

"They'll break the perimeter right here," Vang Pao said, pointing to a 50 caliber machine gun position. "We need Spookies tonight. Enemy come tonight. For sure. You must get Spooky." Vang Pao wanted Spooky gunship coverage because these C-47s, converted to drop flares and to fire side-mounted Gatling guns, often saved positions from being over-run during darkness. Capable of illuminating vast areas and with its concentrated fire power, a Spooky was a formidable night weapon.

Vang Pao's urgent request for C-47 gunships for the past two nights had been denied by the Lao Spooky commander, who told Vang Pao that his Lao crews preferred to stand alert in Vientiane. If needed, the commander explained, they could be on location within an hour. Vang Pao insisted that was not good enough. He needed them overhead all night. But the Lao commander had refused. Now Vang Pao turned to Keeler for help. Keeler knew the Lao Spooky crews did not want to fly night missions on the PDJ. It was too dangerous.

Keeler followed Vang Pao as he walked around the site talking to his men and inspecting bunkers and trenches. He told Keeler that he had helped dig the older trenches many years ago when he was working with the French. He recalled that he had fought the Viet Minh from this very position a quarter of a century earlier, and now, 25 years later, he would fight the communist Vietnamese here again.

Keeler's optimism was evaporating beneath Vang Pao's depressed mood. He tried to lift Vang Pao's spirits by telling him that the PDJ reminded him of his beloved mountains of North Carolina. Vang Pao did not respond. Keeler tried again. He looked toward the west and Muong Soui. "General, I need some land up there to build a golf course. I'll turn that old French fortification into a clubhouse. And the tourists will love all those old jars." Vang Pao turned to Keeler and smiled. "Fine," he said. The solemn mood was momentarily broken. "How much land you need?" Keeler detected a bounce in his voice, sounding more like the Vang Pao Keeler knew. "About a square mile," estimated Keeler. "No problem," the general answered. "I'll let you know which mile I pick out." Both men laughed, knowing that the enemy held the choice golf course terrain.

A soldier carrying a PRC-25 field radio ran toward Vang Pao shouting in Hmong. Vang Pao listened to a FAG on the radio, then announced to the men around him, "Enemy come tonight!" He turned to Keeler: "We need Spooky tonight. For sure!" Keeler flew back to Vientiane to convince the Lao Air Force Spooky commander that Lima Lima needed coverage all night. Stand-by status would not do. At dusk Vang Pao departed for Long Chieng because his SKY advisor insisted he not spend the night on the PDJ. It was too dangerous.

A North Vietnamese commando monitoring Lima Lima's radios heard Vang Pao's departure and signaled his men to move out. Forty soldiers grabbed each of two ropes attached to a Soviet PT-76 tank and pulled while others pushed from behind. Three other tanks, also pulled and pushed, moved through the darkness. Behind the tanks followed about one thousand infantrymen led by NVA commandos. The much-feared NVA offensive on the PDJ had begun.

At Lima Lima, they waited for the ground attack. Radios crackled with reports from patrols and from FAG positions in the encircling mountains.

In Vientiane, night had fallen and Keeler had not yet convinced the Lao Spooky commander that Vang Pao had intelligence that the enemy planned to attack Lima Lima tonight and that the site needed all-night gunship coverage. The Lao commander stood firm; his crews would only operate on a stand-by basis. Not until Keeler mentioned something about reporting this incident to higher authorities did the Lao commander understand that maybe his Spookies could be helpful in defending Lima Lima.

About 10 o'clock, Spooky 1 lifted off from the Vientiane airfield, arriving over Lima Lima about an hour later. Once in place, Spooky 1 dropped flares which drifted downward, eerily lighting the sky and the ground with an orange glow.

About 2 a.m., the Spooky 1 pilot radioed Vientiane that he was leaving station. "I'm breaking off. I'm low on gas. Spooky 2 get ready to come up here. We'll pass you in the air." The comforting hum of the gunship's engines disappeared. The skies grew dark as the flares flickered and went out. There were three more hours of darkness.

The NVA commando leader, monitoring Lima Lima's radios and air-to-ground communications, heard the Spooky depart. The four tanks were in position—two on each side of the airfield. He passed the signal. Tank drivers lowered the long muzzles of their guns. Machine gunners took their places atop the tanks. Soldiers holding floodlights climbed on the backs of the tanks. Others carried horns. Commandos lined up behind the two tanks positioned to rush the perimeter on the northeast side of the site, the area defended by the Hmong. Infantry prepared to follow. The night burst open with screams, blaring horns, whistles, and blinding lights. Tank engines, with their mufflers removed to create frightening noise, cranked up. Gunners fired their long-nosed guns. Positions on the perimeter returned fire. Radiomen begged for help. Spooky 2 dragged through the darkness, about an hour from the besieged site.

Lima Lima's forward positions, defended by mortar crews, fell to the Soviet tanks' big guns. As the tanks moved closer, Lao SGU soldiers panicked and fled. The Hmong did not. Two enemy tanks, followed by commandos, lumbered toward the northeast corner of Lima Lima—the exact spot Vang Pao had predicted the enemy would attack. Here a 13-year-old Hmong boy manned a 50 caliber machine gun. The youth stared at the approaching Soviet tanks, but did not fire. Tank 1, crawling through the first barbed wire defense, hit a land mine, jumped into the air, and turned on its side, its motor growling. The commandos ran from behind the disabled tank and rushed the second barbed wire perimeter with satchel charges to blow it. The boy at the machine gun did not fire. Tank 2 stalled but continued firing.

The enemy was now inside the two main wire defenses. The boy at the machine gun watched as they tried to blow the last wires to get inside the main position. Then he fired, pinning them down. The enemy crawled about trying to use Bangalore torpedoes to blow the last wires. The torpedoes fired but made only small holes. In the light of the fire fight, the boy saw the enemy running, falling, crawling toward him. Then, screaming and yelling, they rushed the perimeter in front of him. He fired and fired, until no more enemy soldiers moved toward him.

When Spooky 2 arrived, the pilot immediately called for Spooky 3 and Spooky 4. Spooky 2 dropped flares and fired its Gatling guns.

Tank 1 smoldered. Tank 2 no longer fired. Reserve enemy troops replaced those who had fallen at the perimeter. Lima Lima had to be taken before dawn when Vang Pao's air force would attack, cutting down their exposed troops. As dawn touched the horizon, the NVA force retreated, leaving behind many dead and wounded as well as two Soviet tanks.

Keeler, alerted shortly after the attack began, had immediately driven to the Vientiane airfield to preflight a C-47 to evacuate casualties at Lima Lima—if he could get in. He waited for the Spookies to return with news of Lima Lima. But the crews were not certain if the site had held. He jumped into the C-47 and took off to see for himself.

Approaching Lima Lima, he saw fires burning and two disabled tanks. It didn't look good. The FAG on the ground insisted that it was safe to land, reporting that White Star had come in earlier by chopper. Keeler circled twice, expecting ground fire. None came, so he landed. He climbed out of the aircraft into the acrid smells of burning equipment and gunpowder, so strong it made him nauseous. As he picked his way through the debris, fearing a delayed grenade explosion, rescue choppers landed to evacuate the friendly wounded and dead.

Keeler found White Star near the 50 caliber machine gun position— the location which he had only yesterday told Keeler would be the point of attack. Vang Pao, smiling broadly, was congratulating his men on their victory and organizing them to search the enemy bodies for intelligence. When he saw Keeler, he pointed to a skinny, black-haired youth less than five feet tall, wearing military fatigues rolled up at the ankles. The boy stood ramrod straight. He seemed embarrassed as Vang Pao pointed at him and proudly announced that this boy, manning a machine gun, had killed over fifty North Vietnamese as they charged his position. Keeler nodded and muttered words of congratulation in the direction of the pencil-stiff boy. Seeing young soldiers like this one fighting battles few grownups could handle brought a lump to Keeler's throat.

Littered about in front of the boy's position were NVA bodies. Keeler walked over for a closer look. Each soldier had a long rope tied to one ankle, used to drag the wounded or dead back from where they had fallen so they could be retrieved after the battle. No one had remained alive or able at this position to retrieve those fallen. Keeler examined the dead soldiers. "I was surprised at their almost new combat boots, their camouflage clothes, and how strong and healthy they looked. They were not children like many Hmong soldiers, but seemed to be in their 20s. Vang Pao's intel teams emptied their pockets, putting the contents on the ground beside the bodies so we could take pictures. Each man carried medical supplies produced in France or Sweden: some carried homemade grenades of gunpowder wrapped in leaves with the fuses carried separately.'' Clearly, these were not ordinary soldiers.

Keeler volunteered to assist the intel team. He passed a bomb crater where the enemy had dragged some wounded before retreating. ''I looked down to see a body sunk into the muddy slime. Then I noticed his lieutenant insignia and decided to go down into the hole for a closer look and, frankly, to take his insignia. As I reached down, he moved. I thought he had a grenade, so I yelled and jumped backwards, falling into the mud. He didn't have a grenade, but he was very much alive and I was covered with mud.

''We searched the lieutenant. He was a commando and the leader of the attack. His diary* provided details of this operation. Lima Lima had been attacked by two elite NVA *Dacon* companies with a third in reserve. Some thought these *Dacon* units were used for suicide missions.'' In 1958, Hanoi had established *Dacon* units, headquartered in Sam Neua Province in Laos, to handle NVA missions inside Laos.[4]

They inspected the two Soviet PT-76 tanks and discovered that one had been disabled by a land mine. The other, loaded with ammunition, had run out of gas and its batteries were dead. Keeler wondered if the NVA had pulled the tanks because they were low on gas or because they wanted total surprise. Or was it a combination of both?

There were 74 NVA dead and three prisoners—one of them the commando lieutenant. Later that day, Keeler flew the three blindfolded prisoners to Vientiane for interrogation by General E Tham, a North Vietnamese defector who worked in intelligence for the Royal Lao government.

That night, enemy forces overran a Lao government position guarding a northern entrance to the PDJ, allowing enemy convoys to once again roll onto the plain. Tanks, armored cars, and trucks were spotted moving along Route 7 heading toward Khang Khay and Lima Lima.

The next day, February 13, Souvanna Phouma formally requested B-52 strikes. By February 16, the NVA and Pathet Lao had driven the government forces out of all major positions protecting the approaches to the PDJ, allowing men and supplies from North Vietnam to pour in.

With the enemy back on the PDJ, Vang Pao withdrew his troops from the eastern side of the plain. Moua Cher Pao, operating near Ban Ban,

---

*The *Dacon* lieutenant's diary is in the possession of Bill Keeler.

withdrew to avoid encirclement. During the next week, Lima Lima and its forward positions came under nightly attack.

As the enemy advanced, Keeler worried that Muong Soui would fall and he would lose his water truck to the enemy. He reminded Vang Pao how difficult it had been to get that truck into Muong Soui and asked him what he should do. "'Drive it as far as you can. Put trees and brush over it. Maybe enemy not find. Don't worry about your truck. If lose Muong Soui, we take back later.'" Keeler did as Vang Pao suggested. He flew to Muong Soui and hid his water truck in a clump of trees not far from the runway.

Kissinger and Nixon also worried about the loss of Muong Soui. On February 16, Kissinger recommended that if the communist forces advanced beyond Muong Soui, President Nixon should authorize B-52 strikes.[5]

Within 24 hours, NVA and Pathet Lao forces attacked Muong Soui. American F-105s, not B-52s, roared off their bases in Thailand to defend the site. In the process they found Bill Keeler's prized water truck: "Those damned 105s hadn't hit anything for days. Then they bombed my water truck at Muong Soui and they cratered our runway. Bombing the runway was really smart since neither the Pathet Lao nor the NVA had airplanes in Laos. Only we had airplanes. They cratered our own landing strip. We lost both Muong Soui and my water truck."

On February 17-18, 1970, Nixon took Kissinger's recommendation. Three U.S. B-52 bombers struck NVA and Pathet Lao positions in northern Laos and on the Plaine des Jarres. While B-52 strikes had been requested as early as March 1968 by Major Richard Secord and on several occasions since then, this was their first use in northern Laos. From February 1970 until April 1973, B-52s would fly several thousand sorties against the communist forces in Laos.

On February 21, General Vang Pao gave the order to abandon Lima Lima and the PDJ—at least temporarily.

16.

Kissinger and Guerrilla Diplomacy

They were specialists in political warfare, determined to move only at their own pace, not to be seduced by charm or goaded by impatience. They pocketed American concessions as their due, admitting no obligation to reciprocate moderation. They saw compromise as a confession of weakness. They were impressed only by their own assessment of Hanoi's self-interest. . . . Their goal was total power in South Vietnam, or at least a solution in which their opponents were so demoralized that they would be easy to destroy in the next round.

—Henry Kissinger in *The White House Years,* describing Hanoi's peace negotiators

On February 21, 1970—the same day that General Vang Pao ordered the evacuation of Lima Lima—Henry Kissinger prepared for another secret meeting with the North Vietnamese in Paris. This time he met with Le Duc Tho, Hanoi's special advisor to its Paris delegation. Hanoi continued to take the high ground, denouncing the U.S. as the aggressor nation and never admitting that it now had an estimated 67,000 combat troops in Laos engaged in overrunning Royal Lao government positions with over 650 antiaircraft guns, radar directed guns, and surface-to-air missiles.

As the Nixon administration had feared, the February B-52 strikes against enemy positions on the Plaine des Jarres and in northern Laos became public. The day after the first B-52 strike in northern Laos, the *New York Times* carried a story on the bombing. Senators Eugene McCarthy, Frank Church, and Mike Mansfield publicly deplored the use of U.S. air power there. On February 25, Senators Mathias, Mansfield, Gore,

Symington, Cooper, and Percy attacked Kissinger and Nixon's secret policies in Laos. Senators Gore and Mansfield demanded that the classified testimony on Laos, given before their Senate Foreign Relations Subcommittee, be released.

Kissinger was furious that these senators made no mention of the North Vietnamese offensive in Laos. He was particularly irked over the senators' self-righteous claims that they did not know about U.S. involvement in Laos. He later wrote: "The issue was not to obtain the facts—they were widely known—but to induce the government to confirm them publicly, which was quite a different matter. The Senate Foreign Relations Committee had substantially full knowledge from its staff investigations as well as from its classified hearings. The issue for us was to what extent an official acknowledgment of our operations in Laos would wreck what was left of the 1962 Accords, give Hanoi a pretext for further stepping up its aggression in Laos, and fuel even more passionate controversy at home."[1]

Responding to Hanoi's successful denial of troops in Laos and to the U.S. senators' silence on the subject of North Vietnamese aggression in Laos, a press conference was called in Vientiane to display captured NVA soldiers, including the commando lieutenant whose company had attacked Lima Lima. Keeler wanted to attend the press briefing, but dared not because of the official secrecy of the U.S. involvement. Instead, he watched the proceedings through a crack in a door from an adjacent room. "One of the reporters asked the commando lieutenant if there were any Americans at Lima Lima. He hesitated. Then, he looked directly at me through the crack. Our eyes froze for an instant. Then he said, 'No. No Americans.'"[2]

The Nixon administration, like those of Kennedy and Johnson, had opted to obfuscate U.S. involvement in Laos. Now, with the B-52 bombing in the limelight and with the attacks on Nixon's credibility, Kissinger thought continued denial was impossible. On February 27 he and his National Security Council staff decided to outmaneuver the senators by preparing a statement on U.S. activities in Laos to be issued by the White House.

On March 6, 1970, after more than a decade of deep involvement in Laos, Nixon revealed for the first time the U.S. presence there. The extent and details of that involvement, however, were not given. Using data prepared by Kissinger's NSC staff—primarily Winston Lord—Nixon explained that there were no American combat ground troops in Laos and that no Americans working officially in Laos had been killed in ground combat operations. He listed the number of Americans working in Laos as 1,040, with 320 serving as military advisors or instructors and another 323 in logistics. He concluded by reiterating: "Our goal in Laos has been and continues to be to reduce American involvement and not to increase it, to bring peace in accordance with the 1962 Accords and not to prolong the war."[3]

The NSC staffers had neglected to mention Army Captain Walter (Wally) Moon, who had been executed at Lat Houang by the communists, the two young kickers from Texas killed at Padong, the USAID worker shot at Na Khang, Army Captain Joe Bush, killed at Muong Soui, the Air Force technicians lost at Phou Pha Thi, or the many American air crews killed or captured. Two days after Nixon's announcement, leaks to the press about American deaths in Laos forced the administration, in some backing and filling, to admit that a few Americans, including six civilians, had been killed over the previous nine years in Laos. The White House announcement on Laos had backfired; it had enlarged the credibility gap.

In Paris on March 16, 1970, in round two of the Kissinger–Le Duc Tho secret meetings, Kissinger proposed "that neither side exert military pressure in Vietnam or in 'related countries' [Laos and Cambodia] during the negotiations—in other words a mutual de-escalation of military operations throughout Indochina." Kissinger's proposal was "contemptuously rejected with a pedantic lecture that every war had its high points with which it was impossible to interfere."[4]

On March 18, Prince Norodom Sihanouk, Cambodia's head of state, was overthrown in a coup by General Lon Nol. Press and public attention shifted from Laos to Cambodia, where the NVA, with equal impunity, disregarded that country's neutrality by maintaining sanctuaries near the border with South Vietnam.

On the day of the Cambodian coup, Hmong patrols spotted NVA troops only a few miles from Sam Thong. While Le Duc Tho jousted brilliantly with Kissinger, his NVA activated plans to take both Long Chieng, Vang Pao's military headquarters, and Sam Thong, a major civilian base for Region II. Sam Thong had a large concentration of civilians, with its hospital and school, but it had no combatants. Except for a few policemen and school superintendent Moua Lia and his teachers, Sam Thong was defenseless.

In early 1970, Moua Lia had sent his wife and their children to Vientiane to live for a few months while doctors there tried to diagnose and treat their youngest son's illness. He had repeatedly warned Vang Pao that the enemy would attack Sam Thong before Long Chieng. "I believed this because at Sam Thong we had no defenses but we had the hospital and the warehouses with the blankets, medicines, salt, food supplies, and the school headquarters. If the enemy could destroy Sam Thong with all its supplies, its schools, and create refugees out of the Sam Thong people, that would be a major victory. I hoped that Sam Thong would not fall to the enemy. But I knew that the enemy would one day try to take it."[5] Months earlier, Moua Lia had asked General Vang Pao for help. "Instead of soldiers, he sent me 100 guns— some carbines and M-16s, a couple of M-60 machine guns, and told me to organize a civilian defense with the teachers. Of my 50 teachers, many were old and none were combatants. They had no experience in fighting. I organized them into groups of 10 to 15 and sent them out to patrol for a week at a time. I rotated them so that our school could still function." Moua Lia knew an attack was imminent when USAID personnel began to leave Sam Thong by air in the late afternoons to spend the nights in Vientiane and the hospital staff evacuated all patients to either Vang Vieng or Vientiane. "I sent another message to General Vang Pao, asking for a battalion of soldiers because my teachers couldn't defend Sam Thong against the NVA."

At 3 p.m. on March 18 about 200 soldiers, Lao and Hmong, landed at Sam Thong airstrip. Moua Lia, the senior official remaining, greeted the major in charge. "I told him that he should deploy his men at the hospital, warehouse area, and the landing strip—the three strategic points. He disagreed with me. He said that he would put his men on the hill so that they could shoot down on the attackers."

That night, Moua Lia and his teachers waited in the darkness of the school, expecting an attack. At 5 a.m., the NVA attacked the hospital with satchel charges. The hospital, built by Pop Buell, the retired Indiana farmer, with USAID funds, burst into flames.

The frightened teachers ran from the school to the governor's office, which seemed more substantial. From there, Moua Lia watched the enemy's movements. "About 8 a.m., I saw about 50 NVA soldiers rush into our school. These soldiers were commando types—*Kamikazes*. There was no way that schoolteachers could defend Sam Thong against them. I tried radioing Vang Pao at Long Chieng to give him their location. I had no map and only a small radio—like a walkie-talkie. I couldn't reach Long Chieng directly. I had to relay my information through another radioman stationed at Skyline who, in turn, talked to Long Chieng.

"Once Vang Pao got my message, he immediately responded with 105mm artillery based at Long Chieng. The first shell hit the runway. I told the radioman to tell Vang Pao to pull back about 500 meters. The second shelling hit in the hills about two kilometers away. The third shot was wild as well. While I was trying to direct the artillery, fighting continued.

"I knew I didn't have the knowledge to direct the artillery, so I asked Long Chieng to send T-28s. When they arrived, I talked to the Hmong pilots, describing the enemy locations. Unfamiliar with calling in air strikes and with no map, I had difficulty in describing the targets. The Hmong pilots, not wanting to hit civilians, flew dangerously low over Sam Thong trying to verify my targets and they took ground fire. Finally, I told them to return to Long Chieng since they might get shot down.

"I asked Vang Pao for reinforcements, but he had none. At noon, I made the decision myself to evacuate Sam Thong. We retreated west with two wounded Lao soldiers, expecting an ambush. By nightfall we had reached the Nam Ngum River. My teachers had all escaped safely. After we left, the NVA blew up the warehouses and all our stores, leveled our school and Sam Thong College. The NVA had destroyed Sam Thong town, home to over 8,000 people."

The Hmong, furious that the enemy had destroyed a civilian town, vowed that the spirit of Sam Thong would live. The hospital staff moved permanently to Ban Sorn, Lima Site 272. Sam Thong College moved temporarily to Vientiane.

With Sam Thong destroyed, General Giap's troops moved toward Vang Pao's military headquarters. In the Air Command Center Quonset hut along the runway at Long Chieng, Vang Chou listened to the radios. Now a major in the Royal Lao Army, he remained disabled. His right hand and arm were almost useless, but that did not stop him from knowing the ground positions of the enemy. He functioned once again as General Direction. His radios crackled with reports from the field: "Snipers on approach to Alternate," "Skyline Ridge positions under attack," "Send medevac chopper, quick!" "Need 'air'!" "Enemy coming!"[6]

Fackee, Coyote, and Vang Seng scrambled their T-28s. Artillery hit the runway near Vang Pao's house, digging a crater. No matter how close the artillery, Vang Pao never flinched. He just talked louder and faster. Angered that enemy gunners had his headquarters in range, he shouted over his radio for his men to kill the enemy guns. His SKY advisors insisted he move into the command bunker. He refused.

The NVA had infiltrated the southern ridge of Skyline, dug in and carefully camouflaged their guns. Enemy spotters high above Alternate directed artillery accurately into the "dreaded valley." On the purple-dusk mountain crags that stood watch at the approach to Alternate, snipers waited to bring down aircraft. Hmong patrols radioed quick messages to Vang Pao warning that sappers were on the move and might try to blow up Alternate. It was feared that the runway at Long Chieng might be knocked out, stranding the Americans; nonessential personnel were evacuated to Vientiane. The SKY men stayed behind, including Jerry "Hog" Daniels. Two American Raven pilots also remained. They would be needed to fly spotter planes to direct air strikes against the enemy. With the heavy enemy shelling of Long Chieng, some of its 30,000 civilians fled to Ban Sorn, Site 272. Others considered going, but since most had no money, they remained at Long Chieng. Those who had some financial means moved to Vientiane, including the families of the pilots.

Washington viewed the communist attack on Long Chieng as a threat to Vientiane and to Thailand. Kissinger wrote in his memoirs that a communist advance to the Mekong was imminent and that Thailand offered to send "volunteers" to help defend Long Chieng, if the Lao government requested them. According to Kissinger, "This proposal was strenuously resisted by the State Department and received only lukewarm support from other agencies at two WSAG meetings. After we received a formal request from both the Laotian and Thai governments, the President overruled the agencies. He was convinced and I agreed that to refuse the offer would raise doubts in Thailand about our commitment to its defense and might panic Souvanna."[7]

On March 19, Thai "volunteers" and Hmong from other positions were helicoptered in to help defend Long Chieng against the two North Vietnamese divisions. For the next two days, A-1 Skyraiders and T-28s from Thailand joined the Hmong T-28s to bomb ridge positions held by the enemy. The extent of the Thai military participation in Laos remained classified. Kissinger did not inform WSAG of the Thai participation until March 26.[8]

On April 1, after receiving a pounding from U.S., Thai, and Lao planes and from the "volunteer" Thai troops, the NVA withdrew from Skyline Ridge with Vang Pao's troops in pursuit. Long Chieng had held, but not without Thai air support, Thai artillery, and Thai ground troops. These Thais who arrived in 1970 to fight in Military Region II were, like the American Raven pilots, "volunteers," working covertly for their country's military. To keep the Thai involvement secret, numbers of Thai volunteers were recruited from northeastern Thailand where Lao was spoken. They often wore their hair long to resemble Hmong soldiers fighting in remote positions. To avoid detection, they frequently staged out of Chiang Rai, a small town in northern Thailand. Commanded by Thai Army Colonel "Thep," the Thai "volunteers" were sent not only to prevent communist forces from taking Laos. Thai commanders believed that combat in Laos would give their men critical battlefield experience. The U.S. supplied all equipment for these volunteers and agreed to evacuate wounded Thai soldiers. It provided the financial aid and equipment to Thailand to pay for those serving in Laos on a one-for-one basis. As a result of this arrangement, the Thai military was able to increase its armed forces at no cost.[9]

In addition to the Thai volunteers, sent to replace the depleted indigenous forces and to expand military operations, the CIA recruited from other tribal groups and from ethnic Lao. Vang Pao's irregulars now organized into Guerrilla Battalions, comprising three 100-man companies, and into Mobile Groups, consisting of three to six battalions. Vang Pao still retained a few small counterinsurgency units. But the days of using the hill people as counterinsurgents were gone. Now they formed conventional battalions expected to defend set positions.

On April 4, 1970, Kissinger met with Le Duc Tho for the last time in this set of secret meetings. Le Duc Tho used this occasion to blame the U.S. for events in Laos. "Le Duc Tho accused us of escalating the war in Laos. When I replied that one good test of who was doing what to whom was to see which side was advancing, Le Duc Tho argued that we had 'provoked' the North Vietnamese offensive and that the fighting was being conducted by Laotian forces in any event. (This caused me to comment that it was remarkable how well the Pathet Lao spoke Vietnamese.)"[10]

While Kissinger's repartee with Le Doc Tho might have scored a verbal point, his reasonable approach to a negotiated settlement was no match for the gray-haired North Vietnamese guerrilla diplomat who waged his own war at the negotiating table. Kissinger was unprepared for the intractability of Hanoi's hard-core, strident Marxist-Leninists, who excelled at psychological warfare at the negotiating table and in the world press. Kissinger's inexperience with guerrilla diplomacy had allowed him to be entrapped by the secrecy of these meetings and their adverse propaganda potential.

It was at Hanoi's suggestion that these meetings between Kissinger and its senior representatives were kept secret. Initially the arrangement seemed to please Kissinger. In time, he realized that this secrecy allowed the guerrilla diplomats to "whipsaw" him and Nixon, to threaten exposure of the contents of these secret meetings, and to gain concessions.

Years later, less naive and with considerably more experience, Kissinger wrote: "I grew to understand that Le Duc Tho considered negotiations as another battle. Any settlement that deprived Hanoi of final victory was by definition in his eyes a ruse. He was there to wear me down. As the representative of the truth he had no category for compromise. Hanoi's proposals were put forward as the sole 'logical and reasonable' framework for negotiations. The North Vietnamese were 'an oppressed people'; in spite of much historical evidence to the contrary he considered them by definition incapable of oppressing others. America bore the entire responsibility for the war. . . . In his view, the sole 'reasonable' way to end the fighting was American acceptance of Hanoi's terms, which were unconditional withdrawal on a fixed deadline and the overthrow of the South Vietnamese government."[11]

In April, a partial transcript of the prior October Symington-chaired Senate Hearings on Laos, including data on American fatalities, was released: "in the period 1962–68 something like under 200 U.S. military personnel were killed in Laos and approximately another 200 can be listed either as missing in action or prisoners of war. . . . Of those killed in Laos up to October 22, 1969, something around one-quarter were killed with respect to operations in northern Laos."[12]

After years of being overlooked, the secret war in Laos exploded in the U.S. media. Coverage was generally negative. The antiwar climate was such that some of the informed senators refused to acknowledge that they had been briefed or that they had once been in favor of the CIA tactics in Laos. Though the lid was partially off Laos, few Americans really knew the situation. Instead of shedding light, the emerging information, often fragmentary and distorted, bred doubt and fueled the growing domestic voice against the war in Southeast Asia.

The secret war in Laos, however, held the news spotlight only briefly. On the evening of April 30, President Nixon explained to the nation over television that for Vietnamization to succeed it was necessary to eliminate the communist sanctuaries inside Cambodia. As he spoke, South Vietnamese armed forces, supported by U.S. air power, fought inside Cambodia. Nixon's decision to expand the war into Cambodia again roused the antiwar community, setting off more demonstrations. On May 4, Ohio National Guardsmen shot into a crowd of antiwar demonstrators at Kent State University, killing four youths. These deaths sent a rush of adrenalin through the antiwar movements. Protests, sometimes violent, broke out across the United States. On May 9, between 75,000 and 100,000 antiwar protesters demonstrated near the White House, which was fortified by 60 buses and many police. Protests, often ending in violence, continued throughout the summer.

The Nixon White House grappled with the spinoffs of the disclosure of years of clandestine involvement in Laos, with the intransigence of Hanoi, and with an increasingly vocal and violent antiwar movement, now joined by Congress.

Nixon continued U.S. troop withdrawal from South Vietnam. In September 1970, the McGovern-Hatfield amendment, which set a December 31, 1971, deadline for U.S. withdrawal of forces, was defeated by a vote of only 55 to 39. Kissinger believed that he had to get a "peace" agreement with Hanoi before Congress legislated a unilateral U.S. withdrawal.

17.

Bouam Loung, SKY Border Base

If all Vietnamese die then the war will stop. Otherwise the war will continue. The Vietnamese like too much to fight and to conquer.

—Hmong Colonel Vang Youa True, who lost many members of his family to the communists at the 1979 massacre on the Mekong River, described in chapter 1

While the NVA had retaken the Plaine des Jarres, it did not have Moua Cher Pao's base at Bouam Loung, now called "the Fortress" by the Americans. Promoted to major in the Lao Army, Moua Cher Pao remained the tough, mercurial, and determined commander who vowed the enemy would never take Lima Site 32.

The Fortress not only provided the U.S. a location from which to intercept critical enemy communications but it was now being considered as a staging area for a highly secret raid against a POW camp in North Vietnam. While the Johnson administration had kept the issue of the POWs and MIAs held by the communist in Vietnam and Laos off the public agenda, antiwar movement leaders Cora Weiss, Tom Hayden, and Ramsey Clark had visited North Vietnam and broadly publicized that American POWs were well treated. Nixon knew that the North Vietnamese brutalized POWs. He decided to rescue some who could tell for themselves of their cruel treatment. Their testimony, he believed, would tarnish the antiwar movement's image of the North Vietnamese as humane heroes.

In early May 1970, U.S. military intelligence believed that it had located two POW camps west of Hanoi—one at Ap Lo and the other near

Son Tay. Intelligence experts estimated that more than 50 men were held at Son Tay. Planning began for a raid against this POW camp, which lay 20 miles west of Hanoi and 105 nautical miles from the Lao border. Such a raid was logistically difficult. Helicopters were essential to ferry commandos and rescued POWs. Since helicopters, at the time, did not have an aerial refueling capability, they had to launch as near the North Vietnamese border as possible. One option was to use Site 32—Bouam Loung. From there, the helicopter-borne rescue team could fly across the border, storm the prison camp, extract the POWs, and return without refueling.[1]

Also in May, the NVA attacked Site 32. The fighting was so fierce that aerial resupply was impossible. Enemy troops stormed the mined and barbed-wired slopes. A few penetrated the bowl. In repeated assaults, many troops were killed. With heavy losses, the enemy withdrew, but did not retreat. Instead, it laid siege to the Fortress.

Supplies were depleted. Major Moua daily radioed General Vang Pao for "air" to drive the enemy from his perimeters, but monsoon clouds and fog banks precluded air strikes. On the morning of May 16, the skies cleared. Vang Pao ordered his T-28s to Bouam Loung. By 11 a.m., Lt. Vang Seng, returning from his second strike of the day, found fog and rain clouds obscuring Alternate. Repeatedly he tried to get beneath the ceiling to land and rearm. The dreaded mountain, sitting on the approach concealed in fog, snagged Vang Seng.

The next day in Vientiane, a grief-stricken Nhia climbed aboard an Air America flight to Long Chieng. Once again the Hmong mourned the loss of one of their pilots. Once again the funeral truck, decorated with plastic and paper flowers, moved along the dirt road beside the airstrip across the approach to Alternate and to the pilots' graveyard. Once again General Vang Pao saluted his pilot as his coffin was lowered into a dark hole.

Nhia, 20 years old and four months pregnant with her third child, grieved for her husband and for herself. "Now I was a widow. I had no experience in making money. Now I was responsible for myself, my children, and my stepmother-in-law and her four young children. I knew the Hmong saying, 'Widows cried to death.' I was very frightened."[2] Repeatedly she tried to collect her "widow's pay." The widows of pilots were supposed to receive a lump-sum payment equivalent to six months of their husband's salary. "Chao Thai, Vang Pao's man responsible for giving the 'widow's pay,' refused to give it to me. He made me beg for it. It made me very angry. He would only give me a little at a time. I spent much time begging. I never did get the six months' widow's pay. He only gave me five.''

By moving into a more humble house in Vientiane, she managed to feed her family and to pay the rent until her third daughter was born in October. Then Nhia had to earn a living. Her stepmother-in-law suggested that she become a vendor. Nhia agreed. There were no alternatives. She thought about vending in Long Chieng, but there was much competition. She decided to try Bouam Loung, where there was little competition because it was so difficult to get to. With a few *kip* saved from her widow's pay, she purchased pieces of cloth and a few tins of condensed milk and meat at the Vientiane market. Leaving her children with her stepmother-in-law, she took her merchandise to the airport to beg a ride on an Air America flight.

Getting aboard a flight into Bouam Loung was extremely difficult, since most flights carried critical military personnel or supplies. Nhia persisted, using her father's name and reminding those in charge of boarding that she was a pilot's widow. Eventually, she arrived at Bouam Loung. It took days for her to sell her goods. With the money earned, she returned to Vientiane to buy more goods. Life was difficult for Nhia. ''Sometimes I had to wait at the airfield seven to ten days to get on a flight from Long Chieng to Bouam Loung. I made just enough money to buy milk for my baby and rice for my children. One time when I was waiting at Long Chieng for a flight to Bouam Loung, I decided to ask General Vang Pao to hire me as a cook. I went to his headquarters, but his men said no.''

Nhia was not the only widow suffering. ''Many widows cried to death. There was no way to feed their children. Sometimes, they had to give their children to their husband's brothers or parents so the children could eat. Widows made little gardens to have something to eat and something to sell in the market. The only hope for a widow with many children was that she could find enough rice to feed them so they could grow up and take care of her.''

At Bouam Loung, so high in the sky that as a little girl Nhia had believed it would always be safe from the communists, she watched her father. He had never been to school. He had taught himself to read and write in Lao and to pursue his interest in astrology. ''My father believed in astrology. He studied carefully a big calendar book which told him the exact times that he would have good luck. Others didn't know that he did this. Only our family knew. This calendar book was on a seven-day cycle and it could tell him what time of day would be good for an important meeting. The astrology calendar worked for him. One time he decided to build a new house. According to astrology, the good time was 10 in the morning. So, he ordered the builders to set the house-poles at exactly 10 so our house would have good luck.''

Nhia met Lo Ma at the Bouam Loung airstrip. With his good English and years of Forward Air Guide experience, Lo Ma was here helping to direct air strikes and interpreting for the SKY men. He also controlled who climbed aboard the Porters and Helios. Nhia, usually desperate to get to Vientiane to buy more goods, often used her best wiles when pleading with Lo Ma to give her permission to fly. He was impressed with her tenacity and resourcefulness, but did not always give in.

With the coming of the 1970 fall dry season, intel teams, looking for signs of the annual NVA offensive, reported large numbers of enemy troops advancing, once again, toward the Fortress. With Site 32 threatened, it was fortunate for the Americans that their elaborate Son Tay POW rescue operation would no longer need to stage from Bouam Loung. Helicopters now had the capability to refuel in flight. A Lao staging base was not necessary. The mission would launch from Udorn Air Base in northern Thailand. Late on the night of November 20, two C-130s and six helicopters, four loaded with highly trained commandos and two empty, took off from Udorn and headed northeast over Long Chieng and Bouam Loung and into North Vietnam. The raid was brilliantly executed, but the commandos retrieved no POWs. Later, it was learned that the 61 American POWs held at Son Tay had been moved in July to another prison.[3]

At the Fortress, Moua Cher Pao's Hmong and Kmhmu defenders and their SKY advisors deepened bunkers, sandbagged another layer of protection around gun positions, laid down more mine fields, and unwound more coils of barbed wire on the slopes leading to the rim positions that protected this three-sided bowl. Twenty-four hours a day men and boys in these positions waited and watched for probes and attacks. Down in the bowl, SKY men and their Hmong liaisons monitored enemy communications and waited.

The increasing number of green body bags delivered for identification to Ban Sorn and Long Chieng, where tens of thousands of civilians now lived, troubled the Hmong. So many Hmong had been killed. Morale was low. Aware of this, Jerry Daniels reached back to his ''growing days'' in Montana to bring a bit of Western Americana to Long Chieng to celebrate the Hmong New Year and to lift spirits.

Daniels and a SKY air operations advisor called ''Shep'' who, like Daniels, had rodeo experience, organized a Western style bull-riding contest. Daniels had spurs in his belongings at Alternate. Shep radioed Vientiane, asking that his spurs be flown up. The soccer field perimetered with concertina wire would hold the rodeo. The bulls, they hoped, would be provided by Colonel Ly Tou Pao, one of Vang Pao's top commanders. Ly Tou Pao owned the best bulls at Long Chieng and usually won the much-coveted New Year bullfighting contests. The colonel was extremely reluctant to allow his champions to be used; he feared they might be hurt in the riding or scarred by the barbed wire. Daniels' repeated attempts to explain to him the thrill and challenge of bull-riding fell short. The colonel was not enthusiastic about American rodeos, particularly for his bulls. Finally, Daniels prevailed and the colonel provided two spirited brown and black bulls—but not his favorites.[4]

On the day of the rodeo a large crowd gathered. Wearing spurs on their jungle boots, Hog and Shep rigged the nervous, sleek bulls. With considerable fanfare, Daniels, in army trousers and a T-shirt, prepared to mount the first bull. The moment he touched the bull's back, he took off bucking. The experienced rodeo bull-rider landed almost immediately on the hard soccer field, injuring his ankle. The spectators laughed at Daniels' spill and at the dangerous and strange idea of riding a bucking bull. The frightened animal jumped the wire and took off. Hmong gave chase. Even General Vang Pao, in full uniform, joined in. The bull evaded capture and headed for the hills.

Now the rodeo was down to one bull. Daniels, determined to demonstrate his ability, wanted Shep's bull. "Jerry almost went down in tears because he hadn't ridden his bull. He wanted mine. 'No,' I said, 'I'm up next. This bull is mine.' I got on and I rode my bull. I eventually got bucked off, but I rode it longer than he did. Afterwards, all the little kids gathered around me rather than Jerry, the king. It really upset Jerry."

Daniels, who had given the impression that he excelled at this sport, felt embarrassed, particularly after the self-effacing Shep hung on to his lunging bull for several serious bucks before being thrown. Many younger Hmong remembered this New Year's celebration as a particularly special occasion because of the SKY rodeo which tried to replace Ly Lue's spectacular New Year's air shows.

Colonel Billy spent a quiet Christmas in the U.S. Now working at CIA headquarters at Langley, Virginia, he monitored Laos. His concept of the Hmong as a counterinsurgency force was now only a memory. Fast-moving jet aircraft dropped 500- and 2,000-pound bombs against small moving targets. Troops were helicoptered to fight pitched battles with enemy forces that were more experienced and better equipped. In his opinion, the Americans had usurped responsibilities that he had envisioned for the Thai. Frustrated over these developments and the cost to the Hmong, he tried not to think about Hmong suffering and the high casualty rate. It was too painful.

Colonel Heine Aderholt, now based at Eglin Air Force Base in Florida, home of Air Force Special Operations, prepared to retire. His unorthodox, "can-do" responses to solving problems in the field were not particularly appreciated by those who recommended colonels for promotion to general. Aderholt would retire as a colonel.

Kissinger was telling the world there was "light at the end of the tunnel" and there would be "peace with honor." Most Americans thought the Vietnam War was almost over. They were wrong.

* * *

An upsurge in communist stockpiling of men and weapons, including tanks, along the Ho Chi Minh Trail in Laos and near the U.S. Marine base at Khe Sanh just over the Lao border in South Vietnam indicated that Hanoi planned another ground attack against South Vietnam's northern provinces. Since an NVA invasion could doom Nixon's "Vietnamization" policy, military strategists believed that this buildup had to be eliminated. But U.S. congressional legislation prohibited the use of U.S. ground troops in Laos. Thus, the South Vietnamese Army would have to make the assault. The U.S. would provide only air support, not yet prohibited by Congress.

On February 8, 1971, South Vietnamese troops in "Operation Lam Son 719," with U.S. air support, crossed the Lao border, heading for Tchepone, a Lao town on the Trail, a known hotbed of NVA activity. To support Lam Son 719, the U.S. Air Force helicoptered in three 100-man Hmong blocking units. This was the first time that Hmong were to fight in southern Laos, out of their Military Region II northern homelands. Positioned northwest of Tchepone, they mined escape routes and waited to interdict enemy soldiers forced west by the Lam Son operation.[5] A few days into the operation, South Vietnamese troops encountered stiff NVA resistance. They stalled and dug in, making themselves vulnerable to NVA artillery.

As the fighting in southern Laos made headlines, an enemy net tightened around Long Chieng. The NVA had again infiltrated the southern ridge of Skyline overlooking Long Chieng, threatening the navigational beacon there. While communist forces waited to attack Vang Pao's headquarters, their big guns nightly pounded Hmong positions around Long Chieng and Long Chieng itself. The NVA's Soviet-made 130mm field guns terrorized the Hmong. With a range of 30 kilometers, these menacing guns destroyed with no concern for retaliation.

A Thai howitzer crew fired 105s and 155s from a banana grove near the king's summer bungalow. Neither had the range to reach the 130 gun positions. Vang Pao's "flying artillery," his T-28s, were useless against the 130 guns hidden in caves. As on Padong in 1961, the Hmong remained outgunned.

Fearing a ground attack at Long Chieng, Vang Pao sent his wives and children to Vientiane. He refused to leave his headquarters, where he monitored squawking radios. Hmong pilots daily scrambled their T-28s to bomb enemy positions on Skyline Ridge, at Bouam Loung, and at other positions in danger of being overrun.

Everywhere Hmong were pinned down and needed constant resupply. At Long Chieng, Shep rigged supplies for aerial drops. Frustrated because he often worked without a full complement of men, he often stormed into the shack of the Lao lieutenant in charge of organizing the resupply workforce to find him high on opium. "After a particularly unfriendly visit from Vang Pao, who demanded to know why I was not resupplying his men properly, I reported my understaffing problem to Jerry Daniels. Daniels told me to tell Vang Pao. I went to Vang Pao's house, told him the situation, and returned to my rigging area. In about thirty minutes, 'V.P.' showed up with an entourage of officers in two jeeps to look at my operation. They looked around and saw that I only had five guys working and I was supposed to have fifty. Vang Pao departed. A few hours later, Vang Pao returned with fifty men and told me, 'No more problem.' Later, I asked Jerry how he had managed to get so many men. Jerry said simply, 'He shot one of them.' I was stunned. I don't know if he shot someone or not, but I never saw that opium-smoking Lao lieutenant again. After this incident I never had a staffing problem. Sometimes more than fifty men showed up to work."[6]

On February 14 at about three in the morning, NVA commandos stormed Alternate, blowing up aircraft, ammunition dumps, and supply stocks. Many defenders were seriously wounded, including Shep, who was hit in the leg and thigh by an enemy B-40 mortar.

At dawn, an American Raven pilot at Long Chieng called in U.S. air strikes. Two fast-moving F-4s responded from Thailand. One carried 500-pound bombs; the other carried CBUs—cluster bomb units. As a result of panic and confusion, the jet carrying the CBUs hit friendly positions, causing fires which swept through several buildings along Alternate. Delayed bomblets exploded sporadically, tearing into unsuspecting defenders as they put out fires and assisted the wounded. More were killed and wounded by the Americans than by the enemy. This debacle would be referred to as the Valentine's Day Massacre.

From its encircling positions, the enemy watched Long Chieng licking its wounds, keeping the pressure on with its shelling. At night, Hmong in mountain positions could see muzzle flashes and hear the initial sounds of the big Soviet guns firing from positions on the Plaine des Jarres. Their assignment was to determine the coordinates of a gun when it fired. They called that information to Cricket, Alley Cat, or White Star. By the time jet fighters arrived, the gun usually had retreated to the sanctuary of a cave. Some pilots realized that the only way to get at these guns was to "force feed" bombs into the mouths of the caves. This would not be easy.

Even if pilots could see a 130mm gun, its sleek, streamlined chassis and delicate muzzle made it a difficult target. Pilots discovered that to render it useless required a direct hit of at least a 2,000-pound bomb. It was a formidable target for U.S. bombing equipment accurate to only 10 meters. To render a 130mm gun temporarily inoperative was difficult; to permanently destroy it required extraordinary skill and luck.

Then Operation Lam Son 719 suffered a setback. In mid-March, the South Vietnamese Army withdrew. Inadequate U.S. air cover exposed units to NVA gunners during this withdrawal. Photos of fleeing South Vietnamese soldiers frantically clinging to helicopter skids as American pilots tried to evacuate them convinced some Americans that the South Vietnamese soldiers were not fighters, but cowards.

The situation at Long Chieng and throughout northern Laos was dismal. During March, Long Chieng remained under siege. Heavy shelling continued. T-28s flew over 1,000 sorties in defense of the base. Enemy ground probes took place at night—the enemy's preference. Flareships dropped flares to illuminate the blackness, outline ridges and karsts, and expose the enemy. Spooky gunships, Gatling guns blazing from their fuselages, held off ground attacks.

General Vang Pao turned to Prince Sisouk na Champassak, recently appointed Lao defense minister, for more troops. He responded by ordering Royal Lao troops and their commanders to Long Chieng. Vang Pao balked: he wanted the troops, but did not want their Lao commanders interfering with his operations; he considered some of them incompetent and unsympathetic to his people. The Lao commanders refused to turn over their troops to him because they thought many would be killed "as a result of what they felt was poor staff work of Vang Pao and his CAS [CIA] advisors."[7]

As a result of the bickering by the Army General Staff, two battalions of Neutralist troops were sent instead of Royal Lao soldiers. The Hmong looked upon the Neutralists with derision and considered their arrival an insult. Since Vang Pao could not get assistance from other Lao commanders, he called in his irregulars from other areas to defend Long Chieng.

American commanders also feuded. The war in Laos, now favoring the enemy, continued to be controlled by the U.S. Ambassador to Laos, as head of the Country Team. He had no U.S. or any other troops under his command. The 7/13th Air Force, headquartered across the river in Thailand, provided the critical air support for operations in Laos. Yet 7/13th Air Force was often not involved, for "security reasons," in the planning of military operations.

"The chain of coordination for air operations over Laos was tenuous at best," wrote an Air Force historian. "It involved aircraft based in Thailand, under the control of a command center in Vietnam (7th AF), responding to the requirements of a Meo [Hmong] ground commander (Maj Gen Vang Pao), who in turn was advised by and responsive to CAS [CIA], which was directed by the American Ambassador to Laos, who made known his air requirements to 7/13th AF (a nonoperational command), which then requested the air assets from 7th AF."[8]

There was intense competition for power and prestige, pitting the State Department and the CIA on one side against the Pentagon on the other. Since the conflict over which agencies were in charge of military operations in Laos could not be resolved in Laos, these matters of operational dispute were passed on to the bureaucracy in Washington for resolution.

*   *   *

On April 15, 1971, Vang Pao attempted to retake the ridges overlooking Long Chieng, sending forces against enemy positions on Skyline and on a mountain behind called Phou Pha Xai. After three days of heavy fighting, he retook Skyline, although the enemy still held Phou Pha Xai. In a series of bold maneuvers, he airlifted his troops over the enemy to conduct hit and run strikes against its supply lines. He sent small units, with Forward Air Guides, behind enemy lines to locate enemy gun positions and call in air strikes.

During this time many Hmong, some of them only children, were deployed on dangerous missions. While the following story may seem extraordinary, it was, as I learned from hundreds of interviews with Hmong soldiers, typical of those in the front lines.

Moua Bee, age 13, had joined the Hmong "special forces" as a cook when he was 11. When he was 12, he was strong enough to carry a gun and became a "carbine soldier." He had four weeks of training in Laos followed by a month's combat training at Pitsanoulok in Thailand. Then Moua Bee was helicoptered behind enemy lines as part of a small unit to support Forward Air Guide Lee Peng. His unit's position was code-named Hotel Echo. Their only contact with Long Chieng was by radio. They had two gun positions, arranged to cover each other. The soldiers spent most of their time underground or lying on their bellies watching the enemy.

By now the U.S. Air Force had withdrawn many aircraft operating in the Lao theatre. Those remaining to cover Laos were assigned to interdiction strikes along the Trail in southern Laos. This left Vang Pao exposed to the largest and certainly the best-equipped and best-supplied enemy force yet to occupy northern Laos. Lee Peng and other Forward Air Guides were lucky when ABCCC could divert a plane to respond to their calls.

There were many NVA guns near Moua Bee's position. "We could see the bullets exploding in the air from antiaircraft guns as they shot at the American and Lao planes, but it was difficult to locate the exact position of these guns. It was our responsibility to locate them and call in air strikes to blow them up."[9]

About a month after Moua Bee arrived at Hotel Echo, he spotted NVA soldiers nearby. "We saw them beneath our position, lower down the mountain, moving toward us. Some of the area had been mined to slow down a ground attack which we knew would come. We were trapped on the top in our bunkers. We could escape only by chopper."

Each gun position at Hotel Echo had fifteen defenders. It was dark, with no moon. Moua Bee watched the blackness: "We knew they were out there. Somehow, they had gotten by the mines. Suddenly, B-40 rockets hit, killing and wounding several. Then B 40s stopped firing. We did not dare fire our M-16s or machine guns. That would show the enemy our exact position and they would kill us all. We waited. Then we heard it: that sound we didn't want to hear—a long, shrill whistle—the NVA signal for attack.

"We heard them running toward us. We waited, watching. We could defend only with hand grenades. As the noises got louder, we shot flares into the darkness to show us the enemy. It was now life or death for us.

In the light, we threw hand grenades at the running figures. Flares, NVA running in the trees, hand grenade explosions, AK-47s and B-40s firing, darkness, moaning, flares, hand grenades, more flares. Pain in my hand. More grenades. Then darkness and quiet. When the shooting stopped, I felt my right hand. My little finger was missing. I wrapped something around my hand to stop the bleeding.

"When light came, the NVA had retreated to their positions. My hand hurt, but the attack was over and we had won. Several of our men were dead. The wounded helped each other with bandages. Then our commander ordered us to check the area for dead soldiers. We picked up twelve bodies and brought them to our bunker. The dead men carried photos of Ho Chi Minh in their pockets. Lee Peng radioed Long Chieng to pick up our dead. Later in the morning an American chopper came in. An American took photographs of the dead NVA while we put our dead soldiers into the big green body bags. The chopper took the Hmong soldiers back to Long Chieng to be buried. No replacements were sent."

Within a few weeks the NVA launched another night attack. This time Hotel Echo killed three NVA and took prisoners. Moua Bee helped secure the prisoners: "We tied the prisoners' hands behind their backs and ordered them to sit on the ground. Some prisoners fell over dead with much saliva coming from their mouths. We noticed that their collars were wet and chewed. We slit open some collars to find five or six very tiny gray dots of poison. This was the first time that Hotel Echo had taken prisoners, so we didn't know about the poison. From then on, when we captured a soldier, we immediately cut his collar off so he couldn't kill himself."

Vang Pao's strategy of leapfrogging his men to the enemy's rear to interdict supply lines and to find and destroy their guns was working. Communist troops fell back, relieving the pressure on Long Chieng.

* * *

During Nixon's first year in office, antiwar protests escalated. Violence, including bombings and vandalism, resulted in millions of dollars of damage. Underground newspapers supported violent acts against the U.S., calling it a "pig nation." Protesters wielding knives and shotguns stormed campus buildings and held administrators hostage.[10] In April and May of 1971, massive antiwar demonstrations took over Washington. A May Day program of civil disobedience and property destruction, intended to disrupt government, frightened the occupants of the White House and captured news headlines. Nixon saw the media as having a double standard that hampered his efforts to conclude the Vietnam War: "Often statements by American and South Vietnamese military authorities were assumed to be lies by the same reporters who printed North Vietnamese lies without question. A hue and cry was raised against the United States when an isolated incident of mass murder by American forces at My Lai was revealed; yet when the West learned of the massacre by the Communists at Hue, where twenty-five times as many civilians as at My Lai died in what was anything but an isolated incident, Amnesty International indulgently chalked the crime up to the 'merciless tradition of war.'"[11] He later wrote that the antiwar critics had been duped "by the Communist PR blitz, the intellectual dream machine that . . . has been tricking western intellectuals into looking at slavery and seeing utopia, looking at aggression and conquest and seeing liberation, looking at ruthless murderers and seeing 'agrarian reformers,' looking at idealized portraits of Ho Chi Minh gazing beneficently upon the children gathered around him and seeing a mythical national father figure rather than the brutal dictator he really was."[12]

The President, however, held firm in his determination to end the war honorably for the United States. "I was convinced that unless we backed up our diplomatic efforts with strong military pressure, the North Vietnamese would continue their strategy of talking and fighting until we tired of the struggle and caved in to their bottom-line demand: that the United States withdraw unilaterally and acquiesce in the overthrow of the South Vietnamese government in exchange for the return of American prisoners of war. I considered it unthinkable that we would fight a bitter war for four years, lose 30,000 men, and spend tens of billions of dollars for the goal of getting our POWs back."[13]

Antiwar sentiment in Congress grew. Kissinger feared that Congress would legislate a dishonorable end to U.S. involvement in Southeast Asia. Entangled in Hanoi's web of secret "guerrilla" negotiations, he was unable to convey to the American public Hanoi's truculence in demanding unconditional surrender by the United States and its South Vietnamese ally. Obviously annoyed with the know-nothing attitude of many antiwar leaders, Kissinger and Nixon decided that the long-term interest of the U.S. had to take precedence over domestic turmoil. "With deep foreboding, but also a prayerful sense of the long-term national interest, the United States government had concluded that the security of free peoples everywhere would be jeopardized by an essentially narcissistic act of abdication. We could not simply turn tens of millions in Southeast Asia over to a Communist rule we knew would be repressive and brutal. We would settle for minimum terms. But we would not dishonor our country by joining our adversary against our friends. And if we would not accept Hanoi's terms, only two possibilities existed: Either we would negotiate a compromise compatible with our values, or else there would be another military test in 1972."[14]

*   *   *

Since 1967, U.S. intelligence intercepts had recorded the NVA use of helicopters to infiltrate troops into Laos and to resupply them. During early May 1971 American pilots spotted NVA helicopters operating at night in Laos and requested permission to attack. The U.S. Embassy in Vientiane denied permission until May 23, by which time the enemy helicopters had retreated to the rear. It was still the Land of Oz.

Intelligence intercepts also indicated that the enemy intended to take Bouam Loung; Pathet Lao radio taunted Site 32 defenders with psychological warfare, trying to destroy their will to fight. Those in the rim positions of the Fortress believed they could not be overrun. Each position, surrounded by ditches too wide to jump and six to seven feet deep, was accessed by ladders thrown over the gaping trenches. Enemy forces on ladders would be easily killed. Early one morning, however, this confidence was shattered. As one young soldier pulled in his ladder, he heard a scratching noise coming from the ground beneath him. He turned toward the noise, pointing his gun. As he did, a NVA soldier popped from a hole, running and firing. The surprised youth fired back. The intruder fell. Another enemy scrambled out of the same hole and ran with his hands over his head toward some stored ammunition. In his hands, he carried dynamite. Another Hmong fired at his hands. Exploding dynamite ripped his body into fragments. The first defender grabbed two boxes of hand grenades, ran to the tunnel opening, and with rhythmic precision dropped one grenade after another down the hole until he had expended two boxes. Then he listened for noises coming from the tunnel. There were none.

News of the enemy tunnel scared the Americans and the defenders. The older Hmong knew about the tunnels at Dien Bien Phu where the Viet Minh had successfully dug under French perimeters to positions beneath the French base. When the final attack came, Viet Minh popped from their tunnels, firing at close range upon the startled French. Did the NVA intend to penetrate this fortified bowl through tunnels like those at Dien Bien Phu? Inspection by binoculars of the bowl's sides indicated that they had indeed been tunneled.

Bouam Loung, with its intelligence gathering capabilities and its vital role as an interdiction staging base, was a worthy prize, as was its boastful commander. Moua Cher Pao, recently promoted to lieutenant colonel, remained confident that Site 32 would hold. The defenders of Bouam Loung had consummated their vow never to surrender or flee with the "drinking of the water" ceremony. In addition, his astrological signs indicated that this was an auspicious time for him. His Bouam Loung would not fall.

On May 20, 1971, cold rain fell on Bouam Loung. The enemy knew that Site 32, isolated from air support because of the bad weather, was vulnerable, and launched an attack with a combined NVA–Pathet Lao force of some 2,500 soldiers. This outnumbered the entire population of Bouam Loung by 500 and the colonel's soldiers by more than three to one. In the gray wetness, enemy troops fought their way up the slopes, foot by foot, with intense gunfire raking their advances. As long as the bad weather held off Vang Pao's "air," the NVA would inch up the slopes, using the ubiquitous tunnels, and eventually overpower Site 32.

Colonel Moua frantically radioed for help. In response to his "May Day," a newly trained Hmong Forward Air Guide equipped with a mobile beacon was dropped into Bouam Loung. He carried with him a new technology, referred to as "offset beacon bombing," which allowed aircraft to lock on to a target without visual contact. Pilots working off this ground beacon could home in on enemy positions in all weather conditions.

On the third day of the battle, clouds still shrouded the bowl. The NVA knew that the cocky Bouam Loung commander could not count on U.S. or Hmong pilots this day. Atop the bowl, soldiers studied the ominous overcast and hoped that the attack would not come. Then they heard the spine-tingling whistles and screams, signaling attack. The enemy rushed the slopes. Bouam Loung immediately called for "air." Spooky gunships, standing alert, lifted off. The Forward Air Guide turned on his battery powered beacon.

As the enemy fought its way up the slopes, the Hmong heard the muffled sounds of approaching aircraft engines. Overhead and out of sight of the enemy, Spooky pilots, working off the beacon and the directions of the ground Forward Air Guide, fired through the overcast. Operating with extraordinary courage and skill, gunship crews, directed by the Forward Air Guide, killed attackers on the slopes. Surprised by the aerial slaughter of its troops, the enemy withdrew.

When the firing ceased, Site 32 defenders looked down the slopes to see hundreds of bodies hanging in the barbed wire coils. Some were trapped in wires, only yards away. The corpses were not removed. The stench of decomposition lingered in the mountain air, a reminder to all that Bouam Loung would be defended to the death.

Bouam Loung had survived the attack, thanks to the offset beacon bombing. By the end of May, the NVA departed the area of Site 32, leaving behind three Pathet Lao battalions to keep Colonel Moua's men from breaking out to return to destroying their supply caches and interdicting their supply lines.

18.

War Bloodies the Land of Oz

To seek peace at any price was no answer to an enemy who sought victory at any price.

—Richard Nixon, *No More Vietnams*

There was more bad news for General Vang Pao and Military Region II. Beginning in July 1971, U.S. Air Force Barrel Roll sorties over northern Laos would again be reduced, this time by almost 50 percent, from 60 to 32 sorties per day. With this further evidence that the U.S. intended to withdraw from Southeast Asia, King Savang Vatthana and Prime Minister Souvanna Phouma ordered Vang Pao to gain as much territory as possible in Xieng Khouang and Sam Neua provinces before the July 1 deadline.

Though he had only two operable forward bases—Long Chieng and Bouam Loung—Vang Pao agreed to go on the offensive. Both towns had recently been under siege and taken heavy losses. Enemy forces lingered around both. Yet he reasoned that it would be better to try to retake lost territory before July 1 while he still could count on 60 U.S. air strikes a day.

On June 11, in a bold move, Vang Pao airlifted irregulars to the southern tip of the Plaine des Jarres in yet another attempt to take the entire plain, now rich with enemy supplies. Since his 8,900 irregulars were outnumbered by an estimated 20,000 enemy soldiers, he would supplement his hit-and-run strikes with his favorite twist—"air." Helicopters airlifted his forces to a location where his men flushed out the enemy.

Once exposed, his T-28s finished them off. His mobile troops would then be airlifted to yet another area to flush out the enemy for "air" to annihilate. Vang Pao was back to waging guerrilla warfare with T-28 close support, as he had done earlier at Lima Lima. T-28 pilot Coyote well remembered those terrifying days: "I didn't want to fly those missions. I was constantly scared during this operation. I flew because my fellow Hmong begged me for help."[1]

Moua Bee's forward position, Hotel Echo, was in the midst of this heavy fighting. His hair was long; he had been here for a long time. Water was scarce, only enough for drinking. Water and food were night-dropped by impact chutes. (These chutes allowed pilots to drop accurately from high altitudes.) One day during this offensive, Moua Bee watched three American F-105 jets with their afterburners firing, flying from Thailand heading for Ban Ban. "Soon I saw them returning; the one in the middle was burning. Fire on its wings and black smoke. The plane circled and turned back toward the enemy. Then it turned again toward us. Lee Peng, who was in the bunker, listening on the radio, shouted: 'Time to get out of the bunker. An American plane is going down. Get ready! Hurry! Hurry! Get up there and watch the plane. See where it's going down.' We ran out of our bunkers. I watched the pilot parachute from his burning plane not far from an area that we had mined.

"As soon as the pilot was on the ground, Peng tried to call him over his radio. Then we heard the American talking to Peng. Peng told him not to move, as the area was mined. He should stand still and we would rescue him. About 20 of us ran toward his location. When we arrived, the tall, blond pilot was trembling and pointing his gun at us. He was also talking on his small radio. We hoped he was still talking to Peng and wouldn't shoot us. Since we couldn't talk English, we raised our M-16s in the air to show we were friends. Over his radio, Peng told him that he had to go with us, and we guided him safely to Hotel Echo.

"When we got there, he was still trembling. Peng greeted him in English, but he continued to shake. Peng had already called White Star for air rescue. Within a short time, many planes circled overhead to protect our position. Then a huge chopper dropped down into our very small area to pick up the pilot. The American seemed happy now. He shook Peng's hand and jumped into the chopper. I stood looking up at the chopper in the wind and the dirt as it took off. The American pilot smiled, waved his hand, and disappeared into the wind and dust. I didn't wave back because I didn't know what a wave meant."[2]

During this daring operation General Vang Pao's forces captured nearly 800 tons of supplies—enough, the experts estimated, to support the enemy in the PDJ for three months. They captured 1,228 rounds of 82mm mortar shells, bomb-damaged 85mm and 122mm field guns, small arms, medicines, and huge amounts of bagged rice.[3] General Vang Pao ordered one of the captured 122mm guns taken back to Long Chieng where he placed it in front of his house as a war trophy.

Vang Pao believed that the NVA around Long Chieng would pursue his units to the PDJ. He was wrong. The NVA had no intention of being distracted from its major goal: taking the secret CIA base and Vang Pao's headquarters. The enemy installed more units along Skyline Ridge.

On June 15, fighting broke out on Skyline once again. Five days later the Hmong retook the ridge. The NVA began to withdraw, leaving behind Pathet Lao forces. The NVA troops headed toward the northern and northeastern portions of the PDJ to protect their supply caches from Vang Pao.

* * *

On June 22, the U.S. Senate passed the Mansfield amendment, calling on the President to withdraw all U.S. forces within nine months if Hanoi agreed to release American POWs. This was a signal to Hanoi that Kissinger's negotiating stance was more bluff than substance. The U.S. Congress now seemed to control negotiations with Hanoi.

Kissinger now regretted entering secret negotiations. "In retrospect, I wonder whether we paid too high a price for secrecy. Hanoi wanted secrecy because it sought to deprive the Administration of the possibility of using the negotiations to rally public opinion. We went along because we thought success was more important than publicity but also because experience had shown that no matter what we proposed, our critics would push us further, undermining our position. There is no doubt that in 1971 secrecy enabled Hanoi to whipsaw us; the question whether more openness would have stopped this or produced an even earlier stalemate must remain in the realm of conjecture."[4]

On June 26, Le Duc Tho and Kissinger met again secretly in Paris. After the usual polemics and a lecture on North Vietnamese superiority, Le Duc Tho said American POWs would be released at the time of U.S. withdrawal, but he stuck to his ultimatum that the U.S. must dismantle the Thieu government in South Vietnam. Then he added a new twist. The North Vietnamese demanded war reparations. Kissinger claimed that he rejected this demand "out of hand" and said that the U.S. would not pay war reparations as "an act of penance." It might, however, agree to do so for other reasons.

Kissinger tried to discuss Laos and Cambodia. "Le Duc Tho would unnervingly point out that Hanoi was 'already' living up to the Geneva Accords (at a time when several hundred thousand North Vietnamese troops were roaming around these countries). When I questioned this, Le Duc Tho would explain coolly that there were Vietnamese in many countries of the world; or if he wanted to be more formalistic, he would argue that the North Vietnamese were there to protect the neutrality of Laos and Cambodia."[5]

Le Duc Tho's riveting concern was to maneuver the U.S. into a position of destroying the Saigon government. He proposed a complete cutoff of U.S. military aid to Saigon. Kissinger recalled in his memoirs that at one point Le Duc Tho, in his eagerness to get the U.S. to overthrow the anticommunist regime in the South, offered advice: "During a break he took me aside and suggested that if we did not know how to replace Thieu by means of the presidential election, assassination would do admirably. The vehemence of my refusal produced one of the few occasions when I saw Le Duc Tho temporarily flustered."[6]

* * *

About a month after the rescue of the F-105 pilot by the soldiers of Hotel Echo, the NVA launched another night attack against their position. Their numbers diminished by lack of replacements for their earlier casualties, the defenders barely prevailed. Moua Bee, wounded in the knees by an AK-47 burst, fought throughout the night. Airlifted out the next day for treatment, he was soon back at his position. Shortly after his return, the NVA attacked again, killing Lt. Yang Cheu, Hotel Echo's commander. The young boys held out until dawn. Then, knowing they could not withstand another assault, they slipped into the jungle. From Long Chieng, a flight of Hmong T-28s rose into the gray dawn to bomb Hotel Echo and its NVA occupiers.

Now Vang Pao knew that though he could count on his T-28s, the U.S. Air Force was not as eager to support him as in the past. He also learned that on July 21 a further reduction of U.S. air sorties would go into effect.

Not everyone had considered General Vang Pao's offensive on the PDJ to be a wise move. A message from General Andrew J. Evans, Jr., Deputy Commander of 7/13th Air Force based at Udorn, to General Lucius Clay, Commander of the 7th Air Force in Saigon, read: "In view of the current policy to wind down the war and decommit air and ground resource wherever possible, I feel the wisdom of a major ground effort by Vang Pao at this time should be questioned."[7]

Always his own man, with or without U.S. support, White Star resolutely launched phase two of his initiative designed to sweep the enemy forces from the Plaine des Jarres. On July 1—the day the U.S. Air Force reduced its air support by half—he ordered his men to move. One force of his three-pronged attack was airlifted to positions near Lima Lima. The other two were already in place on the PDJ.

Even after Vang Pao had committed his troops, the Air Force, the CIA, and the embassy disputed whether or not to support him. The embassy finally decided that it was in its best interests to do so, and limited air support was reluctantly granted. To offset reduced U.S. air support during this offensive, choppers airlifted Thai 105mm howitzer artillery battalions onto the PDJ. To protect the Thai gunners from ground attack, Hmong irregulars dug forward positions. Enemy pressure came against all three prongs of the Hmong attack strategy. Although Vang Pao's forces retook Lima Lima on July 17, they were driven off three days later. Vang Pao needed the Lima Lima airfield as he had needed it two years earlier. After several weeks of fighting, he retook it once more. To sustain the offensive, Air America and Continental Air Services crews rigged, loaded, and dropped supplies by parachute to beleaguered positions on the PDJ and in the surrounding mountains.

That month, the White House announced that Kissinger had secretly traveled to China to talk with Chou En Lai and Mao Zedong, and that Nixon would visit there sometime in 1972.

Colonel Billy had returned to the area, but not to Laos. Reassigned to Thailand, he spent most of his time in Bangkok as a liaison with the Thai government, sometimes discussing Thai military efforts in Laos.

On August 28, the Washington bureaucracy finally responded to the unresolved chain of command problem for operations in Laos which had pitted the Pentagon against State and the CIA over which agency was to run war operations in Laos. This response from the Joint Chiefs of Staff added a distinctly American flourish to the Land of Oz. The Joint Chiefs sent a directive requiring Washington's approval of any multi-battalion operation in Laos. Detailed plans had to be submitted ten days in advance of the operation.[8]

Vang Pao and his SKY advisors were furious when they learned about this. This was a war, not a chess game. Vang Pao often had only minutes or hours to respond to crises, not ten days plus the additional days it would take to write up a battle plan then transmit it to Washington for study by the JCS.

As the monsoon rains ended, Vang Pao was stalled on the Plaine des Jarres. The Hmong knew that they would be defending fixed positions when the Vietnamese launched their fall dry season offensive. The NVA would destroy them. War-weary Hmong were demoralized by the unrelenting deaths of their people, years of fighting, rumors of American withdrawal, and the increased NVA attacks on civilians. Hmong losses had been enormous. According to U.S. official data, "By 1971, many [Hmong] families were down to the last surviving male (often a youth of 13 or 14), and survival of the tribe was becoming a major concern."[9]

That fall, Hmong clan leaders, upset with the extraordinary loss of Hmong life, met with Vang Pao to propose civilian withdrawal from Military Region II. Vang Pao took the clan leaders' petition to Souvanna Phouma. The prime minister convinced the Hmong leaders to wait for the dry season before requesting permission to move the civilians.

The U.S. Embassy in Vientiane now warned the State Department that the Hmong people, on whom the U.S. had counted so heavily for so long, might collapse. "If the Meo [Hmong] suffer severe losses in the PDJ campaign this year, or if Bouam Loung falls to the NVA, massive refugee movements will be generated from north of the PDJ, the Long Tieng [Chieng] area, and the Ban Xon [Sorn] Valley, and impetus behind the Meo desire to pull out of the war completely will grow significantly. If the civilians began to leave . . . heading west, it would be difficult if not impossible for Vang Pao to prevent his troops from joining their dependents in a mass exodus from MR II."[10]

Civilians did not entirely withdraw from Region II. Many sought protection at Ban Sorn, Lima Site 272, where soon over 50,000 people, including the refugees from Sam Thong, would live. Pop Buell's hospital, with its Hmong female nurses, operated here.

In late October, typhoon Hester swept across the PDJ, stalling the enemy's advance. Once Hester passed and the earth dried out, the NVA struck Hmong positions across the PDJ. Because the situation was critical, T-28 pilots slept in Vang Pao's house at Alternate near the flight line.

About 4 a.m. one morning, Vang Pao summoned pilot Fackee. "Vang Pao was pacing and worrying about his men—six companies—pinned down near Lat Sen, Lima Site 276, by NVA soldiers with tanks. Over the radio, I heard the commander shouting and the heavy fighting. Vang Pao asked me, 'Do pilots fly at night?' I answered 'Yes, sir.' He then asked,

'Can all pilots fly at night—even Hmong pilots?' I answered, 'Yes, sir. All pilots can fly at night.' 'OK,' he shouted, 'Let's go.'[11]

"We woke up other pilots and ran to the airstrip. General Vang Pao helped load our planes with bombs. About 4:30, three T-28s lifted off. I flew as Chaophakaow Lead. The night was very dark with clouds. At first, we flew high above the clouds, but we couldn't see the shapes of the mountains to guide us. Then I ordered my wingmen to stay above the clouds and I would go below. Below the clouds, I saw the battle. I could see the red and green tracer bullets—it was like boys throwing stones at each other. It was very funny and very sad at the same time. I flew nearer and nearer, then the enemy spotted my aircraft. Suddenly the enemy stopped attacking our soldiers and started shooting at me with every kind of gun they had. The sky lit up with shells exploding all around me. I knew that I couldn't get through the enemy shelling. I put the plane in a steep dive to gain speed, banked away from the guns, and headed back for Long Chieng. General Vang Pao was furious that we couldn't get in."

Fackee could not stop thinking about the men at Lat Sen and the enemy guns. For a month, he couldn't sleep. He told Vang Pao that he dreamed about Lat Sen and all the men killed there. He asked the general if he could have a vacation. Vang Pao answered crisply, "No. No one can have a vacation. You are a soldier. It is like this. One time you win; one time you lose."

Instead of giving Fackee a vacation, General Vang Pao sent him to attack two positions overrun a few days earlier. Fackee, flying the lead, took off from Alternate with two wingmen, heading toward Route 9 near the North Vietnamese border. "As I neared the site, I could see lots of NVA. I told Chaophakaow 2 and 3 to stand by overhead. I wanted to go in low to drop my bombs and to see what was down there. I rolled in low for my first strike with a good hit. No problem. I circled and came in fast for my second strike. There was an explosion. All the needles passed over the red lines. There was a rushing sound under my feet. I heard Chaophakaow 2 say: 'I'm so sorry that you go so low. Jump out! Jump out!' I looked down at the rudders and smoke was coming up.

"Everything below was enemy, but I had to jump—my plane was on fire and out of control and I still had four bombs on board. I jumped and the enemy opened fire on me as I hung in my parachute. Bullets came very close, but none hit me. Since I was coming down in enemy territory, I knew that I would have to run to escape capture. As I landed in a tree, I heard my T-28 explode. Blood was spurting out of my nose. I cut myself out of my chute, climbed down the tree, and ran in the direction of friendly forces. "Overhead, Chaophakaow 2 and 3 circled, watching me. When they saw my parachute in the tree, they called Long Chieng to report that I was down and the coordinates of my parachute.

"I ran for four hours. The terrain was very difficult, and in four hours I only managed a few kilometers. Then, overhead I heard a chopper. I signaled him and down from the sky dropped 96 Whiskey with Captain Hood. He lowered a rope and pulled me in. Captain Hood saved my life. I had hurt myself jumping, but my wounds weren't serious. General Vang Pao allowed me to rest for one week, then I was back flying."

By autumn, Thai-manned firebases Rossini, Tom Tom, Mustang, King Kong, Cobra, Panther, Sting Ray, and Lion had dug in on the western edge of the PDJ. From these positions, Thai gunners were to protect Long Chieng. Some Thai gun positions had interlocking firing ranges. Others did not, and stood undefended except for the Hmong satellite positions with call-signs Hotel Delta, Hotel Yankee, Fox Bravo, and Fox Echo.

In late fall, the tempo of the war increased. Thai artillery battalions, intended to give backbone to Vang Pao's forces, were instead being hammered by the longer-range NVA 130mm guns. More Hmong were airlifted into positions on the PDJ to protect the Thai. This meant the irregulars might at any time be used in set piece conventional warfare for which they were not trained.

More Hmong were airlifted to mountain positions, often at altitudes of 5,000 to 6,000 feet, to pinpoint enemy guns. These men depended upon Air America or Continental Air Services for drops of water, munitions, and food. One-hundred-gallon red and blue gasoline drums of water, many rigged in Long Chieng, slipped from cargo planes and parachuted to lonely outposts. Directing these air drops were English-speaking Forward Air Guides—mostly Hmong—with call-signs that seemed out of place in Laos—though indeed appropriate for the Land of Oz. Men called Glassman, Smallman, Yellow Dog, Stringbean, Hunter, Badman, Dakota, Blue Boy, Night Fighter, Pressure, Red Hat, Tonto, Hill Billy, Ohio, and Rocket Mobile worked the radios to coax pilots to drop zones. These positions were often surrounded by enemy troops just waiting to pick off airplanes.

Resupply to Bouam Loung was so dangerous now that big Chinook helicopters took over much of the work. Unlike fixed wing aircraft, they could drop straight down into the bowl, avoiding enemy fire.

"Tango Juliet," a SKY expert in aerial resupply, rigged many loads during this intense fighting in Region II. "These were terrible years for Vang Pao and the Hmong. The enemy was on the move everywhere.

Long Chieng was threatened constantly with sappers, rockets, and artillery. I rigged right up on the front—out of Long Chieng and PDJ positions—to get supplies to those pinned down. Often, while we were rigging we came under attack and had to call in air strikes or artillery to save ourselves. I dropped anywhere from 100,000 to 300,000 pounds of cargo a day. My highest day was 309,000 pounds. This went on day after day after day without letup. The only time we got a break on the dropping was when the weather socked us in. Then we worked on rerigging and reordering."[12]

On November 19, two MiGs were spotted over Ban Ban. American pilots speculated that the North Vietnamese pilots might attempt a dogfight with U.S. jets over Laos or bomb Hmong positions which were not armed to defend against aerial attacks. While a dogfight never occurred, Bouam Loung was bombed.

In the midst of this heavy fighting, the CIA decided to drop propaganda leaflets and run "Loud Mouth" missions—airborne loudspeaker night propaganda broadcasts to enemy troops urging them to defect. Both Air America and Continental Air Services crews were pressed into action. Fred Walker, who had transferred recently from Bangkok to Udorn to fly supplies, was tapped to drop propaganda leaflets over the Bolovens Plateau in the south of Laos. Ed Dearborn was assigned to fly Loud Mouth missions in the north.

About midnight, Dearborn climbed into the cockpit of his Twin Otter, checked to see if he had his cotton balls for earplugs, and signaled to the Hmong in the rear, holding a microphone and a notebook, to prepare for takeoff. His target coordinates indicated he was to fly over enemy concentrations not far from Muong Soui, where he knew there were plenty of enemy and big guns. Dearborn hated both Loud Mouth missions and leaflet drops. They were dangerous. They were always in enemy territory.

He was still seething about the "Bubble Gum" leaflet drop he had flown a couple of years earlier. That night, he had circled low and slow over enemy territory while the kicker pushed the bundles out the door and the intended recipients fired at them. Dearborn then swung out to make a second pass, much more dangerous than the first, since gunners, now alerted, were prepared. He signaled to the kicker to bring him one of the leaflets. "I couldn't believe it. There was a picture of a local lady of the evening, standing naked in high-heeled shoes in one of the local taverns in Vientiane. The message was 'Come on down. Surrender and meet Bubble Gum.' I thought: 'I'm risking my ass out here in enemy territory to drop *this!*'"[13]

Tonight, as he approached his last target, he turned out all but an eyebrow light to read the cockpit instruments. He stuck the cotton balls in his ears and began his descent to 2,000 feet. The reader, sitting in the back, turned on his small flashlight used to see the message and picked up his microphone. Dearborn lined up on the coordinates, and about a half mile out, turned on the music. Several giant speakers—five feet high and three feet wide, attached to the fuselage and one in the open doorway of the plane—blared Wagner's *Ride of the Valkyries,* later used in a scene in the movie *Apocalypse Now.* Dearborn's first pass with the blaring music was intended to wake everyone up to listen.

"Actually, waking them up like this made them mad and everyone down there was shooting at us. For more than 20 minutes, I circled the area while the guy in the back is shouting out some message about the benefits of coming down to Vientiane with their guns and maybe getting a night with Bubble Gum and maybe a house or a farm or a goat. While he's talking, the enemy is hammering away at us. A couple of flashes seemed close so I decided to break off and leave. The guy in the back shouts, 'No! No! Go back! No finis! No finis!'

"I had decided that I was 'finis.' I was mad. These unarmed night missions of music and propaganda were dangerous and I doubted they did anything but make the enemy madder. I pulled off the mission and headed straight for Alternate. As I approached Alternate the sun was just coming up. I rolled right down past the old CIA barracks and I turned that thing on so loud it was an ear-splitter. I circled the Agency buildings for about 10 minutes with the music playing and the guy in the back talking. I knew that if there was any glass down there it just blew it clean out. I thought, 'Bastards, I've listened to this damn thing for the last couple of hours. Now *you're* going to listen to it.' When I landed at Long Chieng, there were some angry CIA people."

On the night of December 17, NVA forces launched a full-scale attack against firebase Tom Tom and its satellite positions. Throughout the night, Thai and Hmong radiomen frantically called for help. The next day, three Continental pilots flying Otters left Alternate loaded with ammunition and rations to resupply the pinned down locations. The pilots dropped in heavy ground fire that disabled one Otter, but it made it back to Long Chieng.

That night, enemy 130mm guns near Ban Ban fired on the Thai firebases with deadly accuracy. Some returned fire with their lesser guns, unable to reach the 130s. Crews in Alley Cat listened to men screaming over their radios about being attacked by tanks and ground troops.

By dawn, firebases Tom Tom and Mustang, shelled throughout the night, were no longer firing. In the morning, the enemy turned its guns on King Kong and Rossini. Only days before, Ed Dearborn had landed at these positions to offload his cargo. That was now impossible. Reports of antiaircraft gunners near all the firebases meant that supplies now had to be airdropped from 7,000 to 10,000 feet with impact chutes. Tango Juliet and his crews worked in rigging sheds at Long Chieng, frantically rigging cargo with impact chutes, charged by a primer cord, that detonated at 100 feet off the ground.

Dearborn and other Continental pilots paced nervously as their Otters were loaded with supplies for King Kong, the most desperate position. As Dearborn approached King Kong, he spotted four 12.7 antiaircraft guns in trees about 400 yards from the position, firing so rapidly that clouds of dust gave away their positions. The Otter pilots broke off the drop. It was too dangerous. Dearborn radioed for fire support to silence the antiaircraft guns. ''But neither counter battery fire nor air-cover was available to knock them out. We abandoned trying to supply King Kong. It was too late.''[14]

The Continental Otters dropped their cargoes at alternate sites and returned fast to Long Chieng, where they learned that Tom Tom was encircled by NVA antiaircraft guns and firebase Mustang and two Hmong positions, Fox Bravo and Fox Echo, were about to be overrun. Dearborn and Dan Cloud reloaded and lifted off, heading first for Fox Echo. Cloud reached it first. As he approached, the enemy opened up on him with 12.7 and 37mm antiaircraft guns. Cloud made one pass and dropped, taking a hit in his left wing that exploded inboard of his right engine, putting a hole in his flap. He made a hasty exit with shells exploding around him. Dearborn came under intense ground fire before he reached the drop zones, so he broke off and dropped his cargo at another site.

Once more at Long Chieng, Dearborn learned that his third resupply attempt would be to Hotel Delta and Hotel Yankee helicopter pads near the base of Tom Tom, where survivors reported that 130mm guns continued to pin them down and Soviet tanks were approaching. Don Bomes, flying an Air America Otter, joined Dearborn for this mission. As Dearborn roared off Alternate, he heard the radioman at Tom Tom shout that enemy troops were coming through the barbed wire. His pleas for help brought in U.S. F-4 Phantom fighters from Thailand to ''kill'' the 130mm guns, hidden on the northeastern side of the PDJ. Dearborn asked Cricket for the location of the jet strike, then switched frequencies. ''I heard a pilot say, 'We just lost an F-4. Just augered in out there. You can see the smoke.' I looked to the northeast and there was black smoke. I switched back to Cricket to hear the crew give coordinates for an immediate rescue attempt for the American pilots.''

As he listened to the Cricket crew, Dearborn continued toward the Hmong position at Hotel Delta. ''I came in at 2,000 feet, taking small arms and 37mm fire. I hit the bell to signal the kicker in the back to drop the cargo. I pulled up and away to watch Bomes come in to Hotel Yankee to drop. I went around and dropped a second time. Ground reported that only one of my seven impact chutes had opened. As I was cursing the malfunction, the ground controller interrupted to tell me that his position was under constant attack and they needed help badly. I didn't know what to say. I couldn't promise help.''

Dearborn switched his radio frequency to Tom Tom. ''I could see it taking heavy incoming fire. The Thai controller's voice quivered as he begged for help and resupply. Over half his battery was dead and wounded. As I departed the area, he shouted to me that the NVA were coming 'now—in through the perimeter defenses—they're coming—help us—help us!' Christ, there wasn't anything I could do.''

At Long Chieng, Vang Pao *could* do something. He ordered his T-28 pilots to drop CBUs against friendly positions in a desperate attempt to stop the enemy. The T-28s, braving intense antiaircraft fire, dropped CBUs on friendly perimeters, stalling the enemy advance.

About 5 p.m., Fred Walker, airborne in a C-47 heading for Udorn after a heavy day of ferrying supplies, monitored his radio. ''Suddenly, I heard 'Falcon 82,' an F-4 pilot, shout, 'Oh! No!' I looked for him. I saw flames. He just fell out of the sky. I saw no parachute. I also recorded in my logbook that day: 'One MiG shot down today.'''[15]

December 19 finally ended. During the past two days, enemy MiGs had shot down five F-4s, with no confirmation of any MiGs shot down.[16] One U.S. chopper had crashed. Enemy guns had also shot down two T-28s, one flown by Coyote. He parachuted and was picked up before the enemy could capture him. He flew again the next day.

During the early hours of December 20, Tom Tom and Mustang were overrun. The following day, Lion fell. Survivors headed south, with NVA troops and Soviet PT-76 tanks in hot pursuit. There was a low overcast; it would be another day without fighter support. The only pilots flying the PDJ on the 20th were Continental's pilots Dick Douglas, Al Adolph, and Dearborn.

Orders came to Dearborn to resupply firebase Panther under steady shelling, with Soviet PT-76 tanks moving rapidly toward it. ''While dropping to Panther, I saw a tank only a few hundred yards away from the position, firing at my bundles as they dropped. Then he turned his gun on the drop zone and blasted it. He did this after each pass. When I saw some Thais running away from the position under heavy tank fire, I discontinued dropping.

"By noon on December 20 everything was lost except King Kong and Rossini. Both these firebases were completely surrounded by the enemy with no chance of escape. I stayed airborne and in contact with the Thai radioman at King Kong. During my last radio contact with him, he cried and pleaded to me: 'The tanks are coming over our bunker! Please help! Please help!' I looked toward King Kong. It was true. I looked down to see a Soviet tank crawling up over his bunker. Then his radio went dead."[17]

After the fall of the Thai firebases on the Plaine des Jarres, the enemy attacked the sixteen smaller positions, coded Delta, dug in around Sam Thong and its landing field and eighteen positions, coded Romeo, on Phou Pha Xai. Hmong soldiers on these two mountaintops now were the last defense against the enemy's ground advance. If the enemy could capture these mountaintop positions, they could destroy Long Chieng. Now Vang Pao's strategy focused on resupplying these positions and those protecting Skyline Ridge with its navigational beacons. He gave orders to drop supplies to the survivors of the fallen firebases—if they could be located.

Using Soviet-made tanks and 130mm field guns, the communist attack against the forces defending the approaches to Long Chieng had been completely successful. The enemy had captured several 105mm and 14 155mm howitzers, which it would soon use against Vang Pao's forces. The enemy also took many Thai prisoners—most important political spoils of war.

Later, the enemy claimed that it had "captured or destroyed 34 artillery pieces of 105 and 155mm, 20 armoured cars and military trucks, shot down 17 aircraft and made a big haul of weapons of various kinds and military equipment."[18] While the enemy's tally was an exaggeration, the reality was that Colonel Thep's Thai artillery battalions that were intended to replace the dwindling U.S. air support had been mauled. Significantly, the firebases had been overrun not by a barefoot peasant force but by highly trained and well-equipped North Vietnamese soldiers with far superior weaponry.

With the firebases lost, Dearborn's mission was no longer resupply but rescue—picking up the wounded and the survivors from the firebases who had escaped capture. Some had crawled into the high grasses to wait for darkness; others played dead, waiting for a chance to sneak away. NVA tanks ran down any survivors they found.

On December 21 and 22, Dearborn rescued survivors. "What a pitiful sight. Some of these kids I picked up had blood pouring out of their ears and noses from the concussions they had suffered in the firebases with shells landing on top of them. The majority were shell-shocked after the hundreds of 130 rounds that had hit their positions. Many were suffering shrapnel wounds, exposure, and shock in one form or another. It was terrible."[19]

Dearborn's plans to spend Christmas with his family in California faded. Hesitant about leaving at such a critical time, he delayed his departure. Then on the afternoon of December 23, he put on his cleanest clothes and boarded a Thai Airways flight for Bangkok. There he caught a Pan Am flight to the West Coast that stopped in Hong Kong, where he bought his wife a piece of jewelry as a Christmas present. He arrived in Los Angeles on Christmas Eve day. He spent Christmas with his wife, his parents, and Grandfather Beecher after whom he, a decade earlier, had named the landing strip—Ban Beecher, Lima Site 100.

19.

The Siege of Long Chieng

In my country, Vang Pao is the most stubborn, relentless, and determined man. There is no other Hmong like Vang Pao.

—Lee Blia Chue, who was born in 1916 in Xieng Khouang Province, lived during the time of the French, Japanese, and Americans,
and came to the U.S. as a refugee

After spending only two days over Christmas with his family, Ed
Dearborn boarded a plane to return to Laos. On the evening of December
29, 1971, he stepped off a Thai Airways flight in Vientiane to learn that
the situation at Long Chieng was critical: the enemy had overrun positions at the southern end of Skyline Ridge and captured the navigational
equipment. Snipers controlled the approach to Alternate.

Americans, including Ambassador G. McMurtrie Godley, believed
that Long Chieng could be overrun at any moment. Defying Godley's
orders to evacuate, Vang Pao remained at Alternate. Hog and Bamboo
also remained there. Many thought that a ground attack was imminent—maybe on New Year's Day, since the Vietnamese seemed to prefer
to launch offensives on holidays.

Early the next morning Dearborn, trying to shake off jet lag, dropped
supplies to Hmong positions pinned down on Skyline Ridge. The following morning, he flew out of Pha Khao picking up survivors from the
firebases that had been overrun just before Christmas. He was moved by
the condition of these survivors. "They were torn up and dirty. Most had
defecated in their pants, which is natural when there is such great fear.
They were absolutely filthy from days of being out there, maybe locked
in their bunkers because of the heavy shelling or hiding from the tanks.

They smelled terrible; they looked terrible. Some had sidearms and rifles. Some just had the clothes on their backs. They were all tired, hungry, and thirsty."[1] After nine hours of flying, Dearborn, exhausted, headed for Vientiane.

At Long Chieng, a helicopter carrying radioman Lo Ma landed. Tired, dirty, and loaded down with his M-16, grenades, and radio, he trudged wearily beside Alternate's runway. Suddenly 20 rounds of 130mm artillery hit near the Buddhist temple. "I shouted to a Hmong colonel driving past me in a jeep. 'Let's get out of here! The next ones will be on the runway! I pushed him out of the driver's seat and took control. I sped up the hill to our night command post near the king's house. I looked back and saw Vang Pao's jeep behind me."[2]

As the two jeeps reached the top of the hill, shells hit along the edge of the runway. Everyone jumped out and ran for the command post, with Vang Pao shouting to Lo Ma to contact the front line commanders to locate the gun positions.

Hog and Bamboo rushed into the command bunker, dressed for fighting. No blue jeans tonight. They wore fatigues, heavy boots, and carried M-16s and lots of ammunition. Each had a pistol on his belt. Within minutes, Vang Chou, "General Direction," arrived from the Air Operations Center. By dark about fifteen people were in the command post. For Lo Ma, who was trying to get information from various positions, it was a time of much confusion. "No one seemed to know what was going on. I was certain that a ground attack would start any moment."

Lo Ma talked over a sideband radio to unit commanders while Vang Pao shouted to him to get more information. As intel came in, Lo Ma charted enemy positions on a large military wall map. Daniels, Vang Chou, and General Vang Pao watched as Lo Ma inserted enemy troops among Vang Pao's positions. When Hog saw the situation, he called the SKY Chief in Udorn asking for "air." Udorn refused.

Bamboo called Alley Cat for air strikes. Everyone was asking for "air." Vang Pao wanted "air" against the guns. His T-28s had moved to Vientiane. There was no nearby Hmong "air." The Skyline navigational beacons had been captured or blown up by the enemy, knocking out directional aids for pilots. It was a mess. Everyone was talking at once. Outside, guns ripped up Alternate. As the bombardment became heavier, Vang Pao ordered his men to man the 155 howitzer set up near the western loading ramp and return fire. They were forced to retreat by heavy shelling. He shouted that the enemy must be on Alternate to direct such accurate firing. Lo Ma was afraid. "I asked Vang Pao what was going to happen. He looked at me and shook his head. 'American people,' he said sharply, 'they never do things right. We need 'air!' ''

Dearborn was unaware of the situation at Long Chieng as he prepared to land at Vientiane. He did know that he was extremely tired, but decided to have a drink or two with friends to celebrate New Year's Eve. That was not to be. At the airfield, he learned of the attack on Long Chieng. Few details were available. Instead of drinks tonight, he and Dan Cloud were told to fly night-cover over Alternate for Daniels and the other CIA men, in case the base was overrun and they had to flee on foot.

Enemy gunners increased their shelling of Long Chieng as they became more accurate. Every position was pinned down, including the howitzers and Vang Pao's command post. Vang Pao knew the enemy was on Alternate. The SKY men ordered Vang Pao into the bunker just outside the command post. He resisted, but they insisted. After heated words, he jumped into the bunker with two bodyguards. Almost immediately, the enemy artillery struck again with a thunderous noise, jolting everyone in the command bunker and knocking out a 155 howitzer near the runway. Vang Pao rushed back into his command post. He and the SKY men discussed B-52 strikes. Vang Pao wanted the Americans to use B-52 strikes to wipe out the enemy guns and to cut their supply lines so they couldn't sustain a ground attack. In vain, he repeatedly shouted for "air."

Dearborn, knowing it would be a long, cold night above the mountains flying cover for the CIA men, threw his brown leather jacket and a pair of gloves along with his Thompson submachine gun into his Twin Otter, "Papa Hotel Foxtrot." With his pistol strapped to his side, he carefully conducted his preflight check. Tonight was not the night for engine failure. Two full tanks would give him five to six hours of flying time. About 7 p.m., Dearborn, with Cloud in the right seat, departed Vientiane, knowing little about the situation at Long Chieng.

A B-40 mortar hit near Vang Pao's house. In the headquarters bunker, men prepared to defend against a commando raid. They assembled hand grenades, M-16s, and pistols. Behind the command bunker, they set up mortars.

Papa Hotel Foxtrot came on station just before eight in the evening. Dearborn listened to the radio communications. "We were plugged into Jerry's frequency, but other reports were coming. We could hear two or three conversations—locals talking, Americans talking, and Alley Cat. So was Jerry. All kinds of reports on enemy movements. Alley Cat was reporting movement in this position and that position. Then I heard a FAG [Forward Air Guide] report movement near Jerry's position, along the western side of the runway at Alternate. It didn't sound too good to me. I called Hog. 'Hey, Old Buddy, what's going on down there?' I asked. With his usual irreverence, he told me that they were about to have a New Year's Eve party. Did I want to come? I was invited, if I could find a way to get down there under the low ceiling.

"Both Hog and I knew that we were being monitored by the enemy. I wanted to get down under the cloud cover to take a close look at the situation, but Daniels' report of a low ceiling would be just right for the NVA gunners to get us.

"Since my orders were to keep in constant contact with the Long Chieng command post, Daniels and I, not wanting to say much about the military situation for the listening enemy, bantered on about the girls we knew and about the more spectacular parties we had survived. Our language was not very polite and must have confused the hell out of the listeners.

"Around and around Cloud and I flew in the darkness between 4,000 to 5,000 feet. Sometimes we climbed higher to stay above the cloud cover to see other mountains sticking up through it in the night light. Sometimes we flew through snow showers and rain crystals. We were cold, tired, and miserable. We reminded each other that it was New Year's Eve and that we were in the wrong place. The excitement of driving around at a low altitude at night in the mountains trying to hold a position inside and south of Skyline Ridge kept us awake. We didn't want to wander over into Site 20, Pop Buell's old headquarters just over from Skyline, where the enemy now had radar-controlled guns. We watched for Padong which was much higher than our altitude and the big karst near Pha Khao not more than ten air miles away. We could easily drift into these. Trying to stay in position over Alternate for four hours would be tough.

"Then the chatter on the radio lessened. Hog came on to report that, at the moment, all was quiet on the ground. To confuse the enemy listeners, he announced that the only noise he could hear was the popping of beer bottles."

About 10:30, Dearborn turned the plane over to Cloud and crawled into the cargo area in the back to sleep. It was even colder there, but he immediately fell asleep on the hard floor.

In the command bunker, Lo Ma received a whispered report over his radio from a position along Alternate: "NVA running along the airfield." Lo Ma was asking the radioman the number of enemy when a huge explosion shook Long Chieng. Bamboo shouted: "The bastards are bombing us!"

Dearborn awoke to this huge explosion and his plane twisting and turning. "Shit, they're hittin' Alternate!" Cloud shouted to Dearborn. "I'm going down to see what happened!" Dearborn scrambled back into the cockpit and took over the controls. "This is it!" Dearborn shouted. "They're going to overrun the place." Dearborn tried to raise Hog on the radio. No answer. "I figured they were attacking the place and it was time for Jerry to get out."

Vang Pao grabbed a radio and called frontline positions, out on the perimeters and up on Skyline. Some radios answered, some were silent. Vang Pao couldn't get accurate information. As Lo Ma watched the confusion in the command bunker, it seemed to him that everything was falling apart.

Red and orange glows from exploding shells shot up through the clouds around Dearborn as he tried to get down to help. "We spiraled downward through shells and the ragged holes in the clouds whipping over Long Chieng. Finally, we dropped out of the clouds, expecting to take fire. The ceiling was less than 1,000 feet and the glare from the fires on the ground against the clouds came back down again and lit the place up real nice. We got our bearings. Then we saw the ammo storage area burning. In the fire's glow, dark figures darted about. All I could think about was where are the CIA people? Has Hog been killed? Captured?"

In the bunker, Vang Pao shouted for information. No soldier really knew what was going on except within his local 10- to 15-yard area. More giant explosions rocked Long Chieng. Again, a SKY shouted: "The bastards are bombing us!" A soldier near the airstrip excitedly radioed that his men had caught three NVA sappers from a commando team near an ammo dump.

Dearborn flew around inside the bowl, trying to find out what was going on. "I flew very low—below Skyline Ridge. We stayed down in the bowl for ten to fifteen minutes. Then someone gave warning that the enemy was shooting at us, so we crawled back up to a safer altitude. If they'd had missiles there would have been no way that I would have gone down there. I'm surprised that they didn't catch sight of us in the fire light and use their bigger stuff on Skyline to shoot us down."

Standing outside the bunker to get a better reading on the situation, Lo Ma saw the silhouette of Papa Hotel Foxtrot flying around inside Long Chieng. At first he thought it was an enemy plane. Then he thought it was a FAC plane about to call in an air strike. Daniels came on the radio to Dearborn. "Sappers hit the ammo. We've got casualties. Don't know how many yet. All quiet at the moment except for the fire and the exploding shells at the dump." Later, the captured NVA sappers admitted setting charges to the boxes containing howitzer shells, each of which exploded with more force than a 500-pound bomb.

Cloud and Dearborn returned to the cloud cover and safety. As the night wore on, Hog became less irreverent. Just before midnight, with about an hour's fuel in his tanks, Dearborn prepared to depart. He contacted Daniels. "Watch your butt, old buddy. Take it easy. Someone else is coming to fly cover for you. I'll talk to you later, buddy." Dearborn reasoned there was a good possibility that Daniels might lose his butt tonight. About midnight, another Twin Otter came on station to relieve Dearborn and Cloud. Dearborn had to call Hog one last time. "Don't get your butt shot off! Happy New Year, old buddy." Daniels did not respond.

At the Vientiane airfield, men waited for Dearborn and Cloud to land. "Ambassador 'Mac' Godley, the CIA chief of station, and all our people from Continental were there to debrief. As I got out of the plane, someone handed me a glass of whiskey and said 'Happy New Year.' When I reached for it, I knocked it and spilled most of it down my shirt and my pants, leaving me only a big swallow." With his shirt and pants wet and smelling of whiskey, Dearborn walked over to the waiting Ambassador and the station chief. "I told them it was confusion up there. I told Godley that there was a good possibility that those guys coming down over the ridge and down onto the field might take Jerry's position."[3]

This was New Year's Eve. In downtown Vientiane, senior Lao military and civilian leaders, westernized Lao, and bureaucrats educated abroad joined Europeans and Americans to celebrate on open-air terraces, drink good and inexpensive French champagne, and dance. Long-haired Lao musicians wearing bell-bottomed trousers blared their Western music over loudspeakers turned up full blast. Asians and Westerners, some wearing paper hats, gyrated to the latest hits. Occasionally the band played the *lamvong*, the traditional Lao dance, which brought all Lao to the dance floor. In a circle with the women on the inside and men on the outside, the Lao moved to a sensual, syncopated slow beat. Turning ever so slowly, they shuffled the rhythm and moved their hands and fingers in soft beckoning gestures of elegance and grace. The few Westerners who joined the circle appeared awkward. As the music and the laughter pulsated in the warm, tropical darkness, there seemed to be no awareness among the revelers that only an hour's flight away North Vietnamese commandos had penetrated Long Chieng, the base protecting Vientiane and the dancing merrymakers.

At Long Chieng, everyone expected a ground assault. Exploding shells echoed throughout the night, pinning everyone down. Those in the command bunker could not tell if the explosions were from the ammunition dump or renewed shelling. Vang Pao radioed his troops in the high mountain positions to report gun flashes so he could determine if the explosions were incoming rounds or his own ammunition exploding.

When dawn neared and the attack had not come, men in the command bunker relaxed a bit and ate C-rations. Vang Pao, however, did not relax. He was frustrated that he could not get good information on the situation and furious that the Americans had sent no "air."

By dawn on New Year's Day, the enemy held the southern end of the runway and many positions on Skyline Ridge and along the slope east of the airstrip. NVA gunners and spotters hiding in the peak of the "dreaded mountain" at the approach to Alternate controlled air access. Long Chieng was under siege.

Before the sun touched Long Chieng, Vang Pao paced outside his night command quarters, waiting for a chopper. With Alternate's runway in enemy hands, only helicopters could get in. One whopped over the far ridge and settled down on a helipad. In seconds Vang Pao was aboard, heading for Udorn and SKY headquarters. Daniels remained at Long Chieng, holed up in the command bunker.

The defenders discussed why the enemy had not taken advantage of the situation and overrun Long Chieng. Was it because the enemy was unsure of Vang Pao's strength? Or was it because when Dearborn and Cloud flew into the valley as if they were a FAC operation about to call in air strikes the enemy thought the U.S. intended aerial retaliation and backed off? No one was certain.

Night and day, enemy guns pounded Long Chieng. While Vang Pao was prepared to hit and run and abandon positions when expedient, he vowed he would never abandon his Long Chieng headquarters to the enemy. Ambassador Godley, however, did not agree. They argued. "The NVA had artillery hitting us from the Plaine des Jarres, some 30 kilometers away. Ambassador Godley told me that I must retreat. I told him, 'I must hold Long Chieng; I must stay. I will die here if I have to.' Godley said he couldn't allow me to stay, and ordered me to leave. I told him, 'I'm staying and fighting. If you want to remove me, would you please do it after the battle. Right now, I have to fight.'"[4]

Vang Pao returned to Long Chieng and set up temporary command facilities over the next ridge to the west near a banana grove. From this location, known to the Americans as "the Banana Grove," he directed his ground troops and the air and artillery strikes against the enemy on Skyline and in the mountain notches overlooking the approach to Alternate.

Enemy spotters watched the entrance to Daniels' SKY bunker. During daylight, any movement around his bunker position resulted in shelling. The enemy had Daniels pinned down. Hog, too, was under siege.

The civilians at Long Chieng took a terrible beating. To survive the shelling, they lived in tunnels and caves. Vang Pao worried about them. "At Long Chieng, we could hear the sound of the enemy artillery being fired. Once we heard the firing, we knew that we had a few seconds to run and get into the caves and tunnels. Still we lost 3,000 people."[5]

With Long Chieng under daily attack and the airfield unusable, Ban Sorn, Site 272, was designated as the temporary frontline area for troop redeployment, resupply, and as a search and rescue base. Each morning, the big American rescue choppers from Thailand lumbered over the Mekong River heading for Lima Site 272. Air crews standing alert waited for word to lift off. H-34 helicopters often dropped ominously from the skies to deliver green body bags at a predetermined spot along the runway. Often these pilots only paused long enough for their crews to offload the bags. Women and children rushed to the area to open the body bags to identify a dead relative. In public and in the intense heat of the valley, they touched their loved ones and cried over them. Then they found a place to bury them.

On January 15, Fred Walker flew to Ban Sorn where crews loaded his Caribou with supplies for troops in contact with the enemy. That day he made nine drops to positions around Skyline. That evening he recorded in his logbook: "There's a hell of a lot going on around 20 Alternate."[6]

Also on January 15, 2nd Lt. Yang Pao, nicknamed "Skinny," received his pilot's wings and had his photograph taken wearing his flight suit while standing on the wing of a T-28. This photo was for his wife, child, and parents. It would also be used at his funeral, in case he was killed.[7]

Early the next morning, this 5-foot, 4-inch pilot grabbed his cushion and his helmet to join the other fighter pilots on the flight line at Vientiane. At dawn, he lifted off loaded with six 500-pound bombs. Flying as a wingman, he rolled in to drop his first bombs on enemy positions on Skyline and then over to the 81 and 82 gun positions on Phou Pha Xai from where hidden gunners pounded Long Chieng. As he made his run over Phou Pha Xai, enemy gunners fired nonstop. He dropped, pulled up, and away. This was the first of six missions Yang Pao flew on his first day of combat.

* * *

In Paris, North Vietnamese negotiators hardened their position that there be no treaty unless the U.S. and its allies agreed to unconditional troop withdrawal, cessation of air activity over North Vietnam, immediate resignation of South Vietnamese President Thieu, and the dismantling of the "oppressive machinery" of Thieu's regime.

On January 25, 1972, President Nixon told the American people of Kissinger's secret negotiations with the North Vietnamese, explaining that he had proposed a withdrawal of U.S. and allied forces from South Vietnam within six months of an agreement in principle on an overall settlement. He supported the resignations of both the President and Vice President of South Vietnam with a free, democratic presidential election to be held in the South within six months of the final agreement. The National Liberation Front, the political arm of the Viet Cong, would be allowed to participate.

Nixon made no mention of the withdrawal of NVA forces from South Vietnam or from Laos. "We ask only that Hanoi accept the principle that all armed forces of the countries of Indochina must remain within their national frontiers."[8]

Nixon sought POW release concurrently with U.S. troop withdrawal; a cease fire throughout Indochina beginning when an overall agreement was signed; and a prohibition of further North Vietnamese infiltration into South Vietnam, Cambodia, and Laos. He urged that both North Vietnam and the U.S. abide by the 1954 and 1962 Geneva Accords. Nixon announced that the U.S. would limit its military and economic assistance to South Vietnam if Hanoi accepted limitations on aid it received from its allies. He also proposed grand largesse for a peaceful end to the war. "The U.S. would be prepared to undertake a massive post-war reconstruction program in Indochina of several billion dollars, in which North Vietnam could share."[9] Kissinger and Nixon insisted that providing reconstruction aid would be not an act of penance, but a goodwill gesture. They both regarded aid as a "carrot" to entice Hanoi to abide by any agreement.

On January 26, 1972, Radio Hanoi broadcast a summary rejection of Nixon's proposals. North Vietnam's General Giap, bolstered by the Kissinger-Nixon concessions, intended to continue "fighting to negotiate."

Vang Pao's New Year's Day trip to Udorn had resulted in five battalions of Thai troops assigned to him and assurance of B-52 strikes, but the siege of Long Chieng continued.

In February, while Nixon made diplomatic history by visiting the People's Republic of China, the Pathet Lao held a secret meeting at Vieng Sai in Sam Neua Province. The actions taken at this meeting would not be made public until late in 1975 after the Pathet Lao controlled Laos. While many details still remain secret, it was undoubtedly clear to those few attending that the U.S. was determined to withdraw from Vietnam and Laos and probably under any conditions—as long as it seemed not to be abandoning these countries to communism. The communist leaders knew well the words and phrases needed to soothe concerns and guilt feelings that Washington officialdom might have in urging the Royal Lao government to come to an accord with the Pathet Lao. The words "politburo," "Marxism," and "liberation" were not used. These would scare the Americans and many Lao.

They put into place a governing apparatus with a seven-man politburo to head a central committee. The official name of the Lao communist party was changed from Lao People's Party to Lao People's Revolutionary Party, and strategies were developed for the ultimate takeover of Laos.

The high-ranking members of the Pathet Lao inner circle were not widely known and would emerge only after the takeover. The most visible Pathet Lao leader was Prince Souphanouvong. Married to a militant Vietnamese, he remained the frontman for the "Patriotic Forces." Smiling, optimistic, benign, Souphanouvong, the "Red Prince," lulled those in doubt by projecting himself and his Pathet Lao as patriots who respected the royal family, Lao traditions, Lao neutrality, and independence. Kaysone Phomvihane, a Vietnamese-Lao educated and trained in Hanoi and the real power in the Pathet Lao, would not emerge publicly as the communist leader until the Royal Lao government had fallen.

Air America and Continental crews resupplied Vang Pao's forces pinned down on Skyline and the eastern slopes. Daniels remained at Long Chieng, most of the time underground. In the first week of March, complaints from the SKY at Long Chieng that Continental crews were missing their targets brought Dearborn to Alternate for a first-hand look at the situation. Since the runway was not safe, Dearborn choppered in to a helipad located near the king's summer house. He was picked up in a jeep and driven fast through an artillery barrage to Daniels' bunker.

Daniels, unshaven and tired, wore sweaty, grimy clothes as a result of his days underground. His banter of New Year's Eve was gone. Gone was the chatter about "broads" and "booze." He was depressed and sullen. Dearborn was surprised.

The SKY generator still cranked out enough electricity to run some of the radio equipment and to light a couple of bare bulbs in the bunker. Pockets of darkness filled in around the noisy radio equipment and the bunks. Emergency canned foods, Asahi beer bottles, and a couple of jugs of Mekong whiskey were scattered about on the hard-packed dirt floor.

From Daniels' bunker, Dearborn, through binoculars, watched his crews drop supplies on beleaguered positions under enemy fire. He observed that most drops hit on target. He could not understand the Agency complaints. Angered over what he thought was undue criticism of his pilots, he filmed air drops, showing the enemy shooting at the supply planes.

Before leaving, Dearborn tried to cheer up his friend, but being in that hole for so long had taken a toll on Daniels. "'We're not making it,' he told me. 'Christ, I don't think we can hold on here. If things do go bad here, I'll have to walk out.'"[10]

Daniels did not walk out. Thai troops and T-28 bombing of Skyline Ridge slowly took effect. In almost a month of bitter fighting, Vang Pao's troops moved doggedly some two miles back up the Ridge. It took another two months until the base was resecured and the airstrip operational again, but the enemy remained at nearby Sam Thong and Phou Pha Xai.

*   *   *

On April 20, Henry Kissinger arrived in Moscow for a secret meeting, partly dealing with Vietnam, with Soviet Premier Leonid Brezhnev. Kissinger repeated many previous U.S. demands, but now conceded that North Vietnam had only to withdraw its troops which had invaded South Vietnam in the spring offensive, thus ignoring the large number of NVA troops previously deployed in South Vietnam and in Laos. No longer was "mutual withdrawal" of both U.S. and North Vietnamese forces on the negotiating table. NVA troops could stay in South Vietnam and in Laos.

*   *   *

On June 26, 1972, General Vang Pao ordered his T-28s to hit the radar-directed guns at Sam Thong and the gun emplacements at Phou Pha Xai. Lt. Yang Pao with three other Hmong pilots flew against the NVA gun positions. On his fifth mission of the day, Yang Pao flew into a sky choked with gun bursts. "After I rolled in, I heard a noise near my propeller and then an explosion. Fire everywhere. I pulled the Yankee ejection seat. I heard ground fire shooting at me. I heard my plane explode. I couldn't see well. When I hit the ground, I tried to call for help, but I couldn't speak because my face was so badly burned. I could hear the voices of Vietnamese so I ran away from their voices. I looked for a place to hide. My friends stayed overhead giving me cover. An American chopper came in to rescue me. It got very close. Then enemy guns hit it and it flew away.

"When the chopper left, the Vietnamese soldiers rushed at me, shouting and yelling. There were six of them. All Vietnamese. No Lao. No Hmong. They hit me and tied my hands in the back and then tied a rope around my neck that was tied to my hands. It was very tight and painful.

"I thought they were going to kill me. One put a gun in my back. Another put a knife to my throat and shouted at me as if he were going to kill me. He cut my throat, but I didn't die. Then they pushed me, shouting "Di! Di! Di!" [Go! Go! Go! in Vietnamese.] They marched me to the Vietnamese side of Phou Pha Xai mountain. We followed a small river and before dark we came to a large cave where there were a lot of people, probably more than a thousand. It was like a market. Vietnamese soldiers were sleeping in hammocks, some were cooking, some were talking and walking around. Everyone in the cave spoke Vietnamese. The cave wall had many drawings. Pictures of animals, people, and Buddha. These paintings looked like Lao or Thai paintings. They were very beautiful."[11]

Yang Pao spent two sleepless nights. He was frightened not only for himself, but for the people of Long Chieng. He was terrified that so many North Vietnamese soldiers could be so close to Long Chieng. As far as he knew, General Vang Pao did not know that 1,000 enemy soldiers bivouacked in this religious cave safe from T-28 bombs and B-52 strikes. "On the third day, Pathet Lao soldiers came. They were very angry and shouted at me for bombing their places. We left the cave. They kept me tied neck to hands. We moved day and night, heading northeast."

With hands and neck tied together and surrounded by Pathet Lao guards, Yang Pao walked for two weeks, past Xieng Khouang to the Nong Het area. "West of Nong Het at the bottom of a very steep mountainside, they put me in a small building with no light, no food, no water, no bathroom, no blanket. I had only a bamboo mat and a rice sack. Immediately, they interrogated me. The first Pathet Lao began. 'What is your rank? How many houses did you destroy? How many people did you kill? Who are your relatives? Where is your house?' I remained silent. They tortured me and beat me. Still I remained silent.

"My hands and neck tied tightly together made it impossible to sleep because of the pain. My body was covered with bruises and cuts where they hit and tortured me." Then a Second Pathet Lao asked me the same questions. I remained silent. They tortured and beat me again. I thought that I would die. A third Pathet Lao interrogated me with the same questions. I remained silent. Again, they beat and tortured me. I said nothing."

The next month, Jane Fonda arrived in Hanoi. Here she met up with Tom Hayden, first president of the Students for a Democratic Society (SDS), a prominent New Left leader who had been indicted as one of the Chicago Seven for leading the rioting at the 1968 Democratic Convention. Fonda's visit was a carefully planned and orchestrated public relations and media trip prepared by the North Vietnamese in Paris. While in North Vietnam, Fonda made ten broadcasts over Radio Hanoi to American soldiers serving in Southeast Asia. Later likened to "Tokyo Rose" and "Axis Sally," who during World War II abetted the enemy by trying to convince American fighting men to give up, Jane Fonda with her propaganda broadcasts sought to convince American soldiers to stop fighting. She was photographed frolicking with NVA antiaircraft gunners. While she was insisting that Hanoi treated American POWs humanely, they were being cruelly tortured; some were killed. Some were tortured because they refused to write propaganda, to speak prepared communist rhetoric over the radio, or to meet with antiwar leaders brought to Hanoi to sing the praises of the North Vietnamese.[12]

As Fonda made headlines with her Hanoi trip, in the POW camp near Nong Het the Pathet Lao fed Yang Pao only enough to keep him alive. "They fed me one handful of rice and one small piece of canned meat . . . not bigger than what would fit in a small spoon. They did this at 6 a.m. and 6 p.m. I got a small cup of water twice a day."

The young pilot grew weaker and weaker. The interrogation continued. "The guards wanted to know details about General Vang Pao and his plans. One guard repeatedly asked, 'How much money did the Americans give you to fight? How much money did the Americans give you to kill us?' Another one wanted to know: 'Which Americans were helping you?' I remained silent which made them extremely angry and they tortured me. Thi Noi, Boon Kham, and Thi Yai, all Lao, were extremely cruel to me.

"I was never allowed to talk outside the interrogation room. If I did, they beat me. It was impossible to sleep. The mosquitoes were terrible. I became very sick and skinny. If I ate rice, I would have diarrhea. There was no water to wash myself. I was sick and dirty. There was no medicine, no doctor. Fleas and lice crawled on my body. I had no clothes. I was sick inside. It was very difficult to even stand. A crippled Kmhmu man, who brought me rice and water each day, gave me a tree limb to use as a crutch. I knew that I would never again see my wife, child, and parents.''

Part Five

"Peace"
in Laos:
The Communist
Takeover

20.

The Last Americans

The just struggle and the good-will for peace of Lao patriotic forces and people have constantly enjoyed the sympathy and support of the peace and justice-loving peoples the world over, including the American people. A demonstration of this support is the ever stronger condemnation and opposition of world opinion against the intervention and aggression of the U S imperialists, especially against the present adventurist and criminal policy of the Nixon clique in Laos.

—"Nixon's 'Intensified Special War' in Laos: A Criminal War Doomed to Fail," published in 1972 by the Central Committee of the Lao Patriotic Front in honor of the tenth anniversary of the signing of the 1962 Geneva Agreement on Laos

The Biological and Toxin Convention, which would have enormous impact for Laos, was readied for signature. In spite of the lack of any verification apparatus, Nixon, on April 10, 1972, signed it. Toxins were defined as chemical weapons which can be naturally produced by biological processes or chemically synthesized for use as weapons.

This convention was one of the fruits of Kissinger's efforts since 1969 to negotiate several arms treaties with the Soviets, one of which, to become known as SALT I, sought to limit strategic arms. Having already decided that it wanted these kinds of weapons eliminated from the world's arsenals, the U.S. in November 1969 had unilaterally and unconditionally renounced all methods of biological warfare and extended that to toxin weapons in 1970. "The Department of Defense was ordered to draw up a plan for the disposal of existing stocks of biological agents and weapons. The American action was widely welcomed internationally; however, it was generally recognized that unilateral actions could not take the place of binding international commitment. The next step came on August 5, 1971, at the Conference of the Committee on Disarmament when the United States and the Soviet Union submitted separate but identical texts banning biological and toxin weapons."[1]

In June 1972, only two months after the signing of the Biological and Toxin Convention, *New York Times* reporter Drew Middleton reported a marked increase in Soviet chemical biological warfare capabilities—both defensive and offensive.[2]

The SALT I treaty with the Soviets was signed. Detente was moving ahead. Treaties would be signed on European security and on sales of American grain and technology to the Soviet Union.

On August 1, Le Duc Tho and Henry Kissinger resumed talks in Paris. The North Vietnamese were extremely confident now. They had assurances that the U.S. would allow them to keep their army in South Vietnam and that Nixon desired an end to the Vietnam War before the upcoming November presidential election.

On August 22, the Republican party renominated Nixon for president. A few days later, he announced that the drafting of young men to serve in the armed forces would end the next July. Nixon had almost completed the withdrawal of U.S. troops from South Vietnam. He believed that his policy of Vietnamization was working. U.S. military personnel in South Vietnam now numbered only 47,000.

* * *

By autumn, few Americans stayed overnight at Long Chieng. Now even the Raven pilots bunked in Vientiane. AID personnel flew in only on a daily basis. Only Jerry Daniels, known for his ability to dig in, remained at Alternate.

On September 27, 1972, U.S. Air Force Captain Darrel Whitcomb reported to the American Embassy in Laos. He would be among the last American Ravens to fly in support of General Vang Pao. During his time, 11 Ravens were assigned to Laos; six flew Vang Pao's Region II. Whitcomb was a 1969 Air Force Academy graduate. He was a veteran of a year of flying cargo planes in South Vietnam and a second combat tour as a FAC, flying OV-10s over South Vietnam from the Nakhon Phanom Air Base (NKP) in Thailand.

Even at this late date, the American involvement in Laos remained secret. Whitcomb had been "sheepdipped." Officially, he was assigned to the 56th Special Operations Wing at NKP, which Colonel "Heine" Aderholt had activated in 1966. Whitcomb, like his predecessors, received from the U.S. Embassy in Vientiane a yellow card bearing the official U.S. seal and the words "American Embassy." Everything was in three languages—Lao, French, and English. On the front it bore his name (but no rank), birth date, issue and expiration dates—good for six months—and his organization, AIRA (Air Attaché). The back of the card, bearing a full-color American flag, stated only that the person named "is employed by the United States Government."

For the next six months, Whitcomb would never wear a uniform or a flight suit. He and the other Ravens flew in costumes that could have won prizes at Halloween parties. Their unusual clothes did not, however, alter their seriousness about winning the fight. That was why they had volunteered for Laos.

On October 8, 1972, at a house in the outskirts of Paris, Kissinger and Le Duc Tho met secretly once again. Kissinger agreed to Hanoi's troops—some 160,000—remaining in South Vietnam. He did, however, request that they not be resupplied. They decided that the U.S. and North Vietnam would arrange all the details of the agreement. Neither South Vietnam's Thieu nor any one from Laos or Cambodia was involved in negotiating these major matters. While Thieu was apprised of some aspects of the secret negotiations, the fate of South Vietnam, Cambodia, and Laos was being decided by two men—one from Hanoi and one from Washington.

Soon after, on October 14, Hanoi acknowledged that a Pathet Lao delegation was headed to Vientiane to discuss ending the war in Laos. Two weeks later, Hanoi officially approved the proposed accord, secretly negotiated by Kissinger and Le Duc Tho. Nixon responded by announcing a bombing halt north of the 20th parallel. Four days later, Kissinger told the press: "We believe that peace is at hand. . . . It is inevitable that in a war of such complexity that there would be occasional difficulties in reaching a final solution, but we believe that by far the longest part of the road has been traversed and what stands in the way of an agreement now are issues that are relatively less important than those that have already been settled."[3]

The negotiations in Vientiane between Souvanna Phouma's government and the Pathet Lao moved ahead sporadically. Kissinger had "obtained a private assurance from Le Duc Tho that a cease-fire would follow in Laos within twenty days of the Vietnam cease-fire, which was set for January 23, 1973."[4]

Hanoi pressured Souphanouvong to obtain an immediate cease-fire in Laos. With Hanoi directing the "Red Prince," Washington pressured the

Royal Lao to accept a cease-fire and the peace proposals advanced by the Pathet Lao for yet another coalition government. Kissinger and his staff had apparently overlooked the prior unsuccessful attempts to resolve the Lao problem through a coalition.

On November 7, Nixon was reelected in a landslide victory over George McGovern. A week later, Nixon assured South Vietnam's President Thieu that the U.S. would "take swift and severe retaliatory action" if North Vietnam violated the agreement.

* * *

POW pilot Yang Pao was near death. After five months in dark solitary confinement, starving, with no medicine, and tortured until he could no longer walk or stand, he was moved to another part of the camp. Here he lived in a building with 53 Hmong prisoners. He learned that the camp held 700 to 800 POWs, including Hmong, Lao, Thai, Mien, and Kmhmu. These men, victims themselves, cared for him, nursing him back from the edge of death. This camp held two kinds of prisoners—"inside prisoners" and "outside prisoners." Inside prisoners were those such as Yang Pao who had been kept in isolation. Outside prisoners were those who constituted the forced labor teams. Yang Pao now became an outside prisoner. Labor teams received only enough food to keep them alive, were denied medicine, kept under harsh guard, and beaten or shot for the smallest infractions, such as eating a leaf or an insect. Men died of starvation, forced labor, lack of medicine, and torture. Others were shot for talking back to the guards, stealing food, and trying to escape. Many guards were only children.[5]

* * *

No longer did Raven briefings focus on "truck kills." Trucks had been easy prey compared to the sophisticated Soviet weaponry now in Laos. The NVA's arsenal in Military Region II included mobile antiaircraft guns, radar-controlled 57mm guns, and 85mm, 122mm, and 130mm artillery. Soviet hand-held heat-seeking SA-7 missiles were also reported. When Darrel Whitcomb arrived, the challenge was the "hunting" and destroying of the 130mm guns which caused so much damage.

Pilots, however, had not solved the problem of knocking out guns sheltered in caves. They were still experimenting. Whitcomb was asked to select targets for field-testing of new technologies such as the PAVE MACE, laser-guided bombs. It worked this way: Whitcomb would identify a cave known to house guns. One pilot carrying an illuminator pod would beam his laser on Whitcomb's target. A jet fighter carrying bombs would lock on to the laser beam and drop its bombs. The illuminator pilot would move his laser beam at the last moment so that the bomb, which was headed downward, would turn up just before impact to enter the mouth of a cave. Whitcomb not only selected targets for laser-guided bombs, but he nominated targets for the testing of various missiles, such as the "Maverick" which was also used against the mouth of caves and became part of the Air Force arsenal. Whitcomb was impressed with the amount of military equipment tested in Laos. "The heart of the U.S. Air Force story over there was the development and field testing of precision weapons. As a result of that testing, we now have weapons so precise that we can use them in lieu of nuclear weapons."[6]

Whitcomb always felt more comfortable when Xiong Ly Tou was airborne to back him up if he got into trouble. Ly Tou rarely flew a T-28 these days because he had been trained by the Ravens and certified by the U.S. Embassy as a FAC. With the Americans about to withdraw, local men were needed for all military positions. Once, only American FAC pilots were authorized to call in U.S. air strikes. Now, Ly Tou flew a FAC plane, call-sign "Nockateng 502." While the American FACs called themselves Ravens, conjuring thoughts of Edgar Allan Poe, intrigue, and evil, Hmong called themselves Nockateng, "swooping bird."

On December 10, Whitcomb, wearing his usual blue jeans and camouflage jacket and his special bush hat, given him by Montagnards in South Vietnam and considered a good-luck charm, took off from Long Chieng in the early afternoon. Xiong Ly Tou was FACing near Bouam Loung. Flying as Raven 25, Whitcomb headed alone for the PDJ where Vang Pao was fighting. "I lifted off without a backseater. None was available. Monitoring the common radio frequency, I heard a FAG, call-sign 'Pressure,' calling frantically for help. His position was being overrun by NVA. SKY advisor 'Lumberjack' radioed to me. 'Raven 25, can you help these guys out? They're in a lot of trouble.' I answered 'Affirmative.'"

"I flew toward their location near Ban Sorn. I could see enemy forces attacking in broad daylight. Usually that didn't happen because the enemy knew that if we got them out in the open we would bomb the hell out of them. As I'm orbiting over their position at about 1,000 feet and talking to their FAG, I see this pitched battle going on—the bad guys charging up the hill, hand-to-hand fighting and bayonet stuff. The friendlies were going to be overrun. Quickly I called for air support. None was available. So, I called one of the artillery battalions and began directing their artillery fire into the area. But the ground assault continued. The FAG radioed that they were pulling off their position, heading to the West through a valley up to Romeo Ridge, Lumberjack's position.

"While the friendlies organized to evacuate, I put 'arty' on the bad guys. But it was not enough to stop a slaughter. As the Hmong pulled off the site, they had to leave their wounded behind. As the NVA troops overran the position, I watched them bayonet and kill all the wounded left behind. Since there was no air power available at the time, I continued to direct artillery to pound the attackers. Then my main concern was that something was going to happen to the forces that were evacuating.

"I flew about 500 meters or so ahead of them scouting for a possible ambush. And lo and behold, I saw these guys digging foxholes along the side of the trail in an X fashion which is what one does for an ambush. So, I called the FAG and asked him if he had anyone about 500 meters ahead of his retreating troops. He said 'No.' Just to make certain, I asked him to have his lead guy give me a mirror flash so I could see their location. He did and sure enough these guys were well out ahead of the good guys. I called Lumberjack. He said it was an ambush. So I shifted the artillery fire onto the bad guys. The friendlies changed their direction and started up another valley. Once they did that, the bad guys realized that I had busted their ambush and they started shooting at me. I was at about 1,000 feet to direct the artillery fire so I was taking hits from AK-47 fire. One of the bullets came through the right door and through the back seat, chest high. If a backseater had been with me, he would have been killed—it would have gone through his chest.

"They hit me from every direction, but I continued to direct fire against the enemy so the friendlies could get away. Then, a burst of gunfire hit the bottom of my aircraft. I lost my oil. Then my engine. I was going down. I was lucky—for the valley I was working was so high that I glided to the edge of Alternate and landed. The best part of all this was that the friendlies got out. Afterwards, I met the guys involved. They personally thanked me for that mission. That was great. Most Ravens never had the opportunity to meet the friendlies on the ground whom they had helped."

Captain Darrel Whitcomb received the Silver Star medal for this mission.

Whitcomb was not airborne the day John Carroll was killed. Carroll, an Air Force major, had recently arrived as the Raven Chief. He was a highly trained pilot who had flown as an aerospace test pilot at Edwards Air Force Base. "It was my day off," recalled Whitcomb. "But I was at the airport and watched John leave that morning, heading for the PDJ.

Up there, he got hit with triple-A and radioed he didn't have enough power to get off the PDJ and would spiral down to land where he was and try for a rescue.

"He brought the plane in skillfully, immediately got on his survival radio, and announced his location. He was fine, but the bad guys were all around him and shooting. The first rescue chopper was shot away by enemy fire. Then Steve Neal, the Raven on the scene, ran in some fighters and worked the area so they could get a chopper in. Finally, chopper "12-Foxtrot" got in and hovered over John's plane. The door-loader on the chopper got a good view of the situation before intense ground fire drove them off the crash site."

Whitcomb waited at the airport for the chopper to return. "I talked to the crew who told me that, in their opinion, the man was dead because his body was so badly ripped apart. The bad guys had apparently shot him repeatedly at point blank range; his body was literally in pieces. There was no attempt by the enemy to take him prisoner. No Raven was ever taken prisoner. Lucky downed Raven pilots were rescued by friendlies; unlucky ones didn't come home."

Later that night, intel picked up a radio intercept from an enemy radio site, saying they had recovered the body of an American pilot—and his name was John Carroll.

Whitcomb was the first FAC up the next morning. "When I came upon the crash site, I found enemy troops picking over the wreckage and the remains. I called in some Air Force fighters and put a 2,000-pound bomb on his remains, taking quite a few of them with him. I don't know why I did that, but I did. I had to destroy the wreckage and whatever information they might have found. It was hard to do, but I thought it necessary."

* * *

President Thieu, angered by the Hanoi-Washington agreement, demanded changes. On December 13, Le Duc Tho balked at these changes, canceled the negotiations, and returned to Hanoi. The following day, Nixon responded to Hanoi's walkout: talk or else.

Hanoi continued to stall. Nixon stood by his "or else" option. On December 18, he ordered air strikes, called "Linebacker Two," against Hanoi's power plants, radio towers, and military complexes and against Haiphong's docks and harbor. In the initial days, North Vietnam's MiGs and SAMs shot down many U.S. aircraft, including 15 B-52s. The bombing continued for 11 days, excluding Christmas. On the day after Christmas, Hanoi signaled Washington that if the bombing were stopped, negotiations could resume. The bombing stopped on December 30. In 11 days, the North Vietnamese had shot down 26 U.S. aircraft and ninety-three airmen; 31 had been captured.

*   *   *

In late 1972 as the NVA prepared to launch another major attack against Bouam Loung, the remote mountaintop base deep in NVA territory, a MiG bombed and strafed the site, killing five and wounding 24. The NVA full charge came at night. The dark mountain skies glowed and sparkled from the firepower directed at Bouam Loung. Colonel Moua Cher Pao radioed Alternate for "air." At dawn, Vang Pao scrambled four Hmong, including Fackee and Coyote, and six Lao-piloted T-28s. Since the Lao pilots were unfamiliar with Site 32, one Hmong pilot was assigned to guide each pair of Lao pilots.

As the first flight approached, well-camouflaged enemy gunners opened up, surprising the pilots. Frightened Lao pilots pulled up and away, dropping their bombs wide. All day the Hmong led sorties to dislodge the enemy forces, but the guns scared the Lao pilots, who flew extremely high over the targets and as a result missed them. By nightfall, Vang Pao's "air" had failed to dislodge the enemy guns.

The next afternoon, Fackee and Coyote and the other Hmong pilots who were fed up with the high-flying Lao assembled their own strike force. They managed to cripple or knock out a few guns. This sent morale soaring on the flightline at Alternate, even among the Lao pilots, who later joined the Hmong to bomb enemy positions only yards from friendly ones. But a few T-28 strikes were not nearly enough to dislodge an enemy determined to take this site. To survive, Bouam Loung had to call in air strikes almost upon itself. F-111s, working off a fixed beacon, threw in strikes against the enemy's outer positions.

Air Commando Clyde Howard, who had trained many of the Hmong FAGs, was aboard Alley Cat and Cricket to assist with the beacon-bombing. "On the enemy radio net we heard the enemy refer to the F-111 air strikes as 'Silent Death.' They couldn't hear the planes because they flew at super high altitudes. The guys on the ground would be socked in and then the world would just cave in on them. It could even catch them moving out across a field. They couldn't figure out how we could hit them when it was completely socked in. They looked for something big. They looked for big radar vans like they found at Phou Pha Thi. They looked for everything in the world. They knew it was something electronic; had to be—because of the accuracy. But they never found out what brought the 'Silent Death.' They never caught on that it was a small electronic device, placed by a Hmong FAG in their midst. They never figured it out.''[7] For days, the mountains shook around Bouam Loung—and then it was quiet. The enemy retreated.

Darrel Whitcomb, on leave for Christmas, missed the fireworks at Site 32. He received a phone call from Laos, asking him to return. Ravens Hal Mischler and Skip Jackson were both dead and a couple of others had been shot down.*

Soon after Whitcomb returned, Colonel Moua Cher Pao gave a party at Bouam Loung. Beneath billowing orange and white parachutes and a sign in large Lao script that read "The Day of Victory Celebration at Bouam Loung 1973," soldiers, pilots, SKY advisors, and civilians gathered to hear Pat Landry from CIA headquarters in Udorn, General James Hughes, Commander of 7/13 Air Force at Udorn, and General Vang Pao. Everyone toasted the victorious defense of Site 32, the Fortress. There was a *ba-sii* ceremony for the SKY men and the honored guests. Daniels, his wrists laced with *ba-sii* strings, spoke. Then Vang Pao took the pilots on a tour of the site. There was an extraordinary stench coming from the bodies on the wires lower down on the mountainsides. To Whitcomb, it was a grim warning to anyone who thought about taking Site 32. "To me, it said: 'You attack us and this is what will happen to you.'"

That night there was a party with more speeches, dancing, and drinking. Nockateng pilot Ly Tou told about Whitcomb's heroism, explaining how he had flown low and directed artillery against the enemy—until he was shot down—to save the men in Pressure's unit. Later in the evening, the Hmong coerced Captain Whitcomb, who was quite shy and by this time quite drunk, to dance with several young Hmong maidens. He did— much to the delight of the onlookers. Since few Americans had ever been on the ground at Bouam Loung and since the FAC pilots who flew in its support were usually Hmong, Whitcomb considered his trip to Bouam Loung a special occasion.

A few days after the party, Whitcomb loaded his aircraft with his per-

---

*During the "Secret War" in Laos, 31 U.S. Raven pilots were killed: Robert L. Abbott, Henry L. Allen, John J. Bach, Jr., Charles D. Ballou, Danny L. Berry, Park C. Bunker, Joseph K. Bush, Jr., John L. Carroll, Joseph L. Chestnut, James E. Cross, Daniel R. Davis, Richard H. Defer, Samuel M. Deichelman, David A. Dreier, Richard G. Elzinga, Charles E. Engle, John J. Garritty, Jr., Richard W. Herold, Paul V. Jackson III, Edward E. McBride, Harold L. Mischler, Dennis E. Morgan, Joseph W. Potter, Gomer D. Reese III, John W. Rhodes, James Rostermundt, Charles P. Russell, Marlin L. Siegwalt, George H. Tousley III, W. Grant Uhls, Truman R. Young.

sonal arsenal. Into the back he threw an AR-15 (automatic rifle) with 200 rounds, an M-79 grenade launcher with 40 rounds, and two hand grenades. In addition, he wore 38 and 45 caliber pistols. On several occasions when the situation on the ground was desperate, he had flown down to about 100 feet and fired these weapons out the windows at the enemy. After John Carroll's death, he was determined that if he crashed he would fight it out. This day, he flew alone. Since he did not plan to work with friendlies on the ground, he did not need a backseat interpreter. His targets were far to the north: NVA truck convoys.

"I was flying south of Bouam Loung along Route 7, at about 2,000 feet, looking for convoys. I opened the windows to recon for trucks. Suddenly I heard shells whooshing by the aircraft. I looked down. Along the road I saw a 37mm gun firing at me. Shells exploded above me as I turned and jinked. But I couldn't get away. He was getting closer and closer. I needed help. I called Cricket: 'I need an air strike. I'm taking a lot of fire. I've got a gun that won't let me go.' I considered rolling in and shooting him with a rocket but in order to do that I would have solved his aiming problems."

Xiong Ly Tou, flying nearby, heard Whitcomb call Cricket for help. He radioed Whitcomb. "Raven 25, I see you. I see the gun, too," Ly Tou headed toward Whitcomb's position. "I saw him roll in from the north and hit the gun with two rockets, allowing me to get away," remembered Whitcomb. "He saved my life. A few days later, I saw Ly Tou at Long Chieng. I shook his hand, hugged him, and thanked him for saving my life. He smiled and said, 'Hey, no sweat, Raven 25!'"

*   *   *

At Vang Vieng hospital, a pert young Hmong woman named Moua May Song worked as a nurse. May Song was a product of the untiring efforts of Pop Buell and Moua Lia to educate Hmong girls. Vang Pao, who regularly visited his wounded men there, had met this confident and attractive nurse several times while making hospital rounds. In 1971, in his role of leader, he had counseled May Song when she was depressed over her desire to defy Hmong tradition and not marry the man already chosen for her. He knew the man May Song was to marry and urged her to marry him. But even the general's counsel had not changed her mind. It only made her sadder. Vang Pao saw her periodically at the hospital. He continued to concern himself with her problem and tried to console and further counsel her. May Song, however, prayed to the gods to "cancel her troubles." In 1972, she summoned the courage to take her problem to the local "court." There she was advised that she did not have to accept the arranged marriage. Her parents, however, embittered and embarrassed, disowned her. By now, the man whom she had wanted to marry had left Laos and returned to his native country.[8]

In early 1973, in Vientiane, at a gathering at the anniversary remembrance of T-28 pilot Vang Sue's death, General Vang Pao spoke with May Song and learned that she no longer was obligated to the arranged marriage and was now alone. Soon he asked her to consider marrying him. He promised to take care of her, saying that they would work it out with her family and his other wives. On February 18, 1973, in a *ba-sii* in Vientiane, May Song, age 17, married General Vang Pao.

*   *   *

Many Lao believed that the U.S. was forcing their country into a strange, unworkable, and dangerous situation. In the negotiations in Vientiane, the Pathet Lao acted as coequals in the Royal Lao government, in spite of the fact that about two-thirds of the population lived in the Royal Lao government–controlled areas. The Pathet Lao called themselves the "Patriotic Forces" and referred to the Royal Lao government as the "Vientiane government side." The propaganda value of these labels sought to reduce the Royal Lao government to a group that controlled a city and to present the Patriotic Forces as a country-wide nationalist movement.

Lao Army General Oudone Sananikone—who after World War II had been active in the Lao movement for independence with Prince Souphanouvong and who later joined a more moderate Lao group to press for independence from France—was present at many of these negotiations. He recalled the pressure put on the Royal Lao to reach an agreement with the Pathet Lao by the American Embassy, particularly by the Deputy Chief of Mission, John Gunther Dean, and his staff. "He and his staff frequently urged members of the government to make more concessions to the Neo Lao Hak Sat [the political arm of the Pathet Lao]. Some of these urgings took the form of thinly veiled threats of cuts in American assistance. It was quite difficult for any Lao official, who knew that resistance on his part could put the country on the ropes very quickly, to fail to respond to the embassy pressure. The Pathet Lao negotiators were well aware of what was going on. They already knew that Souvanna Phouma would agree to almost anything; now they knew that the Americans were, in effect, in their corner. Armed with these advantages, they became even more obdurate."[9]

While the Lao argued, the "Agreement on Ending the War and Restoring Peace in Vietnam" was signed in Paris in January. It required major concessions by South Vietnam and asked little of North Vietnam except to return U.S. prisoners of war and account for those listed as missing in action. The U.S. agreed to withdraw all its remaining military personnel within 60 days. Hanoi was not asked to remove its 160,000 troops in South Vietnam and the 70,000 in Laos.

Kissinger later claimed in his memoirs that he had a written commitment from Le Duc Tho that the NVA would be withdrawing from Laos following a cease-fire there, but that Le Duc Tho later revised this to be contingent upon a political settlement in Laos, which, at the time, was months away.

The "peace" agreement negotiated by the Lao, the "Agreement on the Restoration of Peace and Reconciliation in Laos," provided for a cease-fire effective February 22, 1973. It also resulted in "neutralizing" both the royal capital of Luang Prabang and the administrative capital of Vientiane. This was accomplished by importing communist soldiers to co-protect these two cities along with the Royal Lao government police. It also provided an equal say by both sides in running the eventual provisional government, while allowing the Pathet Lao to maintain unilaterally its separate zone where it had operated previously. All of this was designed by the communists to consolidate their political gains, and simultaneously to provide cover for the NVA remaining in strength within Lao borders.

Militarily, the agreement stipulated the withdrawal of all foreign troops within 60 days of the establishment of a provisional government. Very specifically, it mandated "the withdrawal of foreign military personnel, regular and irregular, from Laos, and the dismantling of foreign military and paramilitary organizations. . . . 'Special Forces'—organized, trained, equipped, and controlled by foreigners—must be disbanded; all bases, military installations and positions of these forces must be liquidated."[10]

Special Forces included Vang Pao's irregulars and the other tribal groups such as the Lahu and Mien who were similarly engaged in western Laos. The reference to foreign military personnel clearly meant Americans, Thais, and North Vietnamese. NVA forces in Laos now totaled about 70,000. The agreement favored the Patriotic Forces and their mentors, the North Vietnamese. While it included words about a joint inspection team to monitor, there were no provisions to guarantee realistic verification of troop withdrawal or cease-fire violations.

Few Americans asked if the Lao domino was tumbling into the communist sphere as a result of this treaty. Americans were focused on the end of the Vietnam War and the return of American POWs. Beginning on February 12, the North Vietnamese began releasing Americans held captive in North Vietnam. For the first time, Americans learned of the cruelty inflicted upon POWs by the North Vietnamese. Jane Fonda's earlier assurances that they were well treated by Hanoi exploded when these men described their torture and the death of other POWs. Fonda fought back, denouncing the returning prisoners, calling them "hypocrites and liars," and asking Americans not to hail them as heroes.[11]

While the U.S. focused on the return of its POWs, pilot Yang Pao and hundreds of other Hmong POWs remained imprisoned in slave-labor camps. There had been no attempts by American negotiators to secure the release of these POWs.

As the February 22, 1973, cease-fire deadline drew near, the NVA pushed hard, bloodying Vang Pao's men. Whitcomb remembered with sadness his last meeting with Vang Pao. "It was late in the afternoon and it turned out to be my last operational meeting with Vang Pao—the last war council meeting for me. The Raven pilots and the CIA men were there. There was resignation on Vang Pao's part and on the part of all of us. We realized this 'peace' treaty was a bad turn of events. It did not bode well for the Lao and for the Hmong in particular. We knew that it was just a matter of time until they were going to get the short end of the stick. Vang Pao talked about several operational things and then got up and in a very sad and sorrowful way, said: 'You know, you can sit down with the communists at the table and you can talk to them. They'll nod their heads and smile politely, talk to you, agree to anything but under the table they will always be kicking you.' I've always remembered that and I think that's exactly what happened. We accepted this treaty, this armistice, this peace accord. It gave them everything and gave us nothing. We got our prisoners back and that was basically it. We sold those people out."

Whitcomb listened to the SKY men and others discussing the idea that if things really became bad for the Hmong the U.S. would come back in. "In hindsight," Whitcomb concluded, "that was gross wishful thinking."

On the very last day—February 21—Whitcomb was flying for Vang Pao north of Muong Soui. "We were working with Jerry Daniels who was helping Vang Pao put some of his teams in up there to give them some positions they could hold after the cease-fire. It was sad because as we were leaving, they were calling for help. On that last day, we flew our airplanes back to Vientiane where we normally lived and that was it for us. When we got on the ground, the Hmong guys got into the airplanes and flew back up there and continued to fight. They had no choice."

The cease-fire was to commence at noon on February 22. That morning, Fred Walker, still with Air America, was flying out of Pakse in southern Laos. On his second mission, he aborted because of heavy fighting. In spite of the action, he managed seven air drops that day. That evening, Walker wrote in his logbook: "Red Letter day. Cease-fire at noon. It lasted through the lunch hour."[12] Within hours of the signing of the "peace agreement" in Vientiane, communist forces attacked and seized Pak Song.

Whitcomb was now helpless to assist the Hmong. "I just sat and monitored the news, read the newspapers, and watched those people get hammered day after day."

Author Jane Hamilton-Merritt in South
Vietnam in 1969. As a war correspondent
and photographer, she covered South Vietnam, Laos, Cambodia, and Thailand. (Photo
in the collection of the author)

Vang Seng Vang and his son, 1980. To terrorize those who had been
captured, communist soldiers in a public display crippled this child
because his father had been a soldier with General Vang Pao.
(Photo credit: Jane Hamilton-Merritt)

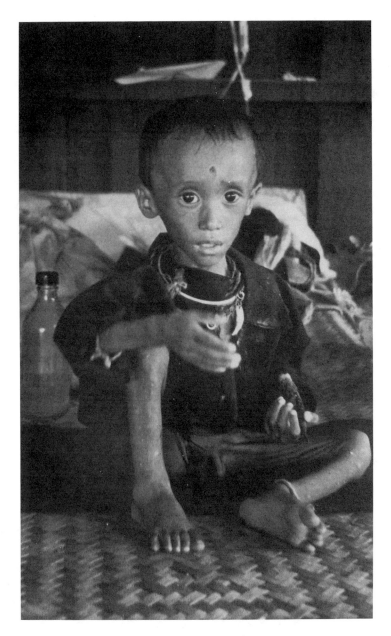

Hmong child, a victim of chemical-biological toxins deployed against his village in Laos, 1979. (Photo credit: Jane Hamilton-Merritt)

Ban Vinai Refugee Camp in northern Thailand in 1979. Hmong fleeing
Laos sought sanctuary in Thailand. At this time Ban Vinai held 43,000
refugees. Tens of thousands were yet to flee. (Photo credit: Jane Hamilton-Merritt)

Hmong refugees at Ban Vinai Camp in northern Thailand. New arrivals
from Laos lived in these long sheds, with each thatch and bamboo unit
of 10x12 feet housing up to 30 people. (Photo credit: Jane Hamilton-
Merritt)

Hmong refugees waiting in line for water at Ban Vinai Camp, 1980.
(Photo credit: Jane Hamilton-Merritt)

Angry Hmong who tried un-
successfully to give the information contained in his
notebook to the U.N. Group
of Experts sent to investigate
allegations of chemical-biological toxin weapons usage
in Laos, telling the author
about the team's behavior at
Ban Vinai Camp, 1981.
(Photo credit: Jane Hamilton-
Merritt)

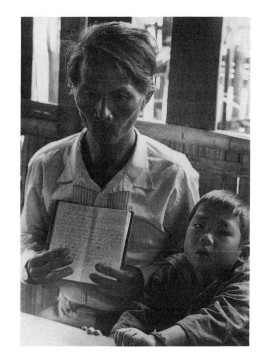

Two Hmong boys in Ban Vinai Refugee Camp drew a picture of the
helicopter that sprayed their village with poisons, 1984. (Photo
credit: Jane Hamilton-Merritt)

Hmong refugee mother and children in Mae Jarim Refugee Camp in Nan Province, Thailand, 1977. Note elaborate traditional baby hats worn by all Hmong children. (Photo credit: Jane Hamilton-Merritt)

Hmong grandmother who made the trek out of Laos in 1977, in
Mae Jarim Refugee Camp, Thailand. (Photo credit: Jane Hamilton-
Merritt)

Refugees from Laos wait behind barbed wire
at Nam Yao Refugee Camp, Thailand, 1978.
(Photo credit: Jane Hamilton-Merritt)

Hmong mother and children. Escapees from Kaysone regime in Laos and its policy of extermination of the ethnic Hmong who sided with the U.S. and the Royal Lao government during the Vietnam War era. (Photo credit: Jane Hamilton-Merritt)

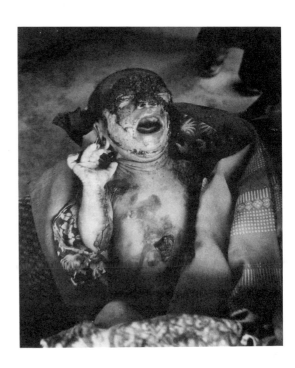

Hmong child, a victim of chemical-biological toxin use in Laos by the Soviet-backed Vietnamese–Pathet Lao regime, 1978. (Photo credit: Jane Hamilton-Merritt)

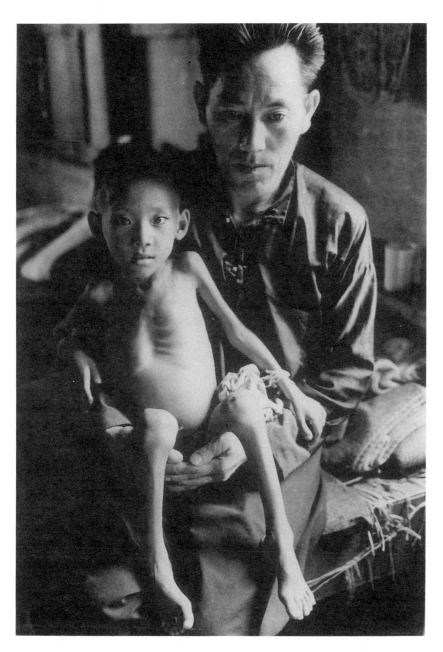

Hmong father and son, escapees from the Lao People's Democratic
Republic (LPDR), in refugee camp in Thailand, 1981. Since the com-
munist takeover in 1975, LPDR authorities have hunted down the
Hmong who allied themselves with the U.S. during the Vietnam
War. (Photo credit: Jane Hamilton-Merritt)

General Vang Pao, left, at a meeting of the Hmong community in Minneapolis-St. Paul, 1982. (Photo credit: Jane Hamilton-Merritt)

General Vang Pao and Ambassador Kenneth L. Adelman (later director of the U.S. Arms Control and Disarmament Agency) at the United Nations, where the general and the author brought evidence of torture, starvation, maiming, slave labor camps, and use of lethal toxins by the LPDR against the Hmong. (Photo credit: Jane Hamilton-Merritt)

Three sketches by Hmong witnesses documenting communist atrocities in Laos, circa 1980. (a) and (b): communist soldiers captured and killed this Hmong farm family in 1978. They raped the women and then killed them. They shot the father in the village. They killed the children by pounding them to death in the rice mortar. (c): On February 4, 1980, communist soldiers captured Hmong men, women, and children near Nam Long and killed them in the ways shown.

Hmong-Americans from across the U.S. demonstrate in Washington,
D.C. on June 10, 1991, protesting the Bush administration's policy
of economic aid to the LPDR and repatriation of Hmong refugees.
(Photo in the collection of the author)

Gravestone created by Montana Hmong to honor their American friend and CIA advisor Jerry Daniels who worked with them for 20 years. Inscription in Lao reads, "Long Chieng." Grave in Missoula, Montana. (Photo credit: T. J. Thompson)

21.

An Ominous Lull

. . . there is a requirement that all foreign troops be withdrawn
from Laos and Cambodia, and it is clearly understood that North
Vietnamese troops are considered foreign with respect to Laos and
Cambodia. . . . It is our firm expectation that within a short period
of time there will be a formal cease-fire in Laos which in turn will
lead to a withdrawal of all foreign forces from Laos and, of course,
to the end of the use of Laos as a corridor of infiltration [to South
Vietnam].

—Henry Kissinger at a press conference on January 24, 1973

As a result of the peace agreement, the U.S. terminated its Raven program and its Thai-based air support of the Royal Lao Armed Forces and
General Vang Pao's irregulars. Once this U.S. support was dismantled,
Pathet Lao officials, using "guerrilla diplomacy," proclaimed that they
did not like the February "Peace and Reconciliation" agreement. First
they stalled on the formation of the new coalition government by announcing that the February agreement was no longer acceptable. They
demanded that a protocol to the basic agreement be negotiated before
they could participate in the formation of a coalition government. Both
the Pathet Lao and the Royal Lao government initially worked on draft
protocols. Then the Pathet Lao insisted that its draft positions be used
exclusively. Souvanna Phouma gave in, and in late April 1973 the Pathet
Lao document became the basis for more negotiations.

This noble-sounding document gave no hint of repression, reprisals, or
the planned destruction of traditional Lao society with its historically pivotal royal family. Instead, it called for "national reconciliation," "national
unity," "neutrality," "independence," "democracy," and "peace." These

high-minded goals were intended to address U.S. officials' concerns in urging the Royal Lao government to co-rule Laos with its Marxist enemies.

Lao General Sananikone remembered the grueling days of final negotiations. "As the days and weeks passed, more hard issues surfaced at the conference table. Heated discussions became the norm, but each time an impasse occurred, Souvanna Phouma ordered his delegation to concede. On the worst of these occasions, the right wing members would threaten to resign. This put Souvanna Phouma in a difficult position which was ameliorated by pressure from the American Embassy. We would find that the weekly shipments of American-supplied rice for the Army would not arrive, or that the American-supplied money to pay the Army would be delayed, or that only part of the fuel needed to run the Army's vehicles would be delivered. Capitulation by the right wing was essential to maintain the NLA [National Lao Army]. The American military attachés made this very clear to all senior officers of the NLA.

"It pleased Souvanna Phouma to see that the right wing leadership—which essentially was the leadership of the NLA—was being rendered impotent by American pressure. In his view, he had suffered for too long the opposition of the right wing during the years when American support had contributed to their strength. He failed to understand or appreciate that he could not have remained in office for the past 13 years without the support of the NLA. Now his actions indicated, 'I don't need you.' The result of all this was an agreement with the Pathet Lao that, as it was implemented, turned the country over to the communists."[1]

On September 14, 1973, the holdouts in the Royal Lao government gave in and signed the protocol known as the Vientiane Agreement. The new agreement pleased the Pathet Lao. The protocol refined and expanded previous provisions, including the spelling out of which side would occupy which ministerial position as the chief minister and which side would be the assistant. More details were worked out on how the two capitals would be occupied by soldiers of both sides and therefore neutralized. Since "landgrabbing" had been going on since the initial days of talk of a cease-fire and peace negotiations, the protocol provided that markers be installed along a temporary cease-fire line. Disputed areas would then be addressed by the Joint Commission on the Implementation of the Agreement.

Although a cease-fire was supposedly in place, the communist forces expanded their control. Vang Teng, a special forces lieutenant in the Royal Lao Army, was stationed at Sala Phou Khoun, a major government position north of Vientiane. It was here that both sides faced each other and cease-fire flag markers would be placed. "From my mountain position, I watched the communists plant their red flags. Our officers told us that tomorrow we would set our markers indicating our boundary, and after both sides had marked their boundaries, then the two sides would talk over the disputed areas.[2]

"At 8 the next morning, over one hundred of our soldiers, armed only with the Royal Lao flag, set out to mark our territory. As the first flag was being pushed into the ground, the communist machine guns opened fire on us, immediately killing more than ten of our men and wounding many more. To escape the ambush the survivors fled into the jungle with their flags.

"The second attack against our position was a ground attack by a force of North Vietnamese, Chinese, Lao, and communist Hmong. We were attacked with hand grenades, machine guns, and mortars. We fought for about two hours, but communist forces were overpowering. My position and two or three other positions were overrun."

As he had done in the past, General Vang Pao warned Lao and American officials that the treaty of 1973 was suicide for Laos. This time, he was not alone in his thinking. Prince Sisouk na Champassak, then minister of defense, agreed. Prince Sisouk resented the "arm-twisting" by General Alexander Haig, Nixon's chief of staff, whom he believed to be under orders from Henry Kissinger to assist in forcing the Lao to sign a treaty with the enemy that was totally in the enemy's favor. In Sisouk's view, signing this treaty was "suicide for the Lao people."[3]

William Colby, director of the CIA at the time of the fall of Laos, also believed that the Royal Lao government was badly advised. In Colby's view the Royal Lao could have negotiated a much better treaty. It could have gotten more time for the various changes to take place. It could have driven a much harder bargain for control of Laos.[4] At the time, many Lao leaders had reached the same conclusion. Later, with the benefit of hindsight, many would be angry with the U.S. for pushing the Royal Lao government into an agreement that favored the communists.

About this time, the Pathet Lao moved T-28 pilot Yang Pao and other "outside" prisoners to a prison camp near Khang Khay on the PDJ where once the French Colonial Army and later the Japanese Imperial Army had headquartered, where the French after Dien Bien Phu had garrisoned and worked with American advisors, where the NVA and the Soviets had received Captain Kong Le after his coup, where Prince Souvanna Phouma had created his own Neutralist capital, and where

General Vang Pao had repeatedly repulsed the NVA. Now, several of Vang Pao's soldiers and one of his pilots worked as slaves at the direction of their captors. Their skeletal bodies, clothed in shreds, moved slowly. Their sunken eyes focused only on the raising of the axe, the shovel of dirt, the next step.[5]

A slogan much bandied about in Laos at this time was: "War Is Finished: Now We Must Turn Another Page." But after fighting the Viet Minh since World War II—some 30 years—many Hmong feared what might be on that next page.

In Long Chieng, while Vang Pao remained commander of Military Region II, he was no longer supplied by the Americans. The U.S. Barrel Roll air support that he had relied on in the past was no more; virtually nothing remained in Southeast Asia of the once mighty U.S. air power.

As stipulated in the "Peace and Reconciliation" treaty, General Vang Pao had disassembled his irregular forces. Since he was a general in the Royal Lao Army, he kept his military position, as did some Hmong soldiers who had held rank with the Royal Lao forces. Many irregulars wanted to sign on with the Royal Lao Army, but budget and political considerations prevented that. Some irregulars, however, did become regular soldiers by transferring to the Royal Lao Army.

Vang Pao, trying to anticipate the future, knew that his soldiers had to be dispersed and given a new life; much land was now occupied by communists, and Long Chieng and Ban Sorn could not support thousands of unemployed soldiers. This disbanding of his forces was troublesome for him. Once dispersed, he knew that it would be difficult—maybe impossible—to reassemble them in a future emergency.

However, resettlement efforts were necessary. To return these farmers-turned-soldiers to the soil was no easy task. Some of the younger soldiers had never farmed full-time; they had been soldiers all of their juvenile and adult lives. The transition required money and suitable land, since many soldiers had abandoned their farms, animals, and implements years ago when the North Vietnamese had invaded. It would be an extraordinarily expensive undertaking and require strong, active leadership. Through Vang Pao's efforts, seeds and livestock were provided. In some cases, Vang Pao ordered his prize bulldozer to assist in flattening lands for fields. His program included making facilities to raise chickens, pigs, water buffaloes, and fish in small ponds. As always, he stressed education, now focusing on adult education for his former soldiers. Though helped by the American aid, Vang Pao personally bore much of the financial burden.[6]

In the summer of 1973, during the lull while the Pathet Lao and the Royal Lao government negotiated the details of implementing the Vientiane Agreement, W. E. Garrett, writer and photographer for *National Geographic* magazine, arrived in Laos to gather information for an article on the Hmong. Garrett's article, which appeared in January 1974, was optimistic. Interviews with French-educated Dr. Yang Dao, the Yang sisters' younger brother and the first Hmong to receive a Ph.D. in France, and LyTeck Ly Nhia Vue, who worked in the Ministry of Interior, exuded confidence in the prospects for the new coalition. LyTeck, who had assisted the government in its negotiations with the Pathet Lao, was photographed by *National Geographic* with his cattle at his "ranch" outside Vientiane at Kilometer 52.

The final photograph in Garrett's article depicted representatives of the two "past enemies"—a government carpenter and a Pathet Lao soldier—posing with a USAID blueprint for a schoolhouse. The caption read: "Such cooperation, here photographed for the first time, may herald better times as killing gives way to learning and building." Garrett had other ideas for Laos. "Even the Ho Chi Minh Trail" he wrote, "could become an artery to new markets [for Hmong products]."[7]

Hmong who read Garrett's article were troubled by his statement that Vang Pao "once tried, without success, to proclaim an independent Hmong nation—anthem, flag, and all."[8] According to teacher Moua Lia, "Mr. Garrett's statement . . . is wrong. It was always Vang Pao who was trying to integrate the Hmong into the Lao society. At meetings, Vang Pao often spoke to us in Lao; he urged our schoolchildren to learn Lao. He disapproved of those who tried to introduce foreign scripts in which Hmong would write their Hmong language."[9]

Garrett's article concluded with the words of Pop Buell, the Indiana farmer, in his 14th year of working with the Hmong: "If anyone offers you a solution [about Laos] and he's speaking English, pay no attention. He probably doesn't even know the problem."[10]

During this lull in the fighting, Ly Neng Tong, who had witnessed the Soviet airlift of supplies to Kong Le in 1960, decided to return to his home village on the Plaine des Jarres. "As the plane circled for a landing, I looked for my village and the grave of my father. Much to my surprise, I could not recognize the terrain. The bombing had changed the earth's appearance so much that it was unfamiliar to me. I could not find my father's grave." Then he added, "After all these years of bombing, fighting, and destruction in my home area, the North Vietnamese were still there."[11]

In October 1973, another early player in the Lao theatre returned. Colonel "Heine" Aderholt, who had been on the scene in 1960 when the U.S. military involvement began in Laos and who, in the 1960s, had flown secret night interdiction flights against the Ho Chi Minh Trail, was recalled to active duty. Secretary of Defense James Schlesinger, aware of the pilfering of U.S. military equipment and supplies in Thailand, activated Aderholt from retirement, conferred upon him the rank of general, named him commander of the U.S. Military Assistance Command in Thailand, and ordered this tough former air commando to oversee the disassembling of the last vestiges of U.S. military presence in Southeast Asia.

At the end of 1973, the Pathet Lao still held T-28 pilot Yang Pao. "The Pathet Lao announced to us that both sides had signed a contract to go home. Some Lao and Lao Teung [Kmhmu] were allowed to leave. I think they were allowed to go home. I'm not certain. They did not release me. They kept me in the Khang Khay area on the PDJ in a jail called Ban Sorn. I was still an outside prisoner.

"There were twenty in my work team—seven Hmong and thirteen Lao. We had five Pathet Lao guards. Daily, we built houses or planted rice—whatever they wanted us to do. We were still fed only twice a day and we were starving. To stay alive we had to eat whatever we could steal while working. If we caught a bug or a butterfly, we ate it quickly before the guards saw us. If they saw us eating an insect, the guards beat us and said: 'Don't eat like that. The Pathet Lao way is not that way.' One day, we were working in a cornfield. I was so hungry so I ate some corn. The guard caught me and beat me very badly. The only way to stay alive was to eat leaves, snakes, butterflies, tree bark. There was a certain tree bark that had some salt in it so we tried to eat that to stay alive.

"The Pathet Lao Commander was Thong Kham. He wore no rank, but he was the boss. The guards were kids. Their guns longer than their legs. These guards forced us to sing communist songs as we worked. If we didn't sing, they tortured us or put us in solitary. We sang these words: 'I am bad. You good. Vang Pao bad. You good.' We sang these songs with tears."[12]

During Hmong New Year, Lo Ma, the former Forward Air Guide, now a lieutenant in the Royal Lao Army, asked Nhia to marry him. On January 14, 1974, in a simple but traditional ceremony, Nhia was married with her uncle again substituting for her father, still the commander at Bouam Loung. After over four years of suffering as a widow, Nhia, 24, started a new life.

Soviet involvement in Laos increased once the U.S. withdrew. Following the Vientiane Agreement in 1973, Soviet planes airlifted into Vientiane 1,000 "policeman," who turned out to be Pathet Lao soldiers, to neutralize the city. China airlifted other Pathet Lao forces to occupy Luang Prabang.

General Sananikone recalled Souvanna Phouma's naivete in dealing with the communists. "Materials and personnel the Pathet Lao brought to Vientiane and Luang Prabang were, under the protocol to the agreement, supposed to be inspected. . . . Despite the protocol . . . the Pathet Lao objected. . . . Characteristically, Souvanna Phouma summoned the officer in charge of the joint security force to his office and ordered him to allow the Pathet Lao and their equipment to enter without any control. His attitude was that it didn't really make any difference how many Pathet Lao entered the city; they considered their mission a sacred one and we must show them our generosity."[13]

Because of the many disputes caused by the unworkable nature of the agreement, the creation of the new provisional government was delayed until April 1974. On June 3 of that year, Captain Fred Walker and Captain Mike Shaver flew the last Air America plane out of Laos. To commemorate this event, a message went out at noon, 1200 Zulu: "Today was AAM's last day in Laos. Udorn based aircraft were all out of Laos as scheduled. The last one being C-7A 2389 piloted by Capt. F. F. Walker and Capt. M. W. Shaver which crossed the border at TE5878 at 1113Z en route from VTE [Vientiane] to UTH [Udorn]. The VTE closeout went well and the departure of AAM from Laos was without incident although some lumps are visible in the throats of those who put so much of themselves into the operation over the years." The message closed with: "And in remembering we will smile and look ahead to the next challenge. We grieve [f]or those missing and dead in Laos and regret that they too could not have enjoyed today."

For Walker there was little joy in this day, other than sentimental pride in piloting the last Air America plane from Laos. As he passed over the "fence" for the last time, he reviewed his days in Asia as a pilot. He had flown one of the last planes out of Yunnan, China, before Mao Zedong's forces took over. He had flown one of the last desperate flights to resupply Dien Bien Phu before it fell to General Giap. Now he flew the last plane from Laos. "I thought: Since 1945, we've been running—the wrong way. We've been retreating. Retreating."[14] Walker did not know then that he was destined to fly in the last desperate days as the communists took over in South Vietnam and Cambodia.

By June 4, 1974, the last U.S. military man had left Laos. Thailand had withdrawn the last of its "volunteer" troops two weeks earlier. No longer did the sleek jets, the gunships, or the fleets of helicopters sit on bases in Thailand to be used against the enemy in Laos. The once-active barracks used by the 7/13th Air Force in Thailand were silent. Grass grew from runway cracks. Air America, Continental Air Services, and the U.S. Air Force had gone home. Some 40,000 (some experts estimated many more) North Vietnamese forces remained in Laos. In addition, there were the Vietnamese cadre, political commissars, advisors, and civilians who worked with the Pathet Lao.

Now, many in the Royal Lao government recognized that they had been fooled. The Americans were gone. The Thai troops were gone. Vang Pao's irregulars were disarmed and dispersed. Only the well-armed, experienced NVA and their bureaucratic cadre remained. Yet neutralist Souvanna Phouma, half-brother to Souphanouvong, the nominal head of the communist Lao, continued to believe that a coalition between the royalists and the communists could work.

Colonel Billy, who had observed Souvanna Phouma for some fifteen years, concluded: "Souvanna Phouma was not a communist as some have said. He was naive and his ego got in the way. He truly believed that with his princely status, his notion that he was so well-liked by so many, and his belief that he had the ability to work out something with his princely half-brother Souphanouvong, he had reason to be confident about the future of Laos. He believed that it would not become communist. He was wrong. First of all, Souphanouvong wasn't in charge of the Pathet Lao as Souvanna Phouma had assumed; Kaysone Phomvihane, Hanoi's tough protege, was."[15]

One Pathet Lao infantry battalion allowed to enter Vientiane, ostensibly to protect its mission, was in fact on a much more important mission—to propagandize the people. It attacked the Lao government as lackeys of the United States, denounced the evils of capitalism, and praised the virtues of the socialist-communist system. General Sananikone observed the Pathet Lao tactics. "Pathet Lao soldiers in mufti became agents provocateur, inciting demonstrations against the government, while others joined the mobs protesting, striking, or otherwise disrupting the functions of government and good order in Vientiane. A group of young university graduates, mostly from French universities, formed an activist association to propel the government as rapidly as possible into a new, liberal, socialist course. They had already absorbed a large dose of socialist doctrine during their student years in Paris and now this was reinforced by their contacts with the Pathet Lao in Vientiane. Their viewpoint was that the leadership in Vientiane was old and reactionary; that only the educated youth of Laos were qualified to shape the destiny of a nation."[16]

LyTeck, whom the *National Geographic* had interviewed in the summer of 1973, was one of these former graduates. He had been the first Hmong to receive a master's degree in political science from France. Upon his return to Laos, Vang Pao assigned him to work on the economic development program at Sam Thong. Vang Pao then sent him to England for a one-year course in English for which Vang Pao had paid. Now, LyTeck spent much time in Vientiane, advising on negotiations with the Pathet Lao, or at Kilometer 52 where ten Hmong families of the Ly clan had moved several years earlier. LyTeck also visited Hmong students at Sisavang Vong University, and urged them to reject General Vang Pao and side with the Pathet Lao. He told them that the Pathet Lao had promised that he, not Dr. Yang Dao, would replace General Vang Pao as the Hmong leader.

Yang Dao, whose older sisters had married Moua Lia and General Direction, had returned from France with a doctorate in political science. He had spent much of his adult life outside of Laos. He now worked with the new government as a member of the National Political Coalition Council and promoted the Vientiane Agreement to the Hmong. Yang Dao believed that an accommodation with the communists was possible and early on had urged the Hmong to abide by the agreement of 1973. According to Ly Neng Tong, a Hmong leader, "Yang Dao went to the Hmong people and told them that the treaty was right; that everyone should resign from fighting. Yang Dao was very naive and very wrong about the communists. He didn't know about the behavior of the Vietnamese."[17]

In July 1974, Moua Lia returned from his educational training in Singapore. "When I returned, the political situation was not good. Yet General Vang Pao insisted that we move forward, that we work hard on economic projects and education. He enthusiastically offered to furnish me with books, kerosene, kerosene lamps and money to pay the teachers who would teach children during the day and adults at night. We worked on adult education until the very end."[18]

In mid-August 1974, strikes by municipal workers and traffic police began in Vientiane. Students entered the political scene as negotiators and stridently promoted their 18-point program of high-minded social goals: elimination of "all sources of foreign cultural vices," including "robbery, homicide, prostitution and gambling." It referred repeatedly to building of a prosperous Kingdom of Laos, implying that there would be a king. It concluded with a stirring call to "all political forces, intellectuals, students, pupils, Buddhist bonzes, soldiers, policemen, and public servants who cherish patriotism, peace, independence, neutrality and democracy to fully implement this political program in order to make the Kingdom of Laos peaceful, independent, neutral, democratic, unified and prosperous."[19]

That same month, Richard Nixon resigned in the wake of the Watergate scandal and was replaced by Gerald Ford. Both the media and public attention for months had focused on the Watergate hearings; the Vietnam War, which had dominated the news for years, had been replaced by the crisis in the White House.

In Laos, municipal workers went on strike; so did hospital orderlies and workers at the electrical plant. The government was in turmoil; workers and military personnel went unpaid; the strikes spread to other towns. Students struck against their schools, against foreign instructors, against the visit of a Thai dignitary. They struck, it seemed, just for the purpose of creating disruption and chaos. On November 1, 1974, Souvanna Phouma, who had suffered a heart attack and had gone to France for treatment, returned to Laos. Unable to quiet the turmoil, he traveled to the royal ceremonial capital of Luang Prabang to convalesce. On December 31, 1974, Souvanna Phouma told visiting American professor Joseph Zasloff that Laos would not go communist.[20]

The new year—1975—was ushered in by more strikes. Now teachers joined the waves of protests. The noncommunist half of the coalition government, referred to as the Vientiane government, was criticized by the communist side as corrupt and incompetent. There were many in the Royal Lao government who believed that the unrest was caused by the communists, but Souvanna Phouma was unable or unwilling to prove it. On February 5, 1975, the Lao People's Revolutionary Army (LPRA), supported by NVA troops, attacked the Royal Lao Army near Sala Phou Khoun. General Vang Pao responded with T-28 bombing strikes. The NVA and LPRA expanded their attacks on government positions throughout Laos. By the end of March 1975, the Vientiane government had lodged 80 protests. None, however, were inspected by the joint commission created by the 1973 agreement to oversee cease-fire violations.

On March 26, the Soviets ratified the convention banning the use, transfer, and stockpiling of biological and toxin weapons which had been negotiated three years earlier and which the U.S. had ratified on January 22.[21]

In Laos, unrest grew. Hmong students were visited frequently by LyTeck, who urged them to overthrow the old ways. He bragged about his future. One night, Yang Chee, then a student at Sisavang Vong University in Vientiane, and another student were picked up by LyTeck. "He drove around and around the houses of Touby LyFong, Vang Pao and Yang Dao in Vientiane, gloating in an evil way about how he would soon replace Vang Pao under the new regime. This happened in late March or early April, just before the school closed. While driving us around, LyTeck said that he and his 'Phi Nong,' his comrades, had organized a force to capture Vang Pao, and Vang Pao would have to be very clever to escape. He also talked about Yang Dao, saying that he was a clever man but had fallen into Vang Pao's hands. He told us, 'I will be the new Hmong chief.' I was scared and said nothing."[22]

Yang Chee remembered that he and other Hmong students were coerced into marching. "To have gone against the Pathet Lao organizers would have been disastrous so I walked silently with the shouting Lao demonstrators. One of the popular Lao banner slogans was: 'Seuk Leo Meo Tay'—'The War Is Ended; The Meo [Hmong] Are Dead.' We Hmong students carried these banners too, We had no choice."

In Vientiane, teachers and civil servants joined the students to protest and strike. Everyone—even those fervently against the proposals that they shouted—carried banners and mouthed slogans calling for "popular uprisings," "people's seizure of power," "purification" of the government by installing the "people's administration." Calls for the elimination of "reactionaries" and "foreign consultants" and for the dissolving of the National Assembly and the Constitution created havoc.

In most towns, mob rule was in effect. Incidents became violent. Mobs struck and sacked United States USIS and USAID offices and threatened Americans. Americans were held hostage in Savannakhet. There was no longer a functioning Royal Lao government. Protesters and agitators were in control, demanding more pay, elimination of foreign teachers, and riddance of the rightist cabinet members.

On March 27 and again on April 11, General Vang Pao's soldiers protecting Sala Phou Khoun came under attack. Lt. Vang Teng, who had earlier attempted to flag-mark the cease-fire boundaries, remained on duty here. To defend this position, the last major stronghold of the Royal Lao government north of Vientiane, Vang Pao ordered his T-28s to bomb the communist force of at least 1,000. Fackee, who had become the T-28

Wing Commander in 1972, led the T-28 attack that halted the communist advance. FAC pilot Xiong Ly Tou, who had saved Darrel Whitcomb's life in 1972, crashed and died during this fighting.

Prime Minister Souvanna Phouma criticized General Vang Pao for protecting Sala Phou Khoun. He suggested that instead of military action, Vang Pao should have allowed the joint cease-fire commission to investigate.[23] On April 12, 1975, the day after the counterattack on Sala Phou Khoun, Cambodia fell to Pol Pot's communist Khmer Rouge, backed by China.

While communist forces moved against government troops in Laos, Dr. Yang Dao toured communist countries in Asia and Europe, seeking support for a coalition government in Laos.

As ordered by Souvanna Phouma, the Royal Lao Army continued to retreat from communist probes. General Vang Pao alone resisted enemy attacks. He considered it his duty to protect government positions. Each time he defended a government position, he was criticized by Vientiane.

Angered by repeated cease-fire violations and by the inspection commission's ineffectiveness, Vang Pao considered a bold plan. He would take over the Lao Air Force and with it defend Royal Lao positions. This was a desperate thought. Vang Pao, throughout his military career, had worked hard to integrate the Hmong into Lao society and to support the Royal Lao government. He had urged respect for Lao traditions. Though he remained basically an animist, he had particularly promoted Buddhism and the king. Vang Pao had been a Lao patriot. He loved the land that since a child of 13 he had fought to protect.

During the last 15 years with the Americans, Vang Pao's men had destroyed a billion dollars' worth of equipment heading for South Vietnam in order to deny this equipment to Hanoi's troops and the Viet Cong there. He and his troops had fought the tough North Vietnamese Army and killed many of them to protect the Hmong homeland and the Lao towns in the Mekong River valley. His men had rescued many American pilots. These efforts had taken a huge toll on the Hmong: some 17,000 soldiers had been killed and uncounted numbers had been wounded. Perhaps as many as 50,000 civilian Hmong had been killed or wounded. Now, in Vang Pao's opinion, Laos was about to be given away without a fight—without even a challenge. The peace agreement was being grossly violated, and the Lao were retreating like cowards. The inspection commission and world opinion seemed ineffectual and uninterested. Vang Pao believed it his duty to protect his country. Beyond being the protector of the Hmong, he was, after all, a general in the Royal Lao Army.

Before initiating his plan to take over the Air Force, he went to Vientiane to convince Prime Minister Souvanna Phouma that the Army had to take action in view of the cease-fire violations. For this meeting, he went as a major general in the Royal Lao Army. He wore his full-dress uniform with his many medals demonstrating his service, valor, and success over many years. Souvanna Phouma was not in his office, so Vang Pao went to his home where he found the prime minister and told him that the NVA continued to attack Sala Phou Khoun and were on their way to Vientiane. Souvanna Phouma responded angrily. He told Vang Pao that he was a troublemaker and that the Vietnamese attacking Sala Phou Khoun and advancing toward Vientiane were his problem, not Vang Pao's. Vang Pao should not worry about it. The Hmong general stood at attention for a moment to consider precisely Souvanna Phouma's words. Then, he ripped off his medals, threw them on the prime minister's desk, and walked out.[24]

Before returning to Long Chieng, he visited Sisouk na Champassak, minister of defense. He asked him if he could obtain munitions to lead an offensive or return to guerrilla tactics. Sisouk, who admired Vang Pao and who was angry over the gift of his country to the communists, confided that although he was minister of defense he really had no authority any longer. He soon would be forced to resign to appease the communists.[25]

A few days later, Lao and Vietnamese communist forces supported by the Soviet Union took Sala Phou Khoun and threatened to move south against Vientiane.

Then with lightning speed the NVA, with Soviet tanks, armored personnel carriers, towed artillery pieces, and convoys of soldiers, rolled across the 17th parallel heading south to Saigon. The South Vietnamese Army fled before this massive conventional invasion by the NVA. It had been left exposed and vulnerable by the congressional passage of the Church-Cooper legislation that denied further funding to resupply the South Vietnamese military. South Vietnamese planes and tanks sat idle due to lack of fuel and spare parts. Once Hanoi understood that the U.S. had no intention of assisting its ally when it was being invaded, divisions of NVA troops and tanks moved in swiftly for the kill.

On April 30, 1975, the last U.S. evacuation helicopter lifted off the roof of the U.S. Embassy in Saigon as North Vietnamese tanks surrounded the Presidential Palace. Liberated Saigon became Ho Chi Minh City. Radio broadcasts of the defeat of the Americans and the South Vietnamese immediately reached Laos. The following day was May Day, the communist workers' holiday—an auspicious day to celebrate the victory of the communist takeover of South Vietnam and the defeat of the Americans. Lao waving the red flags of the Pathet Lao rode in American jeeps through the streets of Lao towns. In Savannakhet, cheering students, many with long hair, Levis, and granny glasses, waved Pathet Lao flags and goaded local citizens as they followed Pathet Lao soldiers and a Soviet PT-76 amphibious tank in a street parade. Revelers, mostly young, beamed as they shouted revolutionary slogans, slandered the U.S., demanded the ouster of rightist cabinet members—particularly Prince Sisouk na Champassak—and taunted anyone who did not seem jubilant. They proclaimed that the evil, neo-colonialist, imperialistic United States had been defeated. Victory had come; peace had arrived. The struggle had been successful in Vietnam. The same would soon be true in Laos.

22.

"Wipe Them Out!"

It has all come back to me very painfully. It now bothers me a
great deal how we just packed up and left those people. We knew
that they were going to suffer. I find it hard to believe that anybody
in this world would ever trust us again. As far as I'm concerned,
our word is no good.

—Darrel Whitcomb, U.S. Air Force Academy graduate who flew
two tours in Vietnam and one in Laos as a Raven spotter pilot,
working with the Hmong

At his headquarters at Long Chieng, General Vang Pao could not
sleep. The Royal Lao government was about to fall to the communists,
and this time there was no one to help—no Frenchmen, no Americans.
Phoumi Vongvichit, the former tax collector who had collaborated with
the Japanese and the Viet Minh and now was a senior official in the
Pathet Lao, had announced on national radio that the Hmong must be
"taken out at the roots." Vang Pao could not stop thinking about what
would happen to those whom he had led in the long and bloody fight
against the communists when the NVA and Pathet Lao came to power.
He paced the floor, sometimes shouting in frustration and frequently
gazing at the silent airstrip. Alternate no longer bustled with excitement.
The Raven FAC pilots had been gone for two years. The CIA compound
with its gangly antennas had been turned over to USAID. Most SKY advisors were gone. Colonel Billy, assigned to the U.S. Embassy in Bangkok,
had lost touch with Vang Pao. Only Jerry Daniels remained.

This crisis required a clan council decision. Following tribal tradition,
Vang Pao summoned the clan leaders and his senior military men to a
meeting in Long Chieng. From outlying villages and remote outposts,

they came to decide the fate of their people. Colonel Moua Cher Pao arrived from Bouam Loung. Tasseng Yang, into whose village Colonel Billy had choppered that day so long ago, and others living in Long Chieng prepared for the meeting.

The heat preceding the monsoon season was oppressive. Temperatures soared to over 100 degrees in the "dreaded valley" as tribal elders and senior military men gathered in early May 1975. Some wore military clothes and carried arms. Others wore parts of uniforms. Others dressed in tribal garb. Some, having hidden or thrown away their uniforms to avoid being identified with Vang Pao, wore Western pants and shirts. Significantly, everyone spoke in Hmong; no one used the Lao language that had so often been promoted by Vang Pao at meetings.

Fourteen years ago this month, many of these men had fought for their lives at Padong when the NVA attacked during a fraudulent cease-fire as diplomats in Geneva negotiated for a "neutralized" Laos. Once again a cease-fire was supposedly in place. Yet NVA 130mm artillery gunners, positioned within range of Long Chieng, fired reverberating rounds to remind those in the valley of their power.

T-28 pilot Coyote (Lt. Moua Chue) had been transferred out of Vang Pao's region to Vientiane. He was one of the Hmong pilots officially absorbed into the Lao military which, importantly, had taken away Vang Pao's Hmong "air," substantially reducing his power. In Vientiane, Coyote listened to Dr. Yang Dao promoting accommodation with the communists. He heard similar talk from his fellow Lao pilots and monitored the pro-communist street demonstrations. By early May, he had concluded that the coalition government was controlled by the communists, and he was afraid. He particularly feared for his people because of their strong association with the Americans. He decided to return to Long Chieng to talk to General Vang Pao.

Lao were very suspicious of Hmong who had worked with Vang Pao, so Coyote had to be careful not to attract attention. When his wife gave birth at Long Chieng, he had a reason to request permission to return. He arrived there on May 8. "As soon as I arrived I went to see Vang Pao. I had only a few words with him, but he told me: 'Be prepared. We are going to re-stock and fight.' That day, I watched Vang Pao's house. I saw many leaders coming and going from his house."[1]

These leaders walked past the Soviet artillery gun captured on the Plaine des Jarres that Vang Pao had installed in front of his headquarters as a monument to Hmong bravery. Men who had often joked about this gun trophy now passed it by as if it did not exist. There was only one thought on their minds, one question to answer: should they resist the hated North Vietnamese or should they surrender?

This was the same question that the Hmong had faced in late 1960—fifteen years earlier—when Colonel Billy asked them if they were prepared to resist the communists. At that time, the Hmong asked for weapons to defend their homelands. Then Vang Pao told Colonel Billy that he, personally, had only two choices—to leave or to fight. He preferred to fight. Now, after all those years and the loss of tens of thousands of Hmong lives, the question remained the same. Those responsible for reaching a decision laboriously reviewed all the facts and debated the answer.

When Moua Lia arrived, the marathon meeting had already commenced. "It was clear that Vang Pao thought that this meeting would decide the Hmong future. It was a life-or-death meeting. When I entered, I heard the people speaking against resistance. The people in attendance were divided into two groups—those who were in favor of resisting and those who were not.[2]

"Since the purpose of the meeting was to decide what the Hmong should do, we first had to carefully analyze the situation. We started with the Paris Agreement of 1973 between Kissinger and Le Duc Tho and how it related to Laos. We hoped that the North Vietnamese would respect the Paris Agreement and withdraw their troops. But the NVA were still in Laos even after the Thai soldiers and the American advisors and aircraft had withdrawn. We noted that the U.S. had withdrawn all its troops from all Indochina. Which country would now force the North Vietnamese to withdraw their troops from Laos? We decided that there was none."

Vang Pao had a copy of the February 21, 1973, "Agreement on the Restoration of Peace and Reconciliation in Laos." Article 3C had been underlined. It read: "All 'sweep' operations, terrorism and suppression which endanger the lives and property of the people, as well as acts of revenge and discrimination against people who have cooperated with the opposite side during the war, are forbidden; one should help the people who were forced to flee from their homes during the war to be free to return and earn a living according to their wishes." Vang Pao had circled the words, "acts of revenge and discrimination against people who have cooperated with the opposite side during the war, are forbidden." Few in the room believed them.

Next they studied the "Vientiane Agreement," the protocol signed on September 14, 1973, modifying the original agreement. Moua Lia listened as man after man concluded that the Vientiane Agreement gave the communists control of Laos, since all authority would be shared. "For example, we knew that if the head of a province was a leftist, his assistant would be from the Lao government side. We noted that the Lao government continued to give everything to the Pathet Lao when they complained, so we knew that this strange method of running a government would be to the advantage of the leftists."

Then the men went over the 18-point policy prepared by the Pathet Lao in May 1974, the policy that demonstrators were demanding. "This was called the 'Program for Achieving Peace, Independence, Neutrality, Democracy, Unification, and Prosperity of the Kingdom of Laos,'" recalled Moua Lia, "but most of us who had experience with the communists knew that the wonderful promises were only propaganda to fool the people and the world."

Most had heard the May 6 Radio Pathet Lao broadcast commentary claiming that "the special forces [meaning those who had fought with General Vang Pao] were the main perpetrators of the barbarous, notorious crimes against the Lao people." The broadcast went on: "The Patriotic Armed Forces, however, have no fear of this handful of special forces. We can wipe them out any time. That is not our primary goal . . . because we want to preserve the spirit of national concord called for in the peace accords. However, if we can no longer tolerate the sinister acts of the reactionary clique, the Patriotic Armed Forces must exercise our right of self-defense and duly punish or wipe them out."[3] Equally disturbing to the Hmong gathered in council, recalled Moua Lia, was that: "We had all heard Souvanna Phouma say over the radio: 'Those who don't like peace, please go and stay outside.' We knew he meant General Vang Pao and his Hmong followers."[4]

Next the Hmong leaders analyzed the Vietnamese military positions and their own. "We knew that the NVA artillery, only a few miles away, had Long Chieng easily in range. The military men estimated that if the Hmong took to the mountains again, they had enough small arms and ammunition to function as guerrillas for at least one year. We decided that we didn't have enough soldiers. We had released some 18,000 men after the Paris peace treaty. They had gone to villages to become farmers. There was no time to call them in and to get organized. If we did succeed in calling them in to fight again, we would be alone in our fight. There would be no air support. All American military assistance was gone. There was only USAID and Jerry Daniels in Long Chieng. The USAID man came in the morning and left in the afternoon. Only Daniels spent the nights at Long Chieng."

In traditional Hmong fashion, the marathon discussions went back and forth, back and forth. To resist or not to resist? Many field commanders wanted to resist even with no outside support. If they did not resist, they asked, where could they go to escape the revenge which they knew would come? There seemed to be no answer to this life-and-death question.

On that same day, Jerry Daniels informed General Vang Pao that he and his key officers would have to leave Laos. They would be taken to Thailand until everything could be sorted out. Daniels told Vang Pao that the U.S. could no longer help the Hmong. He warned that if Vang Pao and his key men did not leave now, the U.S. would leave without helping them. Also on that same day, Dr. Yang Dao and other members of the National Political Coalition Council returned to Laos after what they described as a successful tour of communist capitals where they sought support for a coalition government. That night, the NVA launched a major attack against Sala Phou Khoun. Lt. Vang Teng remembered that it came against all positions at once. "We couldn't resist. We lost radios; we lost men; we lost weapons. We lost. We ran all night to avoid the enemy who chased us. It wasn't until the morning of May 10 that we could radio to Long Chieng to report the defeat of Sala Phou Khoun."[5]

At Long Chieng, the Hmong leaders, many having gone without sleep for several days, were continuing discussions when the news of the fall of Sala Phou Khoun arrived. It was a devastating blow.

Ordinary Hmong observed the grave faces of those coming and going from General Vang Pao's house. It was these ordinary Hmong that concerned Vang Pao. As their leader, he was responsible for them and they in turn needed him to lead and guide them. If Vang Pao left Laos, who would lead? Hmong had to have leaders—that was the custom. If the senior military men and clan leaders were gone, who would protect the Hmong from the communists?

Filled with anger and sadness, Hmong elders now only repeated themselves in their frustration to find a resolution to an unresolvable problem. After the fall of Sala Phou Khoun, they discussed leaving—but where were they to go? How could they live somewhere else? There had been no plans for fleeing their homeland. Over the years, the Americans had repeatedly told them that together they would defeat the communists and that the Hmong, who would be acknowledged for their heroic efforts to save Laos, would be greatly appreciated by the Lao people, resulting in a better life for them. Now, instead, they, the Hmong leaders, were being instructed by the Americans to leave their homeland immediately—perhaps forever. They paced and argued. Some shouted. Some were silent in their torment. General Vang Pao vacillated between periods of somber silence and bursts of shouting. Those who had worked so closely with the Americans for so long could not fathom the idea that the Americans were abandoning them.

Moua Lia remembered that during this time there was great suspicion. "Even good friends did not know what to say to each other. Everyone had to be very careful not to move too fast. We were not certain who among us were now informants, reporting to the communists our names and our plans. Everyone was scared. We knew that the enemy considered everyone at Long Chieng to be CIA—whether we had worked with the CIA or not. We were all afraid."

Daniels pushed for an immediate evacuation of key leaders by air to Udorn. Vang Pao argued that all Hmong who fought in the war should be evacuated, not just a few at the top. The CIA at Udorn refused and counter-offered an airlift of the families of key officers. Angered by this offer, Vang Pao responded with a request for an airlift of 5,000.

While Vang Pao argued with the CIA, Hmong leaders debated. They recalled the promises of Colonel Billy and the repeated pledges by Colonel Billy's successors that the Americans and the Hmong would help each other always. All Hmong assembled had participated in *ba-sii* ceremonies for their American friends. There had been many speeches and toasts of lasting friendship and loyalty.

Daniels urged Vang Pao to draw up a list of his key men and their families—maybe as many as 1,200—to be evacuated.

On May 10, a phone call from the CIA brought the final ultimatum to Vang Pao. The Hmong watched Vang Pao's face as he listened. It was all over. Tasseng Yang remembered that the Hmong leaders "drew up a treaty in which they reminded the Americans of the pledges made over the past 15 years. Then they wrote that they agreed to leave Laos and never return. General Vang Pao and twelve Hmong signed the treaty. As each man signed, he cried. When everyone had signed, General Vang Pao ordered the men to prepare for immediate departure."[6]

That same day, Prime Minister Souvanna Phouma announced that General Vang Pao had been replaced as Commander of Military Region II.

Also on the same day, General "Heine" Aderholt, who had recently arrived in Bangkok, received a call from USAID in Laos requesting a C-130 to evacuate the general from Long Chieng. "I told this USAID fellow that the C-130s and the pilots we had used in the recent Cambodian airlift were deactivated. I didn't think we could assist. The USAID man said, 'See what you can do.' I called Howard Hartley who ran Bird Air and told him of this urgent requirement from Laos. He said there were a couple of C-130s waiting in Thailand to be flown back to Clark Air Force Base in the Philippines. The problem was that there was only one C-130 pilot in country—Matt Hoff—and he was at the airport waiting to board a KLM flight. Howard gave me the flight number and I called the Thais at the airport to find Captain Hoff. I also sent someone out to get him. Then I realized that I didn't have authority to send a C-130 to Laos. I called General Brown, Chairman of the Joint Chiefs. I told him that there was enough money, but I needed authority to divert funds from the Cambodian airlift to make this run into Laos. He approved it. Then Matt Hoff called. He asked me how much I was going to give him. I told him 'Hell, I don't care. How much do you want?' He answered, '$5,000 per crew member.' I agreed, although I knew it was too much. Then Hartley called asking if he could go. I OKed that also."[7]

On the morning of May 11, the sun beat down on the thousands of Hmong waiting on Alternate's runway. Many clutched battered suitcases or cardboard boxes tied with strings, or carried reed back-baskets. Children held tightly to their mothers' clothes. Soldiers with guns stood near the airstrip.

Moua Lia's wife, My, and her six children waited at Alternate with an assortment of hurriedly packed boxes and a battered suitcase. In the baggage were My's silver necklace and some photographs, including one of General Vang Pao, a gift from him. Moua Lia was not certain he could follow her to Thailand. He might be asked to stay and fight.[8]

Lt. Col. Vang Chou (General Direction), who had been ordered by Vang Pao to oversee the evacuation, stood in front of the AOC Quonset hut. On his clipboard was the list of families to be evacuated. There was no pushing, no panic as everyone listened for incoming aircraft.[9]

Word spread in the countryside that Vang Pao was leaving. Frightened people rushed to Long Chieng with their hastily assembled and meager belongings. The crowd at the airport swelled by the hour. About noon the C-130 transport plane flown by Matt Hoff landed at Long Chieng. As he taxied, he opened the cockpit windows to look at the thousands hoping to get on this one plane. Hoff rolled to a stop and dropped the tailgate. People pushed into the plane's dark belly. Soldiers with guns threatened civilians, explaining that this plane was for them and their families. Some Hmong, afraid the soldiers might fire, backed off. Others continued to push, trying to board. To stop the surge, Hoff raced the engines to blow the people back with the prop wash so the tailgate could be shut. Some pushed through the prop wash, dragging themselves into the overloaded plane. The tailgate closed, the C-130 taxied. It lifted ever so slowly, with a record number of passengers carried by a C-130. The Hmong exodus had begun.

After the C-130 departed, people milled around, asking each other when more planes would arrive, and how many. No one seemed to know. Rumors spread that the North Vietnamese were advancing. Hmong continued to arrive at Long Chieng until some 10,000 swarmed Alternate. Leaders knew well that the Vietnamese artillery gunners could at any time kill or wound many of those assembled.

Moua Lia's wife and children, who had not been listed for the C-130, waited in the sweltering sun near the AOC shack. Then a Caribou, flown by two Americans, landed. Vang Chou signaled his family and Moua Lia's family to get ready. They were scheduled to be on this flight, designated for families in the greatest danger. The crowd quieted as General Direction called out the names of those to board. My began to cry. Her younger children clung to her skirt. The others made a tight knot around her. She boarded slowly, tears flowing. Struggling with her belongings and the baby, she pushed her children ahead of her. "I knew for sure that if this plane took off there would be no return. I didn't know if I would ever see my husband again. We had all listened to Lao national radio and Voice of America. We knew of the fall of Saigon and Phnom Penh. I believed that if Laos fell to the communists, there would be no way we could survive in Laos."[10] A few men approached, hoping to board, but Vang Chou stood firm, allowing only women and children on the aircraft.

Aboard, My found her older sister, Mai, Vang Chou's wife, with her children. Once again the Yang sisters had been uprooted, forced to flee the communists. Once again they were refugees, leaving behind most of their possessions. Once again they would be forced to start life over, maybe without their husbands. Ironically, it had been their younger brother, Yang Dao, whom they had worked to send to private school, who had promoted accommodation with the communists and encouraged the coalition government. The Caribou lifted off and headed south for the short flight across the Mekong to touch down at Udorn Air Force Base where the Thais would provide temporary shelter.

Back at Alternate, two old C-47 cargo planes, with Lao and Hmong crews, landed. Hmong pilot Ly Teng flew one of them. Coyote's wife with her days-old infant and her other children managed to board Ly Teng's flight. On departure, both aircraft were so overloaded that the pilots had to abort takeoff to push out dozens of people before trying a second time. Those watching feared they would never be able to get out. The frightened mass of people continued to swell. There were more rumors of approaching enemy forces. Vang Chou, in charge of evacuation, realized that he was losing control of the crowd.

On May 12 Vang Chou observed the last friendly gesture by Prince Sisouk na Champassak: "Two C-47s arrived at Long Chieng loaded with carbines and 20 cases of ammunition. It was our last support. The two planes had been dispatched from Savannakhet by the prince, probably his last official act before fleeing the country. The guns and ammunition were for anyone who wanted them. People just came and took what they wanted."[11]

On that same day, Lo Ma realized that it would be impossible to get himself and his family out of Long Chieng by air; he had to make other plans. About noon he managed to hire a car to drive them to Vientiane. At Ban Sorn, Pathet Lao guards stopped them. No one was allowed to pass through Ban Sorn—on the only road to Vientiane. Afraid for their children, they took the three older ones from Nhia's marriage to pilot Vang Seng to Lo Ma's parents, living at Phou Heh in the mountains near Ban Sorn.[12]

At Long Chieng, Vang Chou, still trying desperately to put some order into the evacuation, was surprised at the lack of air transport. "The Americans sent only a few planes to evacuate the Hmong. There was the one C-130 and a C-123 that took a couple of loads. Most of the flights were not American flights. Ly Teng flew a C-47 cargo plane three trips a day to Udorn and back for two days. Then Coyote took over for him. There were not enough planes to evacuate the Hmong. No one officially told us that: we just knew it."[13] He and the others were correct. The U.S. had no systematic plan to evacuate the Hmong from Long Chieng. The American-crewed C-130, organized by Aderholt, made only one flight to Long Chieng.

As the dawn of May 13 broke across Skyline Ridge, Hmong waiting below continued to hope that planes were on their way to rescue them. Vang Chou vividly remembers that morning. "An American in civilian clothes and not very tall who, I think, was from the U.S. Embassy in Vientiane, arrived at Long Chieng. He came to talk to General Vang Pao. He was very angry and said that the U.S. was washing its hands of the Hmong. He told Vang Pao to evacuate his family. Vang Pao, also angry, answered, 'What about my troops?' They argued and negotiated over the number of Hmong that should be evacuated. Vang Pao insisted that every Hmong soldier should be flown out. The American official said only 1,000 could come out. They argued back and forth. Finally, Vang Pao insisted on at least 2,500 and the American departed. But the planes necessary to fly out that many people never came.

"Vang Pao had told me privately on May 11 that when the time came I should take his Cessna and get out. He told me not to forget to take his 75-pound box of mechanic's tools. After witnessing the performance of the American official early on the morning of the 13th, it was clear to me that it was time to leave."[14]

Fackee stood on the airstrip at Alternate looking at the thousands of people. "There weren't enough aircraft to evacuate those who wanted to go. People were crying and fighting to get on the few planes that came. The enemy was only a few kilometers away. There was a Beechcraft Baron sitting at Alternate, and I decided to use it to get people out. It held only a few people, but I loaded it up with women and children. One woman in each seat and at least one child on her lap. I chose to fly high—about 9,000 feet—to avoid detection. On one flight, a woman gave birth to a girl, which we considered good luck. There was little time to evacuate people, so I made five flights in the Baron, but the plane was so small that I could help only a few people."[15]

Moua Lia was now aware that it was every man for himself. "The communists had long ago labeled me 'the CIA schoolteacher.' I knew that I would be on the list of those to be punished or killed if I stayed, yet I couldn't find any way to get out. There were many Hmong like me with no way to escape. We had been abandoned. I was so very sad that there were not enough planes to take us out." Then Vang Chou, his brother-in-law, told him that Moua Xiong, the mechanic, had just finished repairing Vang Pao's single-engine Cessna, call-sign "Papa Uniform," which had been broken down for two months. They were going to take off soon for Thailand and agreed to take him.

Moua Xiong loaded Vang Pao's heavy toolbox into the back seat of "Papa Uniform," then Moua Lia crawled in. Vang Chou, with his crippled right arm, climbed into the pilot's seat, and the mechanic jumped in beside him. But "Papa Uniform" would not start. Vang Chou could not get the engine to kick at all. Moua Xiong shouted that it must be a dead battery. Hurrying, but trying not to draw attention to himself, Moua Lia brought his old car to the airstrip. They jumpstarted "Papa Uniform" from his car.

Vang Chou knew that a patrol of Lao T-28 pilots were up. He had heard them earlier over the radio. "I thought they might try to shoot us down, so I decided to fly low, about 500 feet, to avoid detection. Once airborne, there were other problems. I could see a major thunderstorm moving toward us, and my gas tank was less than half full.

"I hadn't flown a plane for seven years, since I was hit in June 1968.

My right arm was almost useless and the right arm is necessary to run the cockpit controls. The weather closed in with rain and violent winds throwing us around. At such low altitudes, I was using a lot of fuel and I couldn't find Udorn or Nam Phong. I couldn't find any landmark that I recognized, and my fuel was dangerously low. Moua Lia was scared and repeatedly asked if I knew where we were. Thinking we might crash-land, Xiong, who carried an Air Force–issued 38-special revolver, threw it out the window. I demanded that everyone be quiet. This was the area in which I had learned to fly. I assured Lia and Xiong that I would bring them down safely. I thought back to my training days in Thailand long ago and flew on that memory. As my fuel gauge bounced on empty, I called repeatedly on the emergency frequency, 'Papa Uniform, emergency! No gas! Request emergency landing! Papa Uniform, emergency!' No one answered me. Finally I heard, 'Papa Uniform. Runway 31. Follow the 0-1 ahead of you. Cleared for emergency landing.' I searched the grayness in front of me and saw nothing. Then suddenly I saw the 0-1 and the airfield at Udorn. I followed it down to the runway with no gas left to taxi.'"[16]

The schoolteacher, the mechanic, and the former pilot had landed safely in Thailand. But at Long Chieng, thousands of Hmong still waited for planes. Among them were Vue Sai Long, who had worked both with the French and the Americans, Lt. Xiong Xia Chia ("Alex"), whose luck had allowed him to miss the fall of Phou Pha Thi, and Sgt. Moua Paje and Vang Kai, who had helped rescue downed American airmen.

Coyote flew the last flight out of Long Chieng. "On May 13, I took over Ly Teng's C-47. He had been flying straight for two days. I flew with a Lao copilot and Lao navigator. We flew all day, making three runs between Long Chieng and Udorn. It took more than an hour to reach Udorn because the Lao T-28 patrols were out looking for illegal flights. We had to take evasive action so they couldn't locate us.[17]

"On my last trip to Long Chieng, we arrived about noon to find thousands of Hmong waiting. As soon as I stopped, the fastest, strongest, and those with guns rushed the plane. Colonels with weapons were shouting, 'This plane is mine!' Dr. Yang Dao also got on my flight. An old Dakota holds only 60 people [actually it holds about half that], but more than 80 crowded on my plane. I knew that I couldn't get off the ground with so many. I called for help, demanding that someone take out 20 people. A brave friend inside the Dakota came to my help and pushed out 20 people and slammed the door.

"At the end of the runway, I stood on the brakes, pushed on full power, then let it go down the runway. At the end, I pulled up and, with the stall horn blaring, we slowly lifted out of Long Chieng. When we reached Udorn, the Lao pilot told me the flights would have to stop. He would take this C-47 and fly back to his home base. I begged him to let me make a couple more trips to Long Chieng. He refused. In desperation, I thought of the broken-down C-47 that once belonged to us which now sat at Udorn. I ran to that plane. It seemed in terrible condition, but I climbed into the cockpit anyway. I had to find a way to keep flying Hmong out of Long Chieng. As I was trying to start it, I watched the Lao fly away in the last plane we had available to rescue those stranded at Long Chieng. I tried for hours, but I couldn't start our old C-47.''

Dr. Yang Dao, who had urged accommodation with the communists until the very end, had been among the select few to flee Laos by air.

At Long Chieng, hope faded. The remaining Hmong pilots, knowing that they had to find a way out, decided to fly out in the remaining four T-28s. They doubled up by putting two men in each back seat and roared off, leaving no Hmong pilots behind.

Earlier in the day at Udorn, Thai authorities had loaded the women and children, including the wives and children of Moua Lia and Vang Chou, into covered military trucks. In the backs of the airless, sweltering trucks, women tried to comfort children, most of whom were crying from the intense heat. Under tight security, the Thai moved convoys of refugees to Nam Phong. At one time, Nam Phong had been a secret Thai-U.S. commando training center for Hmong and Lao. Then it was improved to handle F-111s, but never used for that purpose. During the final days of Nixon's withdrawal of troops from South Vietnam, a Marine Air Wing based at Danang had been deployed to Nam Phong for a few months. Women and children moved into the spartan wooden barracks. Moua Lia's wife struggled to keep her fears under control. She might never see her husband again. How would she manage with six children, no money, and no way to earn any?

On the morning of May 14, General Vang Pao, dressed in a short-sleeved khaki jacket and matching trousers, prepared to depart from his headquarters house.* Before leaving, he took all his cash—about $800—and put it into the various pockets of his field clothes. His son drove him

---

*Vang Pao had already sent two of his wives and their children to Thailand under false pretenses. Since he had not told them that he might be forced to leave Laos, they took with them only a few items of clothing. The other wives and children were evacuated during the later stages of the airlift from Long Chieng.

in his jeep through the crowds to the AOC shack. Here he checked for news of more airlift aircraft. There was none. He climbed back into his jeep and headed for SKY headquarters which now housed USAID. He entered the USAID office as if he had a meeting. After spending only a few minutes inside, he exited out the back door and climbed into another jeep. The first jeep remained outside the USAID office, indicating that he was inside, continuing discussions with U.S. officials.

Vang Pao and an aide, carrying an M-16, were driven up the hill to the king's summer house which the Hmong had built for him, and then down the other side to a fishpond. Waiting there, out of sight of those at Long Chieng, was a USAID helicopter. Vang Pao and his aide climbed into the chopper, which quickly lifted into the air. It headed for Phou Khang, a high mountain village with a school and a small Lima Site, only a short flight from Long Chieng. His son would leave Laos later.

At Phou Khang about 500 villagers, many from the Vang clan, rushed to the airstrip and encircled Vang Pao. Overhead a single-engine aircraft circled. The noise of the helicopter rotors mingled with the sobs of those listening to Vang Pao's words: "I must leave Laos for political reasons. I will go for awhile and wait for the opportunity to return. I expect to return one day." These people, all farmers, disturbed that their leader was leaving, implored him to tell them about what to do. Vang Pao had no simple answers. As they begged for direction and a commitment of when he would return, Vang Pao reached into his pockets. While assuring them that he would never forget them and that he would return, he passed out much of his $800.

The helicopter pilot signaled with a thumbs-up sign that he was taking off. Vang Pao turned his back on the dust and debris stirred up by the chopper. He looked across the hills—hills to which many Hmong had moved at his urging after the cease-fire. Before the helicopter dust had completely settled, the circling aircraft, a Porter, landed on the dirt strip. Vang Pao headed for it. At the plane, he turned for a last look at the crying people of Phou Khang, gave a sharp salute, then turned and entered the plane. Within seconds, it roared off, heading for Muang Cha, Lima Site 113.

At Muang Cha, Jerry Daniels waited with another Porter. As the plane with Vang Pao in it approached, the Porter pilot on the ground started his engine. Vang Pao's plane taxied close to the waiting plane. As Vang Pao walked to the second plane, the village chief and several others recognized him. Daniels saw this and over the engine's roar shouted for Vang Pao to get in—they were leaving—now! Daniels, Vang Pao, and the aide scrambled aboard. The pilot surged the engine and started to taxi. The Hmong chased the taxiing plane, trying to catch Vang Pao. The pilot ignored them.

As the Porter rose over Muang Cha, General Vang Pao was flooded with memories. He remembered coming here in 1961 to give encouragement to the survivors of the communists' wild night of disembowelment of civilians. Over the years that sad encampment had developed into an impressive settlement. Below him, he saw the efforts of so many over the past 14 years—Sam Thong College with its 135 students, the Muang Cha United Minorities School with its 125 students, and the fields, livestock, and houses of his former soldiers who had resettled here after the cease-fire, the stone house he used when visiting, which the Hmong called "Vang Pao's House." He looked until Muang Cha was only a small dirt patch.

As the plane gained altitude, Vang Pao could see for miles. Looking to the west, he could see Skyline Ridge just above Long Chieng. He remembered the fierce battles that his men had fought over the years to defend that ridge and Alternate. Looking to the east, he saw the mountain that shielded Ban Sorn, the home of thousands of Hmong displaced by the war. To the northeast, in the mountain vastness where his people had once lived and the communists now waited, he thought he could see Phou Pha Thi. There was Route 7, and the Nam Ngum River meandering through deep valleys into the fertile plains of Vientiane where the Lao lived—the area he had fought so long to protect. To the southeast, clouds hung as usual atop Phou Bia, the highest mountain in Laos, caressing its irregular and massive shape. He remembered all the brave men and women who had fought and died to protect this beautiful land. He remembered the feel of victory when retaking the Plaine des Jarres. He remembered disobeying American Ambassador G. McMurtrie Godley to defend Long Chieng to the death. He remembered the daring American friends who fought by his side. He remembered the pledges of unity, eternal loyalty, and friendship by the Americans. He remembered the numerous aircraft crashes he had survived, and being seriously wounded at Na Khang. He remembered those who died defending the U.S. secret base at Phou Pha Thi, Lima Site 85, and those still at Bouam Loung, defending to the death a now useless site deep in enemy territory. Hmong believe that at grave moments in life, one's heart quivers with emotion. Vang Pao, suddenly aware of his quivering heart, knew he must some day return to Laos.

Late on the afternoon of May 14, the plane carrying General Vang

Pao, his aide, and Jerry "Hog" Daniels arrived at Udorn Air Base. Among the one thousand Hmong who awaited them was Colonel Moua Cher Pao, who, by being evacuated, had broken his sacred pledge not to abandon Bouam Loung. His mountaintop fortress surrounded by the enemy now had no leader and no means of receiving food or supplies—and he was in Thailand. One of Vang Pao's last acts that day was to arrange for the T-28 planes to be flown from Udorn back to Laos because, as he told the Hmong pilots who had escaped in them, "They do not belong to us; they belong to the Lao government." A few days later, in secrecy, the general and some remaining refugees at Udorn were flown to Nam Phong. Waiting wives expressed momentary joy when united with their husbands, though this joy was tempered by the thought that everyone had relatives still trapped inside Laos.

Once in Thailand, General Vang Pao learned that this move was not a temporary relocation but the beginning of permanent exile. White Star was now a refugee, a man without a country. "I never imagined that I would be a refugee, because the United States—the greatest country on earth which had saved Europe from the Nazis and Asia from the Japanese—supported me in my fight against the communist takeover of my country."[18] Not only was he a refugee. He soon discovered that because of the Thai political climate, he was not welcome to stay in Thailand.

Vang Pao was not, after all, the Wizard of Oz. In the end, it was the Royal Lao and the Americans who were the wizards. In Vang Pao's eyes, as the curtain fell, these wizards—festooned in the artificial trappings of show and superficiality, of unkept promises and shifting, opportunistic loyalties—had disappeared into the tropical sky, as if it had all been a fairy tale.

Part Six

The Lao
Gulag

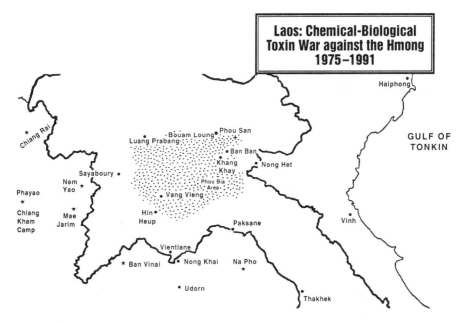

Laos: Chemical-Biological Toxin War against the Hmong 1975–1991

GULF OF TONKIN

Haiphong

Chiang Rai

Luang Prabang
Bouam Loung
Phou San
Ban Ban
Khang Khay
Nong Het
Sayaboury
Nam Yao
Phou Bia Area
Vang Vieng
Phayao
Chiang Kham Camp
Mae Jarim
Hin Heup
Paksane
Vinh
Vientiane
Ban Vinai
Nong Khai
Na Pho
Udorn
Thakhek

+ = Mountain

★ = Refugee camps in Thailand receiving
Hmong who fled LPDR attacks

Hin Heup Massacre at bridge, May 1975

Area of chemical-biological toxin attacks

23.

Exodus

When I heard that General Vang Pao and some of the higher echelon had been pulled out of Alternate, I assumed that the bulk of the
Hmong had been left behind. The first thing that crossed my mind
was that there was going to be a game of hare and hounds with the
Hmong being the hares, poor souls. Knowing the communists, I figured they would hunt the Hmong until they exterminated them.
Who was to complain? And nobody seriously did, as it turned out.

—Captain Fred F. Walker, who flew the last Air America plane out
of Laos in June 1974

Hmong waited at Long Chieng for evacuation planes that never came.
Realizing that they had been abandoned, they made hurried plans to
leave. Some decided to run to the hills, taking with them weapons and
munitions cached at Long Chieng. From the mountains, they would
monitor the communist actions. Others, fearing for their lives, decided to
follow Vang Pao on foot to Thailand.

Before dawn on May 15, 1975, Hmong with tea kettles, U.S. Army
canteens, blankets, crying children, and sacks of rice moved away from
Long Chieng, heading west along the mountainous road to Ban Sorn,
Lima Site 272, the last major Hmong settlement north of Vientiane. By
mid-morning, the milling mass at Alternate had vanished. Only several
thousand remained at Long Chieng, uncertain of what else to do. Most
stayed in their houses, afraid to come out in the uncomfortable silence.

Ly Nai, a Hmong in his 60s who had been a soldier with the French
and a taxi driver during the American time, did not join the exodus. Late
on the morning of the 15th, Ly Nai heard an approaching helicopter. "I
ran to the airstrip thinking it might be another evacuation plane. Out of

the helicopter stepped Touby LyFong and General Chao Manivong, the Lao ordered to replace Vang Pao as commander of Military Region II. Touby came directly to me because we knew each other. We shook hands. He said 'You are here, grandfather, but what about the others?' I told him that they may be gone. Looking directly at me, Touby said, 'We stay. Don't worry. We will stay.'[1]

"As he talked, I looked at his face. He was not the same person that I had known before. He seemed sad and he had little to say. The three of us walked along the airstrip. It was quiet. Only a few curious people came to the airfield. No airplanes. No Vang Pao soldiers. Then we walked back to the helicopter. Touby's parting words were: 'Don't flee. Don't be afraid.'" Ly Nai was afraid. On the 17th, he and his family fled in his old taxi for Ban Sorn.

At Ban Sorn, Hmong met surreptitiously to discuss what to do while awaiting the arrival of family members, particularly those who had been serving in remote military positions. It would take time for them to walk to Ban Sorn.

In Thailand at Nam Phong camp, Hmong worked to make living tolerable in the crowded and spartan facilities. One family, often consisting of a dozen or more people, was assigned to each room, built for only two airmen. Immediately water and sanitation were problems. Refugees stood for hours in lines waiting for a small bucket of water for bathing and drinking. Everyone talked about the dreadful turn of events and worried over relatives and friends left behind. When some heard that Dr. Yang Dao was coming to Nam Phong, they taunted him in absentia, saying, "We have no room for you except a space four meters by six meters." They had a grave in mind.[2]

Six years later, in 1981, Yang Dao presented a paper at the University of Minnesota in which he tried to exonerate himself. "At first, I did not realize that a plan of extermination, carefully set in place by Moscow and its allies, was about to be put into motion against the Hmong of Laos. On May 9, 1975, returning from my trip to the communist countries of Asia and Europe, I received confirmation through the *Khaosane Pathet Lao,* the *Pravda* of the Laotian Communist Party, which wrote: 'We must eradicate the Meo minority completely.'"[3]

Lt. Vang Teng and his unit, whose position had been overrun during the stand for Sala Phou Khoun, were walking to Long Chieng when they received a radio message that Vang Pao had left Laos. The men, exhausted and hungry, changed direction and headed for Ban Sorn. After walking night and day for five days, they arrived, joining tens of thousands of Hmong. The young lieutenant listened to their angry talk. "I learned from those who had walked from Long Chieng that the planes hadn't come to take out Vang Pao's soldiers as promised. Many soldiers felt betrayed, saying they had been left behind to fight and die while those leaders at Long Chieng prepared to leave the country."[4]

Former soldiers hid their weapons, threw away their uniforms, and put on civilian clothes. Many decided Ban Sorn was not safe; Vientiane might be better. Everyone knew that it would be difficult to get there. Already there had been trouble at the Hin Heup Bridge—the bridge that spanned the Nam Ngum, the last major river that separated the Hmong from access to Vientiane. At the bridge, armed Pathet Lao and Royal Lao Army soldiers stood guard. Lao vendors had jeered at the Hmong who crossed earlier, shouting "crazy Meo" and "stupid Meo," chastising them for running away from the Pathet Lao and the new society that was coming.

In Vientiane, Nhia and Lo Ma, who had managed to get out of Ban Sorn, prepared to flee to Thailand with their baby. At the last moment, Nhia cried in despair: she could not abandon her three older children whom she had left with her former in-laws in the mountains near Ban Sorn. No matter how dangerous, she must try to get them out. She would return alone. As a woman with an infant, she had a better chance of getting through the Pathet Lao checkpoints.[5]

Lo Ma had little chance of getting through. His long experience with the Americans as a Forward Air Guide put him in great jeopardy. He knew that his name appeared on a Pathet Lao list of "running dogs of the American imperialists." After the "peace" and the disbanding of irregular units, he had been reaccepted into the Royal Lao Army with the rank of second lieutenant. When Vang Pao was dismissed, Lo Ma destroyed all his military clothing. He knew this was a futile gesture because the Pathet Lao would know from his accent and lighter skin that he was Hmong and conclude he had been a Vang Pao soldier.

Nhia and her baby traveled north, past the Hin Heup Bridge, past Vang Vieng, past Ban Sorn. With her baby tied to her back she walked to the small mountain village of her in-laws to collect her older children.

While waiting for Nhia to return, Lo Ma talked to one of Touby's sons who told him that Touby was worried about the situation and cried every night.

Nhia collected her children from her in-laws and returned to Ban Sorn. To disguise her intentions, she brought only her children, no extra clothing to make guards suspicious. She did carry one item that could betray her—the heavy silver necklace given to her by Vang Seng, her pilot husband now dead. She wrapped her treasured necklace, her only asset, in pieces of cloth she used for diapers and waited for an opportunity to leave for Ban Sorn.

On May 22, Souvanna Phouma ordered Touby LyFong to Ban Sorn to tell the Hmong to stay in Laos and not to flee to Thailand. Touby requested a Hmong driver. Since most Hmong in Vientiane had already fled to Thailand, Touby asked Lo Ma to drive him. Early on May 23, Lo Ma, in civilian clothes and carrying no identification, and Touby, wearing brown pants and jacket and his trademark black gaucho-style hat, climbed into an Army jeep. Security consisted of a jeep of Pathet Lao preceding at some distance and a Volkswagon van–load of Vientiane government soldiers following them.[6]

At sandbagged checkpoints, when Pathet Lao soldiers saw Touby LyFong, they knew that he had been ordered by Souvanna Phouma to talk to the Hmong. At one, Pathet Lao soldiers told Touby that when they ordered the Hmong to return to their villages, many did not listen and continued through the checkpoints. Touby told them to let the Hmong pass to Vientiane to be with Souvanna Phouma. He made a point of repeating this advice to other Pathet Lao along the way, including those guarding the Hin Heup Bridge.

Lo Ma was afraid as a Pathet Lao convoy of 40 to 50 trucks carrying soldiers, 82mm, and 85mm guns passed them. He looked at Touby, who stared at the large military convoy heading for Vientiane. Neither said anything.

About noon, Lo Ma pulled into the Ban Sorn market area. People immediately gathered to hear Touby. He asked for a microphone. None was available, so he climbed on a vegetable vendor's rickety stall. Thousands listened as he, in a flat, unemotional voice, announced: ''Souvanna Phouma has told me to come here to say even though Vang Pao and his high military officials have moved out of the country, don't be afraid. They had to leave. They had no choice. That is their problem. But for you, it's not a big problem. If you are the population and don't have high position, like Colonel or General, you'll be OK. So don't be afraid. Whoever comes to this country, you'll be all right. You are just the population.'' Touby, who knew that the Pathet Lao were listening, explained again and again that if they were only the ''population'' they should have no fear.

As Hmong asked questions, Lo Ma hurried to a small house that he had built earlier. He was delighted to find Nhia and the children. He told her they had to get out now. She and the children would leave in Touby's vehicle. It was the only way out. At checkpoints, he planned to say that his wife and children were traveling to Vientiane to live with him now that peace had come.

Hmong quizzed Touby about the safety of staying in Ban Sorn and about their future in Laos. He issued emotionless, pat responses. Many believed that no matter what Touby said, when the communists came to power they would be punished because they had fought the communists for so long.

About 3 p.m. Touby LyFong climbed back into the jeep for the return trip to Vientiane. Nhia and the four children climbed aboard as if it had all been approved. Touby looked at them, crowded into the back, but said nothing.

With Touby at his side and his family huddled in the back, Lo Ma looked one last time at the Hmong, including his father, standing politely as Touby departed. It was a moment of horror. He wanted to shout a warning, but he could not. Instead, he wheeled the jeep onto the main road. The security van fell in behind. Dust billowed out behind, obscuring it. Nhia held tight to her children as they bounced along the pitted road. At Vang Vieng, Touby stopped to pay his respects to the local Lao authorities. Every few minutes, Lo Ma looked at the sun as it moved lower on the horizon. He wished that Touby would hurry. Finally, Touby returned to the jeep. At the Hin Heup Bridge, guards questioned Nhia and asked for her travel documents. Touby said a few words and the jeep lurched forward. There were more checkpoints. At each one, surly and suspicious guards questioned Nhia. Just after dark, they arrived in Vientiane.

After Touby left Ban Sorn, most Hmong concluded that this major Hmong settlement was a trap. Lt. Vang Teng and his wife, his parents, his three brothers and their wives decided to join those planning an immediate attempt to reach Vientiane. "Our plan was to walk first to a valley about one mile north of the Hin Heup Bridge where we would wait until the thousands of Hmong in Ban Sorn could reach that point. We thought that the Lao government or any government could not shoot thousands of civilians, so we decided that we would all go together. Then we would be safe."[7]

Early on May 25, two days after Touby's speech, Lt. Vang Teng and his family joined the first group to move to the valley. An assortment of ancient and run-down cars and trucks carrying Hmong made repeated trips to the designated valley. Those without money for transportation were walking. Those in the vanguard group were in place about 10 a.m. They would wait until everyone had arrived.

On this same day, Lo Ma paid a Lao boatman 50,000 *kip* (about $100) to take him and his family across the Mekong River to Nong Khai. Once on the Thai side, Lo Ma and Nhia stood for a few minutes looking back and remembering. Only then did they realize the gift Touby LyFong had given them by allowing Nhia and the children to escape. Thai authorities ordered them to Nam Phong refugee camp. Again they were lucky. They were among the last allowed to go there. Those coming later were sent to the makeshift and squalid camp at Nong Khai.

In the valley north of the Hin Heup Bridge, Hmong waited. It was taking longer than expected for everyone to arrive. Many on the road were sick, some were old, some were crippled. Widows with small children struggled to carry them. Relatives took their wounded from the hospital and carried them.

As more and more Hmong arrived in the valley, passing truck drivers slowed to study the swelling encampment. As the Hmong waited, they encouraged each other by saying that if they walked slowly and deliberately, as if crossing the bridge to go to their fields to farm, the Pathet Lao would let them pass. Others felt confident that the soldiers could not shoot down such a large group.

Shortly after sunrise on May 28 almost 10,000 people started walking slowly toward the bridge at Hin Heup. Lt. Vang Teng and his family were near the front of the column. "We were in the 7th or 8th row. As we approached the bridge, I saw soldiers, some in Pathet Lao uniforms and some in the uniforms of the Lao Government Region V troops, lining both sides of the road near the bridge. Many more stood near the bridge. As we approached, soldiers lowered a barricade, blocking the entrance. At the same moment, some soldiers fired into the air; others fired into the crowd with M-16s. Mortars hit us from farther away. Some soldiers charged, bayoneting people. In the screaming and shooting, I turned to run, and jumped over seven or eight bodies lying on the road."[8]

As he was running back to the encampment, he saw his father and mother tending to his sister-in-law. "Blood poured from her stomach. They were trying to stop the bleeding. The only way to save her was to get her back to the hospital at Ban Sorn. I tried desperately to get one of the Lao cars to stop and take her. Some stopped, but they asked for more money than we had so they wouldn't take us. Finally, a truck carrying rice allowed us to put her on top of the rice bags. About twenty miles along the road to Ban Sorn, she died. She was 19 years old and had one daughter."

Most did not have money to pay the Lao to take them back to Ban

Sorn, so they walked for three days. After the massacre at the bridge, Hmong were more frightened.

Late on the afternoon of June 5, Radio Pathet Lao reported its version of the events at the Hin Heup Bridge, very different from Hmong eyewitnesses. Pathet Lao Radio broadcast: "The Vang Pao clique proceeded with its forcible evacuation scheme to force the rest of the Meo tribesmen to evacuate. Over an estimated 1,000 Meo tribesmen were forcibly evacuated on 28 May along the Ban Ton–Hin Heup trail. [Hmong estimated that perhaps 10,000 tried to cross the bridge.] Sai Sivang [labeled earlier by Radio Pathet Lao as a Vang Pao henchman] and his men reportedly destroyed every checkpoint which they encountered on the way. However, when the Meo caravan arrived in the vicinity of Hin Heup—the last checkpoint—the regional forces in the area intercepted and prohibited them from proceeding further. Heated argument ensued between the Sai Sivang team and officials of the people's armed forces. Finally, one of Sai Sivang's men attacked and seriously wounded the officials with his knife. Encountering such a physical assault, the people's armed forces were compelled to act in self-defense in order to keep law and order. Four of Sai Sivang's men were shot dead.

"After the deaths of the reactionary traitors, the Meo tribesmen who were forced to evacuate safely returned to their native villages with great relief. They were grateful to the people's armed forces for promptly saving them from the culprits. At present the Meo people in various areas are rising up to strongly denounce the traitorous crimes of the Vang Pao clique."[9]

While masterful manipulation of the truth beamed over Radio Pathet Lao to explain away the wounding and killing of unarmed Hmong, including women and children, the Hmong trapped at Ban Sorn knew the truth and were fearful.

Also on June 5, Radio Pathet Lao urged those in uniform—both Pathet Lao and National Forces—to follow the "spy activities of the reactionary traitors" and to "completely eliminate the American enemy [it was understood that this meant those who worked closely with the Americans] and make this resounding land of a million elephants beautiful."[10]

Lt. Vang Teng and his brothers, hearing the Pathet Lao explanations of the Hin Heup Bridge incident and the call to eliminate those who had followed Vang Pao, sought a way out of the Ban Sorn trap.

POW pilot Yang Pao, who had been moved to a slave-labor prison camp near Khang Khay in 1973, heard over the guards' radio that Vang Pao had left the country. "At first, I couldn't believe it. Then we heard it again and again. We finally realized that we had no leader. We were very sad. Everything was gone. No one was left to help us."[11]

Xiong Xia Chia (Alex) also listened to the Pathet Lao radio and the repeated calls for the "Meo" to lay down their arms. He and others who had returned to farming decided not to turn in their weapons. They buried them instead—just in case.[12]

Sgt. Moua Paje, who had helped rescue American pilots and who suffered from multiple war wounds as a result of a lifetime of fighting, hoped never to fight again. Since he had no formal education and few skills, he could not imagine life anywhere but in Laos. He decided he had no choice but to live with the communists as a simple farmer. He and his family moved to Nam Fen on the Phou San massif, where many other Hmong had resettled. He too buried his weapons.[13]

Prince Sai Kham, the last prince of Xieng Khouang, who had championed the Hmong for years, and who was now ill and destitute, crossed the Mekong River, and took refuge at a Buddhist temple.

A few days after Lo Ma escaped Laos, Touby LyFong arrived in Udorn to talk to General Vang Pao. The Hmong were shocked that Touby was allowed to come to Thailand. Souvanna Phouma had given official consent. Souvanna Phouma probably did not know that Touby was considering defection and wanted to talk to Vang Pao about it. Touby told Vang Pao he had little money and no way to support his family in another country. He asked Vang Pao if he would give him money and support him. Vang Pao answered that he himself had no money. He did not have enough for his own family. After an emotional meeting, Touby returned to Laos.[14] In 1975 Touby LyFong was sent to Seminar Camp 5, where he reportedly died in 1979.

On June 9, 1975, Radio Pathet Lao announced that Royal Lao Army officers had requested Pathet Lao advisors. On that same day, the radio claimed: "According to foreign news agencies, on 6 June it was reported in Bangkok that the Thai Government plans to move into concentration camps those Lao and Meo tribal evacuees who recently fled into Thailand. If the reports are true, the Lao and Meo tribal evacuees' labor will be exploited. As such, they will eventually face severe difficulties and hardships in their living conditions. . . . most of the belongings brought into Thailand by the Lao and Meo tribal evacuees have been stolen. Several families have only the remaining clothes on their bodies."[15]

Discounting this broadcast as propaganda, more Hmong prepared to slip across the Mekong River to Thailand. Lt. Vang Teng was one of them. But first, he had to get out of Ban Sorn. He was lucky. "I managed to get a Hmong official who was not yet removed from the Ban Sorn police station to sign a travel document for my family to travel to Vientiane. My parents were too afraid so they stayed behind. My three brothers, their wives, and my wife and I decided to escape. Once in Vientiane, we would make a plan to cross the river."

On June 10, Vientiane Domestic Service (the "official" radio in Vientiane) aired Order 904 and reiterated that all weapons must be "urgently returned to arsenal depots in their respective military regions."[16] The new regime's intention of disarming all people frightened many Hmong. Without weapons to defend themselves, they knew they could be slaughtered.

Lt. Vang Teng and his brothers, hiding in Vientiane, heard Order 904 and decided to cross the Mekong that same day. With no possessions, these four brothers and their wives hired a Lao boatman to ferry them across the river. Once on the river, their luck ran out. In the middle of the river, a Pathet Lao patrol boat spotted them and gave chase. A Thai patrol boat noticed the chase and raced toward them. Before the Thai patrol arrived, there was a struggle and the Pathet Lao captured Vang Teng's wife, his brother, and his sister-in-law. The others were rescued by the Thai. In one month, he had lost four members of his immediate family to the Pathet Lao—his sister-in-law, killed at the Hin Heup Bridge, his brother, his brother's wife, and his own 19-year-old wife, Yang Chee, captured by the Pathet Lao on the Mekong River. He never saw any of them again.

Later on this day, official radio in Vientiane issued a warning to those who might be contemplating fleeing Laos. "As is known, the U.S. imperialists recently forced some Vietnamese and Cambodian evacuees to flee to Thailand following their painful defeats in South Vietnam and Cambodia. With the collusion of the Thai reactionary clique, the U.S. imperialists have now forced the Meo tribesmen to flee from Laos into Thailand. The aim of such an evacuation is not based on the so-called humanitarian basis, but is to exploit their labor at cheap prices and to foster them as their henchmen so that they can be sent back to Laos to sabotage peace in this country in the future."[17]

For those who remained at Long Chieng, within a week of Vang Pao's forced departure, their worst fears became reality. Moua Pa Chai, in his 60s, worked in the sanitation department, overseeing water supplies and garbage disposal. Since he had not been a soldier, he thought he might be able to live under the communists. Later, as a refugee living in Bordeaux, France, he recounted grimly those early days of the communist takeover. "Within a week, the Pathet Lao moved into Long Chieng with many soldiers, trucks, and two big tanks. On Skyline Ridge, which the Hmong had protected for years, they placed artillery. The P.L.* took over the CIA headquarters and ordered everyone over age 9 to attend day-long re-education classes.[18]

"The communist teachers wore puffy P.L. hats and green uniforms with no insignia to show their rank. Each man carried a gun while lecturing us. They forced us to call them 'Sa Hai,' comrade. They called us 'Ku Thi,' younger brother. First, they took turns telling us how bad the Americans were and how the Americans had destroyed the land. Then they began shouting questions and giving their own answers: 'Do you know how you have a grand life and grand houses at Long Chieng? I'll tell you. Vang Pao used your blood to create these things. Why did you join the Americans? I'll tell you. They are devils; they look like devils. What have you done to our country? I'll tell you. You allowed the Americans to take our gold, our silver, all our riches. You allowed the Americans to use our blood and our riches in exchange for you to buy these things. You are stupid! That's why you joined with the Americans! You are stupid!'"

The Hmong were not allowed to raise their heads or talk. "Hour after hour, it was like this," remembered Moua Pa Chai. "Day after day. We were told not to talk to each other and to stay in our houses. The Pathet Lao also said some of us would go to 'seminar camp' to learn new ideas." "Seminar" was a euphemism for "concentration camp" where those who posed a potential threat to the new regime would be imprisoned.

Moua Pa Chai recognized many of the Hmong Pathet Lao. Phay Dang, leader of the "Red Hmong," arrived, dressed in black pants, black shoes, white shirt, and a striped tie. Others he knew were Moua Pa Kao, Vue Nhia, Yang Yia Xiong, Teng Ta Tou, and Moua Xiong Ma, who would later appear in a video, "A Journey to Laos," produced in 1986 by Jacqui Chagnon and Roger Rumpf, two American Friends Service Committee workers, that extolled the good life in Laos under communism.[19]

Moua Pa Chai observed the Pathet Lao tactics to snare former Hmong soldiers. "The P.L. found out who the former Vang Pao soldiers were,

---

*While the official name of Laos under the communists changed to the Lao People's Democratic Republic (LPDR) and its army became the Lao People's Liberation Army (LPLA), the Hmong continued to refer to the government as the Kaysone regime and its soldiers as Pathet Lao, P.L., or Reds. Similarly, they continued to refer to the Vietnamese forces as NVA, while their official name was the People's Army of Vietnam (PAVN).

planted guns in their fields, in their houses, or in their belongings. Then the same soldiers found those guns and accused them of still being with Vang Pao. These men were sent to seminar. I saw over 200 Hmong— those who were educated or who had high rank—arrested for possession of weapons planted by the communists. They sent them to seminar at Phong Savan on the Plaine des Jarres. We never saw them again."[20]

Everyone was afraid. Hmong began to mistrust one another. Moua Pa Chai listened carefully as the Pathet Lao began teaching about the new society. "The first concept was that the old tree does not produce anything useful. We must cut down the old tree so that the young tree will grow quickly and produce more fruits for our country. Now I knew that no one was safe, not even the old people like me." The sanitation worker was correct, no one was safe. Not even children escaped the carefully planned takeover of Laos.*

Eleven-year-old Xiong Pao Xe eventually escaped from Laos and was resettled in the U.S. Here he told me what happened to him after the communist takeover. In late May, in Nam Ying Village in Sayaboury Province, Pathet Lao soldiers took away him and other boys to teach them to become part of the new society. "The P.L. soldiers said we had to be big enough to carry a weapon but not older than 17 to go with them. I was 11. In the jungle, the communists armed us with wooden guns and taught us that our parents were the enemy. If we didn't kill them, they would kill us. They told us if we killed our parents, they would give each of us 1,000 *kip* [about $2], a good education, and any woman we wanted for a wife. They told us that in the new society any man had the right to any other man's wife. If the husband objected, we had the right to kill him."[21]

* * *

Old Asia hands previously posted to South Vietnam, Cambodia, and Laos drifted into Bangkok. The sprawling Asian city became a center for jobs. The main business now was not fighting wars or developing countries—it was refugees. Americans, many of them confused, unemployed, and adrift, loaded up bureaucracies and created new ones to handle the

---

*About ten days after the re-education classes began, two jets coming from the east screamed through the air, dove at Long Chieng, and flew away. It scared the Pathet Lao. From that day, re-education classes at Long Chieng were moved from building to building. That first flight may have been a U.S. reconnaissance flight or a MiG overflight. Hmong reported that once or twice a month for four months jets flew over Long Chieng in this fashion. Air Force personnel stationed in Thailand at this time believe that the flights were U.S. RF-4 reconnaissance flights.

flood of refugees flowing into Thailand from Cambodia, Vietnam, and Laos.

Anti-American demonstrations in Thailand frightened those who had worked in covert and overt activities in Laos. Many Americans, traumatized by the communist takeover and the aggressive hatred being vented on the United States and the CIA by both Asians and Americans, burned photographs, letters, and reports dealing with their lives and work in Laos. Some tried to forget their friends in Laos; others poured their energies into refugee work; some returned to the U.S., bitter and silent; some changed their political orientation.

This vigorous anti-American sentiment in Thailand combined with the Thai government's willingness to accommodate the new Lao regime resulted in Thai efforts to get General Vang Pao out of Thailand immediately. But where was he to go?

The CIA had never lost a major long-term covert war. What did the CIA do with defeated leaders whom they had backed for years? And in this case what did they do with the thousands identified with the CIA whose lives and those of their families were in jeopardy? General Vang Pao, White Star, the "big little guy" whom the Americans counted on for so many years, was suddenly *persona non grata* in Thailand, an embarrassment for the CIA, and in general a huge problem for the U.S. What would happen to his large family, including his many children and his five wives? Which country would take a man with multiple wives? The United States? No, certainly not. France? Maybe.

Jerry "Hog" Daniels remained in Thailand. Aware that the Hmong had no place to go, he looked for solutions. He and a Thai general developed plans to buy remote, sparsely populated lands in Nan or Loei provinces in northern Thailand where the soil and climate were similar to that in Laos and where Hmong refugees could settle temporarily. But the idea was ruled out by Thai authorities. Daniels' scheme, although it did not materialize, is one of the few examples of American initiative to help the Hmong in their exodus at this time.

Colonel Billy's original belief that if the communists took over in Laos the Thais would take care of the Hmong was not working out. The rampant anti-American, anti-CIA fervor in Thailand forced Thai officials to distance themselves from General Vang Pao and the Hmong.

Working on Thai issues out of the U.S. Embassy in Bangkok, Colonel Billy made no attempt to visit General Vang Pao at Nam Phong camp in northern Thailand. He tried not to think of the Hmong. It made him sad. Although he saw Daniels occasionally, he asked little about the Hmong situation. He fixed in his mind several images of Vang Pao, dating back to the 1960s, that he was determined to keep. One was a young Vang Pao, with eyes flashing with excitement, close to the action, calling his men together and ordering: "You go there. You go that way. We'll all meet at the top."[22] Other images included Vang Pao in heavy fighting running to frontline positions with armloads of ammunition, Vang Pao insisting that his fighting men receive cooked glutinous rice—rice cooked under Colonel Billy's order and free-dropped in burlap bags into the combat zones. Most vivid of all was the image of Vang Pao in the very early years, dressed in simple khaki pants and shirt with a ranger hat pushed back on his head, sitting atop a high mountain overlooking the PDJ and the enemy forces. With an irresistible, almost pixie-like smile, Vang Pao exuberantly and persuasively had assured him that he and his men, with some help from the Americans, would throw the NVA out and retake their lost lands. If Colonel Billy lingered long enough on this image, he could hear Vang Pao saying, "For me, I can't live with communism. I must either leave or fight. I prefer to fight."

Colonel Billy still believed that Vang Pao should have heeded his early advice to retreat to Sayaboury Province if necessary. In this province, which bordered Thailand in the west, he believed Vang Pao could have consolidated his troops and held out with the help of Thailand.

Vang Pao now wore an odd assortment of uncomfortable-looking civilian clothes. His hairline was receding and he still wore his ring with a light blue stone, given him by a Buddhist monk. Now there were no battles to direct, no flights in a spotter plane to pick out new fields or to catch an enemy patrol, no new weapons to demonstrate, no troops to command or to inspire. He paced the refugee compound, often stopping to talk, to comfort, and to give hope. Never idle, he ordered men and boys to organize this or that to make life easier in the camp. His once-laughing eyes now seemed only sad or angry. He seemed constantly to be looking for someone—a friend maybe from days past, like Colonel Billy, who could give him advice and counsel in these dreadful days. But no one came.

Americans who once bragged of their bravery in flying to Long Chieng to have dinner with General Vang Pao and who had built their reputations on the fighting ability and determination of General Vang Pao and the Hmong now kept their distance and remained silent.

General "Heine" Aderholt, responsible for disassembling the U.S. military presence in Thailand, did remember Vang Pao. When he learned about the crowding and lack of facilities at Nam Phong, he personally delivered 100 cots salvaged from a U.S. hospital that was being closed. He had intended to see Vang Pao, but was told the general was not available.[23]

The CIA, not in the business of resettling refugees or of publicly admitting or discussing its covert activities, left the Hmong to dangle and twist in the wind. These were times when the CIA, traumatized by congressional investigations and by the press, struggled to fend off criticism and to exonerate itself. The Agency was certainly not in a mood to tell the story of its relationship with the Hmong. Revealing details of its covert operation in Laos would give the critics more material. Besides, covert operations, by their very nature, remain secret. There were some who said that official U.S. silence was the path chosen since public discussion of the secret operation in Laos might compromise those individuals who remained in Laos. Others, less generous, concluded that the U.S. intended "to cut and run." The Hmong and the others in Laos who had worked with the U.S. were on their own.

At Kilometer 6, near Vientiane, the Pathet Lao took over the American USAID compound. By the end of June, the U.S. Embassy, bowing to increasing pressure from the Pathet Lao, reduced its staff to 22. Province after province was "liberated" and fell under the control of the "people's administration." In Thailand, the U.S. Air Advisory Group 7/13th Air Force had deactivated. The U.S. "flying artillery" that Vang Pao had counted on so heavily for so many years was gone.

Radio Pathet Lao continued to offer plans for a peaceful, vigorous new country, free of corruption, where all men would be equal. Pathet Lao officials encouraged combatants to turn in all weapons. There was no need for weapons in the glorious new society, they proclaimed.

In mid-June, General Vang Pao left Thailand, heading for France. Later, with CIA assistance, he would go on to the U.S. With Vang Pao no longer a threat, with his senior officers either in exile in Thailand or in seminar camps in Laos, and with the U.S. no longer interested in Laos, the Pathet Lao moved ahead. On July 30, the mixed Pathet Lao and Royal Lao government forces created by Hanoi and Washington to jointly administer Vientiane and Luang Prabang were dismissed. The new minister of defense ordered rightists to lay down their arms and to stop resisting the "liberation" of Laos.

The Pathet Lao were now firmly enough in control of Laos "to cut down the old trees which didn't produce any fruit to allow the new trees to grow," as they had said. It was time to uproot and destroy the old and the traditional to prepare for the glorious new way. At the Vientiane airport, west of the city, Soviet aircraft appeared on the runways. Soviet helicopters and former Royal Lao government planes, given by the United States as part of its aid, collected on the tarmac. On the appointed day, the signal was given. With extraordinary swiftness, high-ranking Lao civilians and military personnel were rounded up under the guise of official meetings with the new government. Throughout the provinces not already controlled by communist officials, provincial governors and their senior administrative staffs disappeared simultaneously in a nation-wide sweep that surprised almost everyone—except the Hmong.

Khamphouei Bouangphosay, Governor of Khong Island in the south of Laos, was a senior Lao official rounded up in this sweep. He survived years in a concentration camp to tell about his experience and the communist takeover.

"Our capture was well organized. Prime Minister Souvanna Phouma signed an official letter ordering all chiefs of provinces, their deputies, and our military commanders and their subdivision commanders to go to Vientiane for a special meeting to receive instructions from the new government. An airplane would be sent to pick us up."[24] For this special meeting, Governor Khamphouei wore his formal uniform, with his ribbons, braid, and award decorations that Lao officials must wear for important meetings. He took along only his briefcase with a few personal items in the event he stayed overnight.

Early on the morning of July 22, a Royal Lao plane arrived to pick up the governor, his two assistants, the local military commander and his deputies. "When we got to the Vientiane airport, we were met by Pathet Lao soldiers who took us by car about 20 kilometers north of Vientiane to a re-education center called Nai Say Thong. Arriving at the same time were six other southern governors with their deputies and military commanders. The next morning we were driven back to the Vientiane airport where we were put on a Royal Lao Air Force plane flown by a Lao to what was described as our special meeting. There were 36 of us on the plane. We were the governors who were still loyal to the Royal Lao government and who had worked hand in hand with the free-world forces.

"We landed on the Plaine des Jarres. About the same time, two more planes arrived with another 70 people—all military—all dressed in their formal uniforms with all their awards and decorations proudly displayed. That evening, there was a party. Vietnamese advisors were also present. They had killed a pig and we had rice, milk, and cake. After eating, we watched a movie of the fighting in Laos, but it only showed the Pathet Lao winning. No communist defeats were shown.

"We stayed here two nights. On the morning of the third day, July 24, two Soviet helicopters landed—one MI-8 and one MI-6—to take us to another meeting place. After three hours of flying, we arrived at Vieng Sai, very close to the North Vietnamese border in northern Laos. Here we were transferred into small buses and driven to a mountain cave. The cave was dark with water leaking in from the top. The communists gave us rice and water and a little oil and some cotton string to make light. The communist officials had electricity in their houses. We were now 106 men, many of us over 50 years old, all dressed in our best uniforms, sleeping on the wet floor of a dark cave on a remote mountain, guarded by communist soldiers. Some cried this night. Everyone was afraid. Now it was clear that we were prisoners. Some of us realized we were prisoners the second night on the Plaine des Jarres, but we didn't want to believe it.''

Early the next morning, they loaded the prisoners on ten Chinese trucks. Around 4 p.m. they arrived at Seminar Camp 6, located between Muong Et and Na Kham. Here they put 25 men into each small bamboo and thatch shelter, measuring 7 by 15 meters. To find space to lie down they had to arrange themselves carefully.

The next morning, July 26, the men were separated into groups of 13 to 15 with no distinction between civilians and military. Then the Pathet Lao announced: ''The local population hates you and if they see you they will kill you since you were with the CIA.'' The prisoners were told never to pass more than one kilometer from the camp or the population would kill them. Khamphouei learned later that it was the guards who would kill them. ''The second order was to turn in our insignia. Many of us tore off our rank emblems and threw them in the open latrines rather than give them to the P.L. They fished them out and saved them.''

The Pathet Lao immediately organized the men into work teams— one to build roads, one to build houses, one to cut trees, another to drag the trees out of the forest to the camp, and another to plough the fields. Teams rotated jobs. All work was done by hand with simple tools. Whenever the communist guards approached the prisoners, they made them kneel and ''whai,'' the Lao gesture of placing the hands in a prayer position to show respect. If they did not do it quickly enough, the guards hit them in the head with their guns.

Khamphouei struggled to stay alive. ''The communists gave us only 500 grams of rice and 20 grams of salt per month—nothing else. We had no medicine, little sleep, soon we would have no shoes and no clothes. After finishing the work and eating the rice and water, we were forced to attend the 'seminar' because they said 'you have not forgotten the American way since you fought so hard for the CIA.'''

By mid-August 1975, about 25,000 Hmong and 16,000 others including Lao, Mien, Kmhmu, and Chinese had fled to Thailand. At Nam Phong refugee camp, men argued over virtually everything. Clan leaders fought for control over their own clans. Conflict erupted between the White Hmong and the Green Hmong. Hmong tried to fix blame for their fate. Some blamed General Vang Pao. Others blamed Dr. Yang Dao because he had urged Hmong to stay and work with the communists. Many who had listened and stayed in Laos were dead, in the seminar camps, or trapped inside Laos. Ly Neng Tong remembered those days and the anger of Hmong toward Yang Dao. "People believed that it was his fault that a lot of Hmong got killed in Laos. They listened to him and didn't flee in time and they were killed."[25]

Many at Nam Phong wanted to return to Laos and fight. Colonel Moua Cher Pao was one of these. He wanted to rejoin his people at Bouam Loung whom he had abandoned, in spite of his pledge, when he fled to Thailand by air from Long Chieng. Others argued that returning to fight was useless unless another country was prepared to assist.

T-28 pilots Fackee and Coyote, angered by the communist diplomatic victory in Laos, spent much time pacing the confines of Nam Phong, reviewing again and again the unfortunate final days and damning the naivete of Souvanna Phouma and of certain "educated" Hmong. Fackee told Coyote that he might return to Laos to resist. Coyote, who loved flying, could not see himself as a ground soldier. He doubted that he would join Fackee.[26]

On August 22, 1975, the Lao border with Thailand closed. The Mekong River, which only months earlier had bustled with boat traffic ferrying loads of teak, bamboo, charcoal, rice, fruits, and vegetables, carried only the flotsam and debris of life further up the river. Behind the eastern banks of this great Asian river, a Marxist-Leninist regime prepared for the creation of a new society.

Orphan Vang Doua was a 13-year-old unofficial soldier when on May 14 his captain told him that Vang Pao had left Laos and the fighting was finished. "My family was dead. I had no place to go. So on May 29, I went to a Pathet Lao village for a meeting. The speakers called all the soldiers to ally with them. 'If you don't come, we will punish you,' the leader said. They took my weapons and told me I would go to Long Chieng for seven days of seminar. But we didn't go to Long Chieng. They took us to the fields to work. They divided us up so that the same clans were not together. They put ten in each work group. After seven days, they told us it would be three months of this kind of work to get us ready for seminar. They fed us only two small cups of rice per day; sometimes each group shared one small tin of canned meat. We worked sunrise to sunset, seven days a week. Guards with guns forced us to work. There were over 100 soldiers—Vietnamese and Pathet Lao—guarding the prisoners in my area. Escape was impossible.''[27]

In August, Vang Doua learned that he and the other prisoners would be held for three more years. ''I knew then I would be a prisoner for a lifetime.'' After witnessing the communists torture and kill the Hmong who worked for the Americans and those who were smart, he decided to act very dumb to survive. He observed their tactics: ''They said to the prisoners, 'We must find out who has the American brains. We know that the CIA gave you American brains. Now, we will have to put those who worked with CIA in the holes so they can get new brains.' The communists selected those they believed had worked for the CIA, usually finding the smart Hmong, put chains on their legs, and worked them all day in the fields. At night, they put them into holes in the ground with no food. The guards only fed them when they were about to die. I saw more than 20 Hmong die from being put in the holes and starved to death.''

Like many other former Hmong soldiers, Vang Kai, the young soldier whose group had lost 60 men to rescue two American pilots, was confused and scared. ''After Vang Pao left I didn't know what to do. I didn't run away to Thailand. My friends and I walked from town to town, village to village, asking other Hmong what to do. Communists attacked and robbed us along the way. The Pathet Lao also went from village to village to collect all weapons. Sometimes, the local people were able to hide some, but many guns were taken.''[28]

Vang Kai decided to stay and protect his village. ''Life in my village was very difficult and dangerous. We were cut off from supplies—we couldn't go to town. They would kill us. But the Lao and Vietnamese soldiers got supplies dropped by air. The Pathet Lao knew which villages had been built by Vang Pao's former soldiers after the Vientiane Agreement. They knew exactly where to find us.''

By September 1975, all high-ranking military, police, and government officials were under arrest or had escaped to Thailand. Now the communists snared the educated and skilled—the teachers, nurses, mapmakers, mechanics, and merchants—and imprisoned them in seminar camps. The people who manned the traditional infrastructure had been eliminated. Many of them would never be heard of again.

Now only the king and the royal family stood in the way of the new society and the new state. During earlier negotiations with the Pathet Lao, the noncommunist Lao had insisted that the constitutional monarchy remain and the king and the royal family be protected. To quiet noncommunist fears that the beloved 700-year-old monarchy might be destroyed, the Pathet Lao always referred to the "Kingdom of Laos," thereby implying the retention of a king.

On November 28, 1975, a rally in Vientiane called for the abdication of the king. This was followed by a secret meeting of the Lao Congress of People's Representatives at K-6, the former American compound outside Vientiane. On December 2, at the conclusion of this meeting, the new government announced that Laos would no longer be known as the Kingdom of Laos. It would be known as the Lao People's Democratic Republic. This call to end a centuries-old kingdom went virtually unnoticed in the Western press.

On the same day, the new regime announced its "Program of Action," intended "to unite the people and the army around the Government, to reinforce all the spheres of life, the most important being the establishment and consolidation of power-wielding organs of the State and the People's Army, to create an atmosphere of revolutionary fervour amongst the masses, to give priority to revolutionary vigilance, to attack the enemy continuously, to resolutely crush the force of the compradors, bureaucrats, militarists, feudal reactionaries and all henchmen of American imperialist[s] who try to wreck our independence and sovereignty, to liquidate the last traces and influences of colonialism and feudalism, the obstacles which have constantly hampered our nation's development and progress."[29] Another goal of the program was "to completely wipe out all traces of the slavish mentality of the depraved imperialist regime, to work for, re-establish and develop the splendid characteristics of our cultural heritage, to spread education, and culture, to improve public health standards and to maintain democracy and progress."

The document called for the "confiscation and nationalization of economic and financial bases," and, in the category of "other tasks," it was decided "to condemn in time and combat resolutely all the new designs and machinations of American Imperialists who, in collusion with the Thai reactionaries, have pushed the Lao reactionaries to perpetrate acts prejudicial to the independence, sovereignty and to the task of national reconstruction of the Lao people; to continuously struggle to force the United States to contribute to the healing of the wounds of war in Laos. . . . ''

Finally, the man behind this document made himself publicly known. This man, the puppeteer guiding Prince Souphanouvong since World War II when he was sent by Hanoi to Laos to recruit Lao and who had operated so successfully behind the scenes, now stepped forward as the new leader of Laos. Kaysone Phomvihane, a tough, dedicated Marxist-Leninist who had been directing the Pathet Lao policies all this time, now openly replaced Prince Souphanouvong, who had only been a figurehead and tool of the North Vietnamese.

With the uprooting and destruction of traditional ways well underway, the communists focused on eliminating lower echelon Hmong and other tribal people who had fought with U.S. assistance during the war. Aided by records left behind by the Americans and Lao officials, lists of those who had worked with USAID, USIS, and the CIA were compiled. Names of Forward Air Guide graduates trained by the Air Commandos in Thailand had been forwarded to agencies in the Lao government and were now in communist hands.

Obsessed with eliminating American influence and thinking, uneducated and maniacal Pathet Lao soldiers sometimes took literally the slogans to eliminate American brains. Chang Cher and his brother Yee, former Vang Pao soldiers with no rank, had returned to their home village in Sayaboury Province after the peace treaty. One day the Pathet Lao surrounded their village demanding those associated with Vang Pao and the Americans. Chang Cher, who years later escaped Laos, explained: ''The Pathet Lao already had our names so we had to come forward. When they tried to tie us up, we fought back. In the confusion, I was able to escape. My brother Yee was taken away behind a nearby hill so that the Pathet Lao could take out his American brains. The next day, my father and my uncle found Yee. He was dead. He was not shot. The Pathet Lao had broken his neck trying to get to his American brains.''[30]

By the hundreds, Hmong of lower military rank were trapped in dragnets. Some were killed. Others were thrown into remote and well-guarded concentration compounds still euphemistically called seminar camps. Hmong children were maimed in public for all to see what happened to those who worked for the American warmongers.[31]

In fear, those Hmong who had a relationship with Vang Pao or the Americans hid in the mountains to avoid the enemy and waited for directions from General Vang Pao. Vang Pao, however, now in Montana, was isolated from his senior military men at Nam Phong refugee camp and in Laos. Vang Pao and his relatives had pooled their money to purchase a 400-acre farm for less than $1,000 per acre, securing it with a modest down payment and a 30-year mortgage. Initially, it seems, the CIA had wanted Vang Pao in a "safe house" in the Washington, D.C. area. The Agency took him to look at several large houses in Virginia, but he and his family decided that Montana would be their home. Jerry Daniels concurred. Near his home town of Missoula, Daniels argued, the general could raise his large family and farm. Besides, Vang Pao knew something about Montana. He had been there to visit a son who, with the assistance of Daniels, had attended high school and college there and now lived in Montana.

*   *   *

At Seminar Camp 6, Governor Khamphouei suffered. "Within three months of our capture we had worn out our shoes. Our clothes were torn. We were weak and many were sick. Occasionally, guards gave us a few tins of canned fish that belonged to the UNHCR [United Nations High Commission for Refugees]. To stay alive it was necessary to eat raw mice, insects, frogs, rodents, and whatever we could find. Some prisoners could not do this, gave up, and starved to death. With my own eyes, I saw ten Lao die of starvation. Many I didn't see also died from hunger, others from sickness. Others were shot trying to escape. By the end of November 1975, I knew of two colonels and a doctor who had been killed while attempting to escape. The doctor was shot about 15 kilometers from the camp. They brought his body back for us to see. When people died, the Pathet Lao said, 'Don't be surprised if you die. Even in the U.S., the big country, people die. So don't worry about dying.' "[32]

If any prisoner was suspected of having wrong ideas, he was put in the deep holes. In Camp 6, a group of 26 men were accused of plotting an escape. The Pathet Lao put them in the holes, with no food, water, or light. Governor Khamphouei watched, and remembered: "The Pathet Lao were uneducated and cruel. If anyone complained or asked for more food for those dying of starvation, he was punished. Immediate punishment was to put the man in a deep hole, cover it up, and keep him there for days. Lao Major Sobhabmixay Khen complained about the treatment of prisoners. They put him in the hole for days. When they took him out, he still complained so they sent him to Sop Hao [also near Vieng Sai] where they imprisoned the highest ranking Lao and where prisoners believed that the worst tortures occurred."

At the work sites, Khamphouei often saw North Vietnamese soldiers, but it was the Pathet Lao who guarded them. He was surprised that much of the equipment used by the Pathet Lao and Vietnamese was Chinese. "The rice sacks had written on them in English, 'Made in China.' The trucks, radio equipment, guns, medical supplies used by our captors came from China. When we became naked, they gave us clothes from China. I don't know for sure how these Chinese goods arrived."

In his camp, the prisoners endured nightly self-criticism and scare tactics. "There was little about Marxist-Leninist theories. Lectures were mostly used to scare us by telling us that since we still had 'American brains' drastic actions would be taken to eliminate our 'American brains.' They tried to make us hate the Americans and to show the greatness of the communist world. Night after night, they lectured us on the fact that in 1917 only the Soviet Union followed Marxism. Now in the 1970s there were many followers. 'Marxism,' they said, 'was very strong and the only country that resisted Marxism was the United States. No longer did the Marxist worry about England, France, or other European countries; they were no longer a threat to Marxism and no longer resisted. Only the United States resisted.'" Khamphouei clung to the hope that his USAID friends knew he was missing and were making efforts to get him released.

As 1975 drew to a close, 11-year-old Xiong Pao Xe who, six months earlier, had been taken by the Pathet Lao to be trained, received a real gun and an assignment. "The P.L. gave each of us a gun—something like a Soviet-made machine gun—and ordered us back to our villages to kill our parents. When I and the other boys from my village returned home, some of us told our parents of the communist plan. A P.L. teacher, a spy in our village, reported this to the P.L. soldiers. The next day, the soldiers attacked our village with B-40 rockets and set fire to our houses. To save our families from death, most of the children, including myself, turned our guns on the Pathet Lao. After the attack, our entire village fled into the forest to hide. We knew they would be looking for us to kill us."[33]

While the macabre and terrifying hunt for Hmong continued in Laos, the Kaysone government spoke convincingly to the outside world about its re-education centers and its seminar camps where citizens had the privilege of learning about Marxism and Leninism, the basis for the glorious new society. Journalists reported positively on the "gentle" communism of Laos and the new society developing under the Kaysone regime.

Fred Walker was right on two counts: the communists were indeed hounding the hares, and no one was complaining.

In the U.S., national attention focused on the presidential election campaigns of Democrat Jimmy Carter and Republican Gerald Ford. Carter campaigned vigorously on the need for the U.S. to pay close attention to human rights violations around the world. According to Carter, a nation's human rights record should influence foreign relations, trade, and economic aid.

24.

Chao Fa: Mystical Warriors

The last word of his [Sin Sai] saying to his all soldiers, "I have to leave you all soldiers in man's world, and you will not forget to stay on the high hill, because when I am not here, there might have many bad giants or spirits will come to make you all trouble; and also you all are my powerful soldiers and have to wait for me until I will come back to stay with your people again!" When Sin Sai he finished his saying he burnt himself away in one minute. So right now all Meo [Hmong] people said they are one kind of Sin Sai soldiers.

—"The Story of Meo People by Maha Thongsar Boupha" as it appears in *Mister Pop*, the story of Edgar "Pop" Buell

Vang Kai had become a diary keeper since his days in commando training in 1972 at Nam Phong. He continued to keep records. On January 18, 1976, he wrote in his diary: "Heard Pathet Lao have sent troops to get us." Four days later he wrote: "Set up ambush to get the P.L. troops sent to kill us. We saw them coming along the road. They had one big tank, 30 Soviet-built trucks, four small Soviet tanks. The big tank had a 127mm gun mounted on it. At about 4 in the afternoon, we hit the convoy. There was heavy fighting. We destroyed one truck which caught fire; one tank came to pull the truck off the road. Still we fought the convoy. The fighting was very heavy. About dark, the communists fired smoke bombs at us. We thought it was from a tank or from a B-40 or both. It made a hissing sound. We felt stunned. Everyone falls down. We are all numb. We can speak but not clearly. Some of us vomit blood; bleeding from the nose; and diarrhea with blood."[1]

Vang Kai had documented the onset of a new and horrible time for the Hmong.

On May 26, 1976—a year after General Vang Pao was forced into exile—life for the Hmong changed forever. A slow-flying biplane appeared over Xiong Xia Chia's area and fired three different kinds of rockets. They exploded at treetop level, releasing clouds of red, yellow, and white smoke. He immediately became dizzy and fell to the ground, bleeding from his nose, mouth, and eyes. "I knew that I was dying; I could not see and could not breathe. I'm unconscious for three days. My body is in agony. Chest pains are terrible. I can't eat. Ten people in my group are dead. I am lucky for I was at the edge of the attack. Ten days later, I'm on patrol not far from our camp site when aircraft return. This time, there are two planes. This time, the strike is a direct hit on our position. Fifty people lay unconscious on the ground for at least 24 hours, fighting for breath. Since I'm on the trail, I can see the attack and I'm also close enough to have chest pains and difficulty in breathing.[2]

"At the end of June 1976, a MiG-21 sprays our area with a yellow substance like rain. I see the residue on the plants and leaves. Within two days, there are holes in the leaves where the 'rain' fell. Hmong in the area have fever, diarrhea, and cannot eat. Very difficult for them to breathe. The diarrhea becomes worse and worse until they die. People who drink the water become sick with diarrhea and heavy fever. Within one month, 39 Hmong in my group are dead."

Xiong Xia Chia, who now forbade anyone to call him by his code name, Alex, dug up his weapons and munitions and joined other Hmong who had decided it was better to fight than to be taken to the "seminar" camps or to be killed by the poisons from the sky. He and others of his former rank now found themselves in charge; most senior officers had either fled or been captured.

These men knew that some Hmong must be reaching Thailand to tell about the atrocities and killings in Laos. Daily, Xiong Xia Chia waited for the arrival of messengers with news that the Americans were returning to help. "We knew the Americans must come. How could they so quickly forget us after working together for so many years? We heard that Vang Pao was living with the Americans in the United States. He would tell the Americans; assistance would come soon."

Such was not to occur. Career diplomats and Carter political appointees turned their efforts to promoting accommodation with the Hanoi government and formulating strategies to finance the rebuilding of Vietnam. The U.S. Embassy in Bangkok turned its attention to the movement of Vietnamese, Cambodian, and Lao refugees to the U.S. Embassy personnel were instructed to massage the Thais, since Thailand was now the front line between the U.S. and communist Southeast Asia. President Carter's attention was focused on his desire to expand Henry Kissinger's detente with the Soviet Union by a SALT II arms treaty, enhancing Nixon's SALT I.

T-28 pilot Yang Pao, a POW now for more than four years, continued to be held near Khang Khay. He and other prisoners knew "that we would be worked and starved to death. We watched as the Pathet Lao killed us one by one. Ly Chue, age about 20, died and we buried him. Sonvilai, a Lao commander and leader at Sala Phou Khoun, was executed. In 1976, they shot Vang Boua Fue, one of our work team, and the prisoners buried him."[3]

On July 24, 1975, a Hmong woman watched as her husband, a major in Vang Pao's forces, was taken away by General Ai Kham, to Dong Ma seminar camp in Sam Neua Province. When she complained about her missing husband, the Pathet Lao told her that she and her family could visit him. One day a Lao named Boonna arrived in a jeep to drive her and her five children to the seminar camp.

"They lied to me. Instead of taking us to Dong Ma, they set up an ambush. They killed three of my children. They took me and my surviving children to Phong Savan. There the Pathet Lao said: 'You are prisoner. Go cut the trees. Your children can't go to school.' There was nothing in Phong Savan—no food, no clothes for the prisoners. The few clothes that I had they took away. They told me to make my own fields; grow my own food. I made a small field of corn and rice but the government took half of it.'"[4]

In Phong Savan, she saw many Soviet pilots and many Vietnamese soldiers. She learned there were at least 3,000 prisoners, including men, women, and children. "They divided the prisoners into groups. Former soldiers were kept separately. They worked hard with little food. They made buildings, dug holes, cut trees, and worked in the saw mill. If anyone tried to escape, they were shot. I saw them shoot one of Vang Pao's colonels. The most suffering men were those with rank of captain or above. One time, they took five Hmong officers and tied their hands behind their backs and beat them. Then they made everyone in the camp come to watch these men dig their graves. With everyone watching, the guards shot them. The Pathet Lao said that it was an example for all of us."

Hmong in Laos had little or no knowledge of what had happened to Vang Pao, their senior military leaders, or some of their clan leaders. When no assistance arrived, many realized that they were totally and pitifully alone against the NVA giant—a giant which would obliterate them with its sophisticated weapons, its well-supplied troops, and its now unchallenged extensive air power.

No longer would Hmong soldiers be moved about by helicopters or cargo planes. No longer would the Hmong FACs or FAGs call Cricket or Alley Cat to launch air strikes to repel advancing enemy forces. No longer would the SKY men make certain they had weapons, radios, and medicine. No longer would Air America or Continental pilots drop food to hungry refugees or move them to safer locations when their camps came under attack. Now it would be as it had been before the Americans. Now the Hmong would be alone, on foot, armed with only their courage, cleverness, and a few hand-held weapons.

In these times of incredible fear, desperate men turned fanatical in their desire to survive. With no military way to defend themselves, some Hmong turned to a mystical group which promised a godlike intervention that would not only protect them from being slain by an evil giant but would give them the power to destroy it. These mystical priests called themselves "Chao Fa"—Prince of the Sky.

Chao Fa priests had incorporated Sin Sai of Lao legend in their beliefs. The Chao Fa version of stories of Sin Sai told how he had protected people from bad giants and evil spirits in times of great troubles. Chao Fa priests proclaimed that Sin Sai would help the Hmong.[5]

Here is part of the Lao legend of Sin Sai as Hmong knew it:

In the olden day, was about five thousand years ago, there was only one land, the land was very small like the trace of the deer. There was only one tree, the tree was very small like the smallest candle. There was also only one hermit who stayed on the land. When the age of that hermit was one thousand years old he took clays to make one man and one woman by his own magic, a man whose name was Phaou Sank See, and a woman whose name was Ya Sank Sar. Both of them stayed together for many and many years. They have had only one son and their son's name was Sin Sai. He was a powerful, grateful and kindly man. . . .

When the age of Sin Sai was about twenty-five years old, his own town was very much trouble about the big bad giant who wants to kill him. . . . So Sin Sai, he sent the message to the big bad giant that he wants to make a war. . . .

Its both eyes were red like the fire hell. On that day the bad giant could not stay on its house. It growled and cried like the bad thunder. It went around the sky and it also transformed itself into thousands and thousands of small giants for making war with a great Sin Sai. . . .

Sin Sai he said in his mind, "Oh, my dear old parents and my dear respecting hermit." So Sin Sai he took grains of rice to put in his mouth and then he spit out all of grains of rice, and all grains of rice became soldiers by his good magical action. . . .

Well, when all of bad giants including the big bad one had died altogether, Sin Sai he said that, "If I shall stay in men's world there is no use at all for me. I have to go to kill bad giant or bad spirits at the other world."[6]

In his last words to his soldiers, Sin Sai warned them to stay on the high hills to avoid bad monsters and evil spirits. Before leaving in a flash of fire, he told his soldiers that one day he would return.

It was this Sin Sai that centered Chao Fa beliefs. While all the details of the origins, plans, and allegiances of the Chao Fa are not fully known, the emergence of this group as a major military force occurred after General Vang Pao's departure. Before 1975, the Chao Fa were a little-known mystical group dating back to the early 1900s. The Chao Fa story probably began with the first Chao Fa, Paj Chai, a Hmong who fought against French colonial rule from 1917 to 1920. Paj Chai, who proclaimed to be in contact with former Hmong kings, held a mystical power over his followers. His force seriously challenged the French. Eventually, with a combination of French victories and disillusionment with Paj Chai, the influence of the Chao Fa waned, but not the memory of their exploits.

In the 1960s, the Chao Fa leader was Yang Shong Lue, who called himself "Nhia Daow," meaning "Mother of Letters," because he had created a special alphabet for the Hmong language. He was reportedly an uneducated man and therefore his amazing ability to create an alphabet impressed many people. He believed that God had sent him to lead the Hmong people to a better life. He could also predict the future. One of his devoted teachers was a youth from North Vietnam from the Her clan, named Pao Kao. The "Mother of Letters" and his teachers not only promoted the Chao Fa alphabet, but also the need for a Hmong king, explaining that when Hmong lived in China, they had a king and an alphabet. They had lost both. Now it was time for Hmong to have their own king and their own alphabet again, not one based on Romanized characters as devised by Westerners.

Initially, Yang Shong Lue had lived in Vietnamese–Pathet Lao–controlled territory in Phong Saly. Later he and some of his teachers, including Her Pao Kao, who would play a leading role in the Chao Fa resistance, defected to join General Vang Pao, who accepted them and allowed the younger men to join the Lao Army. The defectors lived briefly with the general and then moved to a village near Long Chieng.

Rumors spread that the "Mother of Letters" was a communist spy.

School superintendent Moua Lia remembered the problems. "They had a center of education that many people complained to 'V.P.' about because they were teaching a new alphabet. 'V.P.' brought him to Long Chieng and scolded him, telling him he had to stop teaching a written language from Vietnam because Hmong are in Laos and Lao citizens and that the Hmong already have one written language. He warned that if the Lao government found out that he was teaching a Vietnamese Hmong alphabet, they would not like it."[7]

Soon, however, he resumed teaching, conducting classes at night. His followers wore red and blue armbands to identify themselves as Sons of Heaven. Chao Fa teachers taught more than an alphabet. They taught that the Hmong had to dress as Hmong, not as Lao, to indicate that they were sons of a Hmong king. The Chao Fa also urged their followers not to assimilate into Lao culture, warning that if they did not dress like Hmong, they would be eaten by a tiger.

For some time Vang Pao did not believe the rumors about the "Mother of Letters," strongly accusing him of spying and prophesying, but they persisted. He was later found to have radio contact with followers in communist-controlled areas in the north. On September 15, 1967, Yang Shong Lue was jailed in a maximum security facility at Pha Khao. By 1969, he was allowed outside to walk about and to have visitors, and sometime in 1970, with the aid of his followers, he escaped to the jungle to hide. In early January 1971, the "Mother of Letters" was found and shot by men dressed in Vietnamese uniforms. His student, Xiong Nhia Ly, took up his dead leader's cause and built a Chao Fa temple east of Long Chieng near Phou Bia, the highest mountain in Laos, where he reportedly preached incredible and unbelievable things. His miraculous tales of men being able to fly and jump from mountaintop to mountaintop reached General Vang Pao, who ordered a T-28 strike against the temple.

Another of Yang Shong Lue's followers was Her Yong Joua, who commanded a battalion of Chao Fa in Vang Pao's forces. Before each battle, Yong Joua conducted a *ba-sii* ceremony to protect his soldiers. They lined up with outstretched arms as Commander Yong Joua chanted auspicious words and tied strings on their wrists from a "never-ending" ball of white twine that he carried in his jacket pocket. No ball of string was visible, yet he could produce a never-ending supply. He told his troops that his power produced these powerful *ba-sii* strings and there was no end to them. Vang Pao once called him in and asked why he lied to his troops about his magical powers. The Chao Fa commander supposedly answered: "You have trouble getting soldiers to fight. I don't. So forget it. Don't scold me." In spite of his magic and powerful *ba-sii* strings, Yong Joua's Chao Fa battalion, operating on the Plaine des Jarres, was mauled by the NVA in 1970.[8]

After Vang Pao left Laos in 1975, Her Yong Joua promoted himself to a higher rank and preached that the power to fight was given by the gods. According to him, the Hmong no longer needed guns. With the Chao Fa magic, they could kill the enemy with sticks and clubs. They were no longer vulnerable to enemy fire; they were under the protection of Chao Fa.[9] Chao Fa priests espoused the invincibility of those who worshipped properly. True believers could defeat the enemy with magic given by the supernatural intervention of Sin Sai, the great mythological defender, against bad giants such as the Vietnamese and Lao communist forces. As the communist net of terror and death tightened, Hmong, realizing they were doomed, turned in desperation to the Chao Fa priests.

Lo Cheng, a former second lieutenant, knew that it was only a matter of time before the communists captured him. As a "carbine soldier," he had begun his military career as a child, carrying water for the mess cook at Bouam Loung. After Vang Pao's departure, the communists declared that any soldier who had worked for Vang Pao or Jerry Daniels would be eliminated. "I was extremely frightened that I would be rounded up and taken to seminar like the others. One day a Hmong from the Hang clan came and told us about a Chao Fa prophet named Nhia Pao and about the Chao Fa magic. I was so scared that I decided to go to stay with Nhia Pao."[10]

He and three other former lieutenants took their families to live near Nhia Pao. They declared themselves Chao Fa by being "baptized" by a priest using a white stone. The wood, bamboo, and thatch temple was nine-sided; Lo Cheng thought it was beautiful. In this temple where only men were allowed, he learned that the Chao Fa believed that Vaj Chue Chao, appearing in the form of a pig, and Sin Sai were sent to earth to help and to cure the people. With incense and paper the faithful worshipped. The Chao Fa had a red flag that featured a crescent moon next to a sacred pig and other animals, including a rhinoceros. Priests told the men not to cut their hair, warning them if they did they would not be safe.

Nhia Pao impressed Lo Cheng with his prophetic abilities. "He knew when it would be raining and when it would be clear. He meditated and then announced that tomorrow a visitor would come—and always the visitor came."

While most Hmong only heard the fantastic stories about Chao Fa magic, primary school teacher Yang Soua saw some with his own eyes. One Saturday noon, Yang Soua was standing outside his parents' house on a Muang Cha hillside when he saw 20 to 30 armed Hmong soldiers dressed in black, marching in a column heading toward Muang Cha. ''Leading the column was a young Hmong girl carrying a flag with a crescent moon and some animals, including a pig. The soldiers had M-16s, carbines, rifles and one shoulder-held M-72 mortar. I watched, expecting the NVA to shoot them down, but they didn't. A Hmong soldier fired his M-72 mortar and it went through the roof of the former mayor's house. Some NVA ran out and were killed. Other NVA ran to gun positions on the higher ground overlooking the valley. They fired their DK-82 mortars on the Hmong soldiers. Their mortars exploded in mid-air instead of on the ground, so not one Hmong was hit. The girl continued to march around with the flag.[11]

''During this battle many NVA soldiers were killed, including NVA officers in the mayor's house. It took six trucks to take away the dead Vietnamese soldiers. No Hmong died. No Hmong were wounded. After the battle, we learned that these Hmong were Chao Fa. We asked them how they could kill so many Vietnamese and not lose one Hmong. They said that the god looked after them and that their flag protected them. They also told us that the mortar that hit the headquarters was fired at Vang Pao's former office, not at the headquarters building, and that it had turned and hit the building with all the Vietnamese in it. This was the power of the Chao Fa, they said.'' Yang Soua thought the explanation was probably more in faulty weapons than in magic. Yet he had witnessed the successful Chao Fa attack against the NVA and was astonished.

Soon after, Yang Soua asked the Pathet Lao once again for his back salary. He had not been paid since they took over. ''They told me I would have to go to Sam Neua for seminar and get my money. I was scared. I knew that they intended to trick me into going to Sam Neua and take me prisoner. So I took my family, my brothers and sisters, my cousins, and my parents and we went to the jungle to join the resistance of Yang Say Shoua, my uncle. He had been the Tasseng of Pha Khao district and had left there for more remote mountains to escape the communist purges. Now, he led former Vang Pao soldiers and their families. My uncle was a civilian so he was advised by several former colonels.''

In the jungle, the young teacher's brother commanded a group of 100 resistance fighters of which he became the assistant commander even though he had no previous military experience. Life as a jungle fighter posed extreme difficulties. ''The Vietnamese controlled everything—the roads, the markets. The resistance could not get anything to eat—except what we found in the jungle."

The Yang-led resistance did not believe the tales of Chao Fa soldiers battling the enemy unscathed. "Many of us," remembered Yang Soua, "who were educated or who had fought with General Vang Pao, doubted the magic of the Chao Fa. But we had no choice but to fight with them. We needed each other. The Chao Fa had about 8,000 troops and so did we. Our leaders discussed plans for battles with the Chao Fa leaders because together we had a chance to win. Since we did not believe in the Chao Fa religion, we separated from them during their prayers and religious activities, but we often joined together to fight the enemy."

Living with the Chao Fa, Yang Soua learned their ways. "According to Chao Fa thinking, the Lao Teung (Kmhmu) were to be called 'Older Brother' and they should be asked first for their opinions. This was the opposite of the past when they called the Hmong 'Older Brother,' built their houses below the Hmong, and were not the military leaders. In Chao Fa belief the Lao Teung should build their houses above Hmong houses on the mountain slopes and the Lao Teung should go first into battle. This meant that they were killed first."

Chao Fa priests could predict the future. Each Chao Fa commander had a priest who advised him on military tactics and determined the day and hour of attacks. Chao Fa leaders believed that they should never attack at night—only during the daytime when the god could watch and protect them. One famous priest was a boy of about seven years; another was an old man; another was Nhia Pao.

On November 3, 1976—15 months after Laos closed its borders—Kaysone moved against the royal family. King Savang Vatthana, Queen Khamphoui, Crown Prince Vongsavang, the director of protocol at the Luang Prabang palace, and the king's secretary, the son of Prince Khammao, who at one time had been the Lao ambassador to Washington, were arrested and taken to Seminar Camp 1, the infamous Sop Hoa, in the Vieng Sai area. Sop Hoa was reserved for the most important people. It already held generals, ministers, and Touby LyFong, who had been arrested the year before.

In December 1976, Vang Pha and four other families hiding in the jungle were captured near Muang Om. "They accused us of being Vang Pao soldiers and said that they must punish us. They took my six-year-old son and gave him some medicine. From a small red package with Vietnamese letters on it, they took a white powder and mixed it with water and gave it to him. Almost immediately, my son began to scream and cry in pain, holding his stomach. Then he began to jump around and twitch wildly. The soldiers laughed. We could only stand silently and watch my child. In ten minutes he was dead. I asked the Pathet Lao why they did that. They laughed and said, 'Maybe we gave him the wrong medicine.'"[12]

When the Pathet Lao took the five captured families to a permanent prison camp, Vang Pha slipped away and followed to learn the location of the prison. He organized other Hmong to attack the camp to free the prisoners. During the attack in heavy fighting, Vang Pha's only surviving child, a younger son, was killed.

In the final weeks of 1976, the Pathet Lao moved pilot Yang Pao and other "outside" prisoners from near Khang Khay to Phong Savan where, since he was a pilot, he joined the ranks of the "most suffering men." There teams of political prisoners worked fields, built roads, cut lumber, and constructed houses. While most of the prisoners had become docile in their weakened state, they worked with armed guards nearby. Prisoners received little food, no medicine or medical attention, no money, and were treated as pariahs. Escape attempts that failed resulted in torture and death. When detailed to work near the airfield, Yang Pao studied the aircraft. "The communists had 29 T-28s, Raven planes, C-123s, biplanes and the airfield had been lengthened so MiGs could land."[13]

During 1976, LyTeck Ly Nhia Vue, the Hmong who had believed the Pathet Lao promise that he would become the Hmong chief after Vang Pao had been eliminated, was executed at Seminar Camp 6, where Governor Khamphouei was held. The Pathet Lao turned LyTeck's "ranch" at Kilometer 52 into a re-education camp where one purified one's thinking and studied the ways of the new society. Re-education camps were quite different from the seminar camps. Some re-education camps were open to visiting foreign journalists. The seminar–forced labor camps were not; the Kaysone regime denied their existence.

Unlike the Nazi camps which remained fixed, camps in Laos moved often. According to Governor Khamphouei, "The camp was wherever they moved the prisoners. There were base prison camps and satellite work camps. Prisoners were transferred, groups were reorganized, teams were constantly changing work assignments."[14]

Prisoners did escape from these camps, but by the time they got out of Laos and found someone to tell who would believe their experiences, the camp site had probably been moved, or altered, or the prisoners transferred. This mobility allowed the government to say with certainty that there was not a camp at a given location. It also lessened escape attempts since prisoners did not have time to become familiar with the local terrain or habits of local guards.

Forced-labor camps in Laos were similar to those in China introduced under Mao Zedong, where hundreds of thousands of political prisoners mined coal, built roads, and manned factories. Like the labor camps in Laos, they were movable, secret places where torture prevailed to clean the minds of counter-revolutionaries. In China, prisoners were not, however, regularly killed since they were considered a valuable resource—a free labor force.[15]

A continuing flow of refugees—mostly Lao, with some Hmong and other tribal groups—continued to cross into northern Thailand, cramping refugee quarters and causing Thai authorities to worry.

Refugee reports of the miraculous exploits of the Chao Fa fighters were retold in Thailand. Not knowing the situation inside Laos, people began to refer erroneously to all resistance in Laos as "Chao Fa." In time, most resistance fighters—whether they were Chao Fa or followers of another resistance group—who crossed into Thailand responded positively to the Thai authorities' question: "Are you Chao Fa?" They learned that it was easier to deal with the Thai if they said they were Chao Fa, whether they were or not.

The Thai government had rejected Jerry Daniels' idea to buy farmable land in sparsely populated northern Thailand for the Hmong detained at Nam Phong. Another alternative had to be found. In early 1976, Hmong, including Lo Ma, Fackee, and General Direction, had been bused to a valley in northern Loei Province to construct what they believed to be temporary shelters. The camp, less than 10 miles from the Mekong River, was named Ban Vinai—"ban," the Thai word for village, and "Vinai," the name of the Thai general who found the site. Ban Vinai was soon to come under the supervision of the United Nations High Commission for Refugees (UNHCR).

The U.S. was resettling hundreds of thousands of Vietnamese and Chinese-Vietnamese, but it gave little thought to the tribal people of Laos. Most Hmong were not much interested in being sent to the U.S. Almost everyone had relatives in Laos. Many wanted to return to Laos to fight or to find lost family.

Although many Americans working with the refugees in Thailand knew of the dreadful situation in Laos, they did not speak out. Some later excused their timidity in pointing out human rights abuses as a result of being "too afraid" because of the anti-American sentiments in Thailand. The CIA men, Air America, Continental, and Raven pilots, State Department foreign service officers, and USAID personnel kept silent about the horrors perpetrated against those with whom they had worked. Some were bound by secrecy not to talk. Others were intimidated by the labeling of those involved in the Vietnam War as "baby killers." Still others, bitter about what had happened and feeling guilty about abandoning friends, tried to forget Laos. Some, believers in Kaysone's new society, disbelieved or ignored reports of cruelty.

Few in Washington talked about the gross violations of human rights in Laos. While USAID had been expelled, the United States continued to maintain its embassy, now downgraded with only a chargé as the senior person and a small staff, in Vientiane after 1975. For the year 1976, the U.S. Department of State's 143-page report to Congress evaluating human rights practices and abuses of various countries throughout the world did not *list* the country of Laos.

There was little public or government interest in the fact that Eisenhower's original domino—the one that the U.S. had fought so many years to keep upright—had toppled.

25.

Holocaust in the Hills

Reaffirming their [Vietnam and Laos] loyalty to Marxism-Leninism and their will to continue to uphold the banner of national independence and socialism, closely combine genuine patriotism and proletarian internationalism and do their best to defend and develop the Lao-Vietnam special relationship so that the two countries, already bound together in their national liberation struggle, will be forever bound in their national construction and national defence.

—from the "Treaty of Friendship and Cooperation between the Lao People's Democratic Republic and the Socialist Republic of Vietnam," July 18, 1977

Hmong women captured by the Vietnamese and Lao soldiers were publicly and repeatedly raped in view of Hmong male prisoners. This was intended to humiliate the Hmong captives in the Lao Gulag.

Vang Youa Pao, born in 1947, had served in the Hmong "special forces." His last rank was second lieutenant. On May 29, 1975, he was captured by the communists and taken to a slave labor camp near Phong Savan. Here he was terrorized and tortured by his captors. "They asked, 'How many of our people did you kill?' I didn't know if I had ever killed anyone. They torture me for not giving a number. So I have to say a number. I knew that if I say zero I will get the worst punishment. After torture, I say that I killed five. They say that if you kill more than four you must be punished for five to ten years."[1]

After 27 days near Phong Savan, Vang Youa Pao was moved to Nong Het. "Sometimes in our camp, the soldiers bring in our wives and wives of others who worked for the CIA who are prisoners in different camps. They don't let us talk to them. They let us see them. Then the soldiers take these women, play with [fondle] them and rape them. Sometimes the soldiers play with our wives for several days. Many become pregnant. The communists say that these children who are born are the 'government children.'* The government raises these children and turns them into soldiers. They tell these children they have no parents, no relatives. There are many thousands of these 'government children.' One time, I recognized Lou Tou's wife when they brought her into our camp to be raped by the communist soldiers."

Since Hmong consider rape a heinous act, raped women are no longer considered worthy of marriage. Some women who have been forced to become breeders of "government children" try to commit suicide. One woman who had suffered this brutality escaped to confirm this treatment of Hmong female prisoners. She now lives in the U.S. She is terrified of having her name made public because of the stigma of rape. At a Phong Savan prison camp, another Hmong woman was raped by a LPDR soldier while other soldiers watched, laughed, and pointed guns at her so she wouldn't make any noise. From that rape, a child was born. In this case, it was not taken from her, and, when the child was still an infant, she escaped and eventually fled into Thailand and then resettled with that child in the U.S.[2]

Former Governor Khamphouei, still imprisoned in Seminar Camp 6, now weighed only 80 pounds, down from about 165 when he was arrested. Though so weak from starvation that he staggered when he

---

*This effort to create a cadre of "government children" took several forms and was witnessed by women and men of various ethnic groups, including Lao, who were held as political prisoners in the Lao Gulag. Among these witnesses was a Lao grandmother, held in internal exile, whose grandchild was taken at age 10 by the LPDR for the army. She never saw the child again. Another witness was Lieutenant Khampong, arrested in 1975 by the communists and held as a political prisoner under harsh conditions until 1981 when he escaped. He was forced by his captors to build roads, to cut teak trees to be taken to Vietnam, and to pull a plough like a buffalo. He was also terrorized and starved by the guards. "But for me, the worst thing was when the high-ranking Vietnamese officers came. We had to bow and welcome them with flowers. The high-ranking Vietnamese ordered Lao girls into their rooms to have children."

It is the belief of Lieutenant Khampong and others, both Lao and Hmong, that the Vietnamese intend to "Vietnamize" Laos so that if a free election takes place, the Vietnamese will control the votes. Khampong witnessed this strategy. He saw not only the creation of "government children," but the movement of Vietnamese into Laos. "In my area, the Vietnamese were sending Vietnamese in to live, taking Lao names so they would be considered Lao." Interviews with the Lao grandmother and Lieutenant Khampong, California, August 1985. The Lao grandmother requested her name not be used because her grandchild may still be alive and she does not want to jeopardize the child's life.

walked, there was no relief from the forced labor or the nightly self-criticism and propaganda.

On March 17, 1977, President Jimmy Carter addressed the United Nations on human rights: "The search for peace and justice also means respect for human dignity. . . . no member can avoid its responsibilities to review and to speak when torture or unwarranted deprivation occurs in any part of the world."[3]

Carter, believing that "right makes might," had announced he would negotiate with the Soviets in good faith, openness, and truthfulness. In his initial efforts, he found out that these characteristics were not enough; the Soviets were tough bargainers. Carter took the Soviet rejection of his arms control proposal personally and perhaps as a consequence became more determined to promote a SALT II agreement.[4]

During the spring and summer of 1977, Secretary of State Cyrus Vance, National Security Advisor Zbigniew Brzezinski, Secretary of Defense Harold Brown, and staff of the Arms Control and Disarmament Agency [ACDA], Pentagon, CIA, and State Department worked feverishly on details of another arms proposal that might be acceptable to the Soviets. Carter canceled the U.S. B-1 Bomber program to please the Soviets and ordered the withdrawal of U.S. troops from South Korea, although this was later rescinded. Still, however, a SALT II treaty eluded him. Some experts warned that the U.S. must have absolute means of verification of Soviet military installations or a treaty would be meaningless; the Soviets objected to on-site investigations. Bickering and posturing by negotiating teams continued in Geneva. Time was running out for Carter.

Opposition to Carter's SALT II grew as his concessions were perceived as weakness and a lack of understanding of the Soviets. Even if he were able to manage a treaty, there now was the question as to whether or not the U.S. Congress would ratify it if it appeared lopsided to favor the Soviets and particularly if it did not contain provisions for credible inspection. Certainly, ratification of SALT II would not be furthered by public acknowledgment of events taking place in Laos, whose government was actively supported by the Soviets.

In the U.S., little attention was paid to events in Laos or to the far-reaching 25-year Treaty of Friendship between the Lao People's Democratic Republic and the Socialist Republic of Vietnam that was signed on July 18, 1977. This treaty reaffirmed the loyalty of both countries to Marxism-Leninism.[5]

It also sought to coordinate common political and diplomatic actions of the two countries, to manage their resources in common, to insure the common defense of borders, to utilize as it saw fit Lao military installations, and to assure Vietnam the right to intervene in Laos and to speak in the name of Laos. It was also a maneuver to legalize the presence of Hanoi's 60,000 occupation troops and thousands of advisors in Laos—personnel that Hanoi had not withdrawn in violation of the Agreement on the Restoration of Peace and Reconciliation of February 21, 1973. The Vietnamese military presence was confirmed for the first time publicly by a Lao government official in March 1979.[6] This Vietnam-Lao treaty became the legal basis for tragic events unfolding around Phou Bia, the highest mountain in Laos.

Sgt. Moua Paje, who had been a soldier since he was 13 and had helped to rescue several American pilots, was about to discover the meaning of the Treaty of Friendship. About the time it was signed, Vietnamese soldiers occupied his village of about 100 families at Nam Fen. Several Vietnamese soldiers stayed in each house. They slept with the Hmong wives. Husbands could say nothing. If Hmong objected, they were sent to seminar camp. When Sergeant Moua complained, the Vietnamese soldiers told him: "We are now comrades. We share everything. It shouldn't hurt. All is one!"[7]

Sergeant Moua and his wife were terrified. One day while working a field, she and her children slipped away to hide in a cave. Sergeant Moua joined them later. They had heard about the Chao Fa resistance and decided to join. Others did the same. Soon fighting broke out between the resistance and the communists. It was difficult for the enemy to find Sergeant Moua and other resistance fighters in the jungle. "So, the enemy poisoned us," recalled Sergeant Moua. "Sometimes the planes just observed; other times they dropped poisons. There were three kinds used—yellow, black, and blue, the color of the sky. When the yellow poison like rain came people got dizzy with vomiting.

"The black one was used more often and it came in big drops, like a drop of oil. If touched or if breathed it could kill you. If you breathed in hard near the black drop, you couldn't breathe in again. It had a vapor, or steam. It seemed that if people breathed it, they died at the scene if they couldn't get some opium into their bodies. The black poison killed that person within about three hours. We were frightened and ran away. But we had no safe place to go, so we returned. Still the enemy poisoned us. We had no way to resist their poisons. Next we ran to Yellow Rock on Phou San. We were sick and couldn't farm. The vegetables we ate poisoned us. The water poisoned us. Then there was nothing left to eat that was safe. We would all die."

In this life and death struggle in interior Laos, there were three choices—flee, surrender, or resist. For those who decided to flee, the exodus often ended in disaster. Crying babies alerted soldiers who massacred groups of civilians moving along mountain jungle paths. Families had to abandon their weak and dying relatives. Communist patrols shot Hmong down in the Mekong River as they attempted to cross to Thailand. Some refugees did, however, reach Thailand. Others were too weak from starvation or too sick from the poisons to attempt the long and arduous trek out of Laos. Many had no choice but to stay and care for family members unable to escape. They hoped help would arrive before it was too late. Those who surrendered became prisoners. Hunted like animals, poisoned, starved, maimed, tortured, raped, many Hmong, fearful and desperately seeking any means to survive, turned to resistance groups. More and more Hmong—like Sergeant Moua and his wife—turned to the Chao Fa.

As the Vietnamese and Pathet Lao forces squeezed the Hmong, they moved up Phou Bia seeking a safe haven. In the higher reaches of this mountain massif lived Chao Fa leader Yong Joua.

Lo Cheng led a Chao Fa resistance group of 20 men in Nhia Pao's area. Before each battle, he took his men to Nhia Pao's temple: "Before each battle, we burned incense and paper and prayed to Sin Sai and Vaj Chue Chao for protection. After we prayed, the priest told each commander to take a flag for protection. I chose not to carry a flag because it was too big and heavy. Our weapons were already too heavy and we had to move fast. Some people did carry flags because they thought they protected them. But I never did. Just before the battle, a leader again asked Sin Sai and Vaj Chue Chao to protect our men. Then we attacked."[8]

In the fall of 1977, during a major assault against the Hmong in Lo Cheng's area, both Chao Fa and forces led by former Vang Pao soldiers engaged the Vietnamese in heavy fighting.

Lo Cheng, in action near Phou Khan, saw enemy planes drop poisons. "In the first attack I saw two planes fly over our village. They came back a second time and dropped red smoke that started down in a red line and then just above the trees there was an explosion. There was a smell that gave us headaches, dizziness, and vomiting. Many people got very sick. They also dropped poisoned nails that could go through a house.

"We shot at the planes, but they continued to come. One day, our group saw an 0-1 Bird Dog Raven spotter plane. We turned on our PRC-25 radio on the 36-36 channel. We heard the pilot talking in Lao so we listened. 'Drop it! Drop it!' shouted one voice. The other voice said, 'Not yet! Not yet!' Neither man talked exactly like a Lao. Our radioman asked in Hmong, 'Who's the pilot?' In the Hmong language, the pilot answered, 'I'm Hmong. I'm Yang Pao! I'm Yang Pao! Right now, there is a Vietnamese at my back. I will kill you for sure. You must leave your village now. Don't live in villages. Go!'"

The men on the ground were stunned. They knew T-28 pilot Yang Pao had been shot down. They thought he was dead. "Now we believed that he was alive," remembered Lo Cheng. "While it didn't sound exactly like Yang Pao, maybe it was. We didn't know for sure. The next time Yang Pao flew over our area, he dropped something. We could see it fall. We recovered it. It was a package of cigarettes with a message inside. The message written in Lao read: 'I'm Yang Pao. Don't shoot too much. When I shoot, I won't shoot directly at you.'

"The planes with the poisons continued to come. Sometimes we heard the men in them talking over our radio. They spoke Lao. Each plane usually carried one red rocket and one green one on each wing. The red was delivered first. Sometimes other colors were mixed. There were always nails. These poisons brought sickness to our people. Most of our children suffered from the epidemic that the poisons brought. Our people had fever, vomiting, and then they can't eat and get very skinny. They get so skinny from the poisons that death comes. Some people get a disease in their mouths. They get blisters in their mouths that become holes and get bigger and bigger and never end. They can't eat and then they die. A lot die from the big holes in their mouths. My mother died from the poisons. With my own eyes, I saw more than 100 people die."

After the initial radio contact with the pilot of the spotter plane who said he was Yang Pao, their radio batteries lasted two more months. "Before our radio failed, we talked to Hmong pilot Yang Pao one last time. In Hmong, he begged, 'Don't shoot too much; don't be too accurate. I will try not to shoot at you.' He kept his promise not to shoot directly at us, but the problem is that the smell drifted into other areas and others got sick. Yang Pao flew poison flights over our area for one year. Other pilots also dropped poisons on us. Now the planes dropped green and yellow poisons. Many people got sick and died."

Former T-28 pilot Yang Pao remained a prisoner in a Gulag slave-labor camp in Phong Savan. Who, then, was the pilot claiming to be Yang Pao? Was it a Vietnamese or a Lao? It would have to be someone who knew that Yang Pao remained a prisoner, and probably—although not necessarily—someone familiar with the Hmong.

Yang Pao, of course, did not know that an enemy pilot was claiming his name and begging his clansmen not to shoot him down. Yang Pao put all his energies into staying alive. Extremely thin and looking much older than his 29 years, he remained on a starvation diet. When he could, he searched in the Phong Savan market for scraps of food. One time, when scavenging, he saw a Hmong family with a teenage girl. "I talked very briefly to the girl, named Xai, to see if her family was friendly. When they departed the market, I followed them. I wanted to find out about my family and the situation in Laos. This family, named Moua, told me that my family and my wife had escaped to Thailand and that everyone thought I was dead. They told me about the Chao Fa fighting the communists near the Nam Sen River and Phou Bia. I had never heard of this. I returned to my work team before the Pathet Lao knew that I had gone. I began to make a plan to escape."[9]

Soon Yang Pao requested permission to be married. "I asked the Pathet Lao for permission to marry Xai, the daughter of Moua Bee, and to visit my uncle at Khang Kho to get permission to marry. I had been a good prisoner at Phong Savan. They had no reason to suspect I would escape, so they gave me permission to marry and to travel. I was ordered to return in a few days. On December 5, 1977, they allowed me to leave with Xai, who was 14 years old. At Khang Kho, my uncle immediately hid me. Here, the Chao Fa asked me to join them. I couldn't. I was too sick and too weak. I was also very confused. I had two heads—one Pathet Lao and one Chao Fa."

Yang Pao's five-year struggle to survive the extreme physical and psychological abuse had changed him. To stay alive, he had become an obedient, respectful prisoner. Asked to turn against his captors, he psychologically could not—at least not initially in his debilitated physical and mental state.

A few weeks after his arrival at Khang Kho, a combined Vietnamese and Lao force attacked the Chao Fa in Yang Pao's area. He recalled, "The communists had 130mm guns all around the Chao Fa. They fired 130s, 105s, 155s from Long Chieng, from Pha Khao, and from Muang Cha. They brought in troops in green choppers that looked like American choppers. They fired rockets and used Raven airplanes to shoot poison gas on the Hmong." Although the resistance forces were desperately in need of soldiers, Yang Pao did not join them. Instead, he tried to build a small thatch house. His broken body hurt, but he said nothing about the pain.

Desperation made strange bedfellows in the Lao hills. One resistance group of about 8,000, comprised largely of former Vang Pao soldiers, joined a Chao Fa force of about the same size. They planned to attack the Vietnamese at Muang Cha to destroy their big artillery and drive the enemy out of the villages along the Muang Cha River.

Teacher Yang Soua, now a seasoned resistance fighter, prepared for the battle of Muang Cha. "The Chao Fa prayed. The priest predicted the battle should begin at 6 a.m. When dawn came, we were positioned outside Muang Cha. Captain Her Pao Kao, a nephew of Her Yong Joua, was with the Chao Fa troops. My brother and I kept our 100 men at the rear, some distance from the airfield. We didn't trust the Chao Fa. We wanted to stay behind to watch. We knew the Vietnamese were in gun positions in the hills on both sides of the river—just as they had been when the Chao Fa had attacked earlier with a girl carrying their flag.[10]

"This morning, two men carried the flag. The priest had told them to put it at a certain place near the runway and not to move it. With the flag in place, hundreds of Chao Fa, with the Older Brother Lao Teung [Kmhmu] leading the column, marched toward the bridge over the Muang Cha River. As the Chao Fa neared the bridge, the Vietnamese fired on their flag and hit it. The Chao Fa guarding the flag moved it to the far side of the runway. About the same time, the column reached the bridge. With the Chao Fa troops on the bridge, the NVA gunners opened up. Many Lao Tueng were seriously wounded and quickly retreated."

Back at the rear, near Yang Soua's position, Her Pao Kao waited with his "magic sign," which he carried in his rear pocket. "This was a stick about eight inches long wrapped with cloth which, according to Pao Kao, if placed on a wound would make it disappear. The wounded Chao Fa returned to the rear in disbelief. Why had they been wounded? Yong Joua said it was the fault of the Lao Teung. They had worshiped wrong. And the flag had been moved against the priest's instructions. Once it had been moved, it could no longer protect the soldiers."

Yang Soua watched the wounded go to Pao Kao for treatment. "He took out his 'magic sign' and laid it on their wounds. Nothing happened. The wounds continued to bleed. The men were in great pain. The soldiers became very angry. After this incident, many people lost belief in the Chao Fa and split from them. Many went into the jungle to hide. After that we rarely fought together."

Soon after the Muang Cha debacle, Captain Her Pao Kao and some associates moved to Nan Province in northern Thailand, where they lived under the protection of a faction in the Thai military. The Yang-led resistance fighters split into small groups to make it easier to hide and to find food in the jungle. Yang Soua and his brother, their immediate families, and some other fighters and their families—a group of 360 people—moved deep into the jungle.

Farther north in Laos, in dreaded Sop Hoa Internment Camp 1, the king, Savang Vatthana, his wife, the crown prince, and other high-ranking Lao suffered. A former Royal Lao Army lieutenant, himself a prisoner detailed to cook the 100 grams of rice per day allotted the high-ranking prisoners and to bury the dead, escaped to tell a sordid tale. "The 54 prisoners were held in complete darkness in three buildings. One liter of water per person per day was allowed for both drinking and bathing. Each building had one chamber pot for all to use. Prisoners fought to take out the pots because it was the only sunlight they got. The camp was equipped with an interrogator and 24 soldiers armed with AK-47s and grenades."[11]

As the Kaysone regime squeezed life from all traditional vestiges of Lao culture and increased its vengeance against the Hmong, Colonel Billy prepared to leave the area permanently. He had resigned after a quarter century of work with the Agency. He returned to Texas to be near his mother. He did not contact General Vang Pao in Montana.

Vang Kai, who had survived the "smoke" attack during the ambush of the enemy convoy in early 1976, watched repeated aerial attacks using unknown agents near Ta Vieng, the place where Colonel Billy and Vang Pao had met for the first time nearly twenty years before. "Between November 1977 and January 1978, west of Ta Vieng, I often saw aircraft dropping the poisons. The first time it was dropped by a plane that looked like a C-130, but it was a Soviet plane. Along with it was a Raven spotter plane, left behind by the Americans. Two planes always flew together, so there was no way to know which one was dropping the gas. This medicine that they dropped killed all the vegetables, plants, hogs, chickens. If dropped in the river those who drank the water from the river had red diarrhea. In about two hours, the person who drinks the water will die.[12]

"Sometimes it would take 10 to 15 days to die. If we were lucky to have opium, maybe we could survive. For those who had red diarrhea, they would die if they didn't get some opium. After smoking opium for four or five days, it would sometimes slow down the red diarrhea. [Opium had always been used by the Hmong to curtail internal bleeding and diarrhea.] At that time many Hmong did not have opium because General Vang Pao didn't want us to grow it. He was very strong on this point. There was also a white squash we ate that slowed down the red diarrhea.

"Sometimes big planes dropped something that sounded like rain. The chickens, hearing the raindrops fall, jumped up to catch them. When they caught the poison, they run around like crazy and then died. At night when we heard airplanes, we ran into the forest to hide in the caves. In the morning, we would see the poisons like dust on the plants. If the planes came at night, the people didn't always know that the water was poisoned. They would drink it, get sick, and die. The gasses or rains or smoke all seemed to be different. Sometimes it destroyed all the food. If we didn't eat anything we might live for awhile, but we were too weak to fight. If we ate and drank, we got so sick and so skinny that we would die also. Either way, we were not able to fight and we would die.''

It took two years for the enemy to capture Vang Moua, a survivor of the NVA raid on the hi-tech installation at Phou Pha Thi who later worked as a Forward Air Guide. "I was captured in the fall of 1977 when the Vietnamese came to my village asking about the Chao Fa. I didn't know anything about them, but they took me and three other men to Ban Sorn, old Lima Site 272, for interrogation. At Ban Sorn they accused me of being a FAG for the Americans. They said, 'You are a Forward Air Guide, the number one man for the Americans on the Plaine des Jarres. You caused us much trouble.'[13]

"I refused to acknowledge my relationship with the Americans. I also told the Vietnamese interrogators that I was too young to be a leader among the Hmong people; I was not a number one man."

Convinced that he was lying, the Vietnamese sent him to Vang Vieng for a second interrogation. "At Vang Vieng, they bound me with chains. A Lao and a Vietnamese, who spoke Lao, interrogated me. I said nothing. They became very angry and decided to punish me. On December 10, 1977, they put me, with my hands chained, in a metal filing cabinet, measuring about two meters by two meters with three small holes for air. The heat was terrible and breathing almost impossible. Day after day, they kept me like this, demanding to know about the Americans. I denied I knew anything about the Americans. Soon my mind was confused. Then I couldn't talk. I had trouble standing. Still they kept me in the cabinet. My stool was in the cabinet too. Once a day they fed me rice gruel. Then I could no longer stand at all."

Thousands of refugees had fled to Thailand to report torture, disappearances, poisons, rape, and maiming to UNHCR personnel and to American and European refugee workers. Yet their reports were not brought to the attention of the world.

In 1977, under the Carter presidency, the Department of State's annual *Country Reports on Human Rights Practices*, 426 pages long, did not list the country of Laos.

26.

The Giant Slays Sin Sai's Soldiers

Since 1975 the communists killed us in so many ways, but because we have low knowledge we can't make others understand.

—Fang Xe Neng, village defense volunteer in Laos with no rank, who said he was "only the population," yet the communists came after him. California, March 1985

Their increasingly successful attacks against Hmong villages and enclaves and the relentless search for former Vang Pao soldiers whipped the communists into a frenzy for a "final solution." As the enemy net tightened in the interior mountains, more and more Hmong families, defenseless against the superior communist forces and their poisons from the sky, sought sanctuary on Phou Bia, the highest mountain in Laos.

During the American time, the skies around Phou Bia had been active with planes flying between the various Lima Sites around it. This mountain massif, reaching almost 10,000 feet, crested into clouds and fog south of the Plaine des Jarres. Only rarely were its top peaks free of these shrouds. Hmong had never lived high on Phou Bia because it was too cold and there was no water. They considered it inhospitable and generally avoided it, though some inhabited its lower reaches. Although they did not know this mountain well, they reasoned that the Vietnamese would not follow and they would be safe. Besides, Chao Fa chiefs lived there.

On November 22, 1978, enemy forces attacked Lo Cheng's area. In the heavy fighting, his family and others ran to hide in the jungle. There, many women and children were captured and taken away. Outnumbered and outgunned, Lo Cheng and several unit leaders fled, heading for

Phou Bia and Chao Fa leader Yong Joua.[1] By now, tens of thousands of Hmong were in hiding on the slopes of Phou Bia. On the run for years, they had long ago exhausted food supplies. Now, they were eating leaves, bugs, lizards, mice, buds, and bark and desperately digging holes, hoping groundwater would seep in.

Vang Kai and his family came to the Phou Bia area to escape the wrath of the enemy. One of only about 500 men in his area who had a weapon, he carried an M-16, with the last of his ammunition strapped to his body. His group's meager arsenal consisted of several M-79 mortars, a few M-16s, and old carbines. Some men had only crossbows and clubs with which to protect their families. The Hmong were virtually defenseless against the well-supplied Vietnamese artillery, air force, ground troops, and poisons.[2]

During the first week of December, Hmong scouts reported between 6,000 and 7,000 enemy in the area. With the enemy so close, fires for cooking grass or a snared bird or for warming the weary and cold during the near-freezing nights were forbidden. Such life-giving fires only betrayed. Weak and ill from lack of food and medicine, dirty and in tatters, these frightened people, exhausted from years of unrelenting pursuit by the enemy, dug holes and constructed branch and leaf lean-tos to hide from the Goliathan forces.

In early December 1978, communist artillery—85s, 105s, 155s, and 130s—slammed into the jungle, ripping up trees, knocking down jungle protection, exposing Hmong to Vietnamese and Lao gunners and to the sky. Enemy pilots, flying abandoned U.S. spotter planes, attacked with conventional weapons and with poison bombs, darts, and nails. In the ceaseless barrage, Hmong dug deeper for protection. Vang Kai, his brother, and their families shared the same hole. "We were trapped like animals. We dared to come out of the holes only at night to search for leaves and wild plants to feed the children. If we went out in the daylight, the Vietnamese soldiers killed us. If we had a fire, they would see it and kill us. There was no water, no food, no fires."

Day after day, night after night the enemy with its massive artillery and air power bombed, strafed, and pounded the slopes of Phou Bia. Vang Kai knew they were doomed. "There was no way off Phou Bia. There was no way we could survive the communist bombardment. The forest around us was broken and burned. No food. No water. Children dying from starvation. Dead bodies everywhere. Holes with dead Hmong and live Hmong. Still we fought back. There was no choice; we had no place to run."

Two days before Christmas and two days before Vietnam's invasion of Cambodia, the final push came. Vang Kai thought death was near. "December 23, 1978, the attack was so intense that every Hmong knew he would die this day if he did not get away from the attack. Men, women, and children crawled from their holes, trying to run away, to hide somewhere, anywhere, from the fighting. The Vietnamese soldiers chased them. Hmong fought back in hand-to-hand combat with knives, crossbows, and clubs."

Vang Kai shouted to his relatives to run for it. Clutching his gun, he bent over and ran through a communist barrage, trying to reach cover in the forest. Women and children ran behind those with weapons. When a man stopped to shoot at the pursuing enemy, those behind him crouched as he fired. Some shot at the attacking aircraft with crossbows before being mowed down.

Vang Kai, scrambling, clawing, lunging deeper into the forest, found some cover. When he stopped, there were 14 people following him: another man, seven women, one of whom was his wife, with their six children, including a one year-old daughter. "There were only two men in my group. I had an M-16; he had a carbine. We each had less than 30 bullets to protect all these people. My brother was lost. We were separated in the confusion. Vietnamese soldiers were all around us, looking for those who had escaped. The enemy hunted us like animals. A child could not cry. If it cried, we would all be killed. If we had opium we must give it to the babies and children to keep them from crying."

Vang Kai's group watched for enemy soldiers. "When we saw them we hid, hoping they wouldn't find us. For seven days we hid, moving slowly and silently, trying to find a way to get through the Vietnamese." On the seventh day, Vang Kai found his brother and four young men separated from their families. "Now there were 20 of us. We were starving. No food. We knew we had to find a way off Phou Bia, but it seemed impossible. The Vietnamese were everywhere. We were so weak. We knew that we must get into land we knew or we would all die. We hid and ran, hid and ran, making our way down the mountain. Finally we got off the mountain and hid in the forest about five miles south of Phou Bia for three months. There were Vietnamese here, too, but we knew the territory, where to hide, and where the villages were. We ate wild fruit, roots, and leaves. Still there was no rice, no fire, no safety. My baby daughter died of starvation."

During this "final solution," the Vietnamese and Pathet Lao attacked all Hmong encampments, pulverizing them. On foot, the enemy pursued those who had escaped. A Pathet Lao defector later told General Vang Pao that on Phou Bia alone the poisons had killed 50,000; another 45,000 had been shot, died of starvation, or tortured to death. The twentieth-century soldiers of Sin Sai, defeated by the giant, now lived in the jungle like animals, hunted, trapped, and poisoned. Few survivors of Phou Bia remember seeing any Chao Fa leaders during the heavy fighting. Some did recall that they had received word that Chao Fa leaders waited at the top in the clouds. Later, survivors wondered if they had been betrayed—led to this mountain to be trapped and slaughtered.

Lo Cheng and his comrades reached Phou Bia after the big battle: "On the first step of Phou Bia there were some Chao Fa and their families. On the second level about mid-way up, everything was lost. The Vietnamese had destroyed the Chao Fa temple and the houses of Yong Joua and his assistants. This was the first time that I met Yong Joua. He was a big man. He had 40 to 50 men with him. We told him that we had come to ask about the future. We told him that the magical power had transferred. The Pathet Lao and Vietnamese had destroyed all our crops. We had no food, no ammunition. What should we do? Yong Joua said he could not provide anything. We asked him how we were going to get the people off Phou Bia with so many NVA everywhere? We had to have a final answer. Yong Joua gave us his final answer: 'Each man for himself.'"

The power had indeed transferred. Lo Cheng and his comrades discussed how to survive. Some decided to take their groups to Thailand. Some decided to surrender, thinking they could learn the locations of their captured families. Lo Cheng decided not to surrender, but to hide in the jungle and try to locate his wife and children. While Lo Cheng searched for his family, Yong Joua, the Chao Fa high priest, escaped Phou Bia in a group of 30. They were attacked at Muang Om and everyone was killed but Yong Joua and his brother. The magical Chao Fa power had vanished.

A Hmong who had fought with the French at Dien Bien Phu and later with the Americans was not on Phou Bia during the carnage. The aerial poisoning in his village on the Nam Sen River had killed most of the villagers. He took the 60 survivors to a cave near Muang Om at the base of Phou Bia. "We lived on three ears of corn a day and water that trickled through the walls of the cave. After five months, there was nothing to eat. At night, I went outside to dig the roots with my hoe, but roots give little life. Anyone who was pregnant must lose the baby. Little children cannot have life for mothers have no milk. We know that if we stay in the cave without food we must all die. I am so weak from starvation, I am barely able to walk and must use a stick to stand. So we leave the cave. For two more months we try to hide in the jungle to find food. But there are only roots. Then there are no more roots. We have dug up everything. For those who still survive, we know that we must join the communists to live.[3]

"We walk on a road to give ourselves up. We are captured and taken to a place called Nam Phong where there are many prisoners. The Pathet Lao and Vietnamese tell us, 'If you are Chao Fa, we have no food for you.' Then they say, 'If you promise not to go back to Chao Fa or to foreign country, maybe we can feed you.' At first, they only feed a bit of cassava root to the younger ones. No food for the older people. Later, when we promised as they ask, they give us a little cooked cassava. It was the first cooked food I had eaten in months and it was the best food I've ever eaten."

Their captors used these new prisoners like animals, making them pull ploughs while Lao and Vietnamese soldiers kicked them and beat them with guns, shouting at them to hurry. They were taken in groups to the fields to work for five days and five nights continuously and then replaced with other prisoners who worked for five days and five nights. Their only food was cassava root which the prisoners brought to the fields. During his six months in this camp, this man saw six Hmong die of starvation and overwork.

One day, his daughter overheard guards gossiping that their superiors had learned the identity of her father and that plans were being made to "take care of him" the next morning. She got word to her father. He passed the word to escape. Since his group had dutifully obeyed, the guards did not always watch them closely. As soon as darkness came, one by one, they disappeared into the night to meet at a location chosen long ago if escape became possible. Even though they were emaciated and weak, they walked six nights and three days to reach the banks of the Mekong. When they arrived, he looked at those around him. "Of the 60 people I took with me to the cave, only 17 still had life."

At Vang Vieng, Vang Moua had miraculously survived the metal cabinet. "After two months and six days, the communists took me out and put me in a room with 89 other prisoners—three Hmong, ten Kmhmu, and the rest Lao—who helped me recover. Once I learned to stand again—about March 1978—they used me as a slave. To stay alive, I dutifully obeyed the camp soldiers. Laboring all day on only a few grams of rice with vegetable water, I built roads and houses, cleared land, and cut trees that were shipped to Vietnam."[4]

In Seminar Camp 1, the royal family, on starvation rations, with no sunlight and no medical attention, had perished. According to documentation gathered by Prince Sisouk na Champassak, Crown Prince Vongsavang died on February 5, 1978, King Savang Vatthana on June 13, 1978. Thirty-nine other political prisoners had already died from starvation, lack of fresh air and sunlight, and the deplorable hygienic conditions. On September 4, 1978, the surviving 13 prisoners were moved to Seminar Camp 2 at Houei Bao in Houa Phan (formerly Sam Neua) Province. Queen Khamphoui reportedly died shortly thereafter, from the same deprivations as those suffered by her husband, son, and the other 39 prisoners.[5]

These people, some of whom had been feted by President Kennedy and his administration during a royal visit to the U.S. during February 1963 and had later dined with President Johnson at the White House and drunk to his toasts, went to their deaths in great suffering. Their disappearance in 1976 brought no protests from the United States or any other country or from any human rights group. Their deaths in 1978 in concentration camps went unprotested, even unnoticed. Much to the surprise and chagrin of most Lao in exile, Princess Margaret of England paid a royal visit to the Kaysone regime in 1987, sponsored by Save the Children, a U.S. organization based in Connecticut. Did she know that this regime had snuffed out the lives of the Lao royal family?

Lo Xa had fought with the French Army against the Viet Minh following World War II. During the Vietnam War, he served in the Royal Lao Army as a supply captain in Military Region II. In 1975, he was "arrested" by the communists and imprisoned in a seminar camp. In 1978, his forced-labor battalion was working near the governor's office at Phong Savan when the Pathet Lao soldiers brought a Hmong in his mid-20s to the governor. Lo Xa learned from overhearing his guards that the new prisoner had been captured on Phou Bia and that he was a Vang, but he never learned his first name. "The Pathet Lao decided to punish this young man at the governor's office near where my construction battalion was working. When I first noticed him, he had already been beaten. They tied him in a sitting position in the hot sun with his legs tied to a log and his hands and body tied to a pole behind him. Vongsit, chief of the Pathet Lao soldiers, authorized his men to begin the torture. One soldier began chiseling 'meat' from the man's right thigh. He screamed and cried for the Pathet Lao to kill him. Over and over, he screamed: 'Please, kill me!' The soldiers answered: 'We will let you die slowly.' After the soldier had chiseled out several ounces of 'meat' from his right thigh, another soldier cooked it in a nearby fire. Then the guards kicked and beat the Hmong man forcing him to eat his own cooked flesh.[6]

"Later that same day, the Pathet Lao cut several more ounces of 'meat' from his right thigh, cooked it, and forced him to eat it. The Hmong man screamed and pleaded to be shot. The answer was the same as in the morning: 'We will let you die slowly.'

"All of us doing construction could see what they were doing to this man. Our guards told us: 'If you people want to be our enemy, then this is the example. This will happen to you.' As prisoners we could say nothing. We were not allowed to talk. I knew that if I paid too much attention, then I would probably be next. I watched when I could and I remembered."

For the next three days, the soldiers, twice a day, cut flesh from the man's body—first his right thigh, next his right calf, then his left thigh, and then his left calf. "After the second time they cut his flesh out to cook it, he no longer cried or screamed. He was often unconscious so they threw water on him to wake him up. They kicked and beat him until he ate his own flesh. On the fourth day when they cut into his left calf, the young Hmong man died. We prisoners could not talk about what we saw, but as I watched the young man die, I thought to myself: 'He died as a hero with lots of dignity.'"*

At Seminar Camp 6, Governor Khamphouei was hitched to a plough. "By now we were so weak from starvation that it took 25 prisoners on each rope to have the strength to plough."[7]

By the end of 1978, there were scores of seminar, forced labor, camps in the Lao Gulag. These are not to be confused with "re-education" camps where prostitutes, criminals, draft dodgers, drifters, and sometimes students and others labeled social misfits were indoctrinated in the ways of the new society. One re-education camp on the Nam Ngum Reservoir became a showcase camp to which Western journalists were invited.

To disguise its slave-labor program, the Kaysone government initiated payment of prisoners at some camps. In Governor Khamphouei's camp, it worked this way: "The Pathet Lao gave the prisoners 100 *kip* a month. This was good propaganda. By giving us some money, the Kaysone gov-

---

*In October 1983, Lo Xa, bound with ropes, was shot by two guards and left for dead. Although gravely wounded, he survived and eventually escaped from the LPDR. He arrived in the U.S. in 1988.

ernment could say that we were not slave laborers because we were paid for our work. The only place the *kip* was accepted was at the Pathet Lao 'store' for prisoners. Under the communist system, the local population bartered for its needs, so the *kip* was considered useless. At the store for prisoners, we found little to buy. Sometimes there would be small tins of meat or fish. With my 100 *kip*, I could buy only three small tins. Sometimes, the government store had only sugar or cigarettes."

During 1978, prisoners at Seminar Camp 6 were shown a film of American pilots held in captivity somewhere in Laos. Governor Khamphouei watched Americans kept in caves coming out to get sunlight and smoke cigarettes. The camera focused closely on each man's face; each face was very sad. The American prisoners, who were extremely gaunt, wore Western pants and shirts with their hair shoulder length. Khamphouei listened carefully to the narrator say: "The American pilots regretted their actions in bombing Laos, Cambodia, and Vietnam. They didn't like to make these bombings but they followed the instructions of their commander. Now they are glad for very soon they will be Marxists like us." The narrator also proclaimed that every prisoner who could go along with the Soviet doctrine was allowed to have a Vietnamese wife and some liberty. There was no indication of where or when the film was made. The governor thought he recognized the location as somewhere in Khammouane Province. From the narration, he concluded that it might have been produced after the 1973 peace treaty.

Watching this film and listening to other propaganda, Khamphouei concluded that the communists intended to use American POWs. "In my opinion, it was a political necessity for them to keep American prisoners of war. If they wanted to negotiate something with the United States in the future, they needed American prisoners." The governor was correct. The more than 500 Americans missing in action in Laos became big bargaining chips for Kaysone's government and for his "sponsors" in Hanoi.

Treks to find freedom took enormous physical and psychological effort. Sometimes an escape group numbered in the hundreds. Sometimes it was only a few families, or one family. Sometimes the group was composed of strangers bonded together by fear and a desire to survive. Skeletons carried skeletons. With one baby strapped to their backs, one to their breasts, and holding onto one or two other children, men and women struggled on steep mountains. The old, the sick, and the wounded often had to be abandoned so others could live. Relatives and friends wept at parting, but the trek continued. Sometimes abandoned people were found by those who were stronger and able to carry them along with their group. One man found an abandoned, cadaverous child and kept her alive for almost two years while he and his family were running and hiding from the enemy. For weeks and months—for some it was years—these groups moved through the rugged terrain, eating roots and leaves, hiding from enemy patrols and trying to move south and west to the Mekong River.

In power for four years, the communists, not satisfied with their slaughter of Hmong on Phou Bia, continued their maniacal determination to eliminate all "Meo henchmen of the American imperialists."

In February 1979, Vang Ying Pao was captured near Ban Sorn and driven by a Vietnamese to the seminar camp at Long Chieng. There guards told him they wanted to eliminate his brain by washing it in the jail. He immediately decided to escape. Before he did, he witnessed atrocities. "I saw six Hmong prisoners, former officers of Vang Pao, who were in the 'high' category of prisoners. These men had their hands nailed to 11″ x 14″ boards—two nails for each hand; one nail driven through the third finger; the other nail driven through the back of the hand. The guards put small amounts of rice—the only food given them—on the backs of their hands. As the starving men licked the grains of rice from their hands, their captors watched and laughed."[8]

After the slaughter on Phou Bia, a small group of Hmong, hiding in the high jungle, were digging graves to bury two women and a child, recently killed by the communists, when they heard gunfire nearby. They took cover. One grave digger remembered that day. "When we heard the gunfire, everyone hid. We waited many hours, but no more firing. Late in the afternoon, we decided to investigate. We moved silently, heading in the direction of the shooting. We found two women. They were pretty and young—not yet 30. They were naked, tied to trees. From the dirt and bruises on their lower bodies we could see they had been raped. Each woman had a small baby tied to her back with Hmong cloth. Each woman was dead with a bayonet wound through her breast and into the body of her baby on her back."[9]

One night late in March 1979, three months after fleeing Phou Bia, Vang Kai and his wife, equipped only with a gun and a compass, slipped through the Vietnamese net. Their plan was to always follow the compass south. Often, enemy soldiers passed dangerously close. After walking 13 days and almost every night, they reached the Mekong. Neither could swim. They quickly made a small bamboo raft which they clung to and kicked across the river. Thai villagers forced them to turn over all valuables. They only had 10 old French silver coins. Vang Kai begged them not to take their coins, explaining they would have nothing left. The Thais took the silver coins anyway and led them to the local police station, where they were scolded for leaving Laos.

In Thailand, Vang Kai learned that his two sisters lost on Phou Bia had been captured by the Vietnamese. They were never heard from again. His father had been captured by the Vietnamese near Nong Het in 1960 and never seen again. Now the Vietnamese had his sisters. Were they dead? In an internment camp? He never found out.

In fear that the enemy might spot their brightly colored embroidered sashes, women and girls threw them away. No one had shoes. Everyone was in tatters. When crossing a road or nearing an enemy village those with opium mixed small quantities of it with water and gave it to all children. One crying child could alert the enemy and cause all to die. In one group a five-month-old baby boy continued to cry after a dose of opium, so his father gave him another. He had no choice, because the enemy was so near. The baby died in three days. His father dug a hole, piled dirt on top of his baby boy, and walked on.

Throughout the highlands north of the Mekong River, Hmong—in rags with bleeding feet, cadaverous bodies, dying children, and pushed to the limits of human endurance—reached for yet another step—and another step—to escape the holocaust in the hills. Driven to seek sanctuary from the genocide, they surprised their pursuers by their incredible endurance and determination to survive to tell about the horrors in their homelands.

Hmong who reached Thailand repeatedly told Thai, American, and UNHCR officials and refugee workers from several countries about the atrocities and about the poisons that came in red, blue-green, white, gray, black, and yellow, delivered by aircraft, rockets, mortars, and artillery as smoke, dust, rain, and spray. Victims told of blood spurting from all their orifices, of extensive vomiting and diarrhea, often with blood, of chest pains and difficulty breathing, hearing, and seeing. Sometimes they reported that everything looked yellow. They reported sore throats, fevers, coughing up blood, weakness, loss of memory, slowness in thinking. Symptoms differed greatly depending on agent proximity, age and health of the victim, and the kind of agent used. It was said that if victims survived the attack, they often became unable to digest food and starved to death.

Few seemed interested in these reports. For almost four years Hmong had reported the extraordinary brutality of the Lao People's Democratic

Republic and the use of poisons targeted indiscriminately against the Hmong. An investigation by the New York-based Lawyers Committee for Human Rights on the Hmong situation in Laos concluded that between 1975 and 1980, the destruction of the Hmong population of Laos reached staggering proportions. From an estimated population of 350,000 to 400,000 some 100,000 Hmong perished and an equal number fled across the Mekong.*

Yet the U.S. Department of State's annual human rights report submitted to Congress did not mention Laos in 1976 or in 1977 and it failed again in 1978 to mention Laos.

---

*"Forced back and Forgotten: The Human Rights of Laotian Asylum Seekers in Thailand," Lawyers Committee for Human Rights (New York, 1989), p. 8.

Part Seven

A New
Military
Age

27.

"A Conspiracy of Silence"

Laos, which has known forgotten wars which were never its own, silent confrontation, open wounds, and muffled cries, is today forgotten by everyone and sacrificed on the altar of detente, to the rule of the mightiest, far from bothersome witnesses. A kind of conspiracy of silence; a kind of suspect complicity of international opinion preoccupied by other tragedies, concerned with other worries, seems to be plaguing this forgotten, small people, which the storm pushes further into the background.

—Prince Sisouk na Champassak, leader of the United Lao National Liberation Front, in a White Paper on the situation in Laos, 1981

Prince Sisouk na Champassak, former Lao diplomat and minister of defense, who had been forced from Laos just before the communists took over, had since 1976 quietly and diplomatically sought to enlist the support of the noncommunist world—particularly the Carter administration—to take a strong public position against the atrocities in Laos. His attempts had failed totally. By late 1979, frustrated and angry, he accused the world of "a conspiracy of silence."

He talked about the sinister curtain of communism that had dropped over the Mekong River and transformed Laos into the new frontier of the Vietnamese empire. Lao minerals, teak forests, and people were taken to Vietnam to be used for the benefit of Vietnamese overlords. The areas bordering Vietnam were populated not only by Vietnamese soldiers but by tens of thousands of Vietnamese civilians, or "brothers" as the "new settlers" from the "brother" country were called.[1]

Some 60,000 Vietnamese soldiers propped up the Kaysone regime, which had lost much of its appeal, with its 30,000 indigenous forces.

Many flag-waving, slogan-shouting Pathet Lao supporters of the early euphoric days had fled. By 1981, over 200,000 people, both ethnic Lao and minorities, had left. More would have escaped, but the Mekong River had become a Berlin Wall guarded by Vietnamese and Lao patrols, killing those trying to flee.

* * *

Iowa Congressman Jim Leach, who had served as a State Department Foreign Service Officer on the 1972 U.S. Biological and Toxin Weapons Convention negotiating team in Geneva, now sat on the House Intelligence Committee. In January 1979, Leach had quietly traveled to refugee camps in northern Thailand to check on conditions. There, refugees mentioned the "gassing" in Laos. Upon his return, Leach requested the State Department to launch a thorough investigation into the use of lethal agents.

On April 3, 1979, a massive explosion erupted in a secret installation at Sverdlovsk in the Ural Mountains in the Soviet Union. Perhaps as many as 1,000 died from what were believed to be lethal anthrax spores released into the air at the time of the explosion. The Soviets denied there had been a biological warfare factory accident, insisting that the deaths were caused by eating tainted meat. The 1972 convention barring biological and toxin weapons had no verification apparatus, and the Soviets refused to consent to an international investigation. Soviet emigrés reported that Soviet research and development of biological weapons had not ceased with the signing of the 1972 Biological and Toxin Weapons Convention; they pointed to a biological plant housed inside Military Compound 19 at Sverdlovsk. U.S. satellite reconnaissance showed a heavily guarded facility with the type of ventilation equipment associated with biological weapons facilities.

Leach, a supporter of arms control who had been involved in efforts to eliminate biological and toxin agents from all military arsenals, was alarmed about the explosion, satellite information, and refugee reports that Soviet client regimes were using banned toxin weapons to kill their political enemies.

U.S. military experts concluded that neither Hanoi nor Vientiane was capable of producing the lethal agents being used in Laos. The Soviet Union, however, possessed that ability. The 1972 treaty prohibited the transfer of biological and toxin weapons to another country. If these were Soviet agents, then the Soviets had violated the treaty in several ways: production, stockpiling, and transferring of biological and toxin agents.

Leach urged the Carter administration to investigate. "I personally interviewed these refugees. I read State Department and Defense Department reports which are so numerous and so persuasive that they cannot be denied. No one in the White House ever saw a person being gassed in Auschwitz, but we know it occurred. I think this Administration has a moral responsibility to tell the people of the world what is happening."[2]

Instead of heeding his call, the Carter men focused on the President's upcoming June meeting in Vienna with Soviet Prime Minister Leonid Brezhnev. Here Carter and Brezhnev would sign the SALT II Treaty, which Carter considered a cornerstone of his presidency. While Carter believed he could obtain Soviet signature, he worried about congressional ratification. Congressional critics pointed out problems with verification. The continuing reports about use of lethal agents by the Soviet client regime in Laos further threatened congressional approval. If events in Laos received the mass publicity that SALT II was receiving, reasonable people must assume that Americans would question Soviet intent to abide by any arms agreement. Some speculated that the gassing reports and their larger import were consciously ignored by Carter's men.

*   *   *

Yang Nhia, a stern-looking former Vang Pao soldier, was captured in November 1978 along with about 1,200 Hmong, including women and children. Four months later, he and others became human guinea pigs. "On March 25, 1979, two MiG jets flew low over our prison camp and sprayed us with white rain. One hundred people died immediately. The rest of us had diarrhea for two days, then fever: we cannot walk nor raise our arms. Many more people die."[3]

In May 1979, Yang Nhia was given an injection. "It was the color of water. I immediately became dizzy and could not breathe. Blood spurted from my nose and I fell to the ground unconscious. A relative blew opium smoke over me for several hours and finally the bleeding stopped. In 12 hours, I could see again. The next day I could walk. The following day four new medics came. This time they had injections and pills for 40 gassing victims. Some medics gave my people injections and green pills, others got injections and white pills. Nothing happened for 12 hours; then they had trouble seeing, can't speak and black out. Fifteen died, five adults and 10 children; the rest are sick for a long time. The medics wrote reports of these people. Our chief asked them about the medicines. They say they know nothing, only that the government sent the medicines and that they had come from another country. They wouldn't tell us which country."

In April 1979, a cadaverous-looking man, with hair to his waist, crossed the Mekong into Thailand. Lo Cheng had not found his family. He had temporarily abandoned his search in fear that he might be killed or die of starvation if he stayed longer in Laos.

At Ban Vinai, Lo Cheng learned from someone who had escaped a Phong Savan concentration camp that his wife and children were there. That fall, after he regained some strength, he and 32 other men, all looking for lost relatives, returned to Laos. They crossed the Mekong together, then split up. Some walked toward Moung Om. He and seven others headed for Phong Savan. "We walked for 25 days before we could see the Phong Savan airstrip. We learned from Hmong in the jungle that civilian prisoners were held in special villages. Each day the villagers had to work in the fields or in the jungle. It took some time to find the village where they kept my family."[4]

One day in November, he got a message to his wife that he was alive and to come to the jungle the next morning with all the children. She took their four small children and left the prison village to go to the field as usual. When she saw her husband was indeed alive, she cried silently for a few minutes. Then they started walking, heading for the Mekong. "On November 27, 1979—a year after my wife and children had been captured—my men and I crossed the Mekong again. This time with my family."

*   *   *

That same fall, at the instigation of Gary B. Crocker of the State Department's Bureau of Intelligence and Research (INR), the U.S. Army Surgeon General sent a team to Thailand to investigate the allegations of the use of lethal agents in Laos. This team, headed by Colonel Charles W. Lewis, a doctor in the U.S. Army Medical Corps, concluded after interviewing 43 Hmong survivors—40 men, two women, and a 12-year-old girl—that "chemical agents have been used against the Hmong and reported effects of these agents suggest the use of a nerve agent, a riot control agent, and an unidentified combination or compound."[5]

Colonel Lewis' report recommended that a medical team be established on a stand-by basis to be able to react quickly to future CBW attack allegations, interviewing, examining, and rapidly transporting for analysis blood, tissue, or other specimens from reported victims. He urged that every effort be made to identify the chemical agents used and to develop appropriate countermeasures and antidotes.[6]

On December 19, Congressman Leach again criticized the Carter administration. "Unfortunately, the Administration displayed surprising
reluctance to investigate systematically the refugee reports and to apply
any kind of historical perspective to the issue itself. It refused publicly to
confirm that chemical weapons were indeed being used by the Vietnamese and Laotian communist forces, despite the widespread refugee reports and the corroboratory intelligence information available at the
time. I am convinced that far too low a priority has been given to the
issue of chemical weapons. Massive public attention has been accorded
SALT and the control of nuclear weapons, but chemical weapons can be
just as lethal. Unlike nuclear weapons, however, chemical weapons are
being used today."[7]

Leach prophesied, "If Vietnam and its principal weapons supplier—
the Soviet Union—can use lethal chemicals in Indochina with impunity,
the list of other states which may use poison gas will almost certainly
grow." He also warned the administration that Soviet forces included
some 100,000 men trained extensively in chemical weaponry. The
United States, by contrast, had perhaps 2,000 and a military doctrine
reflecting a substantially lower tolerance for chemical weapons usage.

By now, U.S. intelligence had evidence of Soviet direct involvement in
chemical warfare activities in Laos. An estimated 500-man Soviet team
comprised of men from General V. K. Pikolov's Chemical-Warfare Division and other specialists not only provided advanced training to local
personnel in both conventional and chemical warfare, but provided
maintenance and technical support to their client Vietnamese and Lao
and actually ran the Lao Air Force.[8]

In 1979, the international press reported that independent intelligence sources separately confirmed "hard" intelligence that a seven-
man Soviet team headed by a major from Pikolov's Chemical-Warfare
Division visited the Lao towns of Pakse and Seno to inspect four chemical warehouse installations of Soviet standard design. They were reported to have checked on the stocks and reviewed the success of the
operation.[9]

*　*　*

Once again, it was time for the State Department to issue its annual
report on human rights practices. After four years of eyewitness reports
on the atrocities in Laos against both ethnic Lao and minorities, would
the Carter State Department once again ignore Laos?

This time, State *did* include the Lao People's Democratic Republic

(LPDR). The 1979 reporters concluded in their introductory remarks: "There have been some improvements during the past two years in several aspects of human rights in Laos, though notable shortcomings persist in many areas." On the subject of torture, the State Department concurred with the Kaysone regime's pronouncements: "This year, the Department of State has not had any reports of torture." That was followed by: "Lao Government officials have publicly denied reports of mistreatment of persons in re-education camps." On the subject of treatment of minorities, the State Department concluded: "There is no evidence that the government is seeking to destroy any particular ethnic group, per se, such as the Hmong. . . . the main difference between the Hmong and other resistance groups is that the Hmong have attempted to defend specific tribal areas and there is a traditional ethnic antipathy. . . . Also, they [the Hmong] are heavily armed, requiring conventional military operations to dislodge them from their strongholds." On the subject of the use of lethal agents reported by the refugees, "There have been refugee accounts of attacks using some sort of lethal chemical against the Hmong. The Department of State does not have absolute proof of these charges. However, the results of U.S. Government investigations [Colonel Lewis' team] support the conclusion that some chemical agent or agents were being used in Laos from 1974* to as recently as May 1979."[10]

The State Department had disposed of the subject of chemical warfare in 58 words.

Still displeased with the Carter administration's refusal to deal with the chemical weapons threat, Congressman Leach organized a House hearing on the subject. In April 1980, two House Foreign Affairs Subcommittees held joint hearings. One State Department witness, Assistant Secretary of State Matthew Nimetz, took the position that the U.S. government had no responsibility under international law to determine the validity of the evidence of chemical weapons usage. Leach attacked Nimetz's position, calling it "morally derelict."

The House hearings did little more than show that "sides" would be taken. Evidence presented caused little national or international concern. Terrorism, Iran, and the upcoming presidential election consumed the media and its readers.

---

*It is not clear why the year 1974 was used as the beginning of the deployment of agents. Hmong reported the first use of lethal agents against them in the late summer and fall of 1975.

In 1979, a Lao People's Liberation Army (LPLA) pilot defected to Thailand. This officer explained that beginning in late 1976 it was decided to launch special air strikes against areas of Hmong resistance around Phou Bia. This operation, called "Extinct Destruction Operations," was intended to "wipe out the reactionary Hmong people." Initially, he flew his captured American Bird-Dog spotter plane (L-19) with another pilot and a Lao staff officer on board. "After 2 or 3 weeks, however, Vietnamese staff officers, who spoke excellent Lao, began alternating with Lao officers. . . . A new Vietnamese officer was assigned for each strike mission in the H'Mong areas."[11] The pilot defector carried on his aircraft two kinds of weapons: "close support" rockets (ordinary explosives), and "smoke" rockets. Before missions involving "smoke" rockets, his commander warned the pilots to keep the operation secret and to fly above normal altitudes when firing the rockets to avoid hazard to the air crew.

On these missions, he observed that unlike "close support" rockets, "'smoke' rockets detonated in the air and that some produced white smoke, with a mixture of blue, while others produced a red smoke, with a mixture of yellow." He was also told the "smoke" rockets were to be fired at targets far from Lao and Vietnamese troops "to avoid exposing them to the poison smoke."

After each mission in which chemical warfare rockets were used, the pilot was returned to a "rest house" at Phong Savan where a Lao Army doctor and nurse would examine him. He said that after his missions, especially in 1978, he was particularly well treated by the examining doctor and watched very closely by the nurse. He also reported that "smoke" mission pilots received special privileges, including extra flight pay and free meals at the Phong Savan cafeteria.

He said that during June and August 1976, airborne rocket attacks were launched against Moua Cher Pao's position at Bouam Loung where Hmong continued to honor their pledge never to abandon this site, and confirmed that in 1978, Soviet MiG-21s, armed with poison weapons, were used to attack the Hmong in the Phou Bia area.

Significantly, this pilot-defector's description of "Extinct Destruction Operations" with its use of poisonous "smoke" strikes against the Hmong is corroborated by many Hmong who survived this genocidal communist strategy to "wipe them out."

In Washington, ASEAN (Association of Southeast Asian Nations) ambassadors met with high-ranking State Department officials. Prok Amranand, the Thai ambassador to the U.S., who had taken a personal interest in the events in Laos—particularly in the poisoning of the Hmong—raised the Hmong situation. A senior State Department official, irritated that the issue had come up, dismissed it by rhetorically asking the Thai ambassador: Why are the Hmong complaining? Many of them are in the U.S. as refugees driving new Chevrolets.[12]

While the U.S. was reluctant to acknowledge the use of lethal agents against the Hmong by the Soviet-backed regimes in Hanoi and Vientiane, the Vietnamese government applauded its army's chemical warfare branch by awarding it the Ho Chi Minh medal. According to Hanoi radio monitored in Thailand, in April 1980, Vietnamese General Le Trong Tan told the unit: "Chemical weapons contributed to winning the great victory in the great anti-U.S. salvation resistance struggle."[13]

In early December 1980, the United Nations General Assembly, over Soviet-bloc opposition, adopted a resolution calling for an investigation into the use of chemical warfare in Laos, Cambodia, and Afghanistan. The resolution passed by a vote of 78 to 17 with 36 abstentions. Among those voting against the resolution were Laos, Vietnam, Afghanistan, the Soviet Union, and Cuba. The United States, Japan, nearly all the Western industrialized countries, and more than half of the Third World countries voted for the resolution.

* * *

In June 1980 I was again in Ban Vinai. Some 40,000 refugees swelled the depression in which the camp was situated. While many had been resettled in France, Australia, Canada, and the U.S., the refugee population continued to grow. With so many people, the camp had been divided into eight sections, called centers. Each center had a leader or chief, responsible for all those within his center.

This time when I met with the center chiefs and clan heads, I found them and the camp leadership extremely angry with the Americans and the world. They reported that the poisoning of the Hmong continued and that the camp population included many who were ill from those poisons. "Why can no one believe us?" asked Vang Neng, the current chief of the camp.[14]

That anger resulted in stern determination to get more evidence that their people were being killed by poisons. Hmong in Ban Vinai volunteered for suicide missions, returning to areas under attack to retrieve residue samples. It sometimes took months to reach these areas. The chances of being caught or killed were high. After a sample was collected, they had to avoid enemy soldiers and endure the long, dangerous journey on foot back to the Mekong River. Once at the river, they had to elude both Lao and Thai patrols in order to cross safely.

Chief Vang Neng introduced me to a man who had just come from Laos with current news. Vang Seng Vang, a former intelligence officer with Vang Pao's forces, had come to Thailand seeking help for those trapped inside Laos. In July 1975, his family had been captured and his infant son maimed by the Pathet Lao in a public display. "The soldiers forced everyone to watch—including my wife. They rammed needles into his arms while the child screamed in pain. The soldiers, who had forced everyone to attend, announced that this was the punishment for working with the Americans and for resisting the new society. My son's right arm is permanently crippled."[15]

Vang Seng Vang pulled from his pocket a small, tattered diary and read to me from his entries. "On 15 May 1980, two Soviet helicopters dropped yellow powder on a Hmong village of 200 people at coordinate Tango Foxtrot 9376. Thirty-five people died within seven days and the remaining are very sick. On 20 May 1980, two Soviet helicopters hit Ban Loun, near the 15 May coordinate target, with yellow powder. This village had approximately 250 Hmong. Three died immediately, 43 died soon after the attack and 200 are extremely ill."

He paused and looked up. "Since early 1980, people in my area are so hungry that they eat leaves exposed to the chemicals —715 have died. I dig in the ground for roots and water. But many are too weak to do this." He stared at me, apparently deciding whether or not he should say aloud the thought in his mind. Then he did. "Hmong who have escaped from the Vietnamese tell us that their captors said: 'It is the Americans who drop the chemicals on you because the Americans don't want to feed you anymore. It is the Americans who destroy you; not us.'"

I reflected later that he was probably correct. The Americans were indeed destroying the Hmong. Not by dropping lethal agents on them but by not speaking out, by not being outraged at the brutality. When the Hmong were accused of being too primitive and stupid to report on aircraft or ordnance, why didn't someone stand up and announce that the Hmong knew much about aircraft and munitions because they had been trained by Americans to call in air strikes, to monitor enemy equipment and troop movements, to operate everything from sabotage devices, to artillery, to fighter planes?

In Van Vinai "hospital" I watched 18-year-old Vang Chue struggle to breathe. Suffering from edema, his chest heaving with every breath, in a low, hoarse voice, he explained: "I can't eat, I cough blood, it's difficult to breathe. It's from the poisons."[16] His exposure had been recent, in the latter part of May. Many of his group of 19 had been exposed and were ill. Milton Amayun, a Philippine doctor working in the camp as an employee of World Vision, had been one of the first camp doctors to become interested in his patients' reports on lethal agents. He and I discussed Vang Chue's case. We decided he should be examined immediately by experts in Bangkok and have a biopsy, blood tests, and urinalysis. Vang Chue reluctantly agreed "if it would save other Hmong."

That very evening, Dr. Amayun and I boarded an all-night bus to Bangkok to talk with personnel at the U.S. Embassy, headed by Ambassador Morton I. Abramowitz. Though our urgent concern was not shared by the embassy staff, our visit was not totally in vain. The next month, the State Department issued a "Compendium on the Reports of the Use of Chemical Weapons" and nine months later, a March 1981 "Update" to the compendium, which listed Vang Chue with the following remarks: "Vang Chue has a pulmonary infiltration in the right lower lobe with atelectasis and emphysematous changes in the left lobe. Such findings could possibly be the result of a toxic exposure. This refugee is extremely ill."[17]

In October 1980, my article on the Hmong plight appeared as the lead article in all *Reader's Digest* editions around the world, making a major chink in the "conspiracy of silence." The word was out to millions of people that unidentifiable lethal agents were being used in Laos in violation of two international treaties. Infuriated that America's friends, the Hmong, were being persecuted by the communists with lethal agents and that the U.S. had done nothing to stop it, *Digest* readers wrote complaining letters to their senators and representatives who, not knowing anything or very little about this issue, queried the State Department.

The State Department responded with a letter, called in its lexicon "a prepared piece of language." This letter sought not to address the critical issues in Laos but to rebut the concerns raised in my article and to present the Lao government's position. "The Lao Government has used a combination of persuasion and force to bring the Hmong out of their highland homes to new settlements in the lowlands. The Lao Government argues that the Hmong method of agriculture destroys valuable hardwood forests, Laos' principal natural resource. The Lao also argue that, by bringing the Hmong population to the lowlands, the Government can better limit the production of opium, a principal Hmong crop which supplies the heroin markets of the world through illicit channels. The Lao and Vietnamese military forces dealing with Hmong who refuse to resettle under Lao government control reportedly have used very harsh measures, often against civilians. There have been widespread reports that the Lao and Vietnamese forces are using poison gas, or other toxic chemicals, against the Hmong in some remote areas. By 1978, the United States had enough information to bring the matter to the attention of the government of Laos, which denied the validity of the reports. We received the same response when we asked the Soviet and Vietnamese Governments to look into the reports and end the practice if true."[18]

Did State Department officials believe that the Vietnamese, Lao, or Soviets were going to admit to using "poison gas, or other toxic chemicals" against the Hmong?

State's letter ignored the thousands who had died from exposure to lethal agents or had been killed during the siege of Phou Bia. Instead, State focused on the Lao government's explanation, telling concerned people that the Lao government had to act harshly toward this group that "supplies the heroin markets of the world through illicit channels."

While Hmong had traditionally grown opium poppies and had used opium as a medicine, they had never converted opium into heroin nor marketed it to the world. During colonial times, the French opium monopoly purchased the opium which was channeled into the medicinal market as morphine. After independence, this most lucrative business had belonged to influential Lao and Chinese. With the noncommunist Hmong on the run for their lives since mid-1975, few had been able to plant and harvest any kind of crop. The truth was that under the Kaysone regime, drug trafficking had become a main source of hard currency for communist Laos.

Nowhere in this incredibly naive "prepared piece of language" did it mention that the use of toxins was in violation of the 1972 and 1925 conventions. Nowhere did it mention that the U.S. could not identify the agents. Nowhere did it mention that a new generation of chemical-biological-toxin weapons had been developed and was being field-tested against humans in one of the most inaccessible places in the world. And nowhere did it acknowledge that the Hmong had been the effective and loyal allies of the U.S. for almost fifteen years.

*   *   *

In January 1981, the Reagan administration arrived in Washington. American Hmong believed this new regime would listen and take action. Yet nothing seemed to change. In the spring, Eugene Douglas, a member of Secretary of State Alexander Haig's Policy and Planning staff, prepared a position paper on the use of chemical weapons in Laos for Haig. Months went by. More attacks occurred. The Reagan administration did and said nothing.

With great difficulty and risk, Hmong continued to collect residue samples to bring out for analysis. Some were confiscated by Thais who stripped the Hmong of all possessions when they crossed the river into Thailand.

The Hmong community in the U.S. had become outraged by the State Department's continued issuance of its misleading "prepared piece of language," to answer queries regarding the use of lethal agents against the Hmong. They particularly resented the paragraph implying that they were traffickers of heroin. Hmong leaders urged Vang Pao to write to Secretary of State Haig to complain. In a letter dated March 7, 1981, Vang Pao pointed out that the State Department's letter was "misleading, exaggerated, and inaccurate."

Attempting to set the record straight, Vang Pao wrote: "I, myself, was very active in both the Lao government and military affairs. I also worked closely with the United States Embassy in Vientiane to pass a law prohibiting the cultivation of opium in 1971-72. I assisted the United States government, the Thai government, and the Lao government in an effort to control the flow of opium and other narcotics from Burma through the Golden Triangle into Laos and Thailand. Because of those efforts, the cultivation of opium became regarded disdainfully by our people. . . . "[19]

Vang Pao also reminded Haig of an important historical fact. "The Pathet Lao had threatened to wipe out the Hmong ethnic tribe once they were in power. The threat appeared in the Pathet Lao News Bulletin in May 9, 1975. The Bulletin stated that 'the Hmong are the sole enemies of the Pathet Lao. For a long time, the Pathet Lao have tried to get rid of one ethnic group who all the time is endangering them, and who have fought actively and kept them in exile [in the jungle and caves] for more than twenty years. Therefore, such an ethnic group must be destroyed and all roots must be pulled up.'"

In his four-page letter, Vang Pao asked for congressional investigations to "condemn the Pathet Lao and Vietnamese Communists and the Soviet expansionist actions for using chemicals against our people" and to "determine what kinds of chemicals are being used against the Hmong" so that those living in the U.S. "who are chronically ill from gassing can be treated properly by the medical profession in this country."

Vang Pao's letter to Haig was referred to State's John Holdridge, assistant secretary-designate to its East Asian and Pacific Affairs Bureau. In a one-page answer dated April 29, 1981, Holdridge pointed out what Vang Pao already knew—that the United Nations had voted for an investigation and that Congress had held hearings. In spite of the fact that since 1975 U.S. intelligence had developed extensive, consistent, specific evidence that lethal agents were being used against the Hmong in Laos, Holdridge wrote that investigations so far "have not yet yielded sufficient information to permit us to make a firm determination whether such chemical warfare has been waged."[20]

*   *   *

Tens of thousands of Hmong had been resettled in the U.S. Most were shipped to major industrial inner cities. In the ghettos of St. Paul, Providence, Detroit, and Chicago, some Hmong—frightened, homesick, and suffering from the trauma of war and genocide—were cheated, robbed, and raped. Most were unable to speak English. Many adults could not read or write in any language. Culturally afraid of police authorities, they often did not report crimes against them. They suffered in silence.

Then there was the polygamy problem. In Laos, having multiple wives was customary, even a status symbol. If a man had more than one wife, it usually meant more income—more fields could be farmed, more crops marketed, more livestock tended. During the Vietnam war years, so many males were killed that Hmong took second and third wives to compensate for the lack of men. Traditionally, if a man died, a brother would take his widow as a wife. Life for a Hmong widow was not easy; it was often better to be a second wife than to be alone. For Hmong with multiple wives, however, resettlement in the U.S., where polygamy is illegal, was only possible if they divorced all but one. Many, feeling responsibility for all their wives, could not morally do this. Some in this predicament decided to stay in the camps in Thailand, hoping one day to return to Laos with their families intact. Others, fed up with the wretched life in the camps, did divorce second and third wives so they could resettle in the U.S. In Hmong tradition, the children of any broken union remain with the father or the father's family; in many cases, these men took the children and left their divorced wives—now single women with no children—crying in despair.

Almost all Hmong had lost loved ones in Laos. Some were missing, maybe killed in the fighting around Phou Bia; others had been captured and their fates were unknown; some were known to be in concentration camps. Pleas for help and understanding from those in camps in Thailand and in the United States remained unanswered.

Particularly infuriating was the fact that the U.S. government would not acknowledge the Hmong role and relationship with the Americans during the covert war in Laos. After years of reliance on them for their precise military intelligence gathering ability, the U.S. now dismissed their word on events in Laos. Hmong in Asia, France, and the U.S. were shocked and embittered. This anger was not confined to the Hmong leadership; it permeated all levels of Hmong society. None could understand why their honorable friends, the Americans, with whom they had fought, under whom they had served, and for whom they had suffered so many casualties over so many years would not help them.

Hmong pride was badly damaged. Hmong society values honesty. Now, they found themselves disbelieved and ignored by the U.S. government. It is common for victims of torture and of government-authorized terror and brutality to suffer extraordinary despondency when, after revealing their experiences, they are not believed. This was the case for many Hmong. Genevieve A. Cowgill, founder of Survivors International, which educates people in aiding torture victims, has observed, "Survivors need to be loved and understood and, this is fundamental, they need to be believed. One of the most devastating things is not to be believed."[21] Laughed at by many in the medical community who disbelieved their reports of illnesses attributable to "poisons from skies," some Hmong tried to commit suicide. Some were successful. The Hmong blamed General Vang Pao for not making the Hmong situation known to Americans.

With little fanfare, Vang Pao with most of his family and a few other Hmong families had arrived in Montana in 1976. Before being allowed in the U.S., he was forced to legally rid himself of all but one of his wives. He now worked on an isolated farm in Montana's Bitterroot Valley with many of his children and three Hmong women—two now ex-wives— and his mother, who ruled the household. In this remote, beautiful, and cold valley, Vang Pao and his family had difficulty making a living by farming. Jerry Daniels' mother, brother, and friends had joined to assist the newly arrived Hmong, but Vang Pao soon found the isolation unbearable. He spent more and more time in California, where many Hmong refugees were gravitating. Here he would help found a refugee self-help organization to assist in resettlement of refugees from Laos.

It was in an atmosphere of desperation and frustration that Prince Sisouk na Champassak, whose last act as minister of defense before being forced into exile in 1975 had been to order a planeload of weapons to Long Chieng, and General Vang Pao joined together. These two men— one a suave, handsome Western-educated Lao prince, the other the earthy Hmong general who for a lifetime had fought the communists— assembled other Lao and Hmong leaders from around the world to create the United Lao National Liberation Front (ULNLF), also known as *Neo Hom.* Neo Hom had two major goals: to break the "conspiracy of silence" about Laos by informing the world of the atrocities taking place there and to call for world support for military resistance against the Kaysone regime.

In March 1981, I suggested to General Vang Pao that Hmong leaders should state their case directly to elected officials in Washington. I thought that perhaps if General Vang Pao, the president of Lao Family Community, the California-based nonprofit organization that served many Hmong communities in the U.S., and one of his capable English-speaking assistants could meet with key senators, representatives, and their staffs both sides could benefit.

General Vang Pao liked the idea. I agreed to make appointments with senators and congressmen from states with the largest Hmong refugee populations—California, Colorado, and Minnesota. With considerable effort and assistance from friends, I made appointments with Senators David Durenberger and Rudy Boschwitz and Congressman William Frenzel of Minnesota. I also arranged meetings with Senators S. I. Hayakawa and Alan Cranston and Representatives Henry Waxman of California, Patricia Schroeder from Colorado, and Jim Leach from Iowa.

Joining Vang Pao for this March week in Washington was Vang Xeu, who as a teenager had trained as a paratrooper and later as an intelligence officer, and now served as executive director of Lao Family Community.

Congressman Frenzel organized a meeting with his state's representatives who were cordial and expressed concern about the 10,000 Hmong living in the twin cities of St. Paul and Minneapolis, straining the state's social services. Senator Durenberger did not have time to talk with Vang Pao, but did manage to have his photograph taken with the general. Senator Cranston's staff was cordial, but unaware that thousands of Hmong refugees now lived in California and that most were on welfare. His staff was under the impression that most of the Hmong were in Montana. By this time, Vang Pao also lived in California. Waxman's staff expressed interest in refugee health problems. Schroeder was not in when we arrived for our scheduled meeting. Leach invited Center for Disease

Control doctors to join the meeting in his office so they could hear directly from Hmong about the serious health problems suffered by those who had been poisoned in Laos.

Since Senator Boschwitz sat on the Senate Foreign Relations Committee and had been asked by several of his major contributors to help with Vang Pao's visit to Washington, he arranged to have a joint meeting with California Senator Hayakawa, who had been on the same committee. Staffers from both offices were also present. After a few minutes of introductory talk, Senator Hayakawa, who was seated behind his big desk, got up and shuffled behind a screen and presumably out of the room without saying anything. Soon he returned carrying a large atlas. He opened it and searched. Finally, he turned to us to confess he could not find Laos!

There was an awkward moment of silent disbelief. Then Vang Pao quickly moved behind the desk of this member of the Senate Foreign Relations Committee to show him Laos. There was talk of the use of deadly agents against the Hmong in Laos and the resultant terror and suffering of survivors and of the refugee problems that Hmong faced both in camps in Thailand and in resettlement cities in the U.S. We learned that Hayakawa was planning a trip to Laos—his first—in the near future. We asked that he remember the details provided by the general and Vang Xeu when he made his official visit.

After our meeting in Hayakawa's office, I had several detailed phone conversations with Hayakawa's staff who asked me to assist in formulating issues and specific questions that the senator should raise with the Kaysone government during his trip to Laos regarding the use of lethal agents and human rights issues such as torture, starvation, and killing of Hmong in "seminar" camps. I was bouyed by this interest.

In June, I returned to the refugee camps in Thailand where I learned that the attacks continued. Hmong who had crossed into Thailand in February 1981 reported that between January 6 and 20, 1981, they knew of 20 chemical missions flown by Soviet helicopters, deploying several kinds of agents. They documented chemical flights killing 1,260 Hmong who had surrendered to Pathet Lao authorities and were living under their control.

On April 28, 1981, a Soviet MiG-17 dropped yellow chemicals on Ban Thong Hak, killing 24 Hmong outright, including 11 children. Two weeks later, a Hmong party reached Thailand with samples of residue collected from stones, soil, and leaves. These samples were given to U.S.

authorities on April 23, but did not arrive in the United States for analysis until the second week of May.

* * *

Neo Hom leaders believed that genocide committed by the Khmer Rouge in Cambodia, details of which were now becoming known, would renew interest in the neighboring country of Laos. They prepared an eight-page memorandum explaining the takeover of Laos in 1975 by the Kaysone regime, the use of poisons against the Hmong, seminar camps, human rights violations, and the Vietnamese occupation of Laos. The memorandum appealed to the member states of the United Nations to allow them to present Lao problems in the upcoming International Conference on Cambodia.

ULNLF leaders from Australia and France arrived in New York to join U.S. leaders in anticipation of presenting their case. On July 7, 1981, Chao Outhong Souvanavong, the president of the Council of Regents for the ULNLF, wrote to Kurt Waldheim, secretary general of the U.N., sending copies of the Waldheim letter and the memorandum to all members, asking for time to bring the Lao issue before the member states of the U.N. during the conference on Cambodia. Waldheim and the U.N. ignored his request. In 1981, Cambodia was the issue. Laos, where lives still could have been saved in 1981, remained trapped in the "conspiracy of silence."

To blunt criticism of its detention of thousands of political prisoners in seminar camps, the LPDR campaigned to use Westerners in a counteroffensive to convince the world that by late 1980, seminar camps were closed. In 1991, Khamphanh, a Lao victim of this "conspiracy of silence," spoke out. He had been held in seminar camps for almost fourteen years. "In 1981, my wife heard American professor Dr. [MacAlister] Brown give a lecture in Bangkok. Professor Brown said that he had an interview with the officials in the Lao ministry and they told him that all the seminar camps were closed. Dr. Brown told U.S. officials and U.S. officials believed the Lao government but don't accept the word of the people. This was not true; I was in a seminar camp for another eight years."[22]

U.S. interest in Laos focused on the issue of POWs and MIAs. From 1960 to 1975, some 555 Americans, mostly airmen, remained unaccounted for in Laos and were listed as missing in action. Families who believed their loved ones were still alive constantly pressured the U.S.

government for information on the whereabouts and status of these men. If alive, of course, families sought their release; if dead, they requested their remains for burial.

There was some credibility to the assumption that Americans might be alive in Laos. Foreign prisoners were always isolated from indigenous ones, but refugees who had escaped from concentration camps reported seeing Caucasians whom they believed could be Americans. These reported sightings fueled the hopes of families and friends. Efforts to confirm sightings were frustrated because prisoners were regularly moved from camp to camp and from work-site to work-site.

Initially, Hanoi reported that *all* POWs and MIAs had been accounted for. Soon, however, the Kaysone regime recognized that POWs and MIAs were two of its few important bargaining chips in any negotiations with the U.S. Then began what General Vang Pao calls the game of "Bones! Bones! We've Got Bones!" which Kaysone cruelly played with the American government, the American people, and the relatives of men lost in the war. "Bones," according to Vang Pao, is played like this: When a Lao resistance group threatens the Kaysone regime, it responds by screaming, "Bones! Bones! We've Got Bones!" Once the United States government expresses interest in visiting a crash site to collect bones, Kaysone confidentially asks the Thais to call off their support of the resistance in return for access to Laos to retrieve the bones. The Thai comply with the request and then the U.S. government sends a delegation to pick up the bones. Thus, Kaysone's regime has won two victories: the propaganda victory of showing the world its humanitarian concerns and the military victory—without firing a shot—of slowing down the resistance. Then the game starts over again. When the resistance strikes a significant blow, the shout of "Bones!" once again goes out.

As late as 1992, experts who monitor Laos and Vietnam agree that both regimes still use the emotional POW-MIA situation in attempts to entice or "blackmail" the U.S. into providing economic aid and war reparations.

* * *

On August 10, 1981, Senator Hayakawa arrived in Laos. He and his delegation spent approximately 24 hours in Vientiane, where the U.S. Embassy was run only by a chargé. During his short stay, the senator met with officials from Kaysone's Foreign Ministry, representatives of the UNHCR, the U.N. Development Plan, UNICEF, members of the diplomatic community, and members of the Mennonite Central Committee and the American Friends Service Committee. The Mennonites and Friends—the only U.S. private religious groups allowed by the Lao government to work in Laos—had only a few people working in-country.

According to Hayakawa, he was the first U.S. senator to visit Laos since 1976. In his report to the Senate, published in March 1982, he recounted the issues which he discussed with the acting foreign minister of Laos. "I emphasized the need for a safer, orderly means of allowing legal departure for Lao citizens. . . . I stressed . . . that the MIA issue remains of great concern to the American people. . . . I told the Minister that there were seven missing in action that were of particular interest to me. . . . I then went on to indicate the possibility of a U.S. Government sponsored program to remove unexploded ordnance from the Plain of Jars in the context of Lao cooperation in accounting for MIAs in Laos."[23] Further, Senator Hayakawa told the Lao acting foreign minister "that, although the U.S. government was aware of internal armed resist[a]nce to the Lao Government, the United States was not providing support to anti-Lao insurgents. I stressed that there is no official connection between our Government and the insurgents." In his concluding paragraph, he mentioned that he had learned that "there are approximately 4,000 Soviet advisors in the country, in addition to many Vietnamese, some East Germans and even a few Cubans."

Hayakawa made no mention of the cruelties against the Hmong or the use of lethal agents.

28.

"Yellow Rain" and World Councils

You can't say that civilizations don't advance, for in every war they kill you in a new way.

—Will Rogers

On September 13, 1981, Secretary of State Alexander Haig, in a speech before the Berlin Press Association, announced: "We now have physical evidence from Southeast Asia which has been analyzed and found to contain abnormally high levels of three potent mycotoxins—poisonous substances not indigenous to the region and which are highly toxic to man and animals."[1]

Haig's announcement emphasized that military use of lethal trichothecene mycotoxins violated the 1972 Biological and Toxin Weapons Convention and that while Southeast Asia did not have the facilities to produce these agents, the Soviet Union did. Immediately *Tass*, the Soviet press agency, labeled Haig's announcement slanderous, unfounded, and false.

Haig's announcement and two major 1982 reports on the use of chemical-biological toxin weapons in Southeast Asia, one issued by Haig and a second by Secretary of State George Shultz, were based on National Intelligence Estimates. It is important to note that National Intelligence Estimates use only sourced information. In preparing an estimate, all intelligence agencies either agree to the information or take a footnote indicating exception to certain items. The final report then goes to the White House. Significantly, the Haig and Shultz reports were sanitized versions of a National Intelligence Estimate, which had contained no footnotes. The information had been unanimously agreed to by the intelligence community and by the executive branch. The State Department was the vehicle for transmitting these two reports to the United Nations and to Congress.

In spite of extensive, consistent, and specific evidence of the use of chemical-biological toxin weapons in Laos and in Cambodia after the 1979 Vietnamese invasion, elements within the U.S. government, importantly State's East Asia Bureau, consistently refused to publicly acknowledge and address the specifically documented use of such lethal agents. State's "prepared piece of language," written in late 1980, before the Haig Berlin announcement, which falsely implicated the Hmong in heroin trafficking and reinforced the Kaysone regime's propaganda of innocence without comment or explanation, continued to be issued by the State Department.

American Hmong continued to complain bitterly about State's letter and what they believed to be the U.S. government's dishonesty that damaged their reputations and dismissed the ongoing communist genocide against their kinsmen. They asked me to help them persuade the State Department to correct the letter. I made contact with Vice President George Bush, once head of the CIA, who I thought might know something about the Hmong, pointing out the unfairness and naivete of this State Department handout. The Vice President replied on September 25, 1981: "The State Department response you mentioned to inquiries about the H'mong situation has been updated and changed. It no longer includes references to H'mong opium production or to Soviet, Vietnamese, and Laotian government denials of reports about the use of chemical agents."[2] But, contrary to what the Vice President had been told, the State Department continued to send out its "prepared piece of language" without the changes which Bush said had been made. Whether this failure to change the language was simply oversight, incompetence, or belligerence by elements within the department remains unclear.

Several years later, in 1984, columnists Jack Anderson and Dale Van Atta would offer a partial explanation for the surprising lack of official concern in some quarters. "Incredibly, it was not until 1980 that a U.S. President was informed that the Soviets possessed biological-warfare facilities. Part of the reason was the institutional bias of a single CIA analyst, Julian Hoptman, whose power among the intelligence community's tiny group of BW (biological weapons) experts was supreme. So committed was Hoptman to the continuance of the 1972 Biological and Toxin

Weapons Convention . . . that he simply gave no credence to any report suggesting that the Soviets were cheating."[3]

On November 10, 1981, the U.S. Senate Subcommittee on Arms Control scheduled hearings on chemical weapons use in Laos, Cambodia, and Afghanistan, now commonly referred to as "yellow rain"—a misleading misnomer.

I had been asked by the subcommittee to testify on the Lao situation and to show photographs of victims. When I arrived at the Senate hearing room I found it jammed. I had to ask a security guard at the door to help me push through the crowd of TV and newspaper reporters and onlookers so I could reach the seats designated for witnesses.

Richard Burt, Director of the State Department's Bureau of Political-Military Affairs, admitted the difficulty the U.S. had encountered in detecting and identifying trichothecene mycotoxins. He pointed out that this fact enhanced their attractiveness as weapons. According to Burt, it had "taken the U.S. Government, with all the technical resources at its disposal, 5 years, and many thousands of man-hours, to discover the true nature of yellow rain."[4]

Sharon Watson, M.D., an expert on mycotoxins in the Office of the U.S. Army Surgeon General, also testified. Watson had been assigned to solve the mystery of the lethal agents being used against the Hmong. Struck by the fact that victims' symptoms did not match those produced by traditional chemical warfare agents, she decided to look elsewhere. A study of the open literature revealed that the Soviet Union had much experience in the field of trichothecene toxicology, including research into the massive production of trichothecene toxins. Intelligence indicated that the Soviet military was connected with this research. In this open literature, photographs of victims exposed to mycotoxins were also available. On a scientific hunch, Watson requested that attack residue samples be reanalyzed by nongovernmental research facilities for trichothecene mycotoxins—bleeding agents. Her hunch paid off. The Hmong were not being killed and maimed by traditional warfare agents. A new generation of lethal weapons—chemical-biological toxins—had been developed and used.

In her testimony, Watson agreed with Burt that trichothecenes were extremely difficult to detect. Although she did not know the Hmong and their exceptional toughness, she added: "I really think their use in these inaccessible areas was fully expected not to be detected."[5] I wondered if those assembled understood the significance of her remark. Probably not. The Soviets, unfamiliar with the Hmong, probably did not expect these hill people to survive or to escape from Laos to tell of their experiences. Phou Bia had been cordoned off by Lao and Vietnamese soldiers. The crossing points along the Mekong River were heavily patrolled and anyone seen trying to cross into Thailand was shot.

Dr. Chester Mirocha, a professor of plant pathology at the University of Minnesota, was next to testify. Mirocha, who specialized in analyses of mycotoxins, had been chosen by Dr. Watson to perform independent "blind" analyses of attack and control samples. He was told little about the samples and nothing as to their origins. His exhaustive independent analysis led him to report that he had found unnaturally high levels of biologically produced chemical toxins in the attack samples. His work was independently confirmed by Dr. Joseph D. Rosen, professor of food sciences at Rutgers University, who found high levels of trichothecene mycotoxins in a sample from Laos obtained by ABC news. Rosen also found man-made polyethylene glycol, which is used as a propellant in aerosol cans. Rosen believed that this was used as a deliverant for the agents. After peer review, Mirocha's and Rosen's findings were published in separate journals.

Mirocha briefly reviewed his analytical procedure and explained his findings. "We have found unequivocal proof of the presence of these toxins, T-2 toxin, deoxynivalenol, diacetoxyscripenol and nivalenol—four of them—on various substrates sent to our laboratory. They are in combinations which, in my opinion, are high and which, again, based on my experience, we do not find normally in that concentration in natural substrates."[6]

I gave my testimony and showed slides of victims which I had taken over the years. Sterling Seagrave, author of *Yellow Rain*, a book examining recent uses of chemical weapons, and journalist James Coyne, who had brought an attack sample from Laos to the U.S. for analysis, also testified. Then the hearing shifted to the testimonies of those who followed Afghanistan where chemical weapons usage began after the 1979 Soviet invasion. After the hearing, I concluded that the witnesses had provided credible and frightening evidence. Six years after the poison attacks against the Hmong began, the U.S. had at last identified *one* class and a new type of lethal agent—trichothecene mycotoxins. But were there others—alone or in combination—yet to be identified?

Western scientists and doctors had little experience with trichothecene poisoning in humans. Available historical data derived from trichothecene mycotoxicoses occurring mainly in the Soviet Union affecting animals and man depicted symptoms of headache, nausea, vomiting, vertigo, chills, visual disturbances, multiple hemorrhaging, angina, skin inflammation, stomatitis, dermal necrosis, nervous disorders, congestion and hemorrhaging of lungs and intestines. Survivors of poison attacks in Laos, Cambodia, and Afghanistan had reported such symptoms. I was encouraged by a momentum emerging from government agencies and from Congress that might result in action to stop the use of chemical-biological weapons (CBW) in Laos—and in Cambodia and Afghanistan.

I was also very aware that chemical-biological warfare, now being field-tested in these three countries, could change how war is waged. Clearly, CBW weaponry, cheap and relatively easy to produce, is the poor man's equivalent of nuclear capability, and might become the weapon of choice for poor countries.

I was also aware that there was one major disbeliever: Matthew Meselson, professor of biochemistry at Harvard University, who, in 1963, had been hired as a consultant to the U.S. Arms Control and Disarmament Agency. Meselson considered himself the "intellectual father" of the 1972 Convention, intended to ban toxin weapons. In 1979, Meselson was invited by the Soviet Union to investigate the Sverdlovsk anthrax outbreak. He brought Soviet medical experts to the U.S. to testify that this was a result of tainted black-market meat, not an accident at the Soviet biological warfare research facility, Compound 19.

Unlike others who recommended immediate action to stop the poisoning of humans, Meselson urged "caution in concluding whether or not trichothecene mycotoxins have been used in Southeast Asia, although I agree that the preliminary evidence indicates that they have."[7] Seemingly set on discrediting Mirocha's findings and the U.S. position, he asked, "Is there even a remote possibility that the U.S. Government has somehow been provided with samples that are not authentic?"[8]

Shortly after the Senate hearings, I received a cryptic message from Ban Vinai to come as soon as possible. I arrived only days later. Chief Vang Neng explained the reasons for my summons. He wanted to vent his and the Hmong's rage at the U.N.'s CBW investigating team which had visited the camp. The Hmong had concluded that the team was not serious and that the investigation had been useless. Those who had given testimony to the U.N. believed that they had been manipulated. They were now under attack by kinsmen who suggested that those selected to testify had failed to convince the experts of the atrocities taking place in Laos.

Under the U.N. arrangement, its expert team worked under the aegis of the U.N. Center for Disarmament, which in turn reported directly to the Department of Political and Security Council Affairs, headed by Vyacheslav A. Ustinov, a Soviet whose country was accused of providing the lethal agents through its surrogate, the Vietnamese. A conflict of interest was evident.

Biographical data on team members did not indicate expertise in mycotoxins or any third generation evolution of chemical-biological toxin warfare agents. The group consisted of eight people, including two military technical specialists and two medical doctors: an Egyptian Ph.D. who headed the Egyptian Armed Forces Scientific Research Branch; a deputy chief of the Philippines Armed Force Ordnance and Chemical Service; a consulting orthopedic surgeon from Kenya; a professor at the Institute of Tropical Medicine, Lima, Peru; two "Senior Political Affairs Officers" from the U.N. Secretariat staff, an Iranian and a Pole; a secretary to the Iranian, who functioned as secretary for the group, and a consultant from the Pasteur Institute.

Forbidden access to Laos and Cambodia to conduct research at reported attack sites, the U.N. team opted to interview alleged survivors living in refugee camps along Thailand's northern and eastern borders. The U.N. team remained in Thailand only 10 days. Much of that time was spent in transit or in meetings in Bangkok. A Thai army officer who escorted the team observed that some members seemed unprepared for the assignment and demonstrated political and geographical disorientation. While along the Mekong River in northern Thailand, the Iranian looked north toward Laos and asked if that was Vietnam across the river. According to this escort officer, some members were reportedly much more interested in arranging shopping excursions than in questioning survivors. Others expressed homesickness.[9]

Chief Vang Neng told me also that a Hmong team was now attempting to bring out another residue sample from a recent attack and that they wanted me personally to take it out of the camp and give it to a country that promised to analyze it promptly.

While waiting for the team from Laos to arrive, I decided to talk to Hmong who had been interviewed by the U.N. team. Lor Lue, dressed in a refugee-distributed blue and white Hawaiian shirt, seated himself across from me at a hand-hewn wooden table with uneven legs to relate his experience with the team. "They asked me a few questions that needed only one-word answers like, 'Did you see the poison gas?' or 'What is your rank?' So I decided to explain how the people died from the bloody vomiting and bloody diarrhea from the poison gas. Then I startled the U.N. team by producing a sample I helped collect on September 30, 1981, from a September 17 attack at coordinate Tango Foxtrot 83-75. I also gave them photographs I took of a helicopter and Soviet AN-2 plane used in the September 17th attack and of people in Laos suffering and dying from the poisons. I told the panel that when I learned that the U.N. was coming to investigate, I decided to try to come to Thailand with pictures and samples to give to the U.N. The panel expressed disbelief and almost anger that I had a sample and photographs. The Egyptian general seemed quite sure that a Hmong could not use a camera. He ordered me to take a picture with his camera even though it was one I had never seen before.[10]

"The general then wanted to know if I had told any foreigners about the photographs and the sample. I told him 'No.' I should have told him 'Yes,'" blurted out the 33-year-old Hmong, for the first time allowing his anger to show. "I'm angry because the men on the U.N. panel think I'm foolish. They look at me like an animal, not a person. They don't believe me about my sample."

The team had reluctantly taken Lor's sample. He wondered if they had thrown it away. Because his sample was thought to be suspect, his ability to use a camera was questioned, and the authenticity of his photographs was in doubt, he was demoralized. He had "lost face" with his kinsmen. He had let them down.

Others interviewed complained that the U.N. team did not treat them respectfully. Hmong, who are extremely polite and observant of social behavior, were hurt when, as one said, "The U.N. men wouldn't even shake our hands."

Pha Ger Pao, 53, had earned five French medals during his six years with the French fighting the Viet Minh. Then he served as a soldier for the Lao government and later became a soldier under Vang Pao. He proudly told me that he had made two successful parachute jumps during the U.S. time.

He and his son were the only survivors of a family of 15. Thirteen died from the "gas." When he realized that the U.N. did not believe him, he challenged them to get into their helicopter and go with him to Laos, to Lima Site 63, so they could see for themselves. "If," he told them, "you can't use the helicopter, then give me two people you trust and I will take them in to get evidence themselves. If they are killed, I will carry back every bone. So, please, tell me how many bones in each man's body and I will bring them all back to you."[11]

He was further outraged when, apparently insensitive to the agony that this man had suffered in losing most of his family from the poisons, a member of the U.N. team asked him if he had come to Thailand for political or economic reasons. As he described this insult, his lower jaw grew tight, he swallowed hard, he sat up tall, and said, "I told them, I just take only my life from Laos or the Vietnamese will take it."

I asked him to tell me how he and his son had survived an attack. "I saved my boy," he told me with tears in his eyes, "by putting a rag soaked with opium over my face and his face." As he spoke, he demonstrated. "We saw Vietnamese soldiers chewing the corners of their collars when they were near the poisons." I asked why they were chewing their collars. "They have medicine sewn into their collars to protect themselves from the gas," he answered without hesitation.

Since a dawn to dusk curfew remained in effect in the camp, my interviews ended as evening rolled into the valley. Heavy charcoal smoke from cooking fires wafted over hungry children whose black hair showed tints of red, the first stage of chronic malnutrition. A boy with a slingshot in one hand and a dead songbird in the other hurried to his mother to present her with his small prize. It would be the family's evening meal. Some refugees—those who had money sent by relatives resettled abroad—prepared rice which they had bought at the Thai market outside the gate. Some women prepared vegetables grown in small plots near the stream. Some bent over black pots, cooking grass and weeds. Some cooked nothing. They waited for darkness and sleep.

Later after darkness, I thought I heard distant gunfire. I studied the moonlit sky. Would the recovery team try to cross tonight? It seemed far too bright to attempt a crossing of the wide and dangerous Mekong.

When the mosquitoes became too troublesome, I entered my room, a screenless, musty space laced with unkempt cobwebs heavy with dust, loaned to me by camp medical personnel. I sat down on a slab of wood called a bed and with a flashlight checked the grimy mosquito net for holes—only a few small ones. I tried to sleep.

At dawn, I headed for Chief Vang Neng's house. Already men sat on his rickety porch talking in soft tones. He told me that the team had reached the Mekong and was trying to cross. But there were problems. What kind he didn't know. Since they could only cross the river at night, it would be at least another day before they tried again. I decided to continue interviewing those who had met with the U.N.

Her Ge, 36, sat down before me, placing his small notebook of information on the wobbly table. His young son sat next to him. He repeated to me what he had told the U.N. team about the attack during Hmong New Year a year earlier when a helicopter that looked like a "Jolly Green Giant" attacked his area, killing his 6-year-old son and leaving him, his wife, and their surviving children very ill. "I was answering the U.N. questions about the symptoms of the poisoning when they asked me to stop talking," he explained in anger. "They told me they didn't want to hear any more."[12]

I asked him to give me the information the U.N. did not want to hear. "During June 1980, many people very sick," he explained. "They cannot go to the fields. The planes come every other day. The planes drop three different colors: yellow that is like dry powder and people get very drunk and paralyzed; yellow that is sticky and people get fever with vomiting with blood and bloody diarrhea; and the blue color which is sticky and with no smell which gives people the fever, dizziness and vomiting. People die from all these kinds of poisons.

"We Hmong become angry and we take a yellow color gas sample of 'Moscow Medicine' to Pathet Lao authorities and ask, 'What is this?' The Pathet Lao say this belongs to Red Chinese. The planes belong to the Chinese. They steal the gas to kill the people because the Chinese are enemies of the Vietnamese and the Chinese use the gas to poison the people to make problems for Vietnam."

Her Ge still had severe respiratory problems from an attack, which had rendered him unconscious for at least 12 hours. When he awoke, he found it difficult to breathe. "It felt like my chest would break and it feels the same now. I tell the doctor in the camp here about my chest; he says it's T.B. Everyday same problems, always coughing with blood. My wife is still sick with diarrhea with blood and fever. Some days, she is in the toilet all day. Now some days all my children are sick with the fever and diarrhea. My mother is still in Laos and I worry about her. I don't know where she is."

Later that day, I visited Her Ge's family. They lived in a dirt-floored thatch hut. His wife, Chao Thai, age 28, with four children, was lying down in the darkness when I arrived. Slowly she got up from the floor and made her way to the sill of the darkness—with a suckling child at her breast. This was her story: "Very often I go to the fields and see yellow drops. If the drops are on leaves they get dry and die. From April 1980 to February 1981, the planes come and drop the gas and the people get vomiting and fever. Many Hmong die."[13] Her child cried and she jiggled and hugged him as she told me of the attack that took the life of her son. "After the plane that day, my son begins to vomit with green. He vomits for two days until he is dead. I cannot help my son for I am sick. Everyone falls to the ground. I fall to the ground. Go to sleep [become unconscious]. Then there's vomiting. I can't see well. Have difficulty breathing. I vomit for more than ten days—more than ten times each day. My children vomit all day long for a long, long time. For three or four days, I cannot do anything. There is no rice to eat. Nothing to eat. No water. After several days I am still very weak. It's very difficult to even carry water."

I asked her how she felt now—one year later. "I'm still sick. Pain in my arms and legs, pain in all muscles, headache, fever, burning in my eyes. I have diarrhea sometimes with blood. Some days, I have diarrhea ten or twelve times. One child still has diarrhea like me. And when I walk it hurts much in my chest."

Trying to determine how weak she was, I asked, "If you had a field to farm would you be able to go to the field and work?" A smile crossed her drawn face. She looked at me in a way that showed that she, too, knew the importance of a field to help feed the hungry children in this camp. "No," she answered, "I'm too weak. When I walk, I get the pain in my chest. I could not do it."

As I walked the crooked and rutted pathways through the crowded shelters, Hmong I knew approached to tell me of a friend or relative who was sick from the gassing. Would I come to see them and get medical help for them? Sometimes Hmong sent me notes with house numbers of those sick from the gassing and asked me to write their stories for the world to know of their suffering.

Darkness, with its anticipation that the team would cross the river, was soon displaced by the eerie and unwelcome moonlight that cast a whiteness as of snow on trees and barren ground, confusing my eyes. As the cool season pushed away the monsoon cloud cover, dark nights would become scarcer. Those who waited by the Mekong must have searched the heavens as I did, looking for clouds. They must have noticed the moonlight on the Mekong and known that other eyes—eyes behind guns—watched for movement. I hoped they would not try to cross tonight. The night was too still and beautiful to be marred by death.

The next day, I learned from a Hmong interpreter that the U.N. team had interviewed Gideon Regalado, a Philippine doctor who worked for World Vision, a Protestant evangelical relief organization with headquarters in California. He told me that Dr. Gideon, as the Hmong called him, had made problems for the Hmong. Although he had worked in the camp for over a year, he had not told the U.N. investigators about the Hmong who were sick from the poisons. Dr. Gideon would be quoted in the U.N. report that, in essence, there was no medical evidence to suggest poisoning of the Hmong: "No set of signs and symptoms were suggestive of abnormalities associated with chemical warfare agents. There was no consistent laboratory data either."[14]

Yet medical data on Hmong victims of CBW did exist in Ban Vinai medical files. Richard Harruff, a doctor with special training in pathology, spent six months in Ban Vinai and kept records and lab data on a number of Hmong exposed to toxic agents in Laos. Dr. Milton Amayun, who had worked at Ban Vinai during 1979–80, also kept records on patients reporting chemical exposures. Public health nurse Patricia Stuart, who was working at the camp hospital, told me that Harruff's and Amayun's studies were available at the time of the U.N. visit.[15] Neither Harruff's nor Amayun's records were turned over. Later on, their files of medical evidence were stolen. While World Vision was initially reluctant to become involved in the issue of CBW, in May 1982 it issued a manual on trichothecene poisoning for its medical personnel working with refugees in Southeast Asia.

Abandonment also came from the UNHCR representatives in Thailand, charged with the welfare of Hmong refugees. Alan Simmance, regional representative of UNHCR, and Dr. Arcot Rangaraj, health officer, told the team: "they had no report at all on the subject [cases attributable to chemical warfare agents]."[16] This attitude of see-no-evil, hear-no-evil was not oversight. It was policy. On July 30, 1981, when the High Commissioner for Refugees had been asked by the U.N. Group of Experts for help in its investigation, his office had replied, "Owing to its eminently humanitarian and non-political character, UNHCR would not be in a position to participate actively in such an investigation."[17]

As I thought about the men planning to cross the Mekong with yet another CBW attack sample, I wrote in my notebook: "Why should one more Hmong lose his life for a doubting world that apparently does not care that this minority is being systematically eliminated? For years, Hmong have brought sample after sample across the river. Often samples have been confiscated by Thai authorities while body-searching, or they have been lost in the bureaucracy, or left in someone's desk drawer, or worse. Not only have the Hmong provided hard evidence of CBW for years, but Lao pilots who flew chemical raids have defected to confirm it and the Vietnamese have publicly given a medal to honor those who delivered it. Now, a year and a half after that award, a U.N. investigating team conducted a brief perfunctory inquiry. Why aren't Third World countries such as those represented by several members of the U.N. team more interested? They probably have more at stake than Canada and Britain. Is the lack of interest because the Hmong have been identified as the CIA 'secret army' and as a result are considered dupes or worse? If true—and it probably is—what a tragic irony."

I closed the notebook and turned out my flashlight. Sleep seemed impossible with the musty stifling odors. I went outside to stand again on the high spot behind the camp hospital to watch the darkening sky. A few mare's tail clouds scudded by the nearly full moon, creating iridescent pastel circles around it. Below, moonlight turned ordinary shapes into unfamiliar silhouettes. For three nights I had watched this moon and hoped in vain for clouds. Now a few brought hope. Would it be tonight? Would they survive the patrols, high waters, and strong currents?

Lights flickered in Ward 1 and went out. Only the main ward had light—a weak glow from a few tiny fluorescent tubes. Hmong medics moved as dark shadows past unshuttered windows to tend to their most critical patients.

I thought about the human rights organizations, many of which fluttered about looking for causes, about the Western press and its reported keenness to cover human rights, and about Jimmy Carter's pledge to human rights. The Hmong did not even have the right to life. Their plight had not headlined in the Western press or appeared in the countless speeches on human rights violations.

Finally, I lay down under the dusty mosquito net. Sleep was fitful. Twice distant gunfire awakened me. Each time, I listened into the crackling darkness, but I heard nothing unusual. Had I only dreamed about gunfire or had I actually heard it? The third time I wakened with a start. I heard something. Not gunfire, but a shaman's drum beat, calling the soul of a dying person.

Before dawn, I waited for the curfew to pass so I could check in with the chief. As usual, he was surrounded by worried men talking in low tones. When I approached, he shook his head in the negative. "Not here yet, but they will come today—for sure." Then, he leaned close and whispered, "I just get message. There's been a big chemical attack on my people near Muang Phong on Sunday, December 6. Many people die. Many sick."[18]

Those assembled watched me as the chief relayed the news. I looked back at the helplessness in their eyes. I found no words to respond. A wave of nausea filled my body.

Hours passed as I interviewed Hmong ill from CBW attacks. In late morning, I returned to the chief's house for an update on the team. He greeted me by holding up a silver space-age bag, distributed by U.S. officials for collecting samples. He summoned me and several other Hmong to a less public place. There sat a 25-year-old Hmong of slight build. He had brought out the silver bag.

With considerable care, he began his story. "We are a team of ten men who try to get evidence of the gassing. Villagers tell us about a site about four kilometers southeast of Phou Heh. If people pass by it, they become sick. The villagers are sure that the area is poisoned. On October 17, 1981, we go to the area. Six of us scrape the powder from the rocks and leaves. Four stand guard some distance from the area to warn of danger. We begin to scrape the tannish-yellow powder. I have yellow sight, dizzy. Feel like drunk, only different. Everything is moving around. I have headache. All six scrapers are sick like me. We cannot continue to scrape. Our hands become numb. We feel foolish in the mind. But we don't think we have enough for the sample. We must rest. We leave the site and lie down. We smoke some opium and feel better. Then we go back to scrape some more chemicals. Since we are sick, we decide to try to reach a nearby village before dark.[19]

"By early morning, we scrapers are all very sick. Diarrhea with blood begins. We have diarrhea constantly for 24 hours. So many times we cannot count. It is difficult to breathe. Still feel foolish. My eyes feel like they will come out. Three days later, I notice skin blisters on my legs and thighs. First they are black color, then they became swollen and wet and then the sores spread."

He showed me his sores and I photographed them. Then he continued: "We spend three days in the village because we are sick. Then we leave the village for the jungle because the villagers are afraid that the communists will find us. I still have diarrhea and cannot eat for 10 days."

In the following seven weeks, while those exposed to the poisons were recovering, the team twice encountered Lao and Vietnamese soldiers. Both encounters resulted in firefights, but no one from the team was killed.

While he spoke, I studied the delicate features of this extremely thin young man. As he told his story, his expression changed little. During the first week of December 1981, he and another team member, selected to bring out the sample, joined with eight civilians. Together they walked fast for five days to reach the Mekong River. Only the two team members were armed. Once at the river, they spotted communist patrols. Hiding on the banks of the Mekong, they waited to cross. They knew there was no retreat. They were now trapped and afraid. As they waited, he tied the silver bag to his waist.

He lifted a glass of boiled water to his lips. I thought I saw a quivering in his hand. He drank slowly, then continued: "Then we are ready to go. My friend with the other gun goes first into the water to protect the civilians. I must wait. I must protect everyone until they are in the water. I wait and wait. Then, the enemy gun bursts—only 20 meters away. I try to swim hard and the automatic weapon empties around me. I swim harder and harder to get away. For two hours we struggle in the water. Finally we get ashore on the Thai side. The Thai authorities take my gun, my flashlight, my canteen, and my 100 *baht* (U.S. $5). I tell them that the silver bag has poison in it and I must come immediately to Ban Vinai. They let me go. I arrived here this morning."

Had I heard that same gunfire last night or had it only been the gunfire of my dreams?

I told him that he had been brave to risk his life to collect this sample and bring it out. He responded quickly with a trace of emotion. "I am *not* brave. I do it because I am angry. Vietnamese and Pathet Lao try to kill all Hmong. I have to get chemicals to prove it because many Hmong die of the chemicals and unusual diseases. If I die, I die for all Hmong people."

Before I left Ban Vinai, Chief Vang Neng summoned me. He had a message which he wanted me to deliver to the U.N., to the U.S. Congress, and to the White House. He asked that I write it down. "One year ago, in December 1980, the U.N. decided to investigate the use of chemicals against the Hmong in Laos. One year later, a U.N. team comes out here to investigate and finds no conclusive evidence. Please tell everyone that if the U.N. decides to come back one year from now—tell them not to come. There will be no need to come for there will be no Hmong left alive in Laos!"

As I departed the camp with the sample in a worn-out, scarred, and listing blue taxi, Chief Vang Neng stood on the dirt bank outside the hospital complex, waving longer than anyone else.

* * *

In mid-December 1981, 50-year-old Dr. Khamseng Keo Sengsathit, Director of Public Health for the Lao People's Democratic Republic, defected to China, where he denounced the Vietnamese for their occupation of his nation, their expansionist policy, and their use of chemical weapons. "The most brutal thing was that the Le Duan (Vietnamese government) clique practiced a policy of genocide toward national minorities of Laos. They used chemical weapons in the air and on the ground killing thousands upon thousands of people."[20]

In Bangkok, at a meeting with a representative of the British Embassy, who introduced himself as John Greenwood of British Intelligence, and Lt. Col. Dennison Lane, Army military attaché at the U.S. Embassy, I agreed to a dividing of the Phou Heh sample into two parts. One went to the Englishman; the other to the American.

Meanwhile, the U.N. Group of Experts' report dated November 20, 1981, was inconclusive. It acknowledged that it had been unable to conduct on-site investigations in Afghanistan, Cambodia, and Laos, or to analyze samples obtained in Thailand.[21] It did not mention that Vyacheslav A. Ustinov had insisted that the samples, including the one Lor had given them, be analyzed in the Soviet Union. Some members of the team objected. Thus, the samples remained unanalyzed in U.N. custody to be coded by Swedish personnel. The U.N. report indicated that the samples had been tampered with. The U.N. General Assembly—over Soviet objection—voted to extend the investigation for another year.

* * *

On March 22, 1982, Secretary of State Alexander Haig submitted a report to the U.S. Congress entitled "Chemical Warfare in Southeast Asia and Afghanistan." This report, based on National Intelligence Estimates, concluded that " . . . Lao and Vietnamese forces, operating under Soviet supervision, have, since 1975, employed lethal chemical and toxin weapons in Laos: that Vietnamese forces have, since 1978, used lethal chemical and toxin agents in Kampuchea [Cambodia]; and that Soviet forces have used a variety of lethal chemical warfare agents, including nerve agents, in Afghanistan since the Soviet invasion of the country in 1979."[22]

Congressman Stephen Solarz prepared for House hearings on CBW. On March 30, experts and witnesses assembled to give testimony before two House subcommittees—International Security and Scientific Affairs and Asian and Pacific Affairs. Aware of the attacks that had been made on the credibility of the U.S. government's evidence, the committee's staff had assembled doctors with first-hand experience with CBW victims, mycotoxin experts, personnel from State's Bureau of Political-Military Affairs and the Arms Control and Disarmament Agency, and one Hmong—Vang Xeu, who had earlier accompanied General Vang Pao and me to Washington to meet members of Congress. Their adversaries were a professor from the University of Wisconsin and a Mennonite worker allowed by the communist regime to work in Laos.

Solarz opened with a salvo against those who claimed refugee evidence was not credible. He reminded everyone that in 1975, Cambodian refugees who had escaped the murderous Pol Pot regime had not been believed nor had the Chinese refugees in 1962 who told of widespread starvation during Mao Zedong's "Great Leap Forward."[23]

Among the witnesses was Dr. Richard Harruff, the physician specializing in pulmonary problems who had gone to Ban Vinai in early 1980 to work—he thought—on tuberculosis and pulmonary disease cases. He had tested the Hmong for T.B. and found that tuberculosis was not the problem: "Microscopic examination showed no evidence of infection and chest X-rays were normal." Harruff discovered instead that many pulmonary problems were the result of CBW. "I was naive in the beginning," he admitted, "but during my diagnostic evaluation of patients I had contact with many people who complained that their lung disease was caused by exposure to chemical weapons dropped on them in Laos. I interviewed them and examined them and could find no other reason for their pulmonary disease and became convinced that they were telling the truth."[24]

Hmong whom he tried to treat suffered "peripheral neuropathy, nausea, vomiting, anorexia and weight loss." He reported that the agents, whatever they were, caused "a burning sensation of the eyes, nose and lungs, nausea, vomiting with blood and abdominal pain, diarrhea with blood, coughing and chest pain, and blood in the sputum. Exposed persons had periods of unconsciousness with disorientation, dizziness and weakness and occasional convulsions. Skin contact caused blistering. People would treat themselves with opium, either by breathing it or by drinking infusions of it."[25]

Harruff criticized the medical community for not taking the CBW attacks seriously. "The medical staff at Ban Vinai all now accept the Hmong story as truthful, but the group is not speaking out because they have no special interest in pursuing the chemical warfare issue and they are very concerned about the political implications and are careful about making comments. Unfortunately, there are no other groups involved in this camp, so that there has not been a systematic recording of cases. No specialists have come to the camp to assist in case identification, documentation, diagnosis or treatment."[26]

Professor Daniel Cullen from the University of Wisconsin, a believer in the theory that "yellow rain" was not CBW but a natural occurrence, complained, as had Harvard's Meselson in the earlier hearings, that "the analyses lacked adequate control samples" and hinted at a hoax: "the precise identity of the sample collectors remains obscure."[27] When Solarz asked Cullen if the agents previously identified by Professor Mirocha were lethal to someone exposed to them, he said that they were not. When Solarz then asked Mirocha and Watson the same question, they concurred that exposure could indeed cause death.[28]

Vang Xeu angrily reported that somewhere between 50,000 and 70,000 Hmong had died in the Phou Bia area of Laos, many from CBW. He attacked the State Department—although Haig's report had just been released—for its "unwillingness to acknowledge the gas warfare against our people." He shocked the gallery. "Our people don't give samples to the U.S. government because they don't trust the U.S. State Department, because they always refuse to acknowledge this situation. But they gave them [the samples] to the correspondent,* to doctors, and to visitors. . . . We never get any favorable response to the issue. Even when they go to the camps, the U.S. Embassy, all the time they don't seem to understand the Hmong problems and we did not receive any positive action from the U.S. government or State Department."[29]

Solarz cut Vang Xeu's prepared testimony short to go to the next witness. Xeu submitted for the record names, addresses, and, in some cases, home phone numbers of 75 Hmong in the U.S. who spoke English and knew much about CBW and its long-term effect on survivors' health. This was a rich list for doubting journalists and scientists as well as for medical personnel now treating Hmong refugees in the U.S., but few, if any, on this list were contacted.

Frederick Swartzendruber, a representative of the Mennonite Central Committee serving in Laos from late 1979 until the spring of 1981, followed. This tall, bespectacled missionary testified that the Mennonites had been working in Laos "since before the turnover in government, and at a time when other agencies were asked to leave we were asked to stay on because we were able to make a case that we were not supporters of the war. . . . " Swartzendruber told the subcommittee that he had serious misgivings about the State Department data. He found the results of

---

*Reference is to the author and James Coyne, both of whom had brought out residue samples to be analyzed.

its "informal surveys to be rather disturbing. On the basis of that, I twice asked U.S. officials, State Department officials, if it would not be wise to make a systematic survey of refugees to find out what could be learned from a social science type survey of refugees vis-à-vis their knowledge of chemical warfare in Laos."[30]

Vang Xeu squirmed in his seat. He knew about Swartzendruber's current speaking tour in the U.S. and his laudatory comments about the new society in Laos and the advances of the Kaysone regime. Swartzendruber told audiences he doubted the existence of "yellow rain," proclaiming at the hearing that "yellow rain" stemmed, in his opinion, from Hmong confusion about the communist use of pesticides. Vang Xeu and other Hmong denounced him as a mouthpiece and dupe of the Kaysone regime.

Swartzendruber explained that he had visited the Phou Bia area one afternoon and had seen nothing amiss—with Hmong going to market. When questioned by Solarz, Swartzendruber admitted that on this one brief occasion at Phou Bia he had not talked to anyone without LPDR officials present. A few months later, at a conference on CBW in May 1982 at Princeton University, he also admitted that he had flown there on a Soviet helicopter escorted by LPDR officials.

Vang Xeu could not restrain himself. He jumped from his seat, interrupting Swartzendruber. "Excuse me. I would like to say that I am sorry to hear such misleading information. . . . You see, if you [Swartzendruber] are walking on a street where you see Hmong, if you see people with [white] skin [like Swartzendruber] why they look alike, Russian, French and Britain, of course they [the Hmong] are not going to tell you anything. Gas attack? They would say no."[31]

The young Hmong warned Swartzendruber of what should have been obvious for a visitor taken on an official LPDR government tour and seeing nothing amiss among people who fear the government of those officials. "If you say one word wrong," explained Vang Xeu, "then that night, that particular night you will be taken out and taken away from your family. So they can't say anything. . . . They say fine, well, OK. They are just playing very busy going to the market and doing something that people [the communists] feel they are OK."[32]

On December 1, 1982, the U.N. Group of Experts submitted its final report to the General Assembly. During the two years of its existence, this group met only six times and was repeatedly prevented from making on-site investigations. Before its findings were made public, *Pravda* reported on the ambiguities in the team report, but did not mention that the USSR and its client regimes had denied the team access to the countries in question. The U.N. report concluded that "it could not disregard the circumstantial evidence suggestive of the possible use of some sort of toxic chemical substance in some instances."[33]

In the spring of 1982, LAWASIA, an Asian human rights watch organization, asked a distinguished group of Asian lawyers from Pacific-Asian nations to investigate alleged violations of human rights in Cambodia and Laos. This committee concluded: "Evidence of employment of chemical warfare, whether for the purpose of terror, elimination or to force resettlement of people at easily accessible areas, is of such a nature that reasonable men must agree that such weapons have been used against people in Kampuchea [Cambodia] and Laos."[34]

After its investigation and interviews with survivors, the LAWASIA committee had telling words for the skeptics. "Whereas a skeptic might suspect adults of fabricating evidence, the ingenuousness of the very young and old insured their veracity. The common thread of horrific experiences that ran through all their stories could not have been premeditated, and the peculiar symptoms they suffered could not have been caused by any other sources than some virulent chemical-biological agent."[35]

On May 12, 1982, Amnesty International responded to Congressman Solarz' late March request to use its doctors to assist in establishing the credibility of CBW victims in Indochina. Patricia Rengel, director of its Washington office, pointed out that its focus "continues to be a narrow spectrum of human rights violations. Amnesty International works for the release of Prisoners of Conscience, for fair trials for all political prisoners, and for an end to torture and the death penalty." Rengel begged off becoming involved in the atrocities in Laos by shifting the responsibility to other agencies such as the Red Cross, UNHCR, and U.N. bodies "who investigate questions of the violations of humanitarian law and the laws of warfare."[36]

Nearly a year later, in November 1983, Congressman Solarz asked in a statement before the U.N. General Assembly: "If the allies of the Soviet Union are really innocent of the charges, why did they not permit an independent inquiry to clear their name? If United Nations agricultural experts are welcomed in Laos why not chemical weapons experts? The areas involved do not contain vital military installations, knowledge of which would jeopardize the security of those countries. What do they have to hide?" Solarz answered his own question: "It seems clear that they know full well that such investigation would not be exculpatory."[37]

The Helsinki Act had been established in 1975 to deal primarily with security and cooperation in Europe to resolve humanitarian, economic, political, and military issues that divided Europe. While not its initial thrust, the Act did set into motion the concept of Helsinki Monitoring Groups (to become known as Helsinki Watch Committees), whereby individuals could, under its aegis, legitimately form groups to oversee the protection of human rights in NATO and Soviet bloc countries. The U.S. Helsinki Watch Committee was founded in 1979 to promote domestic and international compliance with the human rights provisions of the 1975 Helsinki accords. Its Fifteenth Semiannual Report, issued in November 1983, condemned the Soviet invasion of Afghanistan, and admonished the Soviets for continuing "to provide the Vietnamese with the support necessary to maintain Hanoi's efforts to subjugate and colonize neighboring Kampuchea."[38] Nothing was said about Laos.

Disturbed by this lack of any mention of Laos, I enlisted the aid of Orville H. Schell, Jr., a lawyer very concerned with human rights who was Vice Chairman of the U.S. Helsinki Watch Committee. He had led several groups investigating violations in the Soviet Union, Argentina, Sri Lanka, and Eastern Europe. Schell agreed that something should be done. In mid-1986, he and I jointly presented the Lao case to Aryeh Neier, the other Vice Chairman of U.S. Helsinki Watch in New York. Schell hoped that its newly formed "Asia Watch" would take Laos on as a formal investigation. At that meeting, I was asked to make a formal presentation to the Asia Watch Committee. I prepared such a presentation, but just before that meeting, Eric Schwartz of Asia Watch told me over the phone that there would be no need for me to appear because they were more interested in Burma. That was the last I heard. Eric Schwartz left Asia Watch and moved to the staff of Congressman Solarz, where he is responsible for Laos. From my experience, he remains generally uninterested in the Hmong issue.

Evidence collected by U.S., British, French, Japanese, German, Chinese, Canadian, and Thai governments, and from university scientists, intelligence intercepts, eyewitnesses and defectors confirmed the use of banned toxin weapons in Laos. A 1977 East German military manual on military chemistry describes in detail Soviet bloc weaponry and corroborates Hmong descriptions of deployment.[39] Although elements of the U.S. State Department sought to overlook the issue, the U.S. did more on this critical issue than most of its allies. Canada was the only other government to submit documentation to the U.N. For political reasons, U.S. allies with significant evidence, such as France, Germany, and Japan, decided to remain silent.

A solid body of evidence pointed to the Soviets, who were the only common factor in the CBW being waged in Laos, Cambodia, and faraway Afghanistan. More obviously, in Laos it pointed to the Vietnamese. Both were signatories to the 1972 Biological and Toxin Convention. They had been cheating in a horrible way. They had in their possession toxin weaponry field-tested against the Hmong. This new and frightening weapon had now become a national security concern for the U.S. and for other nations without protective defenses.

29.

Wronged by the Media

The modern imperative . . . is to proceed with arms control negotiations for their own sake. Because allegations of Soviet CBW treaty
violations might disrupt the negotiations, they are considered dangerous and should be opposed. . . . Many individuals with access to
international forums believe that it is the allegations of CBW treaty
violations, rather than the violations themselves, which poison arms
control.

—Mark Storella, *Poisoning Arms Control: The Soviet Union and
Chemical-Biological Weapons,* 1984

"Seeing the World in Red and Yellow," a March 1982 editorial written by a *New York Times* staff writer, asked why any country would want
to make "yellow rain." The writer suggested that maybe it was made "to
perplex the State Department" or as a "home-made poison" to be used
against rats in Southeast Asia. This flip response to CBW usage and death
in Laos, Cambodia, and Afghanistan and the continuing, active, consistent editorial role of this major newspaper would deaden the Hmong
pleas for help in ending the genocide of their people trapped in Laos.
Much of the *Times* readership might have concluded that the charges of
lethal toxins and toxin warfare were but another propaganda ploy in the
bout between two superpowers. Such light-hearted slings at Foggy Bottom bureaucrats and Cold Warriors would continue for several years.

In June 1982, prompted by Nuclear Freeze demonstrations, I submitted to the *Washington Post* an article for its op-ed page titled: "Nuclear War
a Theory: Bio-Chemical War a Reality." As supporting evidence I enclosed one of my photographs of a CBW victim, a child. On June 24, I
received a note from Stephen Rosenfeld, of the *Post*'s editorial depart-

ment: "We're taken by your material but we are curious to know a bit more about you and how do we know what this is a picture of?"[1] I called Rosenfeld and explained that I had taken the photo in 1979 in a refugee camp in Thailand and that scientists familiar with CBW had viewed the photograph and reported that it resembled photos found in Soviet literature of victims accidentally exposed to mycotoxins. In a follow-up letter, I mentioned my background and my testimony on CBW before the Senate Foreign Relations Subcommittee on Arms Control. I enclosed a 1979 *New York Times* op-ed piece which I had written describing a massacre of Hmong on the Mekong River and reprints of my *Reader's Digest* articles on chemical-biological warfare.

I heard nothing more from Rosenfeld. Some time later, I received a standard rejection notice from the *Post*. Still attached to my manuscript was a memo to "Meg" (Greenfield) from "Steve" (Rosenfeld): "I've talked and corresponded with the woman who sent her photo of a Hmong child hit by CW, and I am satisfied she and her material are legit. In her cover letter she says this child resembles photos in Soviet literature of victims accidently [*sic*] exposed to mycotoxins; she called me this morning to say that she now has specific reference in the Soviet literature, i [*sic*] do not see how we can run that picture—her piece should do. steve."[2] There was no indication who had rejected my article, or why.

In the fall of 1982, I met with Philip B. Kunhardt, Jr., managing editor of *Life* magazine, to propose an article on the Hmong and CBW. I showed him a number of photographs of victims. He wanted more evidence, particularly photos of aircraft delivering CBW. I expressed considerable doubt that such photos could be obtained because of the risks of exposure and lack of knowledge of enemy targets. However, I said that I would pursue the idea with Hmong leaders. A few months later, a Hmong managed long-lens photos of an attack by a Soviet helicopter. One photograph clearly showed a mist-cloud near this aircraft. With considerable enthusiasm, I took these photos to the managing editor. He was not impressed: "How do I know that these photos were taken in Laos?"[3] It was obvious that there would be no article in *Life* on the genocide of the Hmong nor on CBW in Laos.

On May 31, 1983, at a Detroit meeting of the American Association for the Advancement of Science, "yellow rain" was on the agenda. There, Matthew Meselson showed photographs depicting bee excrement scraped from his car windshield in Cambridge, Massachusetts, and said that it resembled samples of "yellow rain" collected in Southeast Asia. "It is possible," he was quoted as saying that day, "that yellow rain is bee excrement" and this "opens up the realm of natural explanations for yellow rain in a way not done previously."

With prior organization, Meselson's astonishing supposition was immediately endorsed in a handout distributed at that same meeting by four other scientists, including Julian Perry Robinson of the University of Sussex in England and Thomas D. Seely, a student of bee behavior at Yale University. Seely explained that bees excrete wastes in flight and that these wastes are yellow in color and often contain pollen. Since traces of pollen had been found in some attack samples, yellow rain could be bee dung. Honeybees ingesting fusarium fungus and then excreting toxic wastes might be responsible for the poisoning of people in Southeast Asia.

That May meeting in 1983 in Detroit was significant. The campaign to discredit the U.S. government's contention that mycotoxins had been used as weapons of war had been launched in the popular press. Some prestigious newspapers and magazines accepted the bee feces explanation without rigorous investigation or scientific documentation and began to promote it.

The day after the meeting, Philip M. Boffey's 21-paragraph coverage of Meselson's bee feces theory appeared in the *New York Times*. No one was quoted except Meselson and his supporters. While Meselson apparently only used words such as "a strong hypothesis" and "not conclusive evidence" when referring to his theory, much lineage was given to what were only his speculations.[4] This reporting of Meselson's undocumented pronouncements was a harbinger of things to come. His assertion that bees defecating in flight—not CBW delivered by aircraft or mortars— caused the death of the Hmong, less believable than earlier assertions by the Soviets that these deadly toxins were produced by elephant grasses in southern Vietnam and carried by monsoon winds to Hmong areas in Laos, should have been incredible to reasonable people.

Congressman Stephen Solarz soon fired back at Meselson's bee theory in the *Wall Street Journal* and the *Washington Post*. "The latest effort to explain away the damning evidence asserts that the trichothecenes found in Southeast Asia grew on bee defecations. Since bees have presumably long been indigenous to the region it is odd that these deadly manifestations show up only now. The incredible bee hypothesis, unlike the one advanced by the Soviets, does not even pretend to explain why these poisonous substances did not appear in earlier years or in other places."[5]

In his bee dung theory, Meselson now thought he possessed a natural phenomenon explanation, however weak and unsubstantiated, and he saw that he had found a believing press. Some asked if the press had found him.

The dangerous and horrible issue of the creation and field testing of a new generation of chemical-biological weaponry and of the fate of the Hmong victims changed forever. Attention would now shift from CBW victims to the colorful exploits of the theatrical Meselson.

I had found it very difficult to interest editors in pieces on CBW. There was an extraordinary reluctance to believe this horror. There is, perhaps, an innate human reluctance to acknowledge man's brutality. I also believed other issues were at work. This was the time of the Nuclear Freeze Movement and arms control. Acknowledging the horrors of CBW and the violations of treaties were not compatible with a prevailing public spirit to reduce nuclear weapons and make agreements with the Soviets.

When the Hmong learned of Meselson's Detroit pronouncements and the ensuing *Times* support of his bee feces theory, they were furious. They asked:

- Why are only the Hmong affected?
- Why didn't this happen before 1975, when the Americans were still in Laos; why only after the communists took over and publicly announced that they intended to kill those Hmong who were the "running dogs of the American imperialists"?
- Why is there no mention of agents that are not yellow and do not resemble bee dung; what about the black, blue, red, and white poisons?
- Why hadn't massive numbers of deaths due to bee "cleansing flights" been reported before in Hmong homelands?
- Why not take into account the testimonies of survivors, medical doctors, scientists, defectors, and communications intercepts?
- Why didn't Meselson, when he scraped the bee excrement from his windshield, become dizzy, or fall to the ground unconscious, or find breathing difficult, or vomit, or have bloody diarrhea?

After Meselson's announcement that bees defecating in flight had killed the Hmong, many journalists wanted to know if his bee feces samples collected in 1984 in Thailand had contained mycotoxins. William Kucewicz of the *Wall Street Journal* waited for Meselson to publish the analysis of his samples. When he did not, Kucewicz pursued the matter. He questioned Meselson about the analysis. Meselson finally admitted that his bee feces sample contained no mycotoxins. On September 6, 1985, Kucewicz went public with this critical and startling information. Meselson's own evidence had now disproved his bee feces theory. There were no lethal levels of mycotoxins in his much-publicized bee shower excrement. Kucewicz chastised Meselson and his acolytes for neglecting to mention these negative findings in their recent article in *Scientific American*.[6]

Ban Vinai camp held an immense amount of information about the situation inside Laos. Intelligence brought out by refugees had always been reported to center chiefs who submitted their data to camp leaders. Records were kept on locations and dates of CBW attacks, names and ages of people killed, kinds of aircraft involved, descriptions of poisons, effects on animals and vegetation, and other relevant details. Hmong even performed autopsies on animals killed by CBW.

Because of persistent requests from Hmong around the world for information on missing friends and relatives, there was a constant effort in Ban Vinai to collect data from new arrivals about those missing in the fighting or taken away to seminar camps. Escapees from seminar and internment camps reported the names of those known to be alive and dead and the shocking grimness of life. Some former internees reported sightings of foreign prisoners—some thought to be American POWs. Refugees also reported on local policies of the Kaysone regime, the economy, and movements of Vietnamese troops stationed in Laos.

During 1982 and 1983, several Westerners had come to Ban Vinai claiming falsely to be friends of General Vang Pao and promising to help the Hmong by writing their stories. Some of them had misused and distorted information to promote their own political agendas and to discredit the Hmong. One had found a Hmong teenager who had learned some English while working for a relief agency in the camp. This youngster was a major source of information. The teenager's information was often only partial, or out of date, or hearsay, since he obviously was not at the center of knowledge, but it was often used by foreigners to substantiate preconceived theses. At other times, Hmong interviews were manipulated and twisted. Questions were rigged. On occasion, demeaning and untruthful remarks were made of those interviewed to damage their credibility.

The Hmong learned of the deceptions and trickery only *after* articles and books were published—too late to correct misinformation or rebut misinterpretations. They had no way to respond to a fallacious book about them published in Australia or one-sided articles in U.S. newspapers and magazines. Again, they were victims of those determined to misuse them for their own ends. Hmong painfully learned that not all Americans or Westerners were honest and truthful.

Hmong leadership in Ban Vinai had finally decided that there was only one way to protect Hmong against deceit: all information on the situation in Laos would be confidential. In 1983, Hmong camp leaders had decided that any details of CBW attacks were part of military intelligence and therefore "top secret."

Three months after Meselson had been soundly rebuked at an international conference at Ghent, Belgium, by scientists from the U.S. (including Mirocha and Rosen), Canada, England, and Japan in August 1984, a year and a half after *Life* had rejected my idea for an article on CBW and the Hmong, it ran a special report on Meselson, explaining his bee defecation theory. The *Life* article gave Meselson credit for Nixon's 1979 decision to unilaterally abandon biological weapons. On the question of the Hmong eyewitnesses, Meselson stated, according to *Life,* that "one explanation might be the methods used to question them. Jeanne Guillemin, a Boston College anthropologist who is studying the Hmong interviews, calls them 'an unqualified disaster.'"[7] *Life* did not mention that Jeanne Guillemin was Meselson's wife.

Later, Dr. Chester Mirocha, in the "Letters" section of *Scientific American,* addressed Meselson's and Seeley's data promoted in *Life.* "From the data presented in the article I can only conclude that honeybees in Southeast Asia, like their relatives in other parts of the world, defecate in flight, a fact already well reported in scientific literature and not one that is in the forefront of research. Yellow spots on leaves the authors analyzed were indeed bee feces and had nothing to do with chemical attacks on the Hmong in their villages." Mirocha concluded his attack by calling upon Meselson and his supporters to see "cold scientific data" and to stop writing "prose" which belongs "in the realm of political polemics."[8]

When journalists wanted a quote on CBW, they often turned to the high-profile Meselson. Sterling Seagrave, author of *Yellow Rain,* a study which accuses the Soviets of being responsible for the CBW weapons used in Southeast Asia, understood something about Meselson that most of his colleagues did not. "Journalists take him to be a pure scientist without wondering why he keeps challenging the data. When they need a quote, they hit the Rolodexes, and come up with Matt's name. The problem is, he's also a politician."[9]

Journalists did go to Meselson, the smooth, sophisticated, witty Harvard professor who laughed at his critics' joke: "cagey bees or the

KGBees." Sadly for the Hmong, many prominent journalists did not seek quotes from eyewitnesses or survivors.

The Hmong did not joke about Meselson's bees. Those living in the U.S., now some 75,000, angrily criticized the media for presenting only the bee feces point of view and for neglecting all other data, including the deaths of so many of their people. Hmong victims were not on journalists' Rolodexes. They were not called for print interviews or invited to participate on talk shows.

Public television's prestigious science program *Nova* decided to air a documentary—"The Mystery of Yellow Rain." In the summer of 1984, I spoke with Susanne Simpson, a producer at WGBH in Boston, who was working on this program. According to her, *Nova* had purchased an English film featuring Meselson and Englishman Julian Perry Robinson that promoted the bee feces theory. She explained that because WGBH had paid a high price for this film, it had decided to limit updating or the inclusion of other scientific data or points of view in order to hold down the costs. Trying to be helpful, I sent her some of my writing on the use of CBW, including a series of articles which I had written for the *Bangkok Post*. Having heard nothing from Simpson for several weeks, I called her. I asked if she had read my articles. She said she had not because it was her understanding that the *Bangkok Post* was owned by the CIA.

Eventually, the *Nova* staff did interview a few American and Canadian scientists and toxicologists working on this issue. One was Canadian toxicologist Dr. Bruno Schiefer. Schiefer was interviewed at length by the *Nova* producer, to whom he gave copies of his research findings and reprints of lectures which he had produced while working for Canada's Department of External Affairs.

Nova's "The Mystery of Yellow Rain," aired on PBS stations on October 30, 1984, so angered Schiefer that he protested to PBS President Bruce Christensen, informing him that he had been "abused" by *Nova*. In his ten-page letter to Christensen, Schiefer documented *Nova* manipulation of his data and of data gathered by such a world class toxicologist as Chester Mirocha and the elimination of critical scientific information that had been given to *Nova* that disproved the bee feces theory.

Criticizing the *Nova* production for lack of integrity and professionalism, Dr. Schiefer wrote in his letter to the PBS president, "In the way my comments were used in the broadcast, it sounded like I was endorsing Dr. Meselson's viewpoints," and "I suggest that the lopsided presentation of this issue is as unscientific as possible, and borders on giving false information. . . . In view of this experience, I regret having participated."[10]

Meselson's bizarre bee dung thesis received supportive coverage in many well-regarded magazines and periodicals. Other scientists—and particularly the Hmong—asked, "Why?" The answer lay in Meselson's high profile and his personal political agenda.

Several years after Meselson's bee dung announcement that so captivated the press, Congressman Jim Leach told me about a private conversation with Meselson during the Detroit conference. "Meselson told me personally that he was taking this perspective [that there were no Soviet CBW violations in Southeast Asia or Afghanistan] because he was so apprehensive that in the early days of the Reagan administration antagonism to the Soviets based on violations of CBW could jeopardize the future of arms control which was crucial to our times.[11]

"That's a fair perspective," said Leach, "but a political conjecture on his part that has nothing to do with science or scientific observation. So, he's playing politics as a scientist, not pursuing science as a scientist. That is a major distinction in how one should respect his observations."

Meselson* and his group were, then, manipulating their standing as scientists to further a personal political view. The press joined in and, in the process, by obfuscating the awareness of the use of CBW by the communists in Laos, sacrificed the lives of many Hmong.

Part Eight

Wronged
in War;
Wronged
in Peace

30.

Burial in Montana

Jerry was not only our advisor but our friend as well. He dedicated more than twenty years of his life to us and we grew to know him well, not only in name, but in spirit too. I guess we love Jerry so much because we always knew that he honestly cared for us.

—General Vang Pao at Jerry Daniels' funeral, Missoula, Montana, May 9, 1982

Jerry "Hog" Daniels was dead.

The news spread like a mountain wildfire among the Hmong in Thai refugee camps and Hmong communities across the U.S. They were stunned, as were Daniels' smoke-jumping friends from the U.S. Forest Service, several of whom had served in Laos in aerial resupply and had stayed in touch.

Following the Hmong exodus from Long Chieng in May 1975, Daniels had worked on refugee affairs—particularly Hmong resettlement—at the U.S. Embassy in Bangkok.

In early December 1981, "Tango Juliet" (T.J.), one of Daniels' closest friends who had served as SKY advisor in aerial resupply in Military Region II of Laos, stopped in Bangkok for a three-day visit with him. "In the evenings after Jerry got off work, I joined him at his apartment to talk. He told me that within a year he would be finished in Thailand. He would have done all he could to get the Hmong refugees into the U.S. Then he would go back to the U.S. and try to do something about getting the Hmong off welfare.[1]

"Jerry also mentioned that he had received two death threats from Hmong refugees who wanted to go to the U.S. He had not approved their applications because they had failed their interviews. When Jerry asked them details about certain battles which they claimed to have been involved in, they answered incorrectly. He concluded that they were falsely claiming to be Vang Pao soldiers and to have worked closely with the Americans [criteria for being allowed into the U.S. on the refugee program]. They had threatened to shoot him."

T.J. urged Daniels to "pack it up" and return to the U.S. "Since Jerry had always wanted to prospect for gold, I suggested he should look for gold on his properties in Montana until he found something else to do."

Randolph "Toby" Scott had known Daniels since 1962 when they trained together at Inter-Mountain Aviation, a CIA proprietary company in Marana, Arizona. Scott had talked to Hog on his last home leave and urged him to return to the states, but "Jerry told me he had more work to do with the Hmong resettlement."[2] Daniels told Toby Scott about another mystery man—either a Thai or a Hmong—who called periodically on the phone, warning, "I'm going to get you. I'm going to kill you." During that last conversation, Scott warned Daniels: "If you stay around over there, you're going to get killed." Only months later, Scott's prophecy was fulfilled.

The last time anybody saw Hog alive was on the evening of April 27, 1982. He and two other Americans and their girlfriends had been partying at his apartment on Sukumvit Road in Bangkok. Three days later Daniels' body was discovered in his apartment by Thai police. According to the official investigation, the date of death was April 28, and the cause was asphyxiation due to a gas leak from a faulty bathroom hot water heater. Immediately rumors of foul play began to circulate.

* * *

On May 8, 1982, a chilling spring wind swept across Montana. It seemed particularly sharp as it crossed the runway at the Missoula municipal airport. A small group of men—representing Daniels' family, the State Department, the CIA, and the Hmong—talked in muffled tones and scanned the cloudy skies as they waited for the Northwest Orient flight from Seattle that was carrying Daniels' body. Inside the terminal about 30 Hmong, not allowed through security, also waited.

"Lucky," a Hmong who had held the rank of captain in the Lao Army, had worked closely with Daniels beginning in 1970 when Daniels became chief of operations at Long Chieng. He had been the interpreter-liaison between Daniels and the Lao Army. Lucky had been among the first Hmong refugees to come to the U.S. After living in Idaho and Indiana, he had moved to Montana and lived near Missoula where more than 500 Hmong had settled.[3] He now stood among the mourners.

Moua Cha, who had been "rescued" by Daniels from a disappointing life in another state and brought to Montana, also stood among the mourners. In his sadness, Moua Cha struggled to think of a way to honor his benefactor.

Finally, the plane landed and rolled to a stop. A U.S. government representative stepped from the group waiting outside the terminal, signed the bill of lading, and accepted the coffin.

Inside the terminal, Hmong eyes watched the proceedings on the tarmac. Many did not want to believe Jerry Daniels was dead. They wanted to believe he was needed on another intelligence assignment and his "death" in Bangkok was only a cover. As they watched, they whispered to each other that the coffin was too small to hold Daniels. Maybe he was not dead after all.

The procession moved quickly to the Mountain View Mortuary Chapel, just a block from Lucky's house. Once in the funeral home, Jerry belonged to the Hmong. They intended to honor their favorite SKY advisor with a traditional Hmong funeral. First, they wanted to open the casket. That was not possible. Much to their surprise and chagrin, they learned that it had been sealed by public health authorities. The coffin would remain sealed.

Over the casket, they draped a large piece of pa'ndau, in the traditional colors of black and red accented with whites, greens, and yellows. To this cloth they pinned a blown-up photograph of Daniels framed by a strip of intricate Hmong embroidery. A heart-shaped spray of pink and red carnations outlined Daniels' image. To the left of the casket stood a spray of daisies with a large card that read: "From the Hmong of the Midwestern U.S."

Lucky, a principal organizer, summed up the Hmong intentions. "We Hmong do everything for him. We served him a Hmong ceremony instead of a Western one. Hmong played the pipes and knocked the drum. We have elders to give good wishes to his family." And that they did in the three days to follow.

As Daniels' American and Hmong friends assembled in Missoula, Hmong women and girls prepared feast foods. Hmong men and boys rotated watches by his casket while others butchered two pigs and several chickens.

SKY advisor "Mr. Clean," still sporting a clean shaven head as he had when he worked with Hog in Laos, flew in from Arizona. T.J., wearing cowboy boots, turtleneck, and tweed jacket, and Toby Scott, wearing his Texas string necktie, also flew in. Hmong who had worked with Daniels in Laos arrived by plane and car from other states. Six high school friends from Missoula were chosen by Jerry's mother to carry his casket. Honorary pallbearers, six Hmong—Glassman, Worm, Lucky, Sancho, Judy, and Spider—stood by attentively. Some of them, at the time only teenagers, had worked as ground Forward Air Guides in Laos. All had worked closely with Daniels. All had received their code-names personally from him.

Hmong rituals began. Hmong pipes lamented, drums beat, and Hmong touched the casket and wailed their final words to Daniels. Throughout the night, taking turns, they kept vigil by his side.

Early the next morning, General Vang Pao flew in from California with five Hmong. Mourners were already gathered in the chapel at the funeral home when he arrived. Dressed in a pearl gray suit, Vang Pao started up the aisle of the crowded chapel. Hmong who had not seen the general for years reached out to him as he passed. He paused often, greeting those whom he had not seen for so long.

T.J. stared at Vang Pao. He had never seen him out of military attire, and he had not seen him as a refugee. T.J. was startled: "Vang Pao no longer looked like the dreaded guerrilla leader I had known in Laos."

After many pauses, Vang Pao reached the front of the chapel. The ceremonies began. Wearing a silver necklace and black traditional clothes, a shaman sitting at Daniels' head beat a drum with a pulse that spoke to the soul. Hmong knew the drum talk. Those sitting next to Louise Daniels, Jerry's mother, whispered to her what the drum said. Then, the *khene* player, blowing and sucking on his musical pipe, moved before the coffin, offering a lamenting whine. Women and girls danced, swaying slowly to the hypnotic music, weaving their fingers in beckoning motions. Old French coins and toy coins accompanied their swaying skirts like miniature tambourines.

When the dancers finished, General Vang Pao stepped forward. He stood before Daniels' coffin. Speaking first in Hmong and then in English, he said his final words to Jerry. "From 1961 until the Communist takeover of Laos, our friend Jerry Daniels dedicated every ounce of his strength toward helping us, the Free People of Laos, improve the quality of our lives. Jerry gladly accepted life in our rural villages in order to better understand our problems, hopes, and dreams. Jerry shared with us the dream that one day life would return to normal and we would be able to once again enjoy the beauty and serenity of the high mountains of Laos.

"Sadly, this dream was not to be. In 1975 the anticommunist government of Laos fell to the communist invaders and along with our American friend, we were forced to seek refuge in Thailand.

"Jerry continued to serve our people as a State Department official at the American Embassy in Bangkok. Jerry saw to it that our people were given the opportunity to come to the U.S. to begin a new life. We all have the courage to meet the challenges which we must face because our friend Jerry taught us well. Jerry was not only our advisor, but our friend as well. He dedicated more than twenty years of his life to us and we grew to know him well, not only in name, but in spirit too. I guess we love Jerry so much because we always knew that he honestly cared for us.

"Jerry's life came to a premature end while in Bangkok, still serving the people he had grown to love. We all owe Jerry a lot for all that he did for us and we will miss him very much. Today, each of us in our own way will wish our dear friend a sad farewell."

He paused, turned, and touched the coffin. Then he bid a final farewell to a man whom he had known through the good times and tragic times, by simply saying: "Until we meet again—goodbye, old friend."

Daniels' official eulogy, signed by Secretary of State Alexander Haig and read by State Department representative Jim Schill, referred to Daniels' well-known ability to turn a phrase. "Jerry's inimitable approach to the English language has left its permanent mark on those of us fortunate to have been his cronies with such phrases as 'snaggletooth' which reminds us of his most complicated refugee case—"the Grimm sisters"—different from the other 'patootsies' in Jerry's life. Jerry would enjoin us not to be wetblankets and even after a long day of case work would be ready to put on his moccasins. Indeed, we could go on into the sunset. . . . "

These phrases, sounding so much like Jerry, touched Hog's tough smoke-jumping, goose-hunting, elk-stalking, trout-fishing, beer-drinking comrades. They cried. And they cried again when they heard his final words: "Above all, Jerry would ask that we not grieve, that we rededicate ourselves to the task of caring for the Indochinese refugees and keeping faith with the Hmong people who have given us so much. For all of us, Jerry's heroic example will always be there, over the next hill. He was one of those our pioneers must have had in mind when they coined the phrase: 'Give me men to match the mountains.'"

The Hmong pipes wailed again. Dancing and drumming were interspersed with chants of elders. Ceremonies carried on through the morning and afternoon and into the evening. American and Hmong friends came and went. Food for the hundreds of mourners was available at several Hmong homes. During the night, Hmong took turns sitting with their former SKY advisor. The next day the ceremonies and feasting continued.

That night, men told stories about Jerry. Lucky remembered the mountain climbing he and Hog had done together. "We walked mountains. I never could catch him up. He was best for walking. I don't have to worry about him. He was very tough. He could walk all day. One time, he even helped me carry something. I still cannot catch up. I'm talking about climbing; I'm not talking about walking. I'm talking about going straight up. Hours and hours. We walked up 50 percent of Phou Bia once. We start at 7 a.m. At sundown, we are about two miles before our first station."

Some recalled Hog's boast that he was the rodeo champion of Laos, although there was no competition other than Shep. Then there was the time he had decided to train a rooster that would be the best fighting cock in Laos. Much to his embarrassment, Hog's rooster had refused to fight any opponents.

Scott reminisced about when they both resigned from the CIA and went on a 58-day wilderness trek through the Bob Marshall Wilderness, a journey neither man ever forgot. He and T.J. remembered how they had loaned him money to finish college, after which he had been re-recruited by the Agency and returned to Laos to work in the wilderness for all those years. Hog stories continued far into the night.

His close friends also talked about his untimely death. Scott, like the Hmong, wished Daniels had died in a helicopter crash or a moment of heroism—not in bed killed by a suspicious leaky gas heater. Scott never accepted the accidental theory of his friend's death. He believed that Daniels had been murdered. If the cause of death was asphyxiation due to a malfunctioning gas water heater, then Scott believed that "someone *made* the water heater kill him."

While Hmong funerals traditionally last four or five days, the Missoula Hmong compromised, making it a three-day ceremony. On the third day at 11 a.m., the hearse carrying Jerry Daniels' body moved slowly over the Higgins Street Bridge that crossed the Clark's Fork and headed toward an old cemetery northwest of town. In a car following Daniels rode T.J. and Toby Scott.

As they crossed the river, Scott looked down at the fast, high waters that streamed down from the mountain snows of this vast and beautiful valley. He recalled the pledge that he and Daniels had made in 1964: if, after all their smoke-jumping and other dangerous missions they knew were ahead, they were around at age 40, they would jump off this bridge into the Clark's Fork. Scott thought about that youthful pledge, taken when they were both in their 20s and held an exuberant belief of youth that by age 40 they would have been killed in some heroic action or else be spent men who had done everything. This vow to make a fatal jump off the bridge was not a suicide pact but rather a "marker" on the lives and achievements of two young men determined to live life to the fullest. Scott, a few years older than Daniels, recalled that when he was approaching 40 and working in South Vietnam for Alaska Barge and Transport Company, he received a letter from Daniels, in his mid-30s. It recommended that they change their date with the Higgins Street Bridge by moving it up to 50.

The procession moving so slowly on the Higgins Street Bridge carried Jerry Daniels over it for the last time—at age 40.

At the cemetery, the chilly wind of the past three days blew against those standing under cloudy skies. Around the grave, smoke-jumpers, high school friends, the six honorary Hmong pallbearers, his brothers and mother listened as Hmong elders exorcised the bad influences that had caused Jerry's premature death. Lucky, standing next to T.J., explained: "We usually ask one of our elders to give a short speech—special words—to the dead, telling them they do not want to see any of his relatives or family die the way he did. The elders ask him to carry all those bad things with him and not to leave anything bad behind so the rest of his family will not have the problems like he did or die."

The Hmong insisted that everyone stay until the grave was covered. As a backhoe operator revved up his machine, T.J. tossed into the grave a can of Olympia Golden beer, Daniels' favorite. Scott threw in a can of Cophenhagen snuff and a Louis L'Amour western novel. Others followed with dirt and flowers. Mr. Clean threw in his Seiko watch, a reminder of the days in Laos when all Americans working in covert operations—particularly the SKY advisors—wore expensive Seikos, the first watches to give both time and date. As the backhoe dropped its last scoop of dirt on the casket, Lucky said in accented English just loud enough for T.J. to hear: "Goodbye, Hog. Goodbye, my friend. I'll see you later."

Jerry "Hog" Daniels had been laid to rest. But Lucky and Moua Cha had one more thing to do. They searched for a way to permanently honor him, his relationship with the Hmong, and his work in Laos. They talked incessantly about this. Finally they had the answer.

The next spring, T.J. returned to Missoula and visited Daniels' grave. He was stunned. On the gray headstone were the words "Jerrold Barker Daniels" in large letters. Beneath that was "Jerry" and opposite that "Mr. Hog" with his dates of birth and death below these two words. In the center of the stone was a scene of Long Chieng, the "dreaded valley," Skyline, and the ridges to the east. A moon rose over the far mountain and two Canada geese sat on what might have been the "dreaded mountain" looking down onto the valley and 20 Alternate. Beneath the geese, in Lao script, were the words: "Long Chieng." At the base of the gravestone rested violet pansies, placed there by a Hmong.

As the years pass, the Hmong do not forget. Fresh flowers often rest on his grave. Each Christmas, Hmong make their way to the snowy cemetery to place greens on Mr. Hog's grave.

The Montana Hmong look after Jerry's mother, who lives alone and has Parkinson's disease. Louise Daniels is grateful for their love and attention: "Jerry left me a most precious gift. He gave me the Hmong."[4]

*   *   *

After Daniels' death, T.J. was often asked to explain why Daniels stayed so long in Laos and why he was successful in working with the Hmong. In the beginning, T.J. gave pat answers, but he knew there was more to the explanation. Several years later, he thought he knew; he wrote it all down as if it were the eulogy which he wished he had given at Daniels' funeral.

"Jerry's basic values of honesty and hard work were well ingrained in him by his mother, Louise. Jerry's mother and brothers operated a cafe, maintained the rural telephone lines, and worked on cattle ranches in Helmville, Montana, before moving to Missoula. Jerry excelled at everything he attempted; from playing chess to riding a bad Brahma bull, from smoke-jumping, skiing and wrestling, to being an avid reader and student. Jerry's natural instincts, his mountain-man abilities, coupled with his ability to adapt and learn, made him a very effective advisor to 'V.P.' and Hmong guerrilla units."

He read it over several times and then added two more sentences: "Jerry lived the life that most people only read or hear about. Best of all, he held the respect of his peers."

31.

Abused and Abandoned

Trying to monitor human rights in closed countries is extremely difficult. One has to start with the assumption that one can never do anything about human rights violations until the facts have been assembled and then published. Publishing human rights violations is the enemy of abuses. Silence is acquiescence. The worst abuses take place when no one is paying attention.

—Aryeh Neier, Vice Chairman of Americas Watch, 1985*

A t the end of 1983, Lao People's Democratic Republic (LPDR) officials announced that internment camps had been abolished and repeated this claim to foreign journalists. But Amnesty International's information, which would be published in 1985, was quite different and much more accurate. "According to former camp inmates who subsequently made their way to Thailand and sources in Laos, however, a number of other camps have continued to exist in some form, often as bases for former internees reassigned to heavy labour projects outside. Several new camps, some functioning as high-security prisons, have also reportedly been set up."[1]

Further, since the communists had taken over in 1975, a considerable body of evidence documenting the brutality of the Lao People's Liberation Army (LPLA) and the People's Army of Vietnam (PAVN) against the Hmong and others in Laos was being assembled. Those escaping Laos were keeping records of atrocities in the various camps, whose locations were well-known to escapees, and of life in the Gulag. They had detailed

---

*Aryeh Neier. Interview with author. New York City, 1985.

data on relatives and friends "lost" to the communist guns, poisons, torture, starvation, forced-labor, and imprisonment. Keeping records of family and clan members was nothing new for the Hmong. They were continuing a centuries old tradition of Hmong society wherein it was a clan responsibility to keep records and information on clan members. Unlike the Nazi atrocities of World War II in the extermination camps from which very few inmates ever escaped, the brutalities in camps maintained by the LPDR and in the areas under its control were well-documented by the Hmong whose information was kept current by the numbers escaping Laos into Thailand.

In early 1984, a Hmong leader at Ban Vinai wrote asking if I could come quickly—there was terrible trouble in the camp. I departed immediately.

On the way to the camp, I stopped in Bangkok to meet with members of the new team of experts recently established by the U.S. to gather CBW data. (In the parlance of the time, attacks were referred to as CBW attacks and the team was called the CBW team.) Late the previous year—more than eight years after the chemical-biological toxin attacks began in Laos—this team arrived in Thailand to collect data on CBW usage from both Laos and Cambodia. This team included a State Department foreign service officer who functioned as its titular head, a military weapons expert with knowledge of chemical weapons, and a military doctor. The team served under the overall authority of the U.S. Ambassador to Thailand. Unlike the low profile of past American activities to collect data, this effort was publicized.

Over a hamburger in the embassy cafeteria, I asked the team's medical officer what he had done to prepare himself for this assignment. He answered that he had done little because he wanted to come with an open mind. I was surprised and pointed out that surely such an important and complicated assignment required rigorous study of chemical-biological warfare—particularly trichothecenes, since they had been found in high doses in attack samples—and of the effects of these toxins on humans. I added that cultural and historical knowledge about the Hmong and the political situation in Laos would have been extremely useful to any investigator. He disagreed, insisting that it was much more scientific not to have studied the collected data. He thought it unimportant to know anything about the Hmong. He also told me that, in his opinion, all Hmong sicknesses could be explained by common diseases.

I knew that Washington had asked the team to obtain blood samples from Hmong in Ban Vinai to establish a data base on their blood characteristics. To do this, the team needed the assistance of the Hmong leadership to organize volunteer blood donors. They had refused to cooperate. The team was at an impasse. I offered to intercede on this issue when I arrived in the camp.

Later, at Ban Vinai, I would learn that the Hmong leaders considered the arrival of this team a bittersweet event. They were pleased that the U.S. now apparently had in place a plan to document for the scientific and political communities the events in Laos. Their confidence in this long-awaited effort, however, had been shattered. According to the Hmong, the head of the U.S. team immediately alienated Hmong camp leaders by shouting at them that they had lied about the use of lethal agents. "The American CBW team leader shouted at us: 'It's only bee shit,'" reported a Hmong in charge of keeping CBW data. While one might argue that the American intended this as an investigative technique to get at the truth, such a method did not work with the Hmong. Instead, his attitude and behavior angered and embarrassed them. Reluctantly and sadly, they concluded it would be impossible to work with the head of the U.S. team.

After long discussions and urging on my part, and an offer from the CBW team to compensate each blood donor with 100 Thai *baht* ($5), the Hmong agreed to participate in the blood study if it might help future victims.

*   *   *

As I arrived at the camp, bulldozers climbed the hill behind the refugee huts to the Hmong burial grounds, ripping out fresh bodies of the dead. Hmong families moaned in grief that their relatives' remains were scattered and exposed. Decomposing heads of Hmong stuck up through the red soil. Arms and legs trailing remnants of black Hmong cloth littered the pathways in the new housing area.

United Nations High Commission on Refugees (UNHCR) personnel and Thai officials had ordered new housing constructed for the increasing number of Hmong and Mien refugees who were being transferred from other Thai camps about to close. This new housing was being built on Hmong graves, even though the camp was in a sparsely populated area and there was plenty of other space for building shelters. Hmong leaders had complained strongly to the Thai camp authorities. The official answer was always the same: "You are just refugees. You have no rights."

Thai and UNHCR officials persisted in building upon the graves. When ordered to move into the new shelters, some Hmong refused, explaining only evil would come if they did. Others, afraid of the authorities, did move into the new structures—windowless, tin-roofed, suffocatingly hot, and crowded. The entire camp population was distraught by the forced violations of tribal taboos that prohibit disturbing a body and living with or on the bodies of the dead.

Hmong prayed for foreign visitors to come so they could show them the bulldozers digging up the corpses. But few people came. Those that did come only visited the Thai camp commander and were taken on special tours by him and his staff to see the good things. American visitors never stayed the night nor even long enough to walk through the crowded camp to see the situation.

"No one came to see us living on the graveyard," explained a thin Hmong man. About two feet from the only entrance to his shelter, a skull showed through the soil. He had cut strips of bamboo to make a small fence to protect whoever it was that was buried there and to keep children away. He told me that because so many people had died mysteriously their bodies might be carrying diseases to harm the living.

Once the Hmong knew that I was truly interested in their plight, dozens appeared, asking to take me to their areas to show me bodies. A pretty young mother begged me to follow her. We hurried along the rutted pathways where children with bloated bellies played with human bones sticking through muddy soil. Behind her living quarters was a large mound surrounded by a small split bamboo fence. Around the fenced mound, she grew lettuce and cabbages. Since few vegetables were delivered by the UNHCR contractors, refugees fought for small patches of soil on which to plant a few seeds. She explained that in the mound were several fresh bodies. It was terrible, she said, to live with the bodies and to grow the life-giving vegetables almost on top of them.

Just by looking at the mound, it was not possible to know if it held bodies or not—and I said so. A large crowd quickly gathered. When the onlookers heard my disbelief, they emitted a moaning wail. Several men grabbed sticks and jumped inside the fenced area. Frantically they dug at the mound. Within seconds, one stick caught something. The moan went up again. Slowly, the man worked his stick under something. Slowly, slowly, he brought out of the earth a leg, skin still clinging to the bone, and with it part of the black trouser of a Hmong man. Again the moan.

Now the older man dug deeper to find another body. I stopped him, telling him I believed them. I asked the gathered crowd if anyone knew how many bodies were in this spot. No one knew; when they were forced into this area the graves had already been bulldozed.

After the graveyard visit, I joined a friend to stand in a long line waiting for his meat ration for the week. Hmong teenagers, hired for a few Thai *baht* to chop up the week's meat supply, hacked, sawed, and pulled at the bloody gristle and bone to divide it into small portions. Since obtaining meat for the family was man's business, it was mostly men who waited in the long lines. Each man waited with a stick and some "string" made from vines. At last our turn came. Our meat was mostly slimy gray gristle and smelled bad. With tenderness, he tied the small piece of flesh and bone to his stick, put it on his shoulder as if it were the carcass of a sambur deer, and we walked back down the hill to his family of ten.

Occasionally fish was delivered. However, it was often rotten when it arrived. Doctors at the camp hospital knew that when fish arrived they would be busy with patients ill from eating spoiled food. While Thailand is a land of tropical plenty with abundant and delicious fruits and vegetables, UNHCR food deliveries rarely included fresh fruit. Sometimes there would be leafy cabbages or a kind of bean, but always it was the cheapest vegetable available in the local market.

Ban Vinai was an official refugee camp under the auspices of the UNHCR; those in the camp were to be fed and protected by this agency. The UNHCR contracted with Thai firms to purchase and deliver food supplies to the camp for distribution. The rice was broken and contained stones and rat droppings, indicating it was probably floor sweepings from rice mills, fit only for animal feed. The center chiefs informed me that many in this camp were very hungry and some were starving. Since the early 1980s, these Hmong camp leaders had repeatedly reported not enough food was delivered to adequately feed those living there. Now the chiefs told me that some 5,000 Hmong lived in Ban Vinai illegally because they had escaped Laos and sought sanctuary in Thailand after the refugee camps had been officially closed. Many in this category were starving because they had no food ration at all.*

A camp leader invited me to eat with his family and friends. He was most apologetic about the fare: rice with stones, boiled grasses and weeds, which I had watched his daughters picking earlier from the path-

---

*In the fall of 1987, Lao Family Community, Inc., the Hmong and Lao refugee non-profit organization in the U.S., offered to administer and finance a $300,000 effort to help maintain Hmong refugees in northern Thailand outside the camps and to offer assistance to Thai villagers in the area. This offer was not considered by Thailand.

way leading to the camp hospital, and several extremely small birds. I asked him where he got the birds. He said that his young sons with slingshots had killed these songbirds in my honor.

Because UNHCR food supplies were insufficient, supplemental food had to be purchased by the refugees. That required money, which most of them did not have. There were four ways to obtain this much-needed money for food. A handful of people earned a minuscule amount working for the UNHCR or foreign relief agencies in the camp. Women and children made *pa'ndau,* traditional needlework, and tried to sell pieces to the relief workers or camp visitors. Enterprising women sold vegetables which they had managed to grow in scraps of soil around refugee shelters and along the narrow banks of the stream that passed through the camp. Others received money from relatives resettled in third countries. Those with money supplemented the meager U.N. diet either at the Thai market outside the camp gates or at the small refugee market inside the camp overseen by the Thai authorities.

For the thousands with no money, there was only hunger. Mothers were often too malnourished to nurse their babies. From time to time there were feeding programs for babies and mothers, but there were always those left out. Nightly I could hear hungry children crying and pleading for food.

In the past, I had complained to UNHCR officials in Bangkok who insisted that the food ration would be adequate if those who had the contract to supply the food adhered to it. That was not always the case; inferior, insufficient, and rotten food was often substituted. Refugees went hungry while merchants became rich. Once again, on my return to Bangkok I would meet with UNHCR officials to report the bleak situation in Ban Vinai. Once again they would listen, take notes, and say they would see what could be done.

Refugees who had crossed into Thailand in 1975 and 1976 reported few instances of brutality by Thai people. The somewhat friendly Thai attitude toward tribal refugees began to change in 1978. The Thais discovered refugees as a source of money and valuables. They also discovered that refugees had no rights, no recourse to abuses, no ability to bring charges against thieves, murderers, extortionists, or rapists.

After the slaughter at Phou Bia, those who survived the trek to cross into Thailand often found they were still not safe. Thai villagers and Thai defense forces, armed but untrained, scouted for Hmong crossing into Thailand. Surrounding new arrivals, some *Aw Saw,* local defense forces, made refugees strip naked. Sometimes these men gang-raped the prettiest girls and women. They often took all valuables, particularly silver earrings and necklaces and the ancestral bars of silver, the last store of Hmong family resource. These treasured silver bars, usually owned by families for generations, were often the total inheritance given to a child by his father or mother, to be used only in extreme emergencies.*

If they had nothing of value, the Thais tried extortion. A refugee who did not want to be returned to the communists had to find someone to pay his ransom. Terrified Hmong sent messages with these gangsters to the refugee camps, asking if there were any relatives or friends who could pay. Some had no one to assist. Some had relatives in a camp, but often they had no money. Some who could not pay were pushed back.

When teenager Vang Jue crossed the Mekong in September 1976, she was taken to the Pak Chom police station where she was held for six months while housing was built at Ban Vinai. "Then, the Thai police were nice. They allowed us to be hired by the Thai to work in Thai fields for 20 *baht* ($1 U.S.) per day. I had no children then, so I worked in the field every day for money to buy food.

"In April 1979, things changed for the Hmong coming out of Laos. The police beat my mother and forced her and her small group back across the river. Then the Thai asked, 'How much can you pay to be allowed to cross back to Thailand?' My mother said $300 [a lot of money in northern Thailand in 1979]. My mother had no money, but they allowed her to return. She got the money from relatives and paid the Thai."[2]

Rape in Ban Vinai was rampant. Here the victims knew which Thai soldiers or policemen had raped them. Reports of these rapes to Thai camp authorities rarely resulted in action; this, in turn, subtly sent a message that raping refugee women carried no penalty.

"In 1979, a 14-year-old Hmong girl was raped by 12 Thai in Ban Vinai camp. The Thai came to her 'house' demanding money from her parents. The family had none so the Thai took the beautiful daughter into the night and raped her all night long. They also beat her when she screamed. She couldn't walk; she crawled home the next day. Her parents took her to the camp hospital and reported the rape to the Thai authorities who did nothing."[3]

---

*Videotapes made in 1991 and 1992 of market scenes in Vientiane showed stacks of these precious antique silver bars. When Hmong in the U.S. viewed the tapes and noticed the ingots with their distinctive upturned ends, they were horrified at the large number. "Either the communists killed many Hmong for these bars or they stole them. Hmong would never give these up unless there was no choice" (Vang Ying, California, May 17, 1992).

Refugees learned quickly that if they complained too much about anything, they would be punished severely. The Hmong had little choice but to suffer in silence. Grief, terror, hunger, and frustration filled the camps, particularly Ban Vinai with the largest Hmong population.

When VIPs visited Ban Vinai, they often arrived in a helicopter landing on the playing field, a large dirt area near the Thai camp commander's headquarters. He treated the visitors to refreshments or a meal. That was followed by a briefing on the history of the camp, with charts of numbers of refugees in various relief programs, and a prepared speech by a senior Hmong which was translated into English, often by a Thai on the commander's staff. The Hmong speakers always commended the listening Thai commander and the Thai efforts on their behalf. If there was time, visitors toured the "hospital" with a stop at the market area so they could buy Hmong needlework, the *pa'ndau*. With souvenirs purchased, it was time to depart. In fact, visitors did not see refugee camp life at all. They saw the Thai authorities. Many VIPs were impressed with Ban Vinai. Over the years, many have told me that the Hmong there were "happy as clams," "happy as bugs in a rug," "with no worries."

* * *

Hmong frustration continued to vent itself against Vang Pao. Some blamed him for the acceptance by the media of the bee feces theory of the deadly poison attacks; they blamed him for not being able to convince the U.S. or any government to aid the resistance against the Kaysone regime; they blamed him for the suffering of those in refugee camps and of those trapped inside Laos and for Hmong resettlement problems in the U.S.

Although the U.S. was at that time publicly funding resistance forces in Angola, Afghanistan, Nicaragua, and, significantly, in neighboring Cambodia, Vang Pao and the United Lao National Liberation Front (ULNLF) were unable to obtain U.S. support—even official acknowledgment—for any resistance to the Kaysone regime. In desperation, Neo Hom leaders tried to raise money from Lao and Hmong refugees resettled in the U.S., France, Australia, and Canada.

General Vang Pao was under siege not only by some of his countrymen, but also by some Americans. Former anti–Vietnam War activists, many of whom were now involved in the refugee resettlement business, reported him to federal authorities for raising funds in the U.S. to overthrow a foreign government—a violation of federal statutes. Some harassed him publicly for not encouraging more Hmong to resettle in the

U.S. Vang Pao believed that many of his people would be better off in Southeast Asia—in Laos—in their homeland. He knew all too well of their difficult lives in the U.S. He continued to believe that return to Laos would be possible.

Agents trained by Hanoi, who had entered the U.S. as refugees through a sloppy screening process, trailed Vang Pao, waiting for an opportunity to strike. Death threats became more frequent and more brazen. By 1984, Vang Pao was receiving death threats by phone and letter, promising that he would be poisoned in such a way that authorities could never determine the cause of his death.[4]

Not only were there death threats against Hmong and Lao leaders, there was at the same time an increased effort to create discord and dissension in the Hmong communities in the U.S. It is not totally clear who was behind these successful efforts. Hmong who had more recently escaped from Laos were quite certain that the LPDR was the sponsoring culprit. I interviewed one Hmong who had listened to and recognized both Lao and Hmong in California whom he believed to be part of the LPDR campaign.

Thao Yia was 14 when the communists came to power. In 1975, his father had been captured and taken to a seminar camp at Long Chieng. After his father escaped, 50 communist Lao soldiers came to his village looking for him. He was not there. To terrorize the villagers so that they would not harbor escaped seminar prisoners, the soldiers killed Thao Yia's brother and sister the next morning when they went outside the village. After this, everyone was scared and many moved to the Phou Bia area. For seven years, Thao Yia lived in the mountain jungle in the Phou Bia area under attack by the LPLA and PAVN forces. He escaped Phou Bia in October 1982.

When I interviewed him in March 1985, Thao Yia had been in the U.S. about six months. After telling me about his experiences in Laos, he concluded by saying: "I'm worried that American 'Reds' and the U.S. will make relations with Laos so we can't take back Laos. I see Red [communist] Lao who came here as refugees. In Fresno, I see Red Lao come here to visit, sent by the Lao government to tell the refugees propaganda. They also collect money from refugees here, saying they'll take it to their families in Laos. They are only here to make money for themselves. There were four Red Hmong in Fresno last week. These Red Hmong and Red Lao start rumors in California to cause problems for Hmong living in America."[5]

* * *

In June 1985, I received a report from Northern Warrior Moua Cher Pao, the tough Hmong commander who had broken the pledge with his people and abandoned Bouam Loung to flee to Thailand in the Long Chieng exodus. He had lived with his guilt at Ban Vinai for awhile and then had rejoined the local people in their fight to survive. After so many years hiding in the jungle he had lost all his teeth and his health was not good, but he remained a wiry, determined fighter who had not given up on throwing the communist force out of his homeland. Moua's communique reported: "In May two Vietnamese divisions mixed with four Pathet Lao battalions surround us at UG 337-813 and a big fight took place. Every type of weapon was used, including a rocket with poison. Our side lost 365 dead, 100 wounded. We captured three big weapons, 40.8 used to shoot down air planes. Enemy dead 200. Wounded could not count."

Later that month, I received a chilling report from Laos about a communist massacre of thousands of civilians by using chemicals in a cave in Moua Cher Pao's area. I filed a report with the Defense Intelligence Agency (DIA), giving the coordinates of the cave at UG 332-820 and requesting an immediate investigation. Weeks went by and I heard nothing. In the U.S. and in the camp, Hmong talked incessantly about this massacre and questioned why the U.S. government had not investigated.

Also in June 1985, Her Pa Kao, the Chao Fa soldier, appeared in Angola, billed as the leader of Lao resistance. He shared the podium with Angola's Jonas Savimbi and representatives from the Nicaraguan Democratic Force and the Afghan *mujahedeen*. This meeting was sponsored by American millionaire Lewis Lehrman, who headed an organization called Citizens for America. Here, Pa Kao, who now placed his clan name last so he was known as Pa Kao Her, was honored as one who fights "for independence from Soviet colonialism." Lehrman gave each honoree a copy of the U.S. Constitution.[6] Pa Kao Her left Angola with a videotape of his "coronation" as the head of the Lao freedom fighters and with write-ups and photos in international news magazines.

This was the same Her Pa Kao who as a Chao Fa leader believed that his magic wand could heal wounds. After the Hmong defeat at Phou Bia, he had moved to northern Thailand, where he and former Lao General Boonleurt operated a cross-border resistance effort with the knowledge and support of some portion of the Thai military.

A Lao general actively involved in resistance activities in Laos questioned why Americans supported Pa Kao Her. This general also found it curious that the Americans had even talked to Pa Kao Her when he himself, a well-known high-ranking Lao resistance leader associated with General Vang Pao's efforts, had been prevented by the Thai from meeting with U.S. Embassy officials. The U.S. position had changed after Alexander Haig resigned as secretary of state. The Lao general recalled: "American officials told us that the U.S. wanted nothing to do with Lao resistance. 'The only thing that we can do together,' they explained, 'is the MIA and POW issue.'"[7]

What appeared to be U.S. official endorsement of Pa Kao Her gave this unknown man credibility with some Hmong. It confused others and lessened General Vang Pao's influence. If such was the strategy of those promoting Pa Kao Her with the Americans, it succeeded.

In the U.S., Hmong were startled and fearful when the media reported Pa Kao Her as their leader. Hmong asked each other rhetorically: "How could he be our leader when we don't even know his face?" Some laughed at the absurdity; others did not. Hmong leaders in Asia and in the West were confused about this apparent official U.S. backing of Pa Kao Her and not of General Vang Pao. Impressed with the laudatory world-wide publicity given to Pa Kao Her and disappointed at Vang Pao's inability to solve many of the critical Hmong problems, some Hmong paid attention to the rise of this little-known man.

Pa Kao Her emerged again in August and September 1985 when he came to Dallas to attend a meeting sponsored by the United States Council for World Freedom, an anticommunist organization chaired by retired Army Major General John K. Singlaub. In order to attend this meeting, Pa Kao Her needed a visa as well as a passport. The U.S. Embassy in Bangkok issued him a visa. At the airport, Thai officials recognized his Thai passport as a forgery and detained him. Cables were exchanged between Bangkok and Washington. In the end, he was allowed to proceed to Dallas to attend the conference on condition that he not travel beyond Dallas and return immediately to Thailand after the conclusion of the conference.[8]

As soon as the Dallas conference was over, Pa Kao Her, in defiance of the State Department, held meetings in Hmong communities in California and in Minnesota. His six-hour meeting on September 21, 1985, with Hmong leaders in St. Paul, Minnesota, was taped. Among those attending was Dr. Yang Dao, the Hmong who had earlier urged the Hmong to stay in Laos because accommodation with the communists was possible. According to a Hmong who reviewed that tape, the purpose of the meeting was to present Pa Kao Her's liberation strategies to the Hmong leaders secretly, to discuss the U.S. and China's support for Pa Kao Her's group, and to present Pa Kao Her's plan to run Laos once the country was liberated.

Hmong were impressed with General Singlaub's involvement with Pa Kao Her. Many believed that Singlaub had an official role with the Reagan administration. When Pa Kao Her told them that the Reagan White House had promised to provide him with millions of dollars and with military equipment to liberate Laos, many naturally supported him and his requests for donations. Many Hmong gave generously.

Ethnics Organization Liberation Organization, a newsletter published by Pa Kao Her's organization, in October 1985, reported that the organization was officially recognized by the U.S. Government and that it had received 1,050,000 (not indicating what currency) from the U.S. Government for its 15 politicians' operating costs.[9] This turned out to be untrue. The Reagan White House gave nothing to Pa Kao Her's group and apparently never made any promises. Later, it was widely reported in the press that the People's Republic of China had given them weapons.

In the spring of 1986, Larry H. Tifverberg, executive director of General Singlaub's Council for World Freedom, held a meeting in Fresno, California, with about 900 Hmong. According to one in attendance, "Since only about half of the Hmong at the meeting understood English, Pa Kao Her's group used an interpreter. When Tifverberg came to the stage to talk, he said that he was from a non-profit, private group and that he was NOT President Reagan's assistant. Pa Kao Her's interpreter, however, told the assembled Hmong that Tifverberg WAS an assistant to President Reagan.[10]

"During the evening, Pa Kao Her's supporters told the group that all Hmong should support Pa Kao Her and drop Vang Pao because the U.S. had dropped Vang Pao and picked up Pa Kao Her as the new leader since 152 nations recognized Pa Kao Her as the new resistance leader in Laos. He had the news articles and the Angola video to prove it."[11]

No one in the audience challenged any of this.

* * *

In the summer of 1986, I was in Bangkok before heading north to Ban Vinai and stopped by the U.S. Embassy to talk to the current CBW data collection team. Team members had changed often during its 30-month existence, with most members serving approximately 12 months. The Foreign Service Officer who headed this team was about to leave for an assignment in South America, his area of expertise.

Shortly after our meeting began, the team leader, tapping a folder on his desk, said that the samples his team had forwarded to Washington for analysis had either not yet been analyzed or had been negative—"just like the inquiry that you initiated last year about the cave massacre."

I was surprised that my request for an investigation into a reported massacre in Laos had been turned over to the CBW team in Bangkok. The team leader explained that they had responded to this DIA request in two ways. First, the army captain, the weapons expert on the team, had gone to Ban Vinai and talked to Chong Moua Lee, who spoke English and was often assigned to talk with foreigners. According to the captain, this Hmong knew nothing about the massacre. The second investigative step was to write a letter to *National Geographic* magazine in Washington, asking if there existed in Laos a cave big enough to hold thousands of people.

I don't remember if I was smiling or not, but I thought his comment about contacting *National Geographic* was a joke. I waited for the punchline, but it didn't come. He was serious. The head of the U.S. CBW team had written to *National Geographic* requesting information that any-one with even superficial knowledge of Laos would know: large lime-stone caves are abundant there. Not knowing what to say, I looked at a large, framed image of Mao Zedong on the embassy wall. Andy Warhol's work, I thought, and decided I had no choice but to change the subject.

I asked about the team's current activities. They explained that they monitored events in Laos through two young English-speaking Hmong in Ban Vinai whom they had hired to be their "eyes and ears." I asked why the team did not work directly with the Hmong leadership in the camp since CBW information was considered military information and therefore confidential to this leadership. They thought it better not to work with camp leaders or those involved with resistance because they might be prejudiced. I expressed doubts about their conclusions, pointing out that the resistance had access to current information inside Laos. They assured me that the team's "eyes and ears" worked fine.

I departed the icy air-conditioning of the second floor office where the team headquartered, walked down the stairs, out the iron-grated security door that sealed off the secure areas, past the Marine guard into the torrid heat, then past the gossiping Thai guards at the entrance check point onto the street. It seemed a long walk as I mulled over the team's words. Outside, I looked back through the embassy gate at the gray, squat building from which I had just come, and thought about my dis-turbing meeting with the CBW team.

Americans who had worked in Laos and in Thailand for years had warned me that this CBW team was easily deceived. One American, who had worked in Southeast Asia for years, knew the names and shady histories of several Lao who had repeatedly contacted this team and turned in fraudulent samples and spent ordnance for money or favors. He had summarized the situation: "Once the con-artists and communist agents realized that the CBW team members often knew little about Laos, they knew they could dupe the team on a regular basis—and did."[12]

That night, I headed north for Ban Vinai. After the all-night bus ride to Loei and two more early morning rides on local open-air buses, I arrived at one of the back gates to the camp. Here belligerent Thai soldiers, armed with M-16s, prevented me from entering. I explained that I had come to visit friends and that I was known to the Thai camp commander, Bounmee.

My explanations seemed to anger the guards. At gunpoint, they ordered me to Commander Bounmee's office. As we approached his headquarters compound, Hmong whom I knew sized up the situation. I noticed one of them walk away fast. One irritated Thai soldier rushed into the official compound to get the commander. He returned to announce that Bounmee would not be in the camp today to vouch for me. Soldiers motioned for me to sit down on a wooden bench outside the meeting room used by the camp's current Hmong chief, Vue Mai. I realized I was in a difficult situation, but did not understand why. Over the years, Commander Bounmee had entertained me at his headquarters, inviting me to have lunch with him several times. I had always reciprocated with presents. I had been in and out of this camp for years and only occasionally had Thai soldiers taken any serious interest in my comings and goings. On occasions when Thai guards demanded to see my official permission from the Thai government, which I didn't always have, I explained I was coming to visit Hmong friends and I was usually allowed to enter. These soldiers were acting tough and mean. Not only did I worry about myself but I feared that I was probably compromising Hmong as well.

After what seemed a long time, Chief Vue Mai walked up the hill toward me and the soldiers. Following him was the Hmong whom I had earlier seen walking away fast. As Vue Mai approached, he smiled, greeting me in Thai. His face was flushed and his eyes scanned the circle of armed soldiers. His welcome was uncharacteristically loud; Vue Mai was a quiet man. He grandiloquently gave me the Thai *whai*. We then shook hands Hmong style. Vue Mai ignored the Thai soldiers, who watched us in silence. Then one of them stepped forward to speak to Vue Mai about me. In a loud voice, Vue Mai told everyone listening—and by now a considerable crowd had gathered—that I was an old friend and he had been expecting me. He assured the Thai guards that he, as camp chief, would take personal care of me. The guards need not worry. The tension subsided, but the soldiers demanded that I be brought to Commander Bounmee as soon as he returned.

One by one the soldiers drifted away. When they had all left, Hmong escorted me up the hill where I was given shelter in the house of Vang Tu, a radioman working with the Neo Hom resistance. After putting my gear in a dark corner of an inner room, I set out to talk to Vue Mai. I hoped he would be without Thai guards so I could talk frankly with him to find out why the Thai were so agitated.

Over a glass of hot tea, Vue Mai explained that Ban Vinai had become a closed camp. The Thais wanted no foreigners in the camp who might report on recent tough Thai actions taken against refugees. If I was interested, he could find Hmong who had first-hand information on the Thai crackdown. I was of course interested. My questions about the current situation in Laos and the cave massacre would have to wait.

The first man I interviewed was Vang Cher Pao, 34, who had become a soldier at 16. His "house" was near the market area. About 5:30 a.m. on April 21, 1986, he had heard a commotion outside. He moved in close to watch Thai police from Pak Chom, a nearby Thai town, arrest a small group of White Hmong refugees—children, teenagers, women, and men. "It was easy for the Thai police to find these people in the camp. They had no shoes. Their clothes were torn and dirty. They were hungry and scared. They had crossed the Mekong the night before and walked from the river to the camp."

The Thai police escorted them to Commander Bounmee's office where they took one man inside to talk to Bounmee while many Thai police guarded the others in his compound. Vang Cher Pao stood just outside Bounmee's fence so he could hear and watch.

Word spread quickly that the Thai had arrested new arrivals. This brought a crowd which encircled the camp commander's compound. One of the first to hear the news and join the crowd was Moua Nhia Chou, whose daughter May Song had married General Vang Pao. He had remained in Ban Vinai to assist with refugee problems. He told me that as he stood in the crowd, one arrested man cried out his name. "He knew me. He called to me, as the Thai guards threatened him to be quiet. He begged me: 'If you can help, my cousin, please. They are going to push us back to Laos. Please help us!'"

A "pushback" was the dreaded Thai action of returning escapees to their enemies, the Lao and Vietnamese forces, from whom they had fled.

Moua Nhia Chou told me that he had recognized three men: Moua Xee, Moua Va, and Moua Blia Yang. Moua Blia Yang had been a soldier with the French. The other two men had been with the Hmong resistance since 1975. "I moved closer to the fence so they could speak in Hmong about their problem. They said the communists keep looking for them. They had to flee Laos. While they tried to talk to me, the Thai policemen, who couldn't understand the Hmong language, were very upset about this small group. They shouted at them and made a lot of noise. I tried to talk to the police about these people, but couldn't say too much because I'm sure they will push me back to Laos, too."

Moua Nhia Chou had heard the Thai negotiating over Bounmee's radio with the LPLA army commander at Houei La, across the river from Pak Chom, for the return of these refugees. The swelling crowd pushed each other closer and closer to the fence to find out the names of the people who believed they were about to be sent to their deaths.

After two hours of radio negotiations with the soldiers across the river, Commander Bounmee had ordered this group returned to them. He had told the police to transport the refugees in his red pickup truck to the river and then boat them to the Houei La army commander.

As Moua Nhia Chou talked, he fumbled around in his worn and faded tribal cloth bag and produced a small notebook. "I have written down their names and their ages. May I write them in your notebook so that what happened to them will never be forgotten?" I offered him my notebook and he wrote: "Moua Xee, male, age 33; Song Moua, female, age 9; Lai Moua, male, age 6; Blia Yang Moua, male, age 65; Mai Xiong, female, age 63; Yer Moua, female, age 15; Der Moua, female, age 10, Moua Va, male, age 25; Ying Moua, female, age 22; Moua Vang Pao, male, age 6; Lee Moua, female, age 2 months."

I also learned about a pushback that occurred the following month. On May 4, 1986, a group of 213 Hmong from Na Kha south of Vang Vieng crossed the Mekong near Pak Chom. These refugees were also arrested by the Thai police and pushed back to Laos. After they had been pushed back, Bounmee informed Hmong camp leaders. They immediately radioed Neo Hom forces in Laos and a friendly Thai who watched the river for the freedom fighters, asking them to report on the fate of the men, women, and children turned over to the Lao army commander at Houei La.

Freedom fighter scouts set out to monitor the army camp. Later, they radioed their findings to Ban Vinai: five men were killed upon their return. After that, all surviving men 18 to 45, blindfolded and tied up with ropes, were put on three military boats with big guns and taken toward Vientiane. They did not know the fate of those taken away by boat or of the women and children.

After these two dramatic pushbacks, Hmong camp leaders complained to Commander Bounmee,* who said that he was only following the new refugee policy from the Ministry of Interior in Bangkok.

The Thais also cracked down on refugee vendors by closing the market at noon. Some vendors ignored the ban and continued to try to sell small bunches of lettuce leaves, slices of watermelon, sticky rice in a banana leaf, or eggs to other refugees. Women who sold *pa'ndau*, the intricate needlework made by women and children, were upset with the curtailed market hours because the foreigners who worked in the hospital or in the relief agencies bought these textiles only after lunch or just before their late afternoon vans departed the camp for the day. Most of the *pa'ndau* women defied the ban. Then the Thai police moved in and confiscated their wares, keeping them for themselves. Many of the confiscated textiles had taken months to make and would bring high prices on the Bangkok market.

These women had been so angry about the confiscation of their *pa'ndau* that they forced the Hmong leadership to complain to Bounmee. He explained again that he was only enforcing a new policy and that those who continued to sell beyond noon would be taken to the court at the Pak Chom police station. This threat terrified the refugees. Horrible things had happened to refugees at the Pak Chom police station.

With the Thai limiting outsiders' access to Ban Vinai, the Hmong position, already precarious, became more so. In the past, Hmong had relied on foreigners to carry out information on the worst cases of abuse and corruption. Under the new regulations, they could no longer count on outside contacts.

That night, I shared rice with radioman Vang Tu and his family—his older brother, his wife, their children, and a grandmother. He and I would share a sleeping room. I retired first. By flashlight, I reviewed my day's notes. Overhead, large rats scurried along the bamboo rails that

---

*Later that summer, Bounmee made a month-long USIS-sponsored trip to the U.S. While there, he visited Hmong communities and collected over $10,000. According to Hmong who helped organize his trip, American Hmong considered these gifts as protection money for their relatives in the camp so they would not be pushed back to the LPDR.

held up the thatch roof. I flashed my light on them and they curiously looked down at me. From the outer room, the crackling of a field radio mingled with men's hushed voices. Suddenly an excited voice broke through the crackling noise: "SKY! SKY!" SKY was the code-name for the Neo Hom resistance and, ironically, the name given by the Hmong to their CIA advisors twenty years earlier. The SKY answer was muffled. Long after I turned out my flashlight and crawled beneath the mosquito netting, I listened to the radio static and the clandestine conversations and thought about the situation here.

I had always likened this camp to the American Wild West, where the law was in the hands of those with guns. It was obvious that the Thais did not want me here. I hoped that Commander Bounmee would return tomorrow; then we could settle my problem and I would feel safer. When Bounmee vouched for me, that would take the pressure off the Hmong as well. The radio went quiet. Then I heard Vang Tu slip under his mosquito netting.

The next morning I awoke before the curfew was lifted. As soon as it was safe to move about, I went to see Vue Mai. He seemed nervous, and told me that Bounmee had not yet returned. Late last night, soldiers had instructed him to bring me to Bounmee the moment he returned.

Not knowing how much longer I would be allowed to stay, I decided to continue my research on the May 1985 cave massacre. I asked Vue Mai if he knew anything about it. He did, but suggested that I talk to a man in the camp who knew many details.

With cameras and notebook, I plodded up a hill with a guide to find Thao Neng Xiong. Halfway up, in a clutter of huts, we found him—a thin 28-year-old, who had recently escaped from Laos after years of fighting with the resistance. He had been involved in the battle that led to the cave massacre, and he had also talked to one of its survivors.

He had been involved in the May 1985 fighting near map coordinates UG 337-812. He estimated the Vietnamese forces at two companies. "Our resistance consisted of about 1,000 with weapons and about 8,000 civilians, including about 1,000 Kmhmu, 1,000 Lao, and the rest Hmong. The North Vietnamese fought us hard until May 14. We lost on that day. Many women, children, and old people surrendered to the Vietnamese. Maybe as many as 3,000 people surrendered, including Ly Chue Chia, his family and another family, totaling 16 people. Others had already been captured by the North Vietnamese. After their surrender, the Vietnamese told them they would give them protection in a big cave at location UG 332-820, near the Silver Cave which everyone knows. They told the civilians they would be safe in the cave from fighting and air strikes. Many people went willingly to avoid the fighting. They went into the cave about 6 a.m. on the morning of May 15. After the Vietnamese put the people in the cave, they closed the cave mouth with big tree branches and soldiers with guns stood guard at the entrance. About 10 a.m., the North Vietnamese soldiers fired ordnance into the cave along with approximately five shots of chemicals from a weapon that sounded like a B-40.''

Ly Chue Chia's group were afraid when they saw the entrance being closed and ran to the back of the cave to hide. They heard the shooting, then silence. They waited for hours in the back of the cave, then made their way forward. Near the entrance, they climbed over dead and broken bodies, some face up, some face down. No one guarded the entrance; they fled into the jungle. On May 22, Ly Chue Chia and his group found Thao's position near Bouam Loung and told their story.

The two groups joined, making a total of 50 people. "We discuss what to do," explained Thao Neng Xiong. "We want to photograph the bodies in the cave, but we have no camera. Finally, we decide there is nothing we can do except try to survive to tell the story of the cave. On May 27 at 7 p.m., we are attacked by the Vietnamese. Four people are killed by a B-40. And their big 12.7 gun wounded 14 of our people. We flee to UG 302-905. On June 3 at about 2 p.m., we are attacked again. We couldn't get our radio cable out of the tree when the Vietnamese attacked, so we had to flee without it. We moved to UG 258-962. On June 23, we are attacked again. Sixteen people are killed; eight are wounded. The wounded crawled into the jungle to hide. Our group now has only 17 people—12 men, my wife, and our four children. We flee. The enemy moved away and we returned to find the wounded. We found the wounded and another group of survivors and we join with them. Our group now has more than 70 people. We move again to hide. Three days later, the Vietnamese try to kill us again. They attack and we lost 33 people, including women, children, and men. We hide and the Vietnamese leave. Then we return to bury the dead. We decide that we must move out of the area or we will all die. We moved to an area near Phou Khum where there aren't so many Vietnamese and we hide.''

As Thao drew a map with the cave and battle locations as documentation, Moua Nhia Chou, who earlier had written in my notebook the names of some of those pushed back, arrived. He interrupted to announce he had something important to tell me. "We don't trust the Americans who come to this camp," he explained, his voice rising in anger. "We don't know which ones contact the enemy. We just don't trust Americans anymore. Everything we talk is the truth, but the American Embassy does not trust us. They already know about the cave massacre, they know about the raping, they know about the poisons, they know about the pushbacks, but they don't believe us. All we Hmong can do is cry, and cry, and regret."

I looked at this senior Hmong who had spat the truth at me. His face was flushed as he waited for my answer. What could I say? Should I tell him that the CBW team in Bangkok when asked by the DIA in Washington to investigate the cave massacre had sent a letter to *National Geographic* magazine seeking to know if Laos had big caves? Certainly not. No Hmong would believe such a story. Did he expect me to refute his allegations? I could not. Instead of defending U.S. official behavior, I answered simply, "I know."

As I collected Thao's drawings as documentation of the cave massacre, two of Vue Mai's messengers rushed in. "Bounmee has returned," one announced in an excited voice. "He wants to see you immediately." Something about the terseness of the message and the tenseness of the messengers alarmed me. I folded Thao's map and tucked it in the bottom of my camera bag before setting off with the messengers.

As we neared Commander Bounmee's compound, I recognized the soldiers awaiting my arrival. Bounmee stood inside his compound fence, near his gate. He looked angry and was obviously waiting for me. As I approached him, I "*whai*-ed" and greeted him in Thai. He only stared back. No greeting. No acknowledgment that he knew me. I had told the guards that I knew Bounmee well, yet he was treating me like a stranger. That meant that I had lied to the guards. Did they think I was an informant, a spy? How was I going to get out of this? I switched to English and continued to talk to Bounmee as if we were old friends. He spoke English well and over the years we had discussed refugee problems in this camp and refugee resettlement problems in the U.S. Now, his only response to my chatter was a stern glance. He was not going to acknowledge that he knew me. My next thought was the Pak Chom Jail.

Smiling as if I were having a fine time, I told Bounmee how nice it was to be back in the camp and how glad I was to see him again. Remembering he liked gardening, I admired the pink flowers blooming near his gate. Trying not to reveal my fear, I continued my banter, throwing out names of important Thai people I knew, hoping he might recognize them, and emphasizing that I would be visiting them when I returned to Bangkok.

As the camp commander and I confronted each other in a stand-off in the hot sun, a crowd of refugees formed behind me. Suddenly, Bounmee, without changing his glare, said "OK," while gesturing with his hands in disgust. He said something in Thai about Vue Mai which I did not understand. Then he turned and headed for his office.

Had Bounmee lost face? Had I lost face? Had the soldiers lost face? Maybe everyone had lost face. I did not know, but I did know this was not a good situation for me or for any Hmong who knew me or had been seen with me. Had the Thai seen the two Hmong who knew about the pushbacks talking to me? Would their lives now be in jeopardy? Moua Nhia Chou's fear about saying too much and being returned to Laos now seemed justified. It was time for me to disappear.

I retreated to the darkness of Vue Mai's meeting room for a much-needed glass of boiled water. Not wanting to prejudice Vue Mai any more than I had already, I decided to find the "eyes and ears" of the U.S. CBW team in Bangkok. Commander Bounmee could not object to that if he had someone following me.

I found one member—a pleasant young man who lived with his family far from the offices of the Hmong leaders and thus from information. He had grown up in this camp and knew very little about Laos. So much for the "eyes and ears" of the CBW team. While we talked, a wind kicked up, sending debris swirling about. A monsoon storm threatened. As the sky darkened, I ended our talk and headed for the radioman's house.

The low pressure which precedes monsoon storms and depresses people brought cool, thick mists, concealing this valley. As I scrambled up the wooden steps to the house, chilly rain squalls whipped across our valley, sending everyone, including the armed Thai guards, for shelter.

Radioman Vang Tu listened intently to his small black radio. Around him, young men sitting on hand-hewn benches leaned forward, also listening. A resistance fighter across the river was pleading for "SKY" to grant permission for his team to attempt a crossing. Vang Tu hesitated, looked at those around him, then denied permission to cross with the words, "The cat is watching." "The cat" was Hmong code for the Thai authorities.

With the Thai holed up out of the rain, resistance fighters in the camp moved about with less fear. Within an hour, 19 of them had arrived, introduced themselves, and sat down to listen to the crackling radio, hoping to hear a familiar voice.

I studied the large, round crystalline raindrops clinging to the jagged edges of the roof thatch that framed these extremely gaunt men listening to the resistance radio. As freedom fighters, they knew the fear and frustration of being stranded across the river.

Talking to them, I learned six still carried nasty wounds—some still bleeding, some swollen and red—from the fighting in Laos. They had been unable to find a doctor in Ban Vinai or in neighboring Thai towns who would operate to remove bullet fragments and grenade shrapnel. The Thai government hospital in Loei, the provincial capital, had refused to treat them. No private doctor would treat them because they had no money.

One young, very thin man, wounded in an attack three months earlier, was in great pain. He showed me the shrapnel dotting his mouth and tongue. Any movement was extremely painful. Since speaking was extremely difficult, he tried to talk using only his throat. It was difficult to understand him so his comrade explained. "My friend can only drink broth. Talking to you is extremely painful. He is wasting away and will probably die unless someone operates on his mouth to take out the shrapnel."

Another freedom fighter, wounded in the leg, could no longer walk without the aid of a crutch made from a tree branch, around which he draped his useless leg. He had been young and healthy, he said, before he was wounded, but since no doctor in the camp would treat him because he was wounded in Laos, he was afraid his untreated, shattered leg might mean he would never walk normally again.

By late afternoon, darker skies portended heavier rains. Those across the river knew that a major storm moving quickly toward them would make the treacherous Mekong River crossing more difficult later on. The Neo Hom team leader in Laos pleaded again over the radio static for SKY permission to cross. Vang Tu replied again, "The cat is watching."

The voice from across the river explained that they had no food, no ammunition, and they were certain that the Pathet Lao and Vietnamese patrols had spotted them. They had to cross before the river became impassable. Again, permission was denied. SKY control advised it was working on a plan for them to cross without the cat knowing.

In the minds of the Hmong, the Thais were the cat and they were the mice. For years, the clever cat watched the mice as they scurried about in their normal and clandestine activities. The cat played with the mice, mauled them, and disposed of them as it wished. It was also obvious that the cat needed the mice. The Thai military used the Hmong to run forays into Laos for intelligence gathering. Given only a few guns and a few rounds of ammunition, they were often sent into Laos for weeks at a time.

The mice understood well that to survive and to be allowed to run resistance activities and for refugees to be granted haven in Thailand, the cat had to be acknowledged as supreme. Sacrifices had to be made to the cat. Occasionally, the sacrifices brought such outrage from the refugees that their leaders were forced to report them. This was rare since reprisals against Hmong were certain if atrocities by Thai became known to the outside.

A week earlier, as a Hmong left the camp with several members of his family to look for wild vegetables to supplement the meager UNHCR food, he was shot to death. Outrage over the killing surged through the camp, but no official Hmong report was made. "It is better to forget his death," a Hmong leader explained. "If we made a report, someone else would die. A refugee family must accept death and sorrow. For refugees, there is no justice in this camp."

Throughout the night, chilling, driving rains pelted our valley, gouging deeper ruts in the red clay pathways. Men continued to monitor the clandestine radio, but no more communications came from the team across the river. By morning, the worst of the storm had passed and I ventured out to talk with the man designated by the Hmong for the past four years to collect and record data on CBW in Laos.

He told me that the last time a member of the U.S. CBW team came to see him was in early 1985—over a year earlier. "Since no one came to see the leaders here in the camp about CBW, we assumed that the Americans were not interested in what was happening in Laos."[13]

He then told me of a recent attack, on May 4, 1986, near Phou Heh at coordinates TF 3974-6674-7974. "This was an attack by a Soviet MI-8 helicopter. According to a radio report, the chemical was blue and wet and then it became dry. Eleven people died immediately. Others were ill. This poison was different from others because it took less time to kill. With the red or yellow, it often took four to six hours to die. With this one, people died within 30 minutes. From the radio report, I learned that those who are alive and ill have blistering, vomiting, diarrhea, inability to walk." He had sent a team in to get more details and a sample if possible. "But," as he pointed out, "it is the rainy season and evidence might be washed away with the rains."

He also told me that the previous February, a man—he thought an American—came to the camp and told leaders: "If any person gets wounded from the chemicals, send him to the doctor at the camp hospital for an exam. The doctor will give the results of the exam to the U.S. officials." That sounded good, but it turned out that the doctor did not believe that chemicals were being used. "We sent many people who have chemical wounds. The doctor gives them shots and tells them to come back if they have any more problems. He does not report anything to Bangkok. A Hmong medic told me that the doctor at the hospital said he was not interested in CBW."

In spite of this attitude, the Hmong continued to send victims to the hospital. One day, my informant had sent his assistant with a man wounded by chemicals to the doctor. "My assistant showed the Hmong medic the wounds and asked him to get the doctor to check him and report the findings to the Americans. The doctor would not see the victim so the medic sent him home. So, what's the use of sending those who are wounded to the hospital? That doctor has gone home. Now we have another doctor from Holland. The doctors change often—just like the CBW team. The doctors who come know nothing about the Hmong or how to treat those wounded by the chemicals."[14]

After this interview, I headed for the market. There was about an hour remaining before its noon-mandated closing. I wanted to talk to the women who sold *pa'ndau*. They told me that the Thais had not only ordered their stalls closed at noon, but had forbidden Hmong artisans to make tapestries that depicted the terror and brutality of their lives in Laos. When the women asked why, a Thai official had told them, "Americans say that you are not to make war pictures. No one is interested in buying them. Take them down."

They had taken down their gruesome tapestries of life and death in Laos, folded them into worn and dirty plastic bags, and hidden them. Now they worked on textiles showing Hmong legends and myths. If a buyer like myself happened along who wanted to look at the forbidden textiles, the women, keeping a lookout for Thai police, brought from hiding places needlework depicting rape, murder, Vietnamese and Pathet Lao attacks, enemy aircraft spraying poisons, and dead Hmong littering the scene. I bought several forbidden tapestries. The women said they doubted anyone would have the courage to make more *pa'ndau* depicting life under the communists because such pieces angered the Thai.

The former Tasseng of Khang Kho, Yang Toua Tong, who had met Colonel Billy so long ago when the American was searching for Vang Pao, had remained all these years in Ban Vinai. Some of his children had resettled in the U.S., but he remained behind. "I had to stay here with my people. If I were to leave, then I would have lied to my people. I believed the Americans when they told us in 1960 and all the years in between that they would help the Hmong fight the communists. I believed. I had to stay here." (He also had more than one wife, which made him ineligible for resettlement.)

He recalled in considerable detail those early days when Colonel Billy and Thai Colonel Khouphan had arrived by helicopter to help his beleaguered village. We talked about the war during the American time and the commitments the Americans and the Hmong had made to each other. He remained convinced that the Americans would keep their promise. I told him that, in my opinion, it was unrealistic and extremely doubtful that the U.S. would help because for the past 11 years the U.S. government had expressed no interest in resistance efforts in Laos.

He insisted that the American government had not forgotten its promises to the Hmong. Then he told me he had proof that the Reagan administration knew of the Hmong plight and would help the resistance. He had in his possession something from the White House to confirm this belief. He invited me back the next day so he could show me.

The next morning, in the rain, I walked barefoot through the red sucking mud to the Tasseng's house. Tasseng Yang graciously invited me to join him beneath a thatch overhang extending out from his dirt floor house. We sat around a large tree stump—now smooth after a decade of use as a table. Raindrops edged downward along the tips of roof thatch and dropped into a slender, deep trench created by millions of rain drops from monsoon storms that had passed over his house during the past ten years. He opened a tin canister and took out a small package tightly wrapped in plastic to keep out the unforgiving mold and mildew. With great care, he unwrapped his proof. I could not imagine what he might have from the White House. He handed me an envelope. Slowly I opened it. It was a Christmas card featuring a lovely snow night scene of the Capitol in Washington, D.C., and looked familiar. The Tasseng smiled as he proudly awaited my reaction. I opened it. It was a Christmas card signed by Senator Richard Lugar of Indiana. Suddenly, I recognized the card. It had been used as a Republican National Committee fund-raising mailing. I did not have the courage to tell him that.

In the silence, the rain drops pattered unrelentingly into the trench and I studied the Christmas card, stalling for time to formulate a response. I asked how he had gotten the card. He explained that a Hmong living in Iowa had sent it with the explanation that it had come from the White House. I kept my eyes down, fastened on his cherished card. I dared not look at him.

That night two black rats watched from the thatch overhead as I wrote by a flickering kerosene lamp. "Here, in this camp of sadness, disillusionment, and terror rests the entire panoply of the past and the present abandonment and disposal of the Hmong by their former friends and allies. These people have suffered so much because of the strength of their bonds of trust with others—long departed."

A few days later, I revisited the CBW team at the U.S. Embassy in Bangkok and reported the details of the May 4, 1986, deadly helicopter attack near Phou Heh. The army captain said that he did not want to hear any stories about CBW attacks; he only wanted physical evidence. Did I have the physical evidence? Did I have a piece of clothing or some ordnance from the attack? If not, he was not interested. The head of the team interrupted him to say that he was interested in hearing my report. When I gave the coordinates, he asked the army captain to find Phou Heh on the very large map of Laos on the wall opposite the portrait of Mao Zedong. The army captain stood before this map with its gridded coordinates and searched. He could not find Phou Heh, even though this area had been the site of many chemical-biological toxin attacks over the years.

32.

Requiem

We are on the death road now. . . . the authorities shall force us to go to Laos tomorrow. We lost all the addresses of our relatives in America because the authorities did not allow us to take our property and belongings with us when they arrested us. . . . Our last words to you and people in America are that the authorities used guns and strings [ropes] and wood [sticks] to force us to sign the papers stating we are willing to go to Laos. Please tell the world that there are corruptions and refugees traded in the camp. We will die soon. So you must remember us. We were born in the wrong world and at the wrong time. . . . Our lives are over. We shall die when we arrive in Laos. We shall not meet and see you and our good friends again. We are sorry. We cry now. Goodbye and good luck to all of you in America.

—Moua Cher Xiong, who, along with several hundred other refugees, was arrested on May 17, 1991, by Thai and UNHCR authorities at Chiang Kham refugee camp in northern Thailand to be forcibly repatriated to communist Laos*

B y 1989, *glasnost* and *perestroika* rumbling in the Soviet Union frightened the communist leaders in Hanoi and Vientiane. Without Soviet aid, both the Socialist Republic of Vietnam and the Lao People's Democratic Republic might collapse. Hanoi and Vientiane turned to the West and Japan for aid. To convince potential contributors and investors that the

---

*On May 20, 1991, Moua Cher Xiong recorded this message on a cassette tape for his relatives in the U.S. He and the other refugees were given no advance warning that they would be forced back. There was no time to alert relatives, no time or procedure available to petition their fate. Moua's cassette was received by the U.S.-based Lao Human Rights Council on June 2, 1991.

LPDR was a worthy recipient, the Kaysone regime with the aid of Western lobby groups began an orchestrated effort to convince the U.S. Congress, American businesses, religious groups, and the media that Laos, while maintaining its Marxist-Leninist doctrine, was a regime with which the U.S. could do business. Lobbyists argued that if the U.S. did not promote U.S. business investments there, it would lose out to Japan, Australia, Sweden, and other countries that were actively seeking concessions with the Kaysone government. This would contradict the opinion of many respected scholars that complete intellectual freedom is necessary for entrepreneurial capitalism to succeed.[1]

Little attention was paid to the fact that the LPDR had no constitution, no due process of law, no freedom to assemble or travel, no free press, and no political dissent, and that it continued to hold political prisoners in concentration camps. Amnesty International's 1989 list of 37 political prisoners detained in the LPDR was, according to Lao who had recently escaped these camps, only a fraction of the total.

In response to Amnesty's list and request that political prisoners be released, the Kaysone government successfully double-talked. Some prisoners had indeed been "released," but only to internal exile in the Lao Gulag where local authorities, often the police, gave these broken people work assignments and monitored or guarded them. Little had changed. After years of brainwashing, brutality, and forced obeisance to LPDR guards and officials, even the toughest found their minds and spirits severely damaged. Since they had been stripped of all property when arrested, "released" people were destitute. Some reported that being "released" was even more frightening because they were warned by the LPDR authorities that they would be watched and any mistake might result in severe punishment or death. Since what determined a mistake was unclear, many lived in fear that they would accidentally displease someone.

With the advent of the George Bush presidency, Hmong held great hope that the new president and Secretary of State James Baker would be concerned about the plight of the Hmong, both in the camps in Thailand and in Laos where the armed forces of that totalitarian regime still hunted them. Hmong believed that the Bush administration, in return for aid to the LPDR, would demand some concessions.

Those hopes were soon dashed. Reports to Bush's National Security Council staff on Thai pushbacks of Hmong refugees to Laos went unaddressed, and pushbacks continued. The Bush-Baker "pragmatism" meant that the Hmong would continue to be sacrificed on this altar of the apparent official policy: "negotiate it."

On Capitol Hill the agenda changed also. Congressman Stephen Solarz's office, earlier a champion of Hmong issues, now was silent. Eric
Schwartz, who had moved from Asia Watch to Solarz's staff, was the
congressman's designate on Laos. He showed little interest in human
rights violations against the Hmong or, later, in the Hmong terror that
they might be forced from refugee camps in Thailand back to the LPDR
in the U.S. supported and financed U.N.-Thai-Lao Hmong repatriation
plan.

While Congress held hearings on Vietnam, Cambodia, and the POW-
MIA issue, Laos was ignored by Congress, in spite of the hundreds of
Hmong-American citizens and others aware of the critical situation in
Laos who repeatedly called upon it to address the human rights viola-
tions there.

With the reduction in Soviet aid to Laos and Vietnam and the resulting economic problems in both countries, those opposed to the Kaysone
regime believed that it was an opportune time to go on the offensive in
Laos. On December 6, 1989, in Sayaboury Province, the ULNLF, or Neo
Hom, announced that it had established a provisional democratic government in liberated zones in Xieng Khouang, Luang Prabang,
Sayaboury, Houei Sai, Vang Vieng, and Borikhane provinces. During a
three-day ceremony, this provisional government announced that it
would invite a son of the late Lao king, Prince Suriyavong Vongsavang,
exiled in France, to be the king. Lao Prince Phayaluang Outhong
Souvanavong was designated as prime minister and Hmong General
Vang Pao was named first deputy prime minister. General Vang Pao and
Lao General Tonglith held the top positions in the Defense Ministry, responsible for the Lao Liberation Army (LLA).

The rebels' brazen act infuriated the Kaysone government. The LPDR
recognized the potential of the provisional government to undermine its
campaign for vital noncommunist aid and to encourage the desire for
political change among the many Lao who were unhappy with the
Kaysone regime. On December 6, Kaysone declared that his forces
"would continue to drop bombs and seek to destroy" the Free Lao forces
"until they were totally wiped out."[2]

On January 4, 1990, 20 MiG-21s flying from Vietnam dropped high
explosives and chemicals on several villages in the resistance area. The
next day planes attacked five villages in Xieng Khouang Province. On
January 6, two MiG-21s and three MI-8 helicopters rocketed two villages. On January 7, MiG-21s bombed five villages in Borikhane Province, causing heavy destruction and casualties. On January 9, four MiG-

21s and four MI-8 helicopters bombed and rocketed several villages and ULNLF positions.[3]

On January 10, Vientiane announced that its air force would "continue air raids on all strongholds of the resistance."[4] Two days later, four MiG-21s bombed Neo Hom positions. By January 13, the resistance had taken a terrible pounding from the PAVN (People's Army of Vietnam) and LPDR air forces.[5]

Disillusioned with the Kaysone regime, some field-grade officers of the LPDR forces refused to go on the offensive against their countrymen in the resistance. In some areas, locals continued to shelter and feed the resistance because they, too, wanted reforms. Because of the seriousness of this threat, Vientiane turned to Hanoi for assistance. On January 19, Vietnamese forces were committed to the ground offensive as reinforcements, supported by MI-8 helicopters which used yellow and red powder in the Phou Bia area, killing 32 civilians and injuring another 173.[6]

Later in January, for the first time, Vietnam deployed new aircraft—MiG-23 fighter bombers—to Laos to help in the fight against anticommunist forces. "On site field reports say that they dropped chemical bombs. Reports from the field describe 'invisible gas' that is 'highly toxic and kills on contact.' This fits very close with reported descriptions from both Afghanistan and Angola of the super-lethal cyanogenic agents used there with devastating effectiveness. Reports indicate that the kill zone is approximately 1 km [kilometer]."[7]

Dozens of villagers living just across the Lao border in Sayaboury Province sought treatment in Thai hospitals. The Thai press reported interviews with these patients who complained of severe vomiting, breathing problems, swelling of limbs, and temporary blindness.[8] Similar attacks were to continue throughout 1990.

During this fighting, on January 18, a LPDR spokesman, responding to reports that Thailand was considering unilateral and forced repatriation of refugees from Ban Vinai camp, said, "the Lao side will certainly not take such refugees and will send them back to Thailand."[9] This firm stance would change after the LPDR recognized the potential benefits of such a maneuver.

On March 13, a U.S.-funded road building project began in Houa Phan (Sam Neua) Province in the northeast, part of a U.S. $8.7 million several-year aid package.[10] That same month, at least 35 civilians and seven soldiers were killed during prodemocracy demonstrations in Xieng Khouang Province. The government banned public rallies in the southern province of Savannakhet. The following month, the International

Fund for Agricultural Development approved $5.3 million for an opium substitution program in Xieng Khouang Province, and the U.N. Fund for Drug Abuse Control granted an additional $2.6 million. The next month, Richard Solomon, U.S. Assistant Secretary of State for East Asian and Pacific Affairs, arrived in Vientiane to discuss curtailing heroin production in Laos and improving U.S.-Lao relations. On May 14, while the U.S. delegation was being feted in Vientiane, LPDR forces used chemical rockets in Sayaboury Province, causing the Thai army to warn Thai villagers of "yellow dust" causing skin inflammation, eye irritation, and nausea that was blowing over the Thai border. It was announced that the two countries would join in a ten-day session in early June to discuss drug suppression. Solomon presented the LPDR with $850,000 for the production of artificial limbs.[11] Following Solomon's visit, the LPDR joined with a U.S. team to look for remains of American MIAs lost during the Vietnam War. Vientiane announced that it had smashed efforts to set up a government in Sayaboury Province and killed a number of resistance commando elements.[12]

On June 4, 1990, the LPDR published a draft of its promised constitution in its official newspaper, *Pasason.* An Amnesty International study of the draft concluded that the document "fails to give constitutional recognition to fundamental human rights and lacks comprehensive provisions for human rights protection."[13]

On July 1, in spite of heavy aerial bombardment and use of chemical warfare against the resistance areas, Lao resistance radio, calling itself the "Radio Station of the Government of the Liberation of the Lao Nation," using a mobile transmitter, began broadcasting from the mountains four hours daily in both the Lao and Hmong languages. According to the *Bangkok Post,* the radio station is headed by a former seminar camp prisoner, Somwang Phanthavong, with a staff of 23. Its broadcasts called the Kaysone group "odious" and urged the people to rid the country of the Leninist form of government.[14]

To celebrate the July 4 holiday, the U.S. chargé d'affaires in Vientiane held an Independence Day party. Among the hosted officials was Phoumi Vongvichit, the former cruel tax collector who was now the acting president of the LPDR.

Since the spring of 1990, more than 40 top-level officials of the LPDR, calling themselves the "Social Democrat Group," had openly criticized the Lao government, submitting resignations, returning medals, and calling for fair multiparty elections.[15] On October 8, six LPDR officials, including two former Cabinet vice-ministers, criticized the Lao government and called for a multiparty system. One minister called the Lao political system a "communist monarchy" and a "dynasty of the Politburo." All were jailed.[16] Later, *Pasason* announced that "the arrests were needed to protect national law and order."[17]

In response to the establishment of the provisionary government and the upsurge in antigovernment activities, the LPDR stepped up its attacks against the resistance and against civilian areas suspected of assisting it.

About this time, it became clear that the elimination of one base of the resistance—the refugee camps in Thailand—was now a major LPDR goal. From these camps, Hmong and Lao could cross into Laos to fight and to videotape atrocities committed by the LPDR.

*   *   *

In the spring of 1990, I had discussed with personnel at the Orville H. Schell, Jr., Center for International Human Rights at the Yale University Law School the possibility of holding a conference on human rights in Laos. That summer, Drew S. Days III, Yale law professor and director of the Schell Center, agreed. He and I would co-convene "Laos: Human Rights in a Forgotten Country," in the fall.

On a cold and damp December 8 in New Haven, Connecticut, from across the U.S., hundreds of refugee Hmong and Lao assembled, along with the LPDR chargé d'affaires from Washington, the U.S. Department of State Desk Officer for Laos, a Mennonite Central Committee worker in the LPDR, scholars, and refugee advocates. Initially, Professor Days wondered if anyone would be interested enough in Laos to attend. I repeatedly assured him that many refugees from Laos would attend, particularly since this was the first time that human rights violations in Laos would be singularly addressed at a prestigious conference. But I, too, underestimated the turnout. To accommodate the crowd, we had to reschedule the conference in the more spacious Yale Law School Auditorium.

Hmong, in two chartered buses—one from Wisconsin and one from Minnesota—had traveled 26 hours to attend this one-day conference. Each bus cost $6,000 to charter, a major expense for those who have so little. Concerned about their relatives in Laos, they pooled their scarce resources to send emissaries to Yale to give witness. Representatives brought audio and videotape equipment to record the proceedings for their communities.

Scot Marciel, the Lao Desk Officer at the State Department, who admitted that he had only been on the job for six months, supported the LPDR by giving a most optimistic assessment of Laos. He spoke about the $8.7

million the U.S. had pledged to the LPDR and enthused that the LPDR was progressing so nicely that the U.S. would soon be sending in the Peace Corps. He said nothing about human rights abuses.

The Hmong were obviously upset about these comments. At the break following the first session, several Hmong sought me out to ask why the State Department representative did not mention human rights violations. This was their first direct exposure to the State Department position, and they were stunned.

During the second session, Courtland Robinson, policy analyst for the Washington-based U.S. Committee for Refugees, spoke about the refugee camps in Thailand and noted that they would be closing. This threat had been bandied about since the mid-1980s; few in the auditorium paid attention, particularly since the focus of the conference was on human rights issues.

Linthong Phetsavang, the LPDR chargé d'affaires, gave repetitive exhortations about the victorious communist revolution and how dedicated communist revolutionaries, the people's army, and the party had defeated colonialism and American imperialists and their supporters in wars of aggression. Their revolutionary victory in 1975, he said, was an historic event for the "multi-Lao people," bringing in a new era of peace, democracy, independence, and a unified Laos.

David Merchant, a former Co-Country Representative of the Mennonite Central Committee on Laos, who had recently worked in the LPDR and whose biographical data noted that he was engaged in reconciling and peacemaking between the peoples of Laos and North America, supported the claims of the LPDR official.

Merchant was followed by Pobzeb Vang, the chairman of the U.S.-based Lao Human Rights Committee, who pointed out that the LPDR had killed 300,000 of its own people, including the royal family, and created half a million refugees.

After the second group of speakers, all panelists returned to the podium to field questions from the audience. Survivors and witnesses to LPDR atrocities formed two long lines: a man in a wheelchair who held the LPDR bullet that had paralyzed him; a woman who had witnessed the slaughter of women along a trail and babies pounded to death in rice mortars. Lo Xa, who had been tortured and beaten by the LPDR and who had witnessed the young Hmong being forced to eat his own flesh, also stood in line. One Hmong in line had brought with him videotaped evidence of a recent 1990 CBW attack. He had carried a large TV set all the way from Wisconsin on the bus and set it up in front of the auditorium to show the short tape when his turn came.

In the time allocated for the victims, none of the above had the opportunity to speak. Those who did speak directed most of their questions to the LPDR official, and most questions dealt with the fate of the royal family. Linthong claimed that the king had died of old age, and dodged answering how the queen or the prince had died. The audience booed; most knew that the royal family had been killed slowly by starvation and deprivation. Suddenly someone shouted: "If you can kill the king, then you will kill any of us who are sent back to Laos." The audience erupted with applause. The LPDR official's claims that there were no "seminar camps" in Laos and no political prisoners brought moans from the refugee audience.

Robinson and Merchant said that in large part the violence in Laos was the fault of the resistance. They assured the audience that if the Neo Hom ceased, the LPDR would cease its attacks against the Hmong. They made no mention of why a resistance was formed in the first place.

The emotion of this meeting, in which for the first time those who had been abused faced an official from the abusing side, surged through the crowd. Men and women shouted their rage at those on the podium. It took several minutes to calm them. Questions from the floor continued to be direct and angry. The LPDR representative and State's Marciel, who had traveled together to New Haven on the train from Washington, took offense and both threatened to walk out. Because of this threat, the conference was not extended for another hour or so to allow all victims who wished to give witness to speak for the record. Those who had come so far to tell of their experiences were indignant, but the conference ended on schedule.

While the panelists prepared to leave the podium, the Hmong with the TV set played his videotape taken in Laos depicting civilian victims of a recent attack using lethal agents. When Marciel came near the VCR to pick up his coat, I asked him to view the video with me and the others watching it. He refused. "I see this kind of documentation all the time," he said. I pressed and asked him to please look at the tape, which was only three minutes long. He said that he had already seen it. I asked how he could have seen it, since it had just recently arrived in the U.S. He insisted that he had seen it. Then why hadn't he mentioned it in his official remarks? Why was the U.S. "point man" on Laos more concerned about the feelings of the LPDR representative whose government had for 15 years brutalized its ethnic minorities, incarcerated political opposition, and used toxic agents in contravention of international treaties than about the victims of these tactics and policies? Why, in spite of impressive eyewitness testimony of continuing brutality by the LPDR, did the State Department, counseled by U.S.-based refugee advocacy groups, favor economic aid, urge U.S. companies to do business with the LPDR, support repatriation of refugees without appropriate monitoring apparatus, and recommend sending the Peace Corps to the LPDR?

The anguish of those who had been turned away at Yale permeated the buses as they drove through the darkness back to Wisconsin and Minnesota. I, too, was disturbed, and decided to travel to Wisconsin and Minnesota to collect for myself the testimonies of those denied time to speak at the conference.

*   *   *

On January 4, 1991, two MiG-23s, flying from Vietnam, hit Nhot Sang village, about 100 kilometers east of Paksan, killing 10 and wounding 5. Nhot Sang is a civilian village near the Laos-Vietnam border. No resistance groups operated in its vicinity. Some U.S. military analysts suggested that the MiG-23s, newly arrived in Vietnam, were using Lao villages as target practice.

*   *   *

Over 1,700 Hmong and Lao showed up at the January 19-20 conference organized by the the the St. Paul–Minneapolis Hmong and Lao communities. I took testimony from young and old, from farmers, teachers, and former civilian and military personnel. As was the Hmong custom, they had for years kept detailed records, and now they told of torture, maiming, forced labor, starvation, poisonings, lethal injections, rape, terror, executions, and use of lethal weapons. Victims cried as they told of their suffering, of the deaths and disappearances of their loved ones, and of their fears for those still trapped inside Laos. One child told of the LPDR execution of 33 members of her family after they had been pushed back by Thai authorities. She was seriously wounded and left for dead. There are photos to document this mass murder. I interviewed ten ethnic Lao who had been held as political prisoners in the LPDR Gulag for a total of 91 years. Some had only recently escaped from Laos. They all suffered from depression. They had difficulty remembering. Their personalities had changed, they explained, and it was difficult to learn new skills, although all were educated. Most were on welfare. Most concluded that their minds had been psychologically destroyed. These testimonies were videotaped and audiotaped.[18] It was impossible for me to interview all who came to testify on human rights violations in Laos. Once again, many were disappointed that there was not enough time for them to give witness.

Those who attended were given a "lost and injured" questionnaire on which they could list the name, age, date, and location of those lost or injured and means of death of those killed by the LPDR. This form, hastily assembled by the Minnesota and Wisconsin Hmong, provided startling data on the massive and consistent killing of people in Laos and underscored the extraordinary fear of those in refugee camps that they might be returned to this regime through involuntary repatriation. Attendees at the Minnesota meeting documented personal knowledge of 1,169 people killed by the communist regime in Laos from 1975 to 1990 (see Appendix). At this time, there were in excess of 150,000 refugees from Laos in the U.S. Extrapolation of these figures indicated gross violation of human rights in Laos.

* * *

Under cover of pre-dawn darkness on January 21, 1991, at Chiang Kham refugee camp in northern Thailand, two buses pulled in to take refugees, mostly "highlanders," away. Thai Ministry of Interior (MOI) officials accompanied by men with guns rounded up 59 people and forced them onto the two buses. Other camp residents reported that the refugees were screaming and crying as they were herded aboard. Some were taken from their beds, wearing only skimpy nightclothes. After leaving Chiang Kham camp, the buses traveled for 18 hours to Nong Khai, a Thai town on the Mekong River across from Vientiane. On January 22, these refugees were sent across the river to Laos. These eyewitness accounts were confirmed by both diplomatic sources and U.N. officials in Bangkok.

Upon learning of this incident, the Schell Center for International Human Rights wrote to Secretary of State James Baker urging the State Department to call for a cessation of all repatriation of Lao refugees, particularly "highlanders," to the LPDR until a thorough and extensive investigation could be conducted to make certain that effective mechanisms were in place in Laos to protect them. It further pointed out that, according to a MOI official, of the 1,514 refugees awaiting interviewing, called "screening," only 10% would be accepted for resettlement, or "screened in," and asked how the MOI could give this estimated figure when they had not yet begun interviewing this group.

Although refugees who are rejected for resettlement abroad—"screened out"—have the right to appeal their classification, most are not aware of their status or that they can appeal. As was the case on January 21, 1991, usually no warning is given before they are involuntarily returned. The forced, undignified, and frightening process clearly violates international concepts and laws governing refugees.

In a letter dated February 20, 1991, Sarah E. Moten, Deputy Assistant for International Assistance, Bureau for Refugee Programs for the State Department, replying for Secretary Baker, responded to the Schell Center. "UNHCR officials, who participated in the repatriations, have told United States Government officials in Bangkok and Vientiane, that those repatriated involuntarily were illegal immigrants who had no resistance ties (which might subject them to imprisonment in Laos), had not sought refugee status when originally entering Thailand and had no claim to such. . . . According to UNHCR officials in Vientiane, the Lao government welcomes returnees and does not discriminate against the screened-out. The UNHCR had investigated allegations of human rights violations against returnees and had found them to be without foundation."[19]

Referring to these refugees as "illegal immigrants" reflects a lack of understanding of the situation in Thailand. As early as 1983, I was aware that Ban Vinai refugee camp was closed to those who could not bribe their way in. Since most tribal people fled destitute from Laos, they had no choice but to live in the mountains in northern Thailand or sneak into Ban Vinai to hide themselves. There were thousands of such people in Ban Vinai. Not being entitled to receive the UNHCR food allowance, they had to fend for themselves. Through no fault of their own, life was both difficult and dangerous.

Ironically, the State Department's own *Country Reports on Human Rights Practices* for 1990, released in February 1991, was critical of the LPDR's record on human rights. It noted that the LPDR was an authoritarian, one-party state where the Lao People's Revolutionary Party (LPRP) leadership imposed broad and arbitrary controls on the population. "The Ministry of Interior (MOI) is the main instrument of state control. Although little is known by outsiders about the MOI's police, they are believed to be active in monitoring Lao society and expatriates. . . . The LPRP also has its own system of informants, in workplace and residential communities, who monitor and control events. . . . " Significantly, it pointed out that in the LPDR "People can be arrested on unsupported accusations and without being informed of the charges or of the accusers' identities. Regulations call for judgment to be given in public, however, this is only a public announcement of the sentence and not a true public trial."[20] State's report also pointed out that internal travel still required official permission, that Laos generally did not cooperate with international human rights officials, that domestic human rights groups were prohibited, that the LPDR, threatened by economic and political liberalization in Eastern Europe, tightened some forms of internal control in 1990 to stamp out dissent.[21] Lao students studying in Eastern Europe who demonstrated for reforms in Laos were called home. Many of those who returned were sent to "re-education" camps in Houa Phan Province.[22]

With all of this information, it is difficult to understand why the State Department wanted to forcibly return Hmong political refugees to Laos.

During March 27–29, the LPRP held its Fifth Congress in Vientiane. Videotapes of the proceedings showed a gigantic mural depicting part of the LPDR flag with its top and bottom red stripes representing the blood shed for freedom and a blue middle swath for prosperity in which rests a white circle signifying a bright future. The mural was painted so that a larger flag of the Soviet Union with its hammer and sickle dominated the wall and covered much of the Lao flag. Streamers extending across the top of the mural over both flags ended in cameo-style portraits of Marx and Lenin. In the center of the presidium sat a large white bust of Ho Chi Minh. A much smaller image of Kaysone appeared unpretentiously low and insignificant. The Lao communist party flag and the national coat of arms use the symbol of the hammer and sickle, the only example of such use of the hammer and sickle outside the Soviet Union.[23]

During these proceedings, the Lao communist party reaffirmed its commitment to Marxism and Leninism. Addressing communist representatives from Vietnam, Cambodia, China, the Soviet Union, and North Korea, Kaysone rambled on in a speech filled with contradictions about the failed Lao economy. An American-Hmong watching the video with me commented that it appeared that two people with opposite views had written Kaysone's speech: the author of the first part had written that everything was wonderful; the author of the second had written that everything was terrible. The observer added that Kaysone seemed not to notice that he was contradicting himself. But there was no doubt that the Kaysone regime had no intention of abandoning its Marxist-Leninist commitments— even in the face of a failed economy, the crumbling of communism in Europe, and the blossoming in its stead of *glasnost, perestroika,* reforms, and democracy. The men in Vientiane and their mentors in Hanoi were determined to stay in power and to hold on to communism.[24]

This zealousness was partly driven by fear. The elite in the LPDR were aware of the fate of the corrupt and brutal communist officials in Eastern Europe when those regimes fell. They were undoubtedly also aware that in June 1987 the United Nations agreed to a convention that sought punishment of torturers and compensation for their victims. It called on nations to prevent torture, making it a criminal offense. People suspected of torture could be extradited and torturers barred from defending themselves with the claim that they acted on orders. During 1990–91, international and human rights lawyers vigorously discussed putting on trial under the U.N. Convention on Prevention and Punishment of the Crime of Genocide (see Appendix) those responsible for "acts committed with intent to destroy, in whole or in part, a national, ethical, racial or religious group." Rulers, public officials, and private individuals could be punished for "genocide, conspiracy to commit genocide, direct and public incitement to commit genocide, an attempt to commit genocide or complicity in genocide." Aware that lawyers were preparing such cases against Pol Pot and his cadre in neighboring Cambodia, LPDR officials could justifiably fear that they, too, could be put on trial were they to lose their absolute control. No doubt they feared that those who have documentation—and many do—that could be used in a tribunal might come forward with evidence to convict them.

* * *

In late April 1991, as I prepared to depart for Thailand, some Hmong-Americans called me, upset about reports from relatives in Thai refugee camps that many Hmong would be forcibly repatriated to the LPDR as a result of what they referred to as the "Vue Mai proposal." (Vue Mai was the Hmong administrative chief in Ban Vinai camp.)

Upon arrival in Bangkok, I immediately went to the U.S. Embassy to ask about this Vue Mai repatriation program. "It's revolutionary," a senior U.S. official at the embassy explained. "After 16 years the Hmong refugees in Ban Vinai camp have suddenly decided to return to Laos."[25]

"Revolutionary." His words hung like an exploding grenade in my mind. It would indeed be revolutionary if the Hmong, fiercely independent and extremely anticommunist, would suddenly volunteer to return to a Laos controlled by a regime that had hunted them down with a fanaticism similar to that of the Nazi persecutions and of Pol Pot's mass murder in neighboring Cambodia. As recently as August 1990, every head of family in Ban Vinai had signed a petition begging the UNHCR *not* to send any Hmong back to Laos. Just a few days earlier, the Lao military, using chemical weapons, had attacked a resistance area wounding 24 Hmong and killing five. Why would these Hmong men and boys who had been fighting the Kaysone regime for some 16 years suddenly decide to return to Laos without discussion with their families or their traditional leaders?

I needed to study the "Vue Mai proposal." Another embassy official, Martin Brennan, allowed me to read it and take notes, but denied me a copy. It was dated March 1, 1991, and signed by Vue Mai, who claimed that he represented Lao refugees in Thailand. It was addressed to the United Nations High Commissioner for Refugees in Geneva and sent through Robert Robinson, a UNHCR representative in Ban Vinai. It read: "As the representative of Lao refugees in Thailand, I wish to inform your Excellency that those Lao people having asylum in Thailand wish to repatriate to the home country in Laos under the auspices of your good Office, the United Nations. Attached, please find a statement of 10 elements we feel important to be included in this repatriation program. Therefore, kindly discuss with any authorities as appropriate as our representative in this matter."[26] As an ethnic Hmong, it was impossible for Vue Mai to be the representative of all the Lao refugees in Thailand. I soon learned that he did not seem to represent the majority of the Hmong in Ban Vinai.

The ten points that the Hmong had supposedly agreed to included consent "to live together in a location mutually agreed for the duration of their lives" and to "cease to engage in activities designed to undermine the government authority or destabilize social order." I have not found a Hmong who would agree to live in one location for the duration of his life under any circumstances. The wording "destabilize social order" is significant because this phrase is used by the Kaysone regime when arresting even high-ranking communist party members who speak out. Any real or imagined criticism of the communist regime by any anti-LPDR Hmong could be construed as "destabilizing" and would result in severe punishment.

A third part of this proposal was entitled "Hmong Repatriation." Written on UNHCR stationery, with no signature, it briefly described group repatriation, tripartite meetings, and financing repatriation. Absent was a plan for the security of those returned.

This important letter, dated March 1, 1991, had not been circulated in Hmong communities in the West; it had been withheld for almost two months. Why? Why was something so important—so revolutionary—

withheld from the public and from those whose lives it would greatly affect?

I called Hmong General Vang Pao, who remains the leader of many Hmong in the West and large numbers of Hmong in Ban Vinai, to ask him when he first learned of the Vue Mai proposal. His answer: "April 18, 1991. And I still don't know the details." He added: "For years I worked closely with the Americans. I helped them all the time. Why don't they talk to me about this plan to send Hmong back to Laos?"

A few days later, I was in Ban Vinai to learn from the Hmong leaders why they had so suddenly decided to return to Laos. Although I had a Thai government official camp pass, the Thai guards at the gate confiscated my camera equipment, extorted bribes of money, cigarettes, and liquor, and harassed me. Once again, my presence exposed my Hmong friends in the camp to considerable danger. Vue Mai was not there. It wasn't known where he was. He had told some that he was going to the U.S. to visit relatives.

The camp is divided into nine centers, each with a Hmong chief responsible for those in his center. I interviewed each center chief individually and in depth. I also interviewed the chairman of the Hmong Council that represents the 16 Hmong clans in the camp. Not one of these individuals had been involved in the drafting of the March 1, 1991, Vue Mai letter in which they had purportedly agreed to return to Laos. They explained that in March *after* the letter had been sent to Geneva, Vue Mai called a meeting, which a hundred or more people attended, where he read the letter. Few details were given.

"The idea could not belong to Vue Mai," explained one chief. "It must belong to others." Several chiefs said that they knew Vue Mai very well and they also believed that this idea could not be his. Such proved to be the case. Keisuke Murata, UNHCR representative in Bangkok in charge of Durable Solutions, later personally confirmed to me that UNHCR personnel, American Robert Robinson and Briton Robert Cooper, had worked with Vue Mai on this letter for some time.[27] I also asked Murata if he knew of any precedent for successful UNHCR involuntary repatriation of political refugees as part of a durable solution, with minimal monitoring, to a totalitarian communist regime similar to that of the LPDR. He said that he personally did not know of one, but that this fact did not lessen his enthusiasm for this "durable solution" for the Hmong.

There were reports that U.S. NGOs (nongovernmental organizations) working with refugees as well as the U.S. Embassy were also involved.

The embassy denied this, although it did admit inviting Vue Mai to the embassy to talk about the mass return of refugees to Laos and providing him with documents to go to the U.S. in May 1991 to promote his plan. Hmong with whom I spoke were not aware of these machinations nor even that Vue Mai intended to promote this repatriation plan in the U.S.

One center chief thought that the Vue Mai proposal was the first step in creating a United Nations conference on Laos that would parallel the current one on Cambodia which he believed would result in a U.N. Peace-Keeping Force accompanying the Hmong back to Laos to protect them. I told him that the Vue Mai plan made no mention of a U.N. Peace-Keeping Force but did require that returnees give up their weapons and agree "not to undermine the government authority or destabilize social order."

"Who then will protect us?" he shouted at me. When I answered that this would be the responsibility of the LPDR, he responded with a high-pitched whine that Hmong use to indicate fear and disgust. "No," he said, "if this is the case, we cannot go back. They will kill us."

Several center chiefs mistakenly believed that Vue Mai was working with all Hmong and Lao leaders in France, Australia, and the U.S. and with U.S. and other Western government officials to negotiate a plan with the LPDR that would allow the Hmong to return home safely with international guarantees. I, however, could find no evidence of any such international involvement or negotiations. This plan to repatriate Hmong to Laos seemed to be engineered by the UNHCR in Thailand, Thai authorities, and several U.S.-based NGOs involved in the refugee business.

At Ban Vinai, I walked around the camp, stopping people at random to ask them what they thought about the Vue Mai proposal. I interviewed 37 people. I found only one young couple who knew about it. When they had learned of it, they had immediately made an appointment to be interviewed for resettlement. The others knew nothing about the plan and were horrified that they might be forced back. Most were in the camp illegally, having entered after it was officially closed.

While the plan was not circulated in the West, agencies working with refugees in Thailand knew about it. Energized by the possibility of new funding opportunities, their staffs busily prepared plans, sent delegations to talk to bureaucrats in Vientiane, and made budgets, hoping to compete for the international aid that was expected to flow to support the return of "Lao asylum seekers in Thailand" to Laos.

UNHCR's Murata explained that a Tripartite Meeting of the Lao and

Thai governments and U.N. representation was scheduled for the end of June at Luang Prabang in Laos. At that time, it was his hope that the Lao government would accept a U.N. site-location plan for "villages" to be created for returnees. Hmong returnees would not be allowed to live in their home areas in the mountains but would be resettled in the lowlands. He explained that the budget would include—as a carrot to the Lao government—development funds for existing Lao villages in the areas of the new villages. If the LPDR signed off, according to Murata, then international fund-raising would begin. The hope was that the fund-raising would be completed by the end of the rainy season in September or October. Construction of new sites would begin after the rains. Movement of the first 5,000 Hmong to Laos was planned for December 1991 or early January. In 1992, another 10,000 would be moved to Laos, with another 10,000 resettled there in 1993. This, I was told, would resolve the Hmong refugee problem in Thailand. By 1993, Hmong would either have been returned to the LPDR or would have been scared into resettling in a third country. Murata was firm in his belief that he would accomplish a "durable solution" for the Hmong.

The LPDR's offer to take back anti-LPDR refugees from the camps, funded by the international community with significant promises of additional long-term aid, was ingenious. By doing so, not only would a substantial resistance safe haven provided in the refugee camps be eliminated, but resistance supporters could be neutralized by resettling them inside Laos in camps controlled by LPDR authorities. Point 10 of the Vue Mai plan—"The Hmong will cease to engage in activities designed to undermine the government authority or destabilize social order"— would give the LPDR justification for harsh treatment of any who criticized the government. On a more superficial but equally important level, taking back one's former enemies would be a showcase demonstration of LPDR humanity and goodwill to generate more Western aid and world recognition. (In 1992, Vue Mai moved to the U.S. to live.)

In Thailand, I interviewed both Thai and Westerners sympathetic to the fate of refugees. They concurred that refugee fears were often forgotten as lobby groups worked congressional offices seeking support of repatriation schemes. Those familiar with the situation urged independent congressional inquiries—not investigations prepared by those who seek lucrative resettlement contracts—and congressional oversight, both of which, they lamented, were much needed and long overdue.

*   *   *

A May 2, 1991, letter sent to those inquiring about the U.S. policy toward Laos stated official U.S. policy. Charles H. Twining, Director of the U.S. State Department's Office of Vietnam, Laos, and Cambodian Affairs, wrote: "The United States government has recognized and maintained diplomatic relations with the current government of Laos since it was established in 1975. The Lao Government is widely recognized by the world community and is a member of the United Nations. A few groups have waged a small-scale insurgency against the government for much of the past fifteen years, and in late 1989 they announced the formation of a provisional government. The United States government does not support the insurgents or their cause in any way and does not recognize the provisional government.

"We have been pleased with the developing relationship we are enjoying with the Government of Laos. Increasingly, it is permitting us to meet the bilateral concerns each of us has with the other country. For the United States, areas of particular concern include resolving the cases of American servicemen unaccounted for from the Vietnam War, gaining Lao cooperation on narcotics control, promoting political liberalization and increased respect for human rights and supporting Laos' ambitious economic reforms. The government of Laos has been forthcoming on all these issues."[28]

This letter is one of reconciliation and obfuscation of facts. Why didn't the Twining letter make mention of the human rights violations, as reported in State's own *Country Report on Human Rights Practices* for 1990? Why didn't this official position express concern that Laos had no constitution, no due process, no freedom of assembly, no freedom to criticize the government, and no multiparty system? Why didn't it address the retention of political prisoners or the fact that the LPDR continued to use banned chemical-biological weapons against its own people? Why didn't it mention that people from Laos, in fear of persecution, continued to flee and even re-escape to Thailand?

In addition, the State Department errs in its policy that U.S. officials should follow a strict policy of not having any contact with representatives of these groups. Didn't Twining know that the population in Ban Vinai is anti-LPDR; that the people there have been fighting and fleeing the LPDR regime for years? They are the ones who know from first-hand experience what is currently going on in Laos. They know if it is safe to be repatriated. The American chargé d'affaires residing in Vientiane and the secretary of state, sitting in Washington, D.C., do not have such experience or direct information. It is foolish not to talk to the resistance groups who do have access to information that should be important to the State Department. Claudia Rosett, editorial page editor of the *Asian Wall Street Journal,* agreed; she wrote in June 1990: "In its policy of no official contact with the Lao resistance, the U.S. defers to the Vientiane regime of Kaysone Phomvihane, of which little is known because it ranks among the shadiest totalitarian sinkholes on this planet."[29]

Twining's letter must be construed as a "public relations" campaign for the LPDR and for those individuals and agencies promoting Hmong repatriation—both voluntary and involuntary. Otherwise, it would seem that the State Department would insist on presenting ALL facts and raising concerns rather than skewing information to favor the LPDR.

In early June 1991, communist forces in Laos attacked the resistance forces across the border from Nan Province in Thailand. The Provincial Hospital in Nan Province went on alert to treat victims of chemical warfare. Thai MOI and Military Intelligence officers confirmed that five Hmong were killed and 24 wounded in a "yellow poison gas" attack by the Lao military in a series of recent attacks inside Laos against the resistance.[30]

On June 10, while New York City honored the veterans of the Gulf War with a huge ticker-tape parade, Hmong from across the U.S. came by chartered buses to Washington to demonstrate in front of the Department of State and on Capitol Hill. These protestors, many of them veterans of the U.S.-backed forces in the forgotten Lao theatre of the Vietnam War, marched, they said, to represent their countrymen still fighting the Marxist-Leninist regime and those in refugee camps in Thailand. The protestors called for a stop to the forced repatriation of Lao and Hmong refugees to Laos and a stop to U.S. aid to the LPDR. In frustration and anger, they shouted and thrust their homemade signs of protest and outrage at State's gray silent building, hoping someone in power might take their concerns seriously and propose a long overdue critical examination—not wishful thinking—of the Lao People's Democratic Republic. They carried signs that read: "U.S. Government Stop Aid to Laos," "Don't Trade Refugees for $," "Don't Trade Refugees for Your Own Benefit."

"We've been trying to talk to the State Department and to the Congress about the true situation in Laos, but few will listen," explained Pobzeb Vang, chairman of the U.S.-based Lao Human Rights Council. "When we heard about a secret plan to send our people back to Laos, we had no choice but to come to Washington to protest. . . . Hmong and Lao people have been fighting the Kaysone regime since 1975 when the communists took power. People still fight this regime. There is no freedom. People continue to flee to Thailand to save their lives. Now, the U.S., the U.N. and the Thai government are trying to force them to Laos!''

Other protestors asked why discussions on repatriation were conducted in secrecy, and why most factions of the Hmong communities were excluded from consultation. Why, they asked, would anyone or any agency in the U.S. government want to conspire to keep repatriation information, including the repatriation schedule, from those to be repatriated, from their relatives in the West, and from their leaders?

Any reasonable, informed person would have concluded that to repatriate members of a tribal minority who for almost fifty years have fought the communist forces in their homeland would be a grave decision with potentially enormous negative ramifications for those forced to return. Based on the massive amount of data available on the LPDR's publicly stated policy to "wipe out" the reactionary Hmong, one would have thought that no repatriation would be attempted until there had been consultation with Hmong leaders and with clan chiefs and there was in place a carefully planned, well-financed, publicly discussed plan with some muscle to protect the vulnerable returnees upon their return to Laos. There were also the warnings in the respected Lawyers Committee on Human Rights report, which concluded: "Screening [of refugees in Thailand] is conducted in a haphazard manner with little concern for legal norms. Extortion and bribery are widespread. And despite an observatory role, the office of the United Nations High Commissioner for Refugees (UNHCR) in Thailand has proven incapable of ensuring a reliable and fair procedure."[31]

On June 22, 1991, 1,248 heads of households in Chiang Kham refugee camp either wrote their names or used their thumbprints to sign a petition to UNHCR headquarters in Geneva affirming that they did not want to go back to Laos under current political conditions. As far as I can determine, this petition remains unacknowledged by the UNHCR. (A page from this petition appears in the Appendix.)

In July, I was contacted by Pennsylvania Congressman Don Ritter's office in Washington asking me if I could provide any current evidence of forced repatriation of Hmong to the LPDR. On July 12, I provided Ritter's office with such documentation. On July 25, 1991, Congressman Ritter wrote to several House colleagues asking them to co-sign a letter asking Congress "to act now to stop this forced repatriation [of Hmong] that is likely to result in the execution and deaths of many of these brave people who befriended our nation in the past. . . . We must work to prevent the Thai authorities from sending our Hmong allies back to almost certain oppression and death. It is morally wrong for the United States to turn its backs on our former friends and allies as they are forced back to their executioners."[32]

Although a number of House members did subscribe to Ritter's plea and signed the letter, it never became "official" because Eric Schwartz in powerful Congressman Stephen Solarz's office dissuaded Ritter's staff from pursuing the matter.[33]

Just before Congress recessed for the summer, it approved $1.5 million to finance Hmong repatriation from Thailand to Laos.

* * *

In August 1991, the long-promised Lao Constitution was adopted by the National Assembly. The LPDR, however, remained a one-party state in which the primary source of political authority was the communist party with the Ministry of Interior (MOI) as the main instrument of state control. The MOI police monitored Lao society and expatriates who lived in Laos along with the communist party's own system of informants. Basic freedoms continued to be denied. State's *Country Reports on Human Rights Practices* for 1991 on Laos concluded: "Freedom of speech and press, freedom of assembly, the right of privacy, and the right of citizens to change their government are absent in Laos." State's report also pointed out that under the new penal code, "slandering the State, including distorting party or state policies, and spreading false rumors conducive to disorder" are banned, as are dissemination of books, videos, and other materials which "would infringe on the national culture."[34] It also "expressly prohibits demonstrations or protest marches aimed at causing turmoil and social instability," and it bans "unspecified 'destabilizing subversive activities' . . . with the penalties ranging from house arrest to death."

Particularly ominous for repatriates is the fact that the LPDR allows no domestic or international human rights groups in the country. According to the *Country Reports:* "Any organization wishing to investigate and publicly criticize the Government's human rights policies would face serious obstacles, if it were permitted to operate at all."[35] How then does the State Department or the UNHCR expect to effectively monitor on a continuing basis human rights in Laos not only for repatriated political refugees but for the general population? Will the monitoring depend on Western NGOs that have in the past ignored massive human rights abuses and whose personnel are not trained for this type of work and who are dependent upon the LPDR for contracts and permission to operate in Laos? Surely the U.S. and the U.N. are not that naive.

In late August 1991, Thai authorities began rounding up thousands of Hmong in Ban Vinai to ship them to Na Pho camp. MOI officials told these frightened Hmong, many of them clan leaders, including General Vang Pao's father-in-law and brother-in-law, that being held in Na Pho would not jeopardize their refugee "screened in" status which made them eligible for resettlement. In fact, the Thai intended to forcibly return these men, women, and children to Laos.[36] A congressional inquiry temporarily halted the forced return of some of these refugees.

Others in Ban Vinai, fearing they would be "captured" in another Thai sweep, fled to hide in the forest. Some tried to commit suicide, preferring to die by their own hands rather than be returned to the LPDR. At least one woman and several men were successful. Hmong leaders in Na Pho and Ban Vinai, suspecting deception, alerted relatives in the U.S. of their desperate situations. Hmong-Americans called me with these reports and wrote letters to their congressional representatives asking for help.

I called those in the State Department responsible for overseeing Hmong refugees to tell them of the Na Pho crisis, the numerous reports of forced repatriation, the lack of appropriate screening and review procedures, and the extraordinary fear in both Hmong communities in the U.S. and camps in Thailand. From my conversations with these bureaucrats, I concluded that few were interested enough to follow up aggressively. Some simply told me that if there were such problems, the U.S. Embassy in Bangkok would have alerted them. In fact, some 2,000 of the Hmong shipped to Na Pho had been classified some years earlier as refugees because of their previous involvement with the U.S. or with the Royal Lao government. If they were forced back to Laos, they would be in great danger. Some "captured" in Thai sweeps did not hold refugee status because they had fled Laos and entered the camp more recently after it had officially closed. They, however, considered themselves political refugees terrified of being turned over to their enemies.

In answer to queries about the fate of those shipped to Na Pho, the Thai claimed they were not refugees but "illegal immigrants" and therefore deportable. In September, informants in Thailand reported to me that in contravention of international refugee law, Thai authorities were "arresting" and "imprisoning" those who refused to return to Laos.

Repeated calls for U.S. congressional subcommittees responsible for foreign affairs and foreign aid to hold hearings on Laos failed. Only one congressional opportunity seemed available. Congressman Bill McCollum of Florida, ranking minority member of the House Judiciary Subcommittee on International Law, Immigration, and Refugees, had over the years taken a consistent interest in the Hmong and the situation in Laos. In October, I was invited to appear before this subcommittee to testify.

I testified that the Hmong are unique in that they may be the only refugees in the world that do *not* want to resettle in the U.S. Most Hmong in Thai camps want to return to their homelands in Laos. I stressed that they could not return until the Lao government had in place mechanisms to protect them: due process, a constitution that provides protection for human and civil rights, freedom of travel, assembly, and speech, and the ability on the part of international groups to travel freely on short notice within Laos to monitor civil and human rights. I attempted to point out that it was important that Congress pressure the LPDR to institute change so that the basic human rights declared in the Universal Declaration of Human Rights are protected. I emphasized that such a change in Laos would solve the Lao refugee problems for Thailand and third asylum countries, principally the U.S.

As part of my testimony, I said:

While United Nations High Commission for Refugees (UNHCR) representatives and U.S. State Department personnel in Thailand insist voluntary and involuntary Hmong repatriates have nothing to fear, Hmong know otherwise.

I have with me testimonies of Hmong who volunteered under UNHCR auspices to be repatriated in 1985. Their decision to do so turned into a horrible tragedy.

Mr. Chairman, in the interest of time, may I have permission to include in the record the full transcript of summaries of what happened to some of those who were part of this UNHCR voluntary repatriation program? (Permission was granted.)

Once in Laos, apparently the promised UNHCR aid and monitoring were not provided and volunteer returnees were harassed, beaten, starved, tortured, jailed, chained, raped, used as slave laborers, separated from families. Some were murdered. A few managed to *re-escape,* arriving in Thailand in 1991.

One survivor sent a cassette tape to his son in the U.S. Here is part of that tape. The full transcript is available to you. This survivor asks his son: "Do the Americans know that we [the volunteer returnees] are accused of being the hands and feet of the Americans, of the same flesh, of having drunk from the same breast as the CIA? That the 'Vang Pao people' [those who fought with General Vang Pao against the communists], the 'old hands and feet' of the Americans, are the worst people in the world. That they must look for a way to exterminate them, and not allow there to be any left. That if there is even [a] piece left that the stench will fill the whole country, that there will be trouble in the country, that it will become uninhabitable for them.''

Now listen to a woman survivor of voluntary repatriation, who, with her children, was imprisoned by the LPDR. She re-escaped in February 1991. In Thailand she testified about her life in Laos as a repatriate: ''The 'Red Lao' [LPDR] didn't give our children anything to eat. They didn't give us anything to eat. We just lived and cried, lived and cried. Everyone gathered the yellow leaves growing under the trees to eat. We were that hungry. The 'Red Lao' tortured us so much and they still said that they would imprison the Hmong who had been 'Chao Fa' [resistance] or who had escaped to Thailand until we were all dead. The 'Red Lao' said that one egg was worth more than all the people who had been 'Chao Fa' or who had refugeed to Thailand like us. Though we had come back, it was of no benefit to the 'Red Lao.' They said that the 'Vang Pao people' should not be allowed to live, that they should all be killed.''

She spoke about her life in prison. ''The 'Red Lao' kept us imprisoned all the time. Once a week, they took us away to interrogate us. Women and children cried without end, having nothing to eat, having to live, sleep, and defecate all in one place.'' When the Hmong cried, their guards scolded them, asking, 'Why don't you just keep quiet and be our slaves?'''

She reported that those caught trying to escape were beaten and killed, including four starving Hmong who were only collecting leaves to eat. She provided the names of 21 Hmong she saw being starved, forced to work in an emaciated state, and then taken away to be imprisoned because they had not been working hard enough. When she re-escaped with her two surviving children, she reported at least 40 families in misery at Douan Thao–Douan Nam prisons.

In July 1991, she and other re-escapees learned that they would be deported—involuntarily repatriated—to Laos. In late July, I learned about their possible deportation. Before we could get their I.D. numbers to intervene and stop their repatriation, they were forced back to Laos on August 16, 1991, by Thai and UNHCR officials.

Mr. Chairman, please investigate the fate of these Hmong and other similar cases. Please send a *bi-partisan* team that includes members of the American-Hmong community to Laos to investigate all the events recorded in this document which I am submitting today. This investigation should be completed before any more Hmong are returned to Laos.

Mr. Chairman and members of this Committee, if such has been the treatment of those who *voluntarily* returned to Laos, what will happen to those who are *involuntarily* returned?

Hmong in Thailand know that making a new life in the U.S. is not easy and many prefer to return to their homelands. They, however, do not want to return until democracy returns to Laos and mechanisms are in

place to provide security for them. Until then, they want the repatriation—voluntary and involuntary—stopped.[37]

I emphasized that human rights must never be sacrificed—or compromised—for political and economic expediency and pointed out that since
the LPDR, without Soviet aid and on the verge of economic collapse, now
sought critical economic aid from the U.S. and other countries, it was an
opportune time for the U.S. Congress to pressure the LPDR. I also urged
the subcommittee to send a team, including international human rights
lawyers, to Thailand and Laos to investigate refugee and human rights
issues.

Congressman Romano Mazzoli, chairman of this subcommittee, reminded me that given the jurisdiction of this committee it could not
respond to many of my requests and suggestions. This was true. Many of
the issues which I raised should have been presented before Solarz's Subcommittee on Asian and Pacific Affairs, which does have oversight on
such matters. But that seemed impossible.

During a break in the hearing, an employee of a Washington-based
lobby organization who advises Congress and the media on refugee policy issues, told me and others, including subcommittee "staffers," that
the Hmong who voice concerns about human rights abuses in the LPDR
and the Lao Human Rights Council are only "lunatic fringe" and should
be ignored. Also during this break, Lou Mazel, from State's Bureau of
Refugee Programs, who is "working" the repatriation of Hmong to the
LPDR, told a Washington-based journalist that the Hmong were simply
lying about human rights abuses in Laos. When the journalist questioned
this statement, Mazel proceeded to explain that over there everyone
lies.[38]

Keisuke Murata, the UNHCR Durable Solutions official for Hmong refugees, had been correct in his enthusiasm. Under the auspices of the
UNHCR with support from the U.S., Hmong in large numbers were indeed keeping the repatriation pipeline filled. But the majority were not
voluntary repatriates; they were forced repatriates.

*   *   *

During the fall of 1991, Hmong-American citizens with relatives in
camps in Thailand continued to report that their kinsmen were
"rounded up" by Thai authorities to meet monthly repatriation quotas
established by the Tripartite Repatriation Plan. In Chiang Kham camp,

those who were "screened out" were fenced off and isolated. No outsiders were allowed to visit or counsel them. If these individuals were truly voluntary repatriates eager to return to the LPDR, why should the UNHCR and Thai authorities fence them off and deny free communication and access? Westerners in Chiang Kham involved in the screening process corroborate refugee accusations that the Thai policy is not to give notice to those to be repatriated for fear that they will run away.[39]

Repeated requests to obtain the names and identification numbers of those held in Na Pho and Chiang Kham and those who have been "screened out" are ignored. In early December 1991, the Schell Center wrote to Sadako Ogata, the United Nations High Commissioner for Refugees, ultimately responsible for the repatriation, asking for a hiatus to the repatriation until such time as realistic and reliable mechanisms and guarantees both in law and in practice were in place to provide human and civil rights for all who live in Laos. The Schell Center also asked for the names and identification numbers of those held in Na Pho and Chiang Kham camps, in particular the names and numbers of those who had been "screened out." No response was received.

* * *

On November 12, 1991, President Bush announced that the U.S. and LPDR had agreed to upgrade their diplomatic posts from chargé d'affaires to ambassador.

Many Hmong continued to beg me to help stop the Thai and UNHCR repatriation of their relatives back to Laos. I, in turn, continued to contact people in the State Department and on Capitol Hill, asking for a hiatus in Hmong repatriation until a thorough, detailed investigation had been conducted. Nothing was initiated.

On January 31 and February 5, 1992, respectively, Minnesota Senator Dave Durenberger wrote to David Pierce, Refugee Coordinator in the U.S. Embassy in Bangkok, and to Robert Cooper of the UNHCR in Chiang Kham camp in Thailand, pointing out that many of his constituents had relatives "in Thailand who have been threatened with forced repatriation by the Thai government and the UNHCR office there." Durenberger's letter requested "that action be taken immediately to stop the forced repatriations of the relatives of my constituents." He pointed out: "The U.S. administration has been adamantly opposed to such repatriations." On February 6, Durenberger wrote to Hmong in Minnesota: "The State Department assures me that forced repatriations are not taking place. . . . It is my understanding that the UNHCR has indicated that there is no concrete evidence of forced repatriation or maltreatment of returning refugees."[40]

On the same day, I received a cassette tape from a Hmong refugee in Chiang Kham camp. A Walt Disney logo with a smiling Mickey Mouse holding a Christmas present decorated the sticker which read, "Walt Disney Storyteller: Mickey's Christmas Carol." I played the cassette. It was the plea of Lor Cha Lee begging for his life and that of his family; they were about to be rounded up to be forcibly repatriated to the LPDR.

In late February, David Merkel, a member of Congressman Bill McCollum's staff, Phil Smith of Congressman Don Ritter's staff, and two Hmong-Americans arrived in Thailand to investigate the reports of forced repatriation. In addition to confirming the Thai intent to return to Laos some 2,000 Hmong at Na Pho with refugee status, Merkel discovered that when UNHCR personnel were asked to investigate cases of LPDR mistreatment of returnees, they merely asked LPDR authorities (the abuser) if it were true.[41] Merkel was also shocked to learn that UNHCR had a mandate to visit the thousands of returnees *once a year with a staff of four*—this in a country with few roads and where the communist authorities do not allow freedom of travel and deny both domestic and international human rights monitoring groups.

The UNHCR and the U.S. State Department have always claimed that the LPDR does not know if a returnee is a voluntary repatriate or a forced returnee. This secrecy, they argue, protects returnees from reprisals. The Hmong insist that this is not true. They argue heatedly that the LPDR is given the exact status of each returnee as well as information about those who, in the past, had associations with Americans, had resisted the LPDR, or have anti-LPDR relatives. This deception, involving the UNHCR and Thai officials, has been confirmed by Westerners working in repatriation.

Merkel concluded that during his investigation in Thailand, he was lied to most often about what details were on the lists of returnees given to the LPDR. "I was told that the LPDR did not know whether a returnee was voluntary or involuntary," explained Merkel. "They were lying about this. There is a code in the series of numbers and letters that accompanies each name that signals who are 'screened out' and being forced back and who are volunteers."[42]

On March 3, 1992, the Schell Center sent a letter to Boutros Boutros-Ghali, the newly elected secretary general of the United Nations, pointing out the continuing and pervasive forced repatriation of Hmong from UNHCR camps in Thailand and asking once again for the names of those "screened out" for repatriation to the LPDR. There was no response.

On March 7, the Bush administration offered the LPDR a number of helicopters and pilot training as part of U.S. anti-narcotic aid. Hmong-Americans believe that these helicopters, paid for by their tax dollars, will be used to hunt down and kill their relatives in Laos.

In 1989 Laos was the world's third largest producer of opium, used to make heroin. In 1991, Laos retained its status as a major drug producer. The U.S. government "continues to receive credible reports that a number of LPDR military and government officials actively encourage and facilitate the trafficking of heroin and marijuana."[43]

In October and November of 1991, the LPDR energized its search for Hmong leaders and those who might be potential soldiers in a rebellion. This time the search extended into Hmong villages which had for years sided with the Pathet Lao. Lo Lyfong, now in his 60s, had joined the Pathet Lao in 1961 and remained with them from that time. Then in late 1991, he and others in his village were forced by the LPDR into one of at least two detention camps east of Phong Savan. Lo was held in a camp called Ban Kay, where he and another 1,000 Hmong were under guard and denied a means of making a living.

At 4 p.m. on March 4, 1992, LPDR soldiers arrested him, his son Nao Chao, in his 40s, and a younger cousin, Ly Za Da. The arresting authorities took them away, saying that since they were Hmong they must have connections with the resistance. Their whereabouts remain unknown. Lo's relatives in the Ban Kay camp wrote to clan members in the U.S. giving details of the arrests, the wretched camp life, and the fear that all males in this camp would be arrested and disappear just because they were Hmong. LPDR authorities have threatened to send Hmong females and young children to camps in Houa Phan Province.[44] Other similar reports have reached the West, corroborating the current LPDR effort to force Hmong—even those who have supported the Pathet Lao since the 1960s—out of the highlands into lowland encampments where they are monitored, arrested, and terrorized.

In spite of the State Department's human rights evaluators' continuing analysis that the communist Kaysone regime remains a harsh dictatorship with no due process which denies most basic freedoms, in spite of numerous reports of continuing arrests and disappearances of ethnic Hmong just because they are Hmong, and in spite of involuntarily repatriated Hmong re-escaping to Thailand with horrendous reports on LPDR treatment of returnees, the Bush administration and those in the State Department responsible for refugee programs continue supporting and financing repatriation.

On May 8, 1992, Lou Mazel of State's Bureau of Refugee Programs and the Washington-based point man on Hmong repatriation, criticized the Hmong in the West for calling for a multiparty system in Laos before their relatives were repatriated. Mazel reasoned that Laos with a single-party system was no different from African nations with one-party systems.[45] This specious argument not only confuses and obfuscates the issue, but is not analogous and reflects lack of knowledge of Lao political history—even recent history—when, for many years, those living in Laos indeed had a multiparty democratic system of government, albeit under a titular king. In 1962, when the U.S. prepared to "neutralize" Laos, there were 15 political parties.[46] It was, after all, a three-party "neutralized" Laos that formed the Lao coalition government in the 1960s. It was also a coalition of communists and royal Lao that supposedly were to share joint governance of Laos under the 1973 Agreement on the Restoration of Peace and Reconciliation until Laos was brutally transformed in 1975 into a communist dictatorship.

Is this fallacious argument intended to justify State's current policy to ignore human rights violations in Laos and to blunt the pleas and efforts of those who live in Laos and in exile to regain their stolen political freedoms?

It would seem that at least some in the State Department fear that were those in the West, so concerned with human rights and democracy, to fully realize the heritage of political freedoms so recently usurped in Laos, they could effectively abort current State policy of accommodation with and support of the LPDR. Mazel's revealing remarks might indicate State's attempt, within the larger policy of closing out the Hmong refugee problem, to promote the disinformation that since those living in Laos never had any form of democracy, there is little reason now to push to institute a multiparty form of government there.

* * *

In 1990, Soviet journalists, under *glasnost*, were free enough to begin investigating what had actually happened at Sverdlovsk in the Ural Mountains in April 1979 when something went wrong inside Military Compound 19, a secret military microbiological research institute, and many died. The Soviet official position had always been that the local victims had eaten tainted meat. The U.S. had maintained that victims had died from inhaling anthrax spores from an airborne leak from a laboratory malfunction.

In August 1990, *Literaturnaya Gazeta* published an article by Natalya

Zenova entitled "Military Secret: Reasons for the Tragedy in Sverdlovsk Must Be Investigated" in which the author, after interviewing doctors who treated victims, concluded that it was more than tainted meat. That fall in an article for the *Wall Street Journal,* she asked: "Why, if it was 'simply' anthrax in Sverdlovsk, did people in military uniforms play first violin in the investigation of facts? Why was the whole story of the illness eliminated along with all records and all documentation from 'concerned' institutions?"[47]

In October 1991, Peter Gumbel, the *Wall Street Journal* bureau chief in Moscow, after his own research on the Sverdlovsk incident, wrote: "For the 12 years since the outbreak, the KGB and military have been engaged in a cover-up of the facts of the case," and a " . . . wealth of evidence suggests that the official Soviet version of the anthrax outbreak is false, and that the three-man delegation that visited the U.S. in 1988 engaged in comprehensive disinformation."[48]

On May 27, 1992, Russian President Boris Yeltsin, who in 1979 was head of the communist party in Sverdlovsk and in a position to know what was happening in his area, would settle part of the "yellow rain" argument by admitting Soviet violations of the 1972 Biological and Toxin Weapons Convention. He admitted in an interview with the Russian newspaper *Komsomolskaya Pravda* that the Soviet government had hidden the truth about the cause of deaths in Sverdlovsk in 1979. The truth, he admitted, was that Soviet military researchers had been working on germ warfare weaponry and something went wrong, that many people had died, and that the Soviet military and KGB had covered it up, insisting that the deaths had been caused by tainted meat.

Since the collapse of the Soviet Union, it has been revealed that after the Sverdlovsk explosion, military laboratories were moved to another region, relevant documents were burned, and the base military commander had committed suicide.[49] After the demise of the Soviet Union, arms inspectors have traveled there and have seen the extensive, modern chemical weapons arsenals which the Soviets had developed in violation of existing treaties.

In July 1992, after the people of Kazakhstan complained vigorously upon learning that an island in the Aral Sea was being used as a large biological warfare testing area, the Russian parliament passed a law making it illegal for anyone to be involved in activities that violate the 1972 Biological and Toxin Convention.

In 1991, the debate over the use of chemical-biological toxin weapons in Southeast Asia changed dramatically with Desert Storm and the threat of Iraq's arsenal of chemical-biological weapons. Countries around the world realized that they were threatened by *real* chemical-biological weapons. Government officials woke up to the reality and began acquiring protective equipment and making vaccines against anthrax and mycotoxins.

Beginning in the early 1980s, the *Wall Street Journal* doggedly researched and wrote about the use of chemical-biological toxin warfare, or "yellow rain" as it was commonly called, against the Hmong in Laos and its use in Cambodia and Afghanistan. The *Journal* stood prominent among a small group of the major U.S. media in sticking to its researched position that the Soviets and their surrogates, the communist Vietnamese and Lao, were deploying toxin warfare against the Hmong in Laos. Arrayed in opposition were much of the major media that were quick to publicize the "bee feces" theory actively promoted by Matthew Meselson.

Now that dark secrets held by the Soviet Union are coming to light, *Journal* editors are proud of their often solitary and consistent stand. In June 1992, the *Journal* lamented in an editorial: "We've taken no little heat over the years for publishing material suggesting the Soviets were violating the Biological Weapons Convention of 1972. We and the U.S. Government have long held that Sverdlovsk was a biological warfare accident, but met with withering skepticism from most of the media and the 'scientific community' led by Matthew Meselson."[50]

* * *

It should have been clear and acknowledged in world councils that the Hmong reporting of the use of lethal agents against them in Laos in a genocidal way was accurate. The broader and lasting implications, moral and legal, of this attempted genocide are evident.

In addition to the wording of the convention on genocide, in current usage, genocide can mean the mass extermination of one's political enemies, such as in Democratic Kampuchea (Cambodia) where Pol Pot eliminated his political enemies through mass killings. In Laos, Kaysone attempted to eliminate political enemies in the same fashion. If what Pol Pot did was considered genocide, then what Kaysone did to the Hmong would also be considered genocide. Genocide in Laos has continued longer than the genocide in Cambodia. Also, in Laos, it is more specifically against a distinct group who are distinguished by their ethnicity. The political enemies in Laos, unlike in Cambodia, are ethnically distinct from the people who rule them. In Laos, in fact, most Hmong are under suspicion of having engaged in anti-state activities. They are a minority associated with the enemies of the LPDR regime. Only those Hmong who have been identified as sure friends are not subject to sudden arrest. Suspicion hangs over all other Hmong.

The policy to exterminate the political enemies of the Pathet Lao began in 1975 when on May 9, the Pathet Lao newspaper, according to Dr. Yang Dao, "put in black and white to exterminate the Meo [Hmong] 'to the last root.' "[51] Repeatedly over its official radio, the LPDR stated, beginning in 1975, that it intended to "wipe out" the Hmong and urged others to join in that goal. In 1976, the LPDR launched in the Phou Bia area its "Extinct Destruction Operations" military offensive to "wipe out the reactionary Hmong people," which would last for years. Aircraft deployed "poisonous smokes" against Hmong. To "wipe out the reactionary Hmong people" was LPDR policy. Military operations and police actions implemented this policy which continued for years. Recent Hmong escapees report that though less stridently announced and more carefully camouflaged to the outside world, this policy still exists. In recent years, in an effort to bring highland peoples under closer surveillance, the LPDR has resettled them in lowland areas in the guise of development assistance.[52]

As I wrote the final chapters of *Tragic Mountains*, my eyes often drifted to Hmong mementos hanging on the wall of my computer room. During the final long days and nights culminating the fourteen years of research and writing this book, I often looked at the intricately designed Hmong necklace, no longer made from silver but from aluminum cans in refugee camps in Thailand; soiled and worn Hmong sashes with their jewel-like embroidery still intact and beautiful which had survived long, arduous, and dangerous treks through hostile Laos to at least temporary asylum in Thailand; several dramatic cloth and tasseled baby hats festive in black, red, and white resembling small helmets; photographs of Hmong taken in Laos at New Years' celebrations in the 1960s and 1970s, given to me as gifts when I visited their homes; photographs of new arrivals from Laos, ragged, sick, and frightened, which I had taken in refugee camps in Thailand; and letters from Hmong begging for help in rescuing their relatives from repatriation camps in Thailand.

I often read a poem tacked to that wall, written by a young Hmong woman whose childhood had been spent in Laos and who now lives in the United States. Her haunting poem lamented the death of her father in the fighting in Laos and her bitter realization as she studied the names on the Vietnam War Memorial in Washington, D.C., that her father's sacrifice and death had gone unrecognized and unacknowledged. Her words of anguish speak for many grieving Hmong.

When I was discouraged, frustrated, and tired, I looked at the memorabilia, the stark and poignant photographs, and the sorrowful letters. They prodded me to continue—to finish this tragic saga of loyalty, bravery, honor, and sacrifice of these Hmong whose abandonment resulted in genocide and in a deep sorrow among survivors of that holocaust. This Hmong sorrow was deepened by the refusual in certain quarters within the U.S. government to acknowledge the truthfulness in their reporting the use of lethal toxins against them in Laos and later by the U.S. support and financing of the forced repatriation of Hmong back to the communist regime in Laos. Another great sadness for the Hmong was the loss of their good names. Men like General Vang Pao, who had sacrificed all to defend Hmong homelands against the invading North Vietnamese and to help the Americans in Laos, had suffered egregiously from negative U.S. press coverage which was often based on unidentified sources, rumors, and lack of understanding of Hmong history and culture.

I have known for years that before the healing for Hmong Americans, for Americans who served in the secret war in Laos, for the families of those who were killed or lost there, and for Americans in general to appreciate the Hmong—among the newest Americans—there must be an understanding of the events, sacrifices, abandonment, and heroism that took place in Laos.

As the Hmong tragedy deepened, it became extremely important to me that their story be known beyond the confines of the homes of the 125,000 Hmong who now live in the United States—and beyond the small private spaces remaining to those many Hmong elsewhere in their tragic worlds.

I still have hope that this book might yet change the destiny of those of all ethnic groups in Laos, who, like one Hmong freedom fighter told me, "wait like the sunrise for democracy."

Appendix

1. Text of the U.N. Convention on Genocide, 1948.

2. "Sanitized" classified letter from Richard Helms, director of the CIA, obtained by author through Freedom of Information Act on 4/16/91 and internal White House memorandum to President Johnson. These documents show that General Vang Pao and his Hmong forces suffered high casualties in providing critical assistance to the U.S. war effort during the Vietnam War era and that Vang Pao was personally known to those at the highest levels of the U.S. government.

3.a–f Six representative forms from among hundreds filled out at the January 1991 Minnesota Human Rights Conference. Refugee attendees from just Wisconsin and Minnesota listed more than 1,500 "lost" and "injured" relatives in the LPDR from 1975 through 1990 (see chapter 31). a: Note the November 1975 use of CBW against these Hmong, and the number of locations. b: Note the time span (1977-1987) and the ages of those killed. c: Note the wiping out of an entire Hmong family over the years by communist forces in Laos. d: Note that among those killed was Mrs. Vang Sai, 45, who died in the 1985 cave massacre (see chapter 32). e: Note the ages of those arrested and killed, including six children under the age of 5. f: Note the ages (2-50) of these Hmong killed in Laos as recently as 1990.

4. June 23, 1991, petition signed by 1,248 Hmong heads of households at Chiang Kham refugee camp in Thailand to the UNHCR in Geneva, begging not to be repatriated to the LPDR under current political conditions. Many signed with their thumbprints (see chapter 32).

Convention on the Prevention and Punishment of the Crime of Genocide. Adopted by the U.N. General Assembly (Dec.9, 1948)

Article I. The Contracting Parties confirm that genocide, whether committed in time of peace or in time of war, is a crime under international law which they undertake to prevent and to punish.

Article II. In the present Convention, genocide means any of the following acts committed with intent to destroy, in whole or in part, a national, ethnical, racial or religious group, as such:

(a) Killing members of the group;

(b) Causing serious bodily or mental harm to members of the group;

(c) Deliberately inflicting on the group conditions of life calculated to bring about its physical destruction in whole or in part;

(d) Imposing measures intended to prevent births within the group;

(e) Forcibly transferring children of the group to another group.

Article III. The following acts shall be punishable:

(a) Genocide;

(b) Conspiracy to commit genocide;

(c) Direct and public incitement to commit genocide;

(d) Attempt to commit genocide;

(e) Complicity in genocide.

Article IV. Persons committing genocide or any of the other acts enumerated in Article III shall be punished, whether they are constitutionally responsible rulers, public officials or private individuals.

Article V. The Contracting Parties undertake to enact, in accordance with their respective Constitutions, the necessary legislation to give effect to the provisions of the present Convention and, in particular, to provide effective penalties for persons guilty of genocide or of any of the other acts enumerated in Article III.

Article VI. Persons charged with genocide or any of the other acts enumerated in Article III shall be tried by a competent tribunal of the State in the territory of which the act was committed, or by such international penal tribunal as may have jurisdiction with respect to those Contracting Parties which shall have accepted its jurisdiction.

Article VII. Genocide and the other acts enumerated in Article III shall not be considered as political crimes for the purpose of extradition.

The Contracting Parties pledge themselves in such cases to grant extradition in accordance with their laws and treaties in force.

Article VIII. Any Contracting Party may call upon the competent organs of the United Nations to take such action under the Charter of the United Nations as they consider appropriate for the prevention and suppression of acts of genocide or any of the other acts enumerated in Article III.

Article IX. Disputes between the Contracting Parties relating to the interpretation, application or fulfilment of the present Convention, including those relating to the responsibility of a State for genocide or for any of the other acts enumerated in Article III, shall be submitted to the International Court of Justice at the request of any of the parties to the dispute.

* * *

CENTRAL INTELLIGENCE AGENCY
WASHINGTON, D. C. 20505

OFFICE OF THE DIRECTOR

25 September 1968

The Honorable Walt W. Rostow
Special Assistant to the President
The White House
Washington, D. C.

Dear Walt,

I thought you would be interested to know that General Vang Pao, the Meo General from Laos, will be in the White House from 8:45 o'clock until 9:30 a.m. on 1 October for a private tour of the public rooms. General Vang Pao will also be received in State and Defense. If you have the time I suggest you might find it interesting to take a few minutes to meet with him while he is at the White House.

As you know, Vang Pao is the head of the Meo irregular forces, now consisting of over 22,000 men, which have been the backbone of the resistance to Communist infiltration in Northern Laos. Although Vang Pao and his forces have suffered some considerable loss of territory during the enemy dry season offensive, they are now in the process of regaining a significant amount. They have killed or wounded during the nine months to 1 August 1968 a total of some 3500 of the enemy at losses of 1500 to themselves. Vang Pao is one of the two Lao "fighting generals" as well as being a most effective leader of his people. He is well thought of by both the King and Souvanna Phouma. Although he is primarily interested in the defense of his people and their highland living areas, he recognizes that in the long run the Meo will have to become integrated with the rest of Laos society and has already taken considerable steps to this end, including educating the young children in the Lao language and teaching them allegiance to the King.

General Vang Pao speaks fluent French and understands English, speaking it with a considerable accent.

Sincerely,

Richard Helms
Director

———— 2 ————

MEMORANDUM

THE WHITE HOUSE
WASHINGTON

ACTION

Thursday, November 14, 1968
12:35 p. m.

MEMORANDUM FOR THE PRESIDENT

General VangPao, the leader of the hill-tribe irregulars in Laos, was recently in the United States on a visit. He is a real asset to us, a feisty little fighter who has led his Meo people into a courageous battle against the Communists in Laos. He is an admirer of you -- and of the United States -- and is deeply grateful for the American assistance provided his forces.

As a token of his and the Meo people's appreciation, he has sent to you an old handmade flintlock rifle of the kind commonly used by his soldiers when they first began their resistance. (I think you will find it an interesting gift.) Attached is a letter of thanks which I recommend you sign.

W. W. Rostow

3a.

MINNESOTA HUMAN RIGHT CONFERENCE
JANUARY 19/20, 1991
LOST AND INJURED REPORT FORM
****

I, __Ying Moua__ ,reside at __310 Arundel St.__ city __St Paul__ State __MN__ zip __55103__

from Ban __Pathat__ Taseng __Pakha__ Moung __Hong Noon__ Khuang __Houa Phan__

had the following relatives were poisoned by (yellow rain) (killed) __kepture __taken to reeduc-

cation training camp and never come back by the Lao Communist and Vietnamese Government. Their
names are as follows:

NAMES	AGE	MONTH/YEAR HAPPEN	AREA HAPPEN
01. Youa Vang Moua	37	Nov. 1975 Yellow	Ban Nhot Tou, Xiangkhouang
02. Lee Moua	6	July 1977 Killed	Moung Auo/Moung Om, Xieng khouang
03. You Toua Moua	45	July 1977 "	Moung Auo/Moung Om, Xieng Khouang
04. La Xiong	39	July 1977 "	Moung Auo/Moung Om, Xieng Khouang
05. Vang Moua	25	April 1976 Yellow	Nam Mo, Xieng Khouang
06. Xue Moua	19	Jan 1978 Killed	Phou Hae, Xieng Khouang
07. Ka Moua	7	Jan 1978 "	Phou Hae, Xieng Khouang
08. Cher Neng Moua	42	Aug. 1977 "	Moung Auo/Moung Om, Xieng Khouang
09. Tou Moua	39	Aug. 1977 "	Moung Auo/Moung Om, Xieng Khouang
10.			
11.			
12.			

The above informations are true and can be investigated in the future for more detail with me or
my relatives who do have access toward the actions.

Truly yours

Ying Moua
(Person submitted)

3b.

MINNESOTA HUMAN RIGHT CONFERENCE
JANUARY 19/20, 1991
LOST AND INJURED REPORT FORM
****

I, __Xiong P. Moua__ ,reside at __171 E. Arch St # A__ City __St. Paul__ State __MN__ zip __55101__

from Ban __Namkeng__ Taseng __Phou Xao__ Moung __Ngad__ Khuang __Xiengkhouang__

had the following relatives were poisoned by yellow rain __killed__kepture __taken to reeduc-

cation training camp and never come back by the Lao Communist and Vietnamese Government. Their
names are as follows:

NAMES	AGE	SEX	MONTH/YEAR HAPPEN	AREA HAPPEN	
01. NHIA PAO MOUA	46	m	1977	Phou Bia	(killed)
02. DANG MOUA	26	m	1977	Phou Bia	(killed)
03. YEE MOUA	25	m	1979	phou Bia	(Yellow Rain)
04. Niam YEE MOUA	24	F	1979	phou Bia	(Yellow Rain)
05. Koua MOUA	16	m	1982	phou Bia	(Yellow Rain)
06. NENG THAO MOUA	42	m	1982	phou Bia	(killed)
07. NHIA HOUA MOUA	76	m	1980	phou Bia	(Yellow Rain)
08. YING LOR	74	F	1987	phou Bia	(Yellow Rain)
09. MEE WONG	50	F	1980	Phou Bia	(Yellow Rain)
10. CHA MOUA	17	m	1987	Phou Ma Thao	(killed)
11. XUE MOUA	4	F	1987	Phou Ma Thao	(Yellow Rain)
12. XAI KAO MOUA	49	m	1980	Phou Bia	(Yellow Rain)

The above informations are true and can be investigated in the future for more detail with me or
my relatives who do have access toward the actions.

Truly yours

Xiong Pao Moua.
(Person submitted)

3c.

MINNESOTA HUMAN RIGHT CONFERENCE
JANUARY 19/20, 1991
LOST AND INJURED REPORT FORM
****

I, _Mr. NHIA Chouyang_, reside at _313 Topping St_ city _St paul_ State _MN_ Zip _55117_
from Ban _NAm xou_ Taseng _PHA LAI_ Moung _KHune_ Khuang _Xieng khouang_

had the following relatives were poisoned by yellow rain ✓ killed ✓ kepture _____ taken to reeducation training camp and never come back by the Lao Communist and Vietnamese Government. Their names are as follows:

NAMES	AGE	MONTH/YEAR HAPPEN	AREA HAPPEN
01. YER VANG	42	MAY 23,1979 Killed	PHA BARK
02. KHue yang	14	MAY 23, 1979 killed	PHA BARK
03. PENG yang	12	MAY 23, 1979 Killed	PHA BARK
04. Beo yang	8	MAY 23, 1979 Killed	PHA BARK
05. Mai xo yang	6	MAY 23, 1979 Killed	PHA BARK
06. Mai xai yong	2	MAY 23, 1979 Killed	PHA BARK
07. xian yang	10	June 18, 1976 poisond	BAN nam Khia
08. Choua yong	08	June July 2, 1976 poison	BAN nam Khia
09. NAo kha yong	46	December 14, 1990 killed	BAN hai
10. Song xiong yong	65	Dec 2, 1990 killed	BAN Phou Dong
11. Youa tong	46	MAY 12, 1986 Killed	BAN nam xub.
12. KA vue yang	44	Feb 17, 1985 poisoned	BAN nam xub.

The above informations are true and can be investigated in the future for more detail with me or my relatives who do have access toward the actions.

Truly yours

Nhia Chouyang
(Person submitted)

3d.

MINNESOTA HUMAN RIGHT CONFERENCE
JANUARY 19/20, 1991
LOST AND INJURED REPORT FORM
****

I, _yong kay moua_, reside at _2520 Beverly hills_ City _Eau claire_ State _WI_ Zip _54701_
from Ban _Bouam Long_ Taseng _phou Dou_ Moung _Vieng Fa_ Khuang _xieng Khouang._

had the following relatives were poisoned by yellow rain _x_ killed _x_ kepture _x_ taken to reeducation training camp and never come back by the Lao Communist and Vietnamese Government. Their names are as follows:

NAMES	AGE	MONTH/YEAR HAPPEN	AREA HAPPEN	
01. Xao Moua	15	1982	That chok	die of poison.
02. Mao xiong Moua	14	1979	Haci Home	—"
03. Nou Moua	10	1979	—"	—"
04. Chong Houa Moua	50	1984	Nong Khuang	—"
05. MRS. Xai Vang	45	1985	Nam xai	—" in the cave
06. Phoua Moua	2	1983	That chok	—"
07. Yong yee Moua	1	1983	—"	—"
08. Song Moua	13	1978	Muang out	—"
09. Lia Moua	30	1979	That chot	killed
10.				
11.				
12.				

The above informations are true and can be investigated in the future for more detail with me or my relatives who do have access toward the actions.

Truly yours

Yong moua
(Person submitted)

3e.

MINNESOTA HUMAN RIGHT CONFERENCE
JANUARY 19/20, 1991
LOST AND INJURED REPORT FORM
****

I, _CHIA KAO VANG_ ,reside at _153 Alington_ City _St-Paul_ State _MN_ zip _55117_
from Ban _Oh Hou_ Taseng _Xieng Nguen_ Moung _Xieng Nguen_ Khuang _Luang Phrabang_
had the following relatives were poisoned by yellow rain __killed__kepture ____taken to reeducation training camp and never come back by the Lao Communist and Vietnamese Government.Their names are as follows:

NAMES	AGE	MONTH/YEAR HAPPEN	AREA HAPPEN	
01. Mai Xiong	29	5-14-83	Vientiane	Lao Communist
02. Mai Ker Vang	2	—//—	—//—	
03. Pa Tong Xiong	70	—//—	—//—	Took them from
04. Tou Po Vang	1	—//—	—//—	the family and
05. Ying Yang	66	—//—	—//—	
06. Mai Vang	28	—//—	—//—	Kill all of them.
07. Hue Thao	4	—//—	—//—	
08. Shoua Thao	3	—//—	—//—	
09. Doua Thao	2	—//—	—//—	
10. Nai Thao	1	—//—	—//—	
11. Pang Thao	18	—//—	—//—	
12. Yee Xiong	60	—//—	—//—	

The above informations are true and can be investigated in the future for more detail with me or my relatives who do have access toward the actions.

Truly yours

CHIAKAOVANG
(Person submitted)

3f.

MINNESOTA HUMAN RIGHT CONFERENCE
JANUARY 19/20, 1991
LOST AND INJURED REPORT FORM
****

I, _Tou Lee_ ,reside at _1554 Fellowslone #C_ City _St. Paul_ State _MN_ zip _55106_
from Ban _THAM XON_ Taseng _THAM XON_ Moung _PHONE_ Khuang _VIENTIANE_
had the following relatives were poisoned by yellow rain _killed__kepture ____taken to reeducation training camp and never come back by the Lao Communist and Vietnamese Government.Their names are as follows:

NAMES	AGE	MONTH/YEAR HAPPEN	AREA HAPPEN
01. NAO See Lee	50	8-86	Ban Tham Xon
02. MAIDOUA HER LEE	33	9 - 86	Ban Tham Xon
03. CHOR LEE	5	9 - 86	Ban Tham Xon
04. Peng LEE	4	9 - 86	Ban Tham Xon
05. Ka LEE	2	9 - 86	Ban Tham Xon
06. Vang See Lee	32	8 - 86	Ban Tham Xon
07. Gao Lee	28	9 - 86	Ban Tham Xon
08. Maisee Lee	15	5 - 90	Ban Tham Xon
09. Yangpao Lee	13	5 - 90	Ban Tham Xon
10. Maidoua Lee	9	5 - 90	Ban THAM Xon
11. Pao Lee	7	5 - 90	Ban Tham Xon
12. Huelong Lee	44	5 - 90	Ban Tham Xon

The above informations are true and can be investigated in the future for more detail with me or my relatives who do have access toward the actions.

Truly yours

Tou Lee
(Person submitted)

Nº ລຳ	Names ຊື່ແລະນາມສະກຸນ	ages ອາຍຸປີ	ວ- eA	Address ທີ່ຢູ່	Family mem # ຈຳນວນຄົວ ຄອບຄົວ	signature ລາຍເຊັນ	8. Remark ໝ 600.
01	ນາຍ ໄວລ້າງ	45	3680	ບ້ານດູ່	9		ກະທະນ soldier
02	ນາຍ ລີ ໄລອ້າງ	32	3681	-11-	6		ກະທະນ soldier
2	ນາຍ ຢ່າງອ້າງ	35	3705	-11-	6		ນາຍບ້ານ village chief
04	ນາຍ ຍີ່ອ້າງ	42	3672	-11-	5		ກະທະນ soldier
05	ນາຍ ໜາງລີອ້າງ	30	3383	-11-	5		ກະທະນ soldier
06	ນາຍ ທ້າງລີອ້າງ	28	3403	-11-	7		ຊູລະນ male
07	ນາຍ ເສົ້ອອ້າງ	66	3410	-11-	4		ພນັກງານ provincial govt employee
08	ນາຍ ຍ່າ ອ້າງ	25	3412	-11-	3		ຊູລະນ male
09	ນາຍ ພ່າລືປອ້າງ	60	00426	-11-	2		ກະທະນ soldier
10	ນາຍ ຈ້າງອ້າງ	25	3707	-11-	8		ຊູລະນ male
11	ນາຍ ລີ ອ້າງ	35	3713	-11-	12		ກະທະນ soldier
12	ນາຍ ຈ້າງລີອ້າງ	32	3702	-11-	5		ກະທະນ soldier
13	ນາຍເກົາ ອ້າງ	24	3394	-11-	4		ຊູລະນ male
14	ນາຍຣ່ອ ໄຊອ້າງ	36	4413	-11-	6		soldier
15	ນາຍ ຈ້າລີ ອ້າງ	40	3749	-11-	6		ກະທະນ soldier
16	ນາຍ ລີອ້າງອ້າງ	25	3538	-11-	4		male
17	ນາງ ໄຍ ຢ່າງ	64	3754	-11-	1		ແມ່ໝ້າຍ widow
18	ນາຍ ແດງອ້າງ	23	3921	-11-	3		ຊູລະນ male
19	ນາຍ ລີ ຢ່າງອ້າງ	22	4140	-11-	3		-11- male
20	ນາຍ ຈຳ ປາອອກ	32		-11-	6		-11- male
21	ນາຍ ໜາງ ຕຸ່ອ້າງ	66	2655	-11-	6		ກະທະນ soldier
22	ນາຍ ຈີ່ຢ່າງ	25	ບV-2568	-11-	2		ຊູລະນ male
23	ນາຍໄຊ ຣ່ອ ອ້າງ	63	3872	-11-	10		ກະທະນ soldier
24	ນາຍ ແຈ້ງອ້າງ	40	3490	-11-	8		ພນັກງານ provincial govt employee
25	ນາຍຍລາເຈາ ອ້າງ	40	3426	-11-	9		ກະທະນ soldier
26	ນາຍ ລີອ້າງ	20	4024	-11-	4		ຊູລະນ male
27	ນາຍ ຕົວ ອ້າງ	32		-11-	4		-11- male
28	ນາຍ ເຍັງ ຢ່າງ	25	3246	-11-	3		-11- male
29	ນາຍ ຣ່ອ ອ້າງ	20	3911	-11-	1		-11- male
30	ນາຍ ລີ ອ້າງ	88	3400	-11-	4		ກະທະນ soldier
31	ນາຍເຈາ ໜ່ງ ອ້າງ	40		-11-	7		-11- soldier
32	ນາຍ ເສົ້ນ ຕົວອ້າງ	54	3931	-11-	12		-11- soldier

NOTES

1. Massacre on the Mekong

1. See Yves Bertrais, *Le mariage traditionnel chez les Hmong Blanc du Laos et de la Thailande*. Chiang Mai, Thailand: Hmong Center, 1977. See Jean Larteguy and Yang Dao, *La Fabuleuse Aventure du Peuple de L'Opium* (Paris: Presses de la Cité, 1979).

2. Hugo Adolf Bernatzik, *Akha and Miao: Problems of Applied Ethnography in Farther India*, translated by Alois Nagler (New Haven: Human Relations Area Files, 1970), based on his expedition of 1936-37. The torture and killing of the "Miao" king and his entourage were witnessed by the French missionary Amiot in 1775.

3. General Vang Pao disagrees with this notion. He suggests that mountain isolation might explain these differences.

4. International drug enforcement agencies documented that the current "drug lords" of Laos were the communist government and some of its officials. Data collected by these agencies revealed Lao official complicity with international drug traffickers in supplying raw opium to drug syndicates and operating more than a dozen heroin refining laboratories in Laos, sometimes protected by Lao communist soldiers. This highly lucrative drug trade brings much needed hard currency to the bankrupt Lao economy. A March 1992 report by the Department of State's Bureau of International Narcotics Matters reported: "Laos has long been a major producer of opium and marijuana, with large quantities of both smuggled to the U.S. and other markets." This report adds: "The U.S. government remains concerned over continued reports of the sponsorship of and involvement with marijuana and heroin trafficking by elements of the Lao military." *International Narcotics Control Strategy Report*, U.S. Department of State, Bureau of International Narcotics, March 1992.

2. The Time of the Fackee

1. Historian Arthur Dommen points out that French police records do not indicate that Vongvichit collaborated with the Japanese and later the Viet Minh. Discussion with author, January 1992. Hmong who knew him at the time insist that he was a collaborator.

2. Maurice Gauthier. Interview with author. Connecticut, July 1988.

3. Vue Sai Long. Interview with author. California, January 1987.

4. David K. Wyatt, ed., *Iron Man of Laos: Prince Phetsarath Ratanavongsa* by "3349," trans. John B. Murdoch, Data Paper No. 110, Southeast Asia Program (Ithaca, N.Y.: Cornell University, Nov. 1978), p. 36.

3. The Rise of the Viet Minh

1. Michael Charlton and Anthony Moncrieff, *Many Reasons Why: The American Involvement in Vietnam* (New York: Hill and Wang, 1978), p. 14.
2. Ibid., p. 10.
3. Ibid., p. 15.
4. Arthur J. Dommen, *Conflict in Laos: The Politics of Neutralization* (New York: Praeger, 1971), p. 326.
5. Michel Caply, *Guerrilla au Laos* (Paris: Presses de la Cité, 1966), pp. 315–317.
6. Jean Boucher de Crevecoeur, *La Liberation du Laos 1945–1946* (Chateau de Vincennes: Service Historique de L'Armée de Terre, 1985), the official French military history of the retaking of Xieng Khouang town, places Mutin with Bichelot in the battle, thus giving Mutin credit for the victory.
7. Vue Sai Long. Interview with author. California, January 1987.
8. Nina S. Adams and Alfred W. McCoy, eds., *Laos: War and Revolution* (New York: Harper and Row, 1970), p. 113.
9. Jean Larteguy and Yang Dao, *La Fabuleuse Aventure du Peuple de L'Opium* (Paris: Presses de la Cité, 1979), p. 154.

4. The Time of the Viet Minh

1. Vang Chou, "General Direction." Interview with author. California, August 1987.
2. General Vang Pao. Interview with author. Washington, D.C., March 1982. From spring 1980 until spring 1992, the author has interviewed General Vang Pao numerous times in person, by phone, and in correspondence.
3. Jean Larteguy, *La Fabuleuse Aventure du Peuple de L'opium* (Paris: Presses de la Cité, 1979), p. 204.
4. Col. Jean Sassi. Interview with author. Paris, May 1987.
5. Interviews with Yang Cheng Leng and Moua Tou Lue, Paris, May 1987.
6. Letter to author from Col. Jean Sassi, June 2, 1989.
7. Ibid.
8. Roger Trinquier, *Les Maquis d'Indochine, 1952–1954* (Paris: Société de Production Littéraire, 1976), p. 151.
9. Fred Walker. Interview with author. Maine, June 1988. From June 1988 until 1992, the author frequently corresponded and talked with Walker.
10. Jules Roy, *The Battle of DienBienPhu* (New York: Harper and Row, 1963), p. 268.
11. General Vang Pao. Interview with author. Washington, D.C., March 1982.
12. Moua Tou Lue. Interview with author. France, May 1987. Correspondence from Moua Chia Xang's (Chang) son, Moua Lia, February 10, 1992.
13. Yang Mi Cha. Interview with author. California, January 1988. Yang Mino. Interview with author. France, May 1987.

5. The Time of the Americans

To understand this confusing time, I interviewed many Hmong and Americans, including Colonel Billy, Moua Lia, Tasseng Yang, Vang Chou, General Vang Pao, General Aderholt, Ed Dearborn, Yang My, Bill Chance, Fred Walker, Ly Neng Tong, Josephine Stanton, William Young. Another source was Don A. Schanche's

Mister Pop, about Edgar "Pop" Buell and his life and work with the Hmong during the decade of the 60s (New York: David McKay Co., Inc., 1970).

1. Fred Walker. Interview with author. Maine, May 1989.

2. Lo Moua Nhia. Interview with author. North Carolina, February 1988.

3. Brig. Gen. Harry "Heine" Aderholt. Interview with author. Florida, December 1987. From 1987 until 1992, the author has interviewed Aderholt numerous times in person, by phone, and in correspondence, and received numerous documents and photographs from him.

4. Moua Lia, son of Moua Chia Xang (Chang). Interview with author. France, May 1987. From 1987 through 1992, the author has interviewed and consulted with Moua Lia on numerous occasions in person, by phone, and in correspondence, and received documents and photographs from him.

5. John Lee. Interview with author. California, July 1988. Colonel Billy. Interview with author. Texas, July 1987. Over the years, the author has interviewed Colonel Billy numerous times in person and by phone and received photographs from him.

6. Lo Ma. Interview with author. North Carolina, February 1988.

7. Arthur J. Dommen, *Conflict in Laos: The Politics of Neutralization* (New York: Praeger, 1971), p. 167.

8. Ly Neng Tong. Interview with author. France, May 1987.

9. Yang Mino. Interview with author. France, May 1987. Yang My. Interview with author. Connecticut, July 1989.

10. Former Tasseng Yang Youa Tong. Interview with author. Ban Vinai Camp, Thailand, May 1986.

11. Moua Sue. Interview with author. Georgia, August 1988.

6. Camelot and the Land of Oz

Particularly helpful in piecing together this chapter were Vue Sai Long, Moua Chia, Lo Ma, William Young, Michael V. Forrestal, Brig. Gen. Harry Aderholt, Col. Bill Chance, Colonel Billy, Vang Chou, and Ly Neng Tong. Many Hmong whom I've interviewed remember those days of the North Vietnamese invasion, their flight, the training, fighting, and fleeing. Their memories and reflections were extremely helpful in reconstructing this time.

1. Fred Walker. Interview with author. Maine, May 1989.

2. Ibid.

3. Ambassador Leonard Unger. Interview with author. Washington, D.C., May 1984.

4. Ed Dearborn. Interview with author. January 1988. From 1988 to 1992, the author interviewed Dearborn numerous times in person, by phone, and in correspondence, and received numerous documents and photos from him.

5. Brig. Gen. Harry Aderholt. Interview with author. Florida, January 1988.

6. Walter Isaacson and Evan Thomas, *The Wise Men* (New York: Simon and Schuster, 1986) p. 607.

7. Col. Bill Chance. Telephone interview with author. July 1987.

8. Vue Sai Long. Interview with author. California, January 1987. "Tip." Interview with author. Thailand, August 1980.

9. Michael Forrestal. Interview with author. New York City, September 1986.

10. Vang Chou. Interview with author. California, August 1987.

11. Marek Thee, *Notes of a Witness: Laos and the Second Indochinese War* (New York: Vintage Books, 1973), pp. 127–130.

12. Isaacson and Thomas, *The Wise Men,* p. 618.

7. The Charade of Neutralization

1. Brig. Gen. Harry Aderholt. Telephone interview with author. May 1988.
2. Ed Dearborn. Interview with author. New York, February 1988.
3. Arthur J. Dommen, *Conflict in Laos: The Politics of Neutralization* (New York: Praeger, 1971), p. 232.
4. Michael Forrestal. Interview with author. New York City, September 1986.
5. Ibid.
6. Fred Walker. Interview with author. Maine, May 1989.
7. General Vang Pao. Interview with author. Washington, D.C., March 1989.
8. William Colby. Interview with author. Washington, D.C., June 1987.
9. Roger Hilsman. Telephone interview with author. March 1987.
10. Randolph "Toby" Scott. Telephone interview. February 1988.
11. Don A. Schanche, *Mister Pop* (New York: David McKay Co., Inc., 1970), p. 196.
12. Ibid., p. 197.
13. Lo Moua Nhia. Interview with author. North Carolina, February 1988.
14. Schanche, *Mister Pop,* p. 199.
15. Dommen, *Conflict in Laos,* p. 238.
16. Colonel Billy. Interview with author. Texas, July 1987.
17. Moua Lia. Interview with author. France, May 1987.
18. *New York Times,* December 17, 1963, p. 15.

8. CIA Operations at Long Chieng

1. Fred Walker. Interview with author. Maine, June 1988.
2. Arthur J. Dommen, *Conflict in Laos: The Politics of Neutralization* (New York: Praeger, 1971), p. 259.
3. Ed Dearborn. Telephone interview with author. May 1988.
4. Carol Berger, ed., *The United States Air Force in Southeast Asia, 1961–1973* (Washington, D.C.: Office of Air Force History, 1977), p. 70.
5. Vang Chou. Interview with author. California, August 1988.
6. Vang Chou and Colonel Billy. Interviews with author. California, August 1988.

9. Widening of the "Secret War"

1. Fred Walker. Interview with author. Maine, June 1988.
2. Vang Chou. Interview with author. California, August 1988.
3. Working Paper, HQ 7/13 AF, Udorn RTAFB, Thailand, 7 November 1966 (Washington, D.C.: Office of Air Force History, Bolling Air Force Base).
4. Gen. Harry Aderholt. Telephone interview with author. October 1988.
5. Tom Wickstrom, "The Nimrods," *Air Commando Association, Inc., Newsletter,* July 1988, p. 1.
6. Lo Moua Nhia. Interview with author. North Carolina, February 1988.

10. Phou Pha Thi Falls, "the Alamo Holds"

1. Michael Charlton and Anthony Moncrieff, *Many Reasons Why the American Involvement in Vietnam* (New York: Hill and Wang, 1978), p. 145.

2. Project CHECO Report, *The Fall of Lima Site 85* (Washington, D.C.: Office of Air Force History, Bolling AFB, August 1968), p. 9.

3. Xiong Xia Chia. Interview with author. California, August 1987.

4. Still on active duty so his name cannot be used.

5. Colonel Billy. Telephone interview with author. June 1988.

6. Staunch CIA critic Victor Marchetti, who from 1966 to 1969 served in the Office of the Director of the CIA, where he worked as a special assistant to the Chief of Planning, Programming, and Budgeting, agreed that the Lao war was fought "on the cheap." Comparing other fighting units in Southeast Asia, Marchetti acknowledged: "The Meos [Hmong] fighting in the CIA's L'Armée Clandestine in Laos . . . could be put into the field for less than ten cents per man per day." Victor Marchetti and John D. Marks, *The CIA and the Cult of Intelligence* (New York: Dell Publishing Co., 1974), p. 111.

7. Gen. Richard Secord. Telephone interview with author. August 1989.

8. Some reports indicate the gun was an Uzi submachine gun. See Earl H. Tilford, Jr., *Setup: What the Air Force Did in Vietnam and Why* (Washington, D.C.: Air University Press, 1991), p. 189.

9. CHECO, *Lima Site 85*, p. 36.

10. From Major Sliz's testimony before the U.S. Senate Foreign Relations Subcommittee on Security Agreements and Commitments Abroad, May 1970, classified for 16 years.

11. (Oklahoma City) *Oklahoman*, January 11, 1986.

12. CHECO, *Lima Site 85*, p. 36.

13. Gen. Richard Secord. Telephone interview with author. August 1989.

14. Xiong Xia Chia. Interview with author. California, August 1987.

15. Gen. Richard Secord. Telephone interview with author. August 1989.

16. Ibid.

11. Hmong in the Skies

Interviews with Hmong pilots, Forward Air Controllers (FACs), Forward Air Guides (FAGs), American air advisors, and SKY advisors were most helpful in detailing life for the Hmong pilots based at Alternate.

1. Vang Chou, "General Direction." Interviews with author. California, August 1988.

12. Vang Pao goes to Washington

1. Vang Xeu. Telephone interview with author. January 1979.

2. Colonel Billy. Telephone interview with author. June 1988.

3. Brig. Gen. Harry Aderholt. Interview with author.

4. President Johnson. Letter to General Vang Pao, November 14, 1968.

5. Carol Berger, ed., *The United States Air Force in Southeast Asia, 1961–1973* (Washington, D.C.: Office of Air Force History, 1977), p. 126.

6. Fred Walker. Interview with author. Maine, June 1989.

7. Lo Ma. Interview with author. North Carolina, February 1988.

8. Intelligence officer. Interview with author. Maryland, November 1987. Since he is still on active duty, his name cannot be used.

9. Ibid.

13. Men of Courage

1. *Air War in Northern Laos, 1 April–30 November 1971*, Office of Air Force History, Bolling Air Force Base, Washington, D.C., Project CHECO Report, pp. 46–47.
2. Sgt. Moua Paje. Interview with author. Colorado, August 1987.
3. Lt. Vang Kai. Interview with author. Montana, June 1980.
4. Vang Tou Fu. Interview with author. Illinois, March 1984.
5. Carl Berger, ed., *The United States Air Force in Southeast Asia, 1961–1973* (Washington, D.C.: Office of Air Force History, 1977), p. 37.
6. Col. Bill Keeler. Interview with author. Florida, January 1988.

14. The U.S. Betrays the Hmong

1. U.S. Senate, Subcommittee on U.S. Security Agreements and Commitments Abroad of the Committee on Foreign Relations. Hearings on *United States Security Agreements and Commitments Abroad, Kingdom of Laos*. Part 2, October 20, 22, 28, 1969. U.S. Senate, 91st Cong., 1st sess., 1969.
2. Ibid.

15. Lima Lima

1. Henry Kissinger, *The White House Years* (Boston: Little, Brown and Co., 1979), p. 451.
2. Earl H. Tilford, Jr. Telephone interview with author. January 1989. Tilford was the briefing officer at the time.
3. Col. Bill Keeler. Interview with author. Florida, January 1988.
4. Kenneth Conboy, *The War in Laos, 1960–1975* (London: Osprey Publishing, 1989), p. 37.
5. Kissinger, *White House Years*, p. 452.

16. Kissinger and Guerrilla Diplomacy

1. Henry Kissinger, *The White House Years* (Boston: Little, Brown and Co., 1979), p. 453.
2. Col. Bill Keeler. Interview with author. Florida, January 1988.
3. *Background Information Relating to Southeast Asia and Vietnam*, 7th ed., rev. (Washington, D.C.: U.S. Government Printing Office, 1975), pp. 345–347.
4. Kissinger, *White House Years*, p. 445.
5. Moua Lia. Interview with author. France, May 1987.
6. Vang Chou. Interview with author. California, 1987.
7. Kissinger, *White House Years*, p. 457.
8. Ibid.
9. *Air War in Northern Laos, 1 April–30 November 1971*, Office of Air Force History, Bolling Air Force Base, Washington, D.C., Project CHECO Report, p. 46.
10. Kissinger, *White House Years*, p. 446.
11. Ibid., p. 442.
12. U.S. Senate, Subcommittee on U.S. Security Agreements and Commitments Abroad of the Committee on Foreign Relations. Hearings on *United States Security Agreements and Commitments Abroad, Kingdom of Laos*. Part 2, October 20, 22, 28, 1969. U.S. Senate, 91st Cong., 1st sess., 1969.

17. Bouam Loung: SKY Border Base

1. Earl H. Tilford, Jr., *The United States Search and Rescue in Southeast Asia* (Washington, D.C.: Office of Air Force History, 1980), and Benjamin F. Schemmer, *The Raid* (New York: Harper and Row, Publishers, 1976).
2. Lo Moua Nhia. Interview with author. North Carolina, February 1988.
3. Tilford, *Search and Rescue.*
4. Thomas "Shep" Johnson. Telephone interview with author. October 1988.
5. *USAF Operations in Laos, 1 January 1970–30 June 1971,* Office of Air Force History, Bolling Air Force Base, Washington, D.C., Project CHECO Report, p. 109.
6. Thomas "Shep" Johnson. Telephone interview with author. October 1988.
7. *Air War in Northern Laos, 1 April–30 November 1971,* Office of Air Force History, Bolling Air Force Base, Washington, D.C., Project CHECO Report, p. 40.
8. Major Richard R. Sexton and Captain William M. Hodgson, *OV-1/AC-119 Hunter-Killer Team, HG PACAF,* Project CHECO Report, October 10, 1972. p. 52.
9. Moua Bee. Interview with author. California, August 1987.
10. Richard M. Nixon, *No More Vietnams* (New York: Arbor House, 1985), p. 126.
11. Ibid., p. 21.
12. Ibid., pp. 21–22.
13. Ibid., p. 103.
14. Henry Kissinger, *The White House Years* (Boston: Little, Brown and Co., 1979), p. 1016.

18. War Bloodies the Land of Oz

1. Lt. Moua Chue, "Coyote." Interview with author. France, May 1987.
2. Moua Bee. Interview with author. California, 1989.
3. *Air War in Northern Laos, 1 April–30 November 1971,* Office of Air Force History, Bolling Air Force Base, Washington, D.C. Project CHECO, p. 73.
4. Henry Kissinger, *The White House Years* (Boston: Little, Brown and Co., 1979), pp. 1020 and 1021.
5. Ibid., p. 1028.
6. Ibid., p. 1020.
7. CHECO, *Air War in Northern Laos,* p. 64.
8. Ibid., p. 19.
9. Ibid., p. 44.
10. Ibid., p. 86.
11. Vang Bee, "Fackee." Interview with author. Ban Vinai Camp, Thailand, May 1986.
12. T. J. Thompson. Interview with author. Texas, April 1988. From 1987 until 1992, the author had many conversations with Thompson, both on the telephone and in person.
13. Ed Dearborn. Interview with author. California, July 1988.
14. Ibid.
15. Fred Walker. Interview with author. Maine, June 1988.
16. Air historian Earl H. Tilford, Jr. Letter to author, January 1992.
17. Ed Dearborn. Correspondence with author. February 1988.
18. "Nixon's 'Intensified Special War' in Laos: A Criminal War Doomed to Fail," Central Committee of the Lao Patriotic Front, July 1972, p. 91.
19. Ed Dearborn. Telephone interview with author. February 1988.

19. The Siege of Long Chieng

1. Ed Dearborn. Telephone interview with author. February 1988.
2. Lo Ma. Interview with author. North Carolina, February 1988.
3. Ed Dearborn. Telephone interview with author. February 1988.
4. General Vang Pao. Interview with author. Washington, D.C., March 1982.
5. Ibid.
6. Fred Walker. Interview with author. Maine, June 1988.
7. Lt. Yang Pao. Interview with author. Georgia, August 1988.
8. *Commander's Digest,* Washington, D.C.: Department of Defense, April 6, 1972, p. 3.
9. Ibid., p. 3.
10. Ed Dearborn. Telephone interview with author. February 1988.
11. Lt. Yang Pao. Interview with author. Georgia, August 1988.
12. John G. Hubbell, *P.O.W.: A Definitive History of the American Prisoner-of-War Experience in Vietnam, 1964–1973* (New York: Reader's Digest, 1976). Ernest C. Brace, *A Code to Keep* (New York: St. Martin's Press, 1988). Jeremiah A. Denton, *When Hell Was in Session* (New York: Reader's Digest, 1976).

20. The Last Americans

1. The United States Initiative to Ban Chemical Weapons, Press Book, Department of State, April 1984.
2. "Soviet Nuclear War Gear Said to Be Unequalled in West," *New York Times,* June 2, 1972.
3. Department of State Bulletin, November 13, 1972, p. 549.
4. MacAlister Brown and Joseph J. Zasloff, *Apprentice Revolutionaries: The Communist Movement in Laos, 1930–1985* (Stanford, Calif.: Hoover Institution Press, 1986), p. 104.
5. Lt. Yang Pao. Interview with author. Georgia, August 1988.
6. Darrel Whitcomb. Interview with author. Texas, October 1988. Between 1988 and 1991 the author interviewed Whitcomb numerous times in person and by phone and received documents and photographs from him.
7. Clyde Howard. Interview with author. Florida, January 1988.
8. Moua May Song. Interview with author. Maryland, November 1991.
9. Maj. Gen. Oudone Sananikone, *The Royal Lao Army and the U.S. Army Advice and Support* (Washington, D.C.: U.S. Army Center of Military History, 1981), pp. 149–150.
10. "Agreement on the Restoration of Peace and Reconciliation in Laos," February 21, 1973.
11. John G. Hubbell, *P.O.W.: A Definitive History of the American Prisoner-of-War Experience in Vietnam, 1964–1973* (New York: Reader's Digest, 1976), p. 585. "Jane Fonda's Anti-Americanism Slowly being Accepted by the American Public," *U.S. Veteran News and Report,* February-March 1990, p. 4.
12. Fred Walker. Interview with author. Maine, May 1989.

21. An Ominous Lull

MacAlister Brown and Joseph J. Zasloff, *Apprentice Revolutionaries: The Communist Movement in Laos, 1930–1985* (Stanford, Calif.: Hoover Institution Press, 1986), give a detailed and useful chronology of events from April 1974 to December 1975.

1. Maj. Gen. Oudone Sananikone, *The Royal Lao Army and the U.S. Army Advice and Support* (Washington, D.C.: U.S. Army Center of Military History, 1981), pp. 150–151.

2. Lt. Vang Teng. Interview with author. Colorado, August 1987.

3. Prince Sisouk na Champassak. Interview with author. Connecticut, February 1985.

4. William Colby. Interview with author. Washington, D.C., June 1987.

5. Lt. Yang Pao. Interview with author. Georgia, August 1988.

6. Moua Lia. Interview with author. Connecticut, January 1988.

7. W. E. Garrett, "The Hmong of Laos: No Place to Run," *National Geographic,* Vol. 145, January 1974, p. 111.

8. Ibid., p. 89.

9. Moua Lia. Interview with author. Connecticut, January 1988.

10. Garrett, "The Hmong of Laos: No Place to Run," p. 111.

11. Ly Neng Tong. Interview with author. France, May 1987.

12. Lt. Yang Pao. Interview with author. Georgia, August 1988.

13. Sananikone, *Royal Lao Army,* pp. 151–152.

14. Telex from Air America Base at Udorn, June 3, 1974. Copy in author's possession. Fred Walker. Interview with author. May 1989.

15. Colonel Billy. Telephone interview with author. July 1988.

16. Sananikone, *Royal Lao Army,* p. 154.

17. Ly Neng Tong. Interview with author. France, May 1987.

18. Moua Lia. Interview with author. Connecticut, January 1988.

19. Radio Pathet Lao, May 27, 1974, in Foreign Broadcast Information Service (FBIS). Daily Bulletin, Asia and Pacific, May 30, 1974.

20. Brown and Zasloff, *Apprentice Revolutionaries,* Appendix B, p. 319.

21. *The United States Initiative to Ban Chemical Weapons,* Press Book, Department of State, April 18, 1984.

22. Yang Chee. Interview with author. Colorado, May 1985.

23. Moua Lia. Interview with author. Connecticut, January 1988. This information was also verified by General Vang Pao.

24. General Vang Pao. Interview with author. Washington, March 1982. General Tonglith Chokbengboun. Interview with author. Thailand, July 1986.

25. Prince Sisouk na Champassak. Interview with author. New York City, June 1981.

22. "Wipe Them Out!"

The information that appears in this chapter was provided by the following people: Tasseng Yang Youa Tong, General Aderholt, General Vang Pao, Ly Neng Tong, Moua Yang My, Vang Chou (General Direction), Moua Chue (Coyote), Vang Bee (Fackee), Lo Ma, Lo Moua Nhia, Moua Lia, Ly Nai, Vue Sai Long, Vang Na, Vang Teng, Xiong Xia Chia, Vang Tou Fu, and so many others who waited at Alternate that week in May 1975.

1. Lt. Moua Chue, "Coyote." Interview with author. France, May 1987.

2. Moua Lia. Interview with author. Connecticut, January 1988.

3. Radio Pathet Lao, May 6, 1975, in FBIS-APA, May 9, 1975.

4. Moua Lia. Interview with author. Connecticut, January 1988.

5. Lt. Vang Teng. Interview with author. Colorado, August 1987.

6. Tasseng Yang Youa Tong. Interview with author. Ban Vinai Camp, Thailand, May 1986.

7. Brig. Gen. Harry Aderholt. Interview with author. Florida, 1988.

8. Moua Yang My. Interview with author. Connecticut, May 1989.

9. Vang Chou. Interview with author. California, August 1987.

10. Moua Yang My. Interview with author. Connecticut, May 1989.

11. Vang Chou. Interview with author. California, August 1987.

12. Lo Ma and Lo Moua Nhia. Interviews with author. North Carolina, February 1988.

13. Vang Chou. Interview with author. California, August 1987.

14. Ibid.

15. Vang Bee, "Fackee." Interview with author. Ban Vinai Camp, Thailand, 1986.

16. Vang Chou. Interview with author. California, August 1987.

17. Lt. Moua Chue, "Coyote." Interview with author. France, May 1987.

18. General Vang Pao. Interview with author. California, June 1980.

23. Exodus

1. Ly Nai. Interview with author. France, 1987.

2. Ly Neng Tong. Interview with author. France, 1987.

3. Bruce Downing and Douglas Olney, *The Hmong in the West* (Minneapolis: University of Minnesota Press, 1981), p. 13.

4. Lt. Vang Teng. Interview with author. Colorado, August 1987.

5. Lo Moua Nhia and Lo Ma. Interview with author. North Carolina, February 1988.

6. Lo Ma. Interview with author. North Carolina, February 1988.

7. Lt. Vang Teng. Interview with author. Colorado, August 1987.

8. Ibid.

9. Radio Pathet Lao, June 5, 1975, FBIS-APA-75-109.

10. Ibid.

11. Lt. Yang Pao, Georgia, August 1989.

12. Xiong Xia Chia. Interview with author. California, August 1987.

13. Sgt. Moua Paje. Interview with author. Colorado, August 1987.

14. Vang Tou Fu. Interview with author. Illinois, March 1984.

15. Radio Pathet Lao, FBIS-APA-75-111.

16. Vientiane Domestic Service, FBIS-APA-75-113.

17. Ibid.

18. Moua Pa Chai. Interview with author. France, May 1987.

19. In the 1990s, Chagnon and Rumpf would lobby for Hmong repatriation to Laos.

20. Moua Pa Chai. Interview with author. France, May 1987.

21. Xiong Pao Xe. Interview with author. California, August 1985.

22. Colonel Billy. Interview with author. January 1988.

23. Brig. Gen. Harry Aderholt. Interview with author. May 1988.

24. Gov. Khamphouei Bouangphosay. Interview with author. California, August 1985.

25. Ly Neng Tong. Interview with author. France, May 1987.

26. Lt. Moua Chue, "Coyote." Interview with author. France, May 1987.

27. Vang Doua. Interview with author. Ban Vinai Camp, Thailand, 1981.

28. Lt. Vang Kai. Interview with author. Montana, June 1980.

29. Documents of National Congress of the People's Representatives of Laos,

Meeting on December 1 and 2, 1975; Delhi, India. Embassy of the Lao People's Democratic Republic.

30. Chang Cher. Interview with author. Ban Vinai Camp, Thailand, 1981.
31. Vang Seng Vang and his son, Ban Vinai Camp, Thailand, 1980.
32. Gov. Khamphouei Bouangphosay. Interview with author. California, August 1985.
33. Xiong Pao Xe. Interview with author. California, August 1985.

24. Chao Fa: Mystical Warriors

1. Lt. Vang Kai. Interview with author. Montana, June 1980.
2. Xiong Xia Chia. Interview with author. California, August 1987.
3. Lt. Yang Pao. Interview with author. Georgia, August 1988.
4. She requested that her name be withheld because she is hoping that her husband may still be alive in Laos and fears that speaking out might jeopardize his life.
5. See "The Life of Shong Lue Yang: Hmong 'Mother of Writing,'" *Southeast Asian Refugee Studies,* Occasional Paper no. 9 (Chicago: University of Chicago Press, 1990).
6. "The Story of the Meo People by Maha Thongsar Boupha," a former Lao Buddhist monk who worked with Pop Buell in providing aid to Hmong refugees during the war, as quoted in Don A. Schanche, *Mister Pop* (New York: David McKay Co., Inc., 1970), pp. 50–51.
7. Moua Lia. Interview with author. Connecticut, January 1988.
8. Lo Ma. Interview with author. North Carolina, February 1988.
9. Moua Lia. Interview with author. France, May 1987.
10. Lo Cheng. Interview with author. California, August 1987.
11. Yang Soua. Interview with author. North Carolina, February 1988.
12. Vang Pha. Interview with author. Ban Vinai Camp, Thailand, 1983.
13. Lt. Yang Pao. Interview with author. Georgia, August 1988.
14. Gov. Khamphouei Bouangphosay. Interview with author. California, August 1985.
15. Hongda Harry Wu, a prisoner in China's gulag for 19 years and author of *Lao Gai: Chinese Gulag.* Interview with author. October 28, 1988.

25. Holocaust in the Hills

1. Vang Youa Pao. Interview with author. California, March 1985.
2. The two women whose experiences are related here asked that their names not be used. I have also interviewed other women who experienced similar brutal treatment by the communist soldiers.
3. Department of State, Selected Documents, no. 5, Bureau of Public Affairs, Office of Public Communications, p. 1.
4. Strobe Talbott, *Endgame: The Inside Story of SALT II* (New York: Harper Torchbooks, 1979), pp. 68–75.
5. From the "Treaty of Friendship and Cooperation" between the Lao People's Democratic Republic and the Socialist Republic of Vietnam, July 18, 1977. FBIS, July 19, 1977.
6. *New York Times,* March 23, 1979.

7. Sgt. Moua Paje. Interview with author. Colorado, August 1987.

8. Lo Cheng. Interview with author. California, August 1987.

9. Lt. Yang Pao. Interview with author. Georgia, August 1988.

10. Yang Soua. Interview with author. North Carolina, February 1988.

11. Documents belonging to Prince Sisouk na Champassak.

12. Lt. Vang Kai. Interview with author. Montana, June 1980.

13. Vang Moua. Interview with author. Ban Vinai Camp, Thailand, 1980.

26. The Giant Slays Sin Sai's Soldiers

1. Lo Cheng. Interview with author. California, August 1987.

2. Lt. Vang Kai. Interview with author. Montana, June 1980.

3. Hmong survivor. Interview with author. California, 1982.

4. Vang Moua. Interview with author. Ban Vinai Camp, Thailand, June 1980.

5. Documents provided by Prince Sisouk na Champassak.

6. Lo Xa. Interview with author. Minnesota, January 1991.

7. Gov. Khamphouei Bouangphosay. Interview with author. California, August 1985.

8. Vang Ying Pao. Interview with author. Ban Vinai Camp, Thailand, 1980.

9. Eyewitness. Interview with author. California, 1985. Requests name be withheld; has relatives still in Laos.

27. "A Conspiracy of Silence"

1. Prince Sisouk na Champassak. Interview with author. New York City, June 1981.

2. Iowa Congressman Jim Leach, in a press release after listening to government testimony before the House Committee on Asian and Pacific Affairs. April 1980.

3. Yang Nhia. Interview with author. Ban Vinai Camp, Thailand, June 1980.

4. Lo Cheng. Interview with author. California, August 1987.

5. Statement of Col. Charles W. Lewis, M.D., Medical Corps, U.S. Army, before the House Subcommittee on Asian and Pacific Affairs December 12, 1979.

6. Colonel Lewis. Interview with author. August 1980.

7. Congressman Jim Leach, in press release dated April 1980.

8. *Chemical Warfare in Southeast Asia and Afghanistan,* Report to the Congress from Secretary of State Alexander M. Haig, Jr., March 22, 1982, Special Report No. 98, p. 13.

9. See "The Other Gas Crisis," William Safire, *New York Times,* January 28, 1980. "Congressmen Blast Officials for Silence on Poison Gas," Henry Bradsher, *Washington Star,* December 13, 1979. "Yellow Rain," William Safire, *New York Times,* December 13, 1979.

10. *Country Reports on Human Rights Practices* for 1979, Report Submitted to the Committee on Foreign Relations U.S. Senate and Committee on Foreign Affairs, U.S. House of Representatives, by the Department of State (Washington, D.C.: U.S. Government Printing Office, February 4, 1980), pp. 482–487.

11. Haig, *Chemical Warfare in Southeast Asia and Afghanistan,* pp. 18–19.

12. Ambassador Prok Amranand. Interview with author. 1981.

13. Alan Dawson, "Vietnam and the Poison Gas Issue," *Bangkok Post,* April 30, 1980.

14. Chief Vang Neng. Interview with author. Ban Vinai Camp, Thailand, June 1980.

15. Vang Seng Vang. Interview with author. Ban Vinai Camp, Thailand, 1980. I took a photo of his maimed child.

16. Vang Chue. Interview with author. Ban Vinai Camp, Thailand, 1980.

17. "Update to the Compendium on the Reports of the Use of Chemical Weapons," Department of State, March 1981, p. 24.

18. Letters to U.S. senators, representatives, and others interested in the Hmong from U.S. Department of State. In author's possession.

19. Personal correspondence of General Vang Pao.

20. Letter to General Vang Pao from John H. Holdridge, Dept. of State, Washington, D.C., April 29, 1981.

21. Christopher Wren, "Salvaging Lives After Torture," *New York Times Magazine,* August 17, 1986.

22. Khamphanh. Interview with author. Minnesota, January 1991.

23. "United States Relations with ASEAN (Thailand, Indonesia, Malaysia, Singapore and the Philippines), Hong Kong and Laos," *A Report to the Committee on Foreign Relations, United States Senate,* March 1982, pp. 14–16.

28. "Yellow Rain" and World Councils

From 1975 to 1992, this issue, first introduced by the French government, on the use of chemical-biological toxin weapons in Laos, Cambodia, and Afghanistan resulted in scientific investigations by many nations, a number of scientific conferences around the world, Congressional hearings, United Nations investigations, television documentaries, hundreds of editorials, and countless articles.

Initially, the major concerns centered on identifying the unknown agents, on creating prophylaxis for those who might be exposed to such agents once identified, on finding antidotes for victims, on finding measures to curtail the proliferation of chemical-biological toxin weapons supposedly banned by the 1972 Biological and Toxin Convention, and on inserting teeth into existing or new chemical-biological arms treaties to mandate unannounced on-site inspections and other verification mechanisms.

In 1983, another element was introduced by Matthew Meselson, the intellectual godfather of the 1972 Biological and Toxin Convention, who claimed that the Hmong (and Cambodians and Afghanis) were mistaken about the use of chemical-biological toxin weapons against them by the Vietnamese and Lao in Laos (by the Vietnamese in Cambodia and by the Soviets in Afghanistan). He proposed that bees defecating in flight had killed these people. This theory received considerable media attention.

1. *New York Times,* September 14, 1981, p. A-8.

2. Personal correspondence from Vice President George Bush, September 15, 1987.

3. Jack Anderson and Dale Van Atta, "Poison and Plague: Russia's Secret Terror Weapons," *Reader's Digest,* proof copy only (these lines were never published), June 1984.

4. "Yellow Rain," Hearing before the Subcommittee on Arms Control, Oceans, International Operations and Environment of the Committee on Foreign Relations, U.S. Senate, November 10, 1981, pp. 16–17.

5. Ibid., p. 23.

6. Ibid., p. 34.

7. Ibid., p. 20.

8. Ibid., pp. 30–31.

9. Capt. Chalermsuk Yugala, Royal Thai Army Officer. Interview with author. Bangkok, November 1981.

10. Lor Lue. Interview with author. Ban Vinai Camp, Thailand, December 1981.

11. Pha Ger Pao. Interview with author. Ban Vinai Camp, Thailand, December 1981.

12. Her Ge. Interview with author. Ban Vinai Camp, Thailand, December 1981.

13. Chao Thai. Interview with author. Ban Vinai Camp, Thailand, December 1981.

14. *Chemical and Bacteriological (Biological) Weapons: Report of the Secretary General* (Report of the Group of Experts to Investigate Reports on the Alleged Use of Chemical Weapons), U.N. Document A/36/613, Agenda Item 42, November 20, 1981, p. 47.

15. Patricia Stuart. Interview with author. Ban Vinai Camp, Thailand, December 1981.

16. *Chemical and Bacteriological (Biological) Weapons: Report of the Secretary General,* p. 55.

17. Ibid., p. 37.

18. Chief Vang Neng. Interview with author. Ban Vinai Camp, Thailand, December 1981.

19. Member of a volunteer Hmong team to collect evidence of use of CBW, Ban Vinai Camp, Thailand, December 1981. He asked that his name not be used.

20. FBIS-APA-81-J2.

21. *Chemical and Bacteriological (Biological) Weapons: Report of the Secretary General.*

22. *Chemical Warfare in Southeast Asia and Afghanistan,* Report to the Congress from Secretary of State Alexander M. Haig, Jr., March 22, 1982 (Special Report No. 98), p. 4.

23. "Foreign Policy and Arms Control Implications of Chemical Weapons," Hearings before the Subcommittees on International Security and Scientific Affairs and on Asian and Pacific Affairs, Committee on Foreign Affairs, House of Representatives, March 30 and July 13, 1982, p. 4.

24. Ibid., p. 11.

25. Ibid., p. 10.

26. Ibid., p. 11.

27. Ibid., p. 67.

28. Ibid., pp. 67–69.

29. Ibid., p. 75.

30. Ibid., pp. 101–102.

31. Ibid., p. 104.

32. Ibid.

33. *Chemical and Bacteriological (Biological) Weapons, Report of the Secretary-General,* U.N. General Assembly, December 1, 1982, p. 50.

34. "Asian Lawyers Legal Inquiry Committee on Alleged Violations of Human Rights in Kampuchea and Laos," LAWASIA, Thailand, 1982, p. 6.

35. Ibid.

36. Hearings, "Foreign Policy and Arms Control Implications of Chemical Weapons," p. 213.

37. Statement by Congressman Stephen J. Solarz, U.S. Representative to the 38th Session of the U.N. General Assembly, in the First Committee, on Chemical Weapons Use, November 4, 1983, p. 5.

38. "Implementation of Helsinki Final Act," Special Report No. 113, U.S. Department of State, 1983, p. 17.

39. The following description is taken from the 1977 East German military manual entitled *Textbook of Military Chemistry*. It describes the nature of Soviet bloc toxin weaponry and corroborates the Hmong description of deployment of toxins against them in Laos.

Toxins are designated as toxic agents which are produced by biological organisms such as micro-organisms, plants, and animals, and cannot themselves reproduce. By the middle of 1960 the toxins selected for military purposes were included among the biological warfare agents. In principle, this was understood to mean only the bacterial toxins. Today it is possible to reproduce various toxins synthetically. Toxins with 10–12 amino acids can currently be synthesized in the laboratory. Toxins are not living substances and in this sense are chemicals. They thus differ fundamentally from the biological organisms so that they can be included among chemical warfare agents. As a result of their peculiarities they are designated simply as "toxin warfare agents." They would be used in combat according to the same principles and with the same methods used for chemical warfare agents. When they are used in combat the atmosphere can be contaminated over relatively large areas—we can expect expansion depths of up to 6 kilometers before the toxin concentration drops below lethal concentration 50 . . . the toxin warfare agents can be aerosolized. They can be used primarily in micro-bombs which are launched from the air or in warheads of tactical rockets. Toxin warfare agents concentrates can be applied with aircraft spray equipment and similar dispersion systems. (Excerpted from the March 22, 1982, Haig Report, p. 17)

29. Wronged by the Media

1. Correspondence from Stephen Rosenfeld, *Washington Post,* June 24, 1982.
2. Note in author's possession.
3. Meetings with Philip B. Kunhardt, Jr., managing editor, *Life,* fall 1982.
4. Philip Boffey, "Bee Waste Is Suspected as 'Yellow Rain Source,' " *New York Times,* June 1, 1983.
5. Stephen J. Solarz, "Make No Mistake: They're Using Yellow Rain," *Washington Post,* June 27, 1983.
6. "The 'Bee Feces' Theory Undone," *Wall Street Journal,* September 6, 1985.
7. Anne Fadiman, "Yellow Rain, A Scientific Sherlock Thinks It's All a Tempest in a Beespot," *Life,* August 1984, pp. 23–24, 26–28.
8. Dr. Chester Mirocha, *Scientific American,* January 1986, p. 8.
9. Sterling Seagrave, "The Bees or Not the Bees?" *Washington Post,* May 27, 1983, p. G1.
10. Letter from Dr. Bruno Schiefer to Bruce Christensen, November 20, 1984.
11. Congressman Jim Leach. Telephone interview with author. September 11, 1987.

30. Burial in Montana

Vang Tou Fu and Vang Xeu were helpful in providing the details of Daniels' funeral.
1. T. J. Thompson. Telephone interview with author. January 1988.
2. Randolph "Toby" Scott. Telephone interview with author. February 1988.

556   Notes

3. "Lucky" Yang. Telephone interview with author. November 1989.
4. Louise Daniels. Telephone interview with author. November 1988.

31. Abused and Abandoned

From 1976 to 1992, I made more than 25 visits to Ban Vinai Refugee Camp.

1. "Democratic People's Republic of Laos: Background Paper on the Democratic People's Republic of Laos Describing Current Amnesty International Concerns" (New York: Amnesty International, April 1985), p. 5.

2. Vang Jue. Interview with author. California, March 1985.

3. Ibid.

4. General Vang Pao, Prince Sisouk na Champassak, and Vang Xeu. Interviews with author. 1984 and 1985.

5. Thao Yia. Interview with author. California, March 1985.

6. *Time*, June 17, 1985.

7. Former Royal Lao Army Brig. Gen. Tonglith Chokbengboun. Interview with author. Thailand, July 1986.

8. Ambassador H. Eugene Douglas. Interview with author. Washington, D.C., September 1985.

9. *Ethnics Organization Liberation Organization*, October 1, 1985.

10. J.V. (whose full name cannot be used). Interview with author. June 1987.

11. Ibid.

12. William Young. Interview with author. Thailand, July 1986.

13. Vang Seng. Interview with author. Ban Vinai Camp, May 1986.

14. Ibid.

32. Requiem

1. For example, George B. N. Ayittey, professor of economics at American University, Washington, D.C., and Mortimer Adler, author. Ayittey and Adler lectured on this subject at the 44th annual Conference on World Affairs, University of Colorado, Boulder, April 7–13, 1991. The author also spoke with Ayittey about this issue at the conference.

2. FBIS-EAS 89-29.

3. "Escalation in Laos: Vietnamese Warfare Against the Hmong and Lowland Lao Resistance," Task Force on Terrorism and Unconventional Warfare, House Republican Research Committee, U.S. House of Representatives, January 31, 1990, p. 2.

4. FBIS-EAS 90-60-61.

5. "Escalation in Laos," p. 3.

6. Ibid.

7. Ibid.

8. Reports appearing in the *Bangkok Post* and *The Nation* in April, May and June 1990.

9. Radio Vientiane, January 18. FBIS-EAS 90-013.

10. FBIS-EAS 90-52.

11. Radio Vientiane, May 15, 16, FBIS-EAS 90-95. June 16, FBIS-EAS 90-119.

12. FBIS-EAS 9-71/82/89/109.

13. Amnesty International, "Lao People's Democratic Republic, The Draft Constitution and Human Rights," December 1990, AI INDEX: ASA 26/03/90.

14. Joint Publications Research Service. Dept. of Commerce (Translations on S.E. Asia).

15. *Bangkok Post,* October 20, 1990.

16. Ibid., October 23, 1990.

17. Associated Press, November 4, 1990.

18. The author has a complete collection of these interviews.

19. Letter to Drew S. Days III, Director of the Schell Center, Yale University Law School, from Sarah E. Moten, Ed.D., Bureau of Refugee Programs, Department of State, February 20, 1991.

20. *Country Reports on Human Rights Practices* for 1990, Report Submitted to the Committee on Foreign Relations, U.S. Senate, and to the Committee on Foreign Affairs, House of Representatives, by the Department of State (Washington, D.C., February 1991), p. 943.

21. Ibid., p. 946.

22. "Taught a Lesson," *Far Eastern Economic Review,* April 25, 1991, p. 8.

23. William Crampton, *The Complete Guide to Flags* (New York: Gallery Books, 1989).

24. Laos: Fifth LPRP Congress. A special FBIS-EAS issue: FBIS-EAS 91-71-S.

25. Victor Tomseth, DCM, U.S. Embassy. Discussion with author. Bangkok, Thailand, May 1991.

26. From the Vue Mai proposal, which I later obtained from another source.

27. Keisuke Murata. Interview with author. Bangkok, Thailand, May 1991.

28. Letter from Charles H. Twining, Director of Office of Vietnam, Laos, and Cambodian Affairs. This was State's prepared piece of language on the issue. Others who inquired about Laos received the same letter.

29. "Yellow Rain in Laos: New Reports," *Wall Street Journal,* June 14, 1990.

30. "Thais Say Laos May Be Using Poison Gas Against Hilltribe Rebels," Paul Wedel, UPI, Bangkok, Thailand, June 5, 1991.

31. "Forced Back and Forgotten: The Human Rights of Laotian Asylum Seekers in Thailand," Lawyers Committee for Human Rights (New York, 1989), p. 3.

32. July 25, 1991, letter signed by Rep. Don Ritter.

33. Discussion with staff member in Rep. Don Ritter's office.

34. *Country Reports on Human Rights Practices* for 1991, Report Submitted to the Committee on Foreign Relations, U.S. Senate, and to the Committee on Foreign Affairs, House of Representatives, by the Department of State (Washington, D.C., February 1992), p. 907–910.

35. Ibid., p. 912.

36. Discussion in April 1992 with David Merkel, member of Rep. Bill McCollum's staff, who in late February went as a member of a team to investigate complaints about violations of refugee rights, confirmed this.

37. "Refugee Resettlement Programs," Hearing before the Subcommittee on International Law, Immigration, and Refugees of the Committee on the Judiciary, House of Representatives, October 2, 1991 (Washington, D.C.: U.S. Government Printing Office, 1992), pp. 216–218.

38. Arthur Randall, editor, *Washington Inquirer.* Interview with author. Washington, D.C., October 2, 1991.

39. Discussion with Steve Heder, who had worked with the screening in Chiang Kham. He reported that he had been told by Thai authorities that it was policy not to give more than two days' notice to involuntary repatriates. February 22, 1992, New Haven, Connecticut.

40. Sen. Dave Durenberger's letters. In author's possession.

41. Discussion with David Merkel, Congressman McCollum's staff, April 1992.

42. Ibid.

43. "International Narcotics Control Strategy Report," U.S. Department of State, Bureau of International Narcotics Matters, Publication 9853-A, March 1991. p. 301.

44. Letters from Ban Kay, Laos.

45. Lou Mazel. Telephone discussion with author. May 8, 1992.

46. Arthur J. Dommen, *Conflict in Laos: The Politics of Neutralization* (New York: Praeger, 1971), p. 209.

47. Natalya Zenova, "The Deadly Cloud Over Sverdlovsk," *Wall Street Journal,* November 28, 1990.

48. Peter Gumbel, "Anthrax: The Survivors Speak," *Wall Street Journal,* Oct. 23, 1991.

49. "Yeltsin Blames '79 Anthrax on Germ Warfare Efforts." *Washington Post,* June 16, 1992.

50. "On to Yellow Rain," *Wall Street Journal,* June 17, 1992.

51. Al Santoli, *To Bear Any Burden* (New York: Ballantine, 1986), p. 156.

52. See Carol Ireson and W. Randall Ireson, "Ethnicity and Development in Laos," *Asian Survey* 31, no. 10 (October 1991): 933.

GLOSSARY

Air America: CIA's proprietary airline operating in Laos with fixed-wing aircraft and helicopters under contracts from U.S. agencies.

ABCCC: Pronounced AB-Triple C, airborne control and command center.

Alley Cat: Nighttime ABCCC orbiting over northern Laos to direct air strikes.

ba-sii: Lao ceremony borrowed by Hmong to bestow honor on family, friends, and colleagues and to call on the spirits to protect them. This bonding ceremony borders on the sacred.

ban: Lao and Thai word for village.

Ban Vinai: United Nations High Commission refugee camp in Loei Province, northern Thailand, near the Mekong River.

Bouam Loung, Lima Site 32: Mountaintop base for Hmong warrior Moua Cher Pao. After the fall of Phou Pha Thi, Lima Site 85, it became a critical U.S. intelligence gathering post.

CAS: Controlled American Source. Code-name for the CIA in Laos.

Chao Fa: "Prince of the Sky," originally a mystic sect in northern Laos. After the communist takeover in 1975, a faction of Hmong resistance followed Chao Fa leaders. Later, outsiders often mistakenly called all anticommunist resistance Hmong Chao Fa.

Chaophakaow: "Lord (or Prince) White Buddha." Call-sign for T-28 fighter pilots.

Continental Air Services: Privately owned air operation in Laos under contract to U.S. agencies, including CIA and USAID.

Cricket: Daytime ABCCC orbiting over northern Laos to direct air strikes.

Customers: Term used by American pilots for CIA advisors.

FAC, Forward Air Controller: Airborne observer targeting air strikes.

FAG, Forward Air Guide: Ground observer directing air strikes.

Hmong: (Pronounced Mong with an aspirated h; rhymes with Kong.) Hmong elders say the word means Free People—those who must have their freedom and independence. During the Vietnam War, the Western press called the Hmong "Meo," which the Hmong consider pejorative.

Ho Chi Minh Trail: Complex trail and road system developed by North Vietnamese through Laos, used to infiltrate troops and to supply communist forces in South Vietnam, thereby avoiding the demilitarized zone (DMZ) at the 17th parallel, dividing North and South Vietnam.

Jolly Green Giant: U.S. Air Force HH-3E helicopter often used for search and rescue operations in Laos.

khene: Bamboo and wooden pipe, Hmong musical instrument.

Kmhmu: Also known as Lao Teung. A tribal group in Laos who believe that their ancestors were responsible for the ancient stone jars on the Plaine des Jarres.

Lao Liberation Army (LLA): Military force of the anticommunist United Lao National Liberation Front (ULNLF), also called "Neo Hom," which established a Provisional Democratic Government inside Laos in December 1989.

Lao People's Democratic Republic (LPDR): Name given Laos in 1975 by communist regime. Most anticommunist Hmong continue to refer to LPDR forces as the Pathet Lao and to the regime as the puppet government of Hanoi or the Kaysone regime.

Lao People's Revolutionary Party (LPRP): Communist party in Laos which wields total control.

Luang Prabang: Ancient royal capital of Laos.

Long Chieng or Alternate: General Vang Pao's headquarters and home for tens of thousands of Hmong. Also CIA forward-staging area in Military Region II to support General Vang Pao's forces from 1963 to 1975.

Mien (also known as Yao): A tribal group in western Laos that was trained and armed by the CIA.

Na Khang, Lima Site 36: Forward-staging area for U.S. Air Force search and rescue operations for U.S. air crews.

Nong Het: Major Hmong town on Route 7 and a major pass from North Vietnam into Laos.

North Vietnamese Army (NVA): Well-supplied and trained forces of North Vietnam, operating in Hmong homelands in Laos from the late 1950s to 1992. After 1975, these forces would be called People's Army of Vietnam (PAVN).

Padong, Lima Site 5: Mountain encampment where CIA and U.S. Special Forces teams trained Hmong in 1961.

pa'ndau: "Flowery cloth," Hmong term for their traditional needlework.

Pathet Lao: "Country of Lao," name of communist Lao. Hmong anticommunist resistance continue to call LPDR forces Pathet Lao.

Police Aerial Reinforcement Units (PARU): Elite Thai mobile forces that trained Hmong soldiers.

People's Army of Vietnam (PAVN): Before 1975 called North Vietnamese Army (NVA). Since communist takeover, Hmong resistance fighters still call PAVN forces NVA.

Plaine des Jarres (PDJ): Fertile plateau with moderate climate, named by the French for the ancient stone jars found there. Colonial French built homes here. Lying east of Long Chieng in Xieng Khouang Province, this desirable land, which the Hmong considered part of their homeland, was the site of many bloody battles involving the North Vietnamese Army and Hmong General Vang Pao's forces.

Phong Savan: Town located in Xieng Khouang Province. After 1975, used by communists as staging area for chemical-biological attacks against the Hmong. Also political prisoners held in this area.

phou: Lao word for mountain.

Phou Pha Thi, Lima Site 85: Ultra-secret U.S. navigational site guarded by Hmong. Overrun in March 1968 by North Vietnamese Army.

re-education camps: Intended to reform prostitutes, drug addicts, petty criminals.

Sam Thong: Civilian town where USAID stored supplies; site of "Pop" Buell's hospital and Sam Thong College.

Sam Neua Province: Traditional Hmong territory, bordering Vietnam. Site of communist seminar camps in which many Hmong and Lao were imprisoned.

seminar camps: Internment camps where the LPDR have sent tens of thousands of Hmong and Lao. Here they are starved, tortured, denied medical treatment, and executed. The Lao royal family died in a seminar camp. As of 1992, the LPDR continues to hold political prisoners and to imprison new ones.

SKY: Hmong term for their American CIA advisors and the CIA.

Trichothecene mycotoxins: Bleeding agents identified by scientists as one set of lethal toxins being used in Laos by PAVN and LPDR forces against the Hmong.

Udorn Air Base: Northern Thai air base, location of CIA headquarters for its operations in Laos.

United Lao National Liberation Front (ULNLF): Also called "Neo Hom." Anticommunist group, headed by Lao Prince Outhong Souvanavong as prime minister with General Vang Pao as first deputy prime minister, which proclaimed a Provisional Democratic Government in Laos in December 1989.

Vientiane: Administrative capital of Laos.

Viet Minh: Communist organization formed in 1941 by Ho Chi Minh in Vietnam, which began operating in Laos during the final days of World War II.

White Star: One of General Vang Pao's code-names.

White Star Teams: U.S. Special Forces which trained Lao forces, including General Vang Pao's soldiers.

Xieng Khouang town: Major town on the Plaine des Jarres.

Xieng Khouang Province: Part of the Hmong traditional homeland.

INTERVIEWS AND SOURCES

Between 1976 and 1992, I talked to, interviewed, corresponded with, or received data, documents, and photographs from over 1,000 Frenchmen, Americans, Australians, Filipinos, Chinese, Canadians, Thais, and Lao: ethnic Lao and Lao tribal Mien, Lahu, Kmhmu, and Hmong. These interviews, filling more than 100 large notebooks, numbering more than 9,000 pages, took place on three continents: Asia, Europe, and North America. In addition, I taped more than 500 hours of interviews. I had many further interviews and discussions in refugee camps where notebooks and tape recorders could not be used. For example, in the summer of 1991 in Chiang Kham camp, from which Hmong were being forcibly repatriated, I could not take notes nor seem to be talking about camp conditions and forced repatriation. While discussing serious questions, my interviewees and I had to act as if our conversations were only of a superficial nature. We tried to smile often and to laugh. In one case, the interviewees were visibly shaking because they were so afraid of the Thai authorities who did not want them to talk with me. Over the years, I have taken over 10,000 photographs of Hmong life.

Since 1976, I have traveled to the refugee camps in Thailand more than 25 times where I interviewed many hundreds of men, women, and children who had fled the Lao People's Democratic Republic. In France, I interviewed Frenchmen who had worked with the Hmong during the time of the French involvement in Laos and Hmong who had resettled in France as refugees after they fled their homeland. I interviewed Hmong living in Paris, Grigny, Courcouronnes, Cholet, Bordeaux, Lormont, Limoges, and Nîmes. In the U.S., I have traveled to every major Hmong community where I lived with Hmong families to learn first-hand of their resettlement experiences in this country and to record their experiences of life in Laos during the time of the French, the Americans, and the communists.

The following lists regrettably do not mention everyone who had input into this book. Some people I undoubtedly have forgotten to acknowledge and for that I apologize. Many Hmong with relatives in Laos requested that their names not be used because they feared that their relatives might suffer retribution as a result of their talking about life under the communist regime there. Others who contributed to this book asked that their names not be used because they are either on active duty or are working in Thailand or Laos.

AMERICANS

Ambassador Morton Abramowitz, Kenneth Adelman, Gen. Harry C. Aderholt, Bernard Alter, William Anderson, M.D., Bill Andresevic, Alex Arriaga

Roy Baron, M.D., David Belkis, Paul Jerome Bennett, Col. Carl F. Bernard, Bill Bird, Jeanne L. Blake, Yossef Bodansky, William Bodie, James Boney, Sen. Rudy Boshwitz, Thomas Boyd, Ernest Brace, Martin Brennan, James L. Bruno, Jesse Bunch, Col. David Bunner, M.D., Richard R. Burt, Vice President George W. Bush

Larry Cable, Col. Frank Calillupo, Donald J. Cann, Clay Cartney, James R. Chamberlain, Lt. Col. Bill Chance, John Coakley, William Colby, Joe Coleman, Louis Connick, Thomas Conroy, Sen. Alan Cranston, Rev. Ted Crouch, John Crowley, Comdr. Stephen O. Cunnion

Louise Daniels, Terry Daru, Thomas R. Dashiell, Victor B. David, Karen Davis, Richard Day, Ambassador John Gunther Dean, Ed Dearborn, Patricia M. Derian, Robert P. DeVecchi, Thomas Doubleday, H. Eugene Douglas, Joseph P. Duggan, Peter M. Dunn, Sen. David Durenberger, Capt. Thomas Dwyer, Nancy Dyke

James J. Ehrman, Sandra Ellander, Rep. Arlen Erdahl

Thomas A. Fabyanic, Thomas Fergerson, Carmel Fiske, David Ford, Vaughn Forrest, Michael V. Forrestal, Charles Freeman, Rep. William Frenzell, Robert Funseth

Frank Gaffney, Sherman Garnett, Ambassador G. McMurtrie Godley, Dennis Grace, Dan Grady, D. Warren Gray, Christopher C. Green, M.D.

Lt. Col. James W. Hamerle, William C. Hamilton, Richard Harruff, M.D., Sen. S. I. Hayakawa, Joseph W. Hazen, Robert M. Hearn, Arthur Helton, John Herzberg, Roger Hilsman, Michael Hogan, Mary Elizabeth W. Hoinkes, Neal Holtan, M.D., Douglas Houlcher, Clyde Howard, Sen. Gordon J. Humphrey, Richard A. Hunt, Col. David L. Huxoll

Jeff Jeffries, Thomas C. "Shep" Johnson, David A. Jones, Jr.

Col. Bill Keeler, Ben J. Kelley, Robert Knouss, M.D., William Kucewicz, Carol Kuecker, Philip B. Kunhardt, Jr., W. D. Krueger

Ronald Lagrone, Col. David Lambert, Col. Dennison Lane, Roger Larson, M.D., Rep. Jim Leach, John LeBoutillier, Harlan Lee, John E. Lee, Ernest LeFever, Col. James Leonard, Carol Leviton, Col. Charles W. Lewis, Steve Lindroth, Shepard C. Loman, Rachel Hefland Los Tumbo

Rep. Bill McCollum, Rep. Stuart McKinney, Ferrall McMahon, Ed McWilliams, Sgt. Patrick Mahoney, Philip R. Mayhew, Lou Mazel, Rep. Romano Mazzoli, Michael Meese, David Merkel, Thomas Miller, Dr. Chester Mirocha, Jeffry A. Moon, Larry Moore, Donald J. Morrisey, Craig Morrison, Gayle Morrison, Dr. Sarah Moten, Thomas Mullooly, Blair Murray

Aryeh Neier, John Nides

Terrel R. Otis, Fulton Ousler, Don Overfield

Dr. A. M. Pappenheimer, Henry P. Pendergrass, M.D., Col. Paul Pettigrew, David Pierce, Fred Platt, John Clark Pratt, Charles Preston

Arthur Randall, John Ratigan, Edwin J. Rhein, Jr., Ed Rice, Larry Ropka, Dr. Joseph Rosen, Sonia Rosen, Lionel Rosenblatt, Walt W. Rostow, Stapleton Roy, Jerry Ryan

Al Santoli, Major Michael Sauri, Orville H. Schell, Jr., Mark Schnellbaecher, John R. Schroeder, Robert Schwab, Eric Schwartz, Stuart Schwartzstein, Randolph "Toby" Scott, Sterling Seagrave, Gen. Richard V. Secord, Dr. Barbara Seidersly, Lt. Col. Fred Sellec, Theodore Shackley, Stephen Shapiro, Jean Sibley, John Sibley, M.D., Sen. Alan Simpson, Suzanne Simpson, French N. Smith, Phil Smith, Donald E. Stader, Gregory Stanton, Josephine Stanton, Dale Stone, Patricia Stuart, William B. Stubbs, James Symington

Father Thiel, T. J. Thompson, Earl Hawkins Tilford, Victor Tomseth, Amos R. Townsend, M.D., Charles Trowbridge, Robert Tyrell

John Underriner, Ambassador Leonard Unger

Dr. P. Roy Vagelos, Andrew Vernon, M.D.

Rick Wade, Fred Walker, Patricia Walker, M.D., Susan B. Walker, Gen. Vernon A. Walters, Sharon Watson, M.D., Steven A. Waugh, Sen. Lowell Weicker, Charles "Jiggs" Weldon, M.D., Col. Darrel Whitcomb, Chuck Whitney, Irene Hixon Whitney, Lee Williams, Joseph Winder, Roger Winter

Rep. Bruce Vento

Gordon Young, Harold Young, Stephen B. Young, William M. Young

CANADIANS

Michael Kengin, Bruno Shiefer

CHINESE

Wu Xueqian (Minister of Foreign Affairs, PRC), Hongda Harry Wu (PRC labor camp survivor)

FILIPINOS

Milton Amayun, M.D., Rene Bollozos, M.D., Virginia Garcia, M.D., Gideon Regalado, M.D.

FRENCH

Gen. Paul Aussaresses, Catherine Delcroix, Claire Fajon, Bernard François-Poncet, Maurice Gauthier, Col. Henry-Jean Loustau, Col. Robert Maloubier, Col. Jean Sassi

AUSTRALIANS

Michael Bonney, Peter Hughes, Graeme Lade, John McBeth, Sen. the Rt. Hon. R. G. Withers

ENGLISH

Andrea Crossland, Steve Heder, Dr. Catherine Maddox, Dr. F. C. Maddox

NEW ZEALAND

Richard Martin

UNHCR

Bernard Kerblat, Hitoshi Mise, Eric E. Morris, Keisuke Murata, Philip Nathan, Philip Passmore, Supanya Rohitastire, Nina Schafer, Gerald E. Walzer

HMONG

In the Hmong tradition of placing the clan first, I have grouped those whom I have talked to, interviewed or corresponded with first by clan name, then I list "given" name and then "ordination" or "adult" name. Often Hmong have the same name. For example, I interviewed four Vang Bee's and four Vang Xiong's—and I have listed all of them.

The pronunciation of X equates to the English sound of "s." So the name "Xa" is pronounced "Sa."

Many Hmong whom I've interviewed cannot be named. Many believe that their relatives are still alive in Laos—some held as political prisoners in "seminar" camps and others hiding in the mountains—and they do not want to jeopardize their relatives' lives. They agreed to tell their stories, but asked that their names not be used. To avoid capture and imprisonment by the LPDR and later the repatriation roundups in refugee camps, some Hmong have changed their names.

CHANG (SOMETIMES WRITTEN CHA OR CHING)

Chang Cher, Chang Chia Xang, Chang Choua, Chang Kia, Chang Kia Pao, Chang Kou, Cha John T., Chang Lao Chue, Chang Ma, Cha Neng Yia, Chang True, Chang Xia Chong, Chang Xia Sang, Chang Xiong Leng, Chang Yang, Chang Yer, Chang Ying Songlue, Chang Youa

FANG (OR FENG)

Fang Say Zey, Fang Xe neng, Feng Pao

HANG

Hang Choua, Hang Koua Pao, Hang Neng, Hang Sao

HER

Her Cher Pao, Her Dangy, Her Chue Blong, Her Ge, Her Joua, Her Ju Lue, Her Mao, Her Nay, Her Neng, Her Pa Seu, Her Pao, Her Say Pha, Her Tong, Her Tou Mao, Her Tou Vue, Her Tse, Her Tu, Her Ying, Her Yong Chou, Her Zong Cheng

KHANG (SOMETIMES WRITTEN KHONG OR KONG)

Khang Pia Tia, Khang Shoua Yang, Khang Yong Chue, Khong Neng Yee, Kong Yang

KUE (SOMETIMES WRITTEN KHUE)

Khue Fue Yang Wa, Kue Chaw, Kue Lue, Kue Nou Shoua, Kue Pang, Kue Thu Doua, Kue Tou Doua, Kue Yang, Kue Yia

LEE

Lee Bao, Lee Ber, Lee Blia Cheu, Lee Blong, Lee Chai, Lee Chan Ta, Lee Chong, Lee Chao, Lee Chang Meng, Lee Chong, Lee Chong Cha, Lee Chong Moua, Lee Chue, Lee Dang, Lee Doua Neng, Lee Gary Yia, Lee Geu, Lee Kao, Lee Khoua Cha, Lee Leng, Lee Mai Yang, Lee Mu, Lee Naim Xao Chay, Lee Nau X., Lee Neng Tong, Lee Nu Xiong, Lee Pao, Lee Pha, Lee Sai, Lee Sai S., Lee Sao Pao, Lee Seng, Lee Shoua, Lee Song, Lee Teng, Lee Thao, Lee Tong Leng, Lee Tou, Lee Toua, Lee Vang Pao, Lee Vue, Lee Wang Xao, Lee Xang, Lee Xang Cherta, Lee Yang Moua, Lee Ying

LY

Ly Chai, Ly Chao, Ly Chong, Ly Dang, Ly Fu, Ly Geu (Colonel), Ly Hai, Ly Her, Ly Lee, Ly Leng, Ly Nai, Ly Neng Tong, Ly Nhia Va, Ly Pao, Ly Seum Sop, Ly Shao, Ly Teng, Ly Vang Pao, Ly Xiong

LO (OR LOR)

Lo Fong Chang, Lo Gao, Lor Hang Pao, Lo Houa, Lo Lao Toua, Lo Ma, Lo Mai, Lo May Ly Moua, Lo Maikao, Lo Na, Lo Neng, Lo Neng "Richard," Lo Nhia Moua, Lo Peng, Lo Sai, Lo Sang, Lo Seng, Lo Sia, Lo Teng, Lo Wa, Lo Xa, Lo Yaoy, Lo Yia, Lor Blia, Lor Chang, Lor Chue, Lor Chia Cheng, Lor Hang Pao, Lor Kia, Lor Lue, Lor Mee Yang, Lor Mai Vang, Lor Nao Pao, Lor Nka Neng, Lor Nhia Nao Pao, Lor Tong Cha, Lor Tou Xiong, Lor Xiong

MOUA

Moua Bee, Moua Bla Tua, Moua Blea Vue, Moua Blia Yao, Moua Blong, Moua Cher Chou, Moua Cher Pao, Moua Chia, Moua Chia Xai, Moua Chong Ge, Moua Chong Neng, Moua Chong Toua Toulu, Moua Chou Noua, Moua Chou Toua, Moua Chue "Coyote," Moua Chue Tou, Moue Chue Toua, Moua Dang, Moua Gia Long, Moua Foung, Moua Houa, Moua Ia, Moua Ia Lee, Moua Kee, Moua Kai, Moua Lia, Moua Ly, Moua Maysee, Moua May Song, Moua Me, Moua My Yang, Moua Nhia, Moua Nhia Bee, Moua Nhia Chou, Moua Paje, Moua Pay Chai, Moua Pha Lee, Moua Seng, Moua Song, Moua Soua, Moua Sue, Moua Yer, Moua Ying, Moua Youa Va, Moua Xai, Mouasu Bliaya

PHA

Pha Ger Pao, Pha Vang, Pha Chue

THAO

Thao Bao, Thao Cha Sia, Thao Cha Teng, Thao Chai, Thao Chao, Thao Cher Sue, Thao Chia, Thao Chia, Thao Chong Neng, Thao Chong Yang, Thao Chou Houa, Thao Chue, Thao Dang, Thao Kee, Thao Mai Yia, Thao May, Thao Neng,

Thao Neng, Thao Neng Chue, Thao Noua Chang, Thao Noua Chang, Thao Pang Chong, Thao Pao "Bruce," Thao Pao See, Thao Pavue, Thao Pong Lia, Thao So, Thao Tang, Thao Teng, Thao Theng, Thao Thong, Thao Tong, Thao Toung, Thao Vang Houa, Thao Wa, Thao Xa Moua, Thao Xay, Thao Chong Yang, Thao Yia, Thao Ying

VANG

Vang Bao, Vang Bee "Fackee," Vang Bee, Vang Bee, Vang Bee, Vang Cha, Vang Chang, Vang Chao, Vang Charles Thai, Vang Cheng, Vang Cher, Vang Cher Pao, Vang Cher Yee, Vang Chi Cha, Vang Chia, Vang Cheng, Vang Chong, Vang Chong Cha, Vang Chong Xeng, Vang Chou, "General Direction," Vang Chou, Vang Chou (helped rescue an American F-111 pilot), Vang Chou Ka, Vang Chue, Vang Chu Tue, Vang Da, Vang Dang, Vang Doua (translator), Vang Doua, Vang Doua Pao, Vang Fu Vang, Vang Gao, Vang Genny, Vang Ger, Vang Ger (student), Vang Gnia Pao, Vang H. Yong, Vang Her Plua, Vang Joshua, Vang Jue, Vang Kai, Vang Kayi, Vang Kayi Kashi, Vang Kou, Vang Koua, Vang Lee

Vang Leng Vang, Vang Long Ge, Vang Lu, Vang Lue, Vang Mae Ko, Vang Mai, Vang Mai Chia, Vang Mai Yang, Vang Moua, Vang Mouachia, Vang Na, Vang Nao, Vang Nao Yeng, Vang Nao Ying, Vang Neng (Chief), Vang Neng, Vang Neng Vang, Vang Nhia Yang, Vang Nhai Xiong, Vang Nkajlo V., Vang Noua, Vang Pa Tou, Vang Pao, General, Vang Pao, Vang Pao Youa, Vang Pao Xiong, Vang Peter, Vang Phaa, Vang Phay Dang, Vang Pheng, Vang Plia, Vang Pobzeb, Vang Sai Her, Vang Sao Dua, Vang Seng (T-28 trainee), Vang Seng (CBW chief), Vang Seng (student), Vang Seng Vang, Vang Seng Wang, Vang Shoua Lee, Vang Shoua Vue, Vang So, Vang Song Yang, Vang Sue, Vang Sy, Vang Teng, Lieutenant, Vang Teng, Vang Thay, Vang Thao Nhia

Vang Thor, Vang Tong, Vang Tong Ger, Vang Tong Xiong, Vang Tony, Vang Thor, Vang Tou Fu, Vang Toua, Vang Toushong, Vang True, Vang Vong H., Vang Wa Cheng, Vang Ying Pao, Vang Youa True, Vang Xang, Vang Xeng, Vang Xeu, Vang Xia Kao, Vang Xiong, Vang Xiong, Vang Xiong, Vang Xiong, Vang Xiong Toua, Vang Xo, Vang Xu, Vang Ya, Vang Yang, Vang Yee, Vang Yee Vang, Vang Yia, Vang Ying, Vang Ying, Vang Ying Pao, Vang Ying Pao, Vang Ying Pao, Vang Yong, Vang Youa Pao, Vang Youa True

VUE

Vue Bee, Vue Blia Moua, Vue Bon Nue, Vue Cha Tou, Vue Chao, Vue Cher, Vue Dai Lu, Vue Gai, Vue Geu, Vue Gnia, Vue Ka Ying, Vue Lee, Vue Long, Vue Mai, Vue Xia Moua, Vue Nao Leng, Vue Neng, Vue Ong, Vue Pa Nou, Vue Pao Xiong, Vue Sai Long, Vue Seng, Vue Sia, Vue Sia, Vue Vang Pao, Vue Xia Moua, Vue Yai, Vue Yang, Vue Zue

XIONG

Xiong Ay, Xiong Bee, Xiong Blia, Xiong Boua Lia, Xiong Boua Yia, Xiong Chong Neng, Xiong Dao Voua, Xiong Doua, Xiong Fay Ly, Xiong Foua, Xiong George, Xiong Kao, Xiong Kay, Xiong Khamma, Xiong Khai, Xiong Je Moua, Xiong Leng Xiong, Xiong Lu, Xiong Mai, Xiong Neng, Xiong Nhia Yee, Xiong Paodoua, Xiong Pao Ge, Xiong Pao Xe, Xiong Pasee, Xiong Pe Sa Mai, Xiong Phao, Xiong Sa Lee, Xiong Sai Lee, Xiong Seang Chean, Xiong Seng Xiong,

Xiong Shoua, Xiong Xia Chia, Xiong Sia Shur, Xiong Song Leng, Xiong Song Vue, Xiong Teng, Xiong Tha, Xiong Thai, Xiong Thao, Xiong Tou, Xiong Tu, Xiong Vang, Xiong Vue Pao, Xiong Wang Lue, Xiong Xao Doua, Xiong Xay Ying, Xiong Xia Toua, Xiong Ye, Xiong Yee, Xiong Ying, Xiong Za Neng, Xiong Zona

YANG

Yang Blia, Yang Cha Bee, Yang Chao Noi Lee, Yang Chaw Pao, Yang Chee, Yang Cheng, Yang Cheng Leng, Yang Cher Cha, Yang Cher Cha, Yang Chia Mee, Yang Chong Cha, Yang Chong Toua, Yang Chong Yia, Yang Chou, Yang Dao, Yang Fue, Yang Fong Khang, Yang Ger, Yang Hueson, Yang Kazong, Yang Khang, Yang Khao, Yang Khue, Yang Khou, Yang Kou, Yang Leng Vang, Yang Leng Yang, Yang Long, Yang Lue, Yang "Lucky," Yang LyPao, Yang Ma, Yang Ma Kue, Yang Mai, Yang Mai (grandmother), Yang Mao, Yang May, Yang Mi, Yang Michael, Yang Mino, Yang Mo Cha, Yang My, Yang Neng, Yang Nhia Chou, Yang Paj Houa, Yang Pao
Yang Phia Gao, Yang Pia, Yang Sa, Yang Sao, Yang Sao Her, Yang See, Yang Shao, Yang Shia, Yang Shoa, Yang Shoua, Yang Soua, Yang Toua, Yang Teng T., Yang Teng Yang, Yang Ter, Yang Ter Fong, Yang Tia, Yang Tia, Yang Ton, Yang Tong, Yang Tong Fong, Yang Tou, Yang Tou, Yang Tou Houa, Yang Tou Lue, Yang Va Khue, Yang Vang Leng, Yang Vang Sao, Yang Wa Khue, Yang Wa Lue, Yang Xiong, Yang Xoua, Yang Ya, Yang Kue Yaa, Yang Yia, Yang Youa Tong

LAO

In Lao tradition, these names are listed alphabetically by first names. An asterisk (*) indicates they are survivors of LPDR seminar camps. While *Tragic Mountains* is a book about the Hmong of Laos, the tragedy that took place in Laos beginning in 1975 also greatly affected other ethnic groups, including the Lao. In order to understand the sweeping efforts by the communist LPDR to "rip out" the old in order to create the "new man" and "new society," it was important to interview Lao who had survived the brutality of the Lao Gulag. Many of the individuals listed below spent 12 to 14 years in slave labor internment camps where they were physically and psychologically abused before they either escaped or were "released" to internal exile and then escaped to Thailand.

In 1990, the LPDR arrested former Deputy Minister of Science and Technology Thongsouk Saisangkhi; the former Deputy Agricultrual Minister, Latsami Khamphoui; and Feng Sakchitthaphong, a senior Justice Ministry official because they called for a multiparty system and accused the ruling communist piarty of corruption. In 1992, as I complete this book, they remain in seminar camps in northeast Laos. There are continuing reports of other political arrests as the LPDR continues to arbitrarily imprison and terrorize its citizens.

Amoun Sayaovong, Boonthawee*, Boounkhouang*, Col. Bounmy Sisouvong*, Col. Bounleuth Thiravong*, Gen. Bounleuth Saycocie, Bounthong Senekhamvong*, Bounrath Thatsanaphone*, Champheng, Chanhbounmy*, Col. Eng Amphavannasoukh*, Colonel Heuang*, Colonel Khamboun*, Khamphao*, Col. Khamphone Symoung*, Khampeng*, Khamphet Saycocie*, Major Khamphan*, Khamphanh Khansourivong*, Khamphao*, Lieutenant Khamphong*, Khamphouei Bouangphosay* (Governor of Khong Island), Khamphoui Douangphouxay* (Governor of Sithadone Province)
Khamsone Noudaranouvong* (teacher), Khamsouk Chantahadara (protocol

officer), Khiem Tua Khenetouy*, Ambassador Khientong, Khounkham, Major Kientong*, Kong See*, Col. Langsanh Souvannosoth*, Khamboun* Linthong Phetsavan (LPDR Chargé d'Affaires to Washington, 1990-92) Nham Insisiengmay, Col. Noudue Mala Uham Tanh, Pimpha Daravong, Lt. Col. Phom Phanthavong*, Phuvinh Chanthavongsa*, Pou Keo (held in internal exile), Praphot*, Maj. Phao Rattanakorn*, Chao Prasit, Lt. Col. Prasit Bouvong*, Col. Oudom Vorarat*, Captain Savat*, Prince Sisouk na Champassak

Major Sisouphongreeseung*, Sisouphang, Capt. Somboun Vongsouthi*, General Suchai, Lt. Col. Souphayt Phetcharoen*, Capt. Tak Sirivong*, Capt. Somboun Vongsouthi, Somwang Phanthavong*, Colonel Soom*, Supan Sannikone, Colonel Thamlong*, Thong Phu, Tianethone Chantharasay (Ambassador), Gen. Tonglith Chokbengboun, Tong Suk, Lt. Col. Traymany Oun*, Villam Phraxayavong*, Villian Petsavang, Visit*, Vong Thai, Vorabout Tanhavong*

THAI

Ambassador Prok Amranand, Capt. Chalermsuk Yugala (Royal Thai Army), Ambassador Birapongse Kasemsri, Dr. Thanat Khoman (former Thai Foreign Minister), Field Marshal Thanom Kittikachorn (former Prime Minister), Gen. Charan Kullavanichja, Anand Panyarachun (Deputy Foreign Minister to Khoman and later Prime Minister), Bounmee Vichitrmala (Ban Vinai Camp Commander), Colonel Vinat, Charlerm (Ban Nam Yao Camp Commander), Charoen Vimutkasol (Ban Nam Yao Camp Commander), Dr. Suvit Yodmani (Office of the Prime Minister), Gen. Saiyud Kerdphol, Charonchai Salyapong, Niramit Sirisula, Vivit Muntarbhorn

KMHMU AND MIEN

Over the years, I have interviewed a number of Kmhmu and Mien in refugee camps in Thailand and here in the U.S. I particularly want to mention Chao La, who for years was the Mien leader in Western Laos and later the leader of his people trapped in refugee camps in Thailand.

INDEX

In keeping with Hmong tradition, the author has placed the clan name first with the ordination and given names following the clan name.